Rebirth

*A History of Europe
Since World War II*

REBIRTH

A History of Europe
Since World War II

Cyril E. Black
Jonathan E. Helmreich
Paul C. Helmreich
Charles P. Issawi
A. James McAdams

WESTVIEW PRESS
Boulder • San Francisco • Oxford

Internal design by Jane Raese

Published in 1992 in the United States of America by Westview Press, Inc., 5500 Central Avenue, Boulder, Colorado 80301-2847, and in the United Kingdom by Westview Press, 36 Lonsdale Road, Summertown, Oxford OX2 7EW

Library of Congress Cataloging-in-Publication Data
Rebirth : a history of Europe since World War II / Cyril E. Black . . . [et al.].
   p. cm.
Includes bibliographical references and index.
ISBN 0-8133-1365-1 — ISBN 0-8133-1366-X (pbk.)
  1. Europe—History—1945-   . I. Black, Cyril Edwin, 1915-   .
D1051.R43 1992
940.55—dc20   91-45541
                                                        CIP

Printed and bound in the United States of America

The paper used in this publication meets the requirements of the American National Standard for Permanence of Paper for Printed Library Materials Z39.48-1984.

10   9   8   7   6   5   4   3   2   1

FOR

Cyril Edwin Black
1915-1989
IN MEMORIAM
SCHOLAR, COLLEAGUE, FRIEND

AND

Ernst Christian Helmreich
SCHOLAR, FATHER, MENTOR

Contents

PART FOUR
Conclusion

Maps

Preface

The dramatic events in Europe in 1989, the tumultuous developments that followed, and the growing realization of a single Europe underscore the need for reassessment of the history of Europe since World War II. In this book we seek to meet that need by examining the political and economic history of postwar Europe in both its domestic and international dimensions.

We begin by surveying the rise of Europe from the fourteenth through the nineteenth centuries, analyzing the forces of modernization that led to its preeminence at the beginning of the twentieth century. We then portray the decline of Europe from its pinnacle of strength and optimism through war, depression, and totalitarianism, culminating in the devastation of World War II, which left Europe deprived of both political and economic vitality. In Part Two we take up our central task of analyzing the international aspects of the phenomenal rebirth of Europe, beginning with its shattered state in 1945 and continuing through the revolutionary changes of the early 1990s. It is a story of division, Cold War confrontation, evolving West European integration, and eventual emergence of a reshaped Europe as an independent player on the global stage.

Part Three presents an in-depth examination of the major European nations and of many of the smaller states. The histories of these states do not always correspond with the flow of international events, and their consideration over a sweep of nearly a half-century thus affords a useful comparative analytical perspective. We discuss the main developments in these countries and place them in the larger international context; special attention is given to patterns of modernization, efforts to achieve economic growth and stability, and political responses to issues of social and economic justice. In our final chapter, we reflect upon Europe as a whole, attempt to place its history in a larger setting, discuss the deepening of the European Community, and consider the many challenges and opportunities facing the new Europe.

Rebirth is in some respects a descendant of a well-known text, *Twentieth Century Europe*, coauthored by Cyril E. Black and Ernst C. Helmreich (first edition: 1950). It is, however, a distinct and separate work. Two of the authors—Jonathan Helmreich and Paul Helmreich—are sons of Ernst Helmreich. Cyril Black, another author, did not live to see the final version of this book. He was a prime mover from the start, and the themes that underlie our analysis are in large part the result of his inspiration. Our sense of loss is eased by the knowledge that his work and insights can be found throughout these pages.

Special mention should be made of Corinne Manning Black, widow of Cyril Black and herself an academic. Without her there would be no book. After the death of her husband in 1989 when work had come to a halt, she found a publisher, pulled the authors together to make a revision plan, and stimulated and coordinated our efforts. She worked closely with Peter Kracht, our editor at Westview Press, provided discriminating criticism, and edited the entire manuscript. She sought out the many photographs and contributed to the styling and writing of the captions. Our deepest thanks and appreciation go to her.

Fred Praeger was our initial connection with Westview Press. His ready response to *Rebirth* and his interest throughout its development were of prime importance to us.

Special thanks are also extended to Peter Kracht, Westview's history editor. His assistance with the conceptualization of the book, his outstanding editorial skills, and his keen perceptions enhanced our efforts and helped to shape the book. We are very grateful to him for his sensitive and learned responses to the text, photo selections, and captions and for his encouragement and unswerving commitment.

Thanks also go to Jane Raese, our project editor, for ably overseeing the copyediting and the production of the book and for her excellent work on its internal design. She and the copy editor, Alice Colwell, and the entire staff at Westview Press are to be commended for their extraordinary attention to this book.

We extend our appreciation to Jane Westenfeld and Don Vrabel of Pelletier Library at Allegheny College and to Nancy Shepardson of Wheaton College, who gave beyond the call of duty in secretarial assistance.

The maps were skillfully drawn by Patricia Isaacs of Parrot Graphics, a job all the more praiseworthy because of the changes in boundaries and place-names that occurred so rapidly.

The authors wish to express their appreciation to New Directions Publishing Corporation for permission to quote from Wilfred Owen's "*Dulce et decorum est*" in Chapter 2, and to Fazz Music Ltd. for permission to quote from John Ford and Richard Hudson's "Part of the Union" in Chapter 6.

The authors close with warm expression of deep gratitude to their wives for their support, understanding, and patience throughout this enterprise:

Nancy Moyers Helmreich, Dorothy Heise Helmreich, Janina M. Issawi, and Nancy O'Connell McAdams.

Jonathan E. Helmreich
Paul C. Helmreich
Charles P. Issawi
A. James McAdams

PART ONE
Historical Background

CHAPTER ONE

Europe Triumphant: 1300-1900

❧

The history of modern Europe can be said, rather arbitrarily, to have begun approximately seven centuries ago with the gradual emergence of Europe from a period that historians have called the Medieval or Middle Ages into a new era labeled, equally arbitrarily, the Renaissance. Historians have long since disproved the old characterization of the medieval period as having been some sort of "dark ages." A comparison of the later, or "high," Middle Ages with the earlier, or "low," Middle Ages indicates a great deal of change in many areas: intellectual, architectural, technological, military, political, and economic. But what can be said without contradiction about these eight or nine centuries is that the pace of life, the speed with which change and development occurred, was dramatically slower than it had been in the preceding classical Greek and Roman periods and than it was again in the so-called Renaissance that ushered in Europe's modern age in the fourteenth and fifteenth centuries.

During the six centuries immediately preceding the twentieth, Europe gradually emerged as a global leader in many fields of human endeavor. Intellectually and culturally; in the arenas of economic, scientific, and technological development; in the evolution of new forms of political organization and the concept of human rights; in the overall betterment of the standard of living of its peoples, both in economic and human terms—in all of these and almost any other area one can imagine, Europe by the end of the nineteenth century had assumed uncontested leadership in the world.

So overwhelming was this supremacy that it led, almost inevitably, to ever increasing European mastery and control of the globe. By the end of the nineteenth century, Great Britain ruled one-fifth of the total land mass and Russia controlled another one-sixth. All of Africa, save Abyssinia (today Ethiopia) and Liberia, had fallen under European domination, as had India, Australia, New Zealand, all of Southeast Asia, and Indonesia. The oceans of the world were policed by the British navy, and European trade, commerce, and investment capital dominated the international economic arena. As Europeans entered the twentieth century, it did indeed seem as if they were history's chosen peoples. No wonder that the decades immediately preceding World War I have been characterized by some as Europe's "age of triumphant optimism."

Why? What caused all of this to happen? What led Europe in such a short period of time to establish a superior economic and cultural standard of living, to gain a nearly total global economic, political, and military dominance from which only the United States and Japan (both eager imitators of things European) were excluded? How had Europe achieved so quickly a level of scientific, cultural, and intellectual development that set it apart and led the rest of the world to send its best young minds to study and learn in Europe?

Modernization and European History

The possible answers are many, and their subcomponents countless. Different historians, writing in different times and from different perspectives, have packaged them in varying ways. The present does indeed lend perspective to the past, and we should not expect that solutions to historical questions and problems presented today will be agreed on by all or regarded as equally valid in a future decade or century. But from the vantage point of the final decade of the twentieth century, two broad factors seem to provide jointly the most comprehensive framework for understanding the acceleration of European growth and development that led to its era of dominance in the late nineteenth century.

The first of these elements was a rapid escalation of the pace of accrued scientific knowledge about the world in which humans lived and the concomitant transfer of that knowledge into developments in the field of technology. Second, and second only because it followed after and in some sense derived from the first, was a fundamental shift in people's thinking about their lives, their purpose on earth, their goals, and their capabilities. In other words, along with an enormous acceleration in the development of scientific knowledge and technical application went a fundamental change in humans' attitudes about themselves and about their reason for existence on this earth. The combination of these factors provided the fuel for a driving, motivating force in history that has even been given a name: modernization.

If indeed "modernization" or the "drive toward modernization" constitutes the single most inclusive theme of modern European history, it deserves at least some basic explanation and definition. This is not as easy as it may sound. Many volumes have been written that intensively develop and explicate the concept of modernization. But for our purpose, the relatively straightforward and simple explanation provided by Patricia Branca and Peter Stearns seems particularly satisfactory:

> A modern society is an industrial society, so during the process of modernization most people cease depending on agriculture and do newer kinds of work, often with new machines, in factories, offices, even schools. Modern society is urban. . . . Modernization involves more, however, than simply how people work and where they live; it involves a new state of mind. . . . Many social scientists agree that modern people differ from most historic peoples by believing in progress instead of relying on traditions to guide them. They are more individualistic, making choices by themselves, guided by their own pleasure, rather than referring to a larger family or community. Modern people are secular and materialistic, usually reducing the role of religion in their lives. They are politically conscious, believing that they have rights of participation in the state and that the state owes them attention to their welfare. The modernization of outlook is not necessarily sudden or

complete. It occurs in different stages with different groups in society. And of course it may not be a good thing; individualistic people may be more neurotic, while expectations of progress may simply lead to frustrations. But most social scientists would agree that modern man is fundamentally different, in any industrial society, from his premodern counterpart.[1]

The Medieval World

Although the full effects of modernization did not become apparent until the last half of the nineteenth century, its antecedents can be seen as far back as the fourteenth and fifteenth centuries. To understand the enormity of the change that began at that time, we must at least briefly sketch in some of the main characteristics of the so-called medieval world.

Social Structure and Lifestyles

The basis of medieval life was rural and agricultural. Society and politics were dominated by a feudal, aristocratic, landholding class, whose members waged constant internecine warfare within an ever more fragmented and decentralized political system. The basic social and economic unit was the manor, a fundamentally self-sufficient territorial unit within which the nobility supplied military security and protection. The church and its clergy provided guidance and direction toward the path leading to eternal salvation. Peasant/serfs worked the land, providing sustenance not only for themselves but for members of the other two groups as well. For the masses of peasant/serfs, it was in some sense not too bad a bargain. Through their work they supported the community economically; in turn the nobles protected their bodies and the clergy looked out for their souls.

The role of urban life in all this was very secondary. Towns, such as they were, tended to exist around major cathedrals, where perhaps a bishop or archbishop had his headquarters, or outside the walls of a castle belonging to an important member of the nobility, perhaps a duke, earl, or prince. In both cases the town's residents would be primarily artisans, craftspeople, and laborers who gained their livelihoods by performing the services necessary for building and maintaining the cathedral or castle and supporting the large retinue that surrounded the important persons who inhabited it. There were also occasional market towns, often found at river junctions, where trade in goods brought from various areas or even overseas took place, but these communities served a fringe function and were in no way central to the economic, political, or spiritual needs of the medieval world.

Life on the manor was basically routine, conducive to the preservation of unchanging tradition. It was based on a cooperative method of economic production in which everyone plowed, planted, cultivated, and harvested in

The diversity and energy of a late medieval town is well reflected in this woodcut of a Dutch marketplace: public speakers; a craft guild on parade; archery contests; the bartering of goods; a tavern; and central to and looming over all, the church. The children play ring-around-the-rosy, a singing rhyme and dance game whose Black Death origins were reflected in its final line, "All fall down!" (Photo from the Bettmann Archive.)

the same way and at the same time. Thus it was difficult for individual experimentation or initiative to emerge. The peasant/serfs, protected by a host of long-established traditions known as the "custom of the manor," were hardly slaves, though life for these people was neither comfortable nor pleasant. But the system did provide them security, as well as revenue for the church and the nobility. Undoubtedly, the lack of a larger, centralized governing authority made it the best and most suitable form of living to meet the needs of the time. Yet it also created a society of rich and poor—the manor did not produce middle classes of any type. Only in towns did the first indication of such groups appear.

The Christian Church

The role of religion in the medieval world was enormous, for life on earth was regarded as only a moment in terms of eternal existence. It was a brief "vale of tears" that must be passed through, its purpose the preparation for eternal life. The church was also the repository of knowledge preserved from previous generations and, as such, controlled education and learning. Only late in the medieval period did certain universities, though initially sponsored by the church, begin to act and teach independently.

Fear of hell and hope of heaven dominated the lives of medieval men and women. The wrath, the power, and the mystery of God were all too apparent in the world around them—in thunder and lightning, in famine-inducing droughts, in floods or blizzards, in the suddenness of death from unknown causes, in the recurrent epidemics of the "Black Death" that swept through Europe.

Those who could afford it sought to assuage their fears and assure their salvation by gifts, particularly of land, to the church—with the result that the church came to possess enormous power and wealth, which tended to make it extremely rigid and conservative. Yet historians have also suggested that the total dominance of Christianity in Europe during the medieval period was greatly responsible for the ultimate opening up of the world to scientific investigation and technological experimentation, both of which would be key to Europe's movement away from a society wedded to tradition and resistant to change.

Unlike the pagan religions that it had replaced, Christianity was not animistic in its teaching; it denied the concept of spirits existing in animals or inanimate elements and objects. Because wind, fire, grain, or cows contained in Christian teaching no essence or spirit of their own, human beings might acceptably examine them, experiment with them, and seek rationally to understand natural forces and objects. In fact the teachings of the church through the story of the Creation (and of Adam and Eve, specifically) gave to humans the right to control and manipulate everything else that existed on this earth. The concept that nature existed solely for the use and benefit of mankind, axiomatic in centuries of Christian teaching, became so thoroughly ingrained that even today people have difficulty considering seriously many of the pressing ecological problems that surround us. Yet this attitude also helps explain the fact that a sudden surge in technological development occurred in the last part of the medieval period. Christianity did, as most other religions did not, free humans to tinker with nature.[2]

The Renaissance

Out of the medieval world that had dominated Europe for centuries there emerged in the fourteenth through early seventeenth centuries a new, vitalized Europe, in which the process of change accelerated with ever increasing rapidity. Historians have traditionally labeled this period the Renaissance.

Renaissance means rebirth, reawakening, renewal, rediscovery. As such it seems a concept that looks backward rather than forward. Certainly in a cultural and intellectual sense this was originally true. What initially characterized the period and what gave it its name was a renewed and awakened interest in classical culture, in the mathematics, science, literature, arts, architecture, and philosophical thought of the Greek and Roman civilizations that had dominated the Mediterranean world for centuries preceding the medieval period. The Renaissance, in one very important sense, was clearly a resurrection of the past.

Particularly significant, however, was the fact that this "rediscovered" cultural heritage was primarily secular not religious, earthly and not other-worldly in its emphasis. The dignity of "man," the worthwhileness of the human endeavor on earth, again became the centerpiece or focus of attention. Inevitably this old/new development brought learning, education, the arts, and philosophy out from under the control of the Christian church. Secular-ization in these areas also opened the door for increased interest in science and technology—in the desire by humans to investigate and seek explanations for the natural phenomena in the world rather than merely accept them as mysterious manifestations of the will, power, and authority of God.

Rise of Trade and Commerce

The Renaissance was also characterized by the rapid growth of commercial cities and towns. Ultimately, first in Italy and later in northern Europe, political and economic power became concentrated in these urban centers rather than in the landed, feudal economic and social structure that continued to control the countryside. In Italy this transition manifested itself in the growing wealth and power of city-states like Florence, Genoa, and Venice. In northern Europe what can clearly be called national states were coming into existence by the latter sixteenth century.

What prompted this massive and relatively sudden set of changes? Without question the dynamic, motivating force that triggered all these developments was an enormous revival of trade and commerce, first in the Mediterranean area and subsequently along the North Atlantic seaboard. The wealth generated by these developments flowed to cities and towns that became the centers for economic exchange. It concentrated itself primarily in the hands of new, prosperous, urban business/merchant/banking classes. These classes, whose attention was focused more heavily on the affairs of this world than the next, had money to spend and wanted to spend it on a lavish secular life-style. To achieve this they commissioned work by architects, artists, musicians, goldsmiths, and tapestry weavers. No longer was the church the sole patron of the arts, as it had been for centuries.

The reasons for this revival of trade and commerce are complex and will not be examined in detail here. Suffice it to say that the decline of a once powerful and expansionist Arab-Muslim empire, the demise of the Eastern Christian Byzantine Empire, and the appearance in the Middle East of a new ruling group, the Ottoman Turks, opened the doors that allowed the transference of Mediterranean trade and commerce to the city-states of northern Italy. The Crusades of the eleventh, twelfth, and thirteenth centuries introduced western Europeans to new, exotic spices, fruits, and fabrics from the Middle East and generated subsequent demand for such items among the landed nobility. And the introduction of naval technology that replaced galleys and boarding forces with sails and artillery pieces opened up avenues first for Mediterranean and then for global expansion of trade and commerce.

It was no accident that this first wave of European global exploration, discovery, conquest, and exploitation coincided with the new view of the world and the escalation of technological innovation that characterized the Renaissance. The demand for riches and goods that motivated the expeditions of men such as Vasco da Gama, Christopher Columbus, Hernando Cortés, Ferdinand Magellan, and Richard Chancellor, as well as the ready availability of risk or "venture" capital to fund these projects, accurately reflects the secular spirit and mode of operation of this new era.

Humanism

Both in the city-states of the south and the emerging national states along the Atlantic coastline, there evolved during this period a growing emphasis on individualism and the study of human beings in their secular environment. This movement, aptly called humanism, emphasized the idea that human beings could rely on themselves and their intellect to improve the human condition. As people became more self-reliant and technological and scientific discoveries multiplied, the dominance of religion as a motivating factor in their lives decreased. It was inevitable that in time traditional church authority to pass judgment on matters relating to the secular and physical nature of the universe would be challenged. On no issue was this clearer than the question of whether the earth was the center of the universe.

This issue assumed major import because of the position taken in church tradition that God had created earth, his masterpiece, as the center of the universe and had then placed man (created in God's own image) and his companion, woman, on earth and given them control over it. The trial and condemnation of the Italian scientist and technologist Galileo Galilei by the Roman Catholic Inquisition in the early seventeenth century became symbolic of the conflict between traditional, theological views of the universe and new forces represented by reason, scientific investigation, and technology. Although Galileo was forced to recant his espousal of new theories that removed the earth from its primary position in the universe, theories that had been developed not so much by Galileo as by predecessors such as Nicolaus Copernicus and by contemporaries such as Johannes Kepler, his trial and the issues joined in it clearly reflected the conflict between religious and secular systems of authority, and old and new views of the nature and purpose of the universe.

In this imaginative woodcut, Copernicus and Galileo debate the movement of the galaxies with Ptolemy, the second-century Greco-Egyptian scientist and mathematician whose geocentric interpretation had asserted the special place of humans and earth at the center of the universe. The ultimate acceptance in the late sixteenth and early seventeenth centuries of the heliocentric view of the universe propounded by Copernicus and Galileo did much to undermine the influence of the Roman Catholic church and opened the door to the development of modern science, technology, and a secular view of the purpose and nature of human existence on this planet. (Photo from Zentners Illustrierte Weltgeschichte, Christian Zentner [Munich: Südwest Verlag München, 1972.])

Thus by the middle of the seventeenth century, Europe had in a sense done an about-face from the medieval world. Though the majority of people still lived on the land and remained bound to the traditional economic and social structure, the dynamic forces governing growth and change had shifted almost completely to the urban scene. And in that urban climate a new money- and credit-based economy flourished that was vastly different from the trade in kind that had dominated medieval agrarian society. New business middle classes created a secular, urban society that had minimal time for or inclination to accept the gloomy view of the world presented by medieval church theology. They were far too busy making fortunes on their own, and they looked forward to enjoying their wealth here on earth.

No longer was the nobility a class set totally apart. Wealth, culture, and education now joined family rank and birth to form new bases for social distinction and, more often than not, political power. By the mid-seventeenth century, political power had shifted to cities and national states, whose monarchs found support from emerging middle classes that applauded the end of the territorial fragmentation of the past and welcomed larger, more secure trade and market areas. Business initiative was recognized as a virtue. Ambition was legitimized. The resurrection of interest in both secular antiquity and the present world continued. Religion was no longer the binding force that it had been in the medieval scheme of things, where the purpose of human existence in this world was clearly understood and people's place in God's plan was unalterable and unquestionable.

Traditional Christianity Challenged

This growing emphasis on individualism, combined with the rising power of national monarchies, made it likely that the overarching doctrine and authority of the Roman Catholic church would sooner or later be challenged. The invention and growing use of the printing press in the late fifteenth century allowed ideas to be exchanged and generated more rapidly. Ultimately, during the sixteenth century a series of challenges, particularly those initiated by Martin Luther and John Calvin, splintered the monolithic Western church and led to the creation of a number of new, Protestant religious groups. Although these differed in theology and dogma, they had in common a rejection of the traditional institutional role of the Catholic church as guarantor of salvation through the use of ritual, conformity, and the total acceptance of hierarchical authority. Instead, the Protestants placed much more responsibility and emphasis on the role of the individual in developing a personal relationship with God. Attempts to achieve assurance of personal salvation would proceed from individual effort rather than institutional conformity.

Luther's emphasis on the separation of worldly and spiritual affairs and his willingness to accept the authority of princes or monarchs in secular affairs made his movement appealing to the rulers of the emerging sovereign German states. In a similar vein, the break with the Roman church engineered in England during the reign of King Henry VIII (1509–1547) represented not so much a theological split as the triumph of state authority over that of the church and the bringing of the latter under the direction and control of the former. The theology of Calvin stressed what later came to be known as the "Protestant work ethic," driven by the Calvinistic belief that the surest possible sign that one had been designated for eternal salvation was earthly success and material prosperity. These rewards, it was thought, God surely would bestow only on those predestined for salvation. Thus individualism, competition, capital accumulation, and concern with the secular affairs of this world, all regarded negatively in the medieval world, were now considered positive attributes in the new, "modern" society.

A word of caution must be entered here. If one excludes the religious divisions, the changes that have been presented thus far affected only a small segment of Europe's total population. The vast majority of people continued to live as peasant/serfs on the land in ways that varied only slightly from how their ancestors had lived for centuries. The impact of the new economic, political, scientific, technological, and intellectual forces unleashed during the late medieval and Renaissance periods would only begin to affect the masses in the latter eighteenth century and would culminate only with the triumph of industrialism in the nineteenth century.

The Scientific Revolution and the Enlightenment

The seeds of modernization were planted in the fourteenth through sixteenth centuries. It was only in the latter half of the seventeenth and the eighteenth centuries, however, that they came together in such a way as to revolutionize the European world and create a favorable climate for the rapid industrialization that would propel Europe into a position of global domination and leadership in the last decades of the nineteenth century. Important scientific and mathematical developments in the seventeenth century found themselves reflected in an eighteenth-century intellectual revolution so profound and all-encompassing that it is commonly referred to as the Enlightenment.

The end result was that for the scientific, intellectual, and cultural communities, the transition from the medieval "age of faith" that had begun several centuries earlier was now complete. Belief in traditional religious theology was replaced by a new faith, equally total and equally compelling, a faith in science and reason. It was now thought that human beings, using the analytical tools provided by mathematicians such as René Descartes and Gottfried Wilhelm von Leibniz and the techniques of investigation developed by theorists like Francis Bacon and scientists like Isaac Newton, could come to understand the laws by which nature operated. By putting their lives in harmony with these laws, people could progress toward the creation of a perfect society here on earth, if not immediately, then at some time in the future. In other words, using the tools of science, mathematics, technology, and reason, human beings could in time fully control their own destiny and environment. Hope for the future was essentially a human and secular matter, religious doctrines relating to life in a nonworldly heaven were unnecessary. One lived eternally through one's posterity; in a sense heaven could be created on earth by human beings themselves.

The function of God was relegated to the past, to the role of a creator who made the world, got it running, placed humans on it, and turned its destiny over to them. *Deism*, as it was called, saw God as a great engineer who had created a universe that operated like a perpetual motion machine in accordance with the laws of nature. Human beings, using the rational tools of deduction and induction and applying the scientific method of investigation (hypothesis ⟶ experimentation ⟶ observation ⟶ generalization) should rigorously examine all aspects of the natural world around them. If indeed the world were a sort of machine, running according to "natural law," then humans could discover these laws. Nature could be understood—witness the discovery of the law of falling bodies by Galileo or the demonstration by Newton that the laws of force and motion applied in the heavens in the same way they did on earth. And perhaps nature, once understood, could be tamed by the combination of reason and scientific knowledge applied through technology (for example, Benjamin Franklin's development of the lightning rod).

If all this were true for the environment in which people lived, how equally true must it be for human beings themselves? Thus the intellectuals of the Enlightenment, led by a group of French thinkers who called themselves *philosophes*, advocated that all aspects of the human condition be subjected to careful scrutiny and analysis according to the test of reason and logic. If found wanting, they should be discarded forthwith and replaced by conditions and systems that could pass muster. Political theories and forms of government, religious institutions and the theological principles that supported them, social classes and the traditions and laws that justified them, any and all aspects of human life, endeavor, knowledge, and experience should be put to the test. "The proper study of Mankind," wrote Alexander Pope, "is Man."

Although the thinkers of the Enlightenment had no difficulty finding much to condemn in the world around them, they were not equally clear as to how, and with what, the concepts and systems they denounced should be replaced. One example will suffice. The *philosophes* were agreed in their rejection of the existing, rigid, class structure and the divine-right theory of absolute monarchy that had long justified the rule of the crowned heads of

This romanticized and historically questionable portrayal of the storming of the Bastille, a royal fortress and prison, on July 14, 1789, nonetheless accurately reflects the intensity, emotion, and violence that characterized many of the economic and class conflicts that marked the French Revolution. Bastille Day, as a current national holiday in France, has a comparable significance to the Fourth of July in the United States. (Photo from the Bettmann Archive.)

European continental states. For some, the answer lay in recognizing and delineating certain fundamental, inalienable human rights and in establishing a government that would grant ultimate political power to a large segment of the population, which in turn would exercise its authority through a smaller body of elected representatives. Out of this approach sprang such documents as the American Declaration of Independence and Bill of Rights, and the 1789 French Declaration of the Rights of Man and the Citizen.

Other *philosophes*, distrusting profoundly the political acumen and judgment of the masses, opted instead for a new type of absolute monarchy called "enlightened despotism." The monarch would rule not in the medieval sense of being God's representative on earth with a divine mandate to govern secular affairs, but rather as the first servant of the state, who would govern as an absolute monarch in the best interest of all members of society within guidelines provided by the new rationalist doctrines of the Enlightenment. When asked why he rejected the concept of an elected parliament or assembly, the French philosopher Voltaire is reputed to have replied that he would rather be governed by one lion than a hundred rats. Just as our democratic, representative forms of government in the twentieth century are firmly rooted in the ideas of the Enlightenment, so also are ideas that have often justified modern forms of dictatorship in which the ruling establishment claims the right to govern autocratically in the interest and name of the masses.

The scientific and intellectual revolution that characterized the latter seventeenth and the eighteenth century was very much a middle-class affair. Some members of the nobility did participate, but the generating force came from the rising business and professional classes. By the end of the eighteenth century, they had been able to translate these new ideas, in conjunction with their growing economic power, into new, more representative forms of political authority in Great Britain and its former colony, the United States. The revolutionary and Napoleonic period in France (1789–1815), though at the time regarded as unsuccessful, had left such a strong ideological imprint, not only on France but on much of Europe, that any effort to return permanently to traditional, conservative political and social systems was doomed to failure.

Modern Industrial Society

It was also during the eighteenth century that Europe's permanent transition from an agrarian to an industrialized, urban society began. During the nineteenth century the success of this process eventually led Europe to a position of global economic, political, and cultural dominance. By the end of the century, the benefits of the industrial age were becoming available to an increasingly broad spectrum of society. The widening dissemination of the fruits of modernization, gradual though it was, heralded the advent of mass culture, mass education, and mass political participation—forces that would wield incredible influence in the twentieth-century world.

The Impact of Industrialization

During the nineteenth century the pace of modernization accelerated as the need to adapt institutions to perform new functions required by the expansion of scientific and technical knowledge rapidly grew. Tensions between tradition and modernity caused a wide range of problems, but gradually traditional practices and institutions were altered and new approaches tried. For example, large landowners in Great Britain, responding to an escalating demand for food to feed the urban, industrial population, often decided to "enclose" the land on their estates in order to create large fields on which crops could be grown more efficiently and with a higher yield. In turn, many peasant farmers or laborers, deprived of their traditional rights of free access to pasturage and woodlots on their landlord's estate once these portions were enclosed, found themselves unable to survive and fled to the cities in a desperate search for

Built in 1889 to commemorate the hundredth anniversary of the French Revolution, the Eiffel Tower was also intended to symbolize the dominance and superiority of the new society created by the industrial revolution and the technology of industrial production. The sense of omnipotence implied in the strength of its severe, structural steel architecture accurately reflects the Social Darwinian, elitist arrogance of Europe's age of triumphant optimism. (Photo from the Bettmann Archive.)

industrial employment. On the national level, an economic customs union, known as the Zollverein, was created among the north German states in order to promote trade and provide larger markets for industry. However, it also succeeded in creating an integrative economic environment conducive to helping achieve the subsequent political unification of Germany.

The surge of industrial development that characterized this period was more an evolutionary than a revolutionary process, if one views it only as a rational, progressive development of technological knowledge, invention, and implementation. The revolutionary aspect of industrialization lay not in the development of the reciprocating steam engine or, later, the internal combustion engine or the use of electrical power. Nor did it lie in the creation of machine technology that was hundreds of times more efficient than earlier forms of production that had depended primarily on direct expenditure of human energy. Even the development of the machine tool industry, which permitted the standardization and exchangeability of parts, though it clearly reflected the new spirit of experimentation and innovation, was in itself hardly "revolutionary."

If indeed a "revolution" was created by industrialization in the late eighteenth and the nineteenth centuries, it stemmed from the impact that these new technological developments had on the structure of society and the way a majority of people came to live. Over the centuries, cottage or domestic means of production had become more and more sophisticated and specialized. The advent of a capitalistic, entrepreneurial system that administered and financed commodity production had introduced to the manufacturing and marketing process a managerial class and rudimentary forms of capital investment procedures. But the center of the productive process had remained the home or peasant cottage, and the basic labor unit continued to be the family. By the eighteenth century, specialization had developed to the point where many families performed only one or two of the many tasks required in order to finish a product. Nonetheless, there remained inherent problems resulting from the necessary transfer of goods from one site to another and the inability of those in charge to supervise effectively the work habits and procedures of those performing the labor.

The Factory System

All these problems were solved by the creation of the factory system of production. Now goods remained in one place as they were transformed from raw materials into finished products. Laborers were brought together in large buildings where they could be supervised, their working hours controlled and regulated, and their output and productivity levels constantly watched and evaluated. The availability of energy resources that could run dozens, or even hundreds, of machines placed under one roof made all this possible. In turn, the factory system promoted the production of more goods more efficiently and much more quickly than had ever been the case in the past.

The factory system also meant that instead of material being taken to peasant homes or cottages to be worked on, laborers had to move to where the goods were. Living close to factories, they wound up crowded into industrial urban slums, where housing was wretched and sanitary conditions abominable. No longer able to supplement their income with a garden plot or as hired laborers on landed estates and lacking the facilities to keep a few chickens, a pig, or a cow, working-class families became solely dependent on the hourly wage they received. Loss of work meant starvation. Families therefore regarded it as necessary and important that all members, including young children, seek and gain employment wherever they could find it, working whatever shifts were available. The concept of the family as a cohesive labor unit disappeared.

During this time, nation after nation in Europe experienced a sudden, rapid surge in the development of industry. The first, and the leader throughout most of the period, was Great Britain; the last was the conservative, traditional, autocratic state of Russia, where the acceleration of industrial development only appeared in the last two decades of the nineteenth century. Some states and areas, particularly in what we today refer to as Eastern Europe and the Balkans, did not experience it at all. But for most of the nations of Western Europe—with the exception of Spain and Portugal—the nineteenth century saw a permanent shift from an agrarian to an industrial economy. Peasants left the countryside in droves, both attracted by the potential of jobs in the new urban industrial world and pushed by the enclosures and technological development of more effective and efficient mechanized ways of farming, ways that produced more and required far less human labor than in the past.

Socialism

It was out of the same industrial, urbanized conditions that a new set of economic, social, and political doctrines emerged that attempted to represent the concerns and interests of the industrial working classes. Organizationally manifested in the development of labor unions, these concerns found expression ideologically through a multitude of doctrines that can be loosely grouped under the heading of socialism. Moderate movements, such as Fabian and revisionist socialism, sought to bring about change and reform gradually through education and participation in existing political systems and processes. Extreme, radical, activist doctrines advocated the revolutionary overthrow of the middle classes and seizure of the means of production by the workers. The most terroristic and violent were the Anarchists; the most historical and theoretical the Marxists, with their doctrines of historical materialism, class struggle, and the inevitable triumph of communism and the industrial proletariat over capitalism and the bourgeois middle classes.

The Era of Triumphant Optimism

The economic stimulus generated by the spread of industrialism was also instrumental in bringing about an intensification of nationalism in the nineteenth century. The separate German and Italian states became united into single, major national states. Conversely, a rising tide of nationalist sentiment weakened and threatened the very existence of the ethnically diverse Austro-Hungarian and Ottoman empires. National pride and patriotism replaced old loyalties to one's community, region, or religious denomination as the dominating collective ethos in society. When Charles Darwin developed and publicized his theories of the biological evolution of species, nations were quick to seize on concepts such as the inevitable struggle for survival between species and natural selection within species. Twisting

Europe Prior to World War I

Darwin's theories far beyond legitimacy and almost beyond recognition, national patriotic theorists developed a set of concepts that came to be labeled as Social Darwinism. Domestically, these were often used to support elitist theories of gender, class and social distinctions, and group relationships. Internationally, they justified competition between national states at all levels, including war; legitimized the conquest of "inferior" races by the "fitter" Caucasian race; and even encouraged the totally spurious concept that one could identify and talk seriously about a British, French, or German "race."

The technological superiority, enormous personal and national wealth, and unbridled self-confidence prompted by the scientific, technological, and attitudinal components of triumphant modernization in Europe received its ultimate expression in the wave of European imperial conquest during the late nineteenth century, the results of which were described briefly at the beginning of this chapter. Imperial success seemed to prove beyond any doubt the total superiority of Europe's political, social, military, economic, religious, and cultural systems. Those parts of the world that were not directly controlled by European nations blatantly looked to Europe for leadership and direction in terms of modernizing their own societies. This was especially evident in the efforts of the United States, Japan, and tsarist Russia, though of course Russian leaders had long regarded their nation as being an integral part of, rather than apart from, Europe, and in this they were probably right.

Looking back, historians have been tempted to point out that Europe, as it entered the twentieth century, was indeed headed for a fall. The arrogant, smug complacency with which Europeans collectively viewed themselves and their society in comparison with the rest of the world led them virtually to ignore the rising tide of nationalism that threatened to turn Europe's member states against one another. Indeed, nationalism had already created a cauldron of seething ethnic rivalries in Eastern Europe and the Balkans. The laboring classes had only recently begun to derive some tangible economic benefits from the growth of industrialism, and these limited gains only made them hunger for more. Economic competition; imperial rivalries and ambitions; restless subject ethnic groups; massive arms buildups; a wide and increasing gulf between the economically well-off and the poor; the potentially explosive combination of nationalism and social Darwinism—all these and more can be seen in retrospect as warning signs that all was not well in Europe as it entered the first decades of the twentieth century.

Yet it also must be recognized that the course of European history from the fourteenth through the nineteenth centuries had created a situation in which, viewed from almost any aspect or angle one might choose, European nations did indeed hold preeminent positions of power, wealth, and influence. In European eyes, this patent supremacy thoroughly justified their collective view of themselves as the patricians of the human race, destined permanently to lead and administer the rest of the world. Not only was this their manifest destiny, but it promised a future, they were sure, that would clearly be to the benefit of all concerned.

Notes

1. P. Branca and P. Stearns, *Modernization of Women in the Nineteenth Century* (1973), pp. 1–2.
2. L. White, Jr., "The Historical Roots of Our Ecological Crisis" in *Dynamo and Virgin Reconsidered* (1971), pp. 75–94.

Suggested Readings

Modernization and European History

Apter, D. E., *The Politics of Modernization* (1965).
Black, C. E., *The Dynamics of Modernization* (1966).
––––––– (ed.), *Comparative Modernization: A Reader* (1976).
Eisenstadt, S. N., *Modernization: Growth and Diversity* (1963).
–––––––, *Patterns of Modernity*, 2 vols. (1987).
Levy, M. J., Jr., *Modernization and the Structure of Society: A Setting for International Affairs*, 2 vols. (1966).
–––––––, *Modernization: Latecomers and Survivors* (1972).
Von Laue, T. H., *The World Revolution of Westernization: The Twentieth Century in Global Perspective* (1988).

The Medieval World

Barraclough, G., *The Crucible of Europe: The Ninth and Tenth Centuries in European History* (1976).
Gottfried, R. S., *The Black Death* (1983).
Heer, F., *The Medieval World: Europe, 1100–1350* (1964).
Herrin, J., *The Formation of Christendom* (1987).
Perroy, E., *The Hundred Years' War* (1965).
Tuchman, B., *A Distant Mirror: The Calamitous Fourteenth Century* (1978).
White, L., Jr., *Dynamo and Virgin Reconsidered: Essays in the Dynamism of Western Culture* (1971).
–––––––, *Medieval Technology and Social Change* (1962).

The Renaissance

Bainton, R., *Here I Stand: A Life of Martin Luther* (1955).
Bowsma, W., *John Calvin: A Sixteenth Century Portrait* (1988).

Cipolla, C., *Before the Industrial Revolution: European Society and Economy, 1000–1700* (1980).
―――, *Guns, Sails and Empires: Technological Innovation and the Early Phases of European Expansion, 1400–1700* (1965).
Drake, S., *Galileo* (1980).
Ginzburg, G., *The Cheese and the Worms: The Cosmos of a Sixteenth Century Miller* (1980).
Huizinga, J., *The Waning of the Middle Ages* (1954).
Kristeller, P., *Renaissance Thought and Its Sources* (1979).
Mattingly, G., *Renaissance Diplomacy* (1971).
Plumb, J. H., *The Italian Renaissance* (1965).
Weber, M., *The Protestant Ethic and the Spirit of Capitalism* (1958).

The Scientific Revolution and the Enlightenment

Butterfield, H., *The Origins of Modern Science* (1949).
Gagliardo, J., *Enlightened Despotism* (1967).
Goubert, P., *Louis XIV and Twenty Million Frenchmen* (1970).
Hazard, P., *The European Mind, 1680–1715* (1963).
Krieger, L., *Kings and Philosophers, 1689–1789* (1970).
Kuhn, T., *The Structure of Scientific Revolutions* (1962).

Modern Industrial Society

Ashton, T. S., *The Industrial Revolution* (1968).
Branca, P., and P. Stearns, *Modernization of Women in the Nineteenth Century* (1973).
Gildea, R., *Barricades and Borders: Europe, 1800–1914* (1987).
Hobsbawm, E. J., *The Age of Revolution, 1789–1848* (1962).
Landes, C., *Unbound Prometheus: Technological Change and Industrial Development in Western Europe from 1750 to the Present* (1969).
Mosse, G., *The Culture of Western Europe: The Nineteenth and Twentieth Centuries* (1961).
Schivelbusch, W., *The Railway Journey: The Industrialization of Time and Space in the Nineteenth Century* (1986).
Stromberg, R., *European Intellectual History Since 1789* (1975).
Tilly, L., and J. Scott, *Women, Work and Family* (1978).

The Era of Triumphant Optimism

Betts, R., *The False Dawn: European Imperialism in the Nineteenth Century* (1975).
Headrick, D., *The Tools of Empire: Technology and European Imperialism in the Nineteenth Century* (1981).
Tuchman, B., *The Proud Tower: A Portrait of the World Before the War, 1890–1914* (1966).

CHAPTER TWO

Europe in Crisis:
1900–1945

The Decline of Europe

The First World War
Changing Attitudes Toward War • Postwar Europe

Communism, Fascism, and National Socialism
The Soviet Union • Italy • Germany

The Second World War
Strategic Decisions • Unconditional Surrender
Partition of Germany

Europe Shattered and Destroyed

Notes

Suggested Readings

The Decline of Europe

The year 1945 has often been regarded as the major dividing point in the history of the twentieth century. It was in this year that Europe and the world emerged from the long and desperate struggle that historians have named the Second World War. A war that had begun in Asia in 1937 and in Europe in 1939 finally came to a close, leaving as its legacy not only loss of life and physical destruction unparalleled in the annals of warfare but also the horrors created by the systematic attempt on the part of Nazi Germany to eliminate all Jews in Europe.

Militarily, the war had been fought on a scope and with an intensity and technological capacity for destruction never before experienced. Ushering in the age of air power, the war had completely blurred previous distinctions between combatant and civilian and had eliminated the concept of safety behind the lines. In its waning days it witnessed the dropping of the atomic bomb on Hiroshima, Japan—killing 50,000 persons immediately—and on Nagasaki. Derived from a new and terrifying source of power, the bomb threatened an unlimited capacity for destruction in the future.

Economically, the war had demonstrated that in conflicts between industrialized states the strength of a nation in terms of its resources, industry, transportation, and labor was as important as the specific size of its military establishment. In the world that emerged in 1945, so great was the physical and financial devastation in most of Europe that all meaningful power came to rest in the hands of political and military leaders operating out of Washington and Moscow, capitals of nations closely linked to Europe (and in the case of Moscow, part of Europe) but drawing much of their strength from non-European sources. After having dominated world affairs for centuries, Europe suddenly found itself the puppet rather than the puppeteer, dancing on strings to tunes played by the two powers whose size, industrial development, and economic strength made them simultaneously masters of and rivals for the entire globe.

Small wonder, then, that political analysts and historians in the years following the war tended to regard the history of events prior to its outbreak as having limited relevance to the postwar situation. The impact of the war had been so cataclysmic, they asserted, that the world that had emerged could be understood only as its product. But as years went by and historians gained greater perspective on the war and the world that came out of it, their views began to change. Although no one would argue that the Second World War did not have a shattering impact on European and global history, the majority of scholars now hold that the history of prewar Europe helps greatly to explain the course of events since 1945.

26

The First World War

There is much evidence that for Europe the long-term impact of World War II, great as it was, was not as devastating as that of World War I—the tragic conflict occurring between 1914 and 1918 that Europeans still refer to as "the Great War." Neither the destruction nor the loss of life incurred then came near to that of the Second World War. Yet the manner in which the First World War was fought, the very nature of the conflict and its economic consequences, came as such a shock and surprise to all Europeans, leaders and masses alike, that the psychological impact and reactions brought into question the basic values and axioms that had governed Europe's attitude toward itself and its place in the world for several centuries.

We have already seen that the rise, development, and worldwide influence of the culture, technology, and political structures characteristic of the modern world were created in large measure by the peoples of Europe, especially Western Europe. From the time modern Western civilization emerged out of the medieval world and began its process of global expansion, it was the Europeans, and the nation-states they created, who led the developmental process. They held in their hands not only their own destinies but also those of the peoples and areas they discovered, conquered, and colonized as their wealth, power, and technological expertise steadily grew.

Never was this more true than in the century preceding the outbreak of World War I. The growing economic and political dominance of a new industrial middle class over the traditional landed aristocracy led to an increasing self-confidence among those responsible for directing the affairs of nations. Ultimately, fueled by rapid industrial development, remnants of rationalistic eighteenth-century faith in the perfectibility of humans in their society, and the pseudo-scientific concepts of social Darwinism, this self-confidence turned to self-satisfaction and even arrogance. The result was a belief in the certainty of Europe's destiny to rule the world and to control, for the good of all, the future of its peoples. The success of the late nineteenth-century wave of European imperialistic expansion, resulting in the conquest and partitioning of Africa, parts of southeastern Asia, and the extension of spheres of influence in China, only served to confirm Europe's sense of its own manifest destiny. Even the expansion and growth in power of such peripheral nations as Russia and the United States were regarded positively, for the governing elite of the former was viewed as European and the latter country had derived its culture and most of its people from European sources.

All of this came to a dramatic and sudden end as the result of the great struggle among the nations of Europe between 1914 and 1918. Given Europe's global influence, other nations of the world were drawn in; but the war was in its origins and course essentially a European conflict. Brought on by a rising tide of nationalism that led European states to believe in the legitimacy

Resplendent in uniforms reflecting an age of confidence that within months would be shattered by the unforeseen horrors of industrial-age warfare, German Kaiser Wilhelm II and his six sons march proudly in the annual Berlin New Year's parade in January 1914. (Photo courtesy of the German Information Center.)

of competition for supremacy among themselves, the nation-states were uncertain as to how the rapid industrialization of the nineteenth century had altered the balance of power that had emerged in 1815 out of the French Revolution and Napoleonic conflicts. The rapid development of the newly unified state of Germany, plus the appearance of a united Italy, only served to reduce small-state buffer zones between the large powers, create new rivalries, and increase the general uncertainty.

Changing Attitudes Toward War

Added to this was an almost cavalier attitude toward war itself. War was regarded as a legitimate means of solving problems between states. It was seen as synonymous with adventure, as a cleansing mechanism by which old issues could be settled and "progress" got on with. Populations tended to view wars and military action as the most important, most glorious part of their country's history. War was, after all, an inevitable part of existence—part of the routine struggle for survival that nineteenth-century science seemed to have con-firmed as one of the immutable laws of nature. As Ernst Renan commented:

The horrors of trench warfare during World War I are tragically summed up in this photograph. Mud, rats, lice, and human remains dominated a stagnant battleline where for four years soldiers on both sides dug deep into the earth and tried to survive, leading lives that were a mixture of stultifying boredom and excruciating fear. (Photo from the Bettmann Archive.)

"War is in a way one of the conditions of progress, the cut of the whip which prevents a country from going to sleep, forcing satisfied mediocrity itself to leave its apathy."[1]

There was also the conviction, firmly held at the beginning of the twentieth century, that future wars between industrialized nations would be short, violent contests that could not last long because of the incredible cost of modern weapons and the terrible destruction they would wreak. Thus when war broke out in the summer of 1914, the peoples and nations of Europe entered the conflict with almost a sense of relief, coupled with an enthusiasm that today stretches the bounds of our credibility. Tensions that had plagued Europe for decades would finally be settled, it was thought; in any case, it would all be over by Christmas.

"Now, God be thanked Who has matched us with His hour, / And caught our youth, and wakened us from sleeping," wrote British poet Rupert Brooke in his poem "1914."[2] Four years later, Wilfred Owen, after describing a poison gas attack would write:

If you could hear, at every jolt, the blood
Come gargling from the froth-corrupted lungs,
Bitter as the cud
Of vile, incurable sores on innocent tongues,—
My friend, you would not tell with such high zest
To children ardent for some desperate glory,
The old Lie: *Dulce et decorum est*
Pro patria mori.[3]

In his classic account of trench warfare, *All Quiet on the Western Front*, the German novelist Erich Maria Remarque wrote of the total sense of loss experienced by those who fought in the war—of their complete disillusionment with the values and standards of the past and of the sense of betrayal they felt toward those who had taught them to believe in those values. The psychological impact of the four-year standoff in the west (the eastern front was far more mobile), in which hundreds of thousands of young men on both sides fought and died with no meaningful movement of the lines, created a bitterness and cynicism felt equally by victors and vanquished. In 1922 the French writer Paul Valéry echoed these feelings in a poignant statement:

> The storm has ended, yet we are restless, anxious, as if the storm were about to break. Nearly all human affairs dwell in a state of terrible uncertainty. We reflect on what has disappeared, we are almost destroyed by what has been destroyed; we do not know what will come to pass, and we fear it with good reason. We hope vaguely, we dread precisely; our fears are infinitely more precise than our hopes; we confess that the sweetness of life is behind us, that affluence is behind us, but that disorder and doubt are in us and with us. . . . The Mind has in truth been cruelly wounded; it whimpers in the hearts of men of intellect and sadly judges itself. It doubts itself profoundly.[4]

Britain, France, and Italy, buoyed by the addition in 1917 and 1918 of fresh troops and supplies from the United States, were able ultimately to force Germany and its allies to surrender and to accept a dictated peace settlement. But in a real sense it was Europe as a whole that had lost the war. Four great empires that had ruled Eastern and Central Europe and the Near East for centuries came to an end. The Ottoman and Austro-Hungarian empires were replaced in the name of national self-determination by smaller, struggling states. The German and Russian empires, reduced in size from their prewar territorial configurations, found themselves reconstituted under new forms of government and saddled with enormous economic problems. Even victorious countries such as France, Italy, Belgium, and Great Britain emerged badly shaken by the material, financial, and human damage wrought by the war. What had been destroyed throughout Europe was an outlook, a sense of supremacy, a self-confident belief in the correctness of the ideals, methods, and forms of government that had dominated the growth and development of Europe for centuries.

Postwar Europe

Despite the assertion of U.S. President Woodrow Wilson that the war was fought to "make the world safe for democracy," Europeans in general, and their leaders in particular, remained suspicious of such messianic pronouncements. Thus they tended to view many postwar institutions, including the League of Nations and the Permanent Court of International Justice, with deep-seated skepticism. From the European victors' perspective, peace and security could best be achieved by disarming the losers and forcing them to pay reparations so extensive that their ability to regain economic health would be impaired. With the failure of the United States to join the League of Nations, and that country's subsequent retreat to an isolationist stance in the 1920s, the European search for security through traditional political and military alliances intensified. The idealism of Woodrow Wilson, never really accepted in Europe, vanished like an enticing mirage.

In its place appeared a growing sense of insecurity, pessimism, and disillusionment with past values and standards. Long-term goals, political ideologies, the concept of sacrificing or working for the future—all these became suspect. With the exception of a few idealists who placed perhaps unreasonable hope in the new governments created in the successor states to the old empires, the European peoples rejected the past, feared the future, and believed only in the reality of the present. Distrusting the political institutions and leadership that had dominated before the war, those who had fought and survived were more often than not ready to support any person and any system that could provide them with the only things they knew to be real and important—food, clothing, shelter, comfort—not promised for the future but available in the present.

Nonetheless, had it not been for another major crisis, the wounds of Europe might have healed well enough to allow growth of a liberal, parliamentary, middle-class-dominated society. But in 1929 the great crash in the U.S. stock market triggered a series of events that by 1932–1933 had escalated into a global economic depression of a proportion and scope unique in the annals of modern industrial society. Seeking to combat its effects, every nation in the world moved toward greater centralization of economic and governmental control. National regulatory policies and welfare programs replaced the relatively unfettered free enterprise system that had prevailed until then.

Whatever confidence there had been in existing political systems was severely eroded. In those countries of Central and Eastern Europe where democratic, parliamentary institutions and traditions were relatively new, fragile, and not well entrenched, they routinely succumbed before a swing

The Big Four at Paris: Prime Ministers Vittorio Orlando of Italy, Lloyd George of Great Britain, Georges Clemenceau of France, and President Woodrow Wilson of the United States conferring during the peace conference of 1919. Seeking solutions to post–World War I problems ranging from the German peace treaty to the partition of the Ottoman Empire, these statesmen inaugurated a new era of summit diplomacy. (Photo from Bernard Baruch Papers, Princeton University Libraries.)

toward greater centralization, authority, and control by a single party or individual. The right to vote paled in significance before the right to work and the right to eat. World War I had wrought vast destruction and accelerated many of the inherent authoritarian tendencies of European society. Italy and several other countries fell into patterns of dictatorial control well before the economic crash. It was, however, the depression that dealt the final blow to the way of life Europe had known at the start of the century.

Communism, Fascism, and National Socialism

The Soviet Union

In the opinion of many Europeans, one nation and one nation only seemed impervious to the global economic crisis of the 1930s. That nation was the

Driven by his vision of a Communist Russia, V. I. Lenin, shown here with his family, put his own indelible stamp on Marxist theory and personally engineered a revolution in 1917–1919 that for the first time united Communist theory with a national political and economic power base. (Photo from the Bettmann Archive.)

Soviet Union, where the combination of a revolution, a political ideology, and a ruthless authoritarian governing structure appeared to have created a new, powerful, industrial giant out of a state that at the turn of the century had lagged behind other European societies. Russia had experienced little of the simultaneous movement toward liberalism and industrialism that had characterized the nineteenth century for most of Western Europe. Rapid economic growth after the 1880s had not been matched in Russia by the development of civil liberties and political participation. By the outbreak of the First World War, Russia resembled a pressure cooker under which the flames of revolutionary unrest had been steadily building for decades, but on which the conservative tsarist monarchy up until that time had kept the lid.

The war proved to be the catalyst that brought on a revolution that many historians believe would have occurred in some form sooner or later. The political ineffectiveness and economic inefficiency evidenced by the Russian government in pursuing the war against Germany ultimately triggered a series of revolutionary attempts resulting in the overthrow of the tsar in March 1917 and in the seizure of power eight months later by the Bolshevik wing of the Social Democratic party, under the leadership of V. I. Lenin. For the first time, a party dedicated to the nineteenth-century, antiliberal, Communist ideology of Karl Marx had been able to attain control of the government of a major world nation.

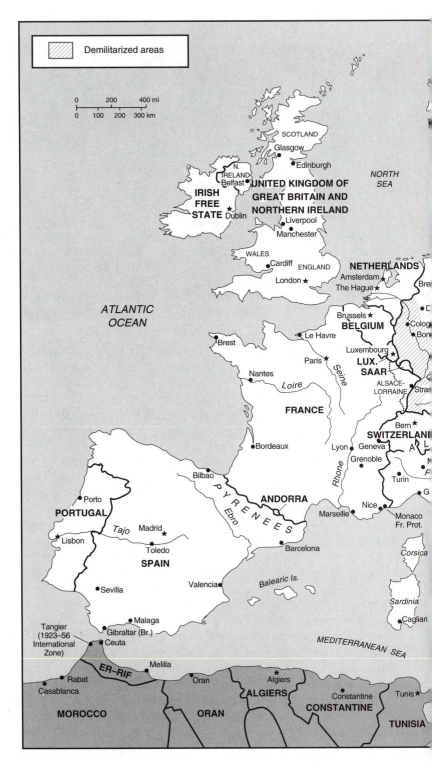

Europe in the Interwar Period

This sequence of events, which gave a power base to a political ideology advocating an economic view of history that called for the elimination of capitalism and the class that dominated it, greatly alarmed both the United States and Western Europe. The result was that in the immediate postwar years, the Western powers provided some limited military and economic support to the anti-Bolshevik forces in the Russian Civil War of 1918–1920. They also consciously supported the creation of a network of nations in Central Europe that ranged from Finland in the north to Romania in the south and included several of the successor states to the old empires. This network formed a barrier, or *cordon sanitaire*, intended to prevent the spread of communism. Today, most historians agree that the Cold War as we know it began in 1919–1920 rather than after the Second World War. The 1941–1945 alliance between the Western democracies and the Soviet Union, created in order to meet the common challenge of fascism and national socialism, is seen as only a temporary, if necessary, hiatus in the larger rivalry that characterized much of world politics in the twentieth century.

The task of seizing and holding control in Russia was not an easy one for the Bolsheviks. Even less so was the goal of the Communist regime to create an industrial base that would allow Russia to proceed along the ideological path toward a classless society, based on industrial production, which was central to the Marxist view of inevitable historical progression. That Russia had not yet experienced the extended period of middle-class, bourgeois, capitalist domination required in Marxist historical theory made the attainment of a communistic society seem doubly difficult.

But the Marxist canon, though remaining true to its Socialist roots in advocating a democratic, nonexploitative society as its ultimate goal, did allow for a period of adjustment under a temporary, authoritarian dictatorship after the proletariat's seizure of power. To adapt this concept to a Russian society still dominated before 1917 by a traditional divine-right monarchy supported by a land-based aristocracy, Lenin argued that it was possible to telescope the historical process during this interim period of temporary authoritarian governance. Instead of a prolonged bourgeois capitalistic period followed by a proletariat takeover of established industrial means of production, the new proletarian dictatorship could simultaneously eradicate the old aristocratic and capitalistic exploiting classes, create the needed industrial base, and educate the workers for their new role as ultimate controllers of the means of production. The mechanism for achieving this would be a comparatively small but well-trained, disciplined, tightly organized, totally loyal, and committed Communist party.

It was this Marxist-Leninist view of the "dictatorship of the proletariat" that enabled the authoritarian regime of Josef Stalin to emerge in the 1930s with a degree of total control perhaps not matched by any society before or since. The creation of the Soviet police state enabled Stalin to change the basic form of landholding to state and communal ownership, thereby eliminating a large and prosperous body of independent peasant landholders. The reorganization also made it possible to put enormous sums of money, expropriated through state control of agricultural production, into the development of heavy industry such as mining, steel, and electricity. Because its political isolation forced the Soviet Union to find capital for its industrial five-year plans solely from internal sources, the country was able in the 1930s to remain apart from the global economic crisis and also to weather severe difficulties within its own planned economy.

The price paid was the disappearance of political and personal freedom within the Soviet Union. Yet for those who could avoid prison and labor camps, there were plenty of jobs available. To millions of workers around the world who were unemployed and facing near starvation for themselves and their families, the Soviet regime therefore became a symbol of apparent economic success at a time when capitalism had been found wanting. The result was the rapid growth in Western Europe of strong, politically active Communist parties, whose avowed aim was the ultimate overthrow of capitalism and the global triumph of communism and the economic system it advocated. Under the aegis of the Communist International (otherwise known as the Comintern or Third International, formed in 1919), all these parties had direct ties with Moscow and were bound to follow directives emanating from the Soviet capital.

The growing strength of Communist parties in Western Europe inevitably spawned a conservative, nationalistic, political reaction. Although this began in the 1920s, the advent of the economic depression in the 1930s greatly accelerated the process. Dissatisfied with existing parliamentary regimes for both political and economic reasons, and apprehensive of growing Communist strength among the working classes, increasing numbers of the middle and upper classes turned toward the political Right and to the authoritarian premises upon which its programs were based. In many areas, including the Iberian Peninsula and most of the smaller countries of Central Europe, this shift resulted in the formation of traditional military or party dictatorships. The most important of these conventional, authoritarian governments was the military regime of General Francisco Franco, who attained control in Spain after a three-year civil war that began in 1936. But in two cases the swing to the right produced new forms of government, governments that justified their existence from ideological bases equally hostile to communism, socialism, and liberal democracy.

Italy

The first to make a major public impact was Italian fascism, under the leadership of Benito Mussolini. The Fascist movement arose out of the chaos in Italy following World War I. It stemmed from national resentment over what Italians regarded as shoddy treatment of Italy at the peace conference, plus apprehension on the part of the Italian upper and middle classes about the growing power of Communist labor unions in the industrial cities of northern Italy.

Taking power in 1922, the Fascists proceeded to create a one-party state, the aim of which was to organize every aspect of Italian life into a corporate state structure based on military precepts and the view that the individual exists only to serve the state. Antidemocratic, the Fascists adopted as their guiding principle the concept of elitism, maintaining that those who were superior should by right rule those who were less capable, unfettered by such practices as representative forms of government, free speech, or freedom of the press.

Germany

Fascism was followed in 1933 by the advent to power in Germany of Adolf Hitler and national socialism. Although the Nazi party had been in existence since the early 1920s, until 1929–1930 it received little support. It was the economic hardship and massive unemployment brought on by the Great Depression that led millions of Germans to repudiate the democratic Weimar government and turn to Hitler's authoritarian one-party state system. Militantly anti-Bolshevik, Hitler promised to quell the Communist movement, end unemployment, and restore Germany to its "rightful" position as a great power. Germany, Hitler maintained, would finally be freed from the disgraceful and illegal conditions wrongfully imposed upon it by the victorious powers in the Treaty of Versailles following the First World War.

Like fascism, nazism was based on antidemocratic, elitist principles. Unlike fascism, which emphasized the corporate state as an organic entity, nazism took as its central purpose the furtherance of the German *Volk*, or nation. By this was meant not the state as a geographical or political unit but rather the German people, a term Hitler defined biologically. Though the concept of a German race was meaningless in any scientific sense, "German blood" became for the Nazis the determining factor for membership in the nation. This meant that those who did not qualify "racially" as Germans could not belong to or be protected by the state, for the state as an institution existed only to serve the *Volk*.

In time the Nazis evolved a complicated hierarchy of national "races" divided into groups referred to as "culture creators," "culture bearers," and "culture destroyers." It was into this last category that Hitler placed Jews, blacks, and Gypsies. This designation allowed the Nazis ultimately to formulate a policy that led to the extermination of 6 million European Jews during World War II. Though this was hardly the first case of mass slaughter or genocide in human history, its uniqueness and special horror lay in its

"Und morgen die Welt!" (And to-
morrow the world!). Preaching a
nationalist doctrine of German elitism and racial supremacy, Adolf
Hitler sought to resurrect Germany
from the ignominy of defeat in
World War I and set his people on
a course that would establish a
"thousand-year Reich," a global hegemony under German leadership.
The fanatical enthusiasm, bordering
on adoration, manifested toward
Hitler by his loyal followers is
clearly evidenced in the salute
given him by the German Reichstag
(Parliament) in 1938 as he announced the annexation of Austria
to Germany. (Photos 242-HB-4547
and 208-N-39843 in the National
Archives.)

scientific execution and in the Nazi attempts to justify this action on ideological grounds that denied the very humanity of those placed in the "culture-
destroyer" category.

By 1939, when Hitler's imperialist ambitions triggered the outbreak of
World War II, Europe found itself divided into three power groupings, each
hostile to the other two. Ideologically they ranged from Nazi Germany and
Fascist Italy on the extreme right to parliamentary Britain and France in the
center and thence to the Communist Soviet Union on the far left. Yet the
desire for total control by the leaders of Germany, Italy, and the Soviet Union
gave their regimes the similar appearance of dictatorships relying more on
the will of one man than on any governmental system. Their common use of
extensive propaganda, police terror, one-party domination, efforts toward
centralization and state planning, and conflicting and competing overlays of
committee structures further strengthened the appearance of similarity. Yet
the administrative processes of the three states, their treatment of ethnic
groups, their relation with the Christian churches, and the ideological
principles that supported their governmental structures and economic systems
all reflected important differences. Whatever the differences and similarities,
these three regimes were equally distant from traditionally democratic, parliamentary forms of government and saw no need of preserving or respecting
them. Their presence rent the body politic of Europe.

The Second World War

The outbreak of war in the autumn of 1939 plunged Europe and eventually
the world into a maelstrom of violence and destruction. Linking with an
Asian conflict that had begun in 1937 upon Japan's invasion of China, the
war spread to include every major national power and a vast number of lesser
ones by the end of 1941. Unlike the western front of World War I, where the
machine gun and miles of barbed wire had produced the defensive horror of
stalemated trench warfare, World War II was characterized by territorial
movement and rapid offensives. In the early years momentum lay with
Germany, Italy, and Japan. However, the European and Pacific territorial
gains carved out by their forces, though enormous, proved transitory. In the
winter of 1942–1943, the Allied forces, led by the Soviet Union, Great
Britain, and the United States, blunted and then turned the enemy advances.
The last two and one-half years of the conflict saw the steady advance of the
Allies, culminating in the unconditional surrender and occupation of Ger-
many in May 1945 and the subsequent surrender of Japan that August.

The difference in form the war took can be attributed primarily to the
development of air technology during the interwar and war years. It was
essentially the use of air power as a form of long-distance artillery, combined
with effective deployment of tank battalions, that kept the military land
fronts flexible and prevented the kind of stagnation that had characterized

the conflict on the western front between 1914 and 1918. Fighter and bomber squadrons could attack roads, bridges, rail depots, and troop and supply movements miles behind enemy lines. This in turn opened corridors for swift advancement of mechanized armored units. Waves of bombers could seek out basic industrial complexes day after day, or lay waste large cities and workers' living quarters in massive nighttime incendiary raids. Some naval battles were fought by fleets that never came within sight of each other—the conflict contested entirely by planes launched from aircraft carriers. Landbased aircraft patrolled vast reaches of the world's oceans. Control of the air became the prime prerequisite for either land or sea advancement.

In turn, problems of transportation, production, and supply became every bit as central to the war effort as the campaigns of military detachments per se. This meant that the worker in a defense industry, the farmer in his fields, and the contractor building civilian housing all came to be viewed as contributors to the war effort—and thus by definition legitimate targets for destruction by the air forces of the various powers. As the war progressed, the technology for delivering these attacks continually changed, always becoming bigger and more destructive. Ultimately this culminated in U.S. use of the atomic bomb on the Japanese cities of Hiroshima and Nagasaki in the waning days of the war. It must be recognized that in terms of military strategy the atomic bomb was basically just the newest technique for escalating destruction and terror. Its use was in accord with a well-established policy, initiated by Nazi Germany in its air attacks on Warsaw, Rotterdam, and London early in the war, and greatly intensified by Britain and the United States in the last years of the war as they hammered at Germany and Japan with round-the-clock bombing raids.

Strategic Decisions

A number of strategic and political decisions made during the course of the war helped to set the stage for events in the postwar period. In general these were taken because they were seen as important to the war itself. Today, their longer-term implications and the impact they had on the postwar world seem at least equally relevant.

The first of these was the decision made by Hitler in the winter of 1940–1941 to undertake a campaign against the Soviet Union. Until the day Germany invaded the USSR in June 1941, Stalin's government conformed carefully to the provisions of the Nazi-Soviet pact of 1939, a pragmatic agreement regarding the disposition of Central Europe between the two powers. The signing of such a pact between the two ideologically opposed regimes had taken many people by surprise, yet it had its own logic. The delay bought Stalin time and at least temporary noninvolvement in what the Soviets considered a war of imperialists; the accord protected Germany from a two-front war (Stalin was also concerned about such a possibility, as Soviet troops had recently clashed with Japanese soldiers in Manchuria); and its division of Poland provided buffer zones between the two powers. Yet by the winter of 1940-1941 there was increasing evidence, which Stalin chose to ignore, that Hitler's primary goals were conquest of the so-called geopolitical heartland of Europe and the establishment of a massive German land empire in Central and Eastern Europe. Although Hitler had failed in his plans to launch a cross-channel invasion of Great Britain, in 1941 the Western European continent lay securely in German control, and Great Britain posed no immediate military threat. Therefore Hitler maintained that he could move against the Soviet Union without making the mistake he had always believed cost Germany the First World War—involvement in a two-front conflict against different powers.

Equally important, and from the German perspective a colossal error, was Hitler's declaration of war against the United States following the Japanese bombing of Pearl Harbor on December 7, 1941, even though the terms of the Tripartite Pact among Germany, Italy, and Japan did not require him to do so. The U.S. government had long since concluded that Germany, rather than Japan, constituted the greatest long-range threat to the United States and the world. However, the nature of the Japanese attack would have made it difficult for President Franklin Roosevelt to obtain a declaration of war against Germany as well as Japan, had not Hitler smoothed the way by declaring war first.

These two actions by Hitler—the first taken to fulfill his long-term ambitions for Germany, the second because he did not believe the war would last long enough for the United States to become a major military factor in Europe (and therefore he could make a no-risk gesture of support for Japan)—united the Asian and European conflicts that had hitherto been separate. Steps were now taken to form a coalition against the Axis powers, as Germany, Italy, Japan, and their allies were called. On January 1, 1942, twenty-six nations signed the Declaration by the United Nations, a document that served as the genesis for what would later become the United Nations Organization (UNO, or simply UN). It also committed all signatories to the principles of the Atlantic Charter, a peace platform put forward by President Roosevelt and Prime Minister Winston Churchill of Britain in August 1941 and accepted by the USSR. As the war widened in scope and lengthened in duration, the victory of the Allied powers became increasingly assured. Access to raw materials and potential for massive industrial production became key to military success, and in both categories the Allied coalition developed marked superiority.

Unconditional Surrender

Next to the decision that the European theater of operations should take precedence over activities in the Pacific, the most important Allied policy formulation came in January 1943. In the wake of a conference between

Roosevelt and Churchill at Casablanca, the president announced to the press that the objective of the war was to obtain the unconditional surrender of Germany, Italy, and Japan. This announcement was primarily designed to bolster popular opinion at home and to commit Britain and the United States publicly to permanent support of their Soviet ally, at that time engaged in a long, bloody battle for the key city of Stalingrad (today Volgograd) on the lower Volga River.

Behind this announcement also lay the realization by Churchill and Roosevelt that for the second year in a row they were not going to be able to fulfill a commitment to the Soviet Union to undertake a cross-channel invasion. This invasion would have established a direct second front against Germany and thus eased considerably German pressure on the USSR. Embarrassed by this decision and mindful that in 1917 Russia had withdrawn from World War I and made a separate peace with Germany, Roosevelt believed that a public statement regarding unconditional surrender was needed in order to reassure the Soviet Union of Allied commitment to see the war to the end.

In later years the decision to adopt publicly such a rigid, no-compromise policy received criticism. Historians have pointed out, correctly, that Nazi propagandists were able to use this announcement effectively for their own purposes. The Allies, Germans were told, meant to wipe Germany off the face of the earth. Germany must either emerge victorious or perish, and any thought of a negotiated settlement was clearly not within the realm of possibility. Full-fledged, total commitment to the war and to the Führer, Adolf Hitler, was therefore the only solution.

In fact, to Roosevelt unconditional surrender did not necessarily mean that the postwar policy of the victors would be ruthless. It meant only that the Allies would make no commitments that the defeated states might subsequently refer to, as Hitler had done so successfully when he argued that the Allied powers after World War I had not lived up to the promises made in the peace platform of President Wilson. What the policy of unconditional surrender did assure was that the defeated states would be occupied and administered for a time after the war by the victorious powers. That the Allied leaders understood this is quite clear, for most were convinced that one of the great mistakes made in 1918 had been the failure to occupy Germany and thus bring home to the civilian population the reality of Germany's defeat. This is not to say that Churchill, Roosevelt, or for that matter Stalin had any clear idea of just what the occupation and administration of these territories would entail or how long it would continue—but they clearly were committed to the implementation of this policy and did not want their hands tied by promises made in order to bring the war to an end.

In the long run, unconditional surrender was virtually ignored in negotiating a settlement with Italy. The Italian government forced out Mussolini and negotiated an armistice in September 1943; fighting against German troops stationed in Italy continued until 1945. In Japan the surrender was total, with the exception of a promise that the person of the emperor would not be harmed and the institution of the imperial throne preserved.

For Germany, though, the principle of unconditional surrender was never altered. Indeed, as knowledge of the Nazi death camps and the mass slaughter we know today as the Holocaust increased, sentiment in favor of a no-compromise surrender steadily hardened. To negotiate with a regime such as that of Hitler seemed a breach of basic moral principles. And so, when Germany surrendered on May 8, 1945, it was without terms and without promises regarding the future of Germany or the actions of those who would take control.

Partition of Germany

The decision to occupy, disarm, and partition Germany also had other long-range implications. Germany is located in the center of Europe. In order to conquer and occupy it, the Allied armies had to cross, from east and west, all of the rest of Europe. They also needed continuing control of lines of communication to Germany in order to provide ready access for the equipment, supplies, and personnel needed to maintain their occupation forces and to govern the people placed under their jurisdiction. Finally, in order to govern the country efficiently, the Allies had to divide Germany into zones of occupation.

All this was accomplished. British, French, and U.S. forces moved eastward following their successful cross-channel landing in Normandy on June 6, 1944. Contact with westward-driving Soviet forces was established at the Elbe River in Germany on April 25, 1945. Subsequently, each nation withdrew its military forces to the prearranged zones of occupation. But the lasting effect of the decision to occupy Germany jointly, coupled with Germany's central location in Europe, was to partition all of Europe into Western and Eastern spheres of influence, spheres that would harden into permanence as the tensions of the Cold War reappeared in the years following 1945. One can only conclude that the geography of the war more than anything else determined the basic political structure of Europe in the postwar era.

Europe Shattered and Destroyed

As hostilities ceased in May 1945, Europe seemed barely to be breathing. The war had wrought far greater damage to life and property than any that had preceded it. It was the first war on record to cause more war-related civilian than military deaths. Estimates of lives lost (including military, civilian, and Holocaust deaths) during the nearly six years of European conflict hover

Cold War tensions were already lurking on the diplomatic and military horizon, but for these two soldiers—one American and one Russian—who embraced each other at Torgau on the Elbe River on April 25, 1945, the meeting symbolized wartime friendship, cooperation, and thankfulness that the task of vanquishing Nazi Germany had been well and successfully completed. The simple sign behind them reads "East Meets West." (Photo 111-SC-205228 in the National Archives.)

around 35 million. The Soviet Union lost between 16 and 20 million people, Germany approximately 4.5 million, Yugoslavia 1.5 million, France between 550,000 and 600,000, Italy and Great Britain around 400,000 each. Polish, Romanian, Hungarian, Czechoslovakian, and Dutch deaths, including those that occurred in Nazi extermination camps, totaled nearly 7.4 million. Poland alone lost 15 percent of its entire population, a higher percentage loss than that incurred by any other country.

Physical damage was equally devastating. In the Central European and Soviet territories over which German and Soviet armies had fought, half of the urban residential areas and three-quarters of the rural homes had been obliterated. Industrial installations and transportation facilities in the same area were also thoroughly destroyed. In Germany and Western Europe, though damage to the countryside was less intense, major cities and towns, subjected to months of round-the-clock bombing and hand-to-hand fighting, lay in total ruin. Major exceptions were Rome and Paris, which had escaped

In an unknown location, a lonely soldier surveys the bleak desolation characteristic of urban destruction in Europe during World War II. Laid waste by months of aerial bombardment, many European cities were subjected to bitter hand-to-hand combat as Allied forces pushed toward Berlin from both east and west in the last months of the war. (Photo 208-AA-207L-1 in the National Archives.)

comparatively unscathed. Waterways, harbors, bridges, rail lines, and power lines all had been systematically laid waste.

This was the Europe of the dead and destroyed. But there was also the Europe of the living. Agricultural and industrial production was half what it had been prior to the outbreak of the war. Necessities needed for shelter, clothing, nutrition—in other words for minimal human survival—were in desperately short supply. National debts had increased astronomically, and the means and methods for dealing with them, or for financing the enormous task of reconstruction, were nowhere in sight.

In addition, between 1939 and 1947, an estimated 50 million Europeans had been uprooted and forced to move from their previous homelands. Of these, some 16 million remained permanently displaced in the postwar era. Eleven million were Germans who had either fled or been expelled from territories in east-central Europe. These population shifts greatly altered the ethnographic map of Eastern Europe and the cultural and social map of Western Europe. Especially important was the 1945-1946 removal of Germans from Czechoslovakia and from lands newly acquired by Poland. The influx of these displaced persons (or DPs) into the remaining portions of Germany resulted in a substantial modification of the radical religious split between the Catholic south and the Protestant north that had characterized and greatly influenced centuries of German history. The "DP problem," as it came to be known, would intensify postwar difficulties of European reconstruction and reconciliation.

Finally, there were the permanent scars and deep psychological trauma generated by the unique horror resulting from Nazi policies and actions in their concentration and extermination camps. Six million European Jews, thousands of Gypsies, and countless numbers of Europeans from many faiths and nations, including Germany, had perished as a result of policies that were fundamentally separate from the war itself, although their implementation was closely connected with the course that the war took. The horror of the Holocaust continues to this day to bewilder, terrify, and shame both Europe and the world.

By the end of 1945 Europe was in a state of total collapse. Even Great Britain and France, which had emerged from the war as part of the victorious coalition of "great powers," were in a state of economic chaos. For some of the states of Europe, prewar overseas colonies seemed to offer potential support that could aid in domestic reconstruction. Yet in many of these areas colonial peoples had made important contributions to the war effort, and now they sought the ending of colonial ties as their reward. In seeking to implement this goal they received the open support of the Soviet Union and the tacit blessing of the United States. It may not have been fully recognized in 1945, but the age of Europe's imperial dominance of the world was over. It would take some years, much anguish, and considerable bloodshed before all concerned came to accept this judgment. But in 1945 the verdict was essentially already in.

Europe, battered, destroyed, and disillusioned, lay prostrate under the direct or indirect influence and control of those who held power in Washington and Moscow. Its future seemed bleak, its problems massive, and its spirit one of deep pessimism. Yet, like the phoenix, Europe would rise again from the ashes to new heights of well-being and prosperity. Countries that formerly possessed primarily agricultural economies would industrialize significantly. More highly developed nations would explore the parameters of advanced or even postindustrial society. New patterns of economic and political relationships would be established in the international arena. In domestic politics leaders and parties would test a variety of arrangements in search of the best tools both for facilitating and controlling the scientific and technological revolution. They would also seek ways of dealing with the tensions of modern mass societies whose governments were expected, despite the size of the societies governed, to be responsive to individual concerns. How all this came about and why certain paths were chosen are the central concerns of this volume.

Notes

1. E. Renan, *La Réforme Intellectuelle et Morale,* as quoted in W. L. Langer, *The Diplomacy of Imperialism* (1935), p. 89.
2. R. Brooke, *1914 and Other Poems* (1916), p. 11.
3. "It is sweet and proper to die for one's country." The poem is entitled *"Dulce et decorum est"* and appears in Wilfred Owen, *The Collected Poems of Wilfred Owen* (1964), p. 55. Copyright © 1964 by Chatto and Windus, Ltd. Reprinted by permission of New Directions Publishing Corporation.
4. P. Valéry, *Variété* (1924), pp. 32–33.

Suggested Readings

Armstrong, A., *Unconditional Surrender: The Impact of the Casablanca Policy upon World War II* (1961).
Baechler, J., J. A. Hall, and M. Mann (eds.), *Europe and the Rise of Capitalism* (1988).
Bullock, A., *Hitler: A Study in Tyranny,* rev. ed. (1964).
Calvocoressi, P., and G. Wint, *Total War: Causes and Courses of the Second World War* (1972).
Dawidowicz, L., *The War Against the Jews, 1933–1945* (1975).
Fest, J., *Hitler* (1974).
Gilbert, M., *The Holocaust: A History of the Jews of Europe During the Second World War* (1986).
Hersey, J., *Hiroshima* (1946).

Jackson, G., *The Spanish Republic and the Civil War, 1931–1939* (1963).
Kennan, G. F., *Russia and the West Under Lenin and Stalin* (1961).
Koestler, A., *Darkness at Noon* (1941).
Kogon, E., *The Theory and Practice of Hell* (1950).
Mack Smith, D., *Mussolini* (1982).
Morgan, M., *Lenin* (1971).
Nicolson, H., *Peacemaking, 1919* (1933).
Orwell, G., *Homage to Catalonia* (1938).
Remarque, E. M., *All Quiet on the Western Front* (1929).
Schmitt, B. E., and H. C. Vedeler, *The World in the Crucible, 1914–1919* (1984).
Sontag, R., *A Broken World, 1919–1939* (1971).
Ulam, A., *Stalin: The Man and His Era* (1973).
Wiesel, E., *Night* (1982).
Wright, G., *The Ordeal of Total War, 1939–1945* (1968).
Zelden, T., *France: 1848 to 1945*, 2 vols. (1973–1977).

PART TWO
The International Scene

CHAPTER THREE

Europe Divided:
1945–1955

❧

The Peace Treaties
Early Great-Power Differences • Italy and the Axis Satellites
The Problem of Central Europe • Other Arenas of Conflict

The Cold War
Growing Division of Germany • The Truman and Marshall Plans
The Treaty of Dunkirk and the Brussels Pact
The Berlin Blockade

Consolidation of the Two Camps
Comecon • The North Atlantic Treaty Organization
The Council of Europe

The Quest for West German Rearmament
War in Korea • The Schuman Plan
The European Defense Community • The Western European Union

The Warsaw Pact

Notes

Suggested Readings

After World War II, the task of reconstruction was so immense and European resources so exhausted that the fate of Europe effectively lay in the hands of the two nations that had emerged as world superpowers: the United States and the Union of Soviet Socialist Republics (USSR). Neither the neutrals nor Great Britain—much as the latter dreamed of power—was in a position to take a definitive lead. The development of Europe therefore became inextricably linked with the struggle between these two superpowers. Decades would pass before Europe could again assert itself strongly and assume control of its own progress.

For the individual European states, the decades following the war were a period of political and economic modernizing and restructuring, as the nations attempted to regain the energy, dynamism, confidence, and prosperity that had been the hallmarks of their civilization. For Europe as a whole, a division developed spurred by three major concerns about political security. The Western states feared Soviet-orchestrated Communist subversion from within and possible Soviet aggression from without. The Soviets and their satellites distrusted Western capitalist encirclement and domination and worried about U.S. superiority in nuclear weaponry and technology. Eastern and Western European states alike were wary of any rebirth of German power.

Fears for political security were no less acute than anxiety about economic survival. The divisions of Europe over security matters led to economic alignments that carried important implications for the defense capabilities of each region. The formulas devised in the West for the joint purposes of defusing the German threat, containing the Communists and Soviets, and rehabilitating the national economies proved effective. In time these strategies brought unprecedented levels of prosperity and international cooperation. In the East, however, political collaboration was of a different nature and economic progress was more limited.

The obvious differences in political and economic development between East and West eventually spurred great changes, especially in the East, during the latter 1980s and early 1990s. The changes were so far-reaching that they amounted to a new restructuring of European relations as a whole and, for Germany, another renaissance. Whether this development marked both the end of a century and a half of wars over German unification and the definitive decline in U.S. and Soviet influence over Europe remained to be seen.

The two major themes of the postwar years—the search for political security and efforts for economic revival—were thus closely related. Often they reinforced each other; occasionally they proceeded independently. Their course, which eventually led to Europe's rebirth, was scarcely direct. Only in retrospect is it possible to impose a tentative model of phases upon the evolution of events. Unfortunately, periodization and models involve artificiality and the doubtful implication that "history was heading in this direction all along." Nevertheless, they may be useful in imposing some coherence on an otherwise kaleidoscopic series of events. Thus the first years following the war could be conceived as a period in which Europe was divided into two blocs, a time of social despair, economic crisis, and the demonstrated impotence of Europe vis-à-vis the power of the United States and the USSR. This era could be seen as followed by nearly two decades of East-West equilibrium, that is, a period of near balance between the two vying power blocs. It was in turn succeeded by a stage that can be considered as culminating in the birth of a new Europe.

The Peace Treaties

Early Great-Power Differences

During World War II, Western Europeans in general hoped that solutions to postwar political problems could be negotiated. The collapse of democratic government and the widespread adoption of authoritarian regimes in the interwar period suggested that this hope might be illusory. Those regimes, however, had become discredited. And though cooperation among the Allies during the war had been difficult, it had been achieved.

By the time of German surrender in May 1945, U.S. military and naval power had given the United States the determining position among the Western democracies. The later use of atomic weapons in the war with Japan further demonstrated the superpower status of the United States. Nonetheless, the principal motive of U.S. policy at this stage was to reduce the nation's military and financial responsibilities in Europe. Soldiers should be brought home and U.S. taxpayers be relieved of the costs of occupation. It was expected that the United Nations, already being planned and organized in the closing months of the war, would handle the larger problems of political security and economic rehabilitation in Europe. The reigning assumption was that free elections could solve the problems of Germany and the Eastern European states and that something resembling the liberal Europe of the 1920s would arise.

The difficulties of economic recovery were recognized, and positive moves were made in this field. In July 1944 a United Nations Monetary and Financial Conference met at Bretton Woods, New Hampshire, to discuss how to stabilize exchange rates and avoid currency disorders. Its financial experts proposed to their governments the creation of an International Monetary Fund (IMF) and an International Bank for Reconstruction and Development (the World Bank). Contributions and loans to these institutions were to be made by those nations able to do so. The institutions were intended to stabilize currency exchange rates and to assist reconstruction. The IMF and World Bank were created the next year, offering what appeared to be an adequate framework for international cooperation in the sphere of economic activities.

Eager to return to the benefits of a peacetime economy and way of life, the United States took two steps that diminished its influence in Europe. The first was to terminate lend-lease aid, an agreement whereby the United States lent to its allies supplies, materials, and credit. (It should be noted that although the United States saw lend-lease as an act of generosity, many Britons considered it a means to subsidize expansion of U.S. industry at the expense of British firms.) The second step was to withdraw U.S. troops from abroad with all possible speed. These and other actions reflected a somewhat unfounded belief that a stable Europe could be restored without major reliance on U.S. help or influence.

Soviet policy was scarcely motivated by faith in postwar stability or automatic adoption of liberal bourgeois political formulas. The official pronouncements of Soviet leaders revealed the expectation that World War II might be followed by a wave of revolutionary movements similar to those that had come in the wake of World War I. The Soviets were prepared to take advantage of such a situation so long as this could be done without significant political and economic risk. Marxist-Leninist doctrine assured that the downfall of capitalism was inevitable and would be accelerated by quarrels for markets and profits among those states that followed capitalistic doctrines. Appropriate Soviet moves and support of Communist opposition groups could assist and even hasten the victory of the proletariat. The Soviets did not expect favorable treatment from the West. Following the Bolshevik Revolution in 1917, agreement between the Soviet Union and the West had been rare. Only the military threat posed by Germany and Japan had forced their cooperation. The Soviet government's intransigence may also have been influenced by domestic instability. The sacrifices needed for postwar reconstruction under the methods employed by the Communist party demanded much from the Soviet peoples. Soviet leaders may have believed that only by evoking an image of the country surrounded by enemies could they reach their goals.

The differences between Western and Soviet expectations soon became evident during the negotiations for a postwar settlement, and these differences formed the basis of future controversies. The central issue then and since has been the question of how Europe would be organized or, put another way, who would control it. This theme was already evident in October 1944, when Churchill, prime minister of the United Kingdom, met in Moscow with Stalin, Communist party secretary and leader of the Soviet Union. President Roosevelt of the United States was busy with his reelection campaign and unable to attend. Churchill was aware that Soviet forces were dominant in Eastern Europe, and he wanted to preserve what Western influence he could

As World War II draws to a close, the Big Three—Winston Churchill, Franklin D. Roosevelt, and Josef Stalin—meet at Yalta in February 1945 to discuss the postwar future of Germany and the rest of Europe. The outcome of the Yalta conference remains controversial. Some have described it as an unfortunate appeasement of the Soviet Union by the West; others see it as a reasonable bargain made under difficult wartime circumstances. But historians agree that the origins of the Cold War cannot be understood without examining this crucial meeting. (Photo courtesy of the British Information Services.)

in that region. He proposed to Stalin that their countries not come to cross-purposes. The Soviets should have 90 percent of "the say" in Romania, 75 percent in Bulgaria, 50 percent in Yugoslavia and Hungary, and 10 percent in Greece. The other Allies would take the balance of influence. Though some critics have called this percentage agreement a capitulation to the Soviets, most historians have recognized it as an act of hard-nosed political realism.

The heads of government of the United States, the Soviet Union, and the United Kingdom held several conferences during the closing stages of the war. Two of the most important took place at Yalta in the Crimea (February 1945) and at Potsdam, Germany (July and August 1945). At these meetings and in subsequent gatherings of their foreign ministers, the powers agreed on certain points but diverged sharply on several key issues. By the time of the Yalta gathering, the Soviet Union exercised a definitive degree of control in Eastern Europe through the presence of its advancing troops. As James F. Byrnes, a member of the U.S. delegation and a future secretary of state, later commented, "It was not a question of what we [the West] would *let* the Russians do, but what we could *get* the Russians to do."

At the Yalta conference, decisions were made regarding the organization of the United Nations, the treatment of Germany, the proposed entry of the USSR into the war of the Allies and China against Japan, and the peace settlement in Asia. Churchill, Stalin, and Roosevelt (the Big Three) had as their principal concern, however, the postwar organization of Eastern Europe. The Soviets were persuaded to assent to a broad statement of policy known as the Yalta Declaration on Liberated Europe. This document proclaimed the powers' desire to assist formation of interim governments "broadly representative of all democratic elements" and pledged early free elections. The statement did not have great influence inasmuch as the relative bargaining power of the parties left the USSR free to assert its own viewpoint in Eastern Europe without effective opposition. The United States and Britain were of course doing much the same in the areas over which they held control. In the specific matter of Poland's borders, it was arranged after months of disagreements that the USSR should receive the regions of Poland east of the old Curzon line (a provisional frontier recommended by a League of Nations commission following the First World War). Poland should in turn be compensated with territory from eastern Germany. This disposition had long been opposed by the Polish government in exile in London. Stalin, however, recognized as the legitimate Polish leaders a group of Communists organized in the city of Lublin, Poland, with Soviet assistance.

During the Potsdam gathering, Harry S Truman, the new president (1945-1953), represented the United States. Clement Attlee, the new British prime minister, replaced Churchill upon the Labour party's victory over Churchill's conservatives in the British elections. The changes made little difference. Germany east of the Oder and Neisse rivers, the former free city of Danzig, and the southern portions of East Prussia were put under Polish administration. Two weeks later Poland ceded its eastern region to the USSR.

The meetings of the foreign ministers brought sharp clashes. The Soviets denied claims that they were interfering in the affairs of Romania, Bulgaria, and Hungary. The West resisted Soviet demands for the cession of Trieste to Yugoslavia, heavy reparations from Italy, and a share in the administration of Italy's North African colonies. Eventually the United States and the United Kingdom made concessions in recognition of Communist-dominated regions in Eastern Europe, sacrificing the substance of the Yalta Declaration though keeping it in form. The Soviets in turn agreed to the calling of a conference in Paris to draft five proposed peace treaties. At Paris, in addition to the five great powers—the United Kingdom, the United States, the USSR, France, and China—the sixteen smaller states that had contributed to the victory in Europe were to be represented.

The conference, which took place from July through October 1946, and related meetings of experts often descended to flagrant forms of propaganda and bargaining. In the end, though the treaties bore little resemblance to the cooperative decisions achieved during the war, they at least represented a reasonably sound resolution of the political forces at work in postwar Europe.

Italy and the Axis Satellites

The peace treaties with Italy, Bulgaria, Hungary, Romania, and Finland were similar in general structure. Many articles dealt with technical details; the most significant focused on territorial, economic, and political terms that were to influence the future roles of these countries.

The most difficult territorial settlement related to Italy. Fiume and much of the surrounding province went to Yugoslavia. The city of Trieste, where 80 percent of the population was Italian, and a small hinterland were established as a free territory under the guarantee of the United Nations Security Council. The region's control remained a political issue for some time. Improved relations between Yugoslavia and the West led to a settlement in 1954 that gave the city to Italy and a major share of the hinterland to Yugoslavia. Italy also ceded islands to Yugoslavia, Greece, and Albania and a small strategic area on its western frontier to France. At Paris the independence of Ethiopia was recognized. The former Italian colonies of Libya, Eritrea, and Somaliland were left under British military rule with the proviso that if no other arrangement were reached within a year they would be referred to the United Nations General Assembly. This is what happened, and under UN auspices the former Italian territories moved toward self-government.

Finland ceded lands to the Soviet Union, including the strategic Karelian Isthmus and the city of Viborg. These regions constituted 12 percent of Finland and held important economic resources. Their loss was a harsh penalty on the Finns for bravely defending their territory and joining the Axis for a number of months.

Romania gave up northern Bukovina and Bessarabia to the USSR and southern Dobrudja to Bulgaria. It did regain northern Transylvania from Hungary, which also ceded to Czechoslovakia a small strip of land along the Danube opposite the city of Bratislava. Czechoslovakia relinquished to the Soviets a portion of Subcarpathian Ruthenia, significant in that its possession afforded the USSR a direct border with Hungary as well as with Czechoslovakia.

Each of the five treaties required the defeated states to reduce their weapons and armed forces and to restore the legal and property rights of the victorious powers. The five countries promised to dissolve Fascist organizations, to guarantee human rights and fundamental freedoms, and to pay reparations to various other countries. All the treaties except that with Finland contained a commitment that the occupying Allied nations would withdraw troops. The Soviets retained the right, however, to maintain

sufficient forces in Romania and Hungary to safeguard their line of communications with Austria until a treaty could be concluded with that country.
The treaties, which in their terms already demonstrated the rigidity of the
line between the Soviet sphere of influence and that of the Western Allies,
were signed in Paris on February 10, 1947. The negotiation of these first
peace treaties clearly revealed both the Soviet tenacity of purpose and the
U.S. intention of supporting the principles of democratic self-determination
held by the Western Allies. Above all, it showed that whatever the desire of
the Europeans to control their own fate, the balance of power had shifted so
greatly that the two superpowers would be the final arbiters of most issues.

The Problem of Central Europe

At the end of the war, Austria was considered neither a satellite nor a
liberated state. Under joint occupation, Austria was in no sense free, despite
the powers' agreement as early as 1943 that Austrian independence should
be restored. Because Austria had not been at war as a separate state, it could
not be expected to sign a peace treaty. This difficulty was circumvented by
referring to the projected settlement as the Austrian State Treaty.

At Potsdam the leaders agreed that Austria should not pay reparations.
But the USSR had the right to appropriate German assets in Axis satellite
states, and Soviet efforts to take Austrian property seized by Germans led to
controversy. So, too, did Yugoslav territorial demands. Ten years and nearly
300 meetings brought little resolution. The obstacle was not particular
substantive issues but the importance of Austria to the general European
settlement. The problem of Austria was subsidiary to that of Germany, and
until progress was made on that issue, the Austrian situation remained
unresolved.

It was in the approaches of the victorious powers toward the German
question that major differences became apparent, especially between Great
Britain and the United States on the one hand and the Soviet Union on the
other. The very resources that gave Germany such strength as an enemy
made it the principal prize sought by the two rival blocs. Germany formed
in many respects the heart of Europe. Each bloc regarded control of Germany
as essential to its security.

The Western Allies were not in full agreement as to Germany's future.
In 1944 Secretary of the Treasury Henry Morgenthau of the United States
proposed the permanent reduction of German power by the destruction or
removal of heavy industry. Certain German provinces would be ceded to
neighboring countries and the remaining territory partitioned into three
states. Long-term controls would be established over Germany's domestic
economy and foreign trade. This extreme Morgenthau Plan to turn Germany
toward a basically agricultural economy was abandoned when its real intent

and the difficulties of its implementation were better known. Yet it continued to influence thinking regarding Germany.

The United Kingdom and France wished a settlement that would permanently restrict the power of Germany. The British did realize that Europe's prosperity depended in considerable measure on Germany's economic health and that some restoration of its economy was necessary if the Allies were to avoid bearing the full costs of feeding the German population. The French, for their part, hoped to pry territories such as the Saar basin and perhaps the Ruhr industrial region completely from German economic control. They resented concessions that might enable German industry to recuperate before French production capacities could be restored. For many months, the French did not see Communist insurrection or Soviet advance as the greatest danger to Europe; rather, they feared the possible renaissance of German power, far-fetched as that seemed, given Germany's utter defeat. France therefore endeavored longer than Britain or the United States to keep a unified policy with the Soviet Union vis-à-vis the hated German enemy.

Early conferences among the powers brought agreement on general principles regarding the surrender and demilitarization of Germany, the punishment of war criminals, and the powers to be exercised by an Allied Control Council. Additional decisions regarding frontiers and reparations were made at Yalta. There it was decided, mostly at the urging of Churchill, that France should participate in the occupation of Germany. Stalin, however, would not relinquish any portion of the previously defined Soviet occupation zone. The United States and Britain consequently agreed to relinquish some of their zones in order to form a French zone located south of the British zone and north of the U.S. zone. A similar arrangement resulted for Greater Berlin, which was to be jointly administered and to host the Allied Control Council. Supreme authority regarding all matters affecting Germany was granted to the four commanders in chief who made up the Control Council.

At Potsdam, the Big Three agreed that Germany should be treated as an economic unit, that war industries should be prohibited, and that large concentrations of economic strength within Germany should be discouraged. Reparations, the key to economic settlement, were to be paid through the removal of Germany's plants and capital equipment and from its external assets. The Soviet share of the reparations bill was to come from the Soviet occupation zone. In addition, one-quarter of the industrial equipment removed from the three Western zones was to go to the USSR. As partial compensation for the latter source of reparations, the Soviet Union was to supply the other zones with food and raw materials from its own sector. The German navy and merchant marine were to be divided among the principal victors.

This broad compromise approach soon spawned conflicts. The French, who had not been invited to the Potsdam conference but could exercise a veto in the Control Council, steadfastly held up implementation of the economic program; they demanded territorial and economic concessions in western Germany, especially in the Saar and Ruhr. The Soviets interpreted the Potsdam accords as permitting levies against current production to obtain reparations. Their actions siphoned to the East production that otherwise would have supported Germans in the West. The German will to produce was sapped. The Western occupying powers, burdened with heavy costs in supporting the populations in their zones, argued that only capital equipment and foreign assets could be seized for reparations.

It quickly became apparent that the regulation of German industry had to be based less on the needs of the German people than on those of the entire European economy. U.S.-British plans to raise the level of German industrial production brought protests from France, still nervous about German resurgence. The French opposed creation of centralized agencies in Germany for the same reason. Although some historians have blamed the failure of the Potsdam system on the French, most still agree that the Soviet authorities were chiefly responsible for its demise. The USSR also refused to cooperate in the establishment of central economic institutions for Germany. Above all, it failed to contribute food and raw materials from its zone in any degree close to the proportions expected.

Efforts to resolve conflicts over interpretation of the Potsdam accords and to move toward some sort of peace settlement with Germany went nowhere. As deadlock developed, the objectives and determination of the Western Allies and the Soviet Union became clear. Both parties understood that the prize at stake was nothing less than control of Germany as a whole and, with it, control of Western and Central Europe. Decades would have to pass and many changes occur in the European context before the German question would be resolved. In the long run, it would be the alteration of Europe that would bring the solution rather than a four-power peace treaty with Germany.

Other Arenas of Conflict

In the closing months of the war, many people assumed that controversial issues could be peaceably debated and resolved in the planned new forum of the United Nations Organization. Tremendous hope was held out for the United Nations. It seemed possible that through this organization the powers would be able to maintain their wartime cooperation. Certainly, the need for collective security had been driven home by the failures of the League of Nations after World War I.

Unfortunately, and perhaps inevitably, the UN became another arena of conflict between the United States and the Soviet Union. Membership in the organization was open to all "peace-loving states" on the recommendation of the Security Council and a two-thirds vote of the General Assembly. Initially the United Nations consisted of the victorious nations in World War II, but soon there was desire to admit new members. Deadlocks in elections arose. The criteria for membership, such as the ability of proposed states to assume the charter obligations regarding maintenance of peace and security, development of friendly relations between nations, and furtherance of international cooperation, were largely lost in the Soviet-U.S. rivalry.

The superpowers' attempts to win the allegiance and support of smaller and newer powers accelerated the entrance of these states into world politics. The process also enhanced the small powers' willingness to demand for themselves a larger share of the world's resources and the largesse of greater states. At the same time, the European nations found their own roles diminished within the UN. They soon had to decide whether to operate independently within the organization or to align themselves with one of the two superpowers. More than the U.S. or Soviet delegates, the European members found themselves in conflict with representatives from Third World states who demanded that colonies receive prompt independence and former colonies receive substantial aid.

Each of the five major powers held permanent seats on the Security Council and an absolute veto on all but procedural matters. Six other members (ten after 1965) were elected by the General Assembly for two-year terms. Soon, many efforts of the council were stymied by multiple Soviet vetoes. The United States was stubborn, too, as witnessed by its successful postponement until 1971 of the substitution of delegates from Communist China for those of Nationalist China (militarily defeated and driven to Taiwan in 1948). The superpower contest was more muted within the important Economic and Social Council, which took as its focus the drafting of reports and recommendations for the well-being of the world's populations; this was also the case for the many specialized agencies dealing with such issues as agriculture, health, science, and tariffs. Some of these, such as the United Nations Relief and Rehabilitation Administration (UNRRA), performed outstanding work. Debate was fierce, however, over the creation and powers of an agency that would deal with the use and control of atomic energy for peaceful purposes.

Originally founded as a tool of victorious major powers for control over a Europe twice ravaged by war brought on by German aggression, the United Nations slowly became a world organization. As such, its global activities in time no longer reflected the Eurocentric concerns of its early years. Its influence became weakened by controversy, limited effectiveness in peace-keeping efforts, and funding problems. As a result, the United Nations came not to shape but to be shaped by the nature and course of international and especially European relations.

The contest between the superpowers was not restricted just to Europe and the United Nations, of course, but gradually encompassed the entire globe. Many new states developed out of great-power colonies immediately after the war, and the superpowers recruited their support. World War II set

The Rush of Decolonization:
Colonial Territories Achieving Independence 1946–1975

Jordan	Great Britain	1946
Lebanon	France	1946
Burma	Great Britain	1947
India	Great Britain	1947
Pakistan	Great Britain	1947
Sri Lanka	Great Britain	1948
Indonesia	Netherlands	1949
Laos	France	1949
Sudan	Great Britain	1950
Egypt	Great Britain	1954
Vietnam	France	1954
Morocco	France	1956
Tunisia	France	1956
Ghana	Great Britain	1957
Guinea	France	1958
Benin	France	1960
Burkina Faso	France	1960
Cameroon	France	1960
Central African Republic	France	1960
Chad	France	1960
Congo	Belgium	1960
Congo	France	1960
Ivory Coast	France	1960
Gabon	France	1960
Mali	France	1960
Mauritania	France	1960
Niger	France	1960
Nigeria	Great Britain	1960
Senegal	France	1960
Somalia	Great Britain	1960

continues

continued

Togo	France	1960
Madagascar	France	1960
Kuwait	Great Britain	1961
Sierra Leone	Great Britain	1961
South Africa	Great Britain	1961
Tanzania	Great Britain	1961
Algeria	France	1962
Burundi	Belgium	1962
Rwanda	Belgium	1962
Uganda	Great Britain	1962
Kenya	Great Britain	1963
Malaysia	Great Britain	1963
Malawi	Great Britain	1964
Malta	Great Britain	1964
Zambia	Great Britain	1964
Gambia	Great Britain	1965
Maldives	Great Britain	1965
Singapore	Great Britain	1965
Zimbabwe	Great Britain	1965
Botswana	Great Britain	1966
South Yemen	Great Britain	1967
Swaziland	Great Britain	1967
Equatorial Guinea	Spain	1968
Nauru	Great Britain	1968
Fiji	Great Britain	1970
Bahrain	Great Britain	1971
Qatar	Great Britain	1971
Bahamas	Great Britain	1973
Guinea Bissau	Netherlands	1974
Angola	Portugal	1975
Comoros	France	1975
Mozambique	Portugal	1975
Papua New Guinea	Australia	1975
Sao Tome and Principe	Portugal	1975

the stage for national liberation by requiring the colonial states to concentrate their military power to a greater extent in Europe. It further encouraged formation of nationalist resistance groups such as that of Ho Chi Minh in Vietnam, upset peacetime commercial relations, and led the colonies to rely more on their own resources. Above all, as the Europeans focused on problems closer to home, political leaders in the colonies who believed that the political, economic, and social development of their peoples was being retarded by colonial policies had opportunity to expand their following.

The rapid pace of decolonization after 1945 reflects clearly the decline of the coercive power and economic leverage of the European states. It may also have indicated a loss of confidence in the right to rule. World War II had been fought to assure basic freedoms. Refusal of the colonies' demands to rule themselves seemed to conflict with the concept of freedom and with democratic beliefs.

For the European nations, the psychological as well as the economic impact of letting go of the colonies was great. This was especially true for France and Portugal, where events in Algeria, Angola, and elsewhere led to political change in the metropole and caused the dissolution of one republic and the formation of another. The ultimate result of the decolonization surge was that by 1975 European colonial empires, which in their heyday had ruled over 500 million people, had virtually ceased to exist, save for a few small regions. Economic and political influence exerted by Europeans in their former colonial territories continued over subsequent decades with both positive effects (seen primarily in terms of investment of funds and technology) and negative aspects (European firms and leaders were accused of neocolonialism).

The breaking away of the colonies gave the Soviets opportunity to fish in troubled waters. Their own ideology scorned imperialism as an extreme form of capitalist exploitation, an appealing stance to many new states. It is not surprising that a number of colonial politicians, anxious to sunder the bonds of imperial rule, turned to their enemy's enemy for support. In time, some new states found Soviet support restrictive and sought to define their own path. The term *Third World* originated in the early 1950s among members of the French non-Communist Left, which hoped to find an alternative to the systems of life and government of the conflicting super-powers. It became the accepted mode for designating states that did not participate in the types of political economies represented by those two powers. With its emphasis on the individual, the First World, as Western Europe and the United States came to be called, stood for an economic structure (no matter how mixed that economy was in practice) based on the concept of private property and a competitive market system. By contrast, the Second World, which included Eastern Europe and the Soviet Union, emphasized collective control of the means of production and relied heavily on economic planning rather than free market forces. Leaders of the Third

World soon found it difficult indeed to steer a completely independent path, so totally did the contest between the United States and the Soviet Union dominate international politics.

The Cold War

At base, the contest between the superpowers was over political control of Europe. It was also, as became manifest in the 1950s and 1960s, between philosophies and ways of life that affected global politics. During the years immediately after the German surrender, the contest found its initial nourishment in events in Eastern Europe and then focused on Germany. Each superpower bloc distrusted the other. Deep tension, characterized by hostility but not shooting, developed between them. This Cold War, as it was called, would last more than forty years. Intermittently calmed by temporary agreements and then refueled by new clashes, it would always be sustained by fear and suspicion.

The concern of the Western countries was that the Soviet Union would gain control of Eastern Europe, then of Germany, and next seek to press its influence farther west. Although Soviet armed forces were reduced from 12 million to perhaps as low as 2.8 million between 1945 and 1948, this was not known in the West at the time. Even the latter figure was substantially higher than that of any of the principal Western powers. For example, U.S. global forces had fallen from 8.3 million troops in 1945 to 1.4 million in 1949, and its defense budget had shrunk from $81 billion to $14 billion in the same period. In both France and Italy, moreover, Communist parties were members of the governing coalitions until 1947, and their potential subversion could not be ignored by Western leaders.

Stalin, for his part, appeared convinced that at the slightest sign of weakness the West would attack the Soviet Union, using nuclear weapons to negate the Soviet superiority in troop numbers. He was not inclined to be moderate in his implementation of established reparations policy, for the reconstruction needs of his country were huge. The history of Allied intervention during the Russian Civil War (1918–1920), the lack of consultation with the Soviets when appeasing Hitler at Munich (1938), and the Allied delays in opening a second front in Europe during World War II only honed his belief in the ultimate hostility and treachery of the Western states.

The Cold War was not really new; rather, it was a resumption of what had been a dominant theme of the interwar years until nazism intervened. The Cold War took on new life and dimensions, however, as a result of events in Eastern Europe and Germany at the end of World War II. It was characterized by ideological struggle, conflict of economic systems, and geographic and national rivalries. The Cold War was a genuine conflict because leaders on both sides were convinced that their opponents had aggressive intentions centering on the control of Europe through the control of Germany. At the same time, neither side recognized that the opposing leaders were motivated more by defensive than offensive considerations.

Though both sides were determined to conduct the conflict short of actual war, the escalation of the Cold War was rapid. Each party took steps, some in response to those of the other, some not. Whatever the immediate cause, a pattern of reciprocal action emerged that increased tensions. There seemed to be an endless number of areas and topics of disagreement. Problems developed over Poland's borders and government and the occupation regimes for Italy, Hungary, and other regions. In the conferences that prepared the creation of the United Nations, sharp differences arose over representation in the General Assembly. These were resolved only when seats were granted to Ukraine and Belarus partially to balance what Stalin insisted would be British puppet votes cast by the dominions. The Soviets delayed withdrawal of their troops from Iran in 1946. There was debate over the occupation and future of Korea. Even as the United States and Britain were proclaiming their interest in international control of atomic energy, the Soviets learned through their spies that the United Kingdom and the United States were secretly endeavoring to obtain a world monopoly of the (then considered scarce) uranium ores that fueled atomic energy. Soviet fears were aroused, as was Soviet anger over the hypocrisy of Western posturing in the UN in support of an international control agency that would actually have little power.

In Germany differences arose over the failure of the Soviets, hard-pressed themselves for foodstuffs and raw materials, to deliver these items to the Western zones of occupation in return for dismantled factory equipment shipped from the West according to the Potsdam accords. And there were disagreements over what the future of Germany should be. At the Yalta meeting, Churchill opposed the dismemberment of Germany, though the Soviets strongly backed such a division of their former enemy. The British prime minister had initially hoped dismemberment would win Stalin's cooperation regarding Poland. When the Communist leader refused to yield on the matter of Poland's eastern border, Churchill changed his position because he feared that Germany's division would turn the Soviet-occupied sections of the country into Soviet puppet states.

Suspicions mounted and fed on each other. In election speeches in February 1946, Stalin and his associates openly described the Western states as enemies. They asserted that Marxism-Leninism predicted the splitting of the capitalist world into warring camps and that war was essentially inevitable as long as capitalism existed. In the West, it was generally believed that Soviet power was prepared to move into any position that the Western states were not willing to defend. In March 1946 Churchill gave a ringing response to the Soviets in a noteworthy address in Fulton, Missouri: "From Stettin in the Baltic to Trieste in the Adriatic, an iron curtain has descended across the

Continent." At the time many thought that Churchill exaggerated the situation, but subsequent events supported his view. The term *Iron Curtain* soon gained wide currency as an apt description of the political and ideological barriers separating East and West.

Growing Division of Germany

The oral conflicts of the politicians were matched by conflicts between the generals in charge of the occupation zones in Germany. The Potsdam accords stated that Germany was to be treated as one economic unit. The dismantling of industries in the West to provide reparations to the Soviets was bankrupting the Western zones, which had to be subsidized by British and U.S. tax revenues (also supplied to help France and the French zone). The Soviets meanwhile were consolidating their power in the Eastern zone. In April 1946 they forced the merger of the Communist and Socialist parties in their zone into a Communist-dominated Socialist Unity party. Pro-Communists were installed in key positions. Without the lever of central administrative organs, the West had no way to slow the takeover of the East and all its institutions by a Communist bureaucracy.

The French, however, feared any move that might rebuild a centrally directed and powerful Germany. They raised roadblocks to the creation of central administrative organs in Germany and refused to acknowledge the Potsdam accords because they had not participated in their drafting. This disruption of Western unity infuriated General Lucius Clay, who commanded the U.S. forces in Germany. Yet Britain and the United States had to tread softly with existing French governments, out of concern that any foreign policy embarrassment for them might lead to Communist victory in French elections. Indeed, the United States in these years sent substantial amounts of grain, coal, and financial aid to bolster democratic French governments (and also clandestine financial support to certain newspapers).

Eventually, Clay and the U.S. War Department took matters into their own hands. In May 1946 Clay announced cessation of the dismantling of industry in the U.S. zone of occupation and halted reparations to the Soviet zone, pending a decision as to whether Germany was really going to be administered as one economic unit. The Soviets retaliated by seizing ownership of 200 key industrial plants in their zone. The British, solicitous for their own economy and distressed by the costs associated with supporting their zone of occupation, needed to find better sources of materials and markets for that zone. A merger of the Western zones would clearly be beneficial to all their economies. France declined to participate, but the merger of the British and U.S. zones into Bizonia took place on January 1, 1947. This time the Soviets responded by holding elections in their own zone and by creating in early 1947 a special administration for internal affairs; in time it would organize the dreaded Stasi (secret police). In short, the reciprocal moves of the superpowers were leading to the consolidation of their particular types of control in their several sectors and to the de facto dismemberment of Germany. This happened despite all the contrary pronouncements that the defeated nation, aside from the lands relinquished to Poland, would remain united.

The Truman and Marshall Plans

The course of events after the war proved strikingly different from what the United States had optimistically expected. The United States was, in fact, more than a little unsure of how to deal with the Soviet Union and the challenge it seemed to be mounting. This puzzlement and lack of ideas in part account for the favorable reception accorded to recommendations forwarded in a long telegram of February 1946 from George Kennan, the first secretary in the U.S. Moscow embassy. Kennan was one of the most experienced U.S. diplomats who had specialized in European and Soviet affairs. He had hitherto played only a minor role in establishing U.S. foreign policy, but that was soon to change for a brief period of years.

In his telegram, Kennan explained the ideological background of the Soviets' policy, their belief in the eventual collapse of capitalism and their use abroad of foreign Communist parties and other pro-Soviet groups to hasten this collapse. At the same time he noted that Soviet foreign policy was not adventuristic. The main aim of the Soviets was to promote the rapid economic and social development of their own country, and they would retreat in foreign policy initiatives when they met with firm resistance.

The conclusion that Kennan drew from this analysis was that the danger to the West was not from Soviet aggression but from Western weakness. The best defense was not in the military sphere but in the health and vigor of Western societies. As Kennan put it, the United States should adopt "an approach aimed at *creating* strength in the West rather than *destroying* strength in Russia." Stalin, he added, could not be bought by promises of aid and would push forward wherever he found weakness. Such tests should be "contained by the adroit and vigilant application of counterforce at a series of constantly shifting geographical and political points."

This was the so-called policy of containment. Its aim was to keep the USSR in its place by strengthening the economies and hence the morale of the countries that might be targets of disruption. It implied the further premise that an extension of communism was equivalent to an extension of Soviet power. Kennan's conception of containment was in later years distorted by U.S. policies designed to encircle the Soviet Union with military bases and nuclear weapons, sometimes at the expense of the economic and social stability of the countries on its border. Kennan, however, did not have in mind creation of a major military force or of alliance systems; these he believed would only be interpreted by the Soviets as aggressive threats.

George F. Kennan, whom many consider to be the father of U.S. foreign policy toward the Soviet Union during the Cold War, is shown here as director of the Policy Planning Staff in the State Department, a post he held from 1947 to 1950. Kennan proposed the concept of "containment" of the Soviet Union as the basis for U.S. foreign policy, but he has since maintained that the West misconstrued and misapplied his notion. Any failure of the policy, he asserts, "consisted in the fact that our own government, finding it difficult to understand a political threat as such and to deal with it in other than military terms, . . . failed to take advantage of the opportunities for useful political discussion . . . [and by] its military preoccupations . . . perpetuate[d] the very division of Europe which it should have been concerned to remove. It was not 'containment' that failed; it was the intended follow-up that never occurred" (Memoirs 1925–1950 [1967], p. 365). Now at the Institute for Advanced Study in Princeton, Kennan is one of the country's leading experts on Soviet history and diplomacy. (Photo courtesy of George F. Kennan.)

U.S. secretary of defense James Forrestal and others saw the telegram as a call for firmness. They soon had opportunity to demonstrate such a stance. The United Kingdom had hitherto taken responsibility for bolstering the Western and democratic cause in the eastern Mediterranean. The British were supporting the Greek government in combating a Communist insurrection (though the West blamed Stalin for nourishing that insurrection, historians would later find that the Greek Communists gained their greatest support from Marshal Tito of Yugoslavia). The United Kingdom had also encouraged the Turks to resist Soviet demands for cession of a small area and for a voice in the defense of the straits leading from the Mediterranean to the Black Sea. But at the beginning of 1947, the economic situation in Great Britain was grim. The British soon informed the United States that they could not find the $250 million in military aid that Greece and Turkey needed. By March a decision was reached in Washington to provide that aid, and the president announced the Truman Doctrine: The United States would send aid to nations threatened by communism.

Truman consciously chose to emphasize the battle against communism rather than quietly transfer old war material to Turkey and Greece. It was the best way to assure the support of Congress and the American people, especially those concerned by the growing strength of the Communists in China. But his phrasing served to build the psychology of the "red scare." The sweeping language also implied that the United States was prepared to shore up countries resisting communism the world over. State Department officials, including Kennan, cringed, worrying that the aid sent to Turkey would upset the Soviets and increase their hostility. However the Soviets did in fact feel, the aid proved timely and successful in strengthening the Greek and Turkish governments.

During the same period, March–April 1947, the foreign ministers of the great powers were in deadlock in Moscow over issues related to Central Europe. The failure of their conference convinced Secretary of State George C. Marshall of the United States that the Soviets would continue to be difficult. The creation of central German administrative agencies would be a long time in coming. Foreign Minister Ernest Bevin of Britain, fretting over the economic drain placed on his country by its occupation zone in Germany, persuaded Marshall that the level of industrial production in Bizonia should be raised, as reunification would not occur in the foreseeable future.

Marshall knew such a move would anger the French, who feared German revival and the possibility that the Germans might achieve a standard of living above that of the French. Marshall therefore asked his new policy-planning staff, headed by Kennan, to work out a program dealing with European economic recovery in general. A plan was badly needed, for the economic situation in Europe in 1947 following two harsh winters was worse than in 1945. The plan produced suggested combining a short-range issue, the production of more coal in the Ruhr area, with a long-range policy of economic assistance for European reconstruction. Two aspects of this plan seemed likely to appease the French: They needed more coal from the Ruhr to fuel their own factories, and the plan provided that the European nations themselves would draw up the rules for allocation of the funds and supervise their administration. The French could thus see to it that German development did not outstrip their own industrial modernization and standard of living.

Marshall announced his proposal for U.S. support for a united economic recovery effort of the European states in an address to Harvard alumni on June 5, 1947. The Marshall Plan, as it came to be known, was a momentous act of statesmanship. The policies initiated under it are generally regarded as the most successful peacetime venture in foreign affairs ever undertaken by the United States. The funding would spark the rebuilding of Western Europe, both in material and psychological terms. The plan would create a foundation for future cooperation that only a few leaders dreamed could really come to pass. Though often described as an act of U.S. generosity, which it was, the Marshall Plan was also a direct offspring of Cold War tensions. These tensions were fueled by events in Eastern Europe, differences over the treatment of Germany, and British and U.S. awareness of the importance of keeping the loyalty of France, which on occasion had tried to hold a mediating position between the Soviet Union and the United States.

Kennan had insisted that the U.S. offer should be made to all of Europe, not just to the Western democracies. If the Soviets did not wish to participate, with the resulting division of Europe, it should be at their initiative and not at that of the United States. The State Department did not expect many Eastern European states to join and no doubt would have had difficulty with Congress if all of them had asked. The gesture did assuage those in Western Europe who initially viewed the U.S. initiative as an attempt to gain economic control of their countries. The Soviets therefore had to make a decision. It is likely that Stalin's thinking was influenced by a series of events that suggested the Soviets were facing a crisis in the spring of 1947. Many of the first secretaries of Communist parties in neighboring countries were evidencing nationalist concerns and an interest in acting independently of Moscow's wishes. Some of these secretaries were even talking of meeting together, in which case they might form a sort of front that could challenge Stalin's leadership. The growing success of Communist troops against the Nationalist Chinese foreshadowed the possibility of a different sort of rivalry for influence among Communist nations. The Truman Doctrine and Marshall Plan showed that Western resistance to Communist advance was stiffening. The position of the Communists within France was slipping somewhat, and the West was clearly gearing up to make a firm challenge to the Communist bid for electoral victory in Italy.

Stalin therefore took a series of related actions intended to strengthen his hold on the international Communist movement. Denouncing the Mar-

Europe in the 1950s

SWEDEN

Uppsala ●

Stockholm ●

öteborg ●

BALTIC SEA

enhagen ●

N.P.

Szczecin ●

Poznan ●

POLAND

Gdansk ●

Warsaw ●

Vistula

Oder

Neisse

Cracow ●

ue

CZECHOSLOVAKIA

Vienna ●

ourg.

TRIA

VENEZIA GIULIA
(to Yugoslavia)

Zagreb ●

CROATIA-
SLAVONIA

BOSNIA

YUGOSLAVIA

Sarajevo ●

BOSNIA

ATIC SEA

Titograd ●

Tirane ★

ALBANIA

s

Messina ●

Budapest ★

HUNGARY

BANAT

Belgrade ●

Skopje ●

MACEDONIA

Salonika ●

GREECE

Athens ★

AEGEAN SEA

Crete

FINLAND

Ceded by Finland to
U.S.S.R. after WW II

Porkkala-Udd
(leased to U.S.S.R.
until 1955)

Helsinki ★

Tallinn ★

ESTONIAN S.S.R.

Riga ★

LATVIAN S.S.R.

LITHUANIAN S.S.R.

Kaliningrad
(Königsbgrg)

Vilnius ●

Minsk ★

BYELORUSSIAN
S.S.R.
(WHITE RUSSIA)

Dniester

UKRAINIAN S.S.R.

NORTHERN
BUKOVINA

SUBCARPATHIAN
RUTHENIA

MOLDAVIAN
S.S.R.

Kishinev ●

Pruth

ROMANIA

WALLACHIA

Bucharest ★

Danube

BULGARIA

★ Sofia

Varna ●

SOUTHERN
DOBRUJA
(to Bulgaria)

Istanbul ●

Smyrna ●

KARELIAN S.S.R.
(1940-56)

Leningrad ●

Volga

★ Moscow

U.S.S.R.

RUSSIAN S.S.R.

Don

Kiev ★

Dnieper

Kharkov ●

Sevastopol ●

Yalta ●

BLACK SEA

TURKEY

★ Ankara

Konya ●

CYPRUS
(British
until 1960)

Nicosia ★

Antalya ●

shall Plan as a capitalist plot to extend Western influence, the Soviets forbade the participation of Czechoslovakia and other Eastern European states that had expressed interest in the plan. Independence of mind among nationalist Communists in several Eastern European states was quashed. Independently thinking leaders were ruthlessly purged and figures loyal to Moscow installed in their places as heads of parties and prime ministers. A new international Communist Information Bureau (Cominform) was created to give direction to the worldwide movement; essentially, it was a replacement for the Third Communist International abolished by Stalin in 1943 in order to improve relations with his allies. The Soviets would now formally characterize Europe as divided between peace-loving Communists and aggressive imperialists.

The Western European response to Marshall's offer was prompt and positive. Under the leadership of the French and British, eighteen nations met in Paris to develop a plan of action. The task was not easy, for the United States made clear that this was not another lend-lease program and that it had no intention of funding duplicative efforts in several countries. Trade barriers and the destructive competition of cartels had to be broken down. Eventually sixteen countries chose to participate and indicated they would need some $22.44 billion worth of food, fuel, raw materials, and capital equipment over and above what they could fund themselves during the next four years. The World Bank and other sources could provide $3 billion of the balance. Truman pared the ultimate request to $17 billion. After much debate, the U.S. Congress appropriated $6.8 billion for the first fifteen months and undertook to make three additional annual grants later. The act establishing the European Recovery Program (ERP) formally passed in April 1948 and created an Economic Cooperation Administration (ECA) to carry out the program from the U.S. side.

In Europe the participating nations set up a permanent body known as the Organization for European Economic Cooperation (OEEC); some years after the end of the Marshall Plan, in 1961, the OEEC was transmuted into the Organization for Economic Cooperation and Development (OECD). The main task of the OEEC was initially to coordinate development planning. It and its successor also moved to reduce trade barriers and to facilitate the transferability of currencies among its members. The OEEC was headed by a council representing the member states; its technical work was implemented by a secretariat and numerous permanent committees. The OEEC presented to the ECA the detailed requests of each country and elaborated a long-term plan for European cooperation and recovery. Most moneys were made available in the form of outright grants that were to be spent on U.S. goods. Each country was required to place in a "counterpart fund" an amount in its own currency equal to these grants. The European states obtained these funds by selling to their own inhabitants the food and material sent to them under the plan. The counterpart funds accumulated and could be spent by the different European countries only with the approval of U.S. authorities. The latter were concerned with seeing that the funds were used to bolster the European nations' economies and to encourage European recovery. Often a small percentage of the funds was set aside to pay for the expenses of the United States in that country or for the U.S. acquisition of scarce raw materials produced by that country.

The European Recovery Program ended officially on December 30, 1951. Some $12.4 billion was granted or loaned to the participating countries. In the years of the ERP, the Western European participants experienced the most rapid economic growth in their history: 10 percent in 1948, 7 to 7.5 percent in the next two years, and 4.7 percent in 1951 (as compared with an average of about 2 percent for the war-ravaged and depressed years of 1913–1938).

Economists still debate how the Europeans might have fared without the ERP, but they agree that its long-term effect was as much institutional as economic. This result occurred in part because U.S. officials, in their implementation of the plan, were heavily committed to persuading Europe to abandon the old rivalries of fragmented political capitalism. In place of the latter they advocated adoption of the associative neoliberal capitalism of the New Deal that had apparently enabled the United States to emerge from the Great Depression. Modern technology and marketing techniques, collaboration between private and public bodies and elites, macroeconomic management, convertible currencies, multilateral free trade, and supranational institutions were intended to overcome ideologic and national rivalries. Free market forces would be balanced by and work cooperatively with institutions of economic coordination.[1] British and occasionally French opposition inhibited full achievement of this agenda, and in the end European economic practices were only "half-Americanized."[2] It is nevertheless evident that the Western European states would have found it much more difficult to develop a structure of cooperation and integration if they had not been confronted by the challenge of the Marshall Plan. It should be given credit for setting Western Europe on a new course.

The Treaty of Dunkirk and the Brussels Pact

The European Recovery Program was directed against "hunger, poverty, desperation, and chaos," as Marshall said. It was intended also to aid "free people who are seeking to preserve their independence and democratic institutions and human freedoms against totalitarian pressures," as Under Secretary of State Dean Acheson explained to U.S. senators. It was a Western economic response to a perceived threat of Soviet expansion. The plan attempted to address long-standing economic problems but found its stimulus in the need to treat immediate problems in Germany in a way acceptable to France.

The French, however, desired more specifically military protection against Germany. They found it in an alliance signed with Great Britain at Dunkirk on March 4, 1947. The Treaty of Dunkirk was a natural outgrowth of the war and reflected recognition that the United Nations was not likely to solve all issues, at least in the near future. The French were reassured; the British viewed the alliance as enhancing their diplomatic position and encouraging Western European cooperation.

Failure of the great powers to reach agreement on Germany the ensuing summer indicated the need for further Western regional collaboration. In December British foreign minister Bevin suggested creation of a "spiritual federation of the west" that would include the United States. But isolationism was still strong in the United States, and its leaders were interested in persuading the Europeans to take more responsibility for their own defense. Washington therefore declined to participate in talks, suggesting that if the Europeans made an alliance that worked, U.S. cooperation would flow to it naturally.

The State Department did, however, urge that the phrasing of the alliance not follow the specifically anti-German terms of the Treaty of Dunkirk. It had been interested in Bevin's proposal because, though meeting French concerns about any possible German attack, it seemed to imply a wider alliance directed against the USSR. Indeed, the United States envisioned the eventual accession of at least the Western-occupied portion of Germany to the pact. The Belgians and British agreed. They saw little use in a pact that did not elicit a favorable U.S. attitude; they also had less fear of Germany and more of the USSR than did France. Concerned that an alliance that might some day include a German state would eventually mean German soldiers, France clung to the formula created in the Treaty of Dunkirk until a major event in Eastern Europe altered its perceptions.

The West was deeply shaken by the Communist coup d'état of February 25, 1948, in Czechoslovakia, the one Eastern European state that had tenaciously clung to democratic processes and friendly relations with both East and West. The Soviets, by sponsoring a takeover of the only government in the Soviet orbit that had not come under Stalinist leadership, clearly demonstrated their determination to resist Western influence. With the news of this assault on Czech democracy, the French no longer saw need for wording an alliance in a way that would not offend the Soviets. They also recognized the necessity of continuing U.S. support against their own domestic Communist threat. Within days, Great Britain, France, Belgium, the Netherlands, and Luxembourg joined in the fifty-year Brussels treaty, directed against any attack on Europe but in reality aimed against the Soviet Union. The Czech coup additionally galvanized the U.S. Congress to pass the long-discussed bill creating the ERP.

The Brussels Pact of March 1948 called for economic, social, and cultural collaboration and collective self-defense. Its breadth recognized that in challenging times the protection of security involved more than just military steps. The treaty, popularly known as the Western Union, made provision for a consultative Council of Foreign Ministers and a permanent commission of ambassadors meeting in London. Under the direction of these bodies, a defense committee and a committee of chiefs of staff were responsible for working out a common defense policy.

The Berlin Blockade

The coup in Czechoslovakia also helped to move the United States closer toward participation in collective arrangements. This departure from traditional U.S. policy was reflected in a resolution adopted by the Senate in June 1948. Authored by the Republican chairman of the Senate Foreign Relations Committee, Arthur Vandenberg, it expressed U.S. determination to make use of "the inherent right of individual or collective self-defense" recognized in Article 51 of the UN Charter; it further proposed U.S. association with regional arrangements based on self-help and mutual aid that would affect national security.

About the same time, the French agreed to merge their occupation zone in Germany with Bizonia. They did so only reluctantly, influenced by the Marshall Plan and after having received assurances regarding their military protection via the Dunkirk and Brussels pacts. The French were also disappointed by the Soviet rejection in the spring of 1947 of French claims for separation of the Rhineland from Germany and for incorporation of the Saar into the French economy (an action Britain and the United States were willing to permit). The French Communists had supported the French claims, but the German Communists had opposed them. The Soviets carried water on both shoulders for some while. They finally decided that the Communists were not likely to win in France and therefore threw their support to the German Communists' position, marking Soviet acknowledgment that the ideological battle lines were moving east.

The merger of the occupation zones occurred on June 18, 1948. Two days later the Western powers instituted a currency reform throughout Trizonia. The Soviets responded with their own new currency in the Eastern zone and Berlin. To prevent that currency from drawing Berlin further into the Soviet orbit, the Western powers introduced the Trizonia currency into the city. The Soviets responded with a blockade of rail and road access to West Berlin. The reciprocal process by which the Cold War escalated was in full swing.

Consolidation of the Two Camps

Even as a Western airlift supplied Berlin until the failed blockade was lifted in May 1949, several developments occurred that further defined the separa-

The Soviet blockade of Berlin in 1948 was an attempt to force the incorporation of Berlin into Soviet-controlled East Germany and a challenge to the resolve of the West. Determined to defend Berlin but anxious to avoid war, the West responded with an unprecedented airlift of millions of tons of food and other necessities to the beleaguered citizens of the city. At the peak of this effort, planes arrived in Berlin every three minutes, around the clock. The airlift became a symbol of the Western world's commitment to defend itself, and the admiration it won among German citizens was a key factor in the Soviet decision to lift the blockade in 1949. (Photo courtesy of the German Information Center.)

tion of Europe into opposing sectors. These events did not come to pass overnight but rather were the result of months of discussion ripened to fruition by the apparently mounting threats.

Comecon

For the Soviets, the immediate postwar concern was rapid economic and social development of their own country and establishment of a sphere of influence regarded as vital to Soviet security. Stress was laid on the exaction of reparations from Eastern Europe. It has been estimated that the transfer of resources from this region to the Soviet Union was in the order of $14 billion, most of which came from East Germany. Thus the Soviets withdrew from Eastern Europe an amount of resources roughly equivalent to that made available by the United States to Western Europe under the Marshall Plan.

In addition, important enterprises that had been acquired by the Germans during the war were reorganized as joint-stock companies in which the Soviets had the controlling interest. Uranium mines in Czechoslovakia and East Germany, coal mines in Poland, and oil wells in Romania, for example, were required to send their products to the Soviet Union at well below world prices.

More important in the long run was the rapid transformation of the economies of the six Eastern European countries from a combination of free markets and central controls to a strictly Stalinist system of central planning. Under this system, the state owned all enterprises and planned in detail the production and distribution of goods. As in the Soviet Union, a policy of extensive growth was imposed. This involved large allocations of resources to investment and a rapid transfer of labor from agriculture to industry. At the same time, agriculture was collectivized, though in varying degrees depending on conditions in the several countries. The result was relatively rapid growth, at an annual rate of about 4 percent in the early postwar years. Emphasis was on investment, and the relatively modest allocations to consumption meant that the standard of living was not significantly improved in this period. The trading pattern of the six Eastern European countries was meanwhile radically altered. On the eve of the war, no more than 1 or 2 percent of their trade had been with the USSR; by 1953 this share was 37 percent.

A Council for Mutual Economic Assistance (known officially as CMEA, but more generally as Comecon) was formed in January 1949. The original members were the USSR, Bulgaria, Czechoslovakia, Hungary, Poland, and Romania. Albania joined later that year. Yugoslavia was not a member, and, until his death in 1953, Stalin unsuccessfully attempted to employ the organization as a lever to keep that country from wandering too far from Soviet leadership. (Albania would be a member from 1949 to 1961; the German Democratic Republic would participate from 1950 to 1990; the Mongolian People's Republic would join in 1962, Cuba in 1972, and Vietnam in 1978.)

Although obviously a response to the economic integration of Western Europe encouraged by the Marshall Plan, Comecon was initially more a mechanism for Soviet economic control than a cooperative enterprise. In time it developed more flexibility. Its organization called for an annual session of all members, with the head of the host country serving as rotating chairperson. An executive committee meeting in Moscow handled week-to-week concerns. As years passed, the structure of Comecon became increasingly complex, with many permanent commissions concerned with different aspects of trade and industry. Seven standing conferences recommended policy in their several fields of competence. These services were all assisted by a Soviet-dominated secretariat.

The North Atlantic Treaty Organization

The Vandenberg Resolution had cleared the way for U.S. participation in a regional alliance structure to protect Europe. The French, now greatly concerned by the immediate Communist threat as well as the more distant possibility of a resurgent Germany, pressed for tangible indications of continuing U.S. concern for European security. Their reluctance to collaborate with the United States and Britain on issues related to administration of German territories only underlined the need for some Western agreement involving the United States. Any future war was expected to be nuclear, for Western policy relied on nuclear weapons to counter large Soviet conventional forces. A defense treaty without the United States (and a congressional commitment rather than just executive promises) seemed to some of the European negotiators like a gun without a bullet.

Complex negotiations culminated in the signing of the North Atlantic Treaty on April 4, 1949, by the United Kingdom, France, Belgium, the Netherlands, Luxembourg, Denmark, Iceland, Norway, Italy, Portugal, Canada, and the United States. (Greece and Turkey acceded in 1951, the German Federal Republic in 1955, and Spain in 1982; France partially withdrew in 1964.) The central thrust of the treaty was that each member would consider an attack on another member in the defined North Atlantic area (thus excluding colonies in Africa, for example) as an attack on itself. In accordance with its constitutional processes, a member should "assist in repelling the attack by all military, economic and other means in its power."

The treaty provided for creation of an executive body, a North Atlantic Council of foreign, defense, and finance ministers. Beneath an overall commander, there were to be three separate commands controlling forces contributed by the member states: an Atlantic Command, a Channel Command, and a Central Command overseeing the forces in Europe, including Turkey but excluding Portugal and Great Britain, under the direction of the Supreme Allied Commander Europe (SACEUR). The treaty also established a U.S.-Canadian regional planning group.

The alliance was unique in its plan for the peacetime creation of a joint military force. The development of NATO forces, although never as extensive as desired, was a remarkable achievement, and NATO made a vital contribution to the security of its members. Yet it had its problems and in many respects fell short of expectations. For example, when NATO was established, it had as its goal the formation of a community of nations with integrated political, social, and economic institutions. Progress on these lines was limited, in part because so much emphasis was placed on military issues and because the alliance membership soon proved too diverse to provide the basis for such a community.

The most difficult issue concerned the nature of the military threat and the means that should be used to counter it. Under the terms of the treaty,

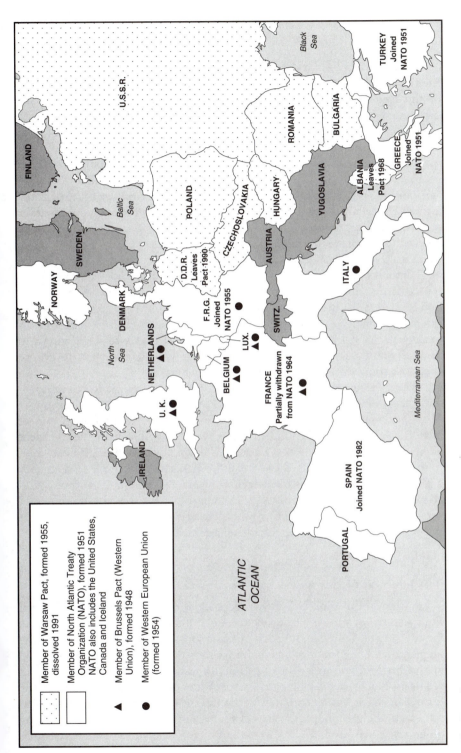

The Two Camps

an attack against one member of NATO was to be considered an attack against them all. This meant that an integrated strategy had to be devised that would take into account the wide diversity of interests and capabilities of the member states. Particularly acute were the differences in outlook between the United States and Western Europe. The Europeans wished to see substantial U.S. forces stationed on the Continent, but it was the U.S. view that the European states ought to be able to provide the bulk of their own forces. European concern arose not only out of uncertainty as to the firmness of the U.S. commitment in Europe, in view of the U.S. tradition of isolationism, but also out of fear that in the event of Soviet aggression the United States might abandon Europe to the Soviet armies and counterattack with nuclear air power. If this occurred, the USSR might ultimately be defeated, but Europe would be destroyed in the process.

The solution NATO finally reached was a strategy that regarded the NATO forces in Europe as a "shield" to deter the USSR from easy conquests on the Continent. U.S. weapons were to be a "sword" available in case the Soviet Union launched an all-out attack. This strategy emphasized the essentially defensive character of NATO, as its forces in Europe were entirely inadequate for an attack on the Soviet Union. In a sense, U.S. troops in Europe would serve as hostages guaranteeing U.S. involvement to avenge their loss should they be annihilated by Soviet attack.

This strategy of "shield" and "sword" had a certain logic to it, but it met with many objections. One was that U.S. strategic air power was not under NATO command, for Congress had decreed in its Atomic Energy Act of 1946 that a decision to use U.S. nuclear weapons rested with the president alone. It was also asserted that because U.S. air power served as a deterrent to the USSR in any event, there was little chance the Soviets would attempt a general offensive. A more likely scenario was a series of limited attacks with conventional weapons in relatively unimportant areas. Such attacks could overwhelm the relatively weak ground forces available to the West but might not be of sufficient gravity to justify a major nuclear reply.

The Council of Europe

While the OEEC and NATO were consolidating a number of the Western European nations in specific economic and military ways, another movement for the general political and social integration of more nations was gaining momentum. The idea of reducing the barriers that separate peoples is an old one in Europe, and indeed Europe's division into discrete nation-states is a relatively modern development. The separateness and exclusiveness of the European states was accentuated in the interwar period, when nations tried to assure their economic welfare by erecting high trade barriers. Many observers considered this effort at autarky—national economic self-sufficiency—as one of the causes of World War II. It was therefore natural that the tragedy of war stimulated plans for creating unity out of diversity.

Several leaders called for greater European cooperation, among them Paul van Zeeland of Belgium and Winston Churchill of Great Britain. With the support of other leaders, a meeting was organized that approved the establishment of a Council of Europe, an action formalized in May 1949. Initial efforts to create a supranational body were unsuccessful, but a consultative Parliamentary Assembly was created. Representatives were to be elected by the parliaments of the member states (ten at the time, and twenty-one by 1978). Representation was proportional to population, and members were to sit alphabetically according to their names, not by national groups. The members were to vote by personal conviction rather than national policy. The parliament had no authority to legislate for the member states. Instead, its recommendations, which required a two-thirds majority of the representatives casting votes, were made to a Council of Ministers. It in turn could make recommendations to the member states. The parliament, at least at its inception, had little clout. In 1951 its first president, Paul-Henri Spaak, resigned, saying, "If a quarter of the energy spent here in saying no were used to say yes to something positive, we should not be in the state we are in today."

Despite the reluctance of member states to relinquish national interests and sovereignty, the council gradually became established as a general policy-formulating body of Europe. It has, for instance, sponsored a number of treaties that bear significantly on the welfare of all Europeans. Of these the most important is the European Convention for the Protection of Human Rights and Fundamental Freedoms, signed in Rome in 1950. The legal guarantees this convention offers are enforced by a Commission of Human Rights empowered to make a friendly settlement of complaints and by a European Court of Human Rights to handle cases the commission is unable to settle. Other conventions sponsored by the Council of Europe were and are concerned with social security, social and medical assistance, patents, and similar subjects. Though the council did not travel far down the road of supranationalism, it showed what cooperation could and might achieve and provided a basis for important shifts toward internationalism in later decades.

All of these events demonstrated the coalescing of Europe into opposing blocs. Further confirmation of this development would be the creation of two different German states. The German Federal Republic (West Germany) would formally come into being in May 1949, the German Democratic Republic (East Germany) in October. This establishment of separate states was the logical culmination of events that had occurred in the occupied German territories since 1945. Still to be resolved would be the manner and extent to which the two German states would be accepted and integrated into the two blocs. In the East, this occurred fairly rapidly under the supervision of the Soviet Union. In the West, the process was more complicated because of the virulent distrust the French held of their former invaders.

The Quest for West German Rearmament

War in Korea

The issue of the Federal Republic's relationship to the rest of Western Europe
was raised with force by the invasion, on June 25, 1950, of South Korea by
troops of Communist North Korea. After World War II, Korea north of the
38th parallel had been placed under Soviet occupation, the territory to the
south under that of the United States. Negotiations for establishing an
independent united democratic Korea broke down, and the matter was
referred to the United Nations. After free elections were held in the south,
the General Assembly recognized the government of that region as legitimate,
and the United States withdrew its occupation force.

It may be that the Soviets did not foresee a strong reaction to the invasion
by the North Koreans, given the withdrawal of U.S. troops. Or perhaps the
North Koreans moved more precipitously than Stalin expected. In Washington and other capitals, the need for prompt action to contain the Soviets was
felt; soon, troops, a great proportion of which were from the United States,
were fighting under the UN flag in defense of South Korea. The U.S. decision
to respond as strongly as it did was motivated to a great extent by the desire
to reassure the members of the new NATO alliance that the United States
would honor its commitments. A major concern plagued the United States,
however. Was the affair a feint to entangle the United States in a war in
distant Asia so that Soviet troops could more freely sweep through Europe?

U.S. involvement in Korea and mounting fears that the Soviets would
soon attempt a military advance in Europe brought immediate pressure from
the United States for increased numbers of Western troops on the Continent.
These could not be supplied entirely by the United States, and it was doubtful
if the French, British, Belgians, and others would be able to do enough by
themselves. What was needed, Washington officials believed, were contingents
of West German troops under NATO command. Their eagerness for German
rearmament revealed a major difference between the U.S. and the French
conceptions of NATO. For France, NATO was a vehicle by which its
preeminent position in the defense of the Continent could be assured. For
the United States, NATO was in part a means for ultimately integrating
German forces into the defense of Europe.

Incorporation of West German troops into the Western Union and
NATO had the possibility of improving the balance of Western forces in
Europe against those of the East, but it could also create an imbalance of

forces within Western Europe upsetting to the French. It was further possible that this step might provoke the Soviets into actions they might otherwise eschew. Paris steadfastly opposed the notion of incorporation of Germany into NATO. But simple opposition was not enough in the face of the perceived Soviet threat.

The Schuman Plan

For several years a remarkable Frenchman, Jean Monnet, head of the Plan for the Modernization and Equipment of France, had been quietly working for international cooperation. He feared German rearmament would escalate the Cold War. He also recognized that NATO was an inadequate tool for integrating Europe inasmuch as it excluded European neutrals and others legitimately concerned with the Continent's welfare. Monnet believed that some form of European union could be devised that would involve West Germany, winning its commitment to the West yet avoiding the critical issue of German rearmament. If customs barriers, especially for such crucial commodities as coal and steel, were broken down, reconstruction could move forward, Western Europe would be strengthened, and joint production of these key commodities would make war between France and West Germany—in Monnet's words—"not only unthinkable but materially impossible." Such an arrangement would also give France some control and say regarding steel and coal production in the Federal Republic. Monnet preferred to work behind the scenes. He soon found a sponsor for his bold proposal, French foreign minister Robert Schuman, for whom the plan was eventually named.

The dream was not new, and the possibility of greater economic collaboration had been suggested by the success of the OEEC and of the European Payments Union created by the OEEC in 1950 to facilitate transferability of currencies. Moreover, Belgium, Luxembourg, and the Netherlands had formed their own Benelux Economic Union that took effect in 1948 and was designed to free controls on 90 percent of all trade among the three countries by 1950 (see Chapter 12).

Monnet was clever enough not to attempt integration on too broad a front. Rather, he chose a sectoral approach that focused on both the key commodities for war and reconstruction—coal and steel—and the geographic area of greatest concern in Western Europe—the French province of Lorraine and the West German Ruhr River valley. The proposal took Europe by storm. The United States, once it was assured Monnet was not suggesting a special, huge cartel, could not help but be supportive of a proposal designed to strengthen Western Europe. The question of German rearmament was temporarily placed on the back burner while the terms of the European Coal and Steel Community (ECSC) were negotiated.

Formally created by the Treaty of Paris of April 1951, the ECSC included France, the German Federal Republic, Italy, Belgium, the Netherlands, and

88

Jean Monnet (left) and Robert Schuman were key architects of the new Europe. Monnet, an international businessman and French government official, contributed creative ideas, a positive approach, and hard work to the goal of a united Europe. Schuman, the French foreign minister, provided the political leadership and flexibility needed to win French and European approval of Monnet's plan to pool Western Europe's coal and steel resources in the European Coal and Steel Community. (Photo 306-PS-52-742 in the National Archives.)

Konrad Adenauer (center), the first postwar chancellor and de facto minister of foreign affairs for the Federal Republic of Germany, at a meeting of the council of the European Coal and Steel Community in 1951. Acceptance of the Federal Republic into the council was a key step in Adenauer's efforts to gain equality of status for Germany. Seated next to him (with water glass) is the state secretary for foreign affairs, Walter Hallstein. Hallstein later became known for his "doctrine" that the Federal Republic would not recognize any country—except the Soviet Union—that granted diplomatic recognition to the German Democratic Republic. That policy was set aside when Social Democrat Willy Brandt took charge of foreign affairs in 1966. (Photo courtesy of the German Information Center.)

Luxembourg—what came to be known as the Europe of the Six. Great Britain declined to join, citing its special relationships with the Commonwealth nations and the United States. More particularly, the British were reluctant to sacrifice any national sovereignty to the ECSC and were unsure how much a part of Europe they wished to be.

Central to the operation of the ECSC was a nine-member administrative high authority in Strasbourg that could make decisions binding on all members. It could do so, however, only regarding the production and sale of coal, iron, and steel. Its power was thus both greater and more circumscribed than that of the Council of Europe. There was also a council of foreign ministers, an assembly elected by the parliaments of the member states, and a court to settle disputes regarding interpretation of the treaty. The purpose of the community was to stimulate the production of coal and steel by creating a free market through the reduction of trade barriers. In this it succeeded. During the first four years of operation, the volume of production of the members of the ECSC increased 23 percent for coal and 145 percent for iron and steel.

In retrospect, creation of the ECSC emerges as a turning point for Western Europe. At the time, perhaps only Monnet and Schuman had such wide-reaching hopes for their project. In many ways, the ECSC was a defensive maneuver—a reaction to war in Korea, U.S. proposals for rearmament of Germany, fears of the USSR that burgeoned following word of the Soviet test of an atomic bomb in late summer 1949, and cessation of the Marshall Plan. The positive economic, social, and even political effects of the plan in the long run, however, both bolstered the West and pointed the way to a new concept of Europe.

The European Defense Community

The perceived Soviet threat and the question of German disarmament did not go away. The United States soon linked increases of its own troop strength in Europe and acceptance of command of Western forces there with participation by German soldiers in the defense of Europe. Rebirth of a German *Wehrmacht* and general staff was far from what France desired. Monnet and René Pleven, the French premier, hastily proposed an alternative to West Germany's creating its own army and joining NATO. It would be a European Defense Community (EDC) of more limited membership. The Federal Republic would contribute multiple units no larger than 1,200 troops that would have no heavy armaments. The contingents would integrate with those from other nations under the leadership of the EDC command; the West Germans would form no separate military establishment. The EDC as a supranational organization thus had the particular aim of providing the means for Germany to rearm without threatening the security of its Western neighbors.

After some hesitancy, the United States threw its support to the so-called Pleven Plan. There were problems, however. The French accepted the plan as a way to avoid true German rearmament; they also liked the further development of European institutions, initiated by the Schuman Plan, that the new proposal seemed to encourage. U.S. officials saw the calls for implementation of European institutions as delaying progress toward their own goal of real German rearmament. Moreover, France, the United States, and Britain had not consulted Germany. When they did, they discovered that the West German public was far from interested in once again supporting a military arm. If it were to do so, Chancellor Konrad Adenauer insisted, there should be a renegotiation of the Federal Republic's contractual relationship with the Western powers.

Two sets of interrelated negotiations were therefore undertaken that culminated in May 1952. The occupying powers first signed a set of contractual agreements with Germany. The next day France, West Germany, Italy, Belgium, the Netherlands, and Luxembourg signed the EDC treaty, which was accompanied by a mutual-defense treaty with the United Kingdom. Continuing French distrust of Germany resulted in a further declaration by the United States, Great Britain, and France that they would treat any action threatening the integrity of the EDC (such as withdrawal of the Federal Republic from the community once German armed units had been created) as a threat to their security.

By the contractual agreements, the occupation statute for the Western zones of Germany was repealed and the High Commission brought to an end. The Federal Republic substantially improved its status, obtaining nearly equal footing with its Western neighbors and about as much sovereignty as possible without requiring Soviet approval. Allied troops in West Germany would now be considered defense rather than occupation forces; four-power rights regarding Berlin, any peace treaty, and possible reunification of Germany were reserved. Adenauer had skillfully used the EDC to enhance the position of his country. In so doing he also made a major commitment to the West that further consolidated the division of Europe and postponed the likelihood of any prompt reunification of Germany even on a basis of neutrality between East and West.

Germany and the United States also had won on the matter of the size of German troop contingents within the EDC. Both insisted that military efficiency required German units be formed in "combat teams" of 5,000 to 6,000 troops, a size far larger than the French initially envisioned. Indeed, enough changes were made to the original EDC proposal that critics claimed it was no longer the true Pleven Plan. Opposition to the EDC within the French National Assembly mounted. Nationalists criticized the expected loss of independent French army units in Europe. Although other countries ratified the pact, political leaders in France delayed putting it before the French legislature. As time passed, a small wave of Germanophobia built within France. Politicians of various persuasions found opportunity to make difficulties over the issue. The death of Stalin in 1953 and a subsequent softening of Soviet rhetoric calmed the fears that had been so strong in 1950. A shaky truce was achieved in Korea in July 1953. French defeat at Dien Bien Phu in Indochina in May 1954 and the retreat of French forces from Southeast Asia caused many French citizens to see surrender of jurisdiction over the country's European army as another disgrace, one especially galling to the military. The French, moreover, wanted a long-term guarantee that Britain would maintain its military contingents on the European continent at the existing level. They believed that only French and British forces together would be adequate to counterbalance those of Germany. In the absence of such a guarantee, the French thought that their security would be better

---

The Building of the Western Alliance System

MARCH 4, 1947   Britain and France sign the Treaty of Dunkirk, creating a fifty-year alliance.

MARCH 17, 1948   Brussels Pact is signed, forming the Western Union among Britain, France, Belgium, the Netherlands, and Luxembourg.

APRIL 4, 1948   North Atlantic Organization treaty is signed.

MAY 27, 1952   European Defense Community treaty is signed.

AUGUST 30, 1954   French National Assembly rejects the European Defense Community treaty.

OCTOBER 21, 1954   Western European Union is formed.

DECEMBER 29–30, 1954   Brussels Pact is modified; West Germany is approved as a member of NATO.

JANUARY 22, 1963   Elysée treaty of Franco-German friendship and reconciliation is signed.

---

served by keeping their defense forces independent rather than by pooling them with those of other members of the EDC. These and other reasons, including the reluctance of Premier Pierre Mendès-France to support the EDC proposal because it was too supranational and anti-Soviet, brought its failure in the French National Assembly in 1954.

The Western European Union

The defeat of the EDC came as a shock to the other proposed members of the community. The French action was, in fact, so disruptive to Western planning that the French position itself was weakened. Under British leadership, the other members of the failed EDC acted with surprising quickness, moving to expand the Brussels Pact by inclusion of Italy and West Germany and to admit the Federal Republic to NATO. The British also finally pledged not to reduce their forces on the Continent below a certain level without the consent of their Brussels-Pact allies. The enlarged Brussels-treaty group, which would remain separate from NATO, was called the Western European Union (WEU). It was not a supranational authority, as had been envisaged in the case of the EDC, but it had the virtue of being an avenue for the "Europeanization" of the Saar basin, the chief price for French acquiescence to all these developments. By the agreements formally reached in October 1954, the Saar was to be Europeanized, independent but under the supervision of the WEU and with economic ties to France. This time the French National

Assembly did not balk. Thus, four years after having proposed the European Defense Community as an alternative to German membership in NATO, the French accepted the Federal Republic into NATO as an alternative to the EDC.

Within West Germany, Adenauer was roundly criticized for seemingly abandoning the Saarlanders. But he had played his cards smoothly, for he had insisted that the arrangement be approved by a Saar plebiscite. The Saar population, tied by heritage and language to Germany and resentful of what it considered French economic exploitation, voted in 1955 to reject its proposed new status. The region eventually rejoined West Germany in 1957, with economic ties to France continuing until 1959. Thus, as Adenauer had no doubt hoped, his concession at the bargaining table was not converted into an actual German loss.

The Warsaw Pact

The Soviet Union did not stand idle while the West consolidated its alliances. The Warsaw Pact of May 1955—signed by Albania, Bulgaria, Czechoslovakia, the German Democratic Republic, Hungary, Poland, Romania, and the USSR—was widely heralded as a reply to the NATO alliance and Germany's entrance into it. In fact, it was no more than a reconfirmation of existing treaty relationships, many of which had been established in 1948 shortly after the original formation of NATO. The pact also reflected the desire of the Soviets to make adjustments prior to the signing of the Austrian State Treaty on May 15, 1955 (see Chapter 12). As long as the occupation of Austria continued, the Soviets had right of passage for their troops through Hungary and Romania to support the occupation. With the achievement of a peace treaty creating an officially neutral Austria and ending its occupation, the Soviets needed new treaty rights to maintain their troops in Hungary and Romania.

The Soviet alliance system in Europe was based initially on mutual assistance treaties concluded with the government-in-exile of Czechoslovakia in December 1943 and with the postwar governments of Yugoslavia and Poland in April 1945. To these were added a series of treaties in spring 1948 with all the states of Eastern Europe. By 1948 an alliance system of similar bilateral treaties had thus been created in Eastern Europe, both between the USSR and the states of this region and among the states themselves. These treaties provided for collaboration and consultation among the signatories, mutual assistance in the event of aggression by Germany or any third state, and the strengthening of political, economic, and cultural ties. They were concluded for a twenty-year period, and it was stipulated that they would be implemented in the spirit of the UN Charter.

Under the terms of the Warsaw Pact, a Soviet marshal was named supreme commander of the Warsaw Pact forces, and a Political Consultative Committee was established to formulate common policies. A major concern of the Soviets was to create unity out of the diversity of Eastern European national identities by stimulating an identity with "socialist internationalism" in the structure of the Warsaw Pact armed forces. This policy had its origins in the experience of seeking to create a Soviet identity in the Red Army: Individuals from different ethnic groups were dispersed throughout the armed forces and ethnic Great Russians were given a disproportionately large role in the command structure. Such a pattern could not be carried out to as full an extent in Eastern Europe. But in the four countries that hosted Soviet occupation troops—the German Democratic Republic, Poland, Czechoslovakia, and Hungary—all six East German divisions and significant elements of the armed forces of the other three countries were combined with Soviet forces to form the Warsaw Pact army. The Eastern European officers learned Russian and were trained in Soviet military academies; many of the Soviet officers were also bilingual. Soviet officers predominated heavily in the command structure, and national regiments were integrated at the division level.

The significance of the Warsaw Pact army was more political than military. Its chief military value was to keep order in Eastern Europe, as a military conflict between NATO and Warsaw Pact forces was really never on the agenda of either alliance. As a political symbol of "socialist internationalism," however, the Warsaw Pact army stood out as a major effort at regional integration in an environment where state and party relations were primarily bilateral.

To say in retrospect that neither alliance truly planned to attack the other does not diminish the authentic fear the alliances stirred at the time. The formation of the two pacts was not a cause but rather a result of the Cold War. Indeed, the Warsaw Pact was something of an afterthought to permit continuing Soviet military control in Eastern Europe even after relaxation of some political controls. Each side believed the other was capable of attacking it and therefore placed great emphasis on defense. Tensions were compounded by the awareness that each alliance's offensive strength corresponded to the weakness of the other's defense. The West, despite moves to draw on West German troops, could not match the extensive conventional forces of the Soviet Union and the Warsaw Pact. Similarly, the Eastern alliance had no good protection against the West's capacity to launch massive atomic air attacks. Moreover, although traditional issues of national vital interests underlay many disputes, such as that over the eastern borders of Poland, an ideological contest paralleled the military confrontation. The age was ideological; nearly all the nations participating in World War II had defined that conflict as a battle of ideologies. Even when political leaders could separate in their minds legitimate national vital interests from proselytizing ideological advancement, their legislatures frequently could not. And often the leaders did not wish to make the separation. One of Stalin's major achievements was the linking of communism with specifically Soviet aims, thus legitimizing his claims on the satellite states.

French fears of a resurgent Germany were grossly unrealistic given that country's damage and disarray, yet the fears were real. In the short run, they hampered efforts to consolidate and strengthen the Western camp. In the long run, they may have helped those efforts. French weakness and insistence that the United States make substantive commitment to the defense of Europe and the strengthening of the economies of the Western states forced accelerated U.S. involvement in Europe. The development of the Marshall and Schuman plans owed much to the linkage of concerns for defense against both the Soviet Union and Germany with the necessity for economic reconstruction. Then, too, the U.S. desire not to spend money refueling old European economic contests and Monnet's effort to reduce economic rivalries fostered a new level of cooperation.

Gestation of a new Europe based on international cooperation was cut short by two developments: the splitting of Europe into two camps and the demise of the EDC, an event that seemingly forced Western European relationships back into more traditional forms even though the ECSC had implied other possibilities. At one time, Stalin apparently hoped that any postwar settlement might provide his nation with a secure sphere of influence buffered from the West by a neutral band of territory ranging from Germany through Austria and Switzerland to Italy. In the most crucial area of Central Europe, that band did not appear, as Germany was divided even as the powers professed their belief in German unification. The victor nations may secretly have been content with that arrangement as a status quo that could be altered in the future. But would the friction of the two camps, made all the more acute by their consolidation and the absence of any buffer zone, lead to escalating tensions and warfare? Or would some sort of equilibrium be achieved? That was the major question at the close of the first decade of the Cold War.

Notes

1. M. J. Hogan, *The Marshall Plan: America, Britain, and the Reconstruction of Western Europe, 1947–1952*, pp. 2, 3.
2. Ibid., p. 440.

Suggested Readings

Angell, R. C., *The Quest for World Order* (1979).
Berezhkov, V., *History in the Making: Memoirs of World War II Diplomacy* (1983).

Chamberlain, M. E., *Decolonization: The Fall of the European Empires* (1985).

Finley, B., *The Structure of the United Nations General Assembly: An Organizational Approach to Its Work, 1974–1980s,* 2 vols. (1987).

———, *The Structure of the United Nations General Assembly: Its Committees, Commissions and Other Organisms, 1946–73* (1977).

Gimbel, J., *The Origins of the Marshall Plan* (1976).

Goodrich, L. M., *The United Nations in a Changing World* (1976).

Hammond, T. T. (ed.), *Witnesses to the Origins of the Cold War* (1982).

Helmreich, J. E., *Gathering Rare Ores: The Diplomacy of Uranium Acquisition, 1943–1954* (1986).

Hogan, M. J., *The Marshall Plan: America, Britain, and the Reconstruction of Western Europe, 1947–1952* (1987).

Holland, R. F., *European Decolonization, 1918–1981: An Introductory Survey* (1985).

Ireland, T. P., *Creating the Entangling Alliance: The Origins of the North Atlantic Treaty Organization* (1981).

Kahler, M., *Decolonization in Britain and France: The Domestic Consequences of International Relations* (1984).

Kertesz, S., *The Last European Peace Conference, Paris, 1946: Conflict of Values* (1985).

McGeehan, R., *The German Rearmament Question: American Diplomacy and European Defense After World War II* (1971).

Mee, C. L., Jr., *The Marshall Plan* (1984).

Milward, A. S., *The Reconstruction of Western Europe, 1945–1951* (1984).

Molotov, V., *U.S.S.R. at the Paris Peace Conference* (1946).

Nogee, J. L., and R. H. Donaldson, *Soviet Foreign Policy Since World War II,* 2d ed. (1985).

Rickhye, I. J., M. Herbotte, and B. Egge, *The Thin Blue Line: International Peacekeeping and Its Future* (1974).

Van der Wee, H., *Prosperity and Upheaval: The World Economy 1945–1980* (1986).

Willis, F. R., *France, Germany, and the New Europe, 1945–1963* (1965).

Yearbook of the United Nations (1947–).

Young, J. W., *Britain, France and the Unity of Europe, 1945–1951* (1984).

———, *France, the Cold War, and the Western Alliance, 1944–49: French Foreign Policy and Post-War Europe* (1990).

CHAPTER FOUR

East-West Equilibrium: 1955–1975

The Situation in the Mid-1950s
The First Summit • The Suez Crisis and Soviet Intervention in Hungary

Integration in Western Europe
Creation of the European Atomic Energy Community
and the European Economic Community
The EEC • The European Free Trade Association
Britain Joins the Economic Community
The Franco-German Treaty of Reconciliation • Developments in NATO

The Soviet Orbit
Cracks in the Bloc • Summit Meetings • The Brezhnev Doctrine

Détente
Willingness to Negotiate • Strategic Arms Limitation Talks
The Helsinki Accords

Notes

Suggested Readings

By the mid-1950s, the Cold War and the division of Europe were established realities to which the European nations had become accustomed. Security and economic development remained dominant concerns on both sides of the Iron Curtain. A modus vivendi that could contain tensions and forestall hot war continued to be elusive. The search for it would be cautious, and shocks along the way would spark pulses of fear. Yet the ability of the East-West blocs eventually to reach a minimal level of agreement at Helsinki in 1975 would attest to the gradual acceptance of the status quo.

An additional major challenge for the Europeans was to find a way to define and express their own concerns and identities while existing in the shadows cast by the conflicting superpowers. In the West an economic approach was developed that had far-reaching implications and improved Franco-German relations. In the East the peoples of several nations resorted to desperate political actions to express their aspirations, actions that would be put down harshly.

The Situation in the Mid-1950s

The First Summit

Not the least of the problems facing European leaders was the mode of negotiating the great issues. The United Nations was the most convenient arena, but in some respects its atmosphere was unsuitable for discussion of matters of the highest importance. The Security Council was governed by rigid rules of procedure, whereas in the General Assembly the presence of over 100 delegations prevented easy and intimate exchange of opinion. Committees of experts performed a useful service, yet their members did not have the authority to make important concessions. Even meetings of foreign ministers tended to be conducted rather formally on the basis of a fixed agenda.

Churchill, who had been returned to power in the elections of 1950, sought to break this deadlock and achieve a more free exchange of opinions on fundamental issues. In 1953 he proposed that a meeting be held "at the summit," that is to say, by heads of state, without an agenda and simply as a means of exploring each other's views. Some criticized this proposal on the ground that little grass grows at the summit; they characterized discussions farther down the slope by seasoned diplomats as more fruitful. But Churchill was aware that during the war decisions by heads of governments had cut through innumerable roadblocks raised by civil service bureaucrats who did not have the breadth of view obtainable only from the heights. The idea

On August 17, 1962, East German Peter Fechter was shot to death at the Berlin Wall while attempting to escape to the West. This photo of Fechter's body being pulled back into East Berlin was a vivid reminder to West Germans of the brutality of the Communist regime imposed in the Eastern half of their country. The pained and frightened look on the face of the young East German border guard emphasized the dilemma faced by all Germans: How could they learn to live with, and perhaps even ease, the suffering caused by the Wall? (Photo courtesy of the German Information Center.)

seemed worth trying, especially as no other procedure had halted the escalation of the Cold War.

The first postwar convocation of heads of state took place in Geneva in
July 1955. The meetings of Dwight Eisenhower (United States), Nikolai
Bulganin (USSR), Anthony Eden (United Kingdom), and Félix Faure (France)
produced some moments of genuine warmth, and a spirit of friendship
prevailed. But on specific issues the heads of state did not move much beyond
the positions their governments had previously set forth. On the unification
of Germany, the West continued to favor free elections in both parts of the
country, whereas the Soviets preferred to maintain the status quo. Various
proposals were presented for a defense treaty linking all the European states,
but until the German problem could be solved, no agreement was possible as
to the terms of such a treaty. Only on the broad issue of improving East-
West relations was some progress made, as measures to reduce barriers to
travel and cultural exchanges were accepted. The greatest significance of the
summit conference therefore was not its specific accomplishments but rather
that the four heads of state had agreed to meet and talk. Discussion was
better than bullets. An avenue of communication was opened that would
eventually play a key role in the dissolution of the Cold War, although more
than a decade passed before it carried much freight.

Not many European heads of state participated in the summit conference,
which resembled more the gatherings of the Big Four after the Potsdam
conference at the end of the war than a true convocation of European leaders
and views. Most Europeans were still playing a secondary role in determining
their own fate. Two other events were soon to symbolize the impotence of
Europe compared with the power of the United States and the Soviet Union.
These events would also affirm the seeming permanence of the division of
Europe.

The Suez Crisis and Soviet Intervention in Hungary

At the close of World War II, as the full horror of the Holocaust became
known, political leaders in many countries felt a moral obligation to support
demands of Zionist leaders for the creation of an independent Jewish state in
the Middle East. The partitioning of Palestine to make room for the state of
Israel, carried out under the UN directives of 1947, was bitterly opposed by
the Arabs who were displaced; their cause was taken up by nearby Arab
nations. The new Israeli government's principal concern in foreign policy
immediately became that of safeguarding Israel's security in a situation in
which its Arab neighbors regarded the country's very existence as an act of
aggression against Arab national rights.

President Gamal Abdel Nasser of Egypt had for some while been attempting leadership of the Arab cause and a foreign policy independent of the
former colonial powers of Europe. Nasser asked to purchase arms from the

West, but Britain and the United States were reluctant to sell for fear the weapons might be used against Israel. The West therefore indicated that it would sell only on conditions (such as cash payment) that Nasser found unacceptable, especially as such requirements were not imposed on other purchasers of U.S. arms. Nasser instead obtained Soviet equipment through Czechoslovakia. The United States in response withdrew its financial and technical support for the building of the Aswan Dam, a project Nasser valued highly, as he counted on it to provide electrification, stimulate industrialization, and revive Egyptian agriculture.

Nasser's own response was to nationalize the Suez Canal Company, promising compensation to its former shareholders. He was in a position to do so because Britain had withdrawn its troops from Suez in accordance with a 1954 treaty with Egypt. In that treaty, Egypt promised to uphold an 1888 convention providing for freedom of traffic through the canal. The canal was to be operated by a company that was technically Egyptian but was actually controlled by international shareholders. Britain retained its right to reenter Suez in case of an emergency affecting Egypt's control of the canal.

At the end of October 1956, Israel attacked Egypt, asserting that its ability to ship through the canal was endangered. The aim was to break Egypt's military power before it was strong enough to threaten Israel. Britain and France had already agreed with Israel to join the invasion, and soon their forces moved to reestablish international control over the Suez Canal Company and to overthrow Nasser. This last goal was of great import to the British and especially the French, who believed Nasser and Egypt were supplying arms to Algerians revolting against French rule.

President Eisenhower (1953–1961) was not told in advance (at least formally) of the British, French, and Israeli actions and refused to endorse behavior that seemed blatantly imperialistic. The United Nations, reflecting world opinion and backed by the policies of the United States and the Soviet Union, compelled the aggressors to withdraw. Repercussions from the Suez affair in Europe were considerable. Prime Minister Anthony Eden of Britain would soon resign following the embarrassing incident. Throughout Europe there were cold homes that winter, as shipment of oil through the canal could not be resumed until the wreckage had been cleared and pressure from the United Nations had forced Egyptian cooperation. The French economy was hurt, unemployment mounted, and the British pound was destabilized. A British appeal to the United States for a loan to shore up the pound was rejected; the U.S. Congress saw no need to finance a military campaign of which it had not been informed and of which it did not approve. The British and French had again discovered that their days of dominant influence were over. They could no longer go it alone in foreign affairs. Consultation with and support from the United States would be a necessity.

When Soviet troops crushed an uprising in Hungary at the peak of the Suez affair, the Suez crisis prevented the West from showing a coordinated front. Nor could the West effectively condemn the Soviet action in Hungary before the eyes of the Third World. The Hungarian people were upset by the economic disasters brought by forced collectivization and trade exploitation by the Soviets. Reformers wanted their country free of Soviet troops, secret police, and political puppets. Dissidents, desirous of more consumer goods and the opportunity to speak their own minds, took to the streets. Strikes and demonstrations brought in new political leaders who announced the restoration of a multiparty political system and their intention to negotiate withdrawal of all Soviet troops from Hungary. They proclaimed their desire to repudiate the Warsaw Pact and declare Hungary's neutrality. Such independence was not acceptable to the Soviets. In response to an appeal by hardline Hungarian Communists who formed an opposition government, Soviet troops bombarded Budapest and "smashed the sinister forces of reaction" during the first days of November (see Chapter 8).

In Suez and in Budapest, Europeans had attempted to take matters into their own hands. Their inability to succeed in the face of opposition from a superpower demonstrated how little control Europe had of its own fate. True, the United States was closely linked to Europe, and it was in European Russia that the governing power of the Soviet Union was concentrated; yet the weight of influence in European—not to mention world—affairs clearly had passed from the center of Europe to other regions.

For some while after the events in Hungary and Suez, tensions between the two superpower blocs remained high, as similar accusations of imperialism were levied. Words were exchanged, but bullets were not. The blocs were becoming accustomed to each other, and, despite oratorical posturing, each was prepared to let the other have its own sphere of influence.

Integration in Western Europe

The events of 1956 signaled to Western European leaders the need to consolidate their position in the face of the Soviet threat and the possibility that the United States could not be counted on in all situations. Spaak of Belgium was among the leaders who had for some while been calling for increased integration. He, Monnet, and others shared the hope that the Coal and Steel Community could be linked with the European Defense Community to form some sort of European political community. Defeat of the EDC indicated that other avenues for cooperation were needed, and the possibility of expanding the areas of common tariffs among the six members of the Coal and Steel Community attracted much attention.

There were precedents for increasing the range of economic integration beyond the sectors of coal and steel. Benelux had proved successful, as had the Organization for European Economic Cooperation and the European Payments Union (EPU). Negotiations in 1947 had led to a General Agreement on Tariffs and Trade (GATT) initially signed by twenty-three countries. The original treaty, reached under UN auspices in Geneva, was intended to be only temporary, until an international trade organization could be formed. A failure to reach agreement on the organization's charter turned the interim agreement into a permanent arrangement that has been adjusted in successive rounds of negotiations. By October 1988, GATT embraced some ninety-six contracting parties, with almost another thirty following its lead.

According to the 1947 Geneva agreement, each country granted the others most-favored-nation status. Thus if one country lowered its tariff on a given product shipped from another nation, all members of GATT could take advantage of that decreased tariff. GATT had improved trade and benefited its signatories. But experience had also shown observers that if industries were truly to prosper, they needed much broader markets, not just cautiously reduced tariffs that opened up export possibilities only slowly and partially.

The integrationists found support in the United States. President Eisenhower had long called for a United States of Europe to build prosperity, to resist Soviet encroachments, and to resolve the German question. Secretary of State John Foster Dulles in early 1957 saw three serious problems facing Europe. First, he worried that German nationalists might trade neutrality for reunification, hoping to seize a controlling position between East and West. Second, he feared French weakness and defeatism. The third problem— Franco-German relations—was related to the first two. Neither Dulles nor his predecessors at the State Department envisioned any solution to these issues until there was some framework of European union into which Germany could be fitted.

The Federal Republic's association with NATO was a start, but more was needed. The European Defense Community had been tried but failed, in part because the Europeans had been prematurely pressured by the United States to agree on sensitive political issues that needed much more time for resolution. Unfortunately, preliminary explorations of the avenue leading to more economic integration suggested that it was a dead end as well; there were simply too many rival interests at stake.

Creation of the European Atomic Energy Community and the European Economic Community

Monnet, always striving to establish linkages, saw only one opening for progress: cooperation on atomic energy matters. The Europeans had long dreamed of the productive and modernized society they thought inexpensive nuclear power could provide. They were also frustrated by the failure of the United States and United Kingdom to provide them with the necessary technology and fuel. The closefistedness of the two powers regarding the

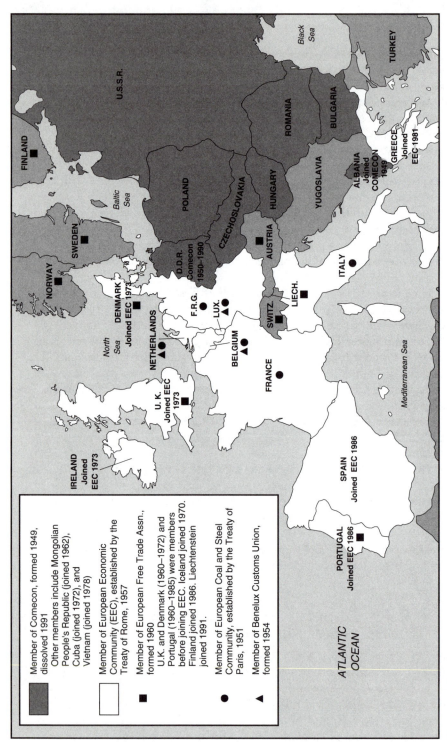

Economic Europe

exchange of scientific information stemmed in part from concern that technologies for peaceful and military uses of the atom were not yet greatly differentiated. Also highly influential was the Atomic Energy Act passed by the U.S. Congress in 1946, limiting U.S. scientific exchange on the atom. Even when the act was amended and then changed, the United States was slow to share information. The cost of nuclear research was enormous and the supply of skilled scientists low. Cooperation by Europeans for their own benefit made sense. Warned by Monnet and Spaak that Europe had to be allowed to reach its own decision, the United States kept a low profile. But it did take helpful steps: It delayed conclusion of bilateral nuclear information treaties with individual states and agreed that Belgium could supply the consortium with Congo uranium previously monopolized by Britain and the United States. The United States also quietly urged the adoption of the integrative model of the ECSC rather than the less supranational cooperative model of the OEEC.

Creation of a European Atomic Energy Community (EURATOM) was thus initially considered a last-ditch effort to retain some momentum for the weakening integration effort. Difficult negotiations led to a surprising development. The West Germans, on the one hand, wanted a common economic market, with its wider opportunities for German industries; they disliked the strong central direction that the French envisaged for EURATOM. The French, on the other hand, were wary of the generalities involved in common-market proposals but liked the concrete advantages offered by EURATOM. They resolved their differences by agreeing on the simultaneous creation of both EURATOM and a European Economic Community (EEC)—often referred to as the Common Market. The Italians were happy to go along, as they were seeking aid for the rehabilitation of southern Italy. The Benelux nations recognized that the new organizations would grant them a more significant voice in Europe and extensive commercial gains as major shipping centers.

By the treaties of Rome of 1957, the six member states of the ECSC formed the European Atomic Energy Community and the European Economic Community. The United Kingdom was invited to participate in both but declined. The British were uncomfortable with the integrative features of the organizations, which implied a certain reduction in individual national sovereignty; they would have much preferred the less binding cooperative approach of the OEEC. They also noted that the British economy had recuperated and seemed to be doing well enough on its own. The United Kingdom wished to protect its commercial relationships with the Commonwealth and its connections with the United States. Indeed, the British were somewhat critical of the EEC as a possible combination that, by means of high tariffs, might try to keep British goods out of Europe.

Though EURATOM was the organization on which the integrationists pinned their most expectant hopes, it did not develop as fully as planned. Its main role was to create a common market for nuclear raw materials and equipment as well as a reservoir of nuclear technicians available to member states. A research center was founded in Switzerland that has attracted skilled physicists and chemists and has achieved much advanced research. But international cooperation did not flourish, in part because several countries— France in particular—felt the need to carry forward their own programs and focused on these instead.

The EEC

The European Economic Community, by contrast, succeeded in a manner much closer to original plans, if somewhat more slowly. Through the creation of a single market, it was intended to stimulate growth in trade and production. The limited sectoral approach of the ECSC was to be broadened to include many more industries than just coal and steel, and the much more difficult issue of agricultural production was to be addressed. The essence of this European economic integration was the surrender by the member states to a common authority of their power to control tariffs, wages, and prices within their own countries.

Initial agreements envisaged elimination of all trade barriers among EEC members in three stages over a period of twelve to fifteen years, involving freedom of movement not only of goods but also of labor and capital; social security systems and wage benefits were to be standardized as well. This was indeed a bold venture, but experience indicated that it was not merely feasible but necessary if Europe were to survive as a center of progress. EURATOM and the EEC, combined with the ECSC, thus provided for the 200 million inhabitants of the Europe of the Six (France, Italy, the Federal Republic of Germany, Belgium, the Netherlands, and Luxembourg) a solid basis for economic integration. All six states were of course members of the OEEC, but there were very significant differences between the approaches of the two organizations. In the case of the OEEC, the member states retained their sovereignty and were free to disregard its recommendations. In the case of the EEC, however, the member states surrendered their sovereignty for certain specific purposes and permitted the community to make decisions for them. Although the community was economic in its functions, it thus called for the pooling of political authority and to this extent laid the foundations for an integrated Europe.

The institutions of the EEC were and are several and have evolved considerably over the years. An important step toward further European integration was taken in 1967, when the executives of the three communities of the EEC, EURATOM, and ECSC were merged into a single European Commission. The members of this commission, though appointed by the participating states, were intended to take a supranational interest and act independently of their governments. Large nations appointed two commissioners each, the small nations one each. The commission supervised in turn a staff that in a few years would number more than 15,000 individuals.

The policies the commission proposes are reviewed by a council composed of the ministers of foreign affairs of the member states; these ministers essentially represent the national interests of those countries. At times the debates within the Council of Ministers have been both difficult and valuable. Their utility was recognized in 1974, when agreement was reached that the heads of state and governments of the members of the EEC should gather for summit meetings three times a year. This offshoot of the Common Market, which only indirectly deals with Common Market affairs, has come to be called the European Council (not to be confused with the Council of Europe formed in 1949—see Chapter 3). It is of considerable import, for it provides the top leaders of key European nations the opportunity to discuss defense and foreign policy matters as well as economic concerns.

There is also a European Parliament of the EEC, delegates to which were initially elected by each of the national parliaments. As early as 1971, the European Parliament and the Consultative Assembly of the Council of Europe held occasional joint meetings. In 1974 a general agreement was reached that the Council of Europe would henceforth focus chiefly on matters relating to human services, whereas the European Parliament would be active in other areas.

The Council of Europe has therefore directed its attention primarily to issues of human rights, youth, education, migrant workers, public health, the environment, and the like. Although the Consultative Assembly of the Council of Europe remained a representation of the parliaments of its member states, the European Parliament of the EEC moved in 1979 to direct election of its members by universal suffrage. The members of this parliament represent their political parties rather than their countries, and election campaigns have begun to have some international significance. The European Parliament can question the commissioners and force their dismissal by a two-thirds vote.

The European Commission oversees several other bodies and activities. The Court of Justice, with one judge from each member country, rules on issues affecting trade. For example, it decided that West German regulations for ingredients used in brewing (banning preservatives, in particular) unfairly prohibited the sale of Belgian and Dutch beers in the Federal Republic. The Court of Auditors monitors expenditures. An Economic and Social Committee with representatives from a large number of interest groups provides advice on many matters. The European Investment Bank promotes development in poor areas, and an extensive social fund helps new member countries to overcome the hardships associated with adjusting to Common Market practices. Most of these organizations have their offices in Brussels, where the European Commission also sits. The European Parliament meets in Strasbourg, and many of the staff of the European Commission work in Luxembourg.

The European Free Trade Association

Nonmembers greeted the development of the EEC with apprehension, as the tariffs erected around the community restricted nonmembers' ability to trade with Common Market countries. The British were especially concerned. They wished to establish strong trade ties with Europe, but, for some of the same reasons that had led them to remain outside of the ECSC, they wished to avoid the binding commitments involved in the Common Market. The United Kingdom therefore took a leadership role in 1960 in forming the European Free Trade Association (EFTA) with Austria, Denmark, Norway (where the association's headquarters were set up), Portugal, Sweden, and Switzerland. This group, soon dubbed the "Outer Seven" in contrast to the "Inner Six" of the EEC, was joined by Finland as an associate member in 1961 and by Iceland in 1970.

EFTA did not envision a common external tariff, as did the Common Market, but rather an easing of internal tariffs through mutual agreements. Original plans called for inter-EFTA tariffs to be removed by 1970. The process was speeded up, and by December 1963 tariffs had been reduced by 60 percent. The target date for complete abolition was set for the end of 1966, when import quotas were also to be eliminated. Agricultural products were not covered; in order to increase trade in this field a series of bilateral agreements, notably one between the United Kingdom and Denmark, were negotiated.

EFTA's joint economic policies were less restrictive than those of the European Economic Community and gave its members more leeway to pursue their separate interests. The main distinction between the EFTA and EEC was that the members of the former did not want to surrender their sovereignty to a common authority; they believed that they would best protect their interests through national policies. The EFTA did not redirect trade substantially, but it did provide some compensation for states that declined membership in the EEC.

Britain Joins the Economic Community

The changes in political orientation called for by the movement for European integration, welcomed by some countries and resisted by others, are best illustrated by the dilemmas the United Kingdom faced. Britain's long tradition of playing a world role was not one that could easily be relinquished, and the Commonwealth of Nations (see Chapter 9) remained a symbol of Britain's special position. Although the Commonwealth was an informal body with no aspirations to integration, it nevertheless included arrangements for pref-

The Acronyms of Negotiation

CAP	Common Agricultural Policy (of the EEC)
CMEA	Council for Mutual Economic Assistance (Comecon)
CSCE	Conference on Security and Cooperation in Europe
ECA	Economic Cooperation Administration
ECSC	European Coal and Steel Community
ECU	European Currency Unit
EDC	European Defense Community
EEA	European Economic Area
EEC	European Economic Community
EFTA	European Free Trade Association
EMU	European Monetary Union
EPU	European Payments Union
ERP	European Recovery Program (Marshall Plan)
EURATOM	European Atomic Energy Community
GATT	General Agreement on Tariffs and Trade
IMF	International Monetary Fund
NATO	North Atlantic Treaty Organization
OECD	Organization for Economic Cooperation and Development
OEEC	Organization for European Economic Cooperation
OPEC	Organization of Petroleum Exporting Countries
SACEUR	Supreme Allied Commander Europe (within NATO)
UNO	United Nations Organization (UN)
UNRRA	UN Relief and Rehabilitation Administration
VAT	value-added tax
WEU	Western European Union

erential tariffs that were in conflict with the requirements for membership in the Common Market. The critical choice facing Britain was whether to retain the remnants of its world role or to become a country with predominantly European concerns.

The British were also aware of their special relationship with the United States. The United States, however, was willing to use that relationship to nudge Britain toward a major goal of U.S. foreign policy: integration of Europe to strengthen it against domestic and external Communist threats. A United Kingdom outside the EEC would always be a weakness. Washington also feared creation of a high tariff barrier between the United States and Europe. Therefore, in a round of GATT discussions begun in 1960 and named after President John F. Kennedy (1961–1963), the United States negotiated a 30 to 50 percent reduction in tariffs between the United States and the EEC; further reductions were promised if Britain joined the EEC.

The success of the Coal and Steel Community was by now obvious, and the British noticed that their industry needed more stimulation than that provided with the small opening of markets achieved through the EFTA and GATT. The record also showed that real earnings in the Common Market countries were growing at about twice the rate as in Britain, largely because of reductions of tariff barriers. Talk of increased political union on the Continent was also disturbing. Though highly wary of such union, the British nevertheless did not want to be left out of early discussions. They thought it better to participate in formulating the ground rules than to discover the necessity of joining after terms inimical to British interests might already have been etched in stone.

The decision to apply for membership in the EEC was a wrenching one in British politics. The Labour party worried that competition might lead to loss of jobs in British industry, and there was concern that merger with a conservative Christian Democratic Europe might endanger socialist domestic policies in Britain. Farmers feared British markets would be flooded with cheap grain from the Continent. When the British finally did apply for membership in the EEC in 1961, they therefore negotiated for terms that would take into account their worldwide interests and protect their agriculture. In particular, they asked for an extended period of years in which to come in line with Common Market regulations on tariffs and agricultural subsidies.

Their application was vetoed by President Charles de Gaulle of France in January 1963. His opposition was stirred not so much by the concessions the British were asking as by concern that the special U.S.-British relationship would come to dominate the community, one area in which French *grandeur* was being maintained even while the French empire was dissolving. De Gaulle's feistiness was further stimulated by word that at a conference in December 1962 the United States had offered Britain use of U.S. Polaris missiles. Was Britain becoming too tied to U.S. policies to act independently? The general argued that European business should be the business of Europeans, perhaps just another way of saying that French influence in Europe should not be reduced.

The abruptness of de Gaulle's veto offended both Britons and other members of the EEC, although many of the latter did oppose granting the extensive concessions the United Kingdom demanded. Other areas of conflict soon appeared. De Gaulle was reluctant to allow decisionmaking within the EEC to slip out of French control. He therefore opposed efforts by the European Commission to expand its power, and he insisted that key decisions be controlled by the Council of Ministers. Though de Gaulle favored economic integration, he was opposed to political integration. He did not wish French sovereignty to be impaired and saw greater likelihood that Eastern European states might at some time adhere to the EEC if its dimensions remained primarily economic. The response of Walter Hallstein, head of the commission, was to try to place the EEC budget in the hands of the European Parliament. This de Gaulle would not accept.

Eventually the other five powers had to give way. In a document signed in Luxembourg in 1966, the six governments agreed that the European Commission must consult the individual member countries before making major proposals. Moreover, there had to be unanimity of opinion in the Council of Ministers on items that any member believed affected its vital interests. The Luxembourg treaty thus negated the clauses of the founding treaty of the EEC that called for decisions within the Council of Ministers to be made by majority vote beginning in 1966. The treaty was therefore a decided blow to the concept of federalism within Europe and slowed the already glacial progress toward some form of political union. But it served its purpose, for France remained within the EEC.

Britain, however, stayed on the outside. De Gaulle vetoed its renewed application in 1967. By the 1970s, however, the prospects for British admission had improved significantly. President de Gaulle retired in 1969, and his successor, Georges Pompidou, was more of a confederationist than the general, emphasized French *grandeur* somewhat less, and was more willing to work matters out with the British. Adenauer, the architect of German rapprochement with France, had also retired. His successor, Willy Brandt, was attempting to build bridges to the East and conducting a more independent foreign policy. In 1968 the West Germans refused to revalue their currency upward so that the French could avoid devaluing their own. Three years later the Germans allowed their strong deutsche mark to float against other currencies, again hurting the French franc. In Paris, the notion grew that British membership in the EEC was needed to balance the rising influence of West Germany.

Within Britain the deep divisions over membership in the Common Market had begun to heal. The advantages of joining seemed greater as British economic woes mounted. Moreover, the possible concomitant loss of sovereignty seemed less serious after de Gaulle had pulled the teeth of the European Parliament. Britain made a renewed application in 1970 and by 1972 had joined the EEC. Ireland and Denmark came along as well, but voters in Norway in 1971 rejected the participation of their country in the EEC. In order to join, the British had to accept a three-year transition to Common Market agricultural policies, rather than the previously requested period of six years. Acceptance of those policies, moreover, meant keeping cheap Commonwealth agricultural goods outside the market.

The political problems of British entry into the Common Market are only one example of individual countries' seeking to adapt their diverse systems to common standards. Proposals have been made to replace national with EEC passports, driving licenses, currencies, and stamps, and progress has been made on several of these. The Social Fund, to which all members contribute, has been used to retrain workers who have been displaced by the

In the early 1970s, West German chancellor Willy Brandt met a twofold challenge that went a long way toward facilitating the normalization of relations between his country and the outside world. By formally renouncing the use of force to challenge prevailing European borders, he helped to convince Soviet leaders like Leonid Brezhnev (pictured above at left with Brandt at a meeting on the Black Sea coast) that the German people no longer represented a threat to continental peace. At the same time, Brandt was also able to reassure his country's skeptical allies, including U.S. president Richard Nixon (pictured below at right with the chancellor), that good relations between the USSR and the FRG did not impair West Germany's vital commitments to the Atlantic Alliance. (Photos courtesy of the German Information Center.)

Chronology of Western European Integration

JANUARY 1, 1947   Bizonia is created in Germany.

APRIL 16, 1947   Organization for European Economic Cooperation is formed.

JANUARY 1, 1948   Benelux Customs Union is inaugurated.

MARCH 17, 1948   Brussels pact is signed; the Western Union is formed.

JUNE 18, 1948   Trizonia is created.

MAY 5, 1949   Statute of Council of Europe is signed.

JULY 25, 1952   European Coal and Steel Community (created by treaty of April 1951) is inaugurated.

OCTOBER 21, 1954   Western European Union is formed.

MARCH 25, 1957   Treaties of Rome create the European Atomic Energy Community and European Economic Community (to enter into effect January 1, 1958).

NOVEMBER 20, 1959   Convention is signed establishing the European Free Trade Association (to enter into effect in 1960).

JANUARY 29, 1963   France vetoes British application to the EEC.

JULY 1, 1967   European Commission of the EEC is formed.

JANUARY 22, 1972   United Kingdom, Ireland, Denmark join the EEC.

JANUARY 3, 1981   Greece joins the EEC.

JANUARY 1, 1986   Spain and Portugal join the EEC.

FEBRUARY 17, 1986   Nine members of the EEC sign the Single Europe Act agreement (to enter into effect December 31, 1992); Denmark, Greece, Italy accede later.

OCTOBER 22, 1991   Representatives of EEC and EFTA states agree on proposal jointly to form the European Economic Area by January 1, 1993, contingent upon approval by the national parliaments.

---

closing of enterprises and by the mechanization of agriculture resulting from Common Market policies. There have also been numerous cases where persons claiming discrimination in individual countries—such as women who are paid less than men for equal work and foreign workers who claim social security benefits in the countries where they are employed—have taken their cases to the European Court of Justice and gained redress of their grievances.

The expansion of the role of the European Community was reflected in a dramatic growth of its budget. Until 1970 the organization derived its income from contributions by its members. Starting in that year, and varying somewhat by country, the national parliaments voted to permit the community to raise its revenues from its own resources derived from the economies of the member states. By the 1980s about two-thirds of the Community's income would come from a 1 percent, later raised to 1.4 percent, share of the value-added tax (VAT) collected by the member states. The VAT is a form of sales tax based on the addition to the value of consumer goods and services achieved at each stage of production and distribution. The VAT has become the principal source of government revenue in the countries of Western Europe. Other sources of community revenue include a share of the levies on the imports of agricultural products and of customs duties on products covered by the Common Market tariffs.

Accomplishment of the Common Market was not an easy task. On many occasions bitter debates arose, especially over the Common Agricultural Policy (CAP). The policy's first aim was creation of a single agricultural market with common prices. Second, it intended to establish the primacy of trade within the community as compared to trade with produce suppliers from outside the EEC. Third, it proposed distribution of the costs of the policy across the entire EEC rather than placing the burden on just the main agricultural states. Farmers in countries where production costs were high resented the competition of cheaper products from neighboring regions. Some countries had technically advanced and efficient farming industries. Others still had systems of farming based on small and relatively inefficient peasant holdings; often such systems were shored up by price supports and export subsidies. Under these circumstances it took long negotiations to reach agreement on common agricultural prices throughout the community. Inequities among the member states were compensated for by a policy of buying surpluses and erecting tariffs to protect the member states from cheap imports from outside the Common Market. The annual total of farm subsidies became quite large and a subject of sharp differences among the membership.

Despite such difficulties, the Common Market, along with EFTA and OEEC, did much for the economies of Western Europe. Indeed, the Western rates of growth in the decades after the Marshall Plan were unprecedented and brought the most prosperous period in Western European history. With this prosperity, which was enhanced not just by tariff reductions but also by technical innovations and a spirit of entrepreneurial initiative, there came a relaxation of tensions between France and Germany.

The Franco-German Treaty of Reconciliation

Admission of West Germany into NATO had occurred to considerable extent against the wishes of the French, and the future of the Saar was resolved by plebiscite in a manner contrary to French hopes. But the success of the ECSC and creation of the EEC greatly reduced the economic hurt of the latter decision. Moreover, Federal Republic chancellor Adenauer was determined to reduce the tensions that lingered between the two states, which were nominally allies through NATO.

Adenauer was well equipped for doing so, as his credentials in terms of advocating better Franco-German relations were long established. He, like de Gaulle in France, was a rigid, self-assured leader who had sufficient support and the confidence of the people to undertake what might initially be considered unpopular policies (witness his gamble on the Saar plebiscite).

The French president, for his part, was intent on lessening U.S. and British influence on the Continent and therefore open to dealing with Adenauer. De Gaulle's relations with the United States had been strained for some while. President Roosevelt had delayed recognizing de Gaulle as leader of the Free French forces during World War II and distrusted the general as not being a "team player." De Gaulle resented both this snub and France's exclusion from critical great-power conferences at the close of the war. There were also numerous particular issues, including explosive colonial affairs, on which France differed with Britain and the United States.

Above all, the Department of State and General de Gaulle held different concepts of international cooperation. The United States envisioned each partner's undertaking a portion of a given task; by such an arrangement, no country could perform alone. De Gaulle believed that cooperation was real only if each partner had a viable choice and could act autonomously. Although both sides endorsed mutual consultation, the United States thought of it in terms of the actions of a joint-stock company, with control proportional to the amount contributed. De Gaulle believed all participants should have an equal voice. Thus the French emphasized equilibrium and the concept of the equality of sovereign nation-states. The United States preached partnership and the idea that the needs of European integration should usually take precedence over the desires of any individual state.

So it was that just a few weeks after de Gaulle vetoed the first British application for membership in the Economic Community, he signed a treaty of reconciliation with the West Germans in January 1963. No specific concessions were made; rather, close cooperation in diplomacy, defense, education, and cultural affairs was promised. The true import of the Elysée treaty was not in its clauses but in the manner in which it signaled a new era of positive Franco-German relations. If it also reflected French desire to build an axis within NATO to counter U.S.-British leadership, that did not seem to be the intention in Bonn, where it was regarded exclusively as a means to lessen Franco-German tensions.

Developments in NATO

De Gaulle's wish to maintain capacity for autonomous action and his dislike for what he considered to be limitations on French sovereignty posed by the North Atlantic treaty soon created problems within NATO. A year after he

The progress of Franco-German rapprochement was symbolized by the visit of French president Charles de Gaulle (left) to Bonn in September 1962. It was the first visit of a French head of state to Germany in the twentieth century. The spirited crowds surrounding de Gaulle and Chancellor Konrad Adenauer of the Federal Republic carry placards calling for European unification. (Photo courtesy of the German Information Center.)

came to power in 1958, de Gaulle refused to place a third of the French Mediterranean fleet under NATO command, as stipulated by the treaty. Later, in 1959, his differences with the United States over stockpiling of nuclear weapons on French soil provoked removal of 200 U.S. planes to other regions. Notwithstanding this development, the NATO council agreed in 1960 to creation of a unified Western European air defense command.

As nuclear weapons began to dominate military thinking, the European countries were increasingly uneasy in a situation in which a U.S. president, over whom they had no control, held a virtual monopoly on the use of nuclear weapons that might vitally affect Europe. The United States was reluctant to let European countries have control over U.S. nuclear weapons stationed in Europe, lest they be used in local conflicts and trigger a major nuclear war. Even less satisfactory was a third alternative, namely, the proliferation of nuclear weapons under national control, such as already had happened in Britain and France. As a possible solution to this dilemma, the United States in 1963 proposed the creation of a multilateral nuclear force

(MLF) consisting of some twenty-five surface vessels, each equipped with eight Polaris missiles and manned by crews of mixed nationalities.

Though the NATO council approved of the multilateral force, France opposed it on the ground that it would perpetuate U.S. military domination of the alliance. France instead favored creation of a European nuclear deterrent, including Britain, that would permit Europe to become a third major nuclear power along with the United States and the USSR. Desiring to keep French naval vessels for his own "third force," de Gaulle withdrew his Atlantic and Channel forces (save for a few submarines) from NATO control and French naval officers from NATO naval commands. He required NATO headquarters to move from France, and they were shortly relocated to a Belgian town south of Brussels. Finally, in 1966 de Gaulle withdrew French military forces totally from NATO's unified command.

The breach was considered serious but not destructive to the alliance. De Gaulle made clear that his forces would defend the West. Though for some while the French did not participate in most formal NATO gatherings, they did maintain contact with their allies and did not formally withdraw from the alliance as such. After de Gaulle's retirement, the French slowly returned to a more active role in the organization.

The debate and French actions reflected, however, that NATO remained a coalition of independent sovereign states. Significant progress in developing a system of political consultation that would serve to integrate national policies would have to occur in some other forum. Yet the possibility that the EEC might provide such a locus seemed remote, given the terms of the Luxembourg treaty of 1966.

Western Europe achieved an unprecedented level of integration and prosperity in the second decade after the war. It had also reached a certain equilibrium. Military and economic collaboration had been forced by necessity and the Soviet threat; Franco-German tensions had been eased. The immediate needs met, there was little energy and, apparently, little desire to push to a new level of self-realization. The realities of nuclear war and of superpower supremacy discouraged such dreams. De Gaulle was the one leader, other than Spaak and Monnet, who occasionally mentioned them. But he also seemed to wish to use European growth as a tool to increase French national *grandeur* and hegemony on the Continent. For his neighbors, this was not a prospect that would inspire them to further action.

The Soviet Orbit

Cracks in the Bloc

Amidst the fears engendered by the Cold War, Westerners often contrasted their own divisions with an Eastern bloc described as a monolith completely

In four languages—English, Russian, French, and German—this sign captures the
stark reality of the East-West division in postwar Europe. Nowhere was the split
more evident than in Berlin, the former German capital partitioned into four zones
of occupation controlled by the United States, Great Britain, France, and the Soviet
Union. Any unauthorized attempt to pass from a Western-occupied zone to the
Soviet side meant risking almost certain death. The smaller notice just behind the
large sign reads, "Attention! The Soviet Zone begins here." (Photo courtesy of the
German Information Center.)

in the service of the Soviet juggernaut. The reality on the other side of the
Iron Curtain was somewhat different. Soviet intervention in Hungary in
1956 demonstrated Soviet willingness to use force. But it also revealed that
all was not well within the Eastern bloc. Soviet troops had previously been
needed to suppress riots in the German Democratic Republic in 1953. Unrest
in Poland in the summer of 1956 was quelled only by a combination of threat
of intervention and promise of concessions, such as the end of collectivization
of farmlands, establishment of workers' councils in Polish industry, provision
of financial aid, and the return to power of Communist leadership that was
more nationalist than Stalinist in orientation. As a result, the Communist
party remained in control and the Poles did not challenge their strategic
bonds with the Soviet Union (see Chapter 8).

Problems with Yugoslavia arose as well, and these were resolved only at
the price of worsening relations with the Chinese Communists. Mao Zedong,

the Chinese leader, was now openly vying for a salient role in world communism. At the same time, he was viciously attacking Marshal Tito of Yugoslavia for abandoning Leninist prerequisites for true communization. The younger Soviet Communist party first secretary, Nikita Khrushchev, found himself caught between these grand old men of communism. He, of course, wished to demonstrate his own leadership. Tito had successfully challenged Stalin, retaining his independence, and Khrushchev for his own reasons had recently denounced Stalin. Mao was espousing certain forms of Stalinism, and Yugoslavia was closer to the important field of European action than China. Khrushchev therefore moved to make peace with Tito.

The general secretary's denunciation of Stalin in early 1956 was well received by the Eastern Europeans, who disliked the dictator for ending their national autonomies and dominating their politics. Khrushchev next abolished the Cominform, which had for so long been used against Tito. In 1956 he signed with Yugoslavia a declaration of "diversity" recognizing the legitimacy of multiple forms of socialist development. Khrushchev thus hoped to steal the wind from the sails of party revisionists for his own benefit.

All this only encouraged revisionists in Poland and Hungary and annoyed the Chinese. The latter had no use for "polycentrism," for they believed that if there were just one general party line, the Chinese would have greater opportunity to influence it. Mao also disagreed with Khrushchev's emphasis on economic competition rather than outright warfare with the West. Nor did the Chinese leader appreciate the Soviets' views on "rhythm of development," which implied the acceptability of inequality of economic development among Communist states. Rather, Mao believed it was the Soviets' duty to provide assistance to less-developed Communist states—assistance in such matters as building atomic bombs. These ideological differences were supplemented by numerous nonideological problems, such as dispute over territories along the Amur River.

As Khrushchev moved to replace Stalinist leaders in various East bloc nations, the Stalinist Enver Hoxha in Albania looked to China for support. He was further motivated to do so because of ideological differences with Tito. These disagreements were aggravated by Albanian irredentist claims on the Yugoslav region of Kosovo-Metohija, heavily populated by Albanians. When Albania sided with the Chinese in the Sino-Soviet dispute, Soviet economic aid was terminated and naval units withdrawn in 1961; Albania broke diplomatic relations with the USSR and left the Warsaw Pact.

Summit Meetings

It was to Khrushchev's advantage to demonstrate to the Eastern bloc the value of his leadership and his interest in resolving the general question of European security without resort to warfare. He therefore accepted the invitation of Eisenhower to meet at the presidential retreat at Camp David in Maryland in 1959. There they agreed that the question of a divided Berlin inside the East German state and disarmament issues should be a matter of continued negotiation and not be allowed to reach a crisis stage. This was essentially an agreement designed to improve the atmosphere of international relations and was not intended to lead to immediate practical results.

The favorable new atmosphere facilitated arrangements for a summit conference of the leaders of the United Kingdom, the United States, France, and the Soviet Union in Paris in May 1960 and for a visit by President Eisenhower to the USSR in June. On the eve of these meetings, however, the USSR announced that a U.S. U-2 aircraft engaged in photographing Soviet military installations had been shot down over the USSR. This event destroyed hopes for any agreement at the summit, and Eisenhower's visit was cancelled. A subsequent investigation by the U.S. Senate Foreign Relations Committee concluded that the U-2 affair had been seriously mishandled, but that it was not the primary cause for the breakdown of the summit conference. Most observers believed that Khrushchev had hoped to use the summit conference to divide the West over the Berlin question. As the time for the conference approached, he realized that this would not be possible, and he seized on the U-2 incident to cover his position. It is also true that the West was pressing Khrushchev, as part of any armaments deal, to persuade the Chinese to forgo development of an atomic bomb. This he knew he could not do, but he did not wish to reveal to the West and others his lack of influence on the Chinese Communists. The U-2 affair strengthened the concerns of Soviets who distrusted the United States and called for increased military strength. In retirement, Khrushchev later asserted that the episode had undermined his ability to achieve domestic reform and to pursue peaceful coexistence.

The problem of Berlin remained, as Khrushchev commented, a "bone in [his] throat." The growing exodus of East Germans to the West through the sector of Berlin administered by the United States, France, and Great Britain threatened the economic stability of the German Democratic Republic. In June 1961 the Soviet prime minister and the new U.S. president, Kennedy, held a brief meeting in Vienna. It proved less a conference than an opportunity for Khrushchev to press vigorously his demands for an immediate conclusion of a German peace settlement on Soviet terms (including German neutrality). No progress was achieved, and Khrushchev departed from the meeting apparently believing that his experience would enable him successfully to challenge the young U.S. leader.

On August 13, 1961, either at the direction of the Soviets or more likely with their acquiescence, the East German government erected a wall throughout Berlin to stem the flow of refugees to the West (see Chapter 6). The Western powers responded with a military buildup but took no overt action to challenge the total partition of the city. With the building of the Wall, the final gap in the Iron Curtain was sealed and the East German emigration problem resolved. The West did continue to reject Khrushchev's frequent insistence, accompanied by an explicit threat of direct action, that a German peace settlement be concluded before the end of the year.

The next fall, in October 1962, the USSR posed a major threat to the United States by preparing to install in Cuba nuclear weapons capable of reaching the major U.S. cities. The United States and its allies stood their ground and the USSR backed down. Subsequent revelations have shown that the superpowers were extremely close to nuclear warfare during the Cuban crisis. The experience may have caused each of them to be more cautious in the future and to work harder for some form of accommodation. The withdrawal of Soviet weapons from Cuba was viewed in both the United States and the Soviet Union as a defeat for Khrushchev. The Soviets did, however, achieve a U.S. pledge not to invade Cuba. If Khrushchev's hope was to exchange withdrawal of Soviet missiles from Cuba for U.S. withdrawal from West Berlin, he had not succeeded.

U.S. toleration of the Berlin Wall and the Soviet retreat in Cuba did ease tensions somewhat and helped to define an equilibrium or stasis in the relationship of the two blocs. Western firmness and the near miss of nuclear war brought on by the Cuban crisis also shifted the arena of confrontation and led to renewed emphasis on Khrushchev's theories of economic competition. In sharp contrast to the situation in Western Europe, where the United States took the leadership in NATO but played no direct role in the European Economic Community, the Soviets dominated Comecon. In order to gain more efficiency, and incidentally further to bolster the Soviet economic position, Khrushchev moved to introduce regional centralized planning throughout Comecon. In particular, the Soviets proposed a system of country specialization under which Albania, Bulgaria, and Romania would concentrate on agricultural products and the other nations would be developed industrially to the extent permitted by their resources. In short, Khrushchev suggested that small agrarian-industrial countries should not aspire to general and universal industrialization. Albanians and other members of Comecon had long resented being told how to plan the future of their economies. The most rebellious were the Romanians, who did not like the idea of suddenly being allotted a permanent agricultural role and were planning a major industrialization drive of their own. In 1963 they rejected Khrushchev's Comecon proposals, turned to the West for financial aid, and received great support from the Chinese. Khrushchev ultimately was forced to back down from his supranational economic proposals. In 1964 the Romanian Communist party declared the equality of all Communist nations and the principle of noninterference in national industrialization programs.

The Romanian setback was an embarrassment and contributed to Khrushchev's overthrow later that year (see Chapter 7). Another contributing factor was Soviet relations with China. By this point, the Chinese Communist leaders were ridiculing the entire range of Soviet policies. They called the Soviet leaders "revisionists" who were betraying Lenin's revolutionary policies

On June 26, 1963, President John F. Kennedy spoke in West Berlin, hailing the city
as a symbol of the spirit of freedom: "All free men, wherever they may live, are
citizens of Berlin. And that is why I, as a free man, am proud to say 'Ich bin ein
Berliner' [I am a Berliner]." Some West Germans had questioned U.S. commitment
to the defense of Western European freedom when the United States failed to make
a strong move to force the dismantling of the Berlin Wall in 1961. Kennedy's now
famous "Ich bin ein Berliner" speech reaffirmed U.S. commitment and brought a
tumultuous ovation. (Photo courtesy of the German Information Center.)

and charged that the Soviet Union was collaborating with the United States
to dominate the United Nations.

These Chinese accusations represented a gross distortion of Soviet
policies. Arising as they did from a heated quarrel within the Communist
family of nations, they nevertheless reflected profound changes in strategic
thinking that had been going on in Soviet military circles. The military
strategy that guided Soviet leaders in the early postwar period was one of
full and balanced development in all branches of the armed services. Nuclear
weapons, the air force, and missiles were developed rapidly, but not at the
expense of the more conventional elements of military power. Throughout
the U.S. presidential campaign of 1960, much was made of an alleged Soviet
superiority in missiles. Kennedy later admitted that he discovered after
becoming president that there was no "missile gap," though the Soviets did
possess larger rockets that could throw more weight into space than could
U.S. missiles. During Khrushchev's administration (1955–1964), however, the

Soviets' attention was devoted very largely to nuclear and rocket weapons, to the neglect of conventional forces. The USSR in 1961 and 1962 tried to use the threat of these powerful weapons to gain concessions from the West without resort to war. But by the mid-1960s, the initial Soviet advantage in rocketry had been more than overcome by the United States, whereas the Soviets had caught up with the United States in possession of numbers of missiles and had expanded their navy substantially. Thus a relative balance between the forces of NATO and the Warsaw Pact was generally acknowledged. The Soviet Union became much more cautious in engaging in policies that might lead to a military and political escalation of international tensions, and it was this new caution that was ridiculed by a China that remained confident that peasant uprisings were capable of overcoming all odds.

Any progress toward relaxation of tensions between the two superpower blocs was slowed by several factors. In the Soviet Union there was a change of leadership as Khrushchev was dismissed and succeeded by Leonid Brezhnev in what proved to be a limited collective leadership with Aleksei Kosygin. The United States became deeply embroiled in bolstering South Vietnam against the Communist North Vietnamese, whom the United States viewed as strongly supported by the USSR. President Lyndon Johnson (1963–1969) and Prime Minister Kosygin met briefly at Glassboro, New Jersey, in 1967. Their talks focused on the Middle East and Vietnam crises, and though they demonstrated the willingness of the leaders to talk, the meeting had little effect on European affairs.

Agreement was reached by the close of 1967 on the main thrust of a nuclear nonproliferation treaty. This treaty, negotiated in conjunction with the United Nations Disarmament Committee, obligated nuclear powers not to transfer nuclear weapons or explosives to nonnuclear states; the latter were required not to construct nuclear weapons. The first formal signings took place in Washington, Moscow, and London in July 1968; within two months the treaty had some sixty-eight adherents. Notably absent from the list, however, were France, China, and Israel.

Achievement of the nuclear nonproliferation treaty was encouraging. But the sudden North Vietnamese Tet offensive of February 1968 brought a cooling of relations. So, too, did the course of events in Czechoslovakia.

The Brezhnev Doctrine

Economic difficulties had mounted steadily in Czechoslovakia since 1962. Reformers protested excessive centralization and neglect of light industry and consumer goods as heavy industry was emphasized in cooperation with Soviet directives. Eventually some economic reforms and even a modest system of profit accountability were installed in 1966. Conservatives were ousted from top posts and leadership given to the reformer Alexander Dubcek (see Chapter 8). Pushed by eager reformers seeking political as well as economic change and stimulated by student demonstrations, Dubcek in the spring of 1968 began talking of allowing political factions within the Czechoslovakian Communist party. He also visited with Tito and Romanian leaders. When an intellectuals' manifesto criticized communism and promised military resistance to any Soviet invasion, Dubcek chose not to denounce it. East German and Polish Communist party leaders reacted in a hostile fashion, fearing that the germ of Czech democratic reforms might infect their countries. Eventually, Brezhnev decided to take action. Forces of the Warsaw Pact (except for Romanian contingents, as Romania had virtually withdrawn from the pact) quickly crushed the "Prague Spring" in August 1968.

Brezhnev, in justifying the crackdown, announced that it was the right and duty of the Soviets to interfere in affairs of other Communist countries whenever the interests of socialism were threatened. Soviet power and Soviet hegemony in Eastern Europe had once again been demonstrated. The Romanians, though they indicated they might fight if ever offered such "fraternal help," became less vocal in their criticisms. The new Soviet leadership had shown its willingness to take action, and dissidents were forced into retreat. The Brezhnev Doctrine was criticized in the West, but the United States could say little, for in some ways it was only the Soviet version of the Truman Doctrine of 1947 and more recent U.S. statements regarding Latin America.

Détente

By the close of the 1960s, a sort of power equilibrium had been reached both within the two superpower blocs and between them. Within both blocs there was debate about domestic reforms yet little suggestion that the basic division of Europe should be altered. True, there were those like George Kennan, the now retired U.S. diplomat, who protested that the presence of U.S. troops in West Germany expected too much of the United States and too little of the Europeans and made permanent that which was intended to be temporary. But most Western political leaders agreed with the position succinctly stated in 1958 by Raymond Aron, a noted French political observer: "The present situation in Europe is abnormal, or absurd. But it is a clearcut one and everyone knows where the demarcation line is and nobody is much afraid of what could happen. If something happens on the other side of the Iron Curtain . . . nothing happens on this side. So a clear partition of Europe is considered, rightly or wrongly, to be less dangerous than any other arrangement."[1]

Willingness to Negotiate

The cost of defense against the opposing bloc was growing rapidly with the increasing complexity of the technology associated with missiles, submarines, and atomic warfare. In both cases the superpowers carried a disproportionate share of the burden. According to some estimates, the United States bore 60 percent of the burden for NATO defense expenditures and the USSR paid 90 percent of the corresponding Warsaw Pact costs. In both alliances the European members used similar arguments to resist increases in their military budgets. The West Europeans argued that if they increased their military budgets they would have to reduce their allocations to investment and consumption. This would permit left-wing political leaders, who usually wished to reduce military expenditures, to raise issues that might bring them success in a future election. The Eastern European leaders claimed in a somewhat similar fashion that granting priority to military over welfare expenditures might provoke the type of social unrest that had already led to domestic strife in Germany, Hungary, and Czechoslovakia. The domestic political problems that arose from the hard decisions of resource allocation among defense, investment, and consumption appeared to be of equal concern in both market and planned economies. Nuclear weapons themselves had become a deterrent to war because their destructive potential exceeded the value of any possible resultant gains. Now it appeared that the welfare state and the sums it required to implement social support policies were also becoming a deterrent to war. The allocations to investment and consumption needed for welfare state programs created constant pressure to keep peacetime military budgets low on both sides of the Iron Curtain.

The cost of armaments, the threat that nuclear war posed for civilization, acceptance of the "abnormal" division of Germany and Europe, desire to focus on domestic issues, and especially the realization that confrontation was not leading to a stable peace, all led by the end of the 1960s to the conclusion that the time had come for negotiations. This new approach came to be known as détente—a French word that means "relaxation of tensions." Détente was initially a European policy that continued into the 1980s. But the term also applies to a shorter-lived and more extensive relaxation of tensions between the United States and the USSR. The U.S.-Soviet détente, which lasted from the summit meeting of Brezhnev with President Richard Nixon (1969–1974) in 1972 to the Soviet occupation of Afghanistan in 1979, was a broadly based relationship that was concerned with global issues of arms control and competition in the less-developed countries, in addition to the question of East-West relations in Europe.

Although relations between the superpowers improved during this period, beneath détente lay an important divergence of outlook. As Marxist-Leninists, the Soviet leaders saw all countries in the world as moving from feudalism through capitalism to socialism and eventually communism. They understood this as an inevitable historical development, quite apart from Soviet policies, and for them détente was a condition under which history would work itself out with a minimum of tensions. Their favorite term for this state of affairs was "peaceful coexistence," by which they meant the gradual victory of socialism over capitalism by means short of military conflict. The U.S. view of détente was significantly different. To the extent that the U.S. leaders held a conception of historical development, it was the pluralistic view that all countries should pursue their own courses of development in the expectation that they would eventually evolve toward free enterprise democracies.

Distinctions between the two viewpoints were blurred or purposely ignored as the pragmatic benefits of at least limited agreements became clear. The possibility of better East-West relations had been steadily raised by the French over the years, and more recently by Willy Brandt, leader of the Social Democratic party in the Federal Republic of Germany. Brandt became foreign minister in the mid-1960s and soon launched his *Ostpolitik*, a policy aimed at improving relations with the East. Subsequently, as chancellor, he achieved a treaty of reconciliation with the USSR in 1970. This was followed by treaties with Poland and the notable Basic Treaty of 1972, which regularized relations between the two Germanys and led to the admission of both into the United Nations the following year (see Chapter 6).

Strategic Arms Limitation Talks

The Soviet Union and the United States were directly and indirectly involved in the settlement of issues affecting the Germanys and Berlin. Progress in this area was paralleled in serious negotiations on arms control. A high point was reached at the Brezhnev-Nixon summit in Moscow in 1972, held to mark the conclusion of the first Strategic Arms Limitation Talks (SALT I). The results were modest, yet they demonstrated the interest of the superpowers in easing nuclear confrontation. The main achievement was a strict limitation on antiballistic missile (ABM) systems, the development of which would have interfered with the existing balance of mutual deterrence. A limit of two ABM systems for each power ended any possibility of either power's launching a "safe" first strike. That attack would not be able to wipe out the opponent's retaliatory power. Nor would the first power's ABM systems be sufficient to save it from severe destruction caused by a retaliatory strike. The "destabilizing" effect of ABMs on the current arrangement of "mutually assured destruction" (MAD) was thus curtailed. The ABM treaty was accompanied by an interim agreement that froze at existing levels the number of strategic missile launchers for a five-year period pending further negotiations.

SALT I did not bring about an actual reduction of armaments but rather agreement not to expand them beyond a rate acceptable to both superpowers (neither at the time actually had two ABM systems, although the Soviets had begun construction of one around Moscow). Yet SALT I was a major turning point in that it demonstrated the possibility of negotiating limits to the arms race. It also marked the acceptance by the United States of an approximate strategic parity with the USSR, after more than two decades in which the

United States had enjoyed and insisted upon a leading position. Despite this achievement, SALT I had a basic weakness in that it did not limit airborne strategic missiles or cruise missile systems. Cruise missiles, in contrast to ballistic missiles, fly close to the earth and are difficult to detect by radar. Though subsonic, they are more accurate than intercontinental ballistic missiles (ICBMs). Moreover, SALT I dealt only with ballistic missiles and not with the number of warheads each missile could carry if converted to multiple, independently targetable reentry vehicles (MIRVs). As a consequence, what was supposed to be a treaty limiting strategic arms became the starting point for a new arms race. Between 1970 and 1985, the number of U.S. strategic warheads and airborne bombs would rise from 3,742 to 10,174, and the corresponding Soviet levels would rise from 1,861 to 10,223. Under SALT I, the Soviet Union would have more ICBMs and submarine-launched ballistic missiles (SLBMs) than the United States, which would have more bombers and, for a while, more warheads.

In November 1974 Prime Minister Brezhnev and President Gerald Ford (1974–1977) held a summit meeting at Vladivostok preparatory to SALT II negotiations. They agreed to an aggregate limit for each country of 2,400 strategic missile launchers with a sublimit of 1,320 of MIRVed missiles. The leaders also banned the construction of new land-based missile launchers and limited deployment of new types of offensive strategic arms. Neither country had as yet constructed two ABM systems, and it was known that many technological hurdles remained before an ABM system would actually provide an impenetrable shield. The number of ABM systems permitted was therefore reduced to one. Disagreement remained, however, on how to verify MIRVed missiles, whether the Soviet bomber known as Backfire was a heavy bomber and therefore to be counted in the 2,400 aggregate, and what to do about cruise missiles. The two leaders, recognizing that these issues would delay any new arrangement, agreed that the previous interim agreement, scheduled to expire in 1977, would be extended through 1985.

The Helsinki Accords

A major policy thrust of the Kremlin was to decouple the United States from Western European planning and to promote East-West détente in Europe without the participation of the United States. Success in this objective would result in a situation in which the Soviet Union would be the dominant power in Europe. To the extent that the United States could be portrayed as interested primarily in promoting military conflict, a notion that was enhanced by the growing U.S. involvement in warfare in Vietnam during the 1960s, the more Europeans might be persuaded of the utility of working out their own relationships with the East bloc.

In spring 1968, the Soviets proposed that a conference solely of European nations be held to discuss general issues of security. The strong-armed actions of the Soviets in Czechoslovakia a few months later and the concern of the members of NATO that their alliance not be divided caused a long snarl in negotiations. Eventually, the United States and its NATO allies successfully insisted that the United States and Canada be included. A preliminary meeting of thirty-five foreign ministers at Helsinki in 1973 constituted the first gathering of what came to be called the Conference on Security and Cooperation in Europe (CSCE). There, Soviet foreign minister Andrei Gromyko proposed creation of a new charter of principles governing European relations.

Negotiations culminated in the Final Act, often referred to as the Helsinki declaration or Helsinki accords, agreed to by thirty-three European states and by the United States and Canada. The act was not a treaty binding the signatories but rather a statement of principles. The principles agreed to were set forth in three categories, known as baskets. Basket I was concerned with security in Europe; it in effect confirmed the political and territorial status quo in Central and Eastern Europe and made provision for confidence-building measures designed further to improve relations. Basket II made provision for cooperation among the signatories in economic relations, science and technology, and environmental problems. Basket III was concerned with cooperation in matters of human rights. In addition, the Final Act provided for regular follow-up meetings to review the implementation of the agreement.

At the time, the East German and Soviet leaders proclaimed that inviolability of frontiers was the "decisive point" of the Helsinki accords. Brezhnev emphasized that the accords affirmed that only the people of each nation had the sovereign right to determine its internal affairs. The East Germans were gratified to have their borders once again acknowledged, and the Soviets were pleased to have gained formal recognition of the status quo in its orbit. The United States had reaffirmed its acceptance of the postwar settlement in Central and Eastern Europe—thus in effect recognizing the legitimacy of the Soviet orbit. But it also had gained Soviet acceptance of certain principles of human rights defined in Basket III.

Some observers believed that the United States, its resolve weakened by the resistance to its involvement in Vietnam that had arisen in previous years both at home and abroad, had abandoned the peoples of Eastern Europe. Yet the concessions granted by the Soviets in Basket III proved to have more significance than was thought at the time. They would become a rallying point for Eastern European reformers, who demanded that the USSR and other satellite governments adhere to these human rights provisions, which were so contrary to their practices.

In 1975 the work of the CSCE was not considered a major achievement. Rather, it was thought to symbolize the manner in which the two armed blocs had gradually eased into an acceptance of the status quo. Like the arms talks, it signified not an end to the Cold War but informal recognition of certain ground rules and limitations. These did not preclude the possibility

Though there was no actual iron curtain dividing Europe, Soviet occupation forces built substantial barriers to prevent East Germans from fleeing
to the West. The 830-mile (1,328-km) zonal border pictured here ran
through the heart of Germany. On its eastern side it was often 3.5 miles
(5.6 km) wide, with a tall steel-mesh fence running along a "death strip"
bordered by bands of plowed earth (to slow the foot speed and reveal the
prints of those trying to escape) and mined fields. These were paralleled by
a patrol road and a security strip devoid of trees and shrubs but dotted
with watchtowers. (Photo courtesy of the German Information Center.)

of eventual victory for either side but did mean to ensure avoidance of nuclear battle. The Helsinki accords, then, epitomized and codified a static European order. Within that order, the European nations might make their own small adjustments, but none was expected to act so independently as to upset the European equilibrium.

As for the expression of views in Europe, the notion in the East was well quashed by the Brezhnev Doctrine, though carefully calibrated statements of autonomy did occasionally drift forth from Albania, Yugoslavia, and Romania. In the West, the Council of Europe, the European Council, EFTA, and the European Economic Community all became vehicles for the expression of European political and economic aspirations. But the two opposing military alliances continued their standoff. The division of Germany remained as a symbol both of the Cold War and of the acceptance as permanent of conditions that initially had been seen as uncomfortable and temporary.

Notes

1. Quoted in G. F. Kennan, *Memoirs: 1950–1963* (1972), p. 253.

Suggested Readings

Arbatov, G. A., and W. Oltmann, *The Soviet Viewpoint* (1981).
Deibel, T. L., and J. L. Gaddis (eds.), *Containment: Concept and Policy* (1986).
Doltrop, A., *Politics and the European Community*, 2d ed. (1986).
Gaddis, J. L., *Strategies of Containment* (1982).
Garthoff, R. L., *Detente and Confrontation: American-Soviet Relations from Nixon to Reagan* (1985).
Grosser, A., *The Western Alliance: European-American Relations Since 1945* (1980).
Ionescu, G., *The Break-up of the Soviet Empire in Eastern Europe* (1965).
LaFeber, W., *America, Russia, and the Cold War, 1945–1990*, 6th ed. (1991).
Monnet, J., *Memoirs* (1978).
Nelson, D. N., *Alliance Behavior in the Warsaw Pact* (1986).
Treverton, G. F., *Making the Alliance Work: The United States and Western Europe* (1985).
Weisberger, B., *Cold War, Cold Peace: The United States and Russia Since 1945* (1984).

CHAPTER FIVE

A New Europe Emerges

❦

Furtherance of Western Integration
Expansion of the EEC • The Move Toward a Single Europe
Franco-German Relations

The Soviet Bloc
Comecon • Reaction and Stagnation

Disarmament Negotiations
SALT II • INF Negotiations • The Deadlock Broken

The Great Change
The Miracle Year • Problems of Transition

The End of the Cold War?
The Charter of Paris • Resetting the Stage

Suggested Readings

E urope in the mid-1970s appeared stable. Its nations had carved spheres of action for themselves, far more limited in the East than in the West, under the aegis of the two superpowers. Tensions between the latter remained. At the same time, there was tacit agreement that these tensions would not be allowed to produce war, at least full-scale warfare directly involving the European nations, the USSR, and the United States. Post-World War II boundaries, save for the division of the two Germanys, were formally accepted. Although some romantics still talked of German reunification, few Germans expected to live to see it and even fewer Europeans thought they wanted once again to live with a large, unified Germany.

Yet beneath the façade of stability, powerful forces were at work that would lead to change as extensive as it was unpredicted. Even in retrospect, the dynamics of this change remain somewhat mystifying. As in biological gestation, much of a critical nature occurred without great notice, only later to conclude in sudden birth. This was the case with the new Europe, the potential and characteristics of which are still to be determined. International conditions contributed to the scenario, but it is clear that the evolution of political and economic modernization within individual nations had much to do with this new European renaissance. So, too, did manifestations of human spirit in defense of basic rights. More perspective and more information is needed before a full analysis and interpretation of the momentous changes that began in the late 1980s are possible. We can, however, identify key milestones along the road to Europe's reformation before we turn our attention to the unfolding of events in the major European states.

Furtherance of Western Integration

Expansion of the EEC

Although French insistence on unanimity within the EEC Council of Ministers on issues of major concern suggested that meaningful progress toward political and economic integration might be terminally slowed, the European Commission found ways to move forward. For example, two conventions signed in 1975 and 1980 in Lomé, capital of the African state of Togo, linked some sixty states in Africa, the Caribbean, and the Pacific (the ACP nations) with the EEC. Under the Lomé agreements, nearly all ACP industrial products and about 96 percent of ACP agricultural goods could be exported to the Common Market tariff-free. Yet the developing countries were allowed to charge import duties so long as these were equal for all EEC members. The 1975 treaty provided grants of $2 billion to the ACP states and credits

The glass pyramid, designed by I. M. Pei and dedicated in 1989, is a dramatic addition to the Louvre Museum. Its striking emphasis on light—received by day, projected at night—symbolizes the new European openness, and its bold originality suggests the creative achievements of present-day France. (Photo from Reuters/Bettmann.)

of an equal amount. Such steps won the Common Market nations not only tons of inexpensive sugar but friends as well.

Pessimism regarding the ability of the institutions of the EEC to achieve true economic and political integration nevertheless remained strong. It weakened only in the early 1980s as a result of several developments. One was the relaxation of French defensiveness. In 1975 France suggested that unanimity might not always be necessary in the Council of Ministers. The establishment of a Regional Development Fund the same year helped to prod national governments to take steps to ease areas of poverty within the EEC. With French objections finally removed, in 1979 direct election of members of the European Parliament was approved. As its proponents hoped, the course of these elections helped to stir interest within the populations of the member states. In many cases, their support of integration and European issues demonstrated to mainline politicians that they might do well to show more interest themselves. A European Monetary System (EMS) was also inaugurated in 1979 to link the several currencies of the EEC. Its development was severely slowed, however, by differences among the states.

The most serious hindrance to forward movement of the EEC was the huge amount of the organization's budget devoted to support of farm prices under the Common Agricultural Policy. The British in particular were aware that they were paying far more in support of agricultural subsidies within the EEC than the United Kingdom was receiving; indeed, the United Kingdom was the largest contributor to the budget though it was the third poorest of the EEC countries. French farmers joked that they were filling their pails with sterling from the British cow. To placate critics, the commissioners increased nonfarm spending to match agricultural spending. The Council of Ministers slashed the nonfarm spending from the budget, whereupon the new popularly elected European Parliament defeated the budget. The assembly had shown its independence and its will. Deadlock ensued, not to be resolved until a reduction in the British contribution was negotiated in 1980. Agriculture subsidy problems would not go away and became the cause of more incidents in the future. The demonstration of the role that might be assumed by the European Parliament and the subsequent negotiations to resolve the crisis did, however, carry encouragement. Moreover, the history of the CAP was not entirely negative. If EEC food prices generally remained above world market prices, the EEC had achieved self-sufficiency and thus security in numerous food commodities, stabilized its domestic food market, and enhanced agricultural workers' incomes.

The interest of other nations in either associated status (as in the case of Austria) or full membership also attested to the apparent worth of the EEC. In 1981 Greece became the tenth member of the organization, and in 1986 Spain and Portugal joined, inaugurating seven-year programs to bring their tariffs in line with those of the EEC. Their accession far outweighed the decision of the Greenland province of Denmark to withdraw from the community in 1982 in order to protect its fisheries. Granted, the admission of three countries whose economies were less developed and more agricultural than those of the other nine was considered something of a gamble. The progress each made, and the benefits each received from access to EEC markets and development funds, proved heartening from many viewpoints. The very acceptance of Spain and Portugal, after their emergence from years of dictatorship and semi-isolation from the rest of the Continent, both undergirded their democratic governments and gave a broader and more inclusive meaning to the concept of a European Community.

Nor should it be forgotten that the EEC was indirectly affecting certain Comecon states, especially the German Democratic Republic. Because the West German government refused to accept the permanent division of Germany, it purposely eschewed any tariff barriers with East Germany on the technical ground that as the two Germanys were supposedly only temporarily divided, a tariff was not required. Thus goods from East Germany could flow into the Federal Republic and vice versa unhindered by tariffs, although the GDR did have to pay duties on its deliveries to other EEC member states. East German materials that received further processing in West Germany might be sold to French or Italian markets without tariffs. Such trade did not reach high levels, in part because of currency problems, but its existence served as a gravitational pull on the East Germans and on the Poles and Czechs, who traded with the Democratic Republic.

The Economic Community also exercised influence on other groups and deliberations, such as those of the Group of Five (France, Germany, Great Britain, Japan, and the United States), which formed in 1985 to deal with international currency issues. This group expanded to include Canada and Italy the following year. In its efforts to improve coordination among the leading industrial nations of the world, it gave further impetus to close European consultation.

The Move Toward a Single Europe

Much cooperation and some real integration had been achieved, yet it was evident that without further changes in rules and stances, creation of an area "without internal frontiers" as envisioned by the treaties of Rome would never take place. The steady growth of U.S. and Japanese exports to Europe was a further warning that the members of the community were missing an opportunity to take advantage of the benefits that integration would provide. So it was that the European Commission in 1985 proposed some 300 changes to bring about a truly complete internal market. The next year the heads of government of the EEC nations agreed to take steps to remove all barriers to a totally free internal market, to streamline voting in the Council of Ministers, and to increase the powers of the European Parliament. Negotiations for trade agreements with Comecon were also to be started. The Single Europe Act was formally approved by the members of the EEC in 1987, and the term *European Community* (EC) replaced—as it already had begun to do—that of *European Economic Community* as a way of emphasizing the intent to move beyond just economic to political and social integration.

The plan was to extinguish *all* existing barriers to trade by the end of 1992. This would mean abolition of restrictions on the flow of unemployed workers from one region to another, equalization of insurance and health benefits, and many other adjustments to social legislation. Regulations on product safety and environmental concerns would have to be coordinated; for example, Denmark forbade the sale of paints containing lead, whereas several Italian companies counted on being able to export such paints. There would be free movement of capital, a step that would ease the cost of capital formation for investment and development purposes. Banking, insurance, and private service firms would have to accept some common rulings; in return, however, they would gain access to a market of 320 million people, by far the largest and most affluent market in the world. Concomitantly, the plan envisaged firm establishment of a complete common external tariff and regulatory system relating to both the export and import of commodities.

The welcome that populations and corporations alike gave to the concept of a single Europe nourished the movement. It seemed unlikely that the goal could be achieved completely by 1993, yet large businesses in Europe, the United States, and Japan could not delay in positioning themselves to take advantage of the great market. Many firms underwent substantial restructuring, opened new offices inside the community, and participated in mergers and takeovers to ready themselves for both new opportunities and competition. Even the Swedes and substantial numbers of Norwegians began to think it would be to their advantage to join the EC, although agricultural interests in Norway continued to oppose the move.

In early 1990 agreement was reached on the creation of a European Community Central Bank that would be responsible for EC monetary policy; it was to be autonomous and answerable only to democratically elected representatives. Planning was directed toward the creation of a European Monetary Union (EMU), and general agreement was reached regarding limits on excessive budget deficits and on upper ranges for government borrowing—all necessary if stable European Currency Units (ECUs) were to be maintained. This unit, on which the finances of the European Community are calculated, is a composite monetary unit based on the gross national products (GNPs) and value of trade of the member states. A merger of the twelve European currencies into a single currency unit would give the new entity great strength; it would surely outweigh both the Japanese yen and the U.S. dollar to become the dominant currency on the world market. The merger would also lead to the transfer of control over national economic policies to a central agency, the nature and policies of which cannot be foreseen. Progress on the EMU was stymied by the opposition of Prime Minister Margaret Thatcher of Great Britain, who objected to the entailed loss of national fiscal sovereignty. But that opposition was in time to become a partial cause for her loss of leadership of the Conservatives and of her personal hold on 10 Downing Street.

Still, the problem of huge agricultural subsidies that benefited some nations much more than others threatened the operations of the community. It also posed the threat of a protectionist tariff war with the United States. European reluctance to decrease farm subsidies and lower tariffs on agricultural imports, thus opening the EC to cheaper U.S. foods, annoyed leaders in the United States. The refusal of the Europeans to make concessions on this issue in GATT negotiations during 1990 demonstrated both the political clout that the farm electorate still held within the EC and the increased willingness of the Europeans to act independently of U.S. wishes and interests. Their behavior also reflected a newfound confidence in Europe's ability to achieve by itself and recognition that the Soviet bloc and communism no longer posed the threat they had in earlier years.

Franco-German Relations

The lessening of French reluctance regarding the European integration movement was linked with France's interest in developing a counterbalance to the influence of the United States, Britain, and NATO, and with continuing to improve relations with the Federal Republic of Germany. The process of rapprochement with the Germans was slow, often accompanied by comments of mistrust. Ironically, as concern about U.S. and NATO influence in Europe waned in France, it was taken up in the Federal Republic. A strong pacifist movement existed there, and many Germans feared that the "cowboy" president of the United States, Ronald Reagan (1981–1989), might lead Europe into a war that would devastate Germany. The strength of the West German currency was significant for French trade planning, and as political and economic conditions in Eastern Europe became more fluid in the mid-1980s, French interest in tying Bonn firmly to the West mounted.

As January 1988, the twenty-fifth anniversary of the Elysée treaty of Franco-German friendship, approached, the two nations began to chart further cooperation. The fiftieth summit meeting of their leaders since the signing of the treaty produced agreement on creation of a security and defense council and a coordinating committee for economic and financial matters. Cooperation in education, telecommunications, and development of a combat helicopter were envisioned. A joint Franco-German brigade of about 3,500 soldiers, stationed in Germany under French command, was also planned. More symbolic than anything else, the brigade demonstrated how far Franco-German relations had moved since U.S. proposals for rearming German soldiers provoked resistance in Paris and French advocacy of programs for controlling German reconstruction.

The Soviet Bloc

Comecon

Although the European Economic Community flourished, save for a recession in 1974, the rate of growth of the gross national products of the six Eastern European members of Comecon declined, according to U.S. estimates, from an annual average of 4.6 percent in 1971–1975 to 0.9 percent in 1983. The corresponding estimates for the Soviet Union were annual growth rates of 5 percent in 1965–1970 and 2.7 percent in 1983. In the case of the USSR, some causes of the decline were temporary—severe droughts affecting agriculture and a West European recession that restricted Soviet exports of oil and gold. Other factors were more long-term. These included a declining birthrate, which reduced the rate of growth of the working-age population; a depletion of oil and coal resources; the burden of armaments; and a failure in efforts to move from extensive to intensive development through the introduction of advanced technology.

As in the case of the Common Market, regulation of trade played an important role in Comecon. The pattern was one of bilateral trade between each country and the Soviet Union rather than the establishment of a common market. In the course of Brezhnev's long administration (1964–1982), the atmosphere of détente that followed the earlier and harsher period of the Cold War led to a greater involvement of Comecon in world trade. By 1980, 40 percent of the imports of the Eastern European members of Comecon came from the Soviet Union, 27 percent from the West, 24 percent from other Eastern European countries, and the balance from Communist Asia. Exports exhibited a somewhat similar pattern, with 34 percent going to the Soviet Union, 26 percent to the West, 25 percent to other Eastern European countries, and the balance to the other, less-developed nations and Communist Asia. This pattern of trade reflected two somewhat contradictory developments that continued to affect the economics of the Eastern European members of Comecon: the significant reliance on trade with the West and thus their involvement in the world economy, and the continuing dominant role of the USSR both as a supplier of raw materials and as a political force with the ultimate authority over economic policies.

The growing Comecon involvement with the West was the result of a Soviet decision in 1971 to embark on an import-led policy of growth, with special emphasis on trade with the Western market economies. This policy was designed to stimulate industrialization by importing advanced technology and improving the quality of Comecon exports so that they could compete on the world market. In this connection loans from the West were encouraged, and the accumulated debt of the Comecon countries rose from $8 billion in 1971 to $95 billion in 1985. Of this total almost $30 billion was incurred by Poland, $26 billion by the Soviet Union, and lesser amounts by the other countries.

Economic theory held that this infusion of capital would permit the development of Comecon industrial exports that would be used both to service the debts and to provide further capital for investment. These hopes were soon disappointed. In many cases mismanagement led to uneconomic uses of the loans. A greater problem was caused by the limitation on oil production and the sharp rise of oil prices imposed by the Organization of Petroleum Exporting Countries (OPEC, founded 1960) following Israel's war with Egypt and Syria in 1973 (sometimes referred to as the Yom Kippur War). The Western European recession caused by the oil crisis greatly reduced the market for Comecon exports. Most of the Comecon countries were forced to use nearly all the profits from their reduced exports to service their loans, thus diminishing the possibility of new investments and growth. Romania did reduce its debt but only by draining its economy to the point of near collapse. Poland, however, with the largest debt and an inefficient system of management, finally had to default. The Western creditors, predominantly German banks, had assumed that the USSR would provide an "umbrella" to cover the loans as a last resort. The Soviets did in fact give some assistance to Poland, for political reasons, but the other countries had to rely on their own resources. Western banks therefore became increasingly hesitant to make further loans to the East, thus dampening prospects there for further growth.

Soviet relations with fellow members of Comecon were complex. On occasion the USSR aided them with trade credits and with investments in enterprises in which it had particular interest. By exporting oil and other raw materials to these countries at lower than world market prices it in effect subsidized them. Yet at times Soviet actions seemed more directed to buying the political loyalties of the countries and their allegiance to Soviet foreign policy initiatives than to their economic development.

The Comecon debt crisis placed in shadow other more positive economic developments in Eastern Europe. With the exception of Poland and Romania, the standard of living in these countries had shown steady improvement, and there were significant experiments in developing policies of market socialism designed to alleviate the rigidities of central planning. The East Germans, in particular, took pride in what they considered their success with their economy and its organization (see Chapter 6). One-third of all world patents were being issued to Comecon countries, and a significant transfer of technology from East to West took place. Soft contact lenses, for example, were first developed in Czechoslovakia; the use of surgical staples in operations originated in the Soviet Union. Some Eastern European products, such as the Icarus buses made in Hungary, competed successfully with those produced in more developed countries.

Reaction and Stagnation

The Brezhnev administration in the Soviet Union had hoped to assist its advance into postindustrial society through imports of Western technology. But recession in the West and the reluctance of NATO-connected countries to release sensitive technology for fear it might be used to support Soviet military development caused disappointing trade results. Particularly annoying to the Soviets was Western insistence that any relaxation of trade restrictions be matched by improvements in human rights within the Soviet Union. An amendment to the 1974 Soviet-U.S. trade agreement, pushed through the U.S. Congress by Senator Henry "Scoop" Jackson (D-Wash.) and Representative Charles Vanik (D-Ohio), that limited trade credits until Soviet emigration permits could be more easily obtained, especially by Jews, notably irritated Brezhnev.

Human rights issues attracted the attention of restless Eastern Europeans as well. For some while after the Soviet invasion of 1968, the population of Czechoslovakia had withdrawn from involvement in political affairs. In return for their "depoliticization" and acquiescence to the leadership of the party elite, aspects of terror were reduced and standards of living were slowly raised as more emphasis was given to production of consumer goods. The Helsinki accords, however, stirred intellectuals in Czechoslovakia to express their concerns. The Final Act called for formal reviews of progress toward establishment of human rights every two years. The government had made many declarations purporting to support human rights. In January 1977 a group of Czech intellectuals, including the noted playwright Václav Havel, issued the Charter 77, calling upon the government to live by its own legislation. Newspapers published documented accounts of violations of laws. For a time the government vacillated in its treatment of the leaders of the Charter 77 movement, for, after all, there were no disruptive street demonstrations and the government was merely being asked to do what it said it would do. Eventually those favoring a hard line won out; Havel and others were imprisoned for a period.

Disappointing results in trade, the inability of U.S. president Jimmy Carter (1977–1981) to persuade Congress to ratify a proposed SALT II treaty, the generally erratic nature of Carter's foreign policy and his heavy emphasis on human rights (an issue Brezhnev considered a matter of private internal affairs), the improvement of U.S. relations with Communist China, plus various domestic pressures led the Soviet party chief to question the value of continued détente. His shift to a harder policy line in foreign affairs became clear with the Soviet invasion of Afghanistan in December 1979 in support of a Communist faction within the government of that nation. The West responded with a Carter-organized boycott of the 1980 summer Olympic Games hosted by the USSR. The effectiveness of the boycott injured Soviet pride, and secretive U.S. shipments of arms to the Afghanistan resistance prevented any rapid conclusion to the Soviet involvement there.

Détente was in retreat, and events in Poland were to signal its death knell. Plagued by food shortages, low production levels, and poor factory efficiency, the Polish government attempted to force price increases and reductions of state food subsidies (see Chapter 8). The result was popular unrest that in part stimulated anticipatory crackdowns by Communist regimes in the German Democratic Republic and in Czechoslovakia, which did not want their countries to be infected by the Polish disease. For a time the Soviets were forbearing regarding events in Poland. Yet the demands of the Polish workers' union, Solidarity, and its leader, Lech Walesa, soon became too great: They called for free formation of trade unions throughout the Eastern bloc, free elections, worker management of factories, and investigation of past wrongs perpetrated by government officials. A mobilization of Soviet troops was called off at the end of 1980, but Defense Minister General

Wojciech Jaruzelski took power in February 1981. By the following December he had established martial law and detention camps, to which arrested Solidarity leaders were soon sent.

The retreat from détente seemed complete, for the elections of 1980 in the United States had brought Reagan to the presidency. Reagan had campaigned on a theme of old-style anticommunism and support of the military; he referred to the Soviet Union as the "evil empire." Although the French distrusted his posturing, he received substantial backing from Conservative Prime Minister Thatcher of Britain. Reagan's emphasis on missiles deployed in Europe and his efforts to prevent construction of a Soviet natural gas pipeline to Western Europe soon stirred opposition on the Continent. Unwilling to let the United States dictate the temperature of their homes or the temperature at which they might be incinerated in war and repulsed by Soviet policies in Eastern Europe, leaders in Western Europe spoke their own minds. Pope John Paul II, himself of Polish extraction, played a key role in support of Solidarity demonstrators in Poland. French and German officials roundly criticized the growing U.S. budget deficits, caused in part by a huge and rapid military buildup. The deficits drained investment moneys from European economies as bankers sought the high interest payments offered by U.S. government notes.

The United States was entering a period of inflexibility. The Soviet Union was entering an interregnum. After a long duration of poor health and accommodation of cronies in a stagnating administration, Brezhnev died in November 1982. He was succeeded by Yuri Andropov. Whether the new general secretary would have revitalized Soviet foreign policy with both the West and within the Eastern bloc can only be conjectured, for he died in February 1984. He in turn was succeeded by an elderly apparatchik, Konstantin Chernenko, obviously elected by the old guard in order not to make any significant changes. Chernenko died only thirteen months later. Soviet policy during these years experienced neither innovation nor revitalization. The bureaucracy stagnated as officials focused on maintaining their positions and perquisites. Meanwhile, the populations of Eastern Europe grew restless. They sensed the lack of a strong hand on the distant reins of power and uncertainty at the national and local levels as politicians endeavored to adjust their relations with the latest newcomers in Moscow. The deterioration of their own environments and economies also became increasingly visible.

Disarmament Negotiations

SALT II

It had been assumed when the first SALT treaty was signed that continuing negotiations would produce a more advanced treaty in a few years. More

Prime Minister Margaret Thatcher of Britain and President Ronald Reagan of the United States stood side by side on many issues, as they did during this November 1988 visit of Thatcher to Washington. Their collaboration, initially based on similar economic political philosophies, was strengthened by personal friendship. Together they led a solid opposition to the Soviet bloc throughout the 1980s. (Photo courtesy of the British Information Services.)

Pope John Paul II traveled widely to encourage the Roman Catholic faithful. His public masses and messages in Poland bolstered support for Solidarity, and he staunchly opposed communism for its professed atheism and its poor record on human rights. The pope's vibrant defense of social justice won him the respect of many Europeans who actively or as a matter of tradition pledge allegiance to the Roman Catholic church. At the same time, his stance on such issues as the role of women in the church provoked criticism. Whatever the reaction, John Paul II demonstrated that the Vatican still had a vital role to play in shaping the new Europe. (Photo courtesy of the Italian Cultural Institute.)

years were required than expected, and the proposed agreement would never be fully ratified as it became a victim of the demise of détente. The SALT II treaty, signed by Brezhnev and Carter in June 1979, accepted the aggregate limits on strategic missiles and the sublimit on MIRVed missiles agreed to at Vladivostok in 1974 and reduced the number of ABM systems from two to one in each country. It also included a variety of other limits, especially on the number of warheads permissible on various types of missiles. The chief thrust of the treaty was to postpone the day when the ICBMs of both sides would be vulnerable to attack. If both sides were vulnerable, then one side might see an incentive to wipe out the other quickly or might think that if the other side were attacked it would not be able to retaliate in a lethal manner. In order to keep the threat of dangerous counterattack real, the negotiators placed a sublimit on seaborne forces (the most difficult to track and eliminate in an attack) but put no limits on submarine launchers (these SALT I had limited).

In the course of the 1970s, although the United States continued to lead the USSR in the number of strategic warheads, the two countries had adopted distinctly different patterns of deployment. The United States placed a quarter of its strategic warheads on land-based missile launchers and put the balance in submarine-launched missiles and airborne bombs. The Soviets, in contrast, deployed some two-thirds to three-quarters of their missiles on land. Because land-based missiles are more accurate than seaborne or airborne—and because Soviet land-based missiles could throw three times the weight that U.S. missiles could—some critics in the United States feared that by the 1990s the Soviets would have enough warheads to place in jeopardy all U.S. land-based missiles as well as command and communications structures. Others complained that SALT II did not really limit the countries' armament programs but rather let them continue to expand as planned until 1985 in any case. Many U.S. senators distrusted Brezhnev's promise, contained in a letter that accompanied the treaty, that the Soviet Backfire bomber was not for intercontinental use, that gas tanks would not be added to increase its range, and that no more than thirty would be produced per year. At the same time, many problems of verification and of control of cruise missiles were raised. In the end the U.S. Senate failed to ratify the SALT II treaty primarily because of the Soviet occupation of Afghanistan, and the SALT process more generally came under heavy criticism in the United States because of perceived Soviet advantages. The Reagan administration initially decided to remain voluntarily within the guidelines of the SALT II treaty but finally denounced it in 1987 on the grounds that the Soviet Union was suspected of violating some of its terms.

Even though arms control formed the centerpiece of U.S.-Soviet détente, the SALT process was accompanied by a continuing tug-of-war between the two superpowers. Throughout the détente era each country sought to weaken the alliance system of the other. Recognizing the Soviet hegemony in Eastern

Europe as the prevailing political condition, the United States nevertheless sought by various means to encourage independent policies in the countries of the region. Through presidential visits to Romania and Poland; the extension of most-favored-nation trading status to Poland, Romania, and Hungary; and the conclusion of cultural and scientific agreements; the United States extended preferred treatment to those countries that exhibited some degree of independence from Soviet policies. The opening of relations with China, symbolized by the visit of Nixon to Mao Zedong in 1972, and the formal establishment of diplomatic relations between the two countries in 1979 led to a major shift in the international balance of power.

Soviet efforts at weakening the Western bloc were directed toward decoupling the Western European countries from the United States. The principal effort in this direction took place during the intermediate-range nuclear force (INF) negotiations in the 1980s. The USSR strongly supported the peace movement in Western Europe designed to prevent the deployment of U.S. nuclear weapons. It also offered negotiating terms designed to separate the United States from Western Europe. These efforts failed to prevent the U.S. deployments, but they did strengthen the forces in the West, especially in West Germany, that might oppose U.S. policies in future crises.

The extensive peace movement in Western Europe arose from two particular issues stemming from the evolution of U.S.-Soviet relations. The first concerned the U.S. commitment to defend Europe. The original strategy, involving a U.S. resort to nuclear weapons if NATO forces were unable to stem a hypothetical Soviet attack at the conventional level, was adopted at a time when the United States was well ahead of the Soviet Union in nuclear weapons. Washington's commitment could therefore be made at no significant risk to U.S. security. As the Soviet nuclear forces reached parity with those of the United States in the 1970s, the Europeans (and many U.S. citizens) began to ask themselves whether a U.S. president would actually resort to the use of intermediate- and short-range nuclear weapons in the European theater. Could a president do this, knowing that a local nuclear exchange would probably escalate to a strategic exchange in which the United States as well as the Soviet Union could be devastated?

An alternative to a resort to nuclear weapons was that the United States adopt a policy of "no first use" of the devices, on condition that the European members of NATO raise the level of their conventional forces to match those of the Soviet Union directed at Europe. Although the European members of NATO were close in population to the members of the Warsaw Pact (364 million to 394 million) and much wealthier, they were reluctant to undertake the additional burden of increasing their military expenditures. The issue of guns versus butter (above all social security and education outlays) was a major one within each country, especially in the frequently close elections between socialist and moderate parties.

The second and more acute issue that stimulated the peace movement, particularly in West Germany, was apprehension that with the deployment of U.S. nuclear weapons, German territory would be the first to be devastated in the event of war. At the same time, most observers were less concerned with the eventuality of nuclear war than with the political uses of Soviet nuclear preponderance. Without deployment of new U.S. nuclear weapons in Western Europe, the Soviets' geographical location and predominance in nuclear capability might well permit them to exert political pressure on European countries. Just as U.S. nuclear predominance in 1962 was a major factor in forcing the Soviets to back down in the Cuban crisis, so in Europe during critical periods the USSR might gain political advantages if its nuclear deployments along its western borders were not countered by U.S. measures.

The two superpowers also competed for influence in the Third World. During the period of détente, the United States intervened actively to oppose socialist regimes in Vietnam, Chile, and Grenada. The Soviet Union took action in Angola, Mozambique, Ethiopia, and South Yemen. Each country sought to use these events to accuse the other of "imperialism" before the forum of world opinion. In Europe, however, distaste grew for what was considered the superpowers' unending preoccupation with the use of force.

INF Negotiations

In the 1980s, East-West relations became especially tense over the issue of intermediate-range nuclear forces in Europe and the USSR. These forces differed from strategic missiles in their shorter range for use within the European theater. By the late 1970s negotiations between NATO and the Warsaw Pact for a multilateral reduction in conventional forces (under the auspices of the Mutual and Balanced Force Reduction talks begun as part of détente in 1973) had made no progress at all. Both sides then decided to replace their existing theater nuclear missiles with more modern weapons. President Carter pressured European leaders to accept the arming of tactical nuclear weapons with neutron bombs (artillery shells) that kill by short-lived radiation. Resistance to this in Western European legislatures was finally overcome just when Carter decided it would be better to defer production of the new weapons. The European politicians were hardly pleased at this vacillation, which raised questions about U.S. commitment. The Soviets, for their part, moved faster than the United States. Their new SS-20 missiles directed against Europe had three warheads each and were mobile; the number deployed (replacing earlier weapons) rose from 18 in 1977 to some 270. The challenge this deployment represented to the West was twofold. Western Europe, especially Germany, was extremely nervous about matching the buildup for fear that it would make a nuclear war on European territory more likely. These fears were enhanced by the U.S. commitment to resort to nuclear weapons if a Soviet attack with conventional weapons should threaten to overrun NATO's defenses.

After much debate, European members of NATO finally agreed that the United States could enhance its nuclear tactical forces in Europe. They accepted a level of 108 Pershing II missiles and 464 cruise missiles on condition that the United States simultaneously undertake negotiations with the USSR looking toward an arms control agreement in Europe. The Soviets were especially concerned about the Pershing II missiles. Even though these missiles had only one warhead each, they were powerful and accurate and could reach vital targets in the USSR in only a few minutes. Complicating the issue were 162 British and French missiles aimed at the USSR. As these were not controlled by NATO, the United States did not consider them subject to negotiation; the Soviets of course did.

A whole series of proposals and counterproposals were exchanged between 1980 and 1983, but no agreement was reached. In 1981 the United States put forth a "zero-zero" option. It would cancel its proposed deployment of nuclear weapons on condition that the Soviets eliminate all of their intermediate-range nuclear weapons. The Soviets rejected the proposal. The U.S. position at this point in the negotiations was weak because the Soviets already had their new missiles in place and the deployment of the U.S. missiles depended on their acceptance by the NATO allies. This problem was solved when a parliamentary vote in West Germany in November 1983 reaffirmed support for the NATO deployments. The other Western countries also agreed to accept U.S. missiles. The Soviets thereupon withdrew from both the INF talks and the Strategic Arms Reduction Talks (START) that had begun in 1982. U.S.-Soviet relations went into a deep freeze, and European leaders on either side of the Iron Curtain seemed unable to bring about a renewal of negotiations.

The Deadlock Broken

In March 1983, Reagan announced plans for a new Strategic Defense Initiative (SDI), popularly known as "Star Wars," designed to provide protection against enemy ballistic missiles by developing new defensive technology in outer space. At the same time, Reagan authorized sharp increases in the U.S. defense budget, conventional forces, and missiles. Soviet scientists were also working on a more modest land-based antiballistic missile program using laser and particle beam weapons. Within the United States, much criticism arose regarding the technical feasibility of SDI and its expense. The Soviets insisted SDI violated the ABM treaty of 1972, which banned the stationing of weapons of mass destruction on other celestial bodies or in outer space. There was no doubt that the proposed development of new levels of ABM systems was destabilizing and added a whole new dimension to the arms control process. Expansion of the U.S. defense program would put strains on the U.S. budget,

Armament Acronyms

ABM	antiballistic missile
ICBM	intercontinental ballistic missile
INF	intermediate-range nuclear force
MAD	mutually assured destruction
MBFR	mutual and balanced force reduction
MIRVs	multiple, independently targetable reentry vehicles
MLF	multilateral nuclear force
SALT	Strategic Arms Limitation Talks
SDI	Strategic Defense Initiative ("Star Wars")
SLBM	submarine-launched ballistic missile
START	Strategic Arms Reduction Talks

which in time would suck more investment capital out of Japan and Europe. The cost seemed worthwhile to Washington planners, who suspected that economic conditions in the Eastern bloc were such that the Soviets might not be able to keep pace. Europeans, however, were shocked by Reagan's comments that a nuclear war might be winnable; they considered any nuclear war unsurvivable. Even in the United States groups advocating a freeze on the building of nuclear weapons gained strength.

The Soviets' decision in 1985 to return to arms control negotiations is generally attributed to their desire to halt the U.S. antiballistic missile program and to reduce defense expenditures. It was closely linked to the accession to power as general secretary of Mikhail Gorbachev. An advocate of "new thinking," which he saw as necessary to get the Soviet Union moving once again, Gorbachev called for "restructuring" in both domestic and foreign affairs. As time passed, it became clear that revitalization of the Soviet domestic economy would require Gorbachev to reduce both foreign affairs challenges and expenses (see Chapter 7).

The new negotiations were held according to an "umbrella" agreement under which three sets of issues—strategic missiles, intermediate-range missiles in Europe, and military use of outer space—were considered by three separate teams of negotiators working together in Geneva. Little progress was made, but there were hopes that a meeting in Geneva between Reagan and Gorbachev in November 1985 would provide a breakthrough. The results of the summit were nevertheless inconclusive. Although the meetings were conducted in a friendly atmosphere, the U.S. president was willing to make no concessions on Star Wars, and the Soviet general secretary was therefore not willing to discuss reductions in the heavy land-based missiles that the United States perceived as threatening its security. On the positive side, a

"process of dialogue" was initiated, with further summit meetings agreed to
in principle. Cultural exchanges and direct New York–Moscow civilian air
flights were renewed; additional consulates were opened, and several other
agreements reflected a greater mutual confidence.

Another summit meeting, held in Reykjavik, the capital of Iceland, in
October 1986, failed to produce any settlement. Though there was much talk
of sharp reductions in nuclear weapons, Reagan would not accept any cuts in
SDI. Although the meeting ended in stalemate, it was in some sense a
propaganda victory for the Soviet side. The United States appeared before
world opinion to be the one opposed to arms reductions; moreover, the
NATO allies were clearly fearful that the security of Western Europe might
be weakened by cuts in nuclear arms that had been discussed without their
participation.

Pressure from European leaders for armament reductions, budgetary
constraints, Reagan's desire to make a historic contribution to peace, and
Gorbachev's need to focus energy and funds on domestic reconstruction all
helped U.S. and Soviet negotiators in Geneva finally to reach agreement on
an INF treaty. It provided for the abolition of intermediate nuclear forces,
with a range of 1,000 to 5,500 kilometers (620 to 3,410 miles), and of shorter-
range intermediate nuclear forces, with a range of 500 to 1,000 kilometers
(310 to 620 miles). The treaty affected in particular the 108 Pershing II missiles
and 208 cruise missiles deployed by the United States in Europe (with a total
of 316 warheads), and the 270 SS-20 and 112 SS-4 Soviet missiles (with a total
of 922 warheads). For the first time in years, an actual reduction in armaments
was agreed upon, rather than limits on what the powers would build. Moreover, new precedents were set in provisions for verification and inspection.

The agreement represented a return to the "zero-zero" formula proposed
by Reagan in 1981 and rejected at that time by the USSR. The Soviets now
accepted the proposal and took the initiative of adding to it the shorter-range
nuclear forces as well, even though they had to destroy or move several times
the number of weapons as did the United States. In adopting this policy the
Soviets were motivated in part by a desire to eliminate the Pershing II
missiles, which threatened Moscow directly, and more generally by their
interest in reducing defense expenditures. They may also have seen the move
as a way to lessen Western European ties with the United States.

The treaty was signed in December 1987 during a summit held in
Washington, in the course of which the people of the United States welcomed
Gorbachev with unprecedented warmth. The exchange of ratifications took
place at a Moscow summit in May 1988. Although not much else was
accomplished in Moscow, this summit meeting had powerful symbolic meaning as a turning point in U.S.-Soviet relations. The prospects of a long-term
normal relationship were raised by the Joint Moscow Statement issued at the
end of the meeting:

The two leaders are convinced that the expanding political dialogue they have established represents an increasingly effective means of resolving issues of mutual interest and concern. They do not minimize the real differences in history, tradition, and ideology which will continue to characterize the Soviet-U.S. relationship. But they believe that the dialogue will endure, because it is based on realism and focussed on the achievement of concrete results.

As if to test this new determination to resolve problems of mutual interest, the negotiators turned to two outstanding issues: the reduction of strategic nuclear weapons and the equalization of conventional forces in Europe. Although agreement in principle was reached on the concept of a 50 percent reduction in long-range nuclear weapons, details could not be easily be worked out, and the SDI program continued to be a roadblock. Other issues did move toward resolution. Agreement was reached in April regarding the withdrawal of Soviet troops from Afghanistan: Most of them were gone within thirteen months, defusing the issue that had most precisely marked the end of détente in the 1970s. In December Gorbachev unilaterally announced his intention to reduce his nation's military forces by a half million troops within two years.

The Great Change

The Miracle Year

Anyone pretending to have predicted the events of 1989 in Eastern Europe (see Chapters 6 and 8) before they occurred would be guilty of untruth. The events were clearly associated with changes introduced by Gorbachev within his country. Also crucial was his willingness to allow the Eastern European Communist leaders and countries to work out their own histories, so that he could concentrate Soviet resources on Soviet restructuring.

Freed—or at least somewhat liberated—from Soviet domination, inspired by what they knew of reforms in the USSR and the prosperity of Western economic life, and filled with anger at years of exploitation and corruption by party leaders, the populations of Eastern Europe reacted. The first signs of rebellion were somewhat tentative, but they soon surged forth in full power.

In June the Polish Communist party was humiliated in national elections. By an agreement reached a few months before, the Solidarity union had been granted legal status and allowed to contest 261 of the parliamentary seats up for election. Solidarity defeated party candidates for all but one of these seats, and by late summer a non-Communist headed the Polish government. A few weeks earlier, in May, Janos Kadar had been forced to resign in Hungary. The barbed wire fences between that nation and Austria were torn down, and in September the Hungarian government announced it would no longer block the passage of East Germans attempting to leave the German Democratic Republic for the West. While demonstrations grew in East German cities and refugees flooded westward, the Soviets asserted that each country should have freedom of choice regarding the path it would follow. Gorbachev announced that the Brezhnev Doctrine of 1968 was dead. The Soviet reformer had little interest in saving the skins of old-line conservatives in East Germany and elsewhere who tended to criticize his restructurings within the Soviet Union. Governmental changes came in a cascade: in Hungary, East Germany, Bulgaria, Czechoslovakia, even Romania. Most startling of all, on November 9, 1989, a new East German government opened the nation's borders and the notorious Berlin Wall came tumbling down.

The tidal change brought a quick December meeting at Malta between Gorbachev and new U.S. president George Bush. Most of their attention was directed toward the German question, for the vox populi in both Germanys was calling for reunification. A particularly thorny issue was the place of any united Germany in the alliance systems. The Soviets were determined that united Germany should not be part of NATO, whereas the West and Chancellor Helmut Kohl of the Federal Republic insisted that Germany would not abandon the alliance that had sustained the Federal Republic for so many years. Throughout Europe the prevailing mood was one of caution. But Kohl did not share the "go slow" mood, nor did most Germans. He met with President François Mitterrand of France and won the French leader's acquiescence, after some cautious hesitation, to the notion of a united Germany. Kohl also carefully assured members of the European Community that German unity should be achieved within the architecture of Europe as a whole; he acknowledged that the many nations lived under one roof and should mutually care for Europe.

If there were Westerners who did not welcome the creation of one large Germany, they knew there was little they could do to stem the obvious desires of the vast majority of the Germans. War was unthinkable, and Germany's economic predominance was such that sanctions—also unthinkable—would little affect Germany but would hamper all of Europe. The best course was that of making virtue out of necessity. To this end Mitterrand worked assiduously to develop closer relations with Kohl, who acknowledged his debt to France for accepting the new Germany. By May 1990 the foreign ministers of the four victorious powers in World War II plus those of the two German states were negotiating the terms of German unification. On July 1 a monetary, economic, and social union between the two republics came into force.

Alliance membership remained a sticking point until Gorbachev withdrew his objections in midsummer. The new Germany would have full sovereignty, would be able to decide for itself its alliance membership, and would reduce its armed forces to a level of 370,000 troops. Poland was reassured about its borders. In the "four plus two" talks, the powers agreed that, instead of a peace treaty, a document dealing with the establishment of German sovereignty and the relinquishment of four-power control would be referred to a meeting of the Conference on Security and Cooperation in Europe. On August 31 the unification treaty was signed, and on October 3 the German Democratic Republic acceded to the territory of application of the Basic Law governing the Federal Republic (see Chapter 6); that is, the territories of East Germany declared themselves henceforth as governed by and subject to the law under which West Germany had operated. There no longer was a German Democratic Republic.

Germany was reunited. Democratic governments were struggling to be born in Poland, Czechoslovakia, Hungary, and with somewhat less success in other regions of Eastern Europe. One after another of the Eastern European nations expunged from their constitutions the famous Article 6, modeled after that of the Soviet constitution of 1977, which granted the Communist party the "leading role" in society. Several parties renamed themselves to eliminate the word *Communist*, to refurbish their image and to gain a new start. Many of the new leaders looked to the West for economic, technological, and spiritual support. A new Europe was in the offing, but the shape it would take was far from clear. More evident were the challenges to be faced.

Problems of Transition

Many Marxist theorists have devoted countless pages to describing the change from capitalism to communism, but very little has been written about the possible transition from a socialist command economy to a free market system. New paths had to be blazed, yet most of the former Soviet bloc countries were in economic crisis.

They faced a multidimensional debt. There was a ruble debt to the USSR and a hard-currency debt to the West. The environmental debt was stupendous, especially in Poland and the former territories of East Germany. The extent of poisoning of the land and water resources had heretofore not been widely known in the West and scarcely measured in the East. The long-term costs for cleanup could hardly be estimated, and the effect on human lives would continue for decades. For example, it was found in one Romanian economic development area that 71 percent of all new male workers in two chemical plants, healthy at the time of employment, had become severely anemic after one year, a symptom of lead poisoning. The environmental debt thus demonstrated another debt, that of health. Again, it was in Romania that the most shocking examples were discovered. There, where birth-control devices were banned in order to increase the population, orphanages were overflowing with children receiving only minimal care despite the desperate efforts of their overworked nurses. Also, the government had denied the existence of acquired immune deficiency syndrome, although AIDS cases had reached nearly epidemic proportions.

The energy debt was equally serious and closely related to the environ-mental debt. The burning of sulfurous coal and the lack of treatment of acid mine runoffs had devastated large areas. The old habit of building new, energy-inefficient plants when existing plants had proved inefficient because of lack of skilled workers, labor unrest, and energy costs, had simply resulted in higher energy demands. Some experts estimated that heavy industries in the East used 2.5 times the amount of energy per unit of production than did factories in Western Europe. The overall inefficiency of Eastern production suggested that many plants would have to close when faced with direct competition from Western manufacturers. This indeed was the experience of numerous East German firms in the first year of reunification.

A debt to the population existed in many forms. For years the people had been asked to sacrifice, to invest for the future. The standard of living had improved somewhat directly after the war, but new shortages developed over the years. The gap between what was experienced in the East and what was known (or imagined) about the West as a result of travel and radio and television reception grew. So, too, did discontent.

The debt to the population had its most serious aspect in the realm of politics. After years of government led by one party that was highly select in its membership, a common political culture and political experience among the population at large was lacking. This deficit was paralleled by widespread resentment at the obvious corruption and cronyism of the party elite and the bullying ways of government bureaucrats. Democratic institutions and an effective system of laws were absent. In some instances, good laws on the books were not enforced. In others, laws were not published or were subject to sudden change. Because individual initiative was discouraged to make way for decisions from the top, there was little coordination of society, most particularly at the local level. The lack of initiative was especially costly within the labor force, where there was little reward for making suggestions or extra effort.

The new governments were faced with two possible courses of action. One was to make reforms and improve performance without changing the identity or the essence of Communist party control of the state. That seemed, in the long run, the course that Gorbachev wished to follow in the Soviet Union through restructuring. The other was to change systems entirely, to move from a command system dominated by a centrally dominant political party to a free market system relying on initiative. This was the course Poland chose (see Chapter 8).

Many of the former Soviet bloc nations of Eastern Europe talked about changing to a market economy. The hurdles were immense, and only a few faced them directly. Market institutions such as banks had to be created. External problems, including tariffs with the Common Market and slowed payment of large foreign debts had to be negotiated. Convertible currencies had to be established, and command economies do not lend themselves well to convertibility. A Western ball-bearing factory might be able to sell its products to the Soviets in return for rubles, for example. But because all Soviet production is planned to capacity, there would be few surplus Soviet goods that the Western firm could buy with its newly obtained rubles: perhaps vodka, furs, tourist items, or natural gas if enough could be tapped. The rubles were therefore considered of little worth internationally and could not be exchanged with other currencies, for their holders could not purchase freely in the Soviet market either.

The monetary, economic, and social union established between the Federal Republic and the German Democratic Republic on July 1, 1990, gave the East Germans a solid and convertible currency. Poland and Czechoslovakia also established such currencies as they moved toward free market economies, and Hungary hastened to follow suit. Bulgaria, Yugoslavia, Albania, and Romania clung to their former systems.

Creation of convertible currencies opened avenues for more active trade with the West. Comecon was undermined. Though inefficient, Comecon nevertheless continued to be of some significance, for 90 percent of Eastern Europe's oil came from the Soviet Union. Were the latter to raise its prices to match those of the world market and demand payment in hard currency, the Eastern European states would be in difficult straits indeed. The surge to create free market economies in the East was so great, however, that it could not be resisted. The German Democratic Republic had already dropped out of Comecon, and at the beginning of 1991 the remaining nine members announced the dissolution of the organization. In its place the Soviet Union, Bulgaria, Cuba, Czechoslovakia, Hungary, Mongolia, Poland, Romania, and Vietnam planned to form an Organization for International Economic Cooperation that could better work with the West. Anxious to proceed with free market economic reforms, the Czechs, Poles, and Hungarians questioned the need of any trade agreement with their former associates who had not yet embraced a free market; negotiations languished.

The demise of the key instrument of Soviet economic planning for Eastern Europe was paralleled by that of military affairs, as the six remaining members of the Warsaw Pact formally announced its dissolution in the summer of 1991, although it had been effectively defunct since its February meeting. Soviet soldiers continued to withdraw from Hungary in accord with an agreement reached the preceding March and accelerated their movement out of Czechoslovakia. Only Poland did not have a formal agreement on Soviet troop removal. Although the number of soldiers was being reduced, the Poles insisted that all be gone by the end of 1991; the Soviets replied that full removal could not be achieved until the middle of 1994. The disappearance of Comecon and the Warsaw Pact marked a decline of Soviet influence in Eastern Europe, yet it did not signal its evanescence, and the potential of future reassertion of Soviet interests in the area remained strong. Meanwhile, the former satellite states charted their own economic courses without the guidance of Comecon.

For the Eastern European states to compete in a free market economy involving all of Europe, their industry would have to be restructured and made more efficient. Price controls would have to be removed, raising the question as to whether such action would result in hyperinflation and strikes that would cut productivity and further accelerate inflation. Capital was necessary but unavailable within the countries. Foreign investment had to be attracted, yet legislation was not in place to facilitate its arrival. Leaders could talk of selling off government-owned industries to private owners. But how was the value of these industries to be assessed? Was it possible to utilize old inefficient plants, or would they simply have to be abandoned for new construction? Who would accept the immense costs of environmental cleanup on the premises of the old plants? Would foreign investors be willing to take responsibility for the housing, health clinics, and stores formerly associated with huge, government-run enterprises? Or would the government have to assume these responsibilities?

Entrepreneurs who were willing to take the risk of investing in the East did exist, but there were not enough of them. Those who did invest worried about Eastern workers, who habitually gave a lackluster effort in return for poor pay. Could they be persuaded to work harder when better pay might not quickly result in a higher standard of living because of the lack of consumer goods? Could slackers be laid off? The populations in the East clamored for a free market economy that they knew had brought prosperity to West Germany. But they were not eager to accept unemployment, reduction of social benefits, or unsubsidized prices. Local governments were still dominated by bureaucrats who knew no other way of doing things than the old way and who were afraid to make changes for fear that former party leaders might regain control and wreak retribution.

The multiple economic, political, social, and environmental challenges were complicated by another concern. Would the ethnic rivalries that so weakened the Eastern European democracies between the wars again undermine political unity and economic progress once the repressive hand of the state was lifted? In Czechoslovakia pressure built for a renaming of the country to acknowledge the autonomy of the linguistic groups of which it was constituted. In Yugoslavia, riots broke out between Albanian minorities and Serbs; Slovenes and Croats threatened to secede. Magyar minorities in Romanian Transylvania agitated for return of their lands to Hungary. In Bulgaria and Poland, ethnic difficulties seemed less severe; yet even there Jewish minorities braced against the current of anti-Semitism that was reappearing throughout Eastern Europe and the Soviet Union.

In the USSR, the ethnic issue became a major force. The Baltic republics demanded the right to secede and soon were joined in claims of sovereignty

This Lithuanian woman is protesting the removal of local government officials by the central authorities in Moscow. Discontent with Soviet rule had regularly erupted in Eastern Europe ever since the imposition of Communist governments after 1945. But until the late 1980s, there had never been any large-scale public protests within the Soviet Union itself. The anger in this woman's face expresses the widespread popular frustration with economic and political conditions in the Soviet Union. In the non-Russian parts of the USSR, like Lithuania, this frustration was combined with a reawakening sense of national identity that further undermined already weakening loyalties to the central Soviet government. (Photo from Reuters/Bettmann.)

by nearly every other republic. Young men drafted into the Soviet army refused to report for service. Within Estonia, Latvia, and Lithuania themselves ethnic conflicts mounted. Fighting between Armenians and Azeries required intervention by Soviet troops. Any breakup of the Soviet Union would have vast implications for Eastern Europeans. Their own revolutions against entrenched and corrupt party leaders were indebted to Gorbachev's original willingness to allow the Eastern European populations freedom of action. A successful Soviet repression of independence movements in the Baltic republics or Moldova might well require that the Soviets dominate the politics of neighboring states.

The future path of Eastern Europe seemed fraught with dangers and surrounded by innumerable pitfalls. Yet there was the possibility that new courses could be chosen. Perhaps new relationships could be established between the leaders and the led, between the Eastern states and their neighbors in the West, and among the nations of a new European Community. Hopeful excitement therefore vied with nervous foreboding, especially in Eastern Europe. Every choice seemed conceivable. Just as the Renaissance in the fourteenth and fifteenth centuries brought renewed confidence in the capabilities of individual humankind and an open-ended conception of society to replace the fixed corporate organization of the Middle Ages, so the events of 1989 and 1990 appeared to signal a dramatic shift in the course of European history.

The End of the Cold War?

The Charter of Paris

The rebirth of Europe was the product of many forces working over many years. The symbol of the former Europe, as it emerged weak and at the mercy of the superpowers following World War II, was a divided Germany. And the theme of the forty-five-year period was the Cold War. Now that Germany was reunited, it was time for the Cold War to be brought to an end.

As in the revolutions of 1989, the pace of events outstripped that of the diplomats. The November 1990 Paris meeting of the leaders of the thirty-four members of the Conference on Security and Cooperation in Europe, originally scheduled to grant permission for German unification, instead became the first international conference at which the already reunited Germany was represented as a single new entity. The heads of state, stirred by the profound and rapid changes in Europe, proclaimed a new era, a recognition of what had been achieved by the peoples of Europe. In their Charter of Paris for a New Europe, they announced

> We . . . have assembled in Paris at a time of profound change and historic expectations. The era of confrontation and division of Europe has ended. We declare that henceforth our relations will be founded on respect and cooperation.
>
> Europe is liberating itself from the legacy of the past. The courage of men and women, the strength of the will of the peoples and the power of the ideas of the Helsinki Final Act have opened a new era of democracy, peace and unity in Europe.

Together they pledged "to build, consolidate and strengthen democracy as the only system of government of our nations."

Just what was meant by *democracy* was made somewhat clear by mention of regular, free, and fair elections; political pluralism; equality of application of law; and freedom of thought, religion, expression, movement, peaceful assembly, and ownership of property. Human rights, economic liberty, social justice, and equal security for all nations were promised. President Mitterrand of France proclaimed the gathering an "anti–Congress of Vienna," contrasting the manner in which the diplomats of 1815 had made decisions affecting all of Europe without concern for the wishes of the population with the way the writers of the charter acknowledged popular actions already taken.

What would result from the charter was less obvious. The CSCE remained primarily a political discussion group, as Thatcher termed it, with no enforcement powers. A small secretariat was to be established in Prague, with a conflict-prevention center in Vienna and an election-monitoring office in Warsaw. The votes of tiny Malta and the Vatican were the equal of those of the Soviet Union and Germany, and it was unlikely that the larger powers would allow their vital interests to be shaped by the myriad of small states unless there was strong concordance of views. It was difficult to expect that democracy was really understood in the same way in Moscow as in Brussels or in Washington. And it was still more difficult to imagine a full-blown, Western-style democracy emerging from the economic and political-ethnic crises erupting in the republics of the Soviet Union. Nevertheless, even if the future was uncertain, most observers did seem to agree with U.S. president George Bush in 1990 when he said, in words that were perhaps more than political hyperbole and wishful thinking, "The Cold War is over. In signing the Charter of Paris we have closed a chapter of history."

A more concrete achievement was the treaty on reducing conventional forces in Europe, signed at the same meeting by the sixteen members of NATO (including Germany) and the remaining six members of the Warsaw Pact. Talks had begun in April 1989. Here again, developments in the individual countries forced the hands of the negotiators. The various Eastern European nations were demanding the prompt withdrawal of Soviet forces. The Soviet Union, anxious to reduce its expenses in maintaining troops abroad, was willing to move them home and pleased to find a way to do so without having the action termed a retreat. Substantially lower limits on military forces were set on both sides, with the Soviets accepting far greater cuts than the West, so that forces could be brought closer to parity. Neither side would station in Europe more than 20,000 artillery pieces or tanks, 30,000 armored vehicles, 2,000 helicopters, and 6,800 combat aircraft.

Even as these agreements were being finalized in Paris, in New York the Soviet Union was supporting the United Nations and the United States in opposition to Iraq's seizure of Kuwait in August 1990. The ability of the two superpowers to work together, rather than oppose each other, signaled the possibility of new life and influence for the United Nations and for European influence throughout the globe. Within weeks, Germany and other European nations were providing food and other economic aid to the Soviet Union in answer to its requests for help. The United States lifted many of its restrictions on trade with its former bitter enemy, now viewed as a longtime rival in temporary distress.

Yet the path to a new relationship between the formerly hostile power blocs would not be smooth or straight. Pressure from conservative, military, and secret police groups within the USSR brought a blocking of certain earlier policies of Gorbachev's *perestroika*, or restructuring. Strong actions against those advocating independence in the Baltic republics, including military raids on key buildings, caused Western European nations to delay their food shipments to the USSR. Reports that the Soviets were sending intermediate-range missiles east of the Ural Mountains rather than destroying them and transferring army divisions to naval bases (outside the purview of the conventional forces treaty) disturbed U.S. leaders. Further difficulties arose over the final terms of a new strategic arms reduction treaty between the two superpowers. Preoccupied also by events in the Persian Gulf, the United States postponed the summit meeting originally scheduled for February 1991 for the purposes of signing that treaty.

The seizure of Kuwait in August 1990 by Iraqi troops met strong condemnation in the United Nations. When economic sanctions failed to make Iraqi leader Saddam Hussein yield, a coalition of twenty-eight countries, led by the United States, launched a military campaign in January 1991 to liberate Kuwait. The Soviets, former long-term allies of Iraq, participated in the coalition, although they did not provide troops. At various points Gorbachev attempted to mediate a cease-fire, and it became evident that the affair put a severe strain on U.S.-Soviet relations. Yet perhaps more important, the Soviet Union, the United States, France, Britain, Italy, Syria, Saudi Arabia, Egypt, and others maintained their front despite whatever disagreements they debated in private. The coalition successfully drove Iraqi forces from Kuwait in a matter of weeks, but the rehabilitation of that country and of political relations in the Middle East seemed destined to take much longer.

Resetting the Stage

In the wake of these events and an apparent return of Gorbachev to his reform ambitions, U.S.-Soviet differences over the conventional arms accord were resolved and progress resumed on START. Gorbachev frankly admitted that agreements were needed so that the Soviets could "reduce the military spending, and make our economy, overburdened with military affairs, turn to human interests." At the same time he offered the possibility of an arms treaty, he angled for his nation to be invited to a July 1991 meeting of the Group of Seven industrialized nations. He was, in fact, granted opportunity to make his case for Western support of his reforms, and the Soviet Union was granted "special association" with the World Bank and the International Monetary Fund.

That same day, Gorbachev and Bush announced their agreement on the terms of a strategic arms reduction treaty that would bring about the first actual reduction of strategic nuclear missiles, by approximately 25 to 35 percent for each power. The U.S. stockpile of nuclear warheads and bombs was to decrease from 12,000 to 9,000, whereas the Soviet count would fall from 11,000 to 7,000. The two leaders signed the Strategic Arms Reduction Treaty on July 31 in Moscow in what was regarded as the first post–Cold War summit (fifteen summit meetings were held during the Cold War).

Western hopes for progress on other difficult issues separating the superpowers fell abruptly with the August 1991 coup attempt by hard-liners in the Soviet Union. Various aid and credit programs were curtailed, and several Western leaders joined Kohl of Germany in decrying that more aid had not been given faster to Gorbachev's regime. The collapse of the coup after four days brought restoration of the aid programs and promises of accelerated assistance in the future. The United States and Britain neverthe-less insisted that before large amounts of aid were provided, the Soviets would have to undertake further economic reforms. The Germans were less de-manding in this regard, for they feared an influx of refugees from Eastern Europe if economic stability and reliable food supplies were not soon estab-lished there. Yet there were limits to what Germany could do by itself. The costs of absorbing the rundown industries of the former German Democratic Republic were proving far higher than expected (many simply had to be closed and extensive environmental cleanups planned). Moreover, Germany was already paying the Soviet Union substantial sums to build housing for troops in order to accelerate their return to the USSR from their previous stations in Germany.

During the first days of the hard-liners' attempted coup, Estonia and Latvia declared their independence from the Soviet Union (Lithuania had made its declaration the previous March). Within days, the three Baltic states won diplomatic recognition from the Nordic Council and the European Community nations as well as from the Russian republic. By mid-September they were members of the United Nations. The Russian republic, under the leadership of Boris Yeltsin, opposed the coup attempt and declared that it would operate independently of the long powerful central government (the "Center").

Gorbachev's desperate efforts to reestablish his own authority in the wake of the coup attempt, to deal with Yeltsin and the leaders of the other restive republics in the Soviet Union, and to obtain Western aid in coping with his country's impending winter food crisis required resolution of international issues. He therefore accepted the secession of the Baltic states as an accomplished fact. Gorbachev also announced his intention to withdraw Soviet troops from Cuba and to return commerce with that nation to a cash basis (rather than trading Soviet oil for Cuban sugar valued at a level well above what it held on the world market). He also reached agreement with the United States on mutual cessation of arms shipments to the vying factions in Afghanistan.

A strong U.S. concern was that Soviet tactical nuclear weapons located in the several republics might fall into the wrong hands during the prevailing political uncertainty—they could be sold, perhaps, to some Near Eastern state or terrorists willing to use them against Israel. This fear stimulated an unexpected round of further disarmament. Even before the treaty signed in July went before the U.S. Senate, President Bush announced a unilateral withdrawal of U.S. ground-based nuclear weapons from Europe and elsewhere in the world, with most such weapons to be destroyed. He further ordered the removal of nuclear weapons from U.S. Navy surface ships and attack submarines, and he ordered the Strategic Air Command's twenty-four-hour bomber alert, which had been maintained continuously since 1957, to stand down. Soviet leaders accepted the president's invitation to reciprocate in a similar manner. They announced elimination of many of their tactical nuclear weapons in Europe. Gorbachev even proposed a further step: the removal of all airborne tactical nuclear weapons. Bush was not prepared to go that far. Even so, a major step had been taken, for now the superpowers were moving toward true disarmament rather than just slowing the pace of nuclear buildup. And they were doing so by decisive individual action, not by tedious and technical negotiation. Gorbachev, anxious to reduce national expenses and aware of the difficulty of obtaining contingents from the independently minded Soviet republics, additionally scheduled a reduction of the standing Soviet army from 4 million to 2 million soldiers.

For the Europeans, the Bush initiative had opened the door to the long-held vision of a Europe free of ground-based nuclear arms, although the issue of storage of plane-delivered missiles remained unresolved. The reduction in the NATO nuclear shield in Europe, though welcome as a sign of the diminishing nature of the Soviet threat, also lent prominence to a growing debate over the future role—or even need—of the North Atlantic alliance. The demise of both the Warsaw Pact and Comecon in the first months of 1991, as the former satellite states of the Eastern bloc asserted their independence of action, had already put the purpose of NATO in question. In response, Britain, Canada, and the United States tried to give new emphasis to the political, economic, and social integrative aspects of the treaty, features that had previously received only limited attention.

Debate also swirled about how a special NATO response force should be formed. The French favored creation of a force that would be primarily European, even continental. Defeated on this within NATO, they soon met with German representatives and announced a mutual interest in expanding the Western European Union as the "defense component" of the EC. To support the concept, Kohl and Mitterrand stated that the German-French joint force would be expanded immediately from its current size of one brigade (4,200 troops) to the nucleus of a corps (about 50,000 soldiers). An invitation was extended to other WEU nations to contribute contingents as well. The exact duties this force would undertake were not spelled out. Possible examples included quick response such as that required during the first days of the occupation of Kuwait, or the protection of truce negotiating and observing teams in such troubled regions as Yugoslavia. The French also talked of forming a joint corps with Spain and Italy to deal with southern European concerns. Whatever role these forces might eventually play, clearly the two greatest powers within Europe intended that Europeans should take a more determining role in defensive preparations, now that the nuclear shield of the United States no longer seemed needed against a divided and weakened Soviet state.

The disunion that reigned to the east became a growing concern, especially for the Germans. The threat of inundation by asylum-seekers was real, and the flow went up steadily in the last months of 1991. So, too, did the number of violent confrontations in Germany between refugees and Neo-Fascist "skinheads," unemployed workers, and other anti-immigrant groups. In the summer of 1991, Italy had its problems with several thousand Albanians who had fled the political chaos of their country. Continuing ethnic warfare between the Serbian-dominated central regime army in Yugoslavia and the breakaway populations of Slovenia, Croatia, and eventually Bosnia brought repeated EC efforts to negotiate a truce. Many were proclaimed; none were kept. By the end of the year, under pressure from Germany, the European Community states were laying plans for recognition of the independent sovereignty of Slovenia and Croatia.

In the Soviet Union, Gorbachev ran into great difficulties in his efforts to construct a new form of economic union that would facilitate reform and economic restructuring. Only eight of the remaining fifteen republics signed an October 18, 1991, treaty embodying the vague terms of the union, and economically important Ukraine was not among them. The futility of the Soviet president's efforts to maintain the Union became evident when, in December, the presidents of the Russian Republic, Belarus, and Ukraine proclaimed the demise of the USSR and the creation of a Commonwealth of Independent States, to which several other former Soviet republics quickly adhered. As the USSR evanesced at the end of 1991 and Gorbachev's influence disappeared, the diplomatic efforts of the West therefore turned energetically from countering the threat of Soviet nuclear weapons to gaining assurance of reliable control of them by Gorbachev's and the USSR's political successors.

From 1988 through the initial years of the next decade, the rebirth of Eastern Europe had taken a far different course than that envisioned by Mikhail Gorbachev when he first launched his programs of *glasnost* and *perestroika*. The unity of Eastern Europe had disintegrated amid disillusion with corrupt one-party governments, shortages, unemployment, calls for establishment of independent currencies for separate states and republics, and ethnic differences.

In Western Europe a critical passage loomed on the path toward integration that had been taken in the name of economic efficiency, clout within world economic and political councils, improvement of living standards, undergirding of democracy, and reduction of ethnic strife. Further progress required concessions in both economic and political sovereignty from all participants. Agreement seemed possible on a monetary union that allowed a common currency and a central bank. But the Germans were loathe to surrender sole control of their stable and powerful mark unless the European Parliament obtained greater powers, thus making EC decisions more democratic. Neither the British nor the French wished to relinquish this sovereignty, and the British strongly insisted that the Strasbourg assembly could not take a decisive role in security and foreign affairs. France and Germany, more willing than Britain or Portugal to see the influence of NATO reduced and U.S. troops withdrawn from Europe, called for a more active EC role on defense matters.

Even discussions on the size of the European Community reflected differing attitudes. The French urged the solidification of the economic and political union before more states, especially those in Eastern Europe, were brought into the EC fold. British prime minister John Major said that the EC should not become an exclusive club, but many observers interpreted this argument as a front for British unwillingness to give up sovereignty and take up a truly active role in the new Europe. Would the UK's reluctance to become genuinely committed to the integration of the EC surrender that organization to the domination of its German and French members? If the EC were to become the vehicle for a German-French condominium of influence, in the growing absence of NATO and U.S. influence and continuing British hesitancy, then the rebirth of Western Europe would take on a meaning far different from what Jean Monnet had originally envisioned.

The decisions of Austria and Sweden to apply for full membership in the EC and the expectation that Finland, Norway, and perhaps even Switzerland would soon follow somewhat diminished the danger of this last possibility. The promise of further progress in Western European economic integration was also enhanced by successful completion in October 1991 of lengthy and difficult negotiations between the twelve nations of the European Community and the seven members of the European Free Trade Association (Austria, Finland, Iceland, Liechtenstein, Norway, Sweden, and Switzerland). Creation of a new, larger common market known as the European Economic Area (EEA) was projected for January 1, 1993, assuming that the parliaments of the several nations would all agree to participate. A free flow of services, capital, and manufactured goods was planned. All nations would accept the financial and labor rules of the EC, as well as laws dealing with consumer and environmental protection. An EEA court modeled after the European Court of Justice was to be created and a joint Council of EEA Ministers formed. As the EC was still struggling to revise its own hotly debated Common Agricultural Policy, no integration of farm production was suggested. That issue, along with fishing rights and similar matters, would eventually pose a difficult challenge. The EC, partly because of its CAP, remained a more tightly knit group inside the EEA. Yet the possibility of integrating into it well over 30 million people who already conducted some 60 percent of their trade with the EC and who boasted a per capita income average almost double that within the EC was exciting. As Jacques Delors, head of the European Commission, commented, proposal of the EEA was an important trial run that would assist the EC's "spiderlike strategy to organize the architecture of a Greater Europe."

In December of 1991, the heads of the EC governments met to examine their organization's progress toward the establishment of a single internal market and to discuss the several problems confronting them. Above all, they needed to establish a more unified diplomatic voice and more semblance of military strength to accompany their economic power in dealing with the unstable situation to the east. The Treaty of Maastricht, signed December 11, 1991, marked significant steps toward political unity. It provided for creation of a common European currency by 1999 at the latest and for an independent European central bank. The EC also agreed to a common defense and security policy, at the center of which would stand the Western European Union; a European police force (Europol) would also be created. Policy guidelines would have to receive unanimous approval, but provision was made for future requirement of only a two-thirds majority in some matters. In order to obtain British assent, the other EC nations granted the United Kingdom option not to participate in the new currency, and any reference to "federalism" was eschewed to placate right-wing British Conservatives. Moreover, the United Kingdom did not take part in an agreement reached by the other eleven members of the community to coordinate resolution of social policy issues such as labor legislation, equal treatment of men and women, and working conditions. Despite the concessions to the British—and it was possible that in a few years the United Kingdom might choose not to "opt out" of the currency arrangement—significant advances had been made.

Thus by 1992, the year of final push toward a Single Europe in the West, it was clear that both there and in the East, where the Soviet Union had so recently joined the ashheap of history, a new Europe was emerging. If its design was not totally clear, all observers recognized that it would be determined by the European nations themselves, within the constraints of the world system rather than being set by the agendas of two competing superpowers. In an amazingly short period, the stage on which the European states were acting had been remarkably altered. The numbers of the European countries had increased, the threat of thousands of refugees replaced the threat of Soviet military invasion, dangers of actual ethnic civil wars now substituted for those of potential nuclear strikes. Changes included unification of Germany, dissolution of the Warsaw Pact and Comecon, nuclear disarmament, independence of the Baltic states, demise of strong Communist parties in several countries, disintegration in Yugoslavia, the end of the Soviet Union, and further economic integration in the West. Much had taken place in a matter of months and even weeks that observers had not expected to occur except over many more years and in some instances with much more bloodshed.

There was irony in the turns history took from 1989 through 1991. The Helsinki Final Act of 1975, instead of legitimatizing Soviet hegemony in Eastern Europe, had sowed the seeds for the growth of human rights movements that changed the shape of European confrontation. The human rights emphasis of Jimmy Carter, considered an ineffectual U.S. president in the battles of the Cold War, became the instrument for significant change. The destabilizing Strategic Defense Initiative of the great Cold Warrior, Ronald Reagan, instead of forcing a new hot confrontation, brought about a disarmament agreement that was a true turning point. And though ethnic bonds undoubtedly helped to bring the two Germanys together once again, the same powerful force of ethnicity tore apart Eastern European states such as Yugoslavia and the USSR. While Western states gave up significant bits of national sovereignty to create a stronger economic and political unity, a reverse process thus gathered headway in Eastern Europe.

Despite Western leaders' countless attempts at peace, it was the new thinking of a Soviet party chief that permitted the change. But his new thinking was stimulated, indeed forced, by domestic considerations not unrelated to the ideological differences that brought about the Cold War and to the immense economic strain caused by that war. Moreover, Gorbachev's thinking was not really new in terms of its overall goal of preserving and modernizing the Soviet Union and protecting the leading role of the Communist party. The results were scarcely what he desired and brought his own obsolescence. Yet his reforms had indeed fostered a rethinking of the organization and economic and political philosophies in Eastern Europe. Perhaps inadvertently, certainly in the uncovering of unexpectedly strong latent nationalisms within his own country, Gorbachev's *perestroika* and *glasnost* created conditions under which Germany, Central Eastern Europe, and the vast lands stretching east from Lvov could redefine themselves and their relationships.

Eastern European discontent with economic shortages and corrupt party governance was certainly connected to awareness of Western European prosperity, pluralism, and freedom of expression. The discrepancy between promises and actuality was too strong, as was the irony of watching relatives just a few miles away, under a very different regime, enjoy the benefits promised but not delivered to the people of Eastern Europe.

The division of Germany had permitted the coexistence of rival ideologies and forces in Europe for decades. What was intended to be temporary had been accepted as permanent by all but a few in the name of assuring peace. The partition represented Soviet-U.S. confrontation, the fears the East and the West held of each other, and the apprehensiveness of Germany's neighbors regarding the Germans themselves. The end of the division did not reflect total disappearance of the distrust that had characterized European international relations in the decades following World War II. But it did show that these suspicions had declined to an extraordinary degree. Simultaneously, the attention and strength of the superpowers were being sapped by budgetary problems and concerns in other areas, ranging from Vietnam to Latin America, from Afghanistan to Central Asia, the Baltic, and the Persian Gulf. Thus the possibility of a new Europe asserting itself emerged.

Europe as of January 1992

Whether or not the Charter of Paris did indeed mark the end of the Cold War, it certainly proclaimed that the forces that brought change came from the peoples of Europe. We must therefore now turn our attention to an examination of the painful revitalization and modernization of each of the major nations of Europe that evolved following the devastation brought by World War II. For it is in the history of these individual peoples and their nations' leaders that the potential for the rebirth of Europe was to be realized.

Suggested Readings

Calvocoressi, P., *Resilient Europe: A Study of the Years 1870–2000* (1991).

Cimbala, S. J., *Extended Deterrence: The United States and NATO Europe* (1987).

Dean, J., *Watershed in Europe: Dismantling the East-West Military Confrontation* (1987).

Freedman, L., *The Evolution of Nuclear Strategy* (1981).

Hackett, C., *Cautious Revolution: The European Community Arrives* (1990).

Kennan, G. F., *The Nuclear Delusion: Soviet-American Relations in the Atomic Age* (1982).

Lodge, J. (ed.), *The European Community and the Challenge of the Future* (1989).

Musto, S. A., and C. F. Pinkele, *Europe at the Crossroads: Agendas of the Crisis* (1985).

Pierre, A. J. (ed.), *The Conventional Defense of Europe: New Technologies and New Strategies* (1986).

Rothschild, J., *Return to Diversity: A Political History of East Central Europe Since World War II* (1989).

Stockton, P., *Strategic Stability Between the Super-Powers* (1986).

PART THREE

The Nation-States

CHAPTER SIX

Germany: West and East

Germany Under Four-Power Control
Territorial Changes • State Governments • Interzonal Relations
Denazification • Education and Religion • Economic Measures

The Federal Republic of Germany
The Bonn Constitution • Establishing Full Sovereignty
Political Events • Economic Recovery
The Remaining German Question

The German Democratic Republic
Establishment of the State • Economic Policy
Upheaval and Fall of the GDR

A New Germany?

Notes

Suggested Readings

T oday, the reality of a unified German nation-state is almost taken for granted. Nevertheless, one does well to remember how recently this was not the case and how implausible the reunification of the long-divided nation once seemed. Until 1990, there were two German states at the heart of Europe, and it would be hard to imagine that their governments could have pursued more contrary paths of political and economic development. The leaders of one polity, the Federal Republic of Germany (FRG), were firmly aligned with the Western world, liberal-democratic in their political orientations, and deeply convinced of the merits of the free market economic system. In contrast, the leaders of the other state, the German Democratic Republic (GDR), were even more tightly bound to the Eastern alliance (they depended on the Soviet Union for their country's very existence), authoritarian in their political proclivities, and firmly committed to Marxism.

These differences provide a striking picture of the contrasting courses of political and economic development that all European states followed in the period after World War II. With the benefit of historical perspective, we can also see that they offer insight into some of the reasons behind the unexpected collapse of the East German state in 1989 and the reunification of the German nation in 1990. To reach the point where we can appreciate these issues, however, we must begin by asking how and why Germany was divided in the first place.

Germany Under Four-Power Control

Territorial Changes

After World War II, the division of Germany that came with Allied military occupation not only disrupted many administrative areas that had been created by Hitler but also cut across long-established state and provincial boundaries. Prussia disappeared from the map; the Königsberg salient (8,184 square miles, or 13,200 sq km) went to the USSR. The rest of former German territory up to the Oder and western Neisse rivers (34,650 square miles, or 55,887 sq km) was given over to Polish administration and thus became de facto a part of Poland. Stettin, on the left bank of the Oder, was handed over to the Poles by the USSR. The surrender of Polish lands in the East and the acquisition of Prussian lands as compensation was in no way acceptable to the Polish national government-in-exile in London but was tolerated by the government that the Soviets had installed in Poland. Berlin, about 100 miles (161 km) from West Germany, became an enclave surrounded by the German Democratic Republic. It was divided into four sections, each administered by one of the occupying powers. It stood legally apart from the Germanys, and any alteration of its status required four-power agreement.

In the four occupation zones, the responsible authorities soon found it expedient to establish new states (*Länder*) to make possible some coordination of local government and some administrative centralization. The Soviet zone (66,447 square miles, or 107,173 sq km; population 17,313,734 according to the 1946 census) was divided into five states. The British, French, and U.S. zones comprised a total of ten states plus the small city-state of Bremen, which served as a U.S. port. The British zone included the rich industrial Ruhr area among its 60,573 square miles (97,699 sq km) and had a population of 22,304,059. The U.S. zone in the southeast was geographically larger (66,625 square miles, or 107,459 sq km) but held a smaller population of 17,254,945. The French zone in the southwest along the upper Rhine was 24,933 square miles (40,215 sq km) and had a population of 5,077,808. The Saar basin, the boundaries of which were considerably extended, was joined economically to France in 1947. This territory, with its own autonomous government, was administered separately from the French zone proper; later events would return it to German control. The establishment of separate occupation zones did not preclude the possibility of a future united German state. Nevertheless, the Allies' previous predilection to countenance the division of Germany combined with the politics of the Cold War to turn temporary occupation-zone boundaries into permanent state borders.

State Governments

In general the United States took the lead in giving governmental functions to the Germans. State constitutional conventions were elected in 1946, their work approved, and legislatures chosen. The British, with their tradition of an unwritten constitution, proceeded with the establishment of state governments in their zone without formulating a written document. All the new state constitutions borrowed heavily from the state and national constitutions of the period of the Weimar Republic; in addition, those in the West incorporated U.S. and French practices, whereas those in the East showed Soviet influences. Titular executives were dispensed with, and cabinets headed by premiers responsible to a popularly elected legislature were the rule. Judicial review made its appearance, particularly in the U.S. zone.

The form and letter of the constitutions are not as important as the freedom (or lack of freedom) that existed under them. In the early postwar years, the states could only do as much as the occupying powers were willing to have them do. The USSR and France exercised the tightest control; Britain came next. The reestablishment of even a limited degree of self-government necessitated the resurrection of political parties. These were not slow in appearing, but because they had to be licensed by the occupying powers, it was always a controlled freedom that they enjoyed. In the Western zones the leading groups were the Social Democratic party (SPD); the Christian Democratic Union (CDU), generally supported on most issues by its predominantly Catholic and somewhat more conservative version in Bavaria, the Christian Social Union (CSU); and the Free Democratic party (FDP), a conservative group standing for free enterprise. The Communist party of Germany (KPD) was quite small; it was banned in 1956 but later resurfaced under a different name (the German Communist party, or DKP).

In the Soviet zone in 1946 the Communist and Socialist parties merged to form the Socialist Unity party (SED). This was the party Soviet authorities largely used to carry out their ends. The SED was not the sole party, however, and did not always control the majority of seats in all the state governments in the Soviet zone. Some minor peasant parties came to be closely allied with the SED. The CDU and FDP in the early years of the occupation always polled a strong vote, but Soviet occupation authorities never allowed them much power. In sum, the political parties of the new Germany quickly became circumscribed by the boundaries of the Western and Soviet occupation zones. None of the great powers was about to let the other side's Germans have influence in its own zone of occupation. Thus one of the key factors that might have worked for the unification of Germany, truly national political parties, did not develop.

Interzonal Relations

When the Allied Control Council failed to set up central administrative agencies for trade and industry, the United States invited the other three occupying powers to form an economic union of all four zones. The devastation of the war and the manner in which zonal boundaries separated industries from previous markets and supplies spelled only a slow and halting recovery of the German economy. Only the British accepted the invitation to union. The Soviets would not collaborate, and the French had fought too hard to obtain an occupation zone to renounce promptly complete economic control of it. The British and U.S. decision to merge the economies of their zones in 1946 created what was to be known as Bizonia. This was a crucial step toward the permanent division of Germany. It also marked a change in the British and U.S. attitude toward the Germans, friendship replacing mistrust. Concomitantly, complaints arose that although the Soviets were quick to claim their share of industrial equipment from the Western zones, they were not paying for it with the food, coal, and other commodities from the East as stated in the terms of reparations. As the gulf between West and East widened, France came to cooperate more closely with Britain and the United States on occupation policy. Thus by mid-1948 a German government for the three Western zones (Trizonia) was established. Allied confidence in the appropriateness of this landmark development in the Cold War was no doubt enhanced by the Communist coup in Czechoslovakia in February.

Up to this time, the one major tie still uniting all of Germany had been a common currency. However, this currency was undermined by an active black market and a proliferation of paper money. A one-dollar carton of cigarettes came to be worth 1,000 reichsmarks (RM), yet the average worker received only 80 RM per week. Believing inflation was destroying any chance to build a sound economy, Western authorities called for currency reform. Nevertheless, arrangements could not be reached with the Soviets, who were unwilling to agree to joint supervision of the amount of paper money to be issued. Hence, the Western nations proceeded with their own reform, striking yet another blow against the prospects for German unity. Citizens in Trizonia were allowed to exchange a total of 600 RM for 60 deutsche marks. Although mortgages, securities, savings, and black market fortunes were wiped out overnight, the draconian measure did restore confidence in the currency by demonstrating that workers' wages would again be of value.

Nevertheless, these steps also led to one of the greatest political-military conflicts of the immediate postwar period. The Western nations had said the currency reform would not apply to Berlin, yet the deutsche mark crept into the city by informal channels. When the Soviets responded by launching their own currency reform in Berlin and the Eastern zone, the West formally backed its currency in Berlin for fear that its part of the city would otherwise be pulled completely into the Eastern orbit. This move led the Soviets to take a major step: a full blockade of land and water access routes to Berlin. A spectacular British and U.S. airlift to the city was begun in June 1948; it finally ended a year later when the Soviets capitulated. But the consequences for the city, and hence for Germany as a whole, were to take four decades to overcome.

During the crisis, the government of Berlin was split into two rival municipal entities, one in East Berlin for the Soviet sector and the other in West Berlin, comprising the U.S., British, and French sectors. These developments also ended in fact if not in theory what little four-power government there had been for all of Germany. There was nothing left to do but establish separate governments for West and East Germany and let them take their separate political and economic paths under the influence of their former occupying powers.

Even as the two governments were established, talks on some definitive German settlement nevertheless continued. One issue was the question of German unity, generally desired by all elements of the German population but regarded with some apprehension by neighboring states. It was recognized that in the long run the solution lay not in a permanent partition but in the integration of Germany into some new form of European organization. Closely related to the unification issue was that of the political complexion of a future Germany. German opinion in the Eastern zone overwhelmingly opposed communism, and it was generally believed that free elections in the Eastern zone would result in a crushing defeat for the Communists. Associ-

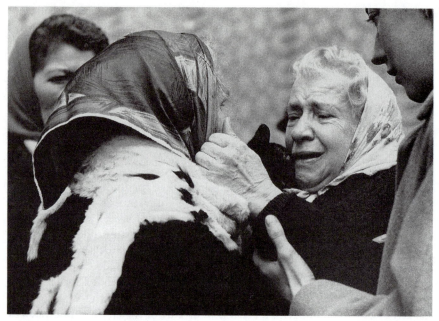

Two sisters, one from East Berlin and the other from West Berlin, meet for a tearful but joyful reunion in the East. Beginning in 1963, citizens of the Western-controlled zone of the divided city were allowed to visit their relatives in the East-ern sector on an irregular basis. Until the signing of the inter-German Basic Treaty of 1972, however, East German citizens were rarely permitted to visit relatives in the West. (Photo courtesy of the German Information Center.)

ated with this was a third issue—whether the future Germany should be demilitarized and neutralized.

In the contest over Germany's fate, the Soviets recognized the German desire for unification, although they insisted that the pursuit of this goal take place on their own narrow terms. At one stage, the USSR proposed that a constitutional council be elected for the whole of Germany, with equal representation from the Soviet and Western zones despite their large differences in size and population; Germany was also to be demilitarized and neutralized.

In contrast, the Western powers wanted a unified Germany free from Communist control and able to participate in plans for the integration of Western Europe. The West felt assured that in any free election the Germans would vote against communism, particularly as the political stability and economic prosperity of the Western zone outstripped the impoverished and politically stifled Eastern zone. Western diplomacy was aided by the awareness that, however much demilitarization and neutralization might appeal to certain sectors of German popular opinion, it was not likely that a great power (like a resurgent Germany) would voluntarily relinquish its freedom of action in foreign policy. Western policy therefore rested on a united Germany based on free elections, in the belief that such a Germany would become an active participant in the security and prosperity of Western Europe. For this reason, following the outbreak of the Korean War in 1950, the use of German troops in the defense of Europe became one of the primary goals of the United States and Great Britain.

The successful negotiation of the Austrian State Treaty in 1955 led to the calling of the highest-level conference on Germany since that of Potsdam ten years earlier. The Western powers defended their vision of a united Germany based on free elections, though in recognition of Soviet security interests they also proposed that mutual security pacts be concluded. The Soviets maintained that Germany could not be unified until overall European security had been established and that this necessarily involved the liquidation of the Western European Union and the North Atlantic Treaty Organization. The problem of Germany was thus once more subordinated to the larger strategy of the Western and Soviet blocs, neither of which was willing to risk losing its existing positions in Europe. As a consequence, any viable German settlement was postponed.

Denazification

Before we explore the histories of the separate German states, we should examine a few other developments during the period of occupation. One issue was that of denazification, which was not only a pressing moral concern but also a practical problem for both German states. It soon became clear that it would be impossible to punish all former Nazis, as many German officials (e.g., teachers) had been forced to join associations that now led them to be classified as Nazis. Yet, here again, the occupying powers had differing approaches to the problem. The USSR from the start struck at only the top-flight personalities; the British and French also never attempted such thoroughgoing denazification as did the United States. In June 1946, responsibility for further denazification in the U.S. zone was passed to German tribunals acting under U.S. supervision. Three years later, over 13 million adults had filed questionnaires, and of those 3.5 million had been considered chargeable. Only 1,635 were judged major offenders, although over 600,000 received some punishment.

In addition to the general denazification procedures, the United States, Britain, France, and the USSR collaborated in the establishment of an International Military Tribunal at Nuremberg that tried the surviving topmost Nazis. These men were indicted on various counts, the chief one being the crime of plotting aggressive warfare. After a long trial, three of the defendants were freed; seven were given prison terms from ten years to life; twelve were sentenced to death. Never before had such a tribunal been established, and there were many differences of opinion as to whether the trials were in accordance with international law, or indeed with the laws of the respective victorious states. Critics of the procedure point out that even if there was a law that applied, it was being enforced only against the defeated countries. For example, many judicial-minded observers were disturbed that the USSR's aggressive action in the Baltic states and Finland had been overlooked. But the procedure's defenders maintained that, although there was no precedent, it was high time to establish a process for trying "war criminals"; the trials were laying the basis for a new world order.

Of course, denazification was also part of a larger historical challenge, that of contending with the Germans' own feelings of historical responsibility for the crimes committed under Nazi rule, and particularly for the Holocaust, the genocide of 6 million European Jews. Although officials in the Eastern zone tended to play down this issue, arguing that they, too, as Communists, had been persecuted under the Nazi dictatorship, in the West there was and would be for decades much public soul-searching. Though some Germans could honestly say they did not know what was happening to the Jews, many others had to admit that they had carefully avoided finding out. Thousands of others, from those running the trains that carried the prisoners to the concentration camps to the actual operators of the gas chambers, were directly involved. The responsibility for specific crimes could perhaps be pinned on Hitler alone or on a few additional officials, but the Holocaust—and the failure to oppose or at least refuse cooperation in the extermination of the Jews—raised painful questions about the character of the German people and the course of its history.

In the immediate postwar years, the issue was too sensitive to be discussed broadly. In time, difficult as it was, parents did admit to their children what had happened. The West German government made reparations payments to the state of Israel and to Jewish individuals and families who had lost property or been deprived of their incomes as a result of the atrocity. (Yet other groups that had also been victimized by the Nazi terror, such as Gypsies, Communists, homosexuals, and Jehovah's Witnesses, did not receive such payments.) To be sure, as prosperity returned in the late 1950s and early 1960s, the question of responsibility became somewhat lost in the busyness of business. Yet political events in the Middle East; the capture in 1960 and subsequent trial and execution in Israel of Adolf Eichmann, a key SS member; and the murder of Jewish athletes at the 1972 Munich Olympics kept the issue from being totally forgotten.

A special catalyst for widespread and probing questions by a new generation of Germans was the 1979 showing in the FRG of a U.S.-made television miniseries entitled "The Holocaust." Several years later, the burden of history and of the Holocaust was frankly addressed by the president of the Federal Republic, Richard von Weizsäcker, in a noteworthy speech commemorating the fortieth anniversary of the German surrender of May 8, 1945:

Today we mourn all the dead of the war and tyranny. In particular, we commemorate the six million Jews who were murdered in German concentration camps. . . . The perpetration of this crime was in the hands of few people. It was concealed from the eyes of the public, but . . . who could remain unsuspecting after the burning of the synagogues, the plundering, the stigmatization with the Star of David, the deprivation of rights, the ceaseless violation of human dignity? . . . When the unspeakable truth of the Holocaust then became known at the end of the war, all too many of us claimed that they had not known anything about it or suspected anything. . . . The vast majority of today's population were either children then or had not been born. They cannot profess a guilt of their own for crimes that they did not commit. . . . But their forefathers have left them a grave legacy. All of us, whether guilty or not, whether old or young, must accept the past.[1]

Education and Religion

After the war, the occupying powers also charged themselves with the reorganization of the whole German educational system, although they interpreted this challenge differently in each zone. In West Germany there was little zonal control; schools were reorganized much as they had been before the Nazi era. Private schools were permitted, and the old pattern of interdenominational and confessional public schools reappeared. Everywhere religion was a regular but not compulsory subject of instruction in elementary and secondary schools.

In East Germany, despite talk about removing Fascist influences from the schools, the education system continued to be developed along lines set by the Nazis. The Soviets, as early as July 1945, created a German Central Administration for People's Education, emphasizing a uniform educational policy. Only interdenominational schools were permitted and religion was not to be taught as part of the curriculum. Although such instruction was left to the churches, which were formally permitted to use schoolrooms for this purpose, state authorities left no doubt about their hostility to such programs, especially to anyone who dared use their religious institution as a platform for standing up to Communist authority.

The changing demographic situation in central Europe, with the loss of the eastern territories to Poland, also brought about a major shift in the religious makeup of postwar Germany. Most of the Protestant Germans who were expelled from Poland were settled in northern Germany (and were later to constitute the principal religious force in the GDR), whereas the Catholic Germans from the Sudeten area went mostly to the south. Yet as the number of Catholics grew nearly to equal that of the Protestants, for the first time many of the religious bases for political conflict in Germany were eliminated. Indeed, the most important divisions between and among the churches now became those caused by politics itself. On the one hand, the Reformed and Lutheran churches, which had been organized on state lines before Hitler and had never been united into one church body under the Nazis, were able to form a loose confederal organization, the Council of the Evangelical Church in Germany. But on the other hand, the pressures of national division (and particularly pressure from the GDR's Communist government) led the eight regional Protestant churches in East Germany to break from the council in 1969 and form their own separate church federation.

Economic Measures

The greatest challenge of all for Germany in the war's aftermath was economic. Rubble and graves were all that remained of great sectors of formerly beautiful cities. Food and pure water, much less paying jobs, were scarcely available. One lived as one could, seeking to deal with the traumatic loss of greatness.

By turning over German territory as far as the Oder-Neisse line to the USSR and Poland, the Allied powers deprived Germany of lands that normally supplied 25 percent of its food; at the same time, millions of German refugees crowded into the rump German state. Thus in spite of 4 million military and civilian dead and the absence of prisoners of war in French or Soviet camps, Germany was left with 4 million more people than it had in 1939, many of whom could not immediately fend for themselves.

Despite these challenges, however, the Allied powers were not always completely sympathetic to the German plight. Although such schemes as the Morgenthau Plan to turn Germany into a purely agricultural country rapidly lost favor, Allied concern to assure Germany's demilitarization dictated strict limitation of German industrial production. In April 1946 the Allied Control Council published its program for the collection of reparations and decreed what the level of the postwar German economy was to be. A list of prohibited industries—synthetic gasoline, oil, rubber, ammonia, heavy tractors, and so forth—was drawn up. Restrictions were placed on other industries, holding them to a certain percentage of prewar production. Germany, even in the best prewar years, had been able to produce only from 70 to 85 percent of its food. Now, with a smaller area, a larger population, and a great lack of fertilizers, it could not approach these figures. The United States and Britain were forced to pour in millions of dollars' worth of food and supplies, leading President Truman in the spring of 1947 to ask one his predecessors, Herbert Hoover, to undertake an economic survey of Germany and Austria. Hoover recommended numerous changes in policy, above all increase of German exports so that U.S. taxpayers might be spared the burdens of relief. In 1947 a new directive was issued to the U.S. occupation authorities, and the United States launched a policy of making the bizonal area self-supporting. Unable to get four-power agreement, Britain and the United States went ahead alone and announced higher industrial levels for Bizonia.

There were other problems as well. The Potsdam agreement called for the dismantling of many industrial plants, which were to be sent to various war-torn countries as reparations. The dismantling program announced in 1947 created resentment among German workers as unemployment figures rose. But there were also problems with this policy for the Allies. To dismantle a synthetic gasoline plant meant that additional U.S. dollars would be needed to pay for imported gasoline, not to mention that relief would also be necessary for the unemployed. Although the United States came to oppose further dismantling, Britain and France held fast until November 1949, when an agreement was reached that virtually halted this destruction of the German economy. Meanwhile, the currency reform of June 1948 was of inestimable value in stimulating recovery and laying a sound basis for the economy of West Germany. So, too, were funds received under the Marshall Plan.

In the East, in contrast, Soviet authorities focused on other priorities, breaking up the largest estates and laying the bases for the collectivization of agriculture. Many industries were nationalized, and socialized control was extended over utilities. Ironically, although the Soviets themselves also carted off the machinery of numerous plants and shipped home carloads of live-stock—even before wounded soldiers—the USSR officially opposed the dismantling of industry when it was discussed among the powers. Nonetheless, the Soviets still milked the East German economy, first under the guise of collecting reparations, then via so-called joint-stock companies, which enabled them to control ownership of key industries and influence production and sales in ways favorable to the USSR.

The financial measures that the USSR undertook at the time of the currency reform in the Western zone did not have the same economic effect as those in the West, primarily because shortages continued and recovery lagged. But the political effect was the same. In 1949 the Soviet Union sponsored the establishment of the GDR as a counter to the West's creation of the FRG earlier, assuring that the two new German republics would take very different paths of economic development.

The Federal Republic of Germany

The Bonn Constitution

In accordance with the agreement reached by the Western Allies at the London conference of 1948, a parliamentary council composed of delegates chosen by the state governments of West Germany met at Bonn. By the time the four powers had reached an agreement to end the Berlin blockade, this council had hammered together the Basic Law for the Federal Republic of Germany. This went into effect on May 24, 1949, upon ratification by two-thirds of the state parliaments in the Western zones. The term *basic law* was used instead of *constitution* to emphasize the provisional character of the document, which it was hoped would be replaced by a true constitution upon the eventual reunification of Germany.

The Basic Law is a lengthy document that draws heavily on former German constitutions. Although there are elaborate safeguards to preserve states' rights, the distribution of power allows for the establishment of a strong central government, for federal law takes precedence over state law. The Basic Law provides for a president elected for five years by the lower house, which for this purpose is augmented by an equal number of delegates from the state parliaments. Yet presidential powers are nominal, for the real executive power is vested in the chancellor and cabinet. In addition to the reduction of the powers of the president from those under the Weimar constitution, other attempts have been made to avoid the cabinet instability that weakened the Weimar Republic. For instance, the lower house on its own initiative cannot dismiss the chancellor without immediately electing his successor ("a constructive vote of no confidence"). If the chancellor asks for but does not receive a vote of confidence, the president may at the chancellor's request dissolve the chamber.

Political stability is also assured by the division of Parliament into two parts. The upper chamber, the Bundesrat, represents the German state governments. Amendments and certain other types of legislation, enumerated in the Basic Law, require the consent of the Bundesrat, and it can exercise a suspensory veto even on ordinary bills. The remainder of the Parliament's business (debates over such fundamental issues as economic policy and foreign affairs), however, is carried out by the much larger lower chamber, the Bundestag, which is reelected every four years in a national vote.

Finally, in an effort to assure the greatest possible public consensus, the national electoral law has been amended several times since the Basic Law was adopted. (For example, the eligible age for voting in national elections was lowered from twenty-one to eighteen.) Under existing procedure, each voter has two votes in the national elections and each ballot has two columns. The voter casts a first vote in the first column directly for the candidate of his or her choice in the voter's electoral district, and the candidate receiving the largest number of votes is the winner. The second vote is cast in the second column for a party that nominates a separate list of candidates in each state. Although the lists of second-ballot candidates are made public, not all of these candidates' names appear on the ticket. Parties can therefore afford to nominate second-ballot candidates who have no particular campaign appeal but are experts in crucial fields such as finance, education, agriculture, or labor relations.

The share of seats that each party receives from the second vote is determined according to the principles of proportional representation. Proportional representation can assure regular compliance with party directives from those who wish to be placed high on the party's list to guarantee election, although it can also stimulate independent splinter parties. Candidates confident of their electoral appeal within their own district, regardless of how their party might fare on the national level, can form their own party. Too many such splinter parties' winning seats could slow political compromise and lead to political instability, again like that which had once engulfed the Weimar Republic. Therefore the law provides that a party must win at least 5 percent of all second votes or carry three electoral districts to be able to enter the Bundestag. Half the seats are filled through the first vote, the other half through the second. This mixture of direct and proportional electoral procedures—in combination with the existence of a constitutional court with the competence to oversee such processes—is one of the most important factors behind the FRG's postwar political development.

Establishing Full Sovereignty

Another reason for the success of West German democracy was the assistance the FRG received from its former Western occupiers, although this support did not come overnight. In April 1949, the three Western powers had negotiated a trizonal fusion agreement establishing an Allied High Commission as the chief Allied agency of control. Each power was represented by a high commissioner, and various administrative departments and agencies were established. The three powers specifically reserved to themselves authority over disarmament and demilitarization, reparations, foreign affairs, foreign trade and exchange, refugees, the protection of the constitution, and a variety of other subjects; the plan was, however, intended eventually to give the prospective new German government wide authority. But it is hard to conceive of anything the occupying powers could not legally do under the rights they assumed. The occupation statute of May 12, which articulated these rights, clearly implied that the Allies reserved much of their sovereignty in the Western zones.

With the end of military government in September 1949, Allied control passed into the hands of a civilian High Commission, although military occupation continued. The commission soon concluded the first negotiated postwar Allied-German agreement, the so-called Petersburg Protocol, which gave West Germany limited powers in foreign-policy making. The outbreak of the Korean War in June 1950 led the Allies to go even further, with the result that in August 1950 the FRG was admitted as an associate member to the Council of Europe and in the following year was accorded full membership. It was not until the spring of 1951 that a revision of the occupation statute permitted Germany to set up a foreign office, and the new chancellor, Konrad Adenauer, took over the duties as de facto minister of foreign affairs. That year also brought the formal termination of the state of war with the Federal Republic by Great Britain, France, and the United States.

On the economic front, plans for a European Coal and Steel Community—later, one of the key foundations for the European Common Market (EEC)—were drawn up in April 1951 and put into effect the following year. Adenauer took a leading part in these negotiations, and Germany became a full partner in the organization. Other changes were made in the occupation statute, reducing limitations formerly placed on West German industry and shipbuilding. The Federal Republic was allowed to strengthen itself economically in various ways, in order to meet what the Western nations perceived as the threat posed by the Soviet Union and Eastern Europe.

Churchill had been one of the first leaders to call for German rearmament, given the danger of Soviet expansion, and the United States soon followed suit. France opposed anything like a purely German army, and the problem devolved into the question of how German units could be integrated into a European army. Finally, the three Western occupying powers and West Germany signed a series of contractual agreements in May 1952. These agreements, designed to restore virtual sovereignty to the Federal Republic, were tied up with the proposed European Defense Community. When the French Parliament refused to ratify the EDC treaties in 1954, Britain called a conference in London, attended by Canada, the United States, France, Germany, Italy, Belgium, the Netherlands, and Luxembourg, at which new agreements were worked out. Germany and Italy were to join the Western European Union, which was to undertake the integration of the German forces into a common defense force. Unlike the EDC treaty, this arrangement provided that Britain, too, would place some troops at the disposal of the new Western European army. West Germany was also admitted to NATO in May 1955, and the whole new military organization was assimilated with the latter's defense schemes.

Political Events

Inside Germany, however, there was considerable hostility toward a policy of rearmament. Arms had brought suffering before, and their cost was a heavy burden, not only financially but also in light of the Germans' sense of historical responsibility. In particular, the Social Democrats maintained that rearmament was unconstitutional. Yet Adenauer insisted on the necessity of German armed forces, both for defense purposes and as an indication of sovereignty. He then mustered enough support to amend the constitution, thus setting aside any doubt as to the legality of German rearmament. The arms question remained understandably controversial, though, and the government moved slowly in establishing a force. Compulsory service for all males was initiated, and a small navy and air force were also created in addition to the army. But Germany did not initially attempt to set up a self-sufficient armament industry, relying instead about equally on purchases at home and abroad. When in December 1962 the United States and Britain

---

Chancellors of the Federal Republic of Germany

Konrad Adenauer	CDU	September 15, 1949–October 16, 1963
Ludwig Erhard	CDU	October 16, 1963–December 1, 1966
Kurt Georg Kiesinger	CDU	December 1, 1966–October 21, 1969
Willy Brandt	SPD	October 21, 1969–May 16, 1974
Helmut Schmidt	SPD	May 16, 1974–October 1, 1982
Helmut Kohl	CDU	October 1, 1982–

---

proposed building a multilateral nuclear naval force within NATO staffed by mixed contingents from the Allies, the FRG at once expressed its willingness to participate. The proposal aroused a great deal of opposition, not only on the part of the USSR but also from some of the NATO allies, notably France; ultimately, the force was not created. Even well into the 1980s and 1990s, however, many Germans, from popular writers to politicians to average citizens, continued to anguish over the meaning and implications of their state's involvement in military alliances. Could other nations, the United States in particular, be counted upon to use force responsibly? And what was the nature and extent of German obligations to turn its own weapons of war and mass destruction to the defense of its alliance partners?

Nevertheless, for all of the uncertainty that colored this and other debates, West Germany's experiment with democracy still proved remarkably successful. For example, in 1957, for the first time in the history of monarchical or republican Germany, a single party (the CDU) achieved an absolute majority of the popular vote and seats in a parliamentary election. This victory was due primarily to the great economic recovery of the preceding years, the architect of which was Minister of Economics Ludwig Erhard. The public also applauded Adenauer's determined effort to restore good relations with the West and especially France. Yet, significantly, this was not to be a throwback to Germany's authoritarian past. Many West Germans disliked Adenauer's high-handed ways and felt nervous about the ease with which he embraced rearmament. They feared that his "chancellor democracy" (Kanzlerdemokratie) might lead to one person's gaining too much power, as had happened in the past. As a result, not long after its huge gains, Adenauer's party experienced significant losses in the 1961 elections, and the CDU had to form a coalition with the Free Democratic party, a moderating influence, to stay in power.

Similar moderating tendencies could also be seen on the West German Left. Up to this time, the CDU's chief rival, the Social Democratic party, had generally showed more strength in state and local balloting than in national elections. To win more support, the SPD needed to widen its appeal, and this meant that it had to move away from some of its more extreme positions. The party gradually abandoned many of the distinct Marxist doctrines that had characterized its policies before 1933. For example, it no longer opposed religious instruction in the schools or advocated an extensive program of nationalization. What had already been the practice throughout much of the 1950s was officially made a part of the party platform at the SPD's annual convention in Bad Godesberg in 1959. Here the party dropped most of its avowedly Marxist aims, endorsing a kind of welfare liberalism, and not much later its leaders also began openly to support the FRG's membership in NATO. On the death of the party's chairman, Erich Ollen-hauer, in 1963, the dynamic pro-Western mayor of West Berlin, Willy Brandt, became chairman of the party.

A controversial incident in 1962 enabled the CDU, restless with the aging Adenauer's leadership, finally to move beyond its early years. *Der Spiegel* (The mirror), a widely read liberal news magazine, had published an article revealing weaknesses shown by German forces in NATO maneuvers. Many of the article's criticisms seemed aimed at Franz-Josef Strauss, defense minister and also head of the Christian Social Union. Adenauer accused the magazine of making money out of treason, and midnight arrests of journalists and conflicting statements from Strauss soon followed. But this was not to be the prelude to a new authoritarian period in the FRG. Under tremendous public criticism, Strauss was forced out of the government and Adenauer, stubborn to the last, was ultimately compelled to go along with an FDP proposal under which he himself would leave his post in time for a new chancellor to build credibility prior to the 1965 elections.

Ludwig Erhard was the choice for the chancellorship obvious to all save the eighty-seven-year-old Adenauer, who commented (with some justice, it would later appear) that Erhard could not handle the complexities of foreign affairs. An economic wonder-worker and a Protestant member of the CDU, Erhard took over in 1963 and won a solid electoral victory two years later. Then his fortunes fell. The economy, hot for so long, began to cool off. U.S.-Soviet détente changed the international climate, making the FRG's previous policy of implacable hostility toward the USSR seem out of date. In the morass of Middle East politics, Erhard managed to get on poor terms with Israel as well as with several Arab nations. Finally, lacking the will and political cunning of his predecessor, Erhard also had difficulty repressing the infighting within his own party and coalition. As a result, in 1966 the Free Democrats withdrew from his government over a tax dispute.

With Erhard's coalition shattered, Strauss in Bavaria threw his support to another CDU leader, Kurt Georg Kiesinger, and the SPD agreed to participate in a heretofore unlikely coalition with the CDU/CSU, so long as Brandt could serve as vice-chancellor and foreign minister. For the first time since pre-Hitler days, Social Democrats again held national cabinet posts, demonstrating a significant degree of political consensus in the FRG. But the

Ludwig Erhard, shown speaking in the Bonn Parliament on his seventy-fifth birthday in 1972, is known as the father of the Federal Republic's miracle of economic recovery and development. As minister of economics (1949–1963) he prepared the way for monetary reform and established a "social market economy" in which free market prices regulated the economic process (except in the housing, social, and farm sectors). Special measures were taken to incorporate lower-income groups into the capitalist system. With somewhat less success, Erhard served as chancellor from 1963 to 1966. (Photo courtesy of the German Information Center.)

coalition of the two largest parties did not continue for long. In the 1969 elections, Brandt's advocacy of efforts to improve relations with Eastern Europe helped the Social Democrats to a substantial gain. Many West German citizens were happy indeed to have communications with the German Democratic Republic improve, for that meant better communication with relatives still in the East. After all, some 2.7 million Germans had fled from the Eastern zone to the West prior to the building of the Berlin Wall in 1961, and they hoped to see their families and friends again. Instead of staying with the CDU/CSU, however, the SPD formed a coalition with the Free Democrats, allowing Brandt to become the first Social Democratic chancellor since 1930 and at the same time forcing the CDU/CSU to regain the trust of the people by first entering the opposition ranks.

Certainly, no one will dispute the Federal Republic's achievements by the early 1970s. In particular, Brandt's *Ostpolitik* and his efforts to improve

Günter Grass came into prominence as a leading German writer
after World War II. In his novels,
The Tin Drum, Cat and Mouse,
and Dog Years, he attempted to
dispel the mythic qualities associated with nazism. The Tin Drum
(eventually also made into a movie)
depicts life during the Hitler era in
scathing detail. Grass and other
writers of the postwar period felt
they should be realistic critics of
Germany's problems and became
deeply involved in political reform.
(Photo courtesy of the German Information Center.)

the quality of East-West relations in general led to a series of breakthrough
treaties with the East—with the Soviet Union and Poland in 1970 and finally
with the GDR (the Basic Treaty) in 1972. In 1973 his government and that
of the GDR were finally welcomed into the United Nations. The successful
insertion of the FRG into international affairs, along with the country's
domestic gains, seemed to suggest that West Germany was at last beginning
to find its place in the modern world.

Nonetheless, if West Germans accepted such truisms without question,
there were others, especially in intellectual and literary circles, who wondered
if something meaningful had been lost amidst these successes. Even before
Brandt's ascendancy, many West German youth, in search of something in
which to believe aside from the material successes of their parents, had flung
themselves into idealistic causes: disarmament, opposition to U.S. policy in
Vietnam, environmental protection. Often they took a sort of doomsday
approach in their angst, asserting that disaster would bring an end to the
prosperity of their land. They argued that economic gains had been made at
too great a price. Demonstrations, sometimes massive, were frequent in the
late 1960s and early 1970s.

Some young Germans purposely headed to West Berlin, for here they
were not subject to military service or, in lieu of it, social service, as they
would have been if they remained in West Germany. Their arrival helped to
counteract the small but steady flow of West Berlin's population to the greater

vistas of the Federal Republic. Additionally, there was also a small minority of young people who turned to direct action. The most extreme styled themselves "Maoists," rejecting both the Soviet-dominated and Euro-Communist wings of the German Communist party and advocating the use of violence. Radical student groups attempted takeovers of universities and claimed that students and maintenance staff had a right to participate in educational decisions. One leftist characterized the uprisings as being "against an apparently senseless life and cynical tutelage by narrow-minded authorities who exercise their autocratic rule in the machinery of state, in the university and school hierarchies, and in factory management."[2] In this context, as student protests and domestic terrorism increased and the government responded with equally tough measures to combat these threats (e.g., passing laws to prevent left-wing radicals from getting jobs in the public sector), many average West Germans worried about the health of their democracy, at least until the political scene had calmed down.

The FRG also faced other major challenges in the 1970s. For example, the Arab oil-shipping boycott of 1973, a by-product of Israel's victory in the seven-weeks' war against Egypt that year, had a serious effect on West Germany's economic health. Energy-related prices skyrocketed, causing anxiety in foreign ministries throughout the world about the political leverage a new energy cartel enjoyed. While the nation shivered, Helmut Schmidt, Brandt's successor, persuaded Parliament that, despite the safety questions involved, the development of nuclear energy should be pursued until other sources of energy could be found. Later, one such source the Germans thought acceptable was natural gas piped from Siberia. The Soviets were eager to sell gas for hard currency, as they were now importing grain, their chief export for so many decades. The U.S. government was not happy at the possibility of West Germany and other states becoming vulnerable to a Soviet turn of a valve, but in the early 1980s U.S. pressure to halt pipeline construction only increased European determination to go ahead. The pipeline was completed in 1984.

One group that opposed Schmidt's willingness to build nuclear plants, not to mention West Germany's larger role in NATO, was the Greens. A loose federation of protest groups ranging from the non-Communist Left to conservative dissidents drawn from the right wing of the Free Democrats, the Greens began to appear as a political factor in northern Germany at the end of the 1970s. The interests that drew them together were diverse and initially focused on local problems, such as housing shortages in Berlin and industrial pollution everywhere. Their strong concern for the environment won them their name. Basic distrust of establishment politics caused them to resist most forms of internal organization and national political campaigns. Increasing public sympathy with their education programs—in the early 1980s many Germans were upset to learn that acid rain and other pollutants were slowly killing their Black Forest—brought them votes. The Greens were

West Germany was the scene of massive demonstrations by youthful protestors throughout the 1980s. Some Germans regarded these demonstrations as a direct threat to the calm and stability that had characterized the country's experiment with democracy throughout much of the postwar period. Others, in contrast, viewed the protests as a healthy expression of differences of opinion that included more citizens in the democratic process. In this picture, activist citizens' groups protest the creation of a radioactive waste dump at Gorleben. (Photo courtesy of the German Information Center.)

also the recipients of protest votes: A NATO plan, carried out in 1983, to station intermediate-range nuclear weapons on West German soil was sup- ported by all the major parties (including the SPD, until Schmidt's fall) in the face of massive counterdemonstrations.

By the mid-1980s, the Greens had achieved a percentage of votes sufficient to gain them seats in the national Parliament; Green idealists even worried that co-optation into regular politics would compromise their ideals. Yet, though some West German citizens were concerned that their democratic system was at risk, the Greens were actually positive proof of the successful realization of the democratic ideal. Unlike many of the student protests of the late 1960s, the Greens' efforts were intended for the most part to be within the system and more long-lasting, demonstrating that the FRG could indeed ably absorb its discontents.

A final sign of the successful functioning of West German democracy was, of course, the stable transfer of power, again effected in 1982, when the

FDP withdrew from its coalition with the SPD and threw its lot in with the CDU/CSU. A constructive vote of no confidence made Christian Democratic Union leader Helmut Kohl chancellor, in keeping with the conservative trend evident in the United States and Great Britain. In Germany this trend was to some extent a product of party politics and to some extent a reaction against the Soviet invasion of Afghanistan in December 1979. Then, too, many middle-class Germans questioned whether so much of their income should be redistributed to others via social service benefits. Nonetheless, whatever party was in power, no one could deny the basic consensus that existed among all of West Germany's contending elites. All of the country's major parties continued to favor economic growth with social responsibility, all desired freedom of action for the entrepreneur within reasonable limits, and all looked to the West for military support.

As in the past, this basis of agreement contributed significantly to the political coherence of the Federal Republic and to the creation of a climate favorable to economic expansion. Fringe parties like the so-called Republikaner, a right-wing movement that flirted with extremist political views bordering on racism, might have won some votes at the end of the 1980s. But their real level of popular support proved to be fleeting, and by 1990 they had largely vanished from the West German political scene. In contrast, the successful integration of a political grouping such as the Greens, advocating alternative social and industrial policies and addressing the new problems of an advanced economy such as pollution and nuclear control—all critiques adopted by the more right-leaning parties like the CDU and the CSU—suggested how far the political parties of the Federal Republic had come since their state's founding. It also showed how far they could go, so long as they were willing to work within the confines of the rule of law.

Economic Recovery

Of course, the FRG's political success always went hand in hand with the extraordinary road it took to economic recovery in the 1950s, thanks to Minister of Economics Erhard's so-called social market economy. This was a system of regulated free economy, based upon a broad program of social insurance and allowing for the free search for profits at the same time that employers were expected to act responsibly toward society.

In part, the Federal Republic's economic progress was tied to a unique relationship among the country's different centers of economic power: the Ministry of Economics, the Ministry of Finance, and the Deutsche Bundesbank (Federal Bank). The government itself controlled fiscal policy, whereas the bank in large part shaped monetary policy. Following the war, financial capital in West Germany became concentrated in just three major banks. Of these, the Bundesbank was the largest. It went well out of its way to hold down the inflationary pressures that had contributed to the fall of the first German democracy, the Weimar Republic.

Banks in the Federal Republic have a tremendous degree of discretionary power; they may hold stock shares, and it is the practice of private stockholders to deposit their shares with banks and to allow them to vote those shares. Banks in the Federal Republic will also lend their voting rights to other banks. Many firms seek large loans from banks that hold or administer quantities of the firms' equity shares. Thus the banks have influence with the firms and often will have their officers on governing boards of industries.

Under these circumstances, it was only natural that banks in the FRG developed an array of technical industrial experts. Bank holdings in a wide range of equities enabled them, and especially the Bundesbank, effectively to plan for an entire geographic region or sector of the economy. Thus difficult decisions, such as those involving layoffs or the closing of inefficient plants, were frequently reached quickly and quietly, away from public political pressure.

In addition, the organization of West German labor was also conducive to the successful management of the economy. Nearly all sixteen unions into which German labor was divided after the war are incorporated into a strong central federation, the German Federation of Trade Unions (DGB), which has proved to be both an effective way of representing the interests of workers and also a powerful source of stability for the West German economy. Collective bargaining is regulated by law. Wildcat strikes are illegal (and are in any case contrary to the German tradition of order).

West German employers clearly benefited from the arrangement for deciding on incomes policy, which is generally the result of tacit tripartite collaboration among the government, the bankers, and the unions. The centralized relationship of the unions means that when a wage bargain is reached in one industry, all members of the DGB will usually abide by it. Laborers exercise restraint because they know that their fellow workers in the DGB will follow suit in their respective trades. Thus no union or group of laborers will be left behind in the growth of general prosperity; each will have a fair share. This situation is unlike that in Great Britain, where local shop stewards will readily strike against the wishes of the weak Trades Union Congress (TUC).

Even though equity was maintained among West German workers, some still considered that they all suffered as consumers because of the final prop of the FRG's economic miracle, a conscious undervaluation of the mark. The currency's low exchange rate supported export industries, whereas consumers paid high prices for imports. In the process, West Germany became the most successful export power in the world. No wonder the French, who traded extensively with Germany, found their own domestic market dominated by German manufacturers. Because the need for trade and jobs in postwar Germany was so great, the mark's undervaluation initially drew little complaint. What was noticeable was that the economy was thriving and the standard of living rising. A 5 percent upward evaluation occurred in 1961, but the Bundesbank vetoed any greater move. During a short period, the Social Democrats allowed upward evaluation in 1969; yet it was only a small concession made as a result of complaints during an electoral campaign. Finally, in 1973, the Bundesbank altered its posture and permitted the free floating of the mark. Given the change in the international monetary regime spurred by oil price increases and the abandonment of the gold standard by the United States, this was the best course the bank could take and still retain control of monetary policy.

It would be easy to cite statistics without end to show Germany's phenomenal postwar industrial expansion. The slowdown of economic growth that embarrassed Erhard in the early 1960s did not become a true recession. And despite a lesser recession in the first half of the 1980s and the nagging problem of continuing high levels of unemployment, by the end of the decade the Federal Republic had taken the lead among its European neighbors in advocating the creation of a totally unified European market. In this market West German products could compete freely with other countries' goods without being held up by protective tariffs, legal obstacles, or other impediments.

The Remaining German Question

It is widely known, however, that there was still one key respect in which the Federal Republic remained less than fully "normal" compared to its continental neighbors. For all of its achievements, West Germany was still only one part of a divided nation, though its leaders did their best to make their country's relations with its counterpart, the German Democratic Republic, as normal as possible. This was clearly the case following the signing of the Basic Treaty in 1972, which dramatically altered the two Germanys' relations with each other by bringing them into regular contact for the first time since the Berlin Wall's construction in 1961. Steady negotiations between the two states produced comprehensive pacts for improving telephone and transit services between the long-separated German populations. Travel restrictions were eased, with the consequence that millions of West Germans were for the first time in years allowed to visit their relatives and friends in the East; in turn, some thousands of East Germans were allowed annually to make short visits to the FRG in cases of "urgent family need," like weddings and funerals. The GDR also granted amnesty to political prisoners (some of them West Germans) and, by releasing them from their East German citizenship, enabled many others who had escaped from East Germany prior to January 1, 1972, to return to visit their families. Naturally, the West German government did what it could to emphasize the still provisional character of Germany's division, refusing to exchange full ambassadors with the GDR and emphasizing its own commitment to national reunification (however improbable this may have seemed at the time). Nonetheless, it is also evident that the Federal Republic, in its desire to do something to alleviate the burdens of those Germans lost to communism, gradually grew accustomed in the process to treating the GDR as a separate state.

This fact fulfilled the basic precondition for a steady improvement in ties between Bonn and East Berlin throughout the 1970s and into the 1980s. Clearly, there were many occasions—the Soviet invasion of Afghanistan in late 1979, the imposition of martial law in Poland in 1981, and the deployment of NATO's new intermediate-range nuclear missiles in 1983—that could have ruined any prospects for inter-German cooperation. But the Germanys were still able to find reasons for communicating and preserving what they called a "coalition of reason" between them. This spirit was perhaps no better captured than in 1987, when Erich Honecker, SED party leader and chairman of the German Democratic Republic's Council of State, undertook a long-postponed trip to the Federal Republic. It was the first such visit to West Germany by an East German head of state. Honecker and Chancellor Kohl vowed that war should never again be started from German soil and pledged to respect each state's independence and to improve economic ties and intra-German travel; three technical accords were signed. Naturally, Kohl reaffirmed his government's long-term commitment to peaceful reunification, whereas Honecker stressed the existence of two separate German states, which in his view had as much in common as "fire and water." The reiteration of old positions seemed, however, to take second place to the concept of closer cooperation and the further de facto recognition of the GDR by Bonn.

Were the Germanys, then, each becoming more normal as they sought to improve their relations? Were they finally, of their own accord, completing the division of Europe that had begun under such difficult circumstances in 1945? In 1987 these were the sorts of conclusions reached by many experts in German affairs. Yet only three short years later, a very different sort of normality had set in—Germany's reunification. To see why this unlikely event might have become possible so quickly, we now turn to the GDR.

The German Democratic Republic

Establishment of the State

From one perspective, the origins of the GDR may actually be said to have preceded its formal founding. In December 1947, Soviet authorities had sponsored a German People's Congress in Berlin at which only the Communist party of the Western zones was officially represented. This congress elected a German People's Council and authorized it to draw up a constitution

After the revolutionary autumn of 1989, the idea of German reunification may have seemed self-evident to many observers. Only a few years earlier, however, nothing could have been further from the minds of the leaders of both the Federal Republic of Germany (West) and the German Democratic Republic (East). In September 1987 East Germany's Communist leader, Erich Honecker, was officially invited to make a state visit to Bonn. At the time, Chancellor Kohl of West Germany (at right) treated his counterpart as though they would long be conducting business as representatives of separate states. (Photo courtesy of the German Information Center.)

for all Germany. Following approval of this document by a German People's Congress, the German Democratic Republic was proclaimed on October 7, 1949. It was a very different kind of "democracy" from that of the Federal Republic.

On paper at least, the GDR's first constitution looked quite like those of the liberal democracies in the West. It provided for a president, a cabinet, and a popularly elected, unicameral legislature (Volkskammer). It contained an elaborate bill of rights, and one of its articles even expressly allowed its citizens the right of emigration. But it was in the fine print that the document's democratic pretensions became obscured. For example, the constitution contained one article (Article 49) that specified that "all basic rights shall remain inviolable, except where this Constitution authorizes their restriction by law or makes their further development subject to legislative action." Under this clause, considering the wide powers given to the government, the bill of rights was deprived of all safeguards. To cite a further example, various political parties were allowed (there was an East-CDU and an Eastern version of the FDP, called the Liberal Democratic party of Germany), yet it is also true that the constitution spelled out the "leading role" of only one of those parties, the Communist Socialist Unity party.

Originally, the GDR's founders had hoped that the decisions they reached within the confines of the SED would be made collectively, allowing for the greatest number of views to be debated. However, when the country's first president, Wilhelm Pieck, died in 1960, these hopes met with a symbolically telling end. Instead of electing a successor, the Parliament amended the constitution, abolishing the presidency and creating a State Council of twenty-four members. But in reality, this council became merely a compliant instrument in the hands of the party's first secretary, Walter Ulbricht, who used it to subordinate all state and administrative affairs to the SED's dictatorship.

In 1968 a new constitution was adopted that only added to the East German government's control over its citizenry. Although the new constitution now referred to the GDR as a "socialist state" rather than just a "democratic republic," with powers stemming from the "working people," in reality the document probably restricted civil liberties even more than before. The old constitution had stated that the economy should ensure an adequate standard of living for all, theoretically also providing room for different types of property ownership; the 1968 version, in contrast, described the economy in much narrower terms, as "based upon the socialist ownership of the means of production." Women's rights were more explicitly guaranteed, but (not surprisingly, given the erection of the Berlin Wall) the right to emigrate was now deleted. The right of a citizen to dwell where he or she pleased was modified to the right to move "within the framework of the laws." Work became a duty in addition to a right, and Article 24 even specified that one's choice of work had to be made "in accordance with social requirements" as well as personal qualifications.

Historians still debate whether such changes occurred more because of the overbearing weight of the Soviet Union on East German policymaking or as a result of internal, antidemocratic tendencies within the long history of German communism. In either case, the effect was the same: The German Democratic Republic was increasingly organized on explicitly Soviet lines. Everywhere—in education, industry, trade—basic Soviet patterns were followed. It was held that as the USSR was the sole successful exemplar of a modern Communist state, its method of modernization was to be imitated in every respect: "To learn from the Soviet Union," the popular slogan went, "is to learn to be victorious."

Actually, such trends had already been evident years earlier throughout the Eastern bloc. What made them even more acute in the GDR, however, was the SED's efforts to construct socialism in only one half, the weaker half, of the German nation. On the one hand, the party leadership undoubtedly would have liked nothing more than to avoid having to compete with the more affluent FRG for the attention and affections of the East German population. Yet, on the other hand, precisely because the West Germans had begun the road back to economic recovery in the early 1950s—and because they had had the Marshall Plan to help them (as many GDR leaders lamented)—the East German regime felt that it had no choice but to press its own population to work harder and longer to demonstrate that the GDR, too, was capable of living up to its leaders' visions of socialist grandeur. The contradiction, of course, was that the more demanding the SED became, the more its relationship with its citizenry deteriorated. And in the 1950s in particular, this very dilemma led to a refugee crisis that was to haunt the GDR's entire history. Between 1949 and 1961, over 3 million people fled East Germany forever.

The East German exodus bore witness to an almost unresolvable tension between leaders and led in the country. Protests had arisen from time to time in the past. In June 1953, following a lifting of curbs on demonstrations as part of the relaxation of state pressures after the death of Soviet general secretary Stalin the preceding March, riots broke out in East Berlin and in other East German cities. Because they were aware that minor reforms had been enacted in the Soviet Union, many of the GDR's citizens were simply anxious that more changes be implemented in their own country. Nevertheless, their protests were brutally suppressed on June 17, when Soviet troops and tanks intervened to crush the demonstrations. For their part, the East German party leaders were deeply embarrassed by these developments and vowed never again to let matters get out of hand.

As the liberalization of the regime no longer seemed possible, East Germans increasingly "voted with their feet." Many more might have left but for the desire to preserve family ties *and* for the many well-known obstacles— mines and police frontiers—created by the regime. To avoid the hindrances, most escapees traveled to East Berlin and simply crossed over to the Western sectors, for Berlin was still only imperfectly divided. Police and economic barriers may have been erected and telephone service broken, but public transport continued to pass from one part of the city to the other, making passage to the West as easy as a subway ride.

To deal with this problem, the East German government gradually extended its control over East Berlin and in 1960 declared it an integral part of the GDR. The Western powers never recognized this, and their occupying forces in West Berlin strove to maintain what few rights they had in the Eastern sector of the city. But ironically, the more publicity the refugee problem received, the more it grew. People of all classes fled, but the refugees included an extraordinarily large percentage from the professional classes and the skilled work force, all necessary to the country's economic recovery. For example, between January 1 and August 31, 1958, a total of 813 doctors, veterinary surgeons, and dentists; 250 professors and lecturers; and 2,300 teachers departed to West Germany.

It was in these tense circumstances that the East German government took the most famous decision of its forty-year history: to erect the Wall between East and West Berlin on August 13, 1961. Henceforth all inter-German traffic was effectively restricted to seven checkpoints. What had been a partially controlled demarcation line was now considered by the East German regime and its Soviet ally as nothing more than a "normal" state frontier. In fact, very few people—fewer than 5,000 by the twenty-fifth anniversary of the Wall's construction—would ever manage to escape its somber confines to get to the West.

Unquestionably, the decision to build the Wall did imply the acknowledgment of the deficiencies of economic, political, and social life in the GDR. Whether it was Ulbricht and the SED or the USSR and the Warsaw Pact nations that proposed this drastic solution is still unclear to Western historians. Yet, embarrassing as it was, the barrier's construction achieved its initial goal of halting the hemorrhage of skilled laborers and professionals and in a larger sense marked the real founding of the German Democratic Republic. The stabilization of the labor force facilitated the stabilization of the economy, just as the tough action itself demonstrated the regime's determination to stay its socialist course. With the alternative of flight to the West gone, the population better directed its attention to its work and to the improvement of local conditions.

Nonetheless, it is also true that recognition that the Communist government had been forced to go to such lengths to assert its control clearly set limits, often debilitating ones, to the aspirations and horizons of the East German population. All too often people simply turned their attentions inward, focusing on matters at home. They prepared for their yearly vacations and retreated to their countryside dachas on the weekend without even giving a passing thought to the mysteries of the political world over which they had so little say. For those in the SED who worried that the population might rise up in revolt, such apolitical attitudes were no doubt comforting. Yet it is quite understandable that for many of the Communist visionaries who had founded the GDR in the first place, a mute and even unthinking acceptance of East German socialism was hardly the stuff of their Marxist dreams. After all, where was the enthusiasm for this, the "first worker's and farmer's state on German soil"?

Accordingly, when Honecker replaced Ulbricht as party leader in 1971, he immediately sought to make the best of a bad situation. There was no hope of removing the Wall. Such a step was unthinkable, for who could tell how the East German population would react? But there was at least some hope of making life more worth living within the barrier's confines. Whereas Ulbricht had often emphasized the far-off benefits of socialism that might one day come to one's children's children, Honecker deliberately concentrated on the here and now. He instituted a campaign to regain the trust of the GDR's long-persecuted intellectual and artistic community, and he gradually improved relations with East Germany's Protestant churches. Most prominently of all, Honecker introduced a comprehensive plan to better the economic fortunes of all of the country's citizens, increasing pensions, improving health care, and dramatically raising the quantity and quality of housing available to the East Germans. By themselves, these gestures were undoubtedly well meant. Yet, as with other Communist states of its type, the only problem with the Honecker regime's efforts to pursue such concrete objectives was that they were all wholly dependent upon the means available to a socialist economy.

Economic Policy

In most respects, the GDR was a classic planned economy, deliberately modeled after the Soviet Union's system of successive five-year plans and increasingly coordinated, on an international basis, with the needs of the USSR-sponsored Council for Mutual Economic Assistance. Each year the long-term plan approved by the Politburo of the party was implemented by specific annual programs developed by the organs of the state. The most important of these was the State Planning Commission, which advised the Council of Ministers and gave directives to the various ministries. Beneath the ministries were 150 to 200 *Kombinate*, centrally directed trusts formed at the end of the 1970s to assure rationality and efficiency for nonagricultural production; they replaced associations that formerly coordinated the activities of individual producing units.

In this wholesale integration of economic planning from the top down, the GDR was probably no different from any of its Eastern European neighbors. But it did have some slight advantages. Although by no means rich in resources, East Germany had large deposits of lignite (useful as a source of energy but terribly polluting), potash, and salt; and rare elements such as uranium, cobalt, bismuth, arsenic, and antimony were exploited in the western Erzgebirge and in Thuringia. A deficiency of oil was remedied somewhat by the construction of a pipeline from Soviet fields, later to be complemented by the construction of large refineries. Yet the country's real advantages undoubtedly derived from its unique cultural and historical situation. A combination of German ingenuity and the GDR's ability to draw on certain prewar markets led the East Germans to excel in select areas of industrial production—in optics (the Zeiss works at Jena), electronics, and the machine-goods industries. At first, the GDR's membership in Comecon restricted the East German regime to selling such products to other Communist states. Gradually—in part because of trade advantages it enjoyed in the European Common Market by virtue of its special relationship with West

Germany—the country emerged as a major exporter to the Western world as well.

Such strengths notwithstanding, there was always something missing. The GDR's planners did not need to be told that highly centralized five-year plans and state directives were not always the best way of stimulating productivity and promoting efficiency. Accordingly, throughout the country's history there were numerous experiments with refining the character of state planning by decentralizing decisionmaking and using bonuses and incentives to spur production. Most famous among these was the so-called New Economic System (NES) of the 1960s, which relied upon the Associations of Nationalized Enterprises, or VVBs, to make the socialist plan more effective. These institutions were created in the spirit of reforms already proposed by the Soviet economist Evsei Liberman and tentatively being considered in the USSR, and they were meant to transfer some of the authority for economic decisionmaking from the center to associations more directly involved with actual production. In the long run, however, few planners or state officials really wished to give up the authority that they had over the enterprises below them, and the NES was abandoned before it was ever fully implemented.

If only the GDR had been totally isolated from its international environs, its government might still have been able to muddle through with all of its old inefficiencies. In the 1970s, however, two dramatic surges in the price of oil, first in 1974 and then in 1979, arrived precisely at the time Honecker wished to demonstrate the concrete benefits of socialism to his population. The SED was forced to reconsider. The cost of the country's raw material imports rose faster than the prices that could successfully be charged for the GDR's manufactured exports. Trade deficits and foreign debt mounted rapidly. Something more had to be done. The state decided not to decentralize but instead merely to improve the effectiveness of central planning and control. The government turned its back on the VVBs and gave new encouragement to the *Kombinate*. These involved the linkage not only of factories within fields of production but also of suppliers, research institutions, and even foreign trade merchandisers. A small number of *Kombinate* had existed for nearly a decade, but now their numbers burgeoned at both the national and local levels. Intended to stimulate innovation, efficiency, and above all exports, *Kombinate* were granted the use of moneys earned above planned profits as incentive funds. Their effectiveness was to be judged more on the basis of net profits and the production of export goods than on quotas or ideological grounds.

Was such a fine-tuning of the GDR's socialist system enough to keep the country's economy up to the standards of the modern world, and particularly up to those standards that were daily being equaled by the rival German state, the capitalist FRG? Some policymakers privately began to worry about this question in the 1980s as a result of two distinct developments in the Soviet bloc. One development was the political chaos that engulfed neighboring Poland during 1980–1981, in part because of the collapse of that country's equally planned economy. Yet even more disturbing was the rise to power in 1985 of a new Soviet leader, Mikhail Gorbachev, who in the name of a novel concept, *perestroika*, deliberately called into question many of the old truisms about Marxist economics. It was not that one should abandon socialism, Gorbachev argued, but only that one should look for new, more innovative ways of making the system competitive with the capitalist West.

Most surprising of all for those who had grown accustomed to viewing the GDR as little more than a compliant executor of Soviet commands, the aging Politburo of the SED flatly refused to take up the new Soviet general secretary's pleas for economic experimentation. In part, this astonishing act of defiance must have had much to do with the GDR's position in the Soviet bloc. The country's economy may not have been a perfectly functioning machine in comparison with the market economics of West Germany. But when placed against its socialist neighbors, East Germany was still a virtual paradise: Consumer goods were still available in its stores, decent housing was accessible for the majority of its citizens, and even the trains ran (more or less) on time. The other reason for the Politburo's rebuff, both to Gorbachev and to some of its own experts, was its own apprehension that any large-scale economic reform, however necessary, might spill over into political challenges to the regime; these could in turn lead to the resurfacing of uncomfortable questions about the division of Germany and the very existence of the GDR. In fact, the totally unexpected fall of Honecker's government in 1989 demonstrated that this fear was fully justified.

Upheaval and Fall of the GDR

For good reason, no one was able to predict the fall of the GDR, because as late as January 1989 the SED regime seemed to have everything under control. The economy was still functioning, if with some signs of difficulty because consumer demands were rising faster than the socialist plan could accommodate. The government still monopolized the means of coercion in the country, and its dissidents found themselves operating under increasingly repressive conditions. Most important, the artificial environment generated by the Wall in Berlin still seemed to guarantee that the East German population had no other option than to live quietly under the Communist regime. Thus, although there were signs of discontent among some segments of the populace about issues as varied as the freedom to voice one's views, the quality of the environment (the GDR's streams and soil were filled with pollutants), and the all-important right to travel, there were simply no organized means of expressing these grievances.

All of this changed abruptly in spring 1989, with a key decision made *outside* of the GDR. At the beginning of the year, with the evident blessing of Gorbachev's Soviet Union, the Parliament of Hungary had voted to allow

Germany

independent political parties. Then in May 1989 it had ousted its longtime Communist leader, Janos Kadar. The Parliament's final step, taken to emphasize its independence and its desire to rejoin all of Europe, was most decisive for the fate of the GDR: It removed the barbed wire along the border with Austria. At first only a trickle of East Germans traveled to Hungary in order to take advantage of this hole in the Iron Curtain to flee to the West. But soon thousands of GDR citizens were crowding into the West German embassies in Hungary and neighboring Czechoslovakia to demonstrate their desire to be allowed to emigrate as well. In September Hungary unilaterally suspended its two-decade-old agreement with East Berlin to block the passage of East Germans going to the Federal Republic, and within weeks some 57,000 East Germans had gone east to migrate west. On October 3, nearly 10,000 East Germans fought with the Volkspolizei (People's Police) in an attempt to board trains carrying East Germans from Czechoslovakia to the Federal Republic. Within days demonstrators were seething through the streets of Dresden and Leipzig. The breaking up of the first demonstrations by security forces only brought larger crowds to the next night's torchlit parade.

Thus on October 7, 1989, even as officials of the German Democratic Republic were celebrating the fortieth anniversary of their state's founding, the country's façade of security, economic success, and domestic tranquility had been shattered. The SED scrambled to regain credibility and control. Honecker was forced from office and replaced as party leader by the more moderate Egon Krenz. But the exodus of East Germans via Hungary and Czechoslovakia continued, the demonstrations grew larger and larger, and the SED was practically driven to despair. In this context, the party took the fateful step from which there would be no return, opening the Berlin Wall on November 9, 1989, and lifting all remaining restrictions on travel to the West.

There can be little doubt that what Krenz and his fellow reform-minded premier, Hans Modrow, had in mind in removing this bloody barrier was an improved GDR, a state that would embody the virtuous side of Marxism (instead of its negative, authoritarian face) and thereby provide East Germans with the right kinds of reasons for wanting to stay voluntarily in their country. Indeed, this was an ideal that the SED's new leaders shared in common with many of their dissident critics, who themselves chose to stay behind to change the GDR for the better, to create a more humane kind of socialism. Yet for at least two reasons, the collapse of the Wall led straightaway to the demise of the East German state itself.

One reason was self-evident: Although the Wall was opened to demonstrate to average East Germans that they could now travel freely outside of their country, this step could not convince them to stay and rebuild the GDR. To many, life was simply easier and (seemingly) more free from worries in the affluent setting of the Federal Republic; the GDR's socialism required

On November 9, 1989, almost three decades after its construction, the wall that once divided Berlin was suddenly opened. The Communist government in East Germany took this momentous step in a desperate effort to gain the confidence of its population. Thousands of East Germans crossed over the former no-man's-land to a jubilant reception in West Berlin. Young people from both East and West defied the orders of East German police and scrambled to the top of the once formidable edifice. Before long, many began to tear it down with hammers and chisels. On the lips of many East Germans, the word Freiheit (freedom) was soon replaced by the term Einheit (unity). (Left photo from Reuters/Bettmann Newsphotos; right photo courtesy of the German Information Center.)

conviction and a readiness to undergo sacrifices, virtues that most people had lost years before in the quiet desperation of life under a dictatorship. Thousands of East Germans thus continued to leave their country on a weekly basis even after November 9, taking with them all of the training and skills that were necessary to keep the GDR's economy functioning. As goods became scarcer and the government's desperation even more pronounced, East Germany's fate became entrapped in the logic of a self-fulfilling prophecy, with still greater numbers of citizens deciding to leave as well.

The other reason for the GDR's fall was, of course, the presence of a clear and active alternative in the FRG. During the October demonstrations in East Germany, Chancellor Kohl had denounced the use of force by GDR police forces as a symptom of the "deep insecurity" of the East Berlin government. Yet it is doubtful that he imagined that what was transpiring would soon lead to the disappearance of communism in East Germany and the reunification of the German nation. Even after the Berlin Wall fell, he limited his vision of the immediate German future to that of a possible

---

General Secretaries (or First Secretaries) of the Socialist Unity Party, German Democratic Republic

Walter Ulbricht	July 25, 1950–May 3, 1971
Erich Honecker	May 3, 1971–October 18, 1989
Egon Krenz	October 18, 1989–December 3, 1989

---

confederation between the two German states under a broad European roof. Nonetheless, as people continued to stream out of the GDR, adding ever new burdens on already strained West German social services, and as the East German government itself called for truly democratic elections in the GDR in March 1990, Kohl and his advisers recognized both the necessity and the manifest advantages of making the case for a speedy path to national unity. Only if they promised the East German population that it would soon enjoy the benefits of a life blessed by capitalist abundance and liberal democracy did West Germany's leaders have a chance of convincing their "fellow countrymen" (Kohl's term) to stay at home. At the same time, Kohl also saw that he personally had the unprecedented opportunity of presenting himself as the new German Bismarck, the unifier of the nation, leading his party to a heroic victory at the polls.

In this fashion, the train of events was set in motion for the one development that had previously been unthinkable. On March 18, 1990, the East German Christian Democrats (sponsored by Kohl) strode to a convincing victory in the first free elections conducted in the GDR since its founding four decades earlier. In July 1990, in an attempt to arrest the further collapse of the East German economy, the West German government sponsored a complete reform of the country's currency, substituting its own deutsche mark for the failed GDR mark. Finally, once the economies of the two states had been linked, in October 1990 a state treaty formally completed the unification of the GDR and the FRG. Germany was one again.

A New Germany?

Will the German nation-state formed in 1990 be essentially the same country that was embodied by the Federal Republic since 1949, or will it instead be a new kind of Germany, qualitatively different from its predecessor? It will probably be a decade before scholars are able to answer this difficult question with any confidence, because there is still so little information to draw upon. On the one hand, acknowledgment that Germany was reunified under liberal-

In a historic meeting between West German chancellor Helmut Kohl (left) and Soviet president Mikhail Gorbachev in the Caucasus on July 15, 1990, the Soviet leader gave his consent to German reunification. Some observers wondered whether the meeting did not also signify a turning point in Soviet-German relations. It seemed as though the Soviet people, who had fought so hard against Nazi Germany, were now prepared to enter into a new friendship with a democratic and reunified Germany. (Photo courtesy of the German Information Center.)

democratic auspices and that freely elected political parties continue to determine the norms of political life in the country (as they did in the first national elections of December 1990) should be enough to give any doubters realistic grounds for confidence about Germany's democratic potential in the coming years. Public-policy making in the FRG is still dominated by the middle-of-the-road parties that brought stability to West Germany in the 1960s and 1970s. Moreover, the country's leaders' continuing espousal in the early 1990s of the ideals that played so great a role in the FRG's early years under Adenauer—of a polity fully integrated into European institutions like the European Common Market and committed to Western values—should also instill confidence that the new Germany will not return to the dictatorial traditions that once led its people into two world wars.

On the other hand, scholars have not yet shed the idea that something fundamental may have changed with the reemergence of the unified German state in central Europe. Many West Germans were prone to say in 1990 that their country had simply "swallowed" the GDR, and with it everything that the GDR had represented. But some observers could still wonder whether Germany's eastern part—a large entity, after all, with over 16 million inhabitants and a sense of political, economic, and cultural priorities very different from that of the FRG—would not somehow manage to have an impact upon its western counterpart as well.

Certainly, the economic trials facing the people of the former GDR in the early 1990s were daunting. For example, there was the necessity of providing jobs for millions of individuals who had either been thrown out of work or put on half-time schedules as a result of the collapse of the East German economy. But this challenge could only be managed if the rotting infrastructure of the old Communist command system were modernized, a task that would clearly take years to accomplish and potentially lead to years of additional sacrifices on the part of the populations of both the former GDR and the former FRG. Was it not possible, some observers wondered, that the prospect of even greater levels of unemployment in eastern Germany and of higher taxes in western Germany would precipitate new tensions between the now united peoples of the German nation-state? Or conversely, if future German governments chose to avert such conflicts by concentrating their energies on their internal affairs alone, how would such a development influence the widely held perception outside of the FRG's borders that the new Germany was bound to be the political and economic power most likely to lead Europe and the Europeans down the path to continental unity? In the early 1990s, it was impossible for any Europeans, Germans or not, to answer these questions. But everyone could agree that the way in which the German people came to terms with the new reality of national unity would be of decisive significance for the Continent's future.

Notes

1. This speech of May 8, 1945, to the Bundestag is printed in translation in *Bulletin* (published by the Press and Information Office of the Federal Republic of Germany), June 1985.

2. Bernd Rabehl, "From Antiauthoritarian Movement to Socialist Opposition," in C. Burdick, H. A. Jacobsen, and W. Kudszus, *Contemporary Germany: Politics and Culture* (1984), p. 75.

Suggested Readings

Adenauer, K., *Memoirs*, trans. B. R. von Oppen (1966).
Castles, S., *Here for Good: Western Europe's New Ethnic Minorities* (1984).
Cioc, M., *Pax Atomica* (1988).
Craig, G. A., *The Germans* (1982).

Geipel, G., The Future of Germany (1990).
Golay, J. F., The Founding of the Federal Republic of Germany (1958).
Haftendorn, H., Security and Detente (1985).
Hallett, G., The Social Economy of West Germany (1974).
Hancock, M. D., West Germany: The Politics of Democratic Corporatism (1989).
Hanrieder, W., Germany, America, Europe (1989).
Helmreich, E. C., Religious Education in German Schools (1959).
Holborn, H., A History of Modern Germany, 3 vols. (1959–1969).
Katzenstein, P., Policy and Politics in West Germany (1987).
Keefe, E. K. (ed.), East Germany: A Country Study (1983).
Koch, H. W., A Constitutional History of Germany: In the Nineteenth and Twentieth Centuries (1984).
McAdams, A. J., East Germany and Detente: Building Authority After the Wall (1985).
———, Germany Divided by a Wall (forthcoming).
Merkl, P., The Origins of the West German Republic (1965).
Nyrop, R. F. (ed.), Federal Republic of Germany: A Country Study (1983).
Orlow, D., A History of Modern Germany: 1870 to the Present (1987).
Ringer, F., Education and Society in Modern Europe (1979).
Sandford, G., From Hitler to Ulbricht (1983).
Schnitzler, M., East and West Germany: A Comparative Economic Analysis (1972).
Turner, H. A., Jr., The Two Germanies Since 1945 (1987).
Tusa, A., and J. Tusa, The Nuremberg Trial (1984).
Willis, F. R., France, Germany and the New Europe, 1945–1967, 2d ed. (1968).
Windsor, P., City on Leave: A History of Berlin, 1945–1962 (1963).
Wolf, C., The Quest for Christa T. (1970).
Wolfe, R., Americans as Proconsuls: United States Military Government in Germany and Japan, 1944–1952 (1984).

CHAPTER SEVEN

The Soviet Union

Evolution of Soviet Policy
Aftermath of War
Stalin's Successors: An Opportunity for Change?

The Soviet Order
The Political System • Economic Policy
Society and Culture

The Gorbachev Era
"New Thinking" About the Soviet Union
Glasnost and Perestroika

The Crisis of Soviet Reform

The End of the Soviet Union

Notes

Suggested Readings

The postwar history of the Soviet Union is one of tremendous contradictions. At war's end, the country's prospects could not have appeared bleaker, following the years of suffering and devastation inflicted upon the Soviet people by the invasion of Nazi Germany. Yet within a decade, the Soviet Union had been reborn as one of two great superpowers. Much of the secret to Soviet successes could be found in a dictatorial command system peculiar to Marxism-Leninism, which allowed the country's leaders to achieve their military and economic goals in a centralized, tightly controlled fashion quite unlike the paths of development pursued by their rivals in the liberal-democratic West. This Soviet path to modernity, however, also had great costs, both in terms of Moscow's ability to compete efficiently with the Western world in the 1970s and 1980s and in human terms as well. Only in the middle of the 1980s, with the rise of a new, dynamic leader, Mikhail Gorbachev, did it appear possible that the Soviet Union might finally begin to embrace the liberal and capitalist ideals that it had once condemned. Nonetheless, one great uncertainty remained: After so many years of dictatorship, would the USSR successfully make the transition to becoming a democratic society, or would its leaders instead fall back on the despotic means that had been so much a part of their country's past?

Evolution of Soviet Policy

Aftermath of War

In the early years of the war, the Communist leaders were profoundly apprehensive of its outcome, knowing as they did the deep distrust in which their leadership was held by the peoples of the Soviet Union. Indeed, in some areas the populace greeted the invading German troops as liberators. The Germans soon made it abundantly clear that this welcome was not justified. They treated the peoples of the USSR with brutality and contempt and demonstrated that rule by the Nazis was worse by far than rule by the Communists. At the same time the Communist leaders changed their tactics to meet the new crisis and made broad concessions to public opinion. They stimulated national feeling wherever possible, ignoring for the time being the idea of class conflict. Accordingly, the war was termed a patriotic struggle for the homeland. In 1943 the Russian Orthodox church was officially recognized again, thus giving the war a religious sanction as well. There was also a return to tradition in the armed forces, with the reestablishment of ranks, medals, and a privileged status for officers. Moreover, the government gave the impression that, after the fighting ceased, a more humane policy would be adopted at home and that special attention would be given to the production of food and consumer goods that had been so seriously neglected in the prewar five-year plans. In short, during the war the peoples of the USSR were in a very real sense partners rather than the servants of the Communist party, and they hoped that this new partnership would survive the war.

The vast destruction the German armies had wrought confronted the Soviet government with an almost overwhelming problem at the end of the war. In human terms, it has been estimated that as many as 17 million died and another 20 million or more were left homeless. In economic terms, the losses in fixed and working capital and in private property equaled two-thirds of the prewar wealth in the occupied territories. As these were in most respects the most productive parts of the Soviet Union, the loss for the country as a whole may have been as much as one-quarter of the total prewar wealth. Owing to the dislocations caused by the war, the decline in national production was fully as great as the destruction of fixed capital. A twofold task thus confronted the Soviet Union in 1945: It had to make good the losses resulting from the war, and it had to resume the program of industrialization that the war had interrupted.

In plotting their course for the postwar world, the Soviet Union's leaders had to take into account an unprecedented situation. The extensive war damage called for a program of reconstruction that would require great effort. At the same time, the mood of the Soviet peoples favored a continuation of the more relaxed policy that had been created to meet the needs of the war. In the last year of the war, many hundreds of thousands had glimpsed what life was like in Central and Eastern Europe. Despite the wreckage left by the Germans, Soviet soldiers had seen with their own eyes that life in the "capitalist" world was a good deal more comfortable than what they had known at home. Moreover, the Soviet government now enjoyed the confidence of the Western democracies, and the atmosphere was favorable to extensive U.S. economic assistance.

As a result of this situation, the Soviet leaders were confronted with a difficult dilemma. On the one hand, if they returned to their prewar methods, they would place a great strain on the people and would again find themselves in conflict with the outside world. On the other hand, to adopt a moderate policy would be to abandon the revolutionary principles of Marxism-Leninism and to set in motion forces that might permanently weaken the grip of the dictatorial state on Soviet affairs. Under these circumstances, the USSR's rulers and Stalin in particular missed what could have been a historic opportunity to fashion a new relationship between the Communist government and the estranged Soviet populace. But of course Stalin, paranoid and single-mindedly tyrannical until the very end, was only interested in one goal—to give himself total control over the USSR and all of the countries that had fallen under its domination at war's end.

Few notables of the twentieth century are as complex as Josef Stalin. As the long-time general secretary of the Soviet Communist party, Stalin was personally responsible for the deaths of tens of millions of his country's citizens. Yet decades after the tyrant's death in 1953, average Soviets still revered Stalin, much as though he were a religious icon. For them, he represented the better and more orderly times before the collapse of the Soviet empire. (Left photo from Bernard Baruch Papers, Princeton University Libraries; right photo courtesy of Paul Christensen.)

As a consequence, the hopes of the people were met not by relaxation of state controls but by a renewed emphasis on Marxist-Leninist doctrine, combined with a continuation of the stress on national patriotism, which had reached a high point during the war. Much effort was devoted to showing that the Soviet way of doing things was better than Western methods. The party claimed that the Soviet army had defeated the Germans practically single-handedly. It also maintained that many modern applications of science, from airplanes to electric light bulbs, had originally been invented by Soviets. In the cultural sphere, all recognition of foreign values and achievements was described as "objectivism," and dialectical materialism was asserted to be the only way of arriving at the truth. In practice, this meant that in peacetime all scholars and artists had to work enthusiastically on the tasks assigned to them by the state, and any lack of interest in such assignments was criticized as "formalism."

There was an even darker side to these events. As Stalin grew older, his suspicion of everyone around him intensified all the more, and what little hope remained that the bloody purges of the 1930s would not be repeated vanished. Some of Stalin's closest cronies during the war, like Vyacheslav Molotov and Nikolai Bulganin, were lucky only to lose their posts. But others, like the economic planner Nikolai Voznesensky, were summarily executed. In January 1953, only months before his death, Stalin seemed to be laying the groundwork for a new wave of purges when a group of Kremlin doctors was wrongly accused of having plotted to kill the entire Soviet leadership. Because most of the doctors were of Jewish origin, it seems likely that Stalin hoped to use the supposed "plot" as a pretext for eliminating the remaining Jewish members of his own leadership.

Of course, Stalin's suspicions also extended beyond the USSR's borders. In the realm of foreign affairs after World War II, an ideological war was declared against the West and all that it stood for, and every effort was made to press the cause of communism abroad. Within the Soviet orbit in Eastern Europe, Soviet policy gave full support to vigorous and occasionally independent-minded Communist leaders in their effort to establish and consolidate revolutionary regimes. Despite the 1944 percentage agreement with Churchill (see Chapter 3), the Soviets tolerated, if they did not actively support, the efforts of Albania, Bulgaria, and Yugoslavia to infiltrate northern Greece and to help set up a Communist government in that war-wracked country. In France and Italy the large Communist parties participated in coalition regimes and did their best to infiltrate the essential organs of government. Similarly, in such countries as Iran, Japan, China, Indochina, Malaya, Korea, and the Philippines, the Soviets gave such assistance as they could to local Communist movements.

In this fashion the Soviet leaders sought to maintain a fighting morale within their country and to take advantage of the many opportunities for extending their influence abroad that were available in the aftermath of a terrible war. In spring 1947, when the United States announced its determination to use the Truman Doctrine and the Marshall Plan to stem the tide of Soviet influence, the Soviet government took up the challenge. A new propaganda weapon, the Communist Information Bureau (Cominform), was established in September 1947, and Stalin's colleague Andrei Zhdanov announced that the world was now divided between the "imperialist" camp of the United States and the "anti-imperialist" camp of the Soviet Union.

Despite this defiant attitude, a significant change occurred in the party line in 1948 in regard to European affairs. The firm Western policy in occupied Germany and the conclusion of the Brussels treaty by the Western European states in March 1948, forming the basis for NATO, showed the Soviets that the West meant business. In the light of this show of determination, Soviet policy in Europe changed from efforts at expansion to the consolidation of gains already made. But the consequences were no less brutal than in the past, as Stalin's paranoia spread throughout the Soviet empire. In Eastern Europe Soviet agents arranged to have the more independent and national-minded Communist leaders eliminated, ordering the execution of many of them on trumped-up charges. In the case of Yugoslavia, which was not directly under Soviet control, the Soviet Union tried to undermine Tito's position by charging him with numerous acts of disloyalty. This policy resulted in a tighter Soviet grip on the Eastern European states already under its control, but it also brought a weakening of Soviet influence in Yugoslavia and in Western Europe. This partial retreat in Europe, however, was matched by a more active policy in Asia. The 1949 victory of the Chinese Communists, who had received extensive Soviet aid, was now used as a springboard for aggression elsewhere. In June 1950, in an effort to take over the entire country, the North Korean Communists, trained and assisted by the Soviets, attacked South Korea, which had been under U.S. occupation. In the ensuing Korean War, a massive propaganda effort was made throughout Asia to identify the Soviet Union with Asian nationalism and the United States with European imperialism.

Stalin's Successors: An Opportunity for Change?

Because so much of what happened in the Soviet Union before and after World War II was tied up with the personality of Stalin, it was to be expected that the dictator's death on March 5, 1953, would create some confusion. However despotic and ruthless Stalin may have been, he was also the only leader that the average Soviet citizen had known. The myth of Stalin was all-pervasive. All victories in the war were attributed to him; all achievements in Soviet science and industry were supposedly due to his inspired leadership and genius; and, in an odd way, the mythic Stalin was even considered a sort of father figure to the Soviet people, much as the czars had once had a fatherly

---

General Secretaries (or First Secretaries) of the Communist Party of the Soviet Union

Josef Stalin	April 1922–March 5, 1953
Georgi Malenkov	March 5, 1953–March 15, 1953
Nikita Khrushchev	March 15, 1953–October 14, 1964
Leonid Brezhnev	October 14, 1964–November 10, 1982
Yuri Andropov	November 11, 1982–February 9, 1984
Konstantin Chernenko	February 13, 1984–March 10, 1985
Mikhail Gorbachev	March 11, 1985–August 24, 1991

---

relationship with Russian peasants a century earlier. He was enigmatic but seemingly wise, tough but supposedly fair, and ostensibly purposeful in the way in which he administered justice throughout Soviet society. Thus when the news of the tyrant's death was released, some Soviet citizens cried openly in the city streets.

Yet for those who had worked closely with Stalin, there was no mystery at all to the dictator's methods. Indeed, many of the Communist party elite welcomed the idea of relaxing their regime's centralized controls at once and ending the state-sponsored purges, if only to save their own skins. Under Georgi Malenkov, who succeeded Stalin as prime minister from 1953 to 1955, a new phase of Soviet politics was therefore introduced that went under the name of the New Course. In economic policy the New Course called for a marked increase in consumer goods and more generous terms for agriculture. This was accompanied by a "thaw" in the cultural sphere, with wider freedom for writers and artists. In politics there was a marked change from the unqualified glorification of Stalin that had characterized the party line. Now politicians decried the cult of Stalin's personality and claimed that the Soviet Union should have a "collective leadership" in which no single individual was dominant.

Malenkov's New Course lasted only two years. By 1955, Communist party First Secretary Nikita Khrushchev had achieved the lead position in Soviet policymaking that lasted until his enforced retirement in 1964 (though Bulganin served as prime minister from 1955 to 1958). In this phase of the party line, heavy industry was again given precedence, but much of the spirit of the New Course still remained. There was a steady improvement in the supply of consumer goods. For the first time, party policy favored economic and social reforms that relaxed somewhat the bureaucratic centralization of Stalin's day and gave a new generation of party leaders around the country greater initiative. Public criticism of the government was permitted within

Nikita Khrushchev, first secretary of the Communist party from 1953 to 1964, was one of the most outspoken Soviet leaders. This photo was taken October 20, 1960, at a meeting of the fifteenth General Assembly of the United Nations, just after Khrushchev had pounded the table with his shoe in order to get the attention of the assembled delegates. Such boorish behavior contributed to Khrushchev's eventual overthrow by other Soviet leaders. In the second photo, Khrushchev (second from right) greets a U.S. delegation sent to observe the "elections" to the Supreme Soviet in 1958. To Khrushchev's right is Cyril Black, Princeton University historian and an author of this book. Also pictured (left to right) are Richard Scammon, an expert on electoral behavior; Hedley Donovan, managing editor of Fortune magazine; and an interpreter. (Top photo from AP/Wide World Photos; bottom photo from Right Places, Right Times by Hedley Donovan. Copyright © 1989 by Hedley Donovan. Reprinted by permission of Henry Holt and Company, Inc.)

certain limits, and foreigners were allowed to visit the country under conditions similar to those that had existed for a short time in the early 1930s.

In the realm of foreign affairs, the Communist party in 1956 formally adopted the view that international war was not inevitable, and Khrushchev himself proclaimed a policy of "peaceful coexistence." Such a policy did not mean that the Soviet Union accepted the coexistence of other social systems on a long-term basis but rather that it expected the worldwide victory of communism to take place gradually by means short of international war—which no one wanted in any case because of the development of nuclear weapons. These other means especially included assistance to Communist parties seeking to gain power in other countries, by peaceful means if possible and by means of domestic revolution if necessary, until the Communist countries achieved a preponderance in world affairs. This policy was successful in Cuba, but in other countries it was confronted by a growing determination on the part of the United States and its allies to support the forces of moderation. The Soviet approach also met an unforeseen obstacle when Communist China demanded more vigorous and aggressive support for Communist revolutions than was contemplated under the policy of "peaceful coexistence." Soviet-Chinese relations were further exacerbated by military clashes in 1968–1969 in the Ussuri River frontier zone in Manchuria and by an understandable Soviet reluctance to share atomic secrets.

For a while Soviet policy was nevertheless successful in winning friends among the uncommitted states. Khrushchev and his colleagues paid official visits to many countries in Europe and Asia in an effort to convince foreign opinion that the image of a relentlessly aggressive policy current in Stalin's later years was a false one. Moreover, Soviet technical achievements, as evidenced by the launching of the first artificial earth satellite in October 1957, contributed to the impression of a strong and self-reliant Soviet state that no longer had to resort to the type of bullying that characterized Stalin's regime. At the same time, there was no change in the underlying Soviet vision of an idealized world still to come. Khrushchev, like Stalin, assumed that the victory of communism all over the world was the ultimate goal. Certain "different roads to socialism" were permitted to the states of Eastern Europe, but when a Hungary revolted or a Yugoslavia insisted on pursuing an independent policy, Khrushchev used all the means at his command to bring such heretics into line or to banish them from the Marxist camp entirely.

There was also an occasional element of adventurism in Khrushchev's foreign policy. In 1962 he sought secretly to establish missile and bomber bases in Cuba, partly to offset similar U.S. bases in Turkey. He apparently failed to predict the U.S. reaction, which was to blockade Cuba. The Soviets agreed to halt the construction of missile bases and withdraw their weapons. Shortly thereafter, the United States removed its missiles from Turkey. This misadventure was one of the arguments Khrushchev's colleagues used when they ousted him in 1964 (see Chapter 4 for further factors contributing to his removal).

The principal change in the party line introduced by Leonid Brezhnev and Aleksei Kosygin when they came to power in October 1964 was a new concentration of effort on the problems of agriculture. For the first time since the inauguration of the five-year plans in 1928, Soviet leaders recognized that the long-term emphasis on heavy industry had resulted in critical imbalances within the Soviet economy. Khrushchev had dealt with these problems by means of temporizing measures and flamboyant administrative reorganization, but the time had now come to make fundamental changes in the pattern of Soviet economic development. This concern with the domestic crisis was reflected in a cautious and conciliatory approach to foreign affairs that sought to prevent the hostilities in Vietnam and the continued antagonism of Communist China from distracting Soviet energies from internal affairs.

The results of the policies launched by Brezhnev and Kosygin did not come up to their hopes, and by 1970 they were facing a major crisis in the form of a serious stagnation of economic growth. The central problem appeared to be that no one in the Soviet leadership was able to make a satisfactory choice in the allocation of their resources among the various goals they were seeking to reach. True, the space program was cut back substantially, and Soviet scientists watched glumly as the U.S. astronauts made two landings on the moon in 1969. But on the really tough questions, such as the difficult choice between investment in defense and investment in economic growth, Soviet leaders continually vacillated. Over the long haul, the record revealed only an ongoing alternation between the two goals that served simply to slow down economic growth without meeting the needs of military security. In a major report to the Central Committee at the end of 1969, Brezhnev announced that relatively lower rates of growth would continue to prevail for the immediate future.

It was around this time, however, that he and his colleagues first began to think that, by taking decisive efforts to reduce outstanding tensions with the West, they might be able to lessen some of the economic burdens of high levels of military spending and simultaneously open their country to an infusion of Western European and U.S. capital and credits. Yet although this idea did lead to the achievements of the détente period of the early 1970s— the signing of the Moscow treaty with West Germany and the beginning of the SALT negotiations—the hoped-for new direction in Soviet domestic policy still eluded the country's leaders. There was much that remained unchangeable about the USSR. One source of the Soviets' problems was that they refused to abandon the notion that the Communist party as such, a highly elitist organization, still had a "leading role" to play in all aspects of Soviet life.

The Soviet Order

The Political System

Since World War II the commanding position of the Communist party had been the central feature of the Soviet political system. To an ever increasing extent, the party served as the brain of the USSR, stimulating a nervous system that reached into every nook and cranny of Soviet life.

In the mid-1980s the membership of the Communist party, including candidate members, numbered about 19 million. This figure represented some 7 percent of the entire population and almost one-third of the specialists working in the national economy. The party was thus kept relatively small in proportion to the population as a whole, for reasons of discipline and cohesion, but it was very strongly represented in all positions involving specialized knowledge and decisionmaking. The great majority of its members had joined the organization after the 1930s, and few of them knew much about the Soviet Union that had existed before World War II. They were mainly young people, who at that time took for granted the predominant role of their party and were concerned primarily with economic and social development.

The war and the death of Stalin had been serious crises for the party, but it emerged from them stronger than ever before. In the later years of Stalin's administration, the formal structure of the party had borne little relation to its actual operation. Although party congresses were supposed to meet at regular intervals, the Nineteenth Congress did not meet until thirteen years after the Eighteenth Congress. Stalin paid little attention to the Central Committee, supposedly the governing body of the party; the Politburo, at the apex of party authority, rarely met as a formal body. Instead, Stalin completely personalized politics and policymaking by handing out assignments to the various members of the Politburo, and he also relied heavily on the agencies of the secret police to effect his command. At the Nineteenth Party Congress in 1952, a year before he died, Stalin made important changes in the governing body of the party. He almost doubled the size of the Central Committee and greatly expanded the Politburo, renaming it the Presidium. It appears Stalin took these steps with a view to bringing new and younger personnel into the two bodies in order to dilute and counterbalance the influence of the party veterans, whose rivalry the aging leader still apparently feared.

In this light, it is not hard to see why the Communist party enjoyed a new lease on life when Stalin finally passed from the scene. The new Presidium of the party may have included all of Stalin's principal associates in his later years, but its method of government changed significantly, symbolized by the restoration of its old name of Politburo. Most important was that, for the time being, no single individual emerged who could take Stalin's place. His successors made much of their "collective leadership," and indeed there was much more general discussion of policy among the top leaders. At the same time, with no predominant leader available to give the orders, the police could not retain the arbitrary power over high party members that it had exercised in Stalin's day. In July 1953 Lavrentii Beria, Stalin's chief of police, was removed from office, and five months later he and several of his principal subordinates were executed. Control of the police was placed in the hands of a Committee on State Security (known from its Russian initials as the KGB), subordinated to the ruling leadership; at least high party members were now free from the type of police supervision to which Stalin had formerly subjected them.

This relative relaxation in the relations of high party officials was accompanied by more orderly procedures in the conduct of party affairs, as reflected in the proceedings of the Twentieth Party Congress in 1956. Indeed, in what was probably the most sensational speech ever made in the Soviet Union, Khrushchev denounced Stalin's methods of government in decisive terms. He cited many examples of Stalin's arbitrary methods, asserting that "Stalin acted not through persuasion, explanation and patient cooperation with people, but by imposing his concepts and demanding absolute submission to his opinion. Whoever opposed this concept or tried to prove his viewpoint and the correctness of his position was doomed to removal from the leader collective and to subsequent moral and physical annihilation." Although this was a powerful statement against the cult of personality that characterized Stalin's regime, no meaningful change could come overnight. The "collective leadership," for example, soon began to look less collective. The elevation of Bulganin to the post of prime minister in February 1955, in place of Malenkov, was obviously carried out at Khrushchev's initiative. In March 1958 Khrushchev himself became prime minister, thus combining for the first time since Stalin's death (except for the initial days of Malenkov's regime) the top executive positions of both party and government. Indeed, it had already become clear from his many speeches and pronouncements at home and abroad that Khrushchev was the dominant personality in the government. Within the party, he had already consolidated his position in 1957 by dropping from the Politburo such veterans as Malenkov and Molotov.

Yet even at the height of his power, Khrushchev's authority within the party was not comparable to that of Stalin. He had some difficulty in winning over the Central Committee when he was outvoted on policy issues in the Politburo in July 1957, and there was much evidence of continuing discussion and disagreement on matters of policy among top leaders. In October 1964 a majority of the Politburo again voted against Khrushchev and this time were supported by the Central Committee. The two key positions held by Khrushchev were once again separated, with Brezhnev becoming general secretary of the party and Kosygin being appointed as prime minister.

Even with these signs of progress for the Soviet system, however, it was clear well into the 1980s that the method of Communist party rule still combined the strengths of centralized and authoritative political leadership with all of the weaknesses and uncertainties of a government by unrestrained individuals rather than by law. This is not to say that there was no method to the Soviet system; in many ways this type of single-party rule, as it existed until recently, was quite straightforward. The party was headed by the Politburo of the Central Committee, an executive body of around fourteen members and six candidate members. Its decisions were implemented by the Secretariat of the Central Committee, of which the general secretary, a Politburo member, was the head. The importance of this post is indicated by the small number of leaders—seven—who have held the position since its establishment in 1922 as the keystone of the party structure: Stalin, Malenkov, Khrushchev, Brezhnev, Andropov, Chernenko, and Gorbachev.

Below the Politburo sat the Central Committee, a body of some 300 members and 170 candidate members, which generally met twice a year and was elected by party congresses. In a purely formal sense, this was supposed to be the body that decided who would sit on the Politburo and the party Secretariat, although the powerful personalities in the latter posts actually guaranteed that the opposite was the case: They decided who would "elect" them. Nevertheless, the members of the Central Committee were virtually omnipotent in comparison to members of other institutions, thanks to the preeminent authority they enjoyed over the legislative and executive branches of the Soviet government: the Supreme Soviet (the country's titular parliament) and the system of state ministries (charged with the complex task of enacting party policy).

Until recently, the Communist party was able to maintain its preponderance in the Soviet Union by both direct and indirect methods. The most important direct control was the appointment of key officials and the formulation and implementation of policy. As all of the major positions in the government were held by leading party members, there was no meaningful distinction between state interests and party interests. Then, too, the Secretariat of the Central Committee exerted control by using its twenty-plus departments to monitor all major appointments in the government and in public organizations, to verify the implementation of all policies, and to censor all publications. In addition to its own staff, the Secretariat was able to draw on the services of 440,000 primary party organizations. These represented party members in all enterprises and institutions and constituted the nerve ends of the party's system of controls and communication.

Other indirect controls available to the party were through the various public organizations that nominally led an autonomous life but in fact served party purposes and were regulated by the party as "transmission belts" for the implementation of its policies. The most important transmission belts were the Supreme Soviet; the Central Council of Trade Unions, with 68 million members, which performed many public functions in addition to its responsibility for labor relations and welfare; and the Komsomol, or Communist Youth League, with 21 million members. These and other bodies served to organize "the masses" and to educate and guide them in the direction the party desired.

This brief description of the party-dominated governmental structure may convey the impression that authority flowed smoothly from party to government and from government to economic, social, and intellectual life. Recognition that this in fact was not always the case helps in understanding the manifold problems that beset the Soviet Union by the 1980s. Once agreement on policy was reached in the Politburo, there did exist a certain simplicity in the chain of command as compared with other forms of government. Yet it was in reaching a policy decision that the degree of centralization of the Soviet system further complicated the problems of decisionmaking inherent in any form of government. Soviet political life was always fraught with controversies, and as the economic and social structures became more complex, the controversies became more profound. In fundamental matters, such as the allocation of resources, the party quite frequently became incapable of meeting all the demands of the wide variety of interest groups that constituted Soviet society—the armed forces, the different branches of heavy and light industry, the state and collective farms, the educational and research institutions, and the various republics with their national subdivisions.

When Stalin was the USSR's undisputed leader, controversies over such trade-offs as those between consumer goods and capital goods, heavy industry and agriculture, and economic rationality and political control were carried on at a lower level and resulted in the purge of many thousands of party members. Yet with every year that passed after his death, these issues were increasingly brought into the open in the public statements of political leaders and interest groups, with the consequence that the party leadership itself became overburdened with the demands put before it. If the Politburo chose to favor the interests of one group over another, it ran the risk of being accused of favoritism. However, if it tried to satisfy all groups simultaneously, it was in danger of quickly exhausting the scarce resources available to solve problems. All too often in the 1970s, during the height of Brezhnev's leadership of the Soviet Union, the party chose to avoid potential conflicts by simply doing nothing, which only aggravated existing problems and tensions.

As a result, the Soviet elite entered the 1980s with an ongoing controversy among its leading members as to the course they should pursue and no clear plan for resolving their differences. The most salient issue was the continuing validity of centralized planning, held to be inviolable by some party members, and the contrasting efforts of others to make the economy more efficient by experimenting with limited forms of market economy and enterprise initiative. Leaders whose main careers had been as Communist party secretaries and whose principal concern was party control often stood in opposition to officials whose careers had been in the central bureaucracy, where the main concern was economic growth and social change. Division also existed between those who wished to pursue an aggressive foreign policy and favored a large military budget and those who believed that the main emphasis should be placed on domestic development. Finally, there was a marked generational difference among the top leaders. The leaders of Brezhnev's generation were proud of the way the Soviet Union had developed, despite its flaws. They compared the achievements of the 1970s with the harsh years of the 1930s and the wartime hardships, and they saw their country on a steady course of improvement. In contrast, a younger generation of leaders, many of whose political careers had started after the Stalin era, was inclined to compare the Soviet Union not with the Soviet past but with Western Europe, the United States, and Japan. These younger leaders realized that the gap between the USSR and the West was growing rather than narrowing, and they were painfully aware that no other countries—including those under Communist leadership—regarded the Soviet Union any longer as a model of successful economic and social development.

Economic Policy

Nothing can have been more difficult for many Soviet leaders than to admit the depth of their economic problems. Throughout the postwar period, the primary concern of the Communist party was the USSR's industrial development. If Marxism-Leninism was supposed to succeed at anything in the great competition with the West, it was in its ability to provide an alternative path to modernity to that represented by the supposedly repressive capitalist system. Rapid economic growth of the kind prophesied by the country's early leaders requires heavy investment, and it was one of the principal achievements of the Soviet system that it was able to enforce such heavy investments over a long period despite the high human costs involved. Under Stalin's leadership, new industrial towns sprang up throughout the country, the central Asian periphery was modernized, and the Soviet people for the first time began to believe that they could successfully catch up with the West. This emphasis on rapid growth had its costs, primarily the draining of resources from other branches of the economy. Agriculture, housing, consumer goods, and the real income of workers were all sacrificed on the pyre of heavy industrial development. Yet most party members happily defended their choice of keeping much of the economy poor in order to make industry prosper. In Communist eyes, the goal of industrial strength justified the means used to obtain it.

As the largest country in the world in area and the third most populous, the USSR could also draw on a wide range of physical and human resources in implementing its policy of rapid industrialization. In gross national product, a popular but not entirely adequate measure, Communist ideologues pointed out with satisfaction that their country had risen from fifth in rank before 1917 to second in the 1970s, following only the United States among the large industrial societies. (In per capita GNP, however, it ranked about twentieth, about the same as before 1917.) Yet it was in the rate of growth that well-intentioned Soviet planners had grounds for concern. For the period 1950–1980, the broad Soviet GNP growth rate of 4.8 percent was in the middle range of the rates of other advanced industrial societies. But this was achieved under a system with rapidly dwindling potential that led to a crisis by 1980. This crisis was reflected in the decline of the annual rate of growth of GNP from almost 6 percent in the 1950s to about 5.1 percent in the 1960s and 3.4 percent in the 1970s. It was down to about 1 percent by 1980.

The failure of the USSR to sustain a higher rate of growth than a considerable number of countries employing much less drastic methods of government led Soviet leaders to an understandable reassessment of their system. This reevaluation was in fact initiated by Khrushchev, and his denunciation of Stalin was a necessary first step in opening the debate. In his insistence on the predominance of heavy industry, however, Khrushchev remained very much a Stalinist himself, claiming that only "pseudo theoreticians" would argue that "at some stage of socialist construction the development of heavy industry ceases to be the main task and that light industry can and should overtake all other branches of industry." Nevertheless, it was not just Khrushchev who was at fault but the whole Soviet system, with its emphasis on bigness and growth at all costs.

The problems facing the economy can be considered under two categories: management and the allocation of resources. The extreme administrative centralization Stalin favored served a useful purpose at a time when the economy was in a relatively early stage of development and a first generation of managers was still being trained. As the economy became more complex, however, centralization became a serious handicap to development. Khrushchev understood this and in 1957 reorganized the system of management, dissolving 141 industrial ministries at the Union and republic levels. In their place he created 104 regional economic councils, each with the authority to regulate the fulfillment of the plan within its region. A further reform in 1962 reduced the number of regional economic councils to forty, and management was reorganized to conform more closely to the governmental pattern. Finally, in 1963 Khrushchev established a Supreme Economic Council as a kind of supercabinet concerned with economic management. These reforms were essentially reorganizations of the party and government agencies, however, and did not mark a departure from the tradition of detailed bureaucratic supervision of the economy. There was some limited experimentation (known as Libermanism, after the economist who proposed the system) with planning production in consumer industries on the basis of market demand rather than on central plans. But this orientation toward a market economy was not widely adopted and did not mark a basic change in Soviet methods of planning and management.

A further complication for the Soviet leaders was their nation's need either to emulate or to borrow Western technology in order to accelerate the productivity of their own economy. Traditionally, less-developed countries have bought the technology of other countries, thus enabling them to modernize their production capacity rapidly. This is of course possible only if a nation's currency is convertible to other currencies on the open market. But the constant challenge for the USSR's leaders was that the Soviet ruble was not convertible. In order for Moscow to obtain Western goods, it either had to acquire them through espionage or had to get foreign hard currencies to use in exchange for those goods. For years, the Soviets sold wheat to the West; then they sought to obtain hard currencies by selling natural gas to European nations, weapons to Third World countries, and tourist trips through their own country. So long as the Soviet Union lacked an open economy, however, currency convertibility was unimaginable, and hence it was almost impossible for the Soviets to trade most of their goods on the world market.

Society and Culture

In October 1957 the Soviets surprised the world with the announcement that they had launched the first artificial earth satellite, or sputnik. For the Communist party, this achievement was naturally a matter of great pride. For the rest of the world, it served as dramatic evidence of the level science and technology had reached in the USSR. Yet here, too, questions could be raised about the costs of centralized control for the social and cultural well-being of the Soviet people.

In exercising its all-embracing controls over Soviet life, the Communist party went to great lengths to support those aspects of society and culture that it considered essential to the development of a powerful state. The most striking feature was the strong position established by the ruling elite, which comprised the bulk of the Communist party membership as well as nonparty technicians in many fields. The contrast between this "new class," as it was often called, and the rest of the population, however, tended to create a glaring contradiction with the egalitarian ideals of early Marxism. Many members of this new class lived comfortably indeed. They were generally the ones who acquired television sets, refrigerators, and other household appliances when Soviet industry began to turn them out in small quantities, and they also enjoyed significant privileges in housing and consumer goods not available to the rest of the population. What was most important from the party's viewpoint, however, was that the benefits they received and the prestige accorded them effectively assured their loyalty to the regime.

Not all aspects of Soviet social policy were negative. Education, and especially technical training, received strong support from the state. Compulsory eight-year schooling was established, and an important effort was made to improve the conditions of study by introducing boarding schools. Greater emphasis was also placed on higher education, which even today remains the principal gate of entry into the privileged elite and is therefore highly prized. Soviet expenditures per student in higher education equal those in most Western countries.

Strong government support was also given to research in all fields, particularly in natural sciences and mathematics. Advanced research was organized under the Academy of Sciences of the USSR, with over 120 institutes and tens of thousands of employees at all levels, allowing a focus on projects applicable in such high-priority areas as national defense and economic development. In the field of nuclear research, for instance, Soviet scholars kept abreast of Western science until World War II interrupted their work. In 1949 they conducted their first nuclear fission test and in 1953 tested thermonuclear fusion weapons. Similarly, in producing industrial atomic power stations, nuclear accelerators, earth satellites, and intercontinental missiles, they matched, and in some cases surpassed, the work of Western scientists. Less attention was paid, however, to biology, medicine, and other fields of science not closely related to state power.

Excellent work was done in the performing arts, which was supported by a large network of training schools and theaters. The Russian Ballet was able to retain the world-renowned quality it held since imperial days and lavished great attention on the production of classical works. Classical ballet techniques were also adapted to folk themes, as exemplified by the famous Moiseyev dancers, who were allowed to tour the United States. In these respects, the performing arts, like the ornate architecture of Soviet public buildings, served to stress the power of the state and to provide in some measure a substitute for the comforts that the masses lacked in their private lives. In the creative arts, in contrast, state support was frequently accompanied by very rigid party controls. Musical themes and forms were literally dictated by the party; compositions failing to adhere to such standards were severely criticized.

Understandably, the Soviets' achievements in creating a strong and generally loyal elite and in developing such fields as technical education, scientific research, and the performing arts received global approbation. At the same time, other countries recognized the high price of these accomplishments. The material restrictions imposed on the great majority of the Soviet people were particularly striking. Although a small proportion could hope to join the elite through the gate of higher education, the conditions for most improved only moderately in the course of a generation of rapid economic growth. The strain of Soviet life was clearly reflected in the evidence that the standard of living, which had been gaining on that of Western Europe in the 1960s, was falling behind again in the 1970s and 1980s. In the 1970s, there was a rise in the death rate. For a variety of reasons, including alcoholism and a broad decline in the quality of medical care, infant mortality was three times as high as in the United States, and the mortality of males aged twenty to forty-four years was three times that of females in the same age group. More generally, the gradual rate of improvement in living standards had slowed considerably by the 1970s and 1980s, and the hopes of earlier decades for a brighter future were significantly dimmed.

Apart from the question of material welfare before the Gorbachev era, there were also sweeping restrictions on human rights that affected the entire Soviet population. In all areas of Soviet life, the Communist party was supreme, and no views could be expressed in public unless they were within the rather limited framework approved by the party. In matters of property and administration, justice may have been theoretically available through recourse to the courts. Yet in matters relating to politics, the interests of the state as perceived by the party took precedence over law. All forms of expression were regarded as instruments of party propaganda, and every effort was made to impose a rigid pattern on people's thinking.

A special problem of human rights was represented by the desire of a substantial number of the 2 million Jews in the Soviet Union to emigrate. This became a particularly acute issue between the Soviet Union and the United States in the 1970s and 1980s. Some 265,000 Jews were allowed to leave between 1968 and 1985, but this emigration was linked to other policy issues. The highest levels of emigration, of between 30,000 and 50,000 people a year, were reached between 1972 and 1974, when the Soviets hoped to get more favorable terms of trade, and between 1978 and 1980, during the period of the SALT II arms control negotiations (see Chapter 5). In later years emigration dropped to as low as 1,000 a year. In the late 1980s, however, a number of prominent Jewish citizens were permitted to emigrate, but a great many more were still languishing in the category of refuseniks—individuals whose visa applications were refused but who had lost their jobs and status in society.

The Gorbachev Era

"New Thinking" About the Soviet Union

Many accounts of the revolutionary changes in the Soviet Union since the rise of Gorbachev in 1985 tend to emphasize only the personality of Gorbachev himself and the paradoxical impact of his vision for Soviet society on

The Soviet Union in 1985

the history and politics of the USSR. Surely Gorbachev's importance should not be understated. However, there is good reason to think that many Soviets were already aware of the manifold challenges facing their country in the period before 1985, even if they had only very tentatively begun to evince the kinds of critiques about their political and economic system that would later become known as "new thinking."

During the Brezhnev era, for example, one of the most important developments had been the gradual but sure erosion of the way in which many Communist intellectuals perceived their ideology. Khrushchev was the last of the top leaders who adhered to the form of Marxism-Leninism that had prevailed during Stalin's administration. This perspective held that the class struggle was the engine of historical change and that, as a result of the 1917 revolution, the Soviet Union was the most advanced society because it was the first in which the working class had come to power. Khrushchev predicted that the Soviet Union would "overtake and surpass" the United States in the economic and social spheres by 1980 and that it would thereafter become the world's most advanced society. He expressed this view more crudely in his typically pungent style when he declared in 1956 at a Kremlin reception for Western ambassadors: "History is on our side. We will bury you." He did not mean kill and bury, of course, but simply that capitalism would in due time give way to socialism and communism.

Soviet leaders of the younger generation were already questioning this view, and they were greatly stimulated by ideological developments in Eastern Europe. In the early postwar years, ideological pressures moved from the Soviet Union to Eastern Europe, as the Soviets imposed their views on the other countries in their sphere of influence. The Eastern European countries were nevertheless closer intellectually as well as physically to developments in Western Europe, and they were more aware of the ways in which science and technology were affecting economic and social change. A particularly influential statement of these trends was set forth in 1966 in *Civilization at the Crossroads: Social and Human Implications of the Scientific and Technological Revolution,* a collaborative work edited by Radovan Richta and published under the auspices of the Czechoslovak Academy of Sciences. This treatise went so far as to conclude that "socialism and communism stand or fall" depending on their ability to harness science and technology. It further stressed that "everyone should realize that without a scientific and technological revolution the new society must perish." No Communist-sponsored publication before this had ever suggested that socialism might "fall." Thus the significance of Western developments in the new technologies came to be recognized in the Soviet Union.

In March 1970 the physicist Andrei Sakharov wrote a letter to party leaders stressing the significance of the second industrial revolution and warned that the Soviet Union was steadily falling behind the West. The challenge was tacitly acknowledged in 1971 when Brezhnev stated in a major speech that "the task we face, comrades, is one of historical importance: *organically to fuse the achievements of the scientific and technical revolution with the advantages of the socialist economic system*, to unfold our own intrinsically socialist forms of fusing science and production" (italics in the original published version). In effect, Brezhnev was admitting that the advancement of knowledge rather than the class struggle was the engine of historical change, a view synonymous with that underlying the concept of economic and political modernization as understood in the West, Japan, and China. The desire to catch up with the more advanced industrial societies now formed the basis for the policy of détente, which involved maintaining good relations with the West as a basis for increasing trade, getting loans, and acquiring Western technology. Détente with the United States broke down after the Soviet occupation of Afghanistan in 1979, but friendly relations continued with Western Europe and Japan.

During his long administration, Brezhnev had led the Soviet Union toward a form of socialism that stressed stability and relative egalitarianism. Prominent political leaders as well as average workers were assured tenure in their jobs. Subsidies for food, housing, and transportation made the standard of living secure at a rather low but still theoretically rising level. There was also much evidence of social development in this period. For example, the number of Soviet citizens with higher education rose from 5.5 million in 1959 to 22 million in 1984. Various forms of economic benefits were offered to the Eastern European members of the Warsaw Pact, and Cuba was subsidized by the purchase of its sugar crop at prices above the world level. Within the Soviet Union, especially in Central Asia, with its large Muslim population, investments in industry, urban development, and education contributed to a tentative sense of well-being. At the same time, the negative manifestations of Brezhnevism also became apparent. Corruption in many forms became much more prevalent than in the Stalin era. More important, this form of socialist welfare state—comparable to that in some Western countries—proved to be such a heavy financial burden that it became one of the most prominent factors contributing to the Soviet Union's steadily declining growth rates.

The first of the Soviet leaders seeking to reform this system was not Gorbachev but Andropov, who was already sixty-eight when he became general secretary in 1982. He brought many younger leaders into top positions and started the country on the road to a searching reevaluation of its old policies. Upon his death of kidney failure two years later, he was succeeded by Chernenko, a member of the older generation, who was scarcely interested in changing anything and died a year later of emphysema. It was only against this background that Gorbachev was selected to be general secretary in 1985 at the age of fifty-four. He had been promoted to the top ranks of Communist party leadership by Andropov, and it was not long before he proceeded to replace most of the members of the old guard with people of his own generation.

The new party line under Gorbachev soon became apparent and was made explicit in his speeches at the Twenty-seventh Party Congress in February 1986 and at the January and June meetings of the Central Committee. It was perhaps no better summarized than in two terms that quickly gained currency in the Soviet Union and abroad: *glasnost* and *perestroika*. As Gorbachev used both of these terms over time, it became clear, perhaps just as much to Gorbachev himself as to those who were observing him, that the new general secretary was embarking on what amounted to a revolution in the Soviet system.

Glasnost *and* Perestroika

Glasnost, which means "openness" or "publicity," is probably the simpler to understand of the two famous terms. It refers to nothing less than the abandonment of many of the control characteristics of Soviet political and cultural life, as it evolved under Stalin, and a concerted effort to discuss the errors of the past and open contemporary problems to public criticism. Under this policy, for example, Sakharov, the Nobel Prize winner and civil rights leader, was brought back from the city of Gorki, where he had been exiled in 1981, and encouraged to appear on television and meet with visiting foreign dignitaries. There were limits to the permissible freedom, but a whole range of long-suppressed views were discussed in the press, literature, the theaters, and films. In Moscow and Leningrad (now known again by its prerevolutionary name, St. Petersburg) first only a few and then numerous political clubs were formed, some of which sought to play the role of a loyal opposition; eventually, these provided the basis for the first non-Communist parties in the Soviet Union. All along, the purpose of *glasnost* was fairly clear: to expose social wounds so that they could be attended to and to give public opinion a larger role in the formulation and implementation of policy. More important, the whole question of openness was central to the Soviet Union's quest to be a modern society. Whereas Brezhnev had recognized that the advancement of human knowledge had become the engine of political and economic power in the modern world, Gorbachev was prepared to go further and let knowledge flow freely in a last-ditch effort to catch up with the Western polities and Japan.

The policy of promoting *glasnost* received an early test in April 1986, when the explosion of a reactor at the Chernobyl nuclear plant resulted in the world's worst nuclear-reactor disaster. The fallout spread across Europe from Scandinavia to Great Britain and as far south as Italy, causing widespread contamination of agriculture and livestock. The Europeans immediately became aware of the fallout, but Moscow remained silent for several days. It seemed as though the traditional Soviet policy of secrecy was still intact. The

The leadership of Mikhail Gorbachev as the head of the Communist party of the Soviet Union supports the theory that individuals do have the power to change the course of history. Although many Western observers were initially skeptical of his policies of perestroika and glasnost, Gorbachev began a full-scale assault on the inefficiency and inhumanity of many aspects of the socialist system. He also unintentionally set in motion a train of events that led to the complete disintegration of the Soviet empire in Eastern Europe and unleashed forces for revolutionary change within the Soviet Union itself. (Photo courtesy of the German Information Center.)

Soviets finally gave wide publicity to the disaster, although critics have claimed that its full extent was not made clear for some years. Since that crisis, and in part because of its undeniable significance, the Soviet media became increasingly bold in reporting such phenomena. Major accidents, public demonstrations against the government, and critical opinions that previously would have been squelched received free play in the media. Indeed, within a matter of one or two years, Soviet television and print media had become almost as open as that of their Western counterparts (and a bit more lively). Virtually no subject was taboo, from crime, sex, and drug addiction to the personality of Gorbachev himself.

The concept of *perestroika*, literally "restructuring" or "reformation," is more complex. When Gorbachev, as well as Andropov, first used the word, it was in reference to the need for short-term measures to improve the functioning of the Soviet economy. It implied such steps as stricter labor discipline, suppression of corruption among the managerial elite, and the need for a campaign against alcoholism. With the new openness in the country's mass media, it was not long before the problems that had been brewing in the Soviet Union since Stalin's death, ranging from the party's arbitrary political practices to the mismanagement of the economy, presented themselves forcefully. If the Soviet Union were really to change its ways, really to "restructure," how could it afford any longer to paper over the manifold difficulties facing the USSR as it moved toward the twenty-first century?

On the eve of the official celebration of the seventieth anniversary of the Bolshevik Revolution in November 1987, Gorbachev himself answered this question with the publication of *Perestroika: New Thinking for Our Country and the World*, in which he set forth the radical philosophy underlying his reform program. On the very first page, Gorbachev asserted that:

> *Perestroika* is an urgent necessity arising from the profound processes of development of our socialist society. This society is ripe for change. It has long been yearning for it. Any delay in beginning perestroika could have led to an exacerbated internal situation in the near future, which, to put it bluntly, would have been fraught with serious social, economic and political crises. (p. 3)

He then went on to list in some detail the reasons why the Soviet rate of growth had declined to almost zero in the 1980s. His criticisms of Soviet failings were even harsher than those of hostile Western analysts. At the same time he predicted that the success of *perestroika* would demonstrate that socialism was the best system after all.

Looking abroad, Gorbachev stressed the complexity of the world today:

> It is diverse, variegated, dynamic and permeated with opposing trends and acute contradictions. It is a world of fundamental social shifts, of an all-embracing scientific and technological revolution, of worsening global problems—problems concerning ecology, natural resources, etc.—and of radical changes in information technology. It is a world in which unheard-of possibilities for development and progress lie side by side with abject poverty, backwardness, and medievalism. It is a world in which there are vast "fields and tension." (p. 121)

Unlike his predecessors, however, Gorbachev did not claim that the USSR had solutions to all of these problems but insisted instead that they called for international cooperation: "We say with full responsibility, casting away false considerations of 'prestige,' that all of us in the present-day world are coming to depend more and more on one another and are becoming increasingly necessary to one another" (p. 123). In particular, he emphasized (and his words are italicized in his book) that all of the states in the modern world needed to find new, safer means of carrying on the competition among them: "Nuclear war cannot be a means of achieving political, economic, ideological or any other goals" (p. 126).

On the international front, we have already seen (see Chapter 5 for details) some of the consequences of Gorbachev's desire to move away from past conflicts. His sudden readiness to meet with U.S. president Reagan, previously the embodiment of the Cold War for the USSR, and his government's willingness to enter into such arms control agreements as the 1987 ban on intermediate-range nuclear missiles, cannot be understood apart from the Soviet Union's desire to reduce its military expenditures. In other ways as well, the Soviets began to distance themselves from many of their international commitments. Starting in 1986 and 1987, for example, the Eastern European members of the Warsaw Pact were warned that they could no longer rely on Moscow to bail them out of their economic and political difficulties.

It was in the domestic challenge of *perestroika*, however, that Gorbachev proved to be most ambitious. Under the policy of restructuring initiated during Andropov's brief administration and pursued more vigorously under Gorbachev's leadership after 1985, far-reaching plans were set in motion to decentralize the economy. The initial steps involved the introduction of price incentives within the planned system and the encouragement of better labor performance with selectively higher wages. Beyond these beginnings loomed the much larger problem of reducing the role of central-planning bodies. It was also necessary to create an environment in which enterprises would respond to domestic and even to international market forces in setting prices, planning production, and controlling quality. Similarly, in agriculture means had to be found to encourage production by permitting a rise in prices to the extent that this could be done without meeting consumer resistance.

Indeed, the mechanism of reform was simple enough—as long as it did not have to take into account the many interests that resisted reform. Important among these was the vast personnel of the state bureaucracy and the parallel party officials who monitored production at all levels. The jobs of many thousands of these individuals were at stake if their functions were reduced or abolished. No less resistant were the industrial workers, whose relative security even at a low level would be threatened if enterprises were allowed to dismiss workers. Finally, the many millions of consumers who had become accustomed to subsidized food, housing, and transportation were distressed by the thought of having to pay the real cost of these services.

All of the economies of the advanced industrial societies are mixed, in the sense that both the government and the market play a role. Among the major countries, the government has played the least role in the United States and the greatest in the Soviet Union. The challenge to Gorbachev's reforms, as he and his advisers saw it, was not to move the Soviet economy from one extreme to the other but rather to move it toward the middle. In view of the great obstacles to reform, no one could realistically expect the Soviet Union to be transformed into a Japan. Even the reforms in China after the death of Mao Zedong were more drastic than anything that seemed possible in the USSR. The challenge to Gorbachev and his colleagues was to do their best given the nature of the Soviet environment. Only a few years after his rise

Regardless of their nationalities, many of the Soviet peoples were united by the common experience of having suffered through the bloodbath of World War II. Decades after the war's end, one still encountered elderly people (like the old man in this photo) who on special occasions wore the medals they had earned in the struggle against Nazi Germany. In the late 1980s these medals still commanded enough respect to permit their wearers a privileged place in the long lines for scarce commodities (such as those displayed in this, by Soviet standards, unusually well-stocked butcher shop). For average Soviet citizens much of the appeal of communism lay in the government's ability to provide them with basic necessities. The regime's growing recognition that it could no longer guarantee such provision was one of the underlying reasons for the success of Gorbachev's campaign for perestroika. (Left photo courtesy of Paul Christensen; bottom photo courtesy of Richard Brody.)

to power, nevertheless, the question widely posed was whether Gorbachev's good intentions were enough.

The Crisis of Soviet Reform

Because so many positive developments emerged during the period of Gorbachev's ascendancy, it does not seem likely that historians will be inclined to draft entirely negative assessments of his leadership of the Soviet Union. During his first five years in power, the Soviet general secretary was the architect of changes that went beyond the wildest dreams of those who had clamored for fundamental reforms in their country's domestic and foreign policy. However, despite the good, productive forces that Gorbachev facilitated by challenging the "old thinking" that had dominated Soviet policy-making, he also set in motion other, darker, and more unpredictable forces that threatened to undermine not only his economic and political reform program but the very existence of the USSR.

At the end of the 1980s and beginning of the 1990s, few Westerners could find much fault with the previously unfathomable changes that had taken place in Soviet foreign policy under Gorbachev. It was thanks to Gorbachev's leadership and the insight of key advisers such as his foreign minister, Eduard Shevardnadze, that the Soviet Union did not intervene in the intensifying pressures for democratic change in Poland and Hungary in the spring and summer of 1989 and in the popular eruptions throughout Eastern Europe that followed in the tumultuous autumn of that year. It was up to the Eastern European states themselves to "decide how to structure their societies and lives," Gorbachev told a surprised French president Mitterrand in July 1989; it was not appropriate for outside powers to get involved. This and other such statements, which effectively signaled the end of the Brezhnev Doctrine, undoubtedly played a major role in motivating hundreds of thousands of Eastern Europeans to go into the streets to protest against their dictatorial regimes. Without the threat that the Soviets would use tanks to keep their bloc allies in power, the Communist governments in Eastern Europe were revealed to be little more than hollow shells, lacking in most signs of popular legitimacy.

Probably the most important consequence of this Soviet hands-off policy was the opening of the Berlin Wall, which in turn set in motion the train of events leading to the reunification of Germany. With regard to the latter, Gorbachev's role was fundamental. He calmed the anxieties of many Soviet officials and average citizens who had experienced the horrors of the Nazi onslaught half a century earlier. In addition, he was instrumental in working out the intricate details of a German settlement (such as the schedule for withdrawal of Soviet troops from the former GDR and the new Germany's incorporation into NATO) at a historic meeting with FRG chancellor Kohl in July 1990 at the Caucasus mountain retreat of Zheleznovodsk.

None of these shifts in Soviet policy was completely magnanimous. Had that been the case, they probably never would have taken place. Gorbachev was clearly gambling that by prodding his country into a new manner of dealing with the outside world, he could help to erase the years of self-imposed isolation under which the USSR had long suffered. Thus when he spoke of constructing a "common European house" with his neighbors, Gorbachev was making a concerted bid to have the Western European democracies willingly accept the Soviet Union as one of their own. In this sense, the liberation of Eastern Europe was basically the price his country was willing to pay to become part of a world that had achieved much more, politically and economically, than had the USSR in its seventy-three-year experiment with socialism.

Gorbachev's other gamble, again positively received in the West, was with the Soviet political system and the attempt to introduce a true reign of law where only the arbitrariness of party governance had prevailed. It is doubtful that when Gorbachev first presided over a special July 1988 conference of party representatives in Moscow he fully appreciated the significance of the developments that he was unleashing. For four days, a wide-ranging public debate was held on problems facing *perestroika*, and numerous criticisms and proposals were aired on public television. By far the most dramatic change that came out of the conference, was the formation of a 2,250-member Congress of People's Deputies. This forum was to be elected by secret ballot and was charged with the task of selecting both a USSR president—Gorbachev assumed this post in 1989—and a smaller, streamlined Supreme Soviet to act as the country's main legislative body. At the time, it was hoped that these new parliamentary instruments would supplement the leading role of the Communist party, giving it new credibility and helping it to perform its complex tasks. Yet by May 1989, when the Congress of People's Deputies first convened, it was apparent that a political revolution was already under way in the USSR. The new body swiftly became a forum for acerbic attacks on the KGB, for the expression of ethnic dissatisfaction, and also for the jockeying for power and influence by rival factions within the official apparatus. Overnight, as Gorbachev himself shifted his attention from his post as party general secretary to the new office of the presidency, traditionally omnipotent Communist bodies, like the Secretariat and the Politburo, declined in importance. Finally, the "leading role" of the Communist party itself was removed from the Soviet constitution to allow for the proliferation of a host of new rival parties.

If these changes had occurred in a climate of economic and social stability, Gorbachev's reform movement might have been secured. But precisely because such challenges to the old order created new uncertainties, a stable and nurturing climate for the reforms was not present. One of the main problems the Soviet leader faced was the impossibility of arranging for the needed economic reforms to keep pace with the weighty political changes that had already occurred. By the end of the 1980s, the majority of Gorbachev's chief advisers were agreed about the desirability of taking radical steps to overhaul the Soviet economy. For example, there was desperate need for the country's price system to be thoroughly revised and for enterprise managers to be allowed greater autonomy. Yet nearly every time the regime sought to implement such reforms, its efforts immediately backfired. This occurred in large part because the reforms undermined other sectors of the economy and also because they almost always threatened the power of one important group or another. In response to rumors of higher prices, anxious consumers drained stores of their products, leading to ever increasing hoarding and shortages. Correspondingly, without reliable prices, enterprises remained as reluctant as ever to make decisions for themselves, with the consequence that they continued to see the socialist state as the sole source of inspiration (as well as subsidies) for what they were to produce. Under these circumstances, it was probably unavoidable that Gorbachev's economic reforms, inspiring at first, soon languished under the weight of governmental indecision and vacillation. By autumn 1990, the USSR even suffered from a food crisis because of private hoarding, inefficiencies in transport and delivery, and rampant black market corruption.

The realm of political reform might have seemed more hopeful were it not, ironically, for the presence of quite opposite tendencies among actual and potential political elites. Whereas Soviet economic planners were more and more uncertain and hesitant about tackling their country's problems, their political counterparts were filled with the ebullience and urgency that came from finding themselves suddenly liberated from the iron grasp of the Communist party. This spirit was hardly conducive to political stability or to the sober articulation of state goals. On his left, Gorbachev was confronted by a spate of new parties, ranging from the Democratic Platform (an offshoot of the old Communist party) to the Constitutional Democrats and to the Interregional Deputies Group of the Congress of People's Deputies, a growing array of popularly elected municipal governments, and even a number of individual challengers from among his closest circle of advisers. All of these forces had one trait in common, the conviction that their government should abandon all caution and immediately break all ties with the old institutional and ideological order of Soviet communism. Above all, this challenge was present in Gorbachev's personal rivalry with Boris Yeltsin, the former Moscow city party chief who in 1990 became the president of the Russian republic and used his independent base of power to revile the Soviet president in populist fashion for betraying the masses' desires for true democracy.

Former Moscow party boss Boris Yeltsin was originally one of Gorbachev's strongest
supporters. When the two men disagreed about the pace of socialist reform, Yeltsin
(who was the popularly elected president of the Russian republic) set out on his own
course, calling for radical changes in the management of the Soviet economy. His
defiance of the August 1991 coup won him enormous public approval, many Soviet
citizens considering Yeltsin to be their best hope for the country to succeed in its
experiment with democracy. Other observers, however, worried about the ominous
implications of Yeltsin's reliance upon old Russian nationalism and populism. (Photo
from Reuters/Bettmann.)

On the right, however, Gorbachev faced equally troubling challenges
from a heretofore unlikely coalition of frustrated Communists and entrenched
party bureaucrats, monarchists, followers of the Orthodox church, and
national extremists (like the anti-Semitic Memory Society, or Pamyat'), who
were united in their distrust of and anxiety about the pace of the Soviet
reforms. Criticism of Gorbachev and his policies was even evinced from
circles that had been at the forefront of attacks on the old Brezhnev regime.
The Nobel Prize–winning author Alexander Solzhenitsyn used a September
1990 article (entitled "How to Revitalize Russia") in the youth daily *Komso-
molskaya Pravda* to warn the Soviet president against, among other things,
unduly exposing his country to the corrupting influences of the "alien" West:
"The Iron Curtain did an excellent job of defending our country against
everything good in the West," Solzhenitsyn wrote, "but the curtain didn't

quite go all the way down, and allowed the liquid drug of a debauched and decadent 'pop mass culture' to ooze underneath, along with the most vulgar fashions and public displays—and our deprived youth greedily devoured this garbage."[1]

Gorbachev also faced the insurmountable challenge of having laid the foundations for nothing less than the disintegration of the USSR, at least as a moderately well functioning federal state. For years, experts knew that the Soviet federation was in trouble. The dominance of ethnic Russians in many key posts throughout the country had become a glaring inequity as the demographic equation had shifted and the number of births in the Central Asian republics had outstripped that of the European USSR. Many of the non-Russian peoples simply wanted to speak for themselves. Unfortunately, the combined impact of the increased level of information availed by the policy of *glasnost* and the Soviet Union's burgeoning economic difficulties, which seemed to hit the provinces even harder than the country's urban centers, proved to make the situation more explosive than anyone had expected.

At first many of the ethnic conflicts were confined to relatively narrow issues. In December 1986, when Moscow sought to replace the native (but also very corrupt) party secretary of Kazakhstan, Dinmukhamed Kunaev, with a Russian functionary, street riots broke out in the capital of Alma-Ata. Then in 1988 a virtual war erupted between the peoples of Azerbaijan and Armenia over the contested territory of Nagorno-Karabakh. It was not long before such disputes became pivotal for the USSR's future. Beginning in November 1988 with the Estonian government's proclamation of sovereignty and following in February 1989 with a like decree by the Lithuanian popular movement, Sajudis, all fifteen of the Soviet republics eventually proclaimed their independence from Moscow's control in one way or another.

Historians may one day conclude that it was these developments above all that led to the unraveling of key aspects of the revolutionary experiment with socialism that Gorbachev began in 1985. For though one might say with justice that the Soviet leader had succeeded in exposing many of the deficiencies of Marxism-Leninism that had dominated the politics and economics of the USSR since the first days of the revolution in 1917, there could also be little question that Gorbachev had led his country into a crisis with little way out. His own desperate efforts in the early 1990s to refashion some of the principles of order that had once held the country together certainly demonstrated that the Soviet president had not been prepared for the tumultuous and paradoxical consequences of his reform ideals. By this time, Gorbachev seemed to have made his peace with the idea that the Soviet Union would be moving beyond socialism as the ideology had traditionally been conceived in his country. But one consequence he could not accept was that the USSR itself might dissolve in the process.

The End of the Soviet Union

It was in this troubling context that most Westerners and not a few Soviet citizens were shocked in 1990 and 1991 by the appearance of a supposedly new and different Gorbachev who, far from living up to his early proclamations about the need for more democracy and openness, increasingly moved to consolidate all power in the USSR into his own hands and within the confines of his own presidential council. This was a Gorbachev who seemed less and less tolerant of his left-wing critics, preferring instead to turn for his counsel to conservative forces in the KGB and the state bureaucracies, a Gorbachev who steadily tightened control over the official media, insisting that they serve only his purposes, and who was ready to empower the secret police with the authority to quash so-called economic crimes, like the black market. It was also a Gorbachev who turned a blind eye on his military's moves to restore order in the republics and among the ethnic minorities, as was the case in early 1991, when Soviet tanks were dispatched to the Baltic states of Lithuania and Latvia in a brutal attempt to reestablish Moscow's control over its dissident nationalities.

Shevardnadze seemed to say it all only a few weeks earlier when he resigned his post as foreign minister, proclaiming that the ugly specter of dictatorship was looming on the Soviet horizon. But was it necessarily Gorbachev who was uppermost in his mind and the Soviet president himself who was principally to blame for the negative political tendencies emerging from Moscow? This type of question will trouble future historians partly because Gorbachev's personal contribution to his country's political and economic reawakening was so great. It will be troubling also because the task of changing the USSR in any fundamental sense was indisputably of a different order than those challenges any of the developed European states had had to meet. The kinds of problems facing a Germany, a France, or a Great Britain in the modern age—the necessity of continuing ethnic integration, the expansion of civil rights, the provision of routine social services, the balancing of leaner budgets—may have seemed difficult on occasion. But they were by no means as daunting as those facing a country on the brink of economic chaos and lacking many of the key traditions and institutions necessary to resolve social and political conflict peacefully.

For this reason, many West Europeans who looked on with despair at Gorbachev's growing authoritarian proclivities in the 1990s were inclined to give the Soviet leader the benefit of the doubt. If Gorbachev himself were not in power, many asked themselves rhetorically, how could one be confident that he would not be replaced by an even more dictatorial personality? Midway through 1991, in fact, these observers found some comfort in their judgment when Gorbachev, ever the tactician, swung back to the course of reform. He endorsed a plan to redefine the nature of the USSR: The plan

Few people were prepared for the events of August 19, 1991, when tanks and troops appeared in Red Square just outside of the Kremlin, signaling an attempted coup against Gorbachev's reform government. Gorbachev was placed under house arrest in the Crimea, while in Moscow Soviet citizens braced themselves for the imposition of a new dictatorship. Less than three days later, though, it became clear that the coup plotters did not have the full backing of the military. The tanks were withdrawn, and Gorbachev returned to the capital, hoping somehow to restore order in his troubled country. (Photo from Reuters/Bettmann.)

promised greater autonomy to the nine Soviet republics that most wanted to stay within the Union (they made up 98 percent of the country's territory and 93 percent of its population) and seemed implicitly to pave the way for the breakaway republics, such as those along the Baltic Sea, to achieve total independence. He once again placed his authority squarely behind the cause of economic reform, calling for the widespread denationalization of state property and increased private ownership. He even, for a time, put aside his feud with Yeltsin, who had secured his own position as president of the Russian republic in June 1991 by winning the first democratic popular election to that office.

Those who were inclined to give Gorbachev the benefit of the doubt had every reason to feel justified, therefore, by the events that transpired in mid-August 1991. Early in the morning of August 19, the Soviet news agency, Tass, shocked the world with the announcement that Gorbachev had been relieved of his duties as president of the USSR. He had been replaced by a quasi-military council known as the State Committee for the State of Emer-

Yevgeny Yevtuschenko will be remembered as one of the leading Soviet poets of the last decades of communism. Although a frequent critic of the Khrushchev and Brezhnev regimes, Yevtuschenko nonetheless managed to enjoy a certain poetic license because he successfully identified himself with efforts to break away from the brutal legacy of Stalinism and revitalize Soviet Marxism. He also made a name for himself as a strong critic of the United States, and particularly of the U.S. role in the Vietnam War. Since the ascendancy of Gorbachev, whose reforms he supported, Yevtuschenko has gained newfound prominence. During the August 1991 coup, he appeared on international television in an emotional reading of a poem directed against the coup plotters. (Photo from Reuters/Bettmann.)

gency, composed exclusively of rebellious members of Gorbachev's own government: Vice-President Gennadi Yanayev, Prime Minister Valentin Pavlov, KGB chief Vladimir Kryuchkov, and Defense Minister Dmitri Yazov. Tanks and troops were moved into Moscow and Leningrad and the capitals of the dissident Baltic republics, and Gorbachev himself was placed under house arrest at his weekend retreat in the Crimea. Apparently, the decision to stage the coup was triggered by the fact that the new treaty to redefine the USSR was scheduled to be signed on the following day, August 20. But the action was clearly about much more than that. For all the plotters, the takeover of the Soviet government was a last-ditch effort to restore the political order and certainty that had existed in those times when the Communist party reigned supreme and almost no one dared to question the principles of socialism that had governed the country since 1917.

For these reasons, when news of the coup was made public, many outside observers braced themselves for what seemed like an inevitable return to the dictatorial policies and politics of Soviet life before Gorbachev's ascendancy in 1985. Yet despite these apprehensions, there were two huge surprises about the course of subsequent events. The first was that many Soviet citizens, having found themselves increasingly emboldened to express their views thanks to five years of *perestroika* and *glasnost,* simply refused to be cowed by the threats of those who organized the coup. Thousands of protesters defied the military's efforts to impose curfews in the Baltics and other republics, like Moldova. Miners and industrial workers went on strike in Siberia. Most prominent of all, the Russian president, Yeltsin, emerged as the symbol of the forces fighting for democracy by courageously standing up to the coup plotters and using the Russian parliament building (known as the White House) as a rallying point for tens of thousands of protesters to assemble to express their opposition to the new regime.

Even more surprising than these developments, though, was that the State Committee of the State of Emergency, for all its proclamations about the need to restore order in the USSR, proved to be hardly more powerful than the handful of individuals who had conspired to replace Gorbachev. In part, the plotters may have been so concerned to keep their actions secret that they were unable to guarantee the unequivocal backing of all segments of the Soviet army and the KGB. Then, too, they may have acted under the mistaken impression that economic and political conditions in the country were so bleak that the majority of Soviet citizens (and perhaps even Gorbachev himself) would have welcomed the return to more stringent and authoritarian policies. What these miscalculations meant, however, was that the coup began to unravel practically at the moment it was declared. Almost immediately, signs of vacillation and disagreement among the plotters became apparent. Foreign powers like the United States made known their view that they were not about to provide any assistance to a government that had come into being by such undemocratic means. Finally, following the defection of key tank units to Yeltsin's ranks, it became clear that the Soviet military could no longer be counted upon to support the coup.

Thus, on August 21, only two days after the revolt against Gorbachev and the whole reform process had begun, the new regime completely evaporated. Yeltsin emerged a popular hero because of his outspoken defiance of the coup plotters, Gorbachev returned to Moscow to assume the presidency (although his prestige was considerably weakened as a result of the attempt to overthrow him), and throughout the Soviet Union, average citizens engaged in what might best be described as an orgy of highly symbolic demonstrations against the Communist system. Everywhere, in cities big and small, statues of Soviet revolutionaries, including those of Lenin, were defaced or toppled. The offices of the Communist party were closed and many of its documents and properties confiscated. Gorbachev himself even conspicuously resigned as the party's general secretary. Tremendous optimism reigned about the possibility of finally making a clean break with the past.

On balance, it was almost as if the history of the USSR in the twentieth century had been reversed. In 1917 a small cadre of individuals, like Lenin, had come to power and gradually laid the foundations for what was to become known as the Union of Soviet Socialist Republics. In contrast, in 1991 the failure of an equally small group of individuals to halt the process of change that had begun under Gorbachev's leadership held out the promise that a truly democratic, truly modern state could be established in the place of seventy-four years of despotism. Nevertheless, the Soviet Union's options were not nearly so straightforward.

On the positive side, there was much that could be said for an approach to the Soviet future that allowed the country's leaders to treat their polity as a blank sheet that could be rewritten according to new principles and goals. Strong-willed personalities like Yeltsin who favored implementing basic changes as quickly as possible could readily benefit from the manner in which the aborted coup had totally discredited many of their former critics in the party, the state bureaucracies, and the military. In the area of economic reform, in particular, a strong case could be made for moving beyond the inhibitions and hesitations of the past and finally embracing all of the defining aspects of a capitalist free market: private property, a stable and realistic price system, and the allocation of goods according to the norms of supply and demand. Moreover, the radicals could also agree that their new circumstances provided an unprecedented opportunity to refashion the federal system of the USSR from the ground up. They were therefore willing to allow dissatisfied republics to leave the Union gracefully—as was the case with the Baltic states (Latvia, Lithuania, and Estonia), all of which were able to achieve full independence in September 1991. At the same time, the radicals assured those that remained of their intention to create a more equitable distribution of power and resources between the federal administration in Moscow and the outlying republican governments.

There was an undeniable problem with instituting such changes, and it was one that would undoubtedly remain with the region well into the 1990s: The collapse of the old Soviet system and demise of Marxist-Leninist ideology did not necessarily mean that a new system could be swiftly introduced in its place to satisfy the diverse interests that had come to the fore during the Gorbachev era. Quite the contrary, as the euphoria that had initially accompanied the successful resistance to the coup subsided, it became apparent that the proponents of radical change had found it easier to make common cause over what was wrong with the old system than to agree on how to replace it.

It was one thing to speak glibly about the virtues of democracy and political tolerance but quite another to live up to these principles in practice; Yeltsin, for example, was subjected to widespread international criticism shortly after the failed coup when he peremptorily moved to outlaw all

The failure of the August 1991 coup unleashed Soviet disdain for the symbols of the Communist past. The offices of the secret police (the KGB) in Moscow and elsewhere were stormed and defaced; prominent Communist party newspapers like Pravda were temporarily banned; and statues of major revolutionary personalities (such as this one of Lenin), representing decades of Communist oppression and dictatorship, were toppled. (Photo from Reuters/Bettmann.)

newspapers that were sympathetic to the Communist cause. Similarly, some supporters of economic reform discovered that it was much easier to embrace the ideal of economic liberalization than to suffer through the consequences that would attend a sudden shift to the free market. Particularly when the Soviet economy was already drifting toward bankruptcy and the country's population was faced with the prospect of serious food shortages, many citizens were simply unwilling to pay the price for such reforms, which would necessarily have entailed huge increases in unemployment and inflation. Finally, and most ominously, as all of the remaining Soviet republics, including Russia, moved quickly to assert their autonomy from the old USSR, it also became clear that the mystique of the Union itself, the idea that the various republics had more to gain by working together than by going their separate routes, had vanished. It was symptomatic of troubles to come that in late October 1991, Gorbachev was able to entice only eight of the fifteen former Soviet republics (notably, these did not include such major entities as Ukraine and Azerbaijan) to sign a treaty on future economic cooperation. Even then, the agreement was painfully lacking in the kinds of economic controls (e.g., commitment to a common monetary policy) to guarantee that the various republics would be able to work together in harmony.

Clearly, the entity that, for seven decades, the world had known as the Soviet Union was rapidly disintegrating. But if Gorbachev was unprepared to accept this fact, three of the republics, Russia, Belarus, and Ukraine, then made it evident for all to see. On December 8, 1991, in a dramatic act of self-determination, they declared that the USSR had ceased to exist and proclaimed in its place a Commonwealth of Independent States. Only a week later, five central Asian republics, including Kazakhstan and Uzbekistan, declared their willingness to join the new entity. There was nothing else for Gorbachev to do—on December 25, 1991, he resigned his post as president of the USSR, removing the one last articulate voice capable of defending the old regime. Still, although much of the Western world had hoped for such independent acts as those taken by the new republics during earlier times while communism had prevailed, few leaders were inclined to regard this situation, particularly Gorbachev's departure, as marking the happy end to old problems. The collapse of the Soviet system only seemed to be the occasion for the introduction of new, perhaps even more frightening dilemmas, not the least of which was the creation of four new nuclear powers, Russia, Ukraine, Belarus, and Kazakhstan. On a less globally threatening scale, there were also such challenging issues as how to divide up the old Soviet military, how to create an effective system of trade and stable monetary relations among the new republics, and how to manage the already troubled post-Soviet economy at a time when its resources would be divided among a group of quarreling republics. Although few people were likely to lament the passing of many of the Soviet Union's most distinctive characteristics—the inefficiency of the socialist economy, its dictatorial political practices, and its erratic international behavior—no one could say with confidence what kind of order (or orders) would rise to replace it.

Notes

1. Cited in M. Scammell, "To the Finland Station," *New Republic*, November 19, 1990, p. 20.

Suggested Readings

Aganbegyan, A. G. (ed.), *Perestroika: A Collection of Essays by Prominent Russians on the Changes Taking Place in the Soviet Union* (1989).
Aslund, A., *Gorbachev's Struggle for Economic Reform* (1989).
Bialer, S., *Stalin's Successors: Leadership, Stability, and Change in the Soviet Union* (1980).
Black, C. E., *Understanding Soviet Politics: The Perspective of Russian History* (1986).

——— (ed.), *The Transformation of Russian Society: Aspects of Social Change Since 1861* (1960).

Breslauer, G., *Khrushchev and Brezhnev as Leaders* (1982).

Cohen, S. F., *Rethinking the Soviet Experience: Politics and History Since 1917* (1985).

Galbraith, J. K., and S. M. Menshikov, *Capitalism, Communism, and Coexistence: From the Bitter Past to a Better Prospect* (1988).

Gorbachev, M. S., *Perestroika: New Thinking for Our Country and the World* (1987).

Gray, F., *Soviet Women: Walking the Tightrope* (1989).

Hewett, E. A., *Reforming the Soviet Economy: Equality Versus Efficiency* (1988).

Hoffmann, E. P., and R. F. Laird, *The Politics of Economic Modernization in the Soviet Union* (1982).

Holland, B. (ed.), *Soviet Sisterhood* (1985).

Hosking, G., *The First Socialist Society: A History of the Soviet Union from Within* (1985).

Hough, J., and M. Fainsod, *How the Soviet Union Is Governed*, rev. ed. (1979).

Kerblay, B., *Modern Soviet Society* (1983).

Khrushchev, N., *Khrushchev Remembers*, 2 vols. (1977).

McAuley, A., *Women's Work and Wages in the Soviet Union* (1981).

Parrott, B., *Politics and Technology in the Soviet Union* (1983).

Scanlon, J. P., *Marxism in the U.S.S.R.* (1985).

Schapiro, L., *The Communist Party of the Soviet Union* (1970).

Tucker, R. C., *Political Culture and Leadership in Soviet Russia* (1987).

——— , *Stalin as Revolutionary, 1879–1919* (1973).

Ulam, A., *A History of Soviet Russia* (1976).

Yedlin, T. (ed.), *Women in Eastern Europe and the Soviet Union* (1983).

CHAPTER EIGHT

Eastern Europe

❧

Postwar Governments
United-Front Regimes • People's Democracies

The New Soviet Orbit
Consolidation of Soviet Controls • Revolts and Repression

Different Roads to Socialism
Unity and Diversity • The New Reform Era

The Crisis of 1989 and Beyond
Revolt Against Communism • The Path Beyond Socialism

Suggested Readings

I n many respects, the history of postwar Eastern Europe may be seen as a grand experiment. It may also be viewed as an ultimately failed effort on the part of the Soviet Union to carve out an alternative path to modernity. Western Europe had already experienced its major revolutions, and most of its constituent countries had made the successful transition to a modern industrial society. Despite Marxist-Leninist theorizing about the coming revolution of the world proletariat, the vast majority of Western Europeans, whether belonging to the working class or not, had accommodated themselves to the basic norms of liberal institutions and the free market. Yet when the Soviet armies poured into the various countries of Eastern Europe at war's end, it must have seemed to Stalin that the USSR and the world Communist movement were finally being offered the raw material they had always needed to prove the merits of their political and economic system. Therefore the Leninist conception of Marxism was slowly imposed on these countries in spite of their major cultural and historical differences and, in many cases, their lack of suitability to the Soviet experience.

That Communist regimes lasted as long as they did in Eastern Europe can be attributed to diverse factors: the ruthlessness of the Soviet occupiers and their local supporters, the idealistic hopes of many early Communists after years of brutality experienced under national socialism and German domination, and in some cases the short-term gains that the Soviet model of forced industrialization represented for the more backward economies in the region. But the fit between the Soviet model and Eastern European reality was always an uncomfortable one, which after years of alternating waves of coercion and periods of limited relaxation finally came undone in the political revolutions of 1989.

Postwar Governments

United-Front Regimes

After World War II, the establishment of a Soviet sphere of influence in the region that we have commonly come to call Eastern Europe was never simply a matter of imposing an alien political regime during a period of military occupation. Countries like Albania and Yugoslavia remained outside the direct sphere of Soviet military occupation. East Germany (see Chapter 6) was of course a special case. And although there was a massive Soviet troop presence in countries like Hungary, Bulgaria, Romania, Poland, and Czechoslovakia, this factor was secondary to the political tactics the Soviet Union employed both within each of the states and toward the Western world.

Population of Albania (1990 estimate) 3,262,000

Population of Bulgaria (1990 estimate) 8,997,400

Population of Czechoslovakia (1990 estimate)
15,664,000

Population of Hungary (1990 estimate) 10,437,000

Population of Poland (1990 estimate) 38,064,000

Population of Romania (1990 estimate) 23,265,000

Population of Yugoslavia (1990 estimate) 23,861,000

Eastern Europe as of January 1992

Three distinct stages can be distinguished in the establishment of this Soviet sphere of influence in Eastern Europe. The first involved the Soviets' efforts to gain the acquiescence, if not the explicit consent, of the Western powers to the establishment of such a sphere. The second stage was concerned with obtaining the participation of the local Communist parties in united-front governments in each of the countries concerned. The third and final stage involved the assertion of predominant political positions by the Communists, after they had succeeded in eliminating or neutralizing their major opponents. In many cases these three stages overlapped, and the point of transition from one to another was not always clear. They nevertheless represented the essential process through which Soviet influence passed before firm control over the region could be asserted.

As we have already seen, the Anglo-U.S.-Soviet coalition tended to settle immediate occupation problems on the basis of spheres of influence. Certainly, the advance of the Soviet armies toward Germany gave them the advantage of overwhelming military force in Eastern Europe that could in turn be directed toward political ends. (The Western powers, it must be stated, had interests of their own that they wished to secure in Italy and Greece.) The first step toward acknowledging a Soviet orbit in Eastern Europe was taken during autumn 1944, when the Soviets agreed to recognize the predominant British interest in Greece and to share an interest in Yugoslavia, in return for British recognition of a predominant Soviet interest in Romania, Hungary, and Bulgaria. This policy was carried further when armistice terms were settled for Romania (August 1944), Finland (September 1944), Bulgaria (September 1944), and Hungary (January 1945). Here again, the Soviet high command was granted a position of almost exclusive influence in political as well as military matters during the period from the signing of armistice terms until the signing of peace treaties.

In the case of the Eastern European states that were already members of the United Nations coalition, the situation was more complicated. Only in Czechoslovakia was Soviet influence established without controversy with the Western states, as the Czech government-in-exile was prepared to accept the establishment of a Soviet sphere of influence, although with the expectation that the small state would be guaranteed a certain amount of sovereignty in return. The Czech-Soviet treaty of alliance of 1943 had already reflected the decision of Edward Benes and his foreign minister, Jan Masaryk, son of the founder of the Czechoslovak republic, to rebuild their country as a bridge between East and West. In contrast, the Yugoslav and Polish governments-in-exile were determined to resist any Soviet interference in their affairs. The Soviets countered by promoting alternative regimes under Marshal Tito in Yugoslavia and Boleslaw Bierut in Poland, regimes that by war's end were in physical control of their respective countries.

Some of the most prominent Eastern European statesmen met in Warsaw in June 1948 to discuss common problems. The Soviet Union had begun to crack down on its Eastern European allies, imposing a harsh Communist discipline and ordering them to undertake Soviet-style crash programs for industrialization and collectiviza-tion. Most of those who dared to challenge Soviet authority, including even the fierce Stalinist Ana Pauker of Romania, were later purged and executed. When the Yugoslav government stood up to the Kremlin's dictate, Stalin branded its leader, Tito, a heretic and expelled Yugoslavia from the Communist bloc. From left to right in this picture: Vassil Kolarov (Bulgaria), Erik Molnar (Hungary), Viacheslav Molo-tov (USSR), Zygmunt Modzelewski (Poland), Ana Pauker (Romania), Vlado Clemen-tis (Czechoslovakia), and Stanoje Simitch (Yugoslavia). (Photo from UPI/Bettmann.)

Faced with this fait accompli, Roosevelt and Churchill agreed at Yalta in February 1945 to transfer their recognition to new coalition governments in which certain members of the governments-in-exile would be admitted to the Soviet-dominated regimes. In return, they obtained from Stalin a pledge of "the earliest possible establishment through free elections of governments responsive to the will of the people." In the view of the Western states, none of these arrangements was intended to signify recognition of a permanent Soviet sphere of influence. The duration of the armistice terms with the satellite states did not extend beyond the signature of peace, and it was expected that in both the defeated and liberated countries excessive Com-munist influence would be moderated by the free elections to be held shortly after the termination of hostilities. As it turned out, the granting of these initial, and in general reluctant, concessions to the Soviet Union had the unintended consequence of taking the initiative out of the hands of the Western states.

The second stage of Soviet control, which involved obtaining key positions for Communist leaders in each government, was accomplished without great difficulty. Somewhat idealistically, Benes voluntarily admitted Communists into the Czechoslovak cabinet, whereas in Poland and Yugoslavia they had a predominant position in the new coalition governments from the start, with the blessing of the Big Three. In Albania, the victory of the partisans under Enver Hoxha after a long civil struggle gave the Communists a leading role. In the former Axis satellite states—Romania, Bulgaria, Hungary, and Finland—Communists were admitted to the coalition governments formed at the end of the war, without much thought given to the consequences of their inclusion. In general they received key positions, such as the ministries of interior and justice, but only later did they gain a free hand in political matters. The new postwar regimes in all these countries were known in Communist terminology as "united-front governments." This was Moscow's way of selling the West on flexible political coalitions within which the Communists could maneuver for position as a minority group until they were prepared to assume full power. It was a subtle technique of infiltration that deceived the Western states for a while and even misled experienced non-Communist leaders in Eastern Europe.

The transition of the Communist parties from minority participation in the united-front governments to a position of complete dominance, the third stage in their assumption of power, varied in method and timing with each country. It was during this stage that the surviving monarchs—Peter of Yugoslavia, Simeon of Bulgaria, and Michael of Romania—were deposed. Only in Yugoslavia and Albania did the Communists have unquestioned authority from the beginning, although less by virtue of their revolutionary credentials and more because they had been at the forefront of the guerrilla struggles against fascism. In Romania and Bulgaria, the leading non-Communists were actually forced out of the government in the spring and summer of 1945. In Poland, however, it was not until January 1947 that the Communists openly asserted their power. A similar process took place in Hungary the following June. Most spectacular of all, insofar as the event revealed to the West Soviet methods and aims more clearly than ever before, was the seizure of the Czechoslovak government in February 1948. In achieving this coup, the Communists shrewdly employed intimidation and demagoguery to distort the country's democratic electoral system to bring themselves to total power. Only in Finland did the Communists fail to make the transition to the third stage and remain without a determining voice in the government. The Soviets were acquainted with the toughness of the Finns from past experience and were satisfied to let well enough alone. They were all the more willing to do so because greater pressure on Finland might well have pushed neutral Sweden into the arms of the West, when it was more desirable to keep the Scandinavian powers unaligned.

People's Democracies

The united-front governments were the primary device the Soviet Union used to neutralize rival political groups in Eastern Europe before local Communists began their final seizure of power. Once they had asserted their full authority, however, they established new constitutional regimes known as "people's democracies." At least initially, these new regimes were not meant to represent the ultimate establishment of the Soviet form of socialism but rather to provide a framework within which the transition from a "capitalist" to a "classless" society could be made. The early Communist leaders foresaw that their countries would have to go through a phase similar to that which the Soviet Union had experienced between 1928 and 1936, during which the state gradually took over all means of production in both industry and agriculture. The early Eastern European constitutions, therefore, made provision for the liquidation of previous political institutions and empowered their governments to muzzle all criticism and suppress all opposition parties. At the same time, constitution framers paid special attention to such causes as appeasing local minorities by providing for national rights that recognized their sentiments without sacrificing any of the state's monopoly on centralized political power. In Yugoslavia, for example, Tito introduced the popular concept of federalism to bring about better working relations among the many rival nationality groups in the country.

In addition, the new constitutions of the people's democracies also provided for a somewhat mixed system of economic management in which the commanding heights of the economy were in the hands of the state and private property and private initiative were permitted to continue for the time being within certain narrow limits. As in the Soviet Union, the real authority was exercised behind the scenes by the Communist party, led by such vigorous figures as Georgi Dimitrov in Bulgaria (until his death in July 1949), Ana Pauker in Romania, Klement Gottwald in Czechoslovakia, Matyas Rakosi in Hungary, Bierut in Poland, Hoxha in Albania, and Tito in Yugoslavia. In each case, as these parties consolidated their authority over time, their central committees came to appoint all important officials and made all policy decisions.

For a while the absolute character of these dictatorships was camouflaged a bit by an elaborate parliamentary system, resembling some Western democracies in form. For example, local party committees nominated candidates who were not necessarily Communists to single electoral lists that were presented to voters. Such deputies then met in unicameral legislatures (except in the case of Yugoslavia, where the federal structure required two chambers)

Marshal Tito (pictured here with his wife) embodied everything that was stable and predictable about Communist Yugoslavia in the long period from World War II until his death in 1980. There can be no doubt that Tito, who had been a heroic fighter in the guerrilla campaigns against his country's Nazi occupiers, was a tough-minded and unforgiving leader. But it is also true that during his lengthy rule the Yugoslav nation-state did enjoy a certain stability, which began to erode after Tito's death, the country erupting into widespread ethnic conflict in 1991. (Photo from AP/Wide World Photos.)

and served for terms of four to six years. Each assembly was headed by a presidium, or steering committee, that exercised all the powers of the assembly between sessions. The president of the presidium was a secondary figure who, as in the Soviet Union, performed the functions of a chief of state. Nonetheless, for those who actually participated in such systems, it was abundantly clear that the real power lay with the Communist party and, behind it, the Soviet Union. Non-Communists might be found in each cabinet, but they were permitted to remain only in their personal capacity as experts or to appease sections of public opinion that had retained some influence.

Because faithful, believing Communists were initially a minority in every country in Eastern Europe, and a very small minority in most of them, the opposition they had to overcome was considerable. Openly pro-Nazi elements were in most cases summarily tried and executed, but there were many other kinds of political leaders who had suffered along with the Communists under Axis rule. These individuals were in many cases willing to share political power with their Marxist-Leninist compatriots, but they refused to submit to Communist dictation. Thus a showdown of some kind was inevitable. In some cases, as with Benes and Masaryk in Czechoslovakia, it was the prewar middle-class liberals who retained the majority. In Albania, though, rival groups of nationalist leaders competed for power. The situation was more complicated in Yugoslavia, where the leaders of the constituent nationalities joined in varying coalitions with the heads of peasant parties. In most of the countries of Eastern Europe, the parliamentary democrats who had been discredited by the economic disorganization following World War I and the nationalist leaders who were tainted by collaboration with the Axis constituted great obstacles to a Western European path of liberal political development.

There remained, nevertheless, two broad groups, the so-called Agrarians and the Socialists, who had behind them a full generation of political activity and who enjoyed a wide following. The Agrarians proved to be the chief source of opposition to Communist rule. With the exception of Czechoslovakia, between 50 and 70 percent of the population in Eastern Europe was engaged in agriculture, and the great majority were independent peasant proprietors. They had, moreover, developed a vigorous agrarian ideology stressing the preeminent role they felt the peasantry should have in the overall economic policy of the state. The Agrarians believed in a land reform that would divide up the remaining large estates, and they favored promoting the modernization of agriculture through the cooperative efforts of peasant proprietors. Yet this program was in direct contrast to the ultimate Communist aim of collectivizing the small farms and turning the independent peasants into an agricultural proletariat.

Communist opposition to the Agrarians, however, was less on theoretical grounds than on practical terms, for in most of these countries the Agrarians had far greater electoral strength. As soon as they had the police and the machinery of government well in hand, local Communists therefore attacked the Agrarians relentlessly. In Yugoslavia Ivan Subasic was thrown out of the government and Dragoljub Jovanovic was jailed, as were Juliu Maniu and Ion Mihalache in Romania. In Bulgaria the Agrarian leader G. M. Dimitrov (not related to the Communist Georgi Dimitrov) was forced into exile, and his successor, Nikola Petkov, was executed. Ferenc Nagy of Hungary and Stanislaw Mikolajczyk of Poland, who had served as prime ministers of their respective countries in the early united-front governments, managed to escape with their lives. In quite the same fashion, the Eastern European Socialist leaders, who had a much smaller following and whose doctrines did not present a clear-cut contrast to those of the Communists, were either suborned or forced out of political life, as we have already seen in the case of the Social Democrats of East Germany.

The New Soviet Orbit

Consolidation of Soviet Controls

Within the framework of these essentially domestic developments, therefore, the Soviet Union was able to exert its control over Eastern Europe through many channels, both meeting its needs for national security in the uncertain postwar period and also flattering the egos of individuals like Stalin who thought that the "class struggle" was finally moving in their direction. It would not be too much to say that the best of all possible worlds in Moscow's view was, for a time, one in which each Eastern European state would become a replica of the Soviet Union.

The Communist party was only one of the devices to which Soviet authorities increasingly turned as a way of achieving this end. Control was also exercised more directly through Soviet diplomatic officials in each country, and through agents of the Soviet secret police, who kept an eye on local Communists as well as on each other. On a more formal level, Moscow established mutual-assistance pacts with all of its new Eastern European partners except Albania. The treaties with Czechoslovakia, Yugoslavia, and Poland were concluded before the end of the war, whereas those with the four former Axis satellites were not signed until 1948. The overt aim of these pacts in every case was to provide for a common defense against a revived and aggressive Germany.

To be sure, a somewhat different form of control over the region was created in September 1947, with the establishment of the Communist Information Bureau (Cominform). Its purpose was to coordinate the activities of all the Communist parties in their efforts to combat "Anglo-American imperialism," and in many respects it resumed the work of the Communist International (Comintern), which had been dissolved in May 1943. But the message for the region was as tough-minded as ever: The Eastern European states were to be reduced to aiding in Moscow's conflict with a new enemy supplanting national socialism—the capitalist West.

When the pressure of the Marshall Plan began to be felt in Eastern Europe, the USSR attempted to counteract its appeal by sponsoring the Council for Mutual Economic Assistance in January 1949. Through the use of Comecon, the Soviet Union derived very substantial economic gains from its dominant position in Eastern Europe. Soon the organization's member countries were taking over one-half of the USSR's exports and supplying over one-third of its commercial imports, whereas on the eve of the war they had shared less than 5 percent of Soviet foreign trade. The Soviet Union's advantage in this trade was more than merely commercial, for it did not hesitate to use its bargaining position to obtain favorable prices. Moreover, it was able on occasion to reexport some of these products at considerable profit. At the same time, the Soviet Union benefited from the reparations payments that it received from Finland, Hungary, and Romania; these almost equaled its commercial imports from the entire region. It also had a very advantageous political arrangement for the import of Polish coal. All of these deals were of necessity only temporary advantages, as the smaller states could not continue indefinitely to support such an unfavorable balance. But in the decade while such arrangements lasted, they provided highly profitable relationships for the Soviet Union.

At the point where the Soviet sphere of influence took on many of the aspects of old-fashioned imperialism, however, even local Communists, the early idealists, began to question some of the USSR's intentions. In Eastern Europe, as elsewhere, many of these individuals had joined the Communist movement after the war because they thought it would provide answers to the social and economic problems their countries had found so difficult to solve under the various parliamentary and authoritarian regimes of the prewar years. What discouraged them was not only the economic benefits the USSR sought from its position in Eastern Europe but also the Soviet insistence that all local problems be solved by methods developed in the Soviet Union, even though a wide variety of problems and interests in these countries differed markedly from those of the Soviet Union.

Key Communist leaders gradually began to raise serious objections to Soviet policy. In almost every instance, the Soviet response was swift and severe. Many of these Communists, like Traicho Kostov in Bulgaria, Koci Xoxe in Albania, and Laszlo Rajk in Hungary, were executed for treason. Yugoslavia's Tito was actually expelled from the Cominform, although he successfully withstood its verbal onslaughts and the political and economic ostracism of the other countries in the Soviet orbit. Nonetheless, even though the Yugoslav leader was favored by geography and possessed an armed force built up during the war without Soviet interference, his exclusion from the Communist camp raised serious doubts about whether Moscow could continue to hold its bloc together.

An important consequence of the centralized Soviet controls in the Stalin era was Moscow's continued belief that its Eastern European allies should be totally transformed in its own image, particularly in economic terms. In agriculture, for example, the first step the Soviet Union mandated was the breakup of all the larger estates. In Poland, Czechoslovakia, and Hungary this measure involved one-third to one-half of all agricultural and forest land. In Bulgaria, Romania, and Yugoslavia, where landholding was already largely in the hands of the peasants, relatively little land was involved. Thereafter all the Eastern European states moved toward collectivization, although in the 1950s both Yugoslavia and Poland managed to reverse their policies and return to some forms of private ownership of land. It was for this reason that in the turbulent 1980s both of these countries at least had the advantage of economies with socialized industry, trade, and services, but with over 85 percent of the land privately owned. In contrast, by collectivizing, Bulgaria, Czechoslovakia, Hungary, and Romania, which obediently copied the Soviet model, were left with less than 15 percent of their agricultural land in private hands.

Western scholars have reached the conclusion that the two countries with remaining private agriculture—Yugoslavia and Poland—performed better than those with socialized agriculture. In due course, the former exceeded the prewar level of agricultural production by a considerable margin, whereas the latter attained that level more gradually. Industrial production, which was oriented toward Stalinist norms throughout East Europe, surpassed the prewar level in all these countries by 1950 and quickly grew to several times that level. Yet, as in the Soviet Union, this industrial growth was purchased at a high price in levels of personal consumption and the average standard of living and could never be matched by similar increases in labor productivity and general economic efficiency. Furthermore, environmental costs were astounding. As many of the people in the region discovered three decades later, all of their efforts to move away from this legacy of Communist dictatorship were necessarily bound up with equally daunting tasks such as cleaning their polluted rivers, removing life-threatening chemicals from their soils, and struggling to control the contaminating emissions of their factories.

Revolts and Repression

The Soviet system of forced industrialization produced great strains in Eastern Europe, and only by the most severe use of police measures were these countries kept under control. When Stalin died in 1953, and when within a short time Lavrentii Beria's position as head of the Soviet police was undermined, the pressure from discontent in this region could no longer be contained; in East Germany the demonstrations proved extremely serious. Among the Soviets' first efforts to quell this protest (besides armed intervention in the GDR) was Georgi Malenkov's "New Course," which promised measures to increase food and consumer goods (see Chapter 7). In Hungary and Poland, where popular pressure was especially great, agriculture was decollectivized. These and other steps brought few immediate benefits, however, and could not counterbalance the great demoralization that occurred in Communist ranks. Soon there was widespread criticism of the Stalinist system, especially in student and literary circles, and extensive riots shook Poland.

Soviet leaders were now faced with the choice of reimposing the toughest aspects of Stalinism or trying to accommodate some of the specific needs of the individual countries. They chose the latter course. As a consequence of this new policy, the Cominform was dissolved in April 1956. This act served especially as a gesture of reconciliation by Khrushchev toward Tito, who had achieved a certain prestige in some circles for standing up to the Soviet behemoth. But at the same time, the dissolution of the Cominform widened the rift between the Soviets and the Chinese, who accused Tito of deviating from proper Leninist prerequisites for revolution. News of Khrushchev's February denunciation of Stalin, though supposedly secret, spread rapidly as a result of U.S. radio broadcasts from West Germany into Eastern European countries. These nations had far more reason to dislike Stalin than the people of the Soviet Union. In Poland and Hungary, where the activities of the Soviet secret police had long been feared and resented, revisionists' hopes were raised by the prospect that Khrushchev would be more tolerant of change.

In Poland Communists favoring a policy slightly independent of Moscow's dictates quickly gained the initiative. Many believed that a basic reorientation of the economy, including the complete abandonment of collectivization and a greater emphasis on the production of consumer goods, was necessary if the Polish economy were to revive. The standard Soviet methods of enforced modernization, they felt, were both outdated and inappropriate for their country. Intellectuals of the so-called Crooked Circle spoke out and found a responsive chord among the workers. Demonstrations for "bread and freedom" took place. The key question was how to achieve substantial change without Soviet intervention. New direction was needed, and the mantle of leadership was passed in October 1956 to Wladyslaw Gomulka, a former Communist leader who years before had been disgraced and jailed as a nationalist deviator. Even though the great majority of the Poles were anti-Communist, they believed that Gomulka was the only alternative to Stalinism. His new Politburo excluded Soviet Marshal Konstantin Rokosovsky, who had for years served as Polish minister of defense and chief of the Polish army.

On October 19 Khrushchev, along with Molotov and other Soviets, paid a surprise visit to Warsaw; at the same time Soviet troops were ordered to move from their camps toward the capital. In crisis negotiation, Gomulka persuaded the Soviet leader that the reforms being undertaken were not intended to harm Poland's relations with the USSR; rather, he argued convincingly, they would give the Soviets a more reliable and stable ally. Khrushchev was mollified, the Soviet troops returned to their barracks, and modest reforms took hold, including the creation of workers' councils in industry and a relaxation of curbs on the church. To the Poles, it was spring in October. For Khrushchev, the main achievement was that Poland remained an ally within the Warsaw Pact; moreover, he had stolen some of Tito's wind of popularity by accepting this modest breath of revisionism. For his part, Gomulka received a resounding majority in the national elections held in January 1957, which well into the 1960s signified the genuine support of the Polish population for his policies.

In Hungary, however, events did not move so smoothly. There the Communist party was weaker than in Poland, and public opinion was less accustomed to the restraints bred by living on the brink of disaster. Economic shortages, a dislike of collectivization, resentment of the secret police, nascent hopes raised by Khrushchev's criticism of Stalin, and excitement over the Polish workers' success all played a part in generating an atmosphere of stubborn defiance. Then, too, there was a major division in the party leadership, as hard-liners continued to oppose those Communists who favored the ending of forced collectivization and a diversion of investment to include light industry.

On October 24, following a demonstration the preceding day in support of the Poles, students seized the main radio building in Budapest and broadcast a number of radical demands. These included free elections, the withdrawal of Soviet troops from Hungary, and a new government under Imre Nagy, a Communist who, like Gomulka, favored an independent policy. In contrast to events in Poland, however, the Hungarian secret police fired upon the students, and, as tensions rose, Soviet forces entered Budapest. For the most part, the Hungarian army then defected to the rebel cause. As fighting spread throughout the nation, the Politburo named Nagy premier. The Soviets went along with the appointment in the hope of seeing the situation stabilize. An appeal for Soviet aid was also sent, probably without Nagy's knowledge; Soviet troops were in any case already on the scene. The presence of these troops further angered the population, especially the newly formed Hungarian workers' councils. Thus the new premier immediately found himself faced with a revolution against any form of Communist rule. He responded by going beyond the Soviets' conception of the limits of any tolerable deviation from Marxism-Leninism.

At the end of October, Nagy announced the restoration of a multiparty political system and the formation of a coalition government with representatives from the illegal Smallholders party and other political groups. Soviet troops briefly withdrew from Budapest, and on November 2 the emboldened Nagy denounced the Warsaw Pact and asked the United Nations to consider the situation of his country. But this was only the calm before the storm, for on November 4 the Soviets stepped into the picture, sending in an army of tanks that reestablished Communist rule after days of bloody street fighting. Nagy himself was replaced by a man who only days earlier had seemed to be a reformer, Janos Kadar, the secretary of the party. He now attempted to rebuild his country by redefining the limits of politically acceptable activities in Hungary. In the meantime these events and a virtual flood of refugees out of the country into the West served to remind the world of the brutality of Soviet methods (which were in part orchestrated by the cold efficiency of the Soviet ambassador in Budapest, Yuri Andropov) and the very real limits on Moscow's readiness to accept any deviation from its model of development.

In retrospect, it appears that the crucial difference between the course of events in Poland and in Hungary lay not so much in the domestic reforms enacted as in the Hungarians' desire to separate from the Warsaw Pact. The

No one in Europe was adequately prepared for the tragic Hungarian revolution of 1956. In a desperate effort to break with the Stalinist experience and the Soviet Union's control over their country, the Hungarian people rose up against communism, embracing the reforms of the government of Imre Nagy. They smashed all symbols of the totalitarian past, such as this statue of Stalin (pictured above, with the inscription "W.C." ["water closet," i.e., toilet] on its face) that once lorded over the city of Budapest. With the whole world watching, however, Soviet tanks (below) descended upon the Hungarian capital, crushing the rebellion, killing thousands, and forcing tens of thousands of Hungarian citizens into exile. (Photos from UPI/Bettmann Newsphotos.)

Soviets had stated on October 30 that a country could build socialism in its own manner, as long as it was a loyal adherent to the Warsaw treaty. But Khrushchev and his colleagues would not tolerate any defection from the pact—as implied by the loss of one-party rule in Hungary—which might have weakened Soviet security and deprived Moscow of the strategic troop locations so crucial to its strategy against NATO.

Not surprisingly, all of the countries of Eastern Europe felt the impact of the events in Poland and Hungary, but Soviet controls were also sufficiently strong to make any further worries in Moscow unnecessary. This is not to say that the Soviets did not learn from the crisis. Throughout the region, economic planning, though maintaining its Soviet model form, was now adapted somewhat more closely to the needs of each of the individual countries. A division of labor among them began to emerge, with more attention devoted to consumer goods and agriculture, and the pace of industrialization slowed as well. At the same time, there was some lessening of police controls, and travel abroad was more readily allowed. Only in Poland was substantial freedom gained. Poles were now at least tacitly permitted to criticize the Soviet system as well as their own. Poland also negotiated a U.S. loan of $98 million and began to send a number of students and scholars to the United States. Indeed, even this degree of freedom irritated the Soviets after they recovered from the blow to their prestige represented by the events of 1956. Many factors, including the difficulty of bringing Tito back into the fold, led the Soviets in 1958 to tighten controls on their Communist neighbors. The signal of this change was the execution in 1958 of Imre Nagy, who had been held in prison since 1956. As an obligatory sign of obedience to his patrons, even Gomulka was compelled to issue a statement approving this act of revenge.

Despite these setbacks, the trend toward a limited differentiation from Soviet policy initiated in 1956 continued to evolve over the next decade. In due course the Communist countries of Eastern Europe exhibited many diverse forms. Hungary was the country that went furthest in relaxing domestic controls. Under Kadar's leadership, its government sought, by balancing Eastern and Western influences, to pursue a policy of socialist economic growth more directly suited to its own particular needs. For a period, Kadar won the support of the population by raising the standard of living, dissolving many of the collective farms, and permitting greater personal freedom. Western travelers visiting Hungary were impressed by the success of these measures.

Equally dramatic were the changes in foreign policy initiated in the otherwise authoritarian state of Romania in the early 1960s, culminating in the declaration of April 1964, which asserted the right of all Communist countries to pursue independent policies within a framework of common institutions and doctrines. Acting according to the declaration, the Romanian government succeeded in encouraging Western investments, adopting a neutral position in the Sino-Soviet dispute, and in various other ways significantly loosening the close ties that had bound it to the USSR.

The most dramatic developments of all were to emerge slowly in Czechoslovakia, the leadership of which also cautiously sought opportunities to loosen the constraints of the Soviet straitjacket. Up to the mid-1960s, the Czechoslovak Communist leadership had followed the Soviet model as consistently as any country in Eastern Europe and shared with Soviet leaders a particular concern for the possible resurgence of German power, for it alone among the Eastern European countries had a common frontier with West Germany. Czechoslovakia expelled some 3 million Sudeten Germans from its western territories at the end of the war. Yet at the same time there were countervailing influences. Czechoslovakia had in effect been an occupied country since 1938, the only state in the region that had not experienced extensive domestic violence within its borders. This was a long period for even such patient peoples as the Czechs and Slovaks to remain passive, and it helps to explain the burst of vitality that occurred in 1968.

In January of that year the leaders of the Czechoslovak party ousted the conservative Antonin Novotny as first secretary and replaced him with a relatively unknown figure who was acceptable to the Soviets, Alexander Dubcek, previously the leader of the Slovak branch of the Communist party in Czechoslovakia. Such changes in the top leadership frequently reflect rumblings arising from the depths of society. With the ascendancy of Dubcek, a large number of Czechs and Slovaks from all walks of life suddenly exploded with criticism of their government's past policies and with proposals for political and economic reform. Stimulated both by the memory of Khrushchev's apparent support for such policies half a decade earlier in the USSR and by the ethnic divisions within Czechoslovakia, the people believed decentralization both in political and economic decisionmaking would be the proper path to modernization. Students demanded better dormitory conditions, and the populace as a whole desired more consumer products from light industry, resenting the emphasis on heavy industry imposed on their country as a result of its participation in Comecon. Earlier, as production goals failed to be met, the regime had resorted to building new factories rather than improving efficiency and worker morale within the old. Yet the creation of these new factories only spread more thinly the scarce supply of good managers and supervisors. Novotny himself had eventually been pressured into allowing some reforms that called for profit accountability, but his support for these measures was half-hearted and incomplete, thus only intensifying the demand for greater change.

In this context Dubcek, though not initially inclined to engage in radical reform, began first to make tentative gestures toward his angry populace— for example, many aspects of press censorship were lifted—and finally stood aside as attacks on a wide range of Soviet-inspired policies were aired. A thoroughgoing decentralization of economic controls was advocated, and even the possibility of a two-party system was discussed. Rumors spread that the "true" story behind the trials of the 1950s that had purged nationalist Communist leaders would be published, exposing the role of the Soviets in modeling the Communist party in their own image. In a particularly daring manifestation of the euphoria that characterized what came to be known as the Prague Spring, intellectuals published a manifesto, "Two Thousand Words," that boasted of military support for Dubcek if the Soviets dared to invade. Dubcek failed to disavow the manifesto, and the press exaggerated the extent of the reforms being contemplated. Even the reorientation of trade from Comecon to the United States was mooted.

At the time, Western observers were inclined to interpret this outburst of reforming zeal as a step in the direction of a new form of democratic socialism. But to the Soviet leaders and to such conservative autocrats as the East Germans, it looked more like the wholesale crumbling of party controls in the face of popular discontent. If Czechoslovakia were allowed to slip away from Communist control, what was to prevent Poland, Hungary, Romania, and others from following its path? Moreover, though Dubcek insisted that he was only promoting "socialism with a human face," there were substantial indications that many intellectuals did indeed favor their country's separation from the Warsaw Pact. Loss of such a key geographic and industrial area could scarcely have been happily contemplated behind the walls of the Kremlin.

In this increasingly uncertain climate, the Soviet leaders and their like-minded colleagues in the neighboring countries met with Dubcek in a series of high-level conferences in the summer of 1968. They sought to convince him to tighten the reins of power in Czechoslovakia. When persuasion failed, Moscow showed that the old rules still applied. On the night of August 20–21, Soviet troops, accompanied by token contingents from Bulgaria, East Germany, Hungary, and Poland, moved into Czechoslovakia and occupied the country without any warning. This action was consonant with the policy enunciated that fall by Soviet leader Brezhnev; the so-called Brezhnev Doctrine emphasized (for what then seemed to be all time) that a threat to the cause of socialism was a concern for *all* socialist countries. It was the right and duty of the USSR, this principle allowed, to intervene whenever the interests of socialism were threatened in any other Communist country.

The blow was swift and virtually bloodless, but it produced a reaction in many ways resembling the cry of outrage that followed the repression of the Hungarian uprising twelve years earlier. The Soviets' speed in reaching the decision to invade did not win them special favor in the West, though the Soviets apparently felt they had exercised patience. Even within the Soviet bloc there were strong negative feelings, as the Romanians refused to participate in the Warsaw Pact action and said they would themselves fight if ever offered such "fraternal" help.

If anyone after the 1956 invasion of Hungary doubted that the Soviet Union would ever again use military force to restore order in its empire, this uncertainty was dispelled in August 1968. On this date the USSR and other members of the Warsaw Pact used their armies to put an end to what was known as the Prague Spring, the Czechoslovak experiment with reform communism. In this photo, a protester expresses his defiance of the invading Soviet troops by holding up a Czech flag soaked in blood. (Photo from UPI/Bettmann Newsphotos.)

The leaders of the Czechoslovak government were taken to Moscow virtually as prisoners, but after negotiations were concluded, Dubcek was allowed to remain temporarily as head of the party, as Soviet authorities sought to minimize the presence of their troops and to undertake only gradual changes in personnel. Throughout the transitional period Soviet policy was firm but relatively subtle compared to the response to the Hungarian uprising, and there were no executions and few arrests. When Dubcek was finally replaced by Gustav Husak as head of the party in April 1969, the change was formally proposed by Dubcek himself. Husak was a supposed moderate who had been jailed by Novotny in the 1950s and who now sought to reestablish the degree of central control necessary to meet Soviet requirements without entirely alienating Czechoslovak opinion. It was by no means certain that such a policy could succeed, however, for citizens in all walks of life resented deeply the character of the Soviet occupation. When Jan Palach, a university student, died after setting fire to himself on St. Wenceslas Square in Prague in January 1969, his sacrifice became the symbol of two decades of quiet defiance on the part of the Czechoslovak population.

Different Roads to Socialism

Unity and Diversity

When in 1956 Khrushchev advanced the doctrine that there were "different roads to socialism" and that all Communist states did not have to follow the Soviet pattern, he was recognizing that even under Stalin there had been considerable diversity among the countries of Eastern Europe despite an outward appearance of conformity. Khrushchev's new doctrine was designed in part to bring Yugoslavia back into the fold, but it also reflected an acknowledgment of a long-term trend that survived the imposition of Soviet authority by military force in Hungary in 1956 and in Czechoslovakia in 1968. It soon became apparent that the Soviet occupation of Czechoslovakia was an event of limited impact that did not portend a general reversal of policy. What had concerned the Soviet leaders was not so much the specific reforms under discussion, for other countries in the orbit had already gone a good deal further in the direction of many of the changes proposed in Prague. Rather, they feared a loss of control over the country by its Communist party, for this was Moscow's primary vehicle for maintaining its own control over the region. Ever since the Second World War, Soviet leaders had been explicit in asserting that their national security depended on having "friendly" governments in power in Eastern Europe, and by "friendly" they meant governments dominated by Communist parties that saw eye to eye with the Soviet Union on the main issues of policy. The occupation of Czechoslovakia in 1968 reasserted this position in a most forceful way. As Brezhnev said in his formal explanation of the occupation in September 1968, "There is no doubt that the peoples of the socialist countries and the Communist parties have, and must have, freedom to determine their countries' paths of development. However, any decision of theirs must damage neither socialism in their own country nor the fundamental interest of the other socialist countries, nor the worldwide workers' movement, which is waging a struggle for socialism."

Yet even Brezhnev must have recognized that such a statement allowed considerable room for interpretation. As the Soviets themselves had continually found, the challenge of safeguarding the cause of socialism required occasional tactical compromises and ways of dealing with the world on a basis other than one of rigid and stereotypical categories. Hence, in their search for a greater degree of leeway within the confines of traditional Marxism-Leninism, the countries of Eastern Europe showed that they were prepared to take advantage of every opportunity the Soviets were willing to allow. One such opportunity was the era of détente that flowered in the 1970s. For although it was true that all Communist regimes had to be wary of the nature of the deals they struck with the capitalist world, the advances of the scientific-technical revolution made some kind of learning, some kind of borrowing from the West, almost compulsory for economic survival, even if such benefits happened to come from adversaries of communism.

In this period, it was widely known in Eastern Europe that the Soviet Union itself had begun to borrow extensively from the West in order to finance the import of advanced technology. As a result, Moscow could hardly prevent its Warsaw Pact allies from doing likewise. Thus by 1985, the USSR had accumulated a debt of $26 billion—not very large in proportion to its economy—whereas the Eastern European countries had extended themselves much further in proportion to their total economic capacity. For example, Poland had a debt of over $30 billion.

The theory behind this heavy borrowing was that it would permit the construction of plants and equipment based on advanced technology. These new plants would, in turn, increase domestic production, much of which would be exported to repay the loans in the long run. This unprecedented effort had varied results depending on differing national policies, but it tended to run into two major difficulties. First, the amounts borrowed were so large that most of these countries lacked the know-how to invest them properly. As a result, many of the undertakings were affected by serious mismanagement and even considerable graft. Second, by the time the Eastern European countries were ready to expand their exports, the economic recession that had prevailed in the West greatly reduced their ability to earn the hard currency needed to service their debts. These problems were counteracted to some extent by what amounted to a Soviet subsidy of Eastern Europe: Moscow sold the region oil below world prices and bought its countries' products above world prices. From 1971 to 1978 alone, this subsidy has been calculated at $14 billion. But in one respect, Moscow's assistance came up short. The USSR could not provide hard currency to help its allies service the debt to the West; as a consequence, by the end of the 1970s the Eastern European countries had to tighten their belts by raising prices on food and other commodities.

This policy of depressing the standard of living in the 1980s, after promoting rapid growth and raising people's hopes in the 1970s, had its most dramatic and best-known consequences in Poland. Despite the high hopes that attended its rise to power in 1956, the Gomulka administration never really managed to solve the country's manifold economic problems, and its decision finally to raise food prices in 1970 led to an outburst of workers' protest and the resignation of the Polish leader. Edward Gierek, Gomulka's successor, promised a more pragmatic effort to achieve economic growth by utilizing advances in modern science and technology to improve industrial productivity, and it was under his leadership that the Polish government sought to solve its problems with the aid of massive borrowing from the West. For half a dozen years, this policy worked well. Yet despite these good intentions, the rise in oil prices and the recession in Western Europe led to new economic difficulties by the end of the decade. The decline of the Western market for Polish industrial goods meant there were fewer funds available for the Polish industrialization program, which was still ineffective by any standard. Labor unrest negatively affected production, further harming government efforts to tame a growing foreign debt that by 1980 amounted to about $20 billion. Finally, food shortages became increasingly severe following a series of poor harvests.

What happened after these developments, however, made the Polish case more than just a great disturbance in Eastern European history. Indeed, it may even be reasonable to say that the Polish events of 1980–1981 were really a harbinger of the fall of communism a decade later. In July 1980 the government chose to cut back its large subsidies of food prices (that for meat alone in 1980 would cost about $3.3 billion), with resulting price increases of 40 to 60 percent. This time the popular reaction, fed by the memory of successful resistance to price hikes in 1970, led to one of the most important crises for the Communist system in the postwar period. More than 800,000 workers went out on strike. This event naturally meant a decline in all areas of production, from industrial goods intended for export to coal for home heating. Shortages increased, stimulating further discontent and demonstrations and further declines in productivity. Not only did the nationwide wave of strikes lead to the overthrow of the Gierek administration, but, even more significant for subsequent developments, workers throughout the country now began to organize an independent trade union movement, Solidarity. It immediately won wide support in Poland and found itself in the astonishing position of being able to negotiate with the government.

This remarkable decline in the authority of the Polish United Workers' party—the formal name of the Polish Communist party—was the result of several factors extending well beyond the collapse of the economy. Unlike Communists in several other Eastern European states, the Polish Communists (apart from certain key individuals) had never really been accepted as the legitimate government of the country. Particularly in the early 1980s, the party found itself badly divided, and there was no one to provide strong leadership and a sense of direction for Poland; meanwhile, the strikers gained popular support and confidence. It is also true that, thanks to its decision to back away from the collectivization of agriculture, the Polish government had never really been able to establish control over the countryside; no wonder, then, that Poland's independent farmers were quick to call for the formation of a rural Solidarity. Finally, the crippling blow for the country's government was its inability to keep the Roman Catholic church unequivocally on its side. In Poland, more so than in any other Eastern European state, the church had retained a significant degree of administrative independence; it also exercised a much stronger hold on Polish opinion than did the Communist party. In 1978 this role was enhanced to incredible dimensions by the election

For the Polish people, no single event since World War II seemed more important than the election of Polish-born Cardinal Karol Wojtyla as Pope John Paul II in October 1978. The Poles suddenly felt they could transcend decades of socialist underdevelopment and subservience before the Soviet Union and aspire to a higher set of ideals beyond communism. At the same time, the new pope's outspoken criticism of the shortcomings and inhumanitarian practices of Marxism-Leninism proved to be a constant thorn in the side of the Communist regime in Warsaw. The pope's ability to celebrate mass before millions of faithful churchgoers in Poland (he is here depicted at the Jasna Gora Monastery in Czestochowa in June 1983) gave many Poles reason to dream about a non-Communist future. The worshipers are holding a sign that reads, "Our Solidarity with the Pope," a reference to the anti-Communist Polish trade union. (Photos © Jerzy Koss, 1983. All rights reserved.)

In this picture Lech Walesa (center), the head of the Polish trade union Solidarity, raises his arm in an optimistic sign of victory while attending a solemn mass at St. Mary's Basilica in Gdansk, Poland, in November 1983. During this period Solidarity was still illegal, and Walesa was barely able to stay out of prison. But only six years later, the Communist Polish government was forced to legalize the trade union and to call for free elections. Walesa himself was elected president of Poland in 1990. Yet much like other popular Eastern European leaders who came to the fore during a time of acute economic crisis and social uncertainty in the early 1990s, Walesa found that opposing communism in the past was quite different from establishing a smoothly functioning democratic and capitalist order. (Photo © Jerzy Koss, 1983. All rights reserved.)

of Polish Cardinal Karol Wojtyla as Pope John Paul II. Masses conducted by the pope during his visits to Poland in 1979 and 1983 attracted hundreds of thousands of believers, including many young people. Thus the pope's visits demonstrated the helplessness of the government in the face of what were in effect anti-Communist demonstrations. They also served to give the future leaders of Solidarity—such as the one figure who more than any other embodied the independent trade union struggle, Lech Walesa—the confidence that they, too, could mobilize opinion on a massive scale.

Initially, Solidarity met with considerable success. As long as the Communist government was weakened, Solidarity was able to obtain its formal recognition as an independent and self-governing trade union with the right to strike—unprecedented in a Communist country. It also succeeded in bringing about the relaxation of censorship and greater freedom for the Catholic church. Accordingly, Gierek resigned as party leader in September 1980 and was replaced by an apparatchik, Stanislaw Kania, who was in turn replaced in October 1981 by a Polish army general, Wojciech Jaruzelski. Looking back on this period, we can see that the eighteen months from August 1980 to December 1981 were among the most exciting in postwar Eastern European history, as they marked an extraordinary degree of collaboration among Solidarity, the Catholic church, and leading intellectuals. Events demonstrated that it really was possible for representatives of mass society in a Communist country to organize themselves, providing that they were willing to put their differences behind them and work together toward a common goal.

Nonetheless, these groups' widely hailed proposals for a democratic Poland—plans for a liberalized political and economic system and a democratic party congress—were not matched by corresponding organizational strengths. This was especially so because the instruments of force, at this time at least, were still not in the hands of the Polish people. Behind the country's government stood the Soviet Union, which, as all Poles recognized, still had the capacity to intervene directly, as in Hungary in 1956 and Czechoslovakia in 1968. There was some hope that the Soviets might be reluctant to undertake the economic and political burden of occupying a hostile country of 38 million people. Doubt as to what course the Soviets would pursue was resolved conclusively on December 13, 1981, when Jaruzelski proclaimed a state of emergency, allowing the Polish army to impose martial law and arrest the leaders of Solidarity. Foreign observers have been divided as to the meaning of this action, with many assuming that Jaruzelski was simply serving as an agent of the Soviets. As events developed, however, most informed analysts came to see Jaruzelski as a patriotic Pole and a moderate Communist who, with indisputable Soviet backing, sought to find a way out of his country's dilemmas. Under military rule, the Polish economy was gradually stabilized, but the political deadlock between the government and the great majority of people represented by the Catholic church and the Solidarity movement was not resolved. It would be less than a decade before the consequences of this unsettled state of affairs were fully spelled out.

While Poland was undergoing such traumas, Hungary and Czechoslovakia, which had experienced Soviet intervention in 1956 and 1968, continued on separate courses that were much less dramatic. The intervention in Hungary had been the bloodiest in the postwar Eastern European experience, but by the 1980s Hungary had become the most prosperous and the most moderate of the countries in the Soviet orbit. This relative success was partly the result of a heritage of independent policymaking typical of Hungarian actions even when these lands were part of the Austro-Hungarian Empire before World War I. Then, too, there was the great skill of Kadar, who led the Hungarian Communist party after 1956. From almost his first years in power, Kadar had established a working relationship with the Soviet authorities that permitted him to implement significant domestic reforms. Of these, the central reform was the New Economic Mechanism, introduced in 1968, which started the country on the road to a kind of "market socialism." This meant less reliance on central planning and the encouragement of enterprises to respond to market needs. The New Economic Mechanism, along with related policies supported by modest borrowing from the West, led to significant economic growth and social change despite the depression that hung over Europe in the late 1970s and early 1980s. Hungary meanwhile moved only a small distance away from a centrally planned economy. The results of its version of market socialism were sufficiently successful to attract the serious attention of other socialist countries. In particular, Hungary served as one of the principal models the People's Republic of China used in designing its economic reform policies in the 1980s.

In contrast to Hungary, the postintervention settlement in Czechoslovakia developed along much more conservative lines. Although Husak, head of the Communist party from 1968 to 1987, favored a reform outlook, the majority of his colleagues and their Soviet advisers insisted on a tightly controlled system based on central planning. One of the main reasons for this approach was that the Communist party, again in contrast to the situation in Hungary, lost the confidence of the Czech and Slovak people after 1968. It therefore had to rule the country more as an occupying force than as a legitimate government. Along with its repression, the government nevertheless sought to appease the opposition by providing more consumer goods and consistently raising the standard of living. The outcome in the 1980s was a relatively prosperous but still sullen population that deeply resented the weight of its oppression.

This continuing alienation was reflected in the fiction of the scores of leading writers to emerge from Czechoslovakia in the post-1968 period, such as Milan Kundera, Josef Skvorecky, and Pavel Kohout, who found their country's history to be a record of constant betrayal, first by the West in 1938 and then by the East in 1968. The opposition was also reflected in the Charter 77 reform program signed by several hundred Czechs and Slovaks in January 1977 (see Chapter 5). The signers were at various times persecuted by state authorities, but their movement continued to press for a more moderate regime, even to the point of establishing formal links in 1981 with the Solidarity movement in Poland.

Bulgaria and Romania, though similar in their general level of development, pursued very different policies. Throughout the Communist period, Bulgaria was generally regarded as the most loyal of the Soviet bloc satellites in Eastern Europe and consistently tried to develop its policies of economic and social change within the context of Moscow's overall plans. Romania, by contrast, was the most rebellious of the Eastern European countries in its relations with the Soviet Union, if by no means politically liberal. It always sought to the extent possible to develop economic and political ties with Western Europe.

Bulgaria, under the leadership of Todor Zhivkov since 1959, was administered by a coterie of relatively young and well-educated party bureaucrats who sought to improve agricultural methods and develop industry along specialized lines adapted to foreign markets. After several earlier experiments, a reform program known (as in Hungary) as the New Economic Mechanism was announced in 1977 and finally implemented in 1982. This reform introduced some elements of the market economy and especially emphasized the need for enterprises to become profitable rather than relying heavily on state subsidies. Furthermore, the reform provided incentives for introducing advanced technology and for stimulating individual initiative within enterprises, although there was no sense in which it ever deviated from the essential features of command planning.

If Bulgaria was generally cautious in the way in which its leaders went about modernizing their economy, it might be said that Romania was quite the opposite. Led by Nicolae Ceausescu since 1967, the country was both the most oppressively ruled of the states of Eastern Europe, except for Albania, and the most independent of the Soviet Union. This apparent contradiction may be explained by the way Soviet security in the old bloc was normally assured by the firm domestic control exercised by the Communist party, whereas the nationalistic policy of the Romanian party was sufficient to assure the country's government of a consistent anti-Sovietism. Ironically, despite its independence, Romania embraced a path of economic development that had previously been epitomized by Stalinism, stressing rapid industrialization above all else.

In addition, the pattern of socialism Ceausescu articulated in the 1970s and 1980s had a number of idiosyncracies that made the country seem more like a developing country in the Third World than the supposedly "developed" socialist experiments in the rest of the bloc. Ceausescu himself acted very much like a tribal prince, allowing every achievement in his society to be attributed to his personal inspiration and genius. Then, too, the upper echelons of his government were almost entirely personalized, as his wife, son, and a dozen or more relatives monopolized all positions of consequence in his government. Local wits even had a phrase for this curious style of governance: "socialism in one family." Finally, even the Romanian Communist party was slightly different from (or more extreme than) its Eastern European counterparts, not only in that it was proportionately much larger than its neighbors but also in the sense that it was a "populist" rather than a "vanguard" party: It ruled in the name of the "people," abstractly conceived, who were held to be morally supreme in contrast to a corrupting and threatening external world.

Still, one of the mysteries that will always attend any investigation of Ceausescu's reign is how he managed to maintain the aura of total power for as long as he did in Romania. There is no doubt some truth to the wisdom that his enforced campaign of industrialization won him many converts from the countryside, as peasants found themselves suddenly thrust into the glittering world of a semiurbanized society. Moreover, much of the success of his long reign must also be attributed to the all-pervasive force of the secret police, whose agents had the capacity to worm their way into every nook and cranny of Romanian private life. So authoritarian had Ceausescu become by the end of his rule that owners of typewriters were even required to register their machines with the police lest they type articles that were defamatory to the regime.

The death in 1985 of Hoxha, who had led Communist Albania since 1941, gave prominence to the country that was the smallest and least known of the Communist-led states in Eastern Europe but also came the closest to rivaling Romania for its sheer brutality. To an extent, the key to understanding Albania is its size, as reflected in a series of changing alignments since World War I. The country was aligned with Yugoslavia until 1937 to avoid domination by the USSR, with the Soviet Union until 1961 to avoid domination by Yugoslavia, and with China until 1976 again to avoid domination by the USSR.

Almost the whole time, Hoxha administered Albania in a way that seemed to suggest that he was trying to make up for his country's size by achieving greatness. With plans and methods reminiscent of Stalin, he sought to drag Albania into the modern world, promoting rapid industrialization, the collectivization of all agriculture, and, most distinctively among all of the Eastern European states, complete suppression of religion. Hoxha's methods were cruel, and he personally was responsible for the execution of a number of his close colleagues when they failed to follow the zigs and zags of his policies. Nor was his infatuation with his own role in the success of the Albanian revolution any less intense than Ceausescu's. Statues and posters of Hoxha could be found in every public spot. Although his policies at times relied heavily on aid from the USSR and China during the periods of his country's alliance with them, Albania was largely (and often deliberately) isolated from the rest of the world until the late 1980s. At that time its leaders began cautiously to develop trade relations with West Germany and other European countries. It was only then, with Hoxha's death in 1985 and his replacement by a younger cadre, Ramiz Alia, that outsiders were able to entertain even modest hopes that the country might abandon its draconian ways.

The New Reform Era

It is not difficult to understand why, against this background of both cautious change and neo-Stalinist dictatorship, the sudden arrival of a new reform program under the auspices of the Gorbachev administration in the Soviet Union after 1985 met with a mixed reception in Eastern Europe. As we have seen, the Soviet goal was to encourage both *perestroika*—a "restructuring" of the economy in the direction of a market system—and *glasnost*—greater "openness" in the discussion of past errors and of alternative solutions to contemporary problems. Yet as glamorous as these terms may have sounded at the time to hopeful innovators, it is important to recognize that Gorbachev was hardly being generous in seeking to move his allies in this direction. The Soviets hoped that as the Eastern European countries followed Moscow's example in moving toward mixed market and socialist economies, they would come to rely less on the USSR's support to keep their economies afloat. This step in turn was supposed to allow the Soviet government to free up more of its economic resources to deal with its own problems.

It must also be said that Gorbachev's manner of conveying his reform communism was initially not that different from the way in which Soviet leaders in the past had dictated their priorities to the captive Eastern European states. According to the signals that Gorbachev sent, the satellites would still have to follow the dictates of the homeland of the Great October Revolution. At least in the early period after Gorbachev came to power, this meant, first, abiding firmly by the basic precepts of Marxism-Leninism as they sought to carve out their distinctive reform paths and, second, keeping in mind that the security interests of the Soviet Union could not be jeopardized.

On balance, adherence to such principles was no problem for the Eastern European leaderships in the period between 1985 and 1987. Most were not even convinced that the new Soviet general secretary would long stay in power, given the seemingly reckless way in which he attacked the traditional manner of economic and political decisionmaking in his country. If Gorbachev were to have a relatively short term in office, most of the Communist leaders reasoned, those who joined him too enthusiastically might find themselves in disfavor with his successors. Further, even if these personalities could recognize the necessity of some kind of change, there was also an even deeper problem in responding to Gorbachev. Except in Poland, all of the top Eastern European leaderships had been marked by an extraordinary degree of continuity in office; the Communist bosses were all, to one extent or another, implicated in the errors of their countries' past. In Bulgaria, Czechoslovakia, Hungary, and Romania—and also in East Germany—the general secretaries of the Communist parties were over seventy years of age and had been in office from seventeen to thirty-four years, until Milos Jakes replaced Husak in Czechoslovakia in 1987 and Karoly Grosz replaced Kadar in Hungary in 1988. This circumstance meant that to criticize the past, a relatively easy task for the younger, fairly unblemished Gorbachev, they would have all, in effect, ended up criticizing themselves, a not too pleasing prospect for those who wanted to retain their grip on power.

For these reasons alone, it is not hard to see why the majority of these governments were inclined, as we have already seen in the East German case, to put some distance between themselves and Gorbachev. If the reforms that the Soviet Union was introducing might be appropriate for the USSR, the Eastern European leaders could argue, they were unsuited to the specific challenges facing socialist construction in their countries. Some critiques of Gorbachev's policies were harsher than others. For the Albanians, there could be little doubt that the new general secretary was the incarnation of everything that had gone awry with Marxism-Leninism since the passing from the scene of Tirana's idea of a revolutionary hero, Stalin. But even for the countries that were closer to Moscow, there was still a scarcely veiled disdain for Gorbachev. Romania's Ceausescu rarely minced his words in criticizing what he termed the Soviet leader's unjustified interference in the sovereign internal affairs of other states. Following Gorbachev's challenges, Ceausescu actually tightened his controls over Romanian society, cracking down on dissidents and introducing draconian measures—food rationing and stringent limits on the use of electricity—designed to insulate the country from the disturbing influences of the outer world.

Elsewhere in the bloc, the leaders of Bulgaria and Czechoslovakia paid lip service to Gorbachev's reforms, but there was little evidence that they were willing to follow the logic of *perestroika* and *glasnost* to quite the extreme limits that the Soviet leader had in mind. Bulgaria did show some innovation in its economic policies, allowing greater self-management of enterprises. Furthermore, the Bulgarian government began to open up the country to the international market of science and technology and to encourage joint-venture agreements with Japanese, U.S., and West German firms, in the hope of acquiring the advanced electronics so crucial to the modernization of production. In the realm of politics, however, the Bulgarian Communist party remained as conservative as ever. The case of Czechoslovakia was little better. Despite the rise of a younger, somewhat more energetic generation of party members into the leading bodies of the Jakes government after 1987 and many words about the need for more efficient methods of economic management, the regime remained bound to the essentially risk-averse per-spective that had governed its thinking since late 1968. Not only was there little substantial economic change, but the Jakes regime also demonstrated that it was as determined as ever to prevent its critics from gaining even a centimeter in their efforts to press for significant reform. Furthermore, numerous opponents of the party dictatorship (e.g., the outspoken writer and Charter 77 advocate Václav Havel) were jailed throughout the late 1980s, often for espousing ideas that were no different from those articulated by Gorbachev.

Knowing as we do what happened to these Communist governments—that is, that they totally collapsed in 1989—we might think that a Jakes and a Ceausescu would have been much wiser simply to have admitted the manifold problems with which they were contending and then sought to enlist the support of the greatest number of their own citizens in seeking resolution of these social and economic dilemmas. A flaw in such an assump-tion is that it underestimates the bind in which these governments found themselves. Communism may have got them all into an economic mess as a result of the inefficiencies that came with the centralization of initiative in the hands of a few state planners, but all of these leaders' personal interests were still linked with the maintenance of centralized power itself, according to the principle that only an elite group of individuals—the Communist party—was really blessed with the capacity to know what was good for the country. Once the avenues to state power were opened to larger segments of the population, the great risk was that the whole Communist system would tumble like a house of cards.

President Václav Havel of Czechoslovakia (left) meets with President Richard von Weizsäcker of West Germany during a short trip to Germany on January 2, 1990. A playwright and prominent cultural figure, Havel took a formal part in politics only with the peaceful Velvet Revolution against communism in Czechoslovakia in late 1989, though he built on a long background of political involvement. For much of the 1970s, Havel had demanded that the old Communist regime present a more human face and live up to its promises to respect basic human rights. Havel was imprisoned for his protests only months before the people finally went into the streets of Prague in 1989 to overthrow the dictatorial government. As president, Havel embodies the liberal-democratic traditions that his country hoped to embrace in its "return to Europe." (Photo courtesy of the German Information Center.)

Just before the revolutions of 1989, the danger of tampering with the established order could be seen in the indirect impact of Gorbachev's reforms, even the *idea* of reform itself, on the Eastern European outcast, Yugoslavia. Given its location outside of the Soviet alliance, Yugoslavia was of course a special case. The principal theme of the country's foreign policy for decades had been nonalignment, and Tito had demonstrated his independence from Moscow by condemning the actions of both the United States in the Dominican Republic and Vietnam and the Soviet Union for its occupation of Czechoslovakia. But in one respect, in his government's reliance on a centralized Communist party, known in Yugoslavia as the League of Communists, Tito's regime was not all that different from its Leninist neighbors. The specific conditions under which the federated state of Yugoslavia had been formed, bringing together a spate of quarreling ethnic groups—Serbians, Croatians, Slovenians, Montenegrans, Albanians, and numerous others— made the kind of authoritarian control associated with communism a virtual necessity for holding the country together.

Naturally, many of Yugoslavia's problems were homegrown. Even after years of effort to counter the problem, there were still great disparities among the country's principal national groups. Yet when attempts were made to redistribute the wealth of the more prosperous republics of Croatia and Slovenia to the more underdeveloped south, the government normally encountered only resentment in return, both from those in the north, who felt that they had been unjustly deprived of their hard-earned wealth, and from their poorer compatriots, who believed they deserved still more. Then, too, throughout the 1980s Yugoslavia was pommeled with aggravating levels of unemployment and inflation. In this climate Gorbachev's arrival was bound to bring new uncertainties, as the precarious balance among the Yugoslav republics was upset and the mystique of ideological obeisance to the central state was shattered. In late 1988, the people's pent-up resentment of the economic hardships of daily life led to an outburst of anger against the ruling party. In the Voivodina region, protestors succeeded in forcing local party leaders to resign. In Titograd, the capital of Montenegro, riot police were used against the demonstrators, who responded with sit-down strikes in factories. In other parts of the country as well, citizens demonstrated to demand the resignation of Communist party leaders. To this widespread protest against economic conditions was added an increase in national tensions. In Serbia, the largest of the republics, political leaders like Slobodan Milosevic sought to use populist and nationalist appeals to dominate the political scene in Montenegro and the Voivodina and to support the Serbian minority against the Albanian majority in the southern Kosovo province.

As they looked on, many of the other Eastern European states may have congratulated themselves that they were able to maintain a modest level of political calm and predictability, in part by successfully insulating themselves and their populations from the Gorbachev phenomenon. In view of what happened only a year thereafter, such self-confidence would prove to be premature. To understand why this was the case, however, we need to turn to the two countries—Poland and Hungary—that did seriously seek to emulate the Soviet leader's example.

The Crisis of 1989 and Beyond

Revolt Against Communism

It is doubtful that the Communist leaderships of Poland and Hungary thought that they were laying the foundation for their own demise when they began to engage in cautious economic and political innovations in the late 1980s. Rather, like Gorbachev himself, they originally thought they were revitalizing their ideology and giving their populations new, more convincing reasons for binding their future hopes and expectations to communism.

At least initially, the cause of reform in Poland was driven by the government. In 1987 General Jaruzelski announced drastic changes in the economic structure of Poland designed to move the country toward a mixture of central planning and market economics. This new program included a rise in the price of consumer goods—a move that had led to strikes in 1980—but also, significantly, a rise in wages. More important, according to Jaruzelski's plan, uneconomical state enterprises were destined to be discontinued and production was for the first time supposed to meet the challenge of the market. Also involved were increases in the costs of health care, entertainment, and other services that for many years had been heavily subsidized by the state. But the assumption was that because Poland was responding to conditions set by the International Monetary Fund and the World Bank in order to secure new loans, not to mention responding to Gorbachev's reforms as well, the population would buy into the rationality of making further sacrifices for the nation's future.

Perhaps if these moves had led to a serious improvement in the Polish economy, Jaruzelski's efforts to find a halfway point between the wisdom of sounder economic planning and the burdens that came with it would have worked. By summer 1988, however, it was clear that Poland had entered into a spiraling economic crisis in which inflation grew apace with foreign indebtedness, finally leading to a series of industrial strikes that threatened to shut down the economy altogether. It had been almost seven years since Jaruzelski had first crushed the Solidarity movement, but the organization had managed to maintain a lively existence underground. Moreover, its leaders had already learned an important lesson from the past: When their government was on the brink of economic catastrophe, even with its monopoly of power, it, too, could be forced to compromise.

Thus it was that Solidarity reemerged in autumn 1988 and spring 1989, with Walesa at its head, to strike a remarkable bargain with the Communist administration. In return for its implicit promise to abide by certain norms set by the Jaruzelski government—primarily to eschew further labor unrest—the trade union was not only legalized but also received the regime's unprecedented promise to conduct free, if carefully circumscribed, national elections and to create a new office of the state presidency. Cynics might have said that very little of substance had changed when Jaruzelski selected himself to fill the latter office, but there can be no contesting that the entire atmosphere of policymaking in Poland was transformed following this agreement. With opposition parties permitted and with an increasingly free and critical press, Solidarity was able to record a landslide victory over its Communist rivals in the June 1989 competition for those seats in the Sejm (the Polish parliament) which were not reserved exclusively for the old regime. So intense was the outpouring of popular support for the independent trade union that Jaruzelski was not even able to arrange for his military ally, Czeslaw Kiszczak, to be appointed prime minister of the new government. The post went instead to Walesa's retiring adviser, Tadeusz Mazowiecki (editor of a Catholic journal and member of the small Catholic party known as Sign), in December 1989.

In comparison to Poland, what happened in Hungary over the same period was considerably less dramatic though, in view of the events it precipitated, equally significant. It would be fair to say that in a way the Hungarian regime had been engaging in the most gradual kind of reforms ever since Kadar took power following the revolt of 1956. It was not that the Communist government altered anything fundamental but only that it had constantly searched for those incremental steps that might somehow repair the lasting damage done to relations between rulers and ruled during the revolution. At first, even Grosz's replacement of Kadar in 1988 had seemed to be merely another of these slight steps, the exchange of an aging representative of the Hungarian art of compromise for a seemingly more vigorous but still ideologically similar younger comrade.

If anything, the example Gorbachev set served to accelerate the pace of change in the country, raising expectations about what might be possible. For years, Hungarian citizens had been inundated with propaganda about the supposed achievements of their New Economic Mechanism. But though their tastes had become more refined with greater access to Western commodities in their stores and an increased ability to travel abroad, the real capacity of the country's economy to meet such expectations had declined. By the end of the 1980s, Hungary had the largest per capita foreign debt in the whole Eastern bloc, yet it had hardly managed to modernize its factories to the extent that its planners had originally hoped when they began the borrowing. Industrial discontent was on the rise, given a widespread perception of growing disparities between the life-styles available to a new middle class of entrepreneurs (e.g., small-business owners, taxi drivers, artisans) and the rougher circumstances that the broader masses of the Hungarian working population faced. The patience of most citizens had simply become exhausted with the daily struggle: Decent housing was fantastically scarce in urban centers, wages were still low, and the quality of social services had declined throughout the decade.

Accordingly, those in the government who styled themselves reformers began to look for suitable symbolic gestures to demonstrate to their population that communism really could have a human face. The most prominent of these was the decision to stage a public funeral to rebury Imre Nagy in June 1989, in the hopes of finally mending the wounds of national humiliation of 1956. Indeed, the event brought out all of the emotions of the Hungarian populace, millions weeping at the memory of their national tragedy three decades earlier. Just as important, although more subdued because of the rights that the Hungarian population already enjoyed, was the government's decision a few weeks earlier finally to remove the barbed wire and fortifications along its border with Austria.

We saw in Chapter 6 what the consequences of this decision were for the German Democratic Republic, which lost tens of thousands of its own citizens through the open Hungarian border and then suffered a political and economic crisis from which it would never recover. Yet the ramifications of the GDR's fall went far beyond even the significance of German reunification. With the demise of the East German state, it was as if the remaining mystique of communism in the region were imploded. In the eyes of many of its neighbors, the GDR had been the epitome of a communism that worked. It was autocratic, its system often coldly formal and impersonal, but when it came to putting food on the shelves and high-tech products in every household—so the mythology went—the country was supposedly competitive with anything the capitalist West could offer. Nevertheless, when hundreds of thousands of its best citizens organized marches in fall 1989 to protest the SED's policies and when the Communist regime was exposed for what it was—shabby, inept, and in many cases corrupt—the populations of the other Communist states could see that even what appeared to be the best that Marxism-Leninism had to offer was flawed. Moreover, they could see that, unlike in 1956 and 1968, the Soviet Union was no longer willing to do anything in its power to keep an ally, in this case the Socialist Unity party, in office.

The Czechoslovak population reacted by staging its own so-called Velvet Revolution, a remarkable few weeks in November 1989 in which masses of people went out into the streets to call for an end to Communist rule. Workers threatened to go on strike in urban areas. Intellectuals, students, and other activists coalesced into a loosely organized citizens' movement known as the Civic Forum. Even dignitaries from the past, like Dubcek, reemerged to hasten the Jakes government's departure. The result was the peaceful formation of a new Government of National Understanding, under the improbable leadership of the former dissident Havel, which promised to reintegrate Czechoslovakia into the liberal democratic traditions of the West.

In Bulgaria, the outcome was somewhat different, but the change was still significant. Not long after the fall of the Berlin Wall, the old Zhivkov leadership was forced out of power and replaced by a group of putative reformers led by a Communist named Petar Mladenov. Discussion groups and independent trade unions sprang up throughout the country, and very swiftly the leading role of the Communist party was supplanted, first by the formation of independent parties and then by the creation of a grand coalition of opposition groups known as the Union of Democratic Forces (UDF). This coalition promptly pressed for immediate democratic reforms and a drastic overhaul of the Bulgarian economy.

Romanian dictator Nicolae Ceausescu was a master of the art of political imagery. For much of the world, at least until the 1980s, he seemed to be something of a political iconoclast, openly challenging the foreign policy of the Soviet Union. In defiance of Moscow's command, he developed a close relationship with the People's Republic of China and its leader, Deng Xiaoping (see above). At home, however, he was one of the most brutal tyrants of the modern age. Thus, when the people of Romania rose up against his government in December 1989, one of the first acts of the revolutionary council that deposed the Romanian leader was to arrest Ceausescu and his wife, Elena. After a summary trial that was televised throughout Romania (see below), they were both executed by firing squad. (Photos from Reuters/Bettmann Newsphotos.)

No doubt the most tragic of the Eastern European transformations, however, transpired in Romania once the country's population was allowed to vent its frustration over the years of brutality it had suffered under Ceausescu. Whereas in the other cases the overthrow of the old regime was accomplished without much or any violence, the Romanian revolution began in mid-December 1990 with government attacks on peaceful demonstrators in the western city of Timisoara. It culminated in several days of open, bloody fighting between opposition elements and large segments of the army on the one hand and Ceausescu's hated security police (Securitate) on the other. In the end, some say on Christmas Day, the Communist tyrant and his wife were executed by the military—but not before countless other Romanian citizens had lost their lives as well. Furthermore, even though the old dictatorship was replaced by a new coalition of reform Communists, the National Salvation Front, there was some doubt whether the individuals at the head of this organization, most prominently the country's new leader, Ion Iliescu, had truly made a complete break with the authoritarian ways of their predecessors.

Nevertheless, despite these varying responses to the era of *glasnost* and democratization, it was hard to deny that the states of Eastern Europe had passed a critical threshold in 1989 and 1990. This was certainly the impression that one had from viewing the elections conducted throughout the region in the latter year, even if the outcome of some of these votes was not always the straightforward vindication of liberal values that many observers may have desired. In March and April 1990, the first free parliamentary elections in over four decades were held in Hungary. In their wake, a nationalist party, the Hungarian Democratic Forum, and two other smaller parties, the agrarian Smallholders and the Christian Democrats, were able to form a governing coalition. In May 1990 the Romanian National Liberation Front won a decisive victory over its opponents after conducting a campaign of dirty tricks and flagrant intimidation. In June elections in Bulgaria, the renamed Communist party, now known as the Bulgarian Socialist party, eked out a victory over its UDF challengers; it did so by taking advantage of the internal differences within the UDF, although the Socialist candidate for president, Mladenov, was eventually replaced by the UDF leader, Zhelyu Zhelev. During the same month, the Civic Forum triumphed over all of its challengers in Czechoslovakia. And finally, in December 1990, the extent to which Poland had changed by going beyond Solidarity's initial achievements was demonstrated in open elections by which Walesa replaced Jaruzelski as the country's president.

Thus at least the form of the Western European experience seemed to have been replicated in each of these cases. Moreover, the new regimes took marked steps to distance themselves from the old Marxist-Leninist model and its Soviet sponsors. All of the new governments, for example, professed to embrace most of the essentials of the capitalist market economy, just as their foreign policies reflected a newfound preference for modeling themselves after the examples of potential trading and commercial partners in the West. Good reason existed to think that the East-West divide in Europe had lost much of the defining simplicity that had characterized the relations among all states on the Continent during the Cold War. The big question, though, was whether the liberation of the "captive nations" of Eastern Europe, as they used to be called, meant that these polities would automatically soon find their place among the developed states in the West, regardless of what their leaders wanted.

The Path Beyond Socialism

One can say that the Eastern European states would like nothing better than to follow up on the various successes of their Western European counterparts, given the best of all possible worlds. Yet for at least four different reasons, this road is bound to be difficult. First, no one will contest the trouble that almost all of the former Leninist regimes will have in the years ahead in transforming their economies into market-oriented systems. A Polish witticism about socialism expresses the problem: Constructing socialism was a lot like making fish soup out of an aquarium: It didn't taste very good, but it could be accomplished. The real challenge will come in transforming fish soup into an aquarium, in constructing capitalism out of the morass that was socialism.

Even in the early 1990s, it was clear to all of the Eastern European regimes that their populations' hopes of living like their more affluent cousins in the West were simply not realizable in the short term, in no small part because of the waste and devastation that forty years of socialism had left in its wake. What could one do with a country like Romania, whose industry was still geared to the times of Stalinist accelerated growth, whose industrial plant and transportation systems were run-down and outmoded, and whose work force lacked even the basic skills and education necessary to make it relevant to the productive needs of a modern world? In addition, how could one motivate populations that had grown used to highly subsidized prices for basic commodities and been socialized into thinking that they would get paid for their jobs even if they did not work? In some countries, like Poland, a kind of economic shock therapy was administered to bring prices up to more realistic levels while simultaneously holding wages steady. This policy did have the consequence of putting more goods into the stores, though people did not have the money to buy them. In other countries, like Hungary and Bulgaria, the watchword still seemed to be caution, as governments were uncertain about which steps to take first. For good reason, they feared the consequences of alienating their constituents by implementing austerity programs. Throughout the region, it is true that one term, *privatization* (the carving up of old state monopolies and their transfer to private hands), had the nearly magical connotation of promising economic revitalization. Nonetheless, nearly everyone could agree that it would be at least a decade before this process was completed. Even then, there was no guarantee that the industries of old could meet the challenge of finding competitive niches in the world economy.

A second problem that the Eastern European states will face has to do with their political transformation, as polities like Hungary and Czechoslovakia found when they first began to hold regular elections. In most Western European countries it would be unusual to find more than a handful of parties competing actively for public office. In the former Soviet satellites, there were initially as many as sixty different parties in the elections of 1990, representing everything from environmental interests to religion to beer. Nor was it always clear that organizations that went under the rubric of parties, such as the Civic Forum in Czechoslovakia or Solidarity in Poland, were even parties in the normal sense of the term. For example, the latter was much more a mass movement than anything else. This was demonstrated during the contest over Walesa's candidacy for the Polish presidency in late fall 1990, when Solidarity splintered into rival factions the moment it was presented with a serious political problem.

These were of course only technical difficulties for countries that had made the transition away from communism without considerable bloodshed; slowly, a smaller number of more mature parties would emerge in any case. But there were other instances where the problems were more severe because more deeply rooted. For example, even the idea of politics—the notion that citizens might participate as autonomous actors in the formulation of public policy—was still considered alien to the region after decades in which Marxist elites had, in effect, done the thinking for those below them. Thus in June 1990 Romania's National Salvation Front showed little compunction in turning loose truckloads of angry miners on student demonstrators in Bucharest, who were demanding nothing more than the rights of free speech and opinion to which Iliescu's government had already professed to subscribe. Similarly, the Albanian regime, which not surprisingly proved to be the slowest of all the Eastern European states to renounce its authoritarian ways, showed in late 1990 and early 1991 that it was prepared to use all available means of coercion to keep itself in power, even to the point of precipitating a mass exodus of its citizens into neighboring Greece and Italy.

Yet if the norm of political tolerance was still in short supply in many parts of Eastern Europe, an even greater source of instability was that presented by a third set of problems, ethnic intolerance and nationalism. For all of the terror that the Communist past had represented for the region, Marxist-Leninist regimes had at least had the virtue of simplicity, demanding that all of the constituent groups of their societies participate in the common struggle for an ideal order that had not quite achieved fruition. Ethnic disorder in particular was relatively rare, if only because these governments had their own selfish ends to pursue. As the 1990s began, Yugoslavia was of course the

It is unlikely that anything could have been done to prevent the violence and carnage that finally erupted in Yugoslavia in 1991. Resentments were deep among the country's divided ethnic groups, which include Serbs, Croats, Slovenes, Albanians, and others. Their mutual grievances were of such long standing that there was little chance that the Yugoslav state could be held together by appeals to reason. In this photo, a masked Albanian demonstrator standing next to a burning barricade in the troubled and impoverished Kosovo province in southern Yugoslavia flashes a victory sign in stubborn defiance of the policies of the central government in Belgrade. In 1991, in the northern part of the country, Slovenia seceded from Yugoslavia as full-scale civil war was waged between Serbs and secessionist Croats. (Photo from Reuters/Bettmann Newsphotos.)

best known of the states facing such conflict because of the way in which the federated state was structured around a crazy quilt of hostile nationalities and ethnic groupings. There, as the veneer of Communist rule was cracked and some of the wealthier northern republics began to elect legislatures according to democratic norms, few observers were surprised as republics like Slovenia and Croatia took steps to declare their sovereign independence from the larger Yugoslav state. It was no matter that in the most rational of all possible worlds, all of the Yugoslav states might have done better to work together to solve their problems collectively. This was nationalism, which, as the events leading up to the First World War in Europe suggested, defied elementary rationality. Thus it was the tragedy of history repeating itself that led to bloody fighting between the Serb-dominated Yugoslav army and the breakaway republic of Slovenia in midsummer 1991 and then quickly escalated into armed conflict between Croats and Serbs. At first, Yugoslavia's neighbors in the European Community sought to resolve the crisis by appealing to the better judgment of the different republican governments. When this approach failed, some (the Germans, for example) threatened to impose santions on the Serbian regime, which they considered the greatest offender. Nonetheless, by fall 1991, all of the stifled frustrations and animosities once concealed just below the surface of Yugoslav society erupted into full-scale war, assuring the demise of the country that had begun as the kingdom of Serbs, Croats, and Slovenes decades before the advent of communism in Eastern Europe.

What was equally thought-provoking about the future of the Eastern European region as a whole was the extent to which, after forty years of Communist dictatorship, ethnic troubles could still be found in other states as well. Bulgarians held animosity toward the over 1 million Turks in their country; Hungarians and Romanians felt tensions over the bitterly contested border region of Transylvania; there were seriously strained relations between Czechs and Slovaks in modern-day Czechoslovakia. These situations presented one of the fundamental contradictions of the fall of communism in the region. Theoretically one of the most important aspects of the democratic revolutions was the bringing of the right of self-determination to Eastern Europe. The prospect that many of the democratic leaders of these states had not anticipated and with which they will have to grapple in the years to come is that this might also translate into a right to self-destruction.

The final problem that all Eastern European states share as they enter into their postrevolutionary periods of development relates to their collective identity. Certainly one of the more invidious aspects of the experience of Soviet domination was the way in which the satellite states were boxed together in the same military and economic alliances, the Warsaw Pact and Comecon, regardless of their different interests and different stages of industrial development. If one were to ask most of the Eastern European peoples today with whom they would like to associate themselves in the future and what kinds of societies they would like to fashion, the overwhelming majority would aspire to the modern identities we associate with Western Europe.

No wonder, then, that shortly after their revolutions countries like Hungary and Czechoslovakia were looking for links to NATO, or that they and still others were struggling to keep from being excluded from the united Western European market of 1992. No wonder, too, that countries like tiny Albania, whose population finally forced its Communist rulers from power in spring 1991, looked longingly to their affluent Western neighbors for the economic and technological magic to bring them instantaneously out of their darker ages. They, too, wanted to be like the Western Europeans, because it was the *West* that had come to define the ideal of European rebirth in the late twentieth century. The big question, though, was whether, after all the years of artificial separation of one part of Europe from the other, the Western states really wanted to include their poorer Eastern cousins, politically and economically, in the new European ideal.

Suggested Readings

General

Ash, T. G., *The Magic Lantern: The Revolutions of '89 Witnessed in Warsaw, Budapest, Berlin, and Prague* (1990).

Black, C. E. (ed.), *Challenge in Eastern Europe* (1954).

Brzezinski, Z., *The Soviet Bloc*, rev. ed. (1967).

Charlton, M., *The Eagle and the Small Birds: Crisis in the Soviet Empire from Yalta to Solidarity* (1984).

Dawisha, K., *Eastern Europe, Gorbachev and Reform: The Great Challenge* (1988).

Gati, C. (ed.), *The Politics of Modernization in Eastern Europe* (1974).

Linden, R. H., *Bear and Foxes: The International Relations of the East European States* (1979).

Lovenduski, J., and J. Woodall, *Politics and Society in Eastern Europe* (1987).

Rakowska-Harmstone, T., and A. Gyorgy (eds.), *Communism in Eastern Europe*, 2d ed. (1984).

Sodaro, M. J., and S. L. Wolchik (eds.), *Foreign and Domestic Policy in Eastern Europe in the 1980s* (1983).

Terry, S. M. (ed.), *Soviet Policy in Eastern Europe* (1985).

Albania

Biberaj, E., *Albania and China: A Study of an Unequal Alliance* (1986).

Frasheri, K., *The History of Albania: A Brief Survey* (1964).

Halliday, J. (ed.), *The Artful Albanian: The Memoirs of Enver Hoxha* (1986).

Pano, N. C., *The People's Republic of Albania* (1969).

Prifti, P. R., *Socialist Albania Since 1944: Domestic and Foreign Developments* (1978).

Skendi, S. (ed.), *Albania* (1956).

Bulgaria

Bell, J. D., *The Bulgarian Communist Party from Blagoev to Zhivkov* (1986).

Boll, M. M., *Cold War in the Balkans: American Foreign Policy and the Emergence of Communist Bulgaria, 1943–1947* (1984).

Brown, J. F., *Bulgaria Under Communist Rule* (1970).

Bulgarian Academy of Science, *Information Bulgaria: A Short Encyclopedia of the People's Republic of Bulgaria* (1985).

Crampton, R. J., *A Short History of Modern Bulgaria* (1987).

Groueff, S., *Crown of Thorns: The Reign of King Boris III, 1918–1943* (1987).

Lampe, J. R., *The Bulgarian Economy in the Twentieth Century* (1986).

Moser, C. A., *Dimitrov of Bulgaria: A Political Biography of Dr. George M. Dimitrov* (1979).

Oren, N., *Bulgarian Communism: The Road to Power, 1934–1944* (1971).

———, *Revolution Administered: Agrarianism and Communism in Bulgaria* (1973).

Czechoslovakia

Bradley, J.F.N., *Politics: Czechoslovakia, 1945–1971* (1981).

Frantisek, A., *Red Star over Prague* (1984).

Heitlinger, A., *Women and State Socialism: Sex Inequality in the Soviet Union and Czechoslovakia* (1979).

Korbel, J., The Communist Subversion of Czechoslovakia, 1938–1948 (1959).
Lettrich, J., History of Modern Slovakia (1955).
Mlynar, Z., Nightfrost in Prague: The End of Humane Socialism (1980).
Skilling, H. G., Czechoslovakia's Interrupted Revolution (1976).
Valenta, J., Soviet Intervention in Czechoslovakia, 1968: Anatomy of a Decision (1979).
Zinner, P. E., Communist Strategy and Tactics in Czechoslovakia, 1918–48 (1963).

Hungary

Berend, I. R., and G. Ranki, The Hungarian Economy in the Twentieth Century (1985).
Gati, C., Hungary and the Soviet Bloc (1986).
Helmreich, E. C. (ed.), Hungary (1957).
Kecskemeti, P., The Unexpected Revolution: Social Forces in the Hungarian Uprising (1961).
Kertesz, S. D., Between Russia and the West: Hungary and the Illusion of Peacemaking, 1945–1947 (1984).
Macartney, C. S., Hungary: A Short History (1962).
Toma, P., and I. Volgyes, Politics in Hungary (1977).
World Bank, Hungary: Economic Development and Reforms (1984).

Poland

Andrews, N. G., Poland, 1980–81: Solidarity Versus the Party (1984).
Ash, T. G., The Polish Revolution: Solidarity (1984).
Bromke, A., Poland: The Protracted Crisis (1983).
Brumberg, A., Poland: Genesis of a Revolution (1983).
Kwasniewski, J., Society and Deviance in Communist Poland (1984).
Misztal, B., Poland After Solidarity: Social Movements Versus the State (1985).
Reddaway, W. F. (ed.), The Cambridge History of Poland, 2 vols. (1941–1950).
Taras, R., Ideology in a Socialist State (1985).
Woodall, J. (ed.), Policy and Politics in Contemporary Poland (1981).

Romania

Braun, A., Romanian Foreign Policy Since 1965 (1978).
Fischer-Galati, S. A., The New Romania: From People's Republic to Socialist Republic (1967).
Graham, L. S., Romania: A Developing Socialist State (1982).
Jowitt, K., Revolutionary Breakthroughs and Nationalist Development: The Case of Romania, 1944–1965 (1971).
Shafir, M., Romania: Politics, Economics, and Society (1985).
Tsantis, A. C., and R. Perrer, Romania: The Industrialization of an Agrarian Economy Under Socialist Planning (1979).

Yugoslavia

Banac, I., *The National Question in Yugoslavia* (1984).

Byrnes, R. F. (ed.), *Yugoslavia* (1957).

Campbell, J. C., *Tito's Separate Road: America and Yugoslavia in World Politics* (1967).

Cohen, L. J., *Political Cohesion in a Fragile Mosaic: The Yugoslav Experience* (1983).

Djilas, M., *The New Class: An Analysis of the Communist System* (1957).

Gruenwald, O., *The Yugoslav Search for Man: Marxist Humanism in Contemporary Yugoslavia* (1983).

Rusinow, D., *The Yugoslav Experiment, 1948–1974* (1977).

Vucinich, W. S. (ed.), *Contemporary Yugoslavia: Twenty Years of Socialist Experiment* (1969).

CHAPTER NINE

The United Kingdom

Political Developments
Alternating Leadership • Northern Ireland
Constitutional Changes

Social Services
Education • Extension of Social Security

Economic Developments
Nationalization • Crisis in Foreign Trade
Thatcher's Policies

Empire and Commonwealth
The New Commonwealth of Nations
The Experience of Decolonization

Notes

Suggested Readings

T he aftereffects of war brought similar problems to both victorious and defeated states. Some countries had been devastated, others occupied; all found their economies strained to the utmost. Governments struggled under obligations that led them in varying measure toward centrally directed policies. These policies aimed to increase efficiency and to improve distribution of economic benefits and social justice to all segments of their countries' populations. Western Europe became more conscious of the need for unity, and this consciousness gave rise to experiments in economic cooperation. Colonial empires underwent metamorphosis; some did so peacefully; others experienced substantial bloodshed. The colonial conflicts were intensified by the great division in ideas between Communists and anti-Communists.

For the United Kingdom (England, Scotland, and Wales, plus Northern Ireland and the Channel Islands), adjustment to the challenges of peace was difficult. It was all the more so because victory in the war and Prime Minister Winston Churchill's compelling leadership effectively camouflaged the decline of Britain as a world power. Few perceived the extent of the problem, fewer wished to admit it, and still fewer initially had the determination to face it. Britain's factories were worn out, its treasury exhausted. During the war many of its markets had been lost to neutral countries or to the burgeoning U.S. industrial enterprise. The indigenous populations of the colonies called for independence. At home conviction grew that the calamities of the war had not been endured so that old patterns of economic, social, and political privilege could continue. Change was accepted as something that would definitely occur. The key questions were how great and how fast. Behind these lay a debate about the basic nature of social justice, the proper extent of personal freedom (including freedom from heavy taxation), and the role of government.

These issues in turn rested on a larger one, that of defining just what an advanced industrial society would be and the proper avenue toward it. The British population as a whole recognized only slowly the impact of the technological revolution upon the processes of production and the nature of employment. The importance of education and of trained specialists in management, engineering, and the like increased; the influence of industrial laborers and the lower middle class waned. Service activities, such as design, sales, personnel and distribution work, and eventually computer operation, in time employed growing numbers of white-collar workers. Blue-collar workers, through training and technology, moved toward becoming skilled machine operators. Many individuals would have to change careers two or three times. Such shifts—sometimes necessitated by the decline of one industry and the rise of another in a different location—made the population increasingly mobile. Automation and innovative means of information service rendered traditional jobs obsolete; workers unable to adapt to new require-

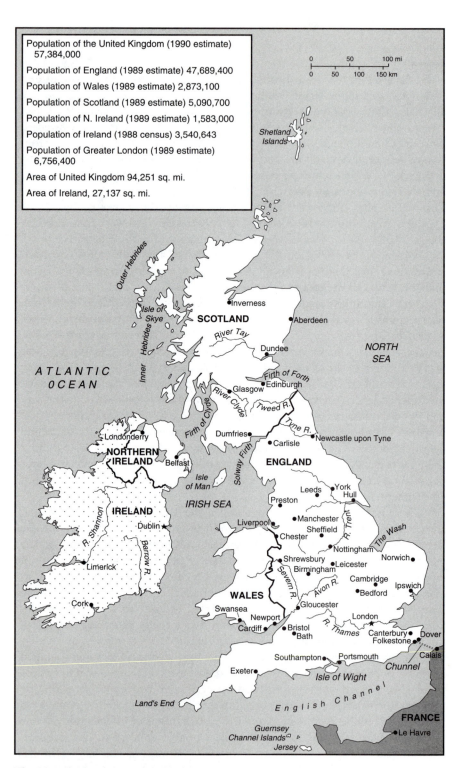

Population of the United Kingdom (1990 estimate)
57,384,000

Population of England (1989 estimate) 47,689,400

Population of Wales (1989 estimate) 2,873,100

Population of Scotland (1989 estimate) 5,090,700

Population of N. Ireland (1989 estimate) 1,583,000

Population of Ireland (1988 census) 3,540,643

Population of Greater London (1989 estimate)
6,756,400

Area of United Kingdom 94,251 sq. mi.

Area of Ireland, 27,137 sq. mi.

The United Kingdom and Ireland

ments were out of luck. The rural and urban poor, as well as the uneducated, straggled behind, bitter and bewildered about their lot. The slow but significant progress of the women's liberation movement, joined with the greater cost of the more sophisticated goods the new society made available to consumers, led to many women taking wage-based careers outside the home. Traditional roles and patterns of life changed. Leisure time expanded, and advances in medical care brought greater longevity. Longer periods of aging meant increased overall medical costs and posed adjustment challenges for families. In addition the youth, freed of the dominance of local tutelage and customs by increased channels of communication, rejected the standards of their parents.

The magnitude and rapidity of the changes brought about by modernization—the adaption of the advances of the technological revolution to the benefit of society at large—were unsuspected at war's end. Yet the war itself had spurred the development of technical knowledge that, when turned to peacetime uses, brought great change. An initial thrust of legislation was intended to reduce the gap between the standards of living of the rich and the poor, that is, to lessen the differences between the privileged and the unprivileged. The means chosen to reach this end of course affected the outcome. Differences of opinion were therefore bound to arise over political programs, no matter how wide the consensus regarding the eventual goal of social justice. Should equality of treatment or equality of opportunity prevail? Did minimum economic security for all imply also a voice for·all in the direction of the general economy and of individual industries and factories? Should reliance be placed on stale yet proven methods of the past, on totally new approaches, or on new technologies to revive aging formulas?

On the Continent, vying political parties in some Western European nations grew closer in their views on the nature of advanced industrial society and how to achieve it. In Britain these issues gradually redefined the language and constituencies of political debate and brought, by the middle 1970s, sharper divisions as well. The debate even encompassed the continuing role of nationalism and empire. Earlier these had served well the advancement of modernization. But did not postmodern or advanced industrial society require a more cooperative and global approach? Was the empire an asset—or perhaps a liability? To what extent should a country so proud of its heritage of splendid isolation accept alliances and make concessions of sovereignty to participate in the United Nations or a common European market?

Discussion of the proper nature of society and the roles of the state and of individuals within it became a primary theme of the postwar decades in Britain. It was complemented and complicated by a second theme: decline. Before World War II, Britain was the most powerful European country and easily the wealthiest. Its basic monetary unit, the pound sterling, served as the world's leading currency. Even in 1945 the British Empire was by far the largest and most populous political entity in the world.

The jubilation U.S. servicemen and British citizens shared in Piccadilly Circus, London, on V-E Day (May 7, 1945) soon gave way to the realization that Britain faced grim economic conditions. A harsh winter was expected, but after the strain of war only limited supplies were available, and Britain clearly lacked the means to carry out its traditional global responsibilities. (Photo 111-SC-205398 from the National Archives.)

The most evident signs of Britain's decline in the following years were the liquidation of its empire and the shrinkage of its influence in both its "informal empire" (e.g., the Middle East) and the sterling area (which included Scandinavia and parts of Latin America). On the whole the process was carried out with great diplomacy and dignity, though some difficult moments occurred, as at Suez in 1956 and in releasing control of Cyprus (see Chapters 4 and 13).

Britain's political decline has also been emphasized both by the rise of the superpowers and by the gradual consolidation of Western Europe, a process it opposed and repeatedly tried to hinder. A parallel economic decline is also witnessed by the slippage in Britain's per capita income, from first place to about thirteenth among the nineteen European countries of the Organization for Cooperation and Development, below Belgium and Finland. Today Britain carries less weight, in Europe and outside it, than Germany or France. At the same time, however, Britain did lead the way in social policy and experienced a marked cultural revival. It laid the basis of the welfare state, a model that has been copied by most advanced countries. Its achievements in science, literature, the theater, music, ballet, and the visual arts rivaled the best.

The day-by-day politics of Britain of course revolved about specific issues. The cumulative impact of these slowly revealed the larger themes of the postwar years. Immediately upon the achievement of peace, the British held two chief goals in particular. First, they wished to regain their former leading position in world trade and industry. Second, they desired progress toward a more just society, with better distribution of wealth and a broader range of social services for all. Unfortunately, the need for investment capital to revitalize industry and for moneys to finance broader services meant that these goals were in competition for scarce resources.[1]

Political Developments

During the grim war years the British people needed to look forward to a better life. The national government, in which Conservatives played a leading role, therefore made plans for the future. In 1942 a far-reaching report was issued. Drawn up by Sir William Beveridge, it aimed to bring freedom with security to all British citizens by the elimination of "want, ignorance, idleness, squalor, and disease." Establishment of a program of social insurance to cover everybody from the "cradle to the grave" was left to further legislation, and in 1944 the government submitted a general scheme to Parliament. That same year reports also appeared on full employment in a free society and on proposed changes in the education system. Implementation of these three reports became the source of intense political debate and the fulcrum of societal change over the next several decades.

Alternating Leadership

The wartime government, however, was not left to carry out postwar reconstruction. With the surrender of Germany, the question arose of the continuation of the coalition cabinet. Labour representatives refused to participate further, which led to the dissolution of Parliament and a general election (the first in ten years) in July 1945.

Labour won a clear majority in an upset that stunned political observers at home and abroad as well as the Conservatives. The old Liberal party, which had dominated the scene before World War I, declined so drastically that it held only twelve seats. Prime Minister Churchill, who was attending the Potsdam conference, resigned as soon as the election results were announced. Clement Attlee, head of the Labour party, took his place. The rejection of the war victor appeared harsh. Yet the people now wanted leadership for social change rather than a war lord, and the Labour party appeared more likely to provide this than did the Conservative party.

The new Labour government pushed through its reconstruction plans. It nationalized key industries, installed a national health insurance plan, and expanded social services. These domestic reforms were not as radical as they first appeared. All measures had precedents. Labour essentially carried to a logical conclusion previous policy of both Liberals and Conservatives (as well as Labour). Though disputes arose over modalities, consensus held that Britons had a right to be properly cared for in the areas of health, education, and legal justice. Similar agreement supported steps to assure the extension and protection of these rights to all segments of the population regardless of their economic status or geographic location. As expenses for the programs mounted and the value of the pound declined on world money markets, Britain's overseas commitments had to be reduced.

Domestic and especially foreign events slowly brought division within the Labour party and eroded public support. An adverse trade balance created an acute financial situation aggravated by the nationalization of the oil industry in Iran. The latter led to a bitter dispute and the forced withdrawal of English technicians from that country. British opposition to nationalization virtually closed down Iranian oil production; this reduction cut both British profits and oil supplies. The Korean War, which brought Britain to the side of the United States on behalf of United Nations policy, was not popular, especially among the members of Labour's far Left.

The placement of defense needs ahead of social services and production of domestic consumer goods caused a rift in Labour party ranks. A deflationary budget attempted to compensate for rearmament costs in part by making the people pay a nominal one-shilling charge for each prescription and for false teeth and eyeglasses supplied through the National Health Service. The funds at stake were not huge, but because of them the fiery Aneurin Bevan resigned his cabinet post, and others joined in his rebellion. When Prime

Winston Churchill, charismatic prime minister of Britain during the war years, is shown here at his desk at 10 Downing Street in 1941. Churchill's unflagging spirit and determination to win symbolized the British will to resist Hitler. A successful leader in wartime, Churchill was not considered by the public to be the right leader for the peace that followed. He and the Conservatives were defeated by the Labour party in the summer elections of 1945. He returned to the premiership from 1951 to 1955. Famous for his inspiring oratory, Churchill also won the Nobel Prize in literature. (Photo by Cecil Beaton, courtesy of the British Information Services.)

Prime Ministers of Great Britain Since 1945

Winston Churchill	Conservative	May 10, 1940–July 26, 1945
Clement Attlee	Labour	July 26, 1945–October 26, 1951
Winston Churchill	Conservative	October 26, 1951–April 6, 1955
Anthony Eden	Conservative	April 6, 1955–January 10, 1957
Harold Macmillan	Conservative	January 10, 1957–October 19, 1963
Alec Douglas-Home	Conservative	October 19, 1963–October 16, 1964
Harold Wilson	Labour	October 16, 1964–June 19, 1970
Edward Heath	Conservative	June 19, 1970–March 4, 1974
Harold Wilson	Labour	March 4, 1974–April 5, 1976
James Callaghan	Labour	April 5, 1976–May 4, 1979
Margaret Thatcher	Conservative	May 4, 1979–November 28, 1990
John Major	Conservative	November 28, 1990–

Minister Attlee sought a new mandate from the people, his party was in disarray. Some of its younger figures saw the calm leadership of Attlee as reflecting not skill but reluctance to take strong action. In elections held in 1951, the Conservatives and allied groups won a majority of seats. Winston Churchill again became prime minister.

For some while the Conservatives profited from Labour's discord, growing British prosperity, and the easing of international tension that had resulted from the more conciliatory Soviet policy and the winding down of the Korean War. The change from Labour to Conservative leadership did not alter the basic lines of British foreign policy. It continued to center on the retention of Commonwealth ties and on close cooperation with the United States and the countries of Western Europe. Although Britain recognized Communist China in 1950, it cooperated with most U.S. policies designed to stop the expansion of communism in both Asia and Europe. Pragmatists in foreign policy, the British were ready to negotiate and trade with the Communist world, more so than was the United States.

Britain became a leading member of the Western European Union, the North Atlantic Treaty Organization, the Council of Europe, the Organization for European Economic Cooperation, the European Payments Union, and other Western European movements (see Chapter 3). Although they accepted the necessity of military alliance, British leaders remained hesitant about economic agreements that might impinge upon their freedom of action and independent decisionmaking. The need to make binding economic commitments to continental nations did not appear pressing. British industry had recovered more rapidly after the war than that of France, Germany, and Italy, where many factories had been reduced to rubble. In 1954, however, Britain

Kingsley Amis was one of the young novelists and playwrights of the 1950s known as the Angry Young Men. Critics of life in postwar Britain, they portrayed the British as self-centered and having no great causes to espouse. They attacked the privilege of the upper class and the stodginess of the middle class. Of the welfare state Amis deplored, he once remarked, "More will mean worse." (Photo from Bettmann/Hulton.)

did sign an agreement for close cooperation with the European Coal and Steel Community, though it did not seek to become a member.

The U.S. attitude toward British and French armed intervention in Egypt in 1956 led to a brief divergence of policy (see Chapter 4). Prime Minister Anthony Eden, Churchill's longtime foreign secretary who had succeeded to the prime minister's post in 1955, resigned in 1957, his health shattered. The spring of that year, under the leadership of another Conservative, Harold Macmillan, Britain drastically revised its defense forces. The armed forces shrank over a five-year period, and the remainder was scheduled for modernization and adaption to the nuclear age.

Though originally opposed to a European free trade area linking the European Economic Community with other members of the OEEC, Britain changed its attitude in 1957. The vitality of the Coal and Steel Community was evident, and British industries were now at a disadvantage in competing with newer plants that had come on-line on the Continent. When negotiations to join the EEC failed, the United Kingdom joined with Austria,

Denmark, Norway, Portugal, Sweden, and Switzerland to form the European Free Trade Association (see Chapter 4).

Positive as these achievements were, they did not serve the suffering British economy well enough. To survive and, more especially, to prosper and provide more employment, the industry of the United Kingdom needed access to the markets in the heart of Europe. These it could currently penetrate only partly because of the tariff boundary of the EEC. In July 1961 the British government announced that it would again seek membership in the Common Market. Opposition arose at home, as some Labour party leaders feared that lowering of tariffs would mean loss of jobs to continental industrial competition. Some Labourites were also concerned that if British economic policies became closely linked with those of a Europe dominated by Christian Democratic parties, Socialist domestic programs might suffer. Fears spread regarding a possible increase in food costs if prices in Britain rose to the level of those on the Continent, where farmers' expenses were higher. A few Conservatives questioned such a major change, and objections came from some Commonwealth countries. To ease the adjustment process and reduce Commonwealth and domestic concerns, British leaders asked for numerous concessions from the Common Market countries. These concessions, especially the extensive ones pertaining to agriculture, were to be eliminated over a period of years. Yet to EEC members they gave pause because of their breadth, duration, and the expenses they implied for the other EEC countries. Several members dragged their feet in acting on the British application; it was still moving forward when French president de Gaulle's unexpectedly abrupt veto ended negotiations in January 1963.

Repeated later attempts by Britain to gain membership in the Common Market finally met with success in the summer of 1971. By this time circumstances had changed. The British were more convinced that they were missing out on a good thing and therefore asked for fewer special dispensations. De Gaulle, who as a matter of principle wished to reduce Anglo-Saxon influence in Europe, was no longer in office. New French leaders themselves took more interest in British membership in the EEC as a counter to the growing influence of the burgeoning West German economy. Then, too, several of the EEC states had become more supportive of the entry of the United Kingdom as a balance to both French and West German domination within the Community.

Prime Minister Macmillan resigned for health reasons in 1963. His successor, Sir Alec Douglas-Home, soon found rivals within the Conservative party and was not as skilled as his predecessor in serenely negotiating choppy political waters. The Conservatives were hard hit by mounting trade deficits, an ethics scandal involving War Minister John Profumo, and general unrest in the country. Elections in 1964 gave the Labour party and its new leader, Harold Wilson, a slim majority that he expanded in later elections.

Wilson believed that new technology, computers and the like, would enable traditional socialist economic planning to work more effectively than in the past. He intended to "reforge Britain in the white heat of the scientific revolution." At first, Wilson's modernizing efforts found some success. Industrial productivity increased and the balance of payments stabilized. In spite of a continuing inflationary trend, the overall situation seemed so favorable that he again dissolved Parliament ahead of schedule. Contrary to all opinion polls, the Conservatives swept the election of June 1970. Wilson's political future appeared dubious; few were to guess that over his lifetime he would serve more months as a peacetime prime minister than any of his predecessors in British history.

The new prime minister, Edward Heath, espoused a conservative economic philosophy, concentrating less on new technology than on government-industry labor relations. A key feature of his program was the Industrial Relations Act of 1971: It required a cooling-off period prior to a strike, secret balloting on strike votes, and open shops. (This last aspect forbade unions to require union membership of all workers in a given plant or industry.) Heath's efforts to force businesses to stand on their own feet with less government subsidy also proved controversial. Success in negotiating entry into the Common Market was countered by failure to stem inflation and unemployment. Arab limitation of oil shipments led to a temporary three-day work week and a freeze of wages and prices at the end of 1973. Confrontation with the miners' union caused Heath in February 1974 to call a general election in the hope of strengthening the government's mandate. Right-wing Conservatives who were opposed to membership in the EEC defected, led by Enoch Powell; the party narrowly lost the elections.

Though Harold Wilson again became prime minister, the role of Liberals and other groupings prevented a Labour majority government until after another round of elections. Once that government was established, the Industrial Relations Act of 1971, so unpopular with the unions, was repealed. An inflation rate at times as high as 26 percent, rising unemployment, and budget deficits forced Wilson both to borrow heavily from the IMF and to bargain with the unions for restraint in the search for wage increases. Agreement reached on wages and the coming on-line of North Sea oil production were encouraging steps toward economic stability. Yet the left wings of the Labour party and of the powerful unions grew increasingly restless. Wilson, who favored continued British membership in the EEC but was opposed by a majority of his party, took the issue to the public in the first-ever British national referendum; the June 1975 vote was more than two to one in favor of staying with the Common Market.

Party problems also afflicted the Conservatives. Heath, loser of two general elections, was vulnerable. So, too, was his heir apparent, the moderate Conservative William Whitelaw. Margaret Thatcher, a grocer's daughter sensitive to the concerns of the lower middle class, an established worker in the party, and a former cabinet minister, skillfully built upon the feelings already stirred by Powell. Her challenge for party leadership was upheld in February 1975 by the Conservative members of Parliament. The first woman leader of a major political party in Britain, she quickly moved the party to the right, ousting Heath followers from key posts and declaring that state involvement in social and industrial matters must decrease.

Wilson unexpectedly resigned as prime minister in March 1976. His successor, James Callaghan, continued to struggle with the failing economy. The falling pound made imports more expensive and increased the balance-of-payments deficit. In order to fund its debts, the government increased rates offered on its securities. This in turn reinforced the general upward swing in interest rates that discouraged private investments and new industrial expansion. Losses in by-elections forced Callaghan to negotiate agreements with the small Liberal party (thirteen seats) and even with Welsh and Scottish separatist members of Parliament. A bill granting substantial domestic autonomy to Wales and Scotland passed in Parliament but did not receive sufficient support in the referenda held in those regions to become law (1979). This gravely weakened the cabinet's position. It had also been undermined by a series of strikes in the preceding months that resulted in violation of the government's 5 percent wage increase guidelines and damaged the mild economic recovery. Public wrath mounted in measure with the accumulation of garbage in the streets caused by the strike of sanitation workers. Callaghan denounced what he called "free collective vandalism." Outsiders spoke of a "second Battle of Britain" regarding who would gain control—the unions, the strikers, the street demonstrators, or the elected representatives. A popular song of the time touted the strength of the unions and the inability of management or government to influence them:

> Now I'm a union man, amazed at what I am.
> I say what I thinks: the company stinks.
> Yes I'm a union man.

>   *   *   *

> And I always get my way if I strike for higher pay.
> When I show my card to the Scotland Yard,
> This is what I say.
> You can't get me, I'm part of the union.
> You can't get me, I'm part of the union.
> You can't get me, I'm part of the union.
> 'Till the day I die; 'till the day I die.[2]

In retrospect, it appears that the failures of the economic and societal formulas of both Labour and the Conservatives in the 1970s had brought Britain to the brink of economic and even civil chaos. Economic isolation had not worked; membership in the EEC had proved helpful but was not a cure-all. Old socialism mounted on new technology had not succeeded either. Tough labor-control measures and nurturing of uninspired management had merely brought strikes, downturns in production, and division. Political, social, and economic difficulties prevented any of the programs from being tried for very long. This abridging of their chance to be effective brought derisive criticism from both sides of the House of Commons. An old adage comes to mind: "What is good politics is bad economics, and what is good economics is bad politics." A key question remained: What formula was the right one for achieving a peaceful and productive advanced industrialized society?

The failed prescriptions and mounting discontent also brought the United Kingdom to an important political divide. Many people believed that further economic tinkering would not work. Convinced that fundamental restructuring was needed in the economy and that groups trying to influence governmental policies should be given a greater say, radical spokespeople came to the fore in both the Labour and Conservative camps. The result was an increasingly bitter tone in political debates and a drawing away from the center, the traditional lodestone of British politics.

Collapse of the autonomy legislation meant withdrawal of the support of the Welsh and Scottish separatist members for the government. Labour, forced to a general election in 1979, was defeated. Thatcher successfully beat back the Heath followers in her own party and welded a new Conservative bulwark. Her support came not so much from the traditional locus of Conservative backers, the upper classes and landed gentry, but more from the middle classes and skilled workers who felt sandwiched between the wealthy and the union-dominated Labour groups. These people sensed that it was their taxes and bodies that supported Britain in peace and war. Yet they had gained little in recent years and saw their status threatened because they held no influential positions and had no organizations with political clout equal to that of the unions. They liked Thatcher's assertion that Labour (and even Conservatives prior to Thatcher) had focused too much on redistribution of wealth rather than on its creation. They agreed that the proper course was to reduce government regulation and subsidies of industry and to allow market forces to operate freely.

Upon taking power, Thatcher cut income taxes, raised indirect taxes, removed price and wage restrictions, and took steps to denationalize several industries. Choosing monetarists as her chief advisers, she attempted to squeeze inflation by manipulating the money supply. Though increasing oil production strengthened the pound and the balance of payments, unemployment mounted and Thatcher faced rebellion in her own party. Her cabinet balked at the size of Britain's contribution to the budget of the Common Market. After bitter negotiating, a reduction of nearly 30 percent was achieved.

The prime minister's emphasis on economic policy naturally stimulated questions regarding her political philosophy. To these she replied:

> What's irritated me about the whole direction of politics in the last thirty years is that it's always been towards the collectivist society. People have forgotten about the personal society. And they say: do I count, do I matter? To which the short answer is, Yes. And therefore, it isn't that I set out on economic policies; it's that I set out really to change the approach, and changing the economics is the means of changing that approach. If you change the approach you really are after the heart and soul of the nation. Economics are the method; the object is to change the heart and soul.[3]

On April 2, 1982, an unexpected event presented Thatcher a grave challenge and ultimately the path to an astounding reversal of her waning popularity. Her defense of British interests in the wake of the Argentine seizure of the Falkland Islands (which the Argentines called the Malvinas) in the South Atlantic brought applause from Britons tired of what were considered foreign humiliations. Thatcher's resolution in pursuit of military victory (the British dispatched an armada to recapture the islands) was cited as proof that she could overcome economic problems as well. Her popularity soared; she seemed more than ever able to ignore critics in her own party and Parliament, pursue her own policies, and appeal directly to the people. This last she did in elections called for June 1983. The results were overwhelmingly in favor of the Iron Lady, as she had become known. In the biggest electoral sweep since 1945, the Conservatives garnered 397 out of the 650 seats in Parliament.

The Labour party contributed to the lopsidedness of the election by its own divisiveness. Leaders of the left wing, such as Michael Foot and Anthony Wedgwood Benn, had steadily asserted themselves since Callaghan's defeat. Calling for British withdrawal from the Common Market, they also favored unilateral renunciation of nuclear arms, further nationalizations, and a huge jobs program.

To some of the more moderate Labour party members, such policies seemed irresponsible, given current international and economic conditions. In 1981 several former Labour ministers formed the Social Democratic party, intended to constitute a "responsible" Left—or even Center. Agreement was struck with the remnants of the old Liberal party, and these various groups combined as the Social Democratic Alliance in the 1983 election. The alliance won about 25 percent of the popular vote, but the single-member constituency electoral system (winner take all in each district) rewarded them with only twenty-three seats. No wonder the alliance had as part of its platform a shift to proportional representation. Labour received a popular vote only 3 percent larger but garnered 209 seats. In the face of Thatcher's newfound popularity, neither group could have much influence.

Margaret Thatcher, the first woman to be elected prime minister in Britain, held that office longer than any predecessor, from May 1979 to November 1990. Possessing grace, skill in articulate expression and debate, and a strong sense of propriety, Thatcher also displayed such single-minded political determination that she won the title of Iron Lady in the popular press. She re-fashioned the Conservative party along her own monetarist and right-wing views, granting moderate Conservatives few concessions and waging an all-out battle against the Labourites and socialism. (Photo courtesy of the British Information Services.)

With the leadership of the Labour party holding to radical positions, isolating themselves and their diminished party in the process, the ability of the Social Democrats and Liberals to forge their alliance into a new, unified, major opposition party became a significant political question. Success might spell the end of the polarization in British political parties that had developed so rapidly since the 1970s. Failure might assure continued Conservative dominance for some while. It would mean, too, the prevalence of the Conservative notion that establishment of broader government social welfare programs in postwar advanced industrialized society did not necessarily imply extensive restructuring of status relationships. The Conservatives instead advocated continuation of more traditional employer-employee and class relationships. Yet the struggling economy and the faltering of British industry in the competitive world market raised doubts as to how successfully Britain had achieved entry into postmodern society. Could this entry truly be accomplished without the changing of relationships that the new Conservatives were determined to avoid?

The presence of opportunity did not mean the leaders of the alliance could automatically seize it. The alliance was still more a coalition than a unified party. In 1986 a split arose between the Social Democrats, who on the whole favored continued reliance upon nuclear weapons, and the Liberals, whose stance was more antinuclear. Thatcher's Conservative forces harped on the defense issue, well aware that it was the source of her victory in 1983.

Neil Kinnock emerged as a new leader of the Labour party during its dark years in the 1980s. By skilled oratory, energy, and reasonableness, he was able to regroup the party and win the confidence of at least some of the electorate that had despaired over the radical divisiveness within the party. Although his efforts won Labour more seats, they did not earn it control of Parliament. (Photo courtesy of the British Information Services.)

Meanwhile, the Labour party, shocked by the extremism of Benn and Foot on the one hand and the defection of Social Democrats on the other, reordered its camp. It elected as party leader the young and dynamic Neil Kinnock. He achieved better party discipline and moved Labour toward the center, away from the brink of the anarchic left on which it earlier seemed poised. At its 1986 convention, the party did take a nonnuclear stance, thus breaking a forty-year tradition of bipartisan defense policy in Britain.

These developments all had their effect in the 1987 general elections, which gave the Conservatives a majority of 101 seats, some 43 less than in 1983 but still the second largest majority achieved since 1945. Labour regained only 21 seats. More significant was the failure of the alliance to improve its position, raising once more the question of the viability of a strong third party in British politics. The British still seemed to accept Thatcher's notion of what was needed to modernize British politics and society, although audible complaints mounted that her policies did little to make available to the masses the benefits of the new scientific and other developments.

The prime minister timed the election well, setting it shortly after her return from a much-publicized series of talks in Moscow with Soviet leader Gorbachev. Moreover, the opposition seemed to self-destruct. Labour's program of high spending, high taxation of incomes over $42,500 per year, and restoration of union powers appeared as worn-out remedies. Its unilateral nuclear disarmament posture led an alliance leader to comment: "On defense,

Labour remains a menace to its allies and the answer to the Russians' prayer." Thatcher's supporters pointed to her firm policies in both foreign and domestic affairs as cause for her success. The economy prospered. Productivity was greater than in the United States and much of Europe; interest rates were down, the pound strong, the stock market up, and workers noted an increase in their pay because of a 2 percent tax cut. Some observers also discerned a tendency for the British public to recoil from the irresponsible behavior of some sectors of society. Incidents such as drunken rioting by British fans at the World Cup soccer match in Belgium in 1986 not only shocked the world and embarrassed Britain but also led voters to support those politicians who identified themselves, as did Prime Minister Thatcher, with the old British virtues. The soccer vandalism, which was not an isolated instance, and recurring ethnic riots suggest that more than a few British were angry and discontent with society. If not rebellious in the normal political sense, they nevertheless were not committed to the existing standards.

Encouraged by her reelection, which soon made her the longest-serving peacetime prime minister in British history, Thatcher pursued her program to end socialism and roll back state control with such fervor that the "wets," or moderates, of her own party murmured caution. Thatcher nevertheless pressed on with a campaign to revive inner cities (where the Conservatives fared badly in the voting). She also moved to deregulate the private housing market, to introduce a national core curriculum in the schools, and to substitute a flat poll tax for taxes based on local property values.

The Liberals and Social Democratic Alliance meanwhile endeavored to create a more unified party. Compromises failed, and David Owen and his followers created an independent party, the Campaign for Social Democracy. Even the pressure of Thatcher's continuing victories could not force a unified Center.

Labour itself noted this and responded by perceptibly shifting its pro-grams toward the center, hoping to pick up the votes of some alliance followers, despite the protests of outspoken leftist leaders who seemed adrift from the mainstream of British politics. At the annual party conference in 1989, it rejected renationalization of industries privatized by the Thatcher administration, much to the dismay of hard leftists who saw this posture as a move away from socialism. Labour also abandoned insistence on unilateral disarmament in favor of negotiated multilateral disarmament. The party nevertheless continued to advocate a sharp reduction in defense expenditures.

Division of the opposition into three parties, two of which still had severe internal differences, bode well for the Conservatives; it gave the prime minister additional leverage in her efforts to prevent the moderates of her own party from separating from her loyalists (the "dries"). Yet time itself would have a negative effect on Thatcher's popularity. Citizens and politicians tired of her high-handed and strong-willed ways and vaunted inflexibility. Opposition to the alleged unfairness of a poll tax substituted for property taxes at the local level would not go away (see the subsection below on Thatcher's Policies). As 1990 drew to a close, the economy stagnated, dashing hopes for the economic miracle that seemed possible in earlier years. The prime minister's reluctance to support further integration within the European Community and to cooperate with the European Monetary Union did not correspond with the attitude of most Britons toward the EC. By-elections were lost, and polls increasingly showed that voters might turn to Labour in the next general election if Thatcher continued to lead the Conservatives. Ministers in disagreement with her policies resigned and received public acclaim. Finally challenged by one of them at the party conference toward the end of 1990, she failed reelection as leader on the first ballot. Aware that many backbenchers saw her as a liability to their own campaigns, Thatcher resigned as party leader and thus as prime minister after eleven and a half years in office. She retained sufficient clout to assist the election of her own choice as successor, John Major.

A relatively young and likable politician with a common touch and experience as foreign secretary and chancellor of the exchequer, Major vowed to maintain Thatcher's policies but to conduct them in a less confrontational manner. The most immediate foreign policy issue that he faced was the Persian Gulf situation (see Chapter 5). Major quickly confirmed his solidarity with the United States in foreign policy matters, a solidarity that had been well strengthened through the years of obvious agreement and friendship between Thatcher and Reagan. Britain firmly supported United Nations and U.S. efforts to remove Iraq from its occupation of Kuwait, and significant British forces participated in the Gulf War that broke out in January 1991. The prime minister was supportive, if pessimistic, regarding EC efforts to mediate the Slovenia-Croatia secession crisis in Yugoslavia. When the Baltic republics of Estonia, Latvia, and Lithuania asserted their independence in August 1991, he moved with alacrity to grant them diplomatic recognition.

Major's comments about wanting Britain to be "in the heart of Europe" seemed to demonstrate a change in the official attitude of Britain toward efforts to achieve a single Europe. Negotiations for a European Monetary Union began to move more positively. Major, however, did not hesitate to object to Dutch proposals for expansion of the powers of the European Parliament. Such a step, the British argued, would infringe on their national sovereignty and create the sort of federal Europe the Conservatives still opposed. Therefore, while signing the 1991 EC Treaty of Maastricht that planned a common European currency and central bank, Major held firm that only the British parliament could make the final decision on such matters; he obtained the United Kingdom's right to "opt out," although experts doubted that course would be taken. Similarly, to protect himself from criticism by Thatcherites, Major refused to make Britain part of an agreement on labor legislation reached by the eleven other EC members.

Prime Minister John Major visits with British troops in Saudi Arabia during the 1991 Gulf War. His former experience as minister of foreign affairs enabled Major to maintain an activist role in this area as he took over leadership of his country from Thatcher. Major's strong performance throughout the Gulf War and in promptly recognizing the independence of Estonia, Latvia, and Lithuania from the Soviet Union won him praise at home and abroad. (Photo courtesy of the British Information Services.)

On the domestic front, Major backed away from the poll tax only slowly, for to do so too quickly would offend those Conservatives, including the still influential Thatcher, who supported it. He did offer measures that softened its impact for 1991–1992 and indicated that the following year it would be replaced by a local tax only vaguely defined for the time being.

Northern Ireland

The decades of animosity between the Irish and the English were punctuated by the total breaking away of the Republic of Ireland from the United Kingdom and Commonwealth on April 18, 1949. The six counties of Northern Ireland known as Ulster, which had not been part of the Irish Free State (1920) or Eire (1937), continued as part of the United Kingdom. Predominantly Protestant, Ulster's citizens had fought alongside the English in World War II, whereas the chiefly Roman Catholic Eire had remained neutral. The Irish Republican Army (IRA), a sizable irregular force originally based mainly in the south, determined to unite both Irish states and waged an extensive terrorist effort to this end. The Border Campaign that it carried on from approximately 1956 to 1961 did not experience a great deal of success. Many northern Catholics at this time appeared to concentrate more on gaining civil rights as citizens in Northern Ireland than on Irish unification. In 1962 the IRA eased its tactics in order to improve relations between the Irish republic and Northern Ireland. In fact what happened was that the cross-border warfare turned into a civil war in Northern Ireland as the IRA became more firmly entrenched in that region.

Catholics in the northern counties believed they were discriminated against in various ways. Property ownership or rent-level qualifications limited the franchise in local elections to only about three-quarters the number of electors for the Stormont (Ulster) or Westminster parliaments. Moreover, plural votes were granted to businesspeople at the rate of one for every £10 of value of their business premises up to a total of six votes. Such a system enabled the Protestants, who controlled much of the property and generally held more wealth than the Catholics, to assert their views out of proportion to their number. Only in 1969, after considerable wrangling and some pressure from London, was the one-person–one-vote system installed for local elections. Catholics also claimed that their civil rights were abridged by gerrymandered districts and the unfair influence of the Protestant Orange Order that controlled job and housing allocation in sections of Ulster.

A Northern Ireland Civil Rights Association, consisting primarily of Roman Catholics but with some Protestant members, formed in 1967 to press for civil rights reforms. Protestants, who considered the group a front for the IRA, resisted. Demonstration marches took place and militant leaders of the Catholic cause emerged, among them Bernadette Devlin, the youngest woman ever elected to the British Parliament. The IRA itself experienced schism, as some members objected to the interest of others in possible negotiation and lessening of conflict by compromise. The militants created their own group, the Provisional IRA, dedicated to energetic battle for unification of Ulster with the Irish republic by whatever means, including military tactics and terror. The "official" IRA was left to concentrate on civil rights and civil disobedience.

Extremism on the part of the Roman Catholics was matched and further stimulated by Protestant extremism. Ian Paisley, pastor of an independent Presbyterian church, built a huge following determined to resist concessions to Catholics and to overthrow any Northern Irish ministry that advocated compromise. Though asserting they were speaking for a Protestant majority, the true interest of some of the extremist Protestants in democratic rule appeared suspect: Various counts and surveys indicated that in at least some counties of Ulster the Catholics outnumbered Protestants and would outvote them if given opportunity.

As terrorism turned into near warfare in the cities of Northern Ireland, the British sent troops and in 1971 began interning IRA leaders without trial. In 1972 British prime minister Heath suspended the provincial government of Northern Ireland and placed the region under the supervision of a British secretary of state for Northern Ireland. In this post William Whitelaw attempted conciliation, as did the republic's prime minister, Jack Lynch, who saw the growing force of the Provisional IRA as destabilizing his own government.

Proposed peaceful solutions were rejected by both Protestant and Catholic militants. In 1973, under reinstated provincial rule, elections occured for a New Assembly, a key proposal of a British white paper on Northern Irish reform. The results did not strengthen the moderates' hands as much as London hoped, but Catholics did for the first time gain representation somewhat commensurate with their share of the population. The chief British, Irish, and Northern Irish political leaders next agreed in December 1973 to create a Council of Ireland that would have representatives from both the republic and Ulster and would thus serve as a link between the two. The Irish republic further recognized that Ulster's ties with Britain could not be altered without the approval of a majority of the Northern Irish population.

Northern Protestants remained obdurate, stirred by fears that the council might lead to some sort of union of the two states. The Northern Irish government coalition that favored power sharing between Catholics and Protestants was brought down by a 1974 general strike led by Protestant trade unionists. British prime minister Wilson denounced the strike as a "calculated attempt to use every undemocratic and unparliamentary means for the purpose of bringing down the whole constitution of Northern Ireland so as to set up there a sectarian and undemocratic state." He therefore announced that Westminster would resume direct rule of Ulster.

To allow the people of Northern Ireland to shape their own government, Wilson called elections for a constitutional convention. In the 1975 balloting, the United Ulster Unionist Council gained nearly three times the votes won by the Catholic parties. The Protestant parties promptly made such demands and rejected collaboration with southern Ireland to the point that the IRA canceled a brief cease-fire; the constitutional convention was not held. A large Northern Irish investment program initiated in Westminster did not reduce the number of bombings. A Women's Peace Movement, led by Betty Williams (Protestant) and Mairead Corrigan (Catholic) briefly had effect and in 1977 won the women the Nobel Peace Prize. Yet in 1979 Airey Neave, a Conservative party specialist on Northern Ireland; the retired war hero Lord Mountbatten; and others were assassinated by Irish terrorists and the Provisional IRA. Catholic demonstrations were matched by larger demonstrations led by Reverend Paisley. In 1982 Sinn Fein (Ourselves Alone), the political wing of the Provisional IRA, contested and won seats in a specially called assembly in the north. Intended to promote dialogue and serve as a path toward provincial self-government, the assembly promptly experienced difficulties as hard-line Catholic and Protestant groups refused to participate despite election to seats. Thatcher herself took a firm line toward Irish political prisoners staging hunger strikes. A bomb blast at a Conservative party gathering in Brighton, England, in 1984 came close, but for a matter of timing, to killing Thatcher and other key officials.

Catholics, Protestants, northerners, southerners, and leaders in London alike seemed caught in the antagonisms of the past and the enmities of the present. Blood spilled on both sides raised the level of determination of the extremists, compromise was orphaned, and the prospect of peace was nowhere to be found. Yet every bomb blast evidenced the need for some solution. Therefore Thatcher and Prime Minister Garret FitzGerald of the Irish republic continued the search via lengthy negotiations that resulted in a new agreement signed in November 1985 at Hillsborough Castle. For the first time in years a formal role was granted to the south in the affairs of Northern Ireland, by means of a new British-Irish Intergovernmental Conference intended to focus on Protestant-Catholic relations in Northern Ireland. FitzGerald in return acknowledged the desire of the Protestants of Ulster to remain under British rule. Though the accord was approved at Dublin and Westminster, extremists on both sides fulminated against the arrangement. Despite threats, the Intergovernmental Conference met on nearly a monthly basis, discussing such matters as impartial enforcement of the law in the north, security of the joint Irish borders, and subsidies of Irish industries. Moderates hoped that in time such small steps would improve Protestant-Catholic relations in the north. Indeed, for a while terrorist attacks decreased. Then in 1988 the bombings resumed and the death toll again mounted. Once more, extensive diplomatic efforts were launched to bring more peaceful relations. A special conference gathered in the late spring of 1991 was unable to reach agreement even on technical aspects of further talks; it disbanded without achieving progress on any of the substantive issues.

Constitutional Changes

In the postwar years, some innovations took place in British constitutional practice. The Representation of the People Act (1948) ended the university and business-premise franchises, and the United Kingdom finally joined those countries where no person has more than one vote. In 1970 the voting age in parliamentary elections (as well as the age of full legal capacity in general) was reduced from twenty-one to eighteen years. In 1949, in order to avoid delays in its nationalization program, the Labour party revised the Parliament Act of 1911: The House of Lord's power to hold up a bill favored by the House of Commons was limited to one instead of two years. In an effort to strengthen the House of Lords by bringing in specially qualified people, the

The British royal couple, Queen Elizabeth II and Prince Philip. The powers of the British monarch are fairly limited, still consisting, as the historian Walter Bagehot wrote in 1867, of the right to be consulted, to encourage, and to warn. Nevertheless, Queen Elizabeth is an important
symbol of the nation, and her experience as head of state and her personal qualities have won her both influence and her subjects' respect.
(Photo courtesy of the British Information Services.)

Conservative government in 1958 sponsored a measure that permitted the
appointment of life peers. For the first time women were to be admitted to
the upper chamber. An act passed in 1963 permits peers to renounce their
peerages for life; that is, peers can resign their peerages in order to run for
election to the House of Commons without affecting the rights of their heirs
(this was done by the Earl of Home, who became Prime Minister Sir Alec
Douglas-Home).

Elizabeth II succeeded to the throne upon the death in February 1952 of her father, King George VI. The royal family maintains its mystique, popularity, and some influence, although its duties are limited mostly to the ceremonial rather than the governmental. In 1981 Prince Charles, Queen Elizabeth's son and heir apparent, wed Lady Diana Spencer, a commoner at law but of noble lineage. The royal couple travels widely, and Charles has served as an extraordinarily effective ambassador of goodwill within the Commonwealth.

Social Services

Education

Even before the close of World War II, Parliament enacted far-reaching educational reform. The Education Act of 1944 struck a blow at ignorance and drastically reconstructed the primary and secondary educational system of England and Wales. Not later than 1947, children were to attend school through age fifteen rather than fourteen and eventually through age sixteen, as sufficient buildings and teachers became available. For the first time all children over eleven would receive a secondary education without charge. The school-meals plan, dating from 1906, was expanded, and all children in public primary and secondary schools received subsidized lunches free of charge if necessary. The Family Allowance Act of 1945, which provided allowance for each child after the first, did much to further education.

Sharp discussion arose over what sort of schools should be built. Should they be grammar schools concentrating on classical subjects and primarily serving those planning to attend universities? Or should they be comprehensive schools with technical training? The battle had overtones of class conflict and raised a popular political question: How much should be taken from the few to help the many? The trend was toward more comprehensive schools. In 1974 the Labour government abolished the dread examination taken shortly after a child turned eleven, which previously had determined the sort of school the child could attend and thus profoundly affected her or his social status and economic future.

Although elementary and more especially secondary enrollments experienced a steady upswing in the postwar years, that in higher education grew even more rapidly. The many new "plate-glass" universities founded in cities formerly noted only for industrial production did not have the prestige of ivy-covered Oxford or Cambridge. They did, however, greatly expand opportunities for higher education and soon attracted able and innovative faculty.

Costs also rose. Though total funding for university student aid increased, by the mid-1980s individual grants often were insufficient to meet a student's needs. The Thatcher government, already providing about 70 percent of all university funding, was unwilling to come up with more moneys for what it considered a poorly managed system; faculty positions went unfilled, struggling departments closed their doors, and young talent searched for employment in business or overseas. In the summer of 1988, the Conservatives passed "GERBIL," the Great Education Reform Bill. Tenure for faculty hired or promoted after November 1987 was abolished, and two new government councils were created to control funding of higher education. In the view of Education Secretary Kenneth Baker, "the past 30 years' curriculum development has been too free-form, everyone doing their [sic] own thing," and therefore the bill prescribed an explicit framework of a "back-to-basics" curriculum for elementary and secondary schools funded by the public.

Extension of Social Security

The Labour government of 1945 set itself at once to the task of implementing the promises made during the war for a general extension of social services. In 1946 three major bills passed: The National Insurance Act combined health, old age, and unemployment benefits, the cost of which was met through a single weekly payment by the employer, the employee, and the state; the National Health (Industrial Injuries) Act provided benefits beyond those furnished when the employer alone was liable; the National Health Service Act granted free medical service and supplies, hospital care, and nursing aid to every Briton. These acts were supplemented by the National Assistance Act of 1948, which superseded the old Poor Law and provided for assistance to any person whose needs were not met under the National Insurance provisions. The above four broad measures, which were on the whole extensions of previous practices, took effect in 1948. The most radical innovation was the extension of free medical aid to every Briton, a measure that in the United States was commonly referred to as the socialization of medicine. Each doctor who adhered to the program received a fixed salary plus an additional fee according to the number of families who selected him or her as their physician. Doctors could also continue their private practices. People were free to choose their own doctors, and provision was made for specialized surgical care.

Over 95 percent of the population soon registered for the popular health insurance plan. Practically all British dentists and over 90 percent of the doctors participated in providing service. To the large group of the underprivileged, the act brought long-needed assistance, as is well attested by the great demand for eyeglasses, dental plates, artificial limbs, and other such items. Adequate prenatal care, maternity aid, and child care meant much to the poor. Since the 1951–1952 budget, there has been a nominal charge for dentures, eyeglasses, and certain other appliances and services. In 1968 abortions were made available on broad social and medical grounds under the National Health Service.

Critics of the National Health Service have pointed to the tremendous costs involved and the burden these place upon governmental revenues. Almost from the outset, funds received from the Health Service insurance fees had to be supplemented by subsidies from national taxation. The first years of the program witnessed soaring costs, as many individuals sought treatment for chronic problems previously only sporadically cared for, and hospitals and clinics became overcrowded. Some doctors left the country, as much to escape what they considered excessive governmental regulation and paperwork as to obtain greater income. The need to provide basic services to the entire range of population and the cost associated with it led to policy decisions limiting the extent and kinds of services that the Health Service would provide. For example, kidney dialysis would not be offered to persons over fifty-five years of age. Therefore only those persons who could privately afford the full cost of such treatment and could travel to a locus where they could receive it regularly would have their lives prolonged in this manner. Because of crowded hospitals and overworked staff, the waiting time for approved elective surgery could be several months. Despite these obvious problems, many people considered the program successful and viewed it as altering British society for the better. The difference between a society where treatment of basic human medical needs is guaranteed for all, as compared to a society where it is not, was seen as fundamental.

This premise has been accepted by the numerous administrations since Attlee's Labour ministries. Although they adjusted fee structures and regulations, the Conservatives did not attempt to dismantle the Health Service or indeed most of the social welfare programs instituted by Labour immediately after the war. The challenge has first been to make the programs more efficient and less costly. Second, debate has raged over the issue of whether differing levels of service (such as unemployment compensation) should be offered to individuals who have paid—or whose employers have paid—higher fees for a longer time or whether instead all should receive the same benefits regardless of how much has been paid on their behalf over the years. Initially, most programs provided the same benefit for all, but the trend has been toward the establishment of varying levels of benefits contingent upon the levels of payment received. Critics of these adjustments argue that variation of benefits perpetuates class distinctions and diminishes the equalization effects of the insurance programs.

In 1967 Parliament passed a private member bill (that is, one not proposed by the government) providing that homosexual behavior between consenting adults in private should no longer be a criminal offense. Another much-debated measure was enacted in 1969: the abolition of the death penalty. The period of the late 1960s and early 1970s also witnessed substantive administrative changes in the British legal system that improved access to and delivery of a fuller range of legal services in rural areas especially.

Economic Developments

Nationalization

In the election campaign of 1945, foreign policy had not been an issue, and all parties emphasized the need for more housing, social security, improved health measures, and full employment. The Fabian Socialists, who greatly influenced the philosophy of the Labour party, had long stressed municipal ownership. With one municipality merging into another, local areas losing their importance in practically all factors that affected the life of the people, the increased mobility of the population, the development of large-scale industries, and the increased nationalization of the revenue and taxation system, there was a growing demand for public ownership on a national basis.

In Britain nationalization of certain industries was an old story. The telegraph and telephone systems had long been run by the Post Office Department. The formation of a National Grid System in 1926 inaugurated government sale of electricity on a wholesale basis; the British Broadcasting System took over the radio in 1927; the London transport system was nationalized in 1933, and so, too, were the mineral rights of the coal mines in 1938. Pledged to a policy of furthering public ownership, the Labour government nationalized the Bank of England (1946); the overseas cable and wireless services (1946); civil aviation (1946); the operation of the coal mines (1947); the railroads, road haulage, canals, and docks (1947); and the electrical supply and gas works (1948).

Nationalization was achieved by various procedures. In each case the government did not confiscate but gave fair compensation to the previous owners. Generally, government corporations were established to run the new industries. In some cases, as in coal mining, where capital investment had long been postponed, the owners showed little reluctance in parting with their companies at a fair price. Indeed, the government took over a number of industries that were unable to stand on their own feet. Not surprisingly, these did not furnish good returns immediately and proved costly invest-ments. The losses incurred by these industries were spotlighted by critics. A more fair criticism was that many industry owners, unsure of whether the government would soon be buying them out, delayed in making capital investments and failed to provide the aggressive leadership the British econ-omy sorely needed in the postwar years.

Unlike the health care reforms, the nationalizations had far less bipartisan support. Iron and steel, a healthier industry than some of the others first taken over by the government, was nationalized in February 1951. It was denationalized by the Conservatives following their electoral victory that fall and then renationalized by Labour in 1967. Truck haulage was also briefly denationalized. The Conservatives did not attempt further denationalizations until the 1980s, when Thatcher stepped in that direction by selling off a publicly owned radioisotope firm, the state oil firm (Britoil), British Airways, and other companies as part of her program of reprivatizing the economy.

Crisis in Foreign Trade

Instead of immediately removing World War II controls, the government was for a time forced to extend them. The rationing of clothing was not lifted until the spring of 1949 and food rationing not completely ended until July 1954. The austerity program was made necessary by the excess of imports over exports, which had come about through the need to replace wartime losses and deteriorated machinery.

British industries made a rapid recovery, and the shipping fleet was enlarged through an active building program. In this reconstruction, loans from the United States were helpful. U.S. insistence on equal access to Commonwealth markets meant that inefficient and war-damaged British industries had to compete with better-equipped and better-managed U.S. firms in what was formerly considered Britain's private yard. Britain participated in the U.S.-sponsored European Recovery Program (the Marshall Plan), and loans were also forthcoming from the dominions. In spite of an increase in exports, the balance of trade remained unfavorable. Cutbacks were made in military commitments and expenses, especially in the Mediterranean. One consequence was the need for the United States to supplant British aid to Greece and Turkey with the Truman Plan of 1947.

A possible remedy for an ailing export trade is devaluation of the nation's currency. Devaluation (an official act, unlike depreciation, which is brought about by market forces) of one country's currency compared with those of other nations can suddenly lower the cost of that nation's goods on the international market. It can enhance sales abroad, improve exports, cut imports, and lead to higher employment at home. Such a move may not necessarily be viewed favorably by other nations, as it threatens the stability of their own exports. If they oppose the move, they can protect themselves by such actions as raising tariffs to increase the cost of imported goods or devalue their currencies as well.

The British were loathe to devalue, perhaps more for reasons of pride than because they feared retaliatory measures. There were legitimate concerns as well. The financial resources of many nations of the Commonwealth and former empire were held in sterling. British devaluation would affect the financial status of these countries and have diplomatic consequences. The capacity of developing countries to purchase needed machine tools and to attract investment funds would be weakened. Foreign investors, who in the aggregate held several billion pounds of sterling, would most likely sell their holdings at the first hint of a decline in the exchange rate. Such a vast sell-off could stimulate a greater fall in the value of the currency than desired. Confidence in the British financial market would plummet and impede the ability of British banks to lend abroad.

Concern for a high exchange rate dominated British economic policies for some while after the war. It had a negative impact on export trade, but even so the overall balance of payments would have been positive or close to it but for the outflow of military expenditures. Other factors associated with Britain's prior industrial and imperial successes also caused Britain's postwar economic recovery to suffer. The first great nation to undergo industrialization, Britain had moved slowly. Much of the process was based on the textile industry, and many firms could rely on internally generated funds for their incremental investment needs. Family banks and small, short-term loans were the rule. France and Germany industrialized later, at a faster pace, with the movement based on steel. There the need for large sums of money all at once to meet huge start-up costs stimulated growth of great national banks, long-term loans, and bank involvement in the management decisions of their client firms.[4]

Britain's early pattern meant that after the war the nation experienced difficulties in capital formation for capital-intensive industries. There was a failure to keep pace with foreign competition in newer fields such as light machine tools and electricity. British investors tended to send their money abroad, where returns were high; if they invested at home, they usually chose safe government bonds rather than private industrial paper.

Because Britain had industrialized early, much of its domestic demand for traditional industrial products (rails, locomotives) had already been met. With only modest local demand available and the high value of sterling depressing exports, British managers were reluctant to make modernizing investments. In time, this meant they would be increasingly vulnerable to foreign competition. The British skill at producing small customized orders was formerly a plus. Now it meant that British firms operated at higher costs per unit produced than did their competitors, who took advantage of the scale savings associated with large-batch, long-run production.

Old management systems had served well for decades. They were preserved and new approaches ignored. No full-time graduate schools of management were established in Britain until the 1960s. The spheres of engineers (chiefly educated through the apprentice system) and management (products of Oxford and Cambridge) remained isolated from each other. The tradition or myth of British gradualism further reinforced the notion that sudden change and decisive response to new conditions were not warranted.

Because Britain had been industrialized for so long, by 1950 only 5 percent of the population was involved in agriculture. The flow of agricultural workers to the urban industrial labor market still occurring on the Continent did not exist in England. The shortage of skilled labor and presence of many small firms granted key influence to union stewards. They could organize factory floors tightly. Often the stewards would resist technological innovation in order to protect jobs. The multiplicity of labor unions led to competitive wildcat strikes, with shop stewards fiercely defending their local work-rule or wage advantages. A gain in one shop might stimulate a strike in another. As the nation moved toward full employment, the power of the unions grew proportionately, especially at the local level.

There were, then, a number of linked factors that worked against rapid British economic recovery: lagging investment, a slow rate of adaptation to new technology, and inefficient organization of both work and management. High employment rates spelled the necessity of investment in expense-saving technology if profit ratios were to improve. But capital for this purpose was not easily attainable, and the posture of union shop stewards was another disincentive. Foreign competition remained strong, even after devaluation was undertaken in 1949 and again in 1964. Profits remained low, discouraging investors and moves toward modernization. In brief, in industry short-range interests dominated and prevented long-range growth; in the banking world long-range interests stalled adaptations that might have provided more short-range flexibility.

In the years immediately following the war, both Labourites and Conservatives adhered to the view of noted British economist John Maynard Keynes that the best way to manage an economy is through fiscal policy. In particular, they acepted the version of Keynesianism that saw the key to stimulating industrial development as demand. If consumers do not provide that demand, then it is appropriate for governments to prime the pump and create demand. This should be done even at the risk of creating short-term debt, for the prosperity induced by government expenditures will in the long run engender tax revenues that will more than compensate for the debt created. In other words, government debts or fiscal surpluses should be used to balance the normal business cycle, creating a stable economy with little inflation or fluctuation in employment levels. The existence of a government debt is not nearly as important as the costs of servicing that debt, for it is the latter that actually affects the government's cash flow.

Application of this theory proved difficult because of the desire to achieve both full employment and a high exchange rate. Stimulation of demand brought increased imports as well as some industrial expansion. The imports fostered trade and balance-of-payments deficits. Reluctant to devalue, the government attempted to deflate the economy by cutting back government purchases and increasing interest rates. Thus the country fell into a pattern of what critics derisively termed "stop-go" economic policies.

Why did the government not adopt more interventionist policies in order to achieve increased industrial development? There are several reasons.

Attlee's Labour cabinet was deeply involved in its nationalization program. Little funding and energy were available for development of industrial policy. Unions financed about 80 percent of the expenditures of the Labour party, and they strongly opposed any planning of labor distribution. Industrialists also demanded autonomy. The Bank of England was nationalized, but other banks were not. Few personnel at the Bank of England were changed. For the most part, they saw themselves as part of the international financial community and opposed devaluation. Communication between the Bank and the Treasury was poor. The latter reviewed all government proposals with primary concern for expenditure control rather than industrial stimulation; its civil servants worked in secrecy, paying little attention to new theories or outside advice.

Above all, the promise of Keynesianism seemed to be that full employment could be achieved without extensive or detailed intervention in each industrial sector; it could be done simply by maintenance of aggregate demand. Full employment for the working class, with managers and owners retaining control of industrial decisions and investment funds, pleased both political parties. Hence, especially after the victory of moderates over left-wingers in the Labour party, there was a convergence of economic politics.

Only small funding became available to industry, usually in the form of tax relief. Private pressure against intervention remained strong despite the growth of governmental apparatus in other sectors of society. Aggregate demand management did help to create full employment. But that in time led to inflation, and Keynes's theory was designed to damp excessive swings in a cyclical economy, not to address this different problem.

The link between inflation and full employment soon became obvious. Shortages of labor beget higher wage settlements that force higher prices. At the beginning of the 1960s, the government therefore turned to controlling incomes, rather than stimulating demand, as a way of curbing inflation. Government employees were forced to accept a "pay pause." Unions resisted wage guidelines and often achieved settlements that violated these guidelines; other unions or shops then struck to obtain similar improvements in benefits. High prices brought decline in exports, increase of trade deficits, and calls for devaluation. The government (whether Conservative or Labour) would bargain with the Trades Union Congress (TUC). But the TUC's hold over its member unions was tenuous at best. Wildcat strikes again occurred. Indeed, as the national union leadership was criticized for its agreements with the government, more power passed to shop-floor stewards, who did not hesitate to exercise it. Their chief interest was wages, and the incomes policy pushed them into public antagonism toward the state. Thus the incomes policy nourished what was already a key long-range problem.

By the time a Labour government took over in 1964, the balance-of-payments deficit exceeded $2 billion. Austerity measures were inaugurated, including increases of taxes on all imports save food, on gasoline, and on incomes. Further loans were arranged, and the pound was again devalued. Defense outlays were cut. West Germany agreed to pay for most of the costs of British forces in its territory. Military and naval bases abroad were reduced, and plans were made to recall all forces east of Suez except those in Hong Kong. One of only a few encouraging developments was discovery of natural gas and oil under the North Sea. These fields began production in 1967, but by the time production costs were met and profits made by foreign oil firms involved in the find, government revenues fell to less than expected. Demand for energy remained high, and Britain pushed the development of atomic power for industrial purposes.

The turn from a demand-management approach to an incomes approach involved a shift toward more direct government intervention in the private sector. Industrial firms gradually received more subsidies. Funds were mostly provided on a geographic basis, in an attempt to transfer resources and improve employment in depressed regions. Preservation of selected unprofitable enterprises took priority over stimulation of profitable firms with strong export capabilities (the latter policy was followed in France and Germany). Investments focused on an essentially narrow spectrum of industry—nuclear, aircraft, aerospace—whereas France, Germany, and Japan funded a wider range of endeavors, including machine tools and chemicals. The tentativeness of the government's industrial policy, plus its "rescue" emphasis, meant that in the long run its effect in stimulating a growth economy was only limited.

In the early 1970s, Conservative prime minister Heath endeavored to reduce government expenditures and to revive the economy by curtailing the power of unions. His efforts were not much more successful than Labour's attempt of the second half of the 1960s to make socialist dogma work through technical efficiency. The unions openly defied the Industrial Relations Act. Though the Industrial Relations Court sometimes rendered guilty verdicts, the fines imposed were often ignored and the court's initial rulings overturned on technicalities. Failure to reach an understanding with the Trades Union Congress on wage and price increases led to government-imposed restraints on wages and prices in 1972. When the United States left the gold standard that same year, Heath allowed the pound to float (find its own level on the international currency market) rather than maintain it at an artificially high level that would in turn hurt exports and the mild economic expansion then under way.

Boldly confronted by his opponents, Heath obtained insufficient effort from his allies. Frustrated by the reluctance of entrepreneurs to invest, he complained to a gathering of business leaders: "When we came in we were told there weren't sufficient inducements to invest. So we provided the inducements. Then we were told people were scared of balance of payments difficulties leading to stop-go. So we floated the pound. Then we were told of fears of inflation: and now we're dealing with that. And still you aren't investing enough."[5]

Labor restlessness and work stoppages by wildcat strikes spread. The prevalent attitude of "I'm all right, Jack" demonstrated a self-centeredness far different from the World War II spirit of common sacrifice. The lyrics of the songs of the popular Liverpool singing group the Beatles reflected an apparently widely held perception that because the "establishment" was "ripping off" the rest of society, individuals had the right to take whatever they wanted for themselves in return. It was, for example, commonly recognized that British industries had failed to keep pace in the modernization race with those in the United States, Europe, and Japan. There were allegations that owners had been more interested in pocketing profits than in reinvestment, whereas the government had failed to make unpopular decisions in the industries it controlled. If everything was coming apart, then the natural response was for everyone—employee, employer, and union—to go it alone. Disillusioned over what they thought were insufficient efforts toward world peace and specifically opposed to the actions of Britain's U.S. ally in Vietnam, many British youth turned inward and became part of a drug culture simultaneously narcissistic, rebellious, and occasionally violent.

In the face of the visible disintegration of societal cohesiveness, a cohesiveness recognized as more myth than reality because Britain had long been two nations—the rich and the poor—the policies of both Conservatives and Labour seemed ineffectual. The Conservatives did attempt some modernizing steps, including entry into the Common Market and a switch to decimal currency. But the benefits of these moves did not become immediately evident, and each stirred emotional debate. Though opposing subsidies to industry in principle, in order to protect employment, the Conservatives nationalized the gas-turbine and aeroengine sectors of the failing Rolls Royce firm and aided the declining shipbuilding industry. A value-added tax appeared in 1973. It was quickly denounced as regressive, that is, bearing more heavily on those of low income than on those with high income; yet the government soon relied on it as a major source of revenue. The personal income tax and investment taxes increased sharply also, in part to narrow the great gap in the distribution of wealth. Such steps reduced incentives at the top and stimulated criticism of Heath within his own party. The Labour government that succeeded to power in 1974 eased wage restraints, but it obtained only a brief breathing period from the unions. Their demands joined with the continuing impact of the Arab oil embargo of 1973 (provoked by the Arab-Israeli War in October of that year) to produce high rates of inflation and unemployment.

Strikes and social disruption continued, taxes and prices skyrocketed, unemployment burgeoned, and British influence in world affairs declined further. Combined with the seeming tiredness of the current approaches of both major parties, these factors stimulated within the populace both an instinctive drawing back from the threat of continuing disintegration and a search for new alternatives. This was especially true among the middle classes, which had long been squeezed between the privileged upper classes and the organized labor movement.

Thatcher's Policies

Among economists, monetarism gained an increased following. Its advocates held that the best way to stimulate an economy is through firm control of the money supply. The monetarists opposed their views to those of the Keynesians, arguing that the fiscal policy and demand-management approach of the latter contributed to the possibility of a large government's becoming involved in many areas of business activity. This practice, they suggested, leads to rational expectation on the part of the private sector that the government will always intervene. The result will be that the private sector does less and the government must become continually interventionist, further substantiating the rational expectation.

Such a governmental role is not acceptable to the conservative monetarists, who suggest that changes in economic activity follow changes in the money supply. They believe that easy credit and government investment to the point of budget deficits, though appearing to strengthen an economy as wage increases initially lag behind price increases, will in the long run lead to inflationary spirals harmful to investment. In place of government demand-management policies, they advocate letting markets work on their own; the government should stand aside, albeit assuring a steady monetary supply, predictable credit, and free trade. The market, left to its internal dynamics, will regulate itself more rapidly and more finely than can bureaucrats with no matter how many computers.

Monetarists point out that increasing demand will decrease employment and stimulate the economy only as long as that increase can be easily met within the aggregate productive capacity of a nation or marketing area. Once demand has passed about the 90 percent level of productive capacity, then costs will rise (because of the difficulty of finding the one more skilled laborer needed, the necessity of using all available raw materials rather than those stored closest by, and so forth). Inflation will result. Reduction of demand— for example, by cutting down on government purchases—will not necessarily reduce the increased price levels because of the psychology of anticipated inflation, even if decreased production does lead to layoffs in the working force. Thus is created the anomaly of "stagflation," a stagnant economy with some unemployment coexisting with inflation; some workers are without jobs whereas others have higher wages than ever.

The monetarists' prescription is not to adjust the demand side of the economy but the supply side. If supplies increase, there will be less pressure for goods. Inflation, though it may continue, will not be as severe. To increase supplies, aggregate productive capacity must be increased. This requires investment funding, which is not likely to be obtained from the less affluent segments of society; any additional moneys that segment receives will not be invested but rather spent, simply boosting demand and inflation. The monetarists therefore advise reduced taxes for the affluent sector of society, those individuals who will use their newly available funds for investment. As the building of new factories and utilization of new machines increases the supply of goods, theoretically prices will fall, providing a "trickle-down" benefit for the poor. Consumption and demand will rise without provoking inflation.

Keynesians, influenced by the Great Depression, view the economy as basically cyclical; monetarists see it as stable. Unemployment is not the result of too little demand but of too high wages, say the latter. Unions, when they understood the rules affecting money supply, would recognize that wage contracts that are too high create unemployment; they would therefore reduce their demands. A stable money supply would create a stable exchange rate. Short-term fluctuations of the economy should be ignored. All focus should be on long-term targets, with strict obedience to monetarist economic rules.

Both Keynesianism and monetarism have their strong and weak points. Both may be equally right or wrong in given situations. Each has important political and ideological implications for the role of government. The limitations of the Keynesian formulas were by now well apparent, and restive Conservatives were ready to try a less shopworn approach.

At the beginning of the 1980s, Prime Minister Thatcher's endorsement of a more liberal political economy (in the nineteenth-century classical British sense of liberalism) was clear and ideological. It won her support. Some of the former policies of Keynesian supply and demand management had already been laid aside in previous years. Global interdependence and inflation, as reflected in the oil price increases in 1973, further demonstrated the inadequacies of demand management. In defeating Heath for leadership of the Conservatives, Thatcher had also beaten the Old Tories who accepted limited state intervention in the economy. Now, in following her monetarist advisers, Thatcher quickly turned to management of the money supply as the key to controlling inflation. The banking industry welcomed the move as congenial to its desire for a restrictive, anti-inflation money supply. Some employers were happy no longer to be urged to bargain with the unions and to be allowed to make layoffs, using unemployment as a lever to discipline labor.

Efforts to cut public spending and allow the economy to adjust to the market were, however, counterbalanced by increased defense spending and the costs of the war with Argentina over control of the Falkland Islands. North Sea oil supplies aided the economy, yet interest rates and unemployment continued to rise. Recession was accentuated by the effect of economic problems in the United States and industrial competition from Korea and Japan. Thatcher continued with her monetarist policy of limiting the amount of money in circulation. She expected that economic progress would be achieved as she built a more solid political basis for a market economy stimulated by private initiative that was unafraid of the threat of inflation.

When monetary policy failed to hold unions in line, the prime minister challenged them by pushing through the House of Commons legislation curbing the rights of picketers and making national union organizations financially responsible for actions taken by local units.

In 1985 the prime minister won a major victory when coal miners, who had been on strike for fifty-one weeks in protest of government plans to close unprofitable pits, returned to work without achieving any concessions. A teachers' strike the following year also collapsed when confronted by Thatcher's determination. By 1986, working days lost due to union disputes had fallen to 1.9 million as compared with 29.5 million seven years earlier. The retreat of the unions reflected the diminished influence of the old-line industrial labor groups, a decline further reflected in a nearly 20 percent reduction in the membership of the Trades Union Congress from that of the previous six years.

Public-sector borrowing fell so that funds would be available for private investment. One major privately funded venture was joint Anglo-French construction of a 31-mile (50-km) tunnel under the English Channel, a long-deferred project abandoned several times and once again begun in 1986. Public borrowing did not decline as much as expected because of reluctance to cut welfare programs more sharply than seemed politically feasible. To lessen government borrowing and facilitate reductions in the income tax, Thatcher balanced cuts in the latter with increases in consumer taxes. These were promptly criticized as regressive, bearing hardest on those least able to pay. Assistance for troubled industries decreased, primarily only selected high-technology firms obtaining aid. Intervention did occur in British Steel, British Leyland, and British Shipbuilders, public enterprises over which the prime minister appointed "ruthless industrialists" who abolished more than a quarter of a million jobs.

As part of her policy to reduce the role of the government, Thatcher implemented a privatization program. Criticism of this action centered on loss of public control and increasing costs of services. In 1986 the percentage of Britons owning stocks and shares had risen to 17 percent from a figure of 6 in 1979, even prior to the government's huge stock flotation of British Gas. The Conservatives' election victory in 1987 encouraged the prime minister to continue her modernization plan to further "people's capitalism" through more sales of government stockholdings. She also pressed legislation limiting the power of unions.

Beginning in 1979, Thatcher altered the method of government reimbursement of local expenses so that the national government could influence the expenditures of municipal councils. Those that spent too much had their government grants cut. Some Labour-dominated councils nevertheless maintained or expanded programs simply by raising property taxes, thus undermining Thatcher's effort to free more funds for consumer spending and private investment. In 1988 the government imposed strict controls on unemployment and welfare benefits. The new budget projected a sizable surplus, much of which was used to achieve a tax reduction for the top 5 percent of the nation's payers. More controversial was initiation of a flat-rate tax of $600 per adult scheduled to replace the variable local property taxes in 1990. Based on voter lists, the tax discouraged poorer citizens from registering and seemed to favor the rich over the poor. As Lord Chelwood protested, "A millionaire will pay half as much as a pensioner couple." Moderate backbenchers among the Conservatives were only reluctantly brought to support the bill. The prime minister had them "whipped" into line, as she interpreted the legislation as necessary to her campaign to improve the British economy by cutting taxes. It also strengthened her hand over Labour-dominated councils by denying them the ability to raise property taxes and to expand services. The populace reacted negatively; street demonstrations against the tax rumbled over many months. To a number of observers, Thatcher's earlier insistence on closing unprofitable pits despite the objections of striking coal miners had made common sense. But her treatment of local taxing privileges now seemed unreasonable, unfair, and vindictive; it weakened her political support.

The prime minister held to her monetarist plans. Despite controversy, she kept to her intention to continue privatization by selling government ownership of the country's ten great water supply authorities. Thatcher's inflexibility regarding the domestic economy was paralleled by her attitude toward the EEC's drive for a complete common market in 1992. She was willing to enter into bilateral agreements, and she insisted that she supported the idea that the nations of Europe should attempt to speak as one on many important issues. But Thatcher had no use for European federalism or any developments that might "suppress nationhood and concentrate power at the center of a European conglomerate." On the national scene, she had questioned whether modernization required a war against local differences and against a multiplicity of private enterprises (although her tiff with Labour-dominated municipal councils somewhat belied this). In 1988 as she observed the willingness of some continental leaders to follow domestic decentralization while advocating international federalization, she questioned the latter as the best path to modernization. The prime minister opposed moves to eliminate border controls as undermining efforts to control terrorism and the drug trade. Nor did she support plans for "harmonization" of excise and sales taxes or creation of a European central bank, a bank that would no doubt be based on the Continent and thus further reduce the influence of British banks.

English reluctance to proceed rapidly toward a European Economic and Monetary Union was reflected when Common Market representatives met to consider the posture the European Community should take toward Eastern Europe during the events of 1989. Although positions were not firmly drawn, some nations favored accelerated integration among the existing members of the EC. Thatcher, however, advocated a reaching out for relationships with the Eastern European nations rather than concentration of effort on deeper integration. It was clear that Thatcher took a more nationally oriented approach toward the adaption of the benefits of the scientific and technological revolution for commercial developments and trade than did her continental colleagues. Difficult negotiations loomed if Britain were to remain within the EEC and that organization were to achieve its goals by 1992 or even later.

As political leaders in other countries talked about the need for restructuring their societies, Thatcher was bringing about significant restructuring in hers. Politically speaking, this reconstruction was not accepted across the board, yet more and more the debate was over the scope of the reconstruction rather than its institution or character. Complaints remained, even though the size of the British middle class seemed once again to be growing. Was the distance between rich and poor expanding too greatly? Under Labour, the burdens of austerity were distributed across the population; under Thatcher, the poor seemed to carry a greater portion of the burden. Were health and education services suffering as Thatcher attacked socialism? Did long-standing high unemployment threaten the economy? What of the difference in prosperity between the south and east and the struggling regions of the north, Wales, and Scotland? Was Thatcher's strong role in enforcing less reliance on government and more on private initiative the most effective path to modernization? With her resignation, the time had arrived for determining whether the changes she had wrought had rooted permanently or were dependent upon her strong personality and persuasive will. The first intimations from Major's succeeding administration were that the basic principles of Thatcher's programs would be maintained, with great efforts made to soften their harshest edges. But would such compromise be possible in the long run?

Empire and Commonwealth

In 1929, in the face of the Great Depression, the British government had appropriated £1 million a year for the economic development of outlying regions of the empire. A department within the colonial office served as a center for economic planning in the colonies. An act of 1940 increased the development appropriation fivefold, and the British Colonial Development and Welfare Acts of 1945, 1950, and 1955 provided for £220 million to be spent by 1960 on colonial improvement. These sums were materially increased by grants from the treasuries of the respective colonies. Such measures were in line with Churchill's famous wartime statement that he had not become His Majesty's prime minister in order to preside over the dissolution of the British Empire.

The New Commonwealth of Nations

It was soon clear, however, that the concepts of empire and Commonwealth were changing. The most devastating blow to old relationships came when Britain officially withdrew from India on August 15, 1947, and the two self-governing dominions of Pakistan and the Union of India were established. In June 1948 King George VI dropped "emperor of India" from his titles, at the same time that Lord Mountbatten was succeeded as governor general of India by a native Indian. Prime Minister Jawaharlal Nehru insisted that the Union of India have a republican constitution with an elective head. This required some change in Commonwealth practice, as before the king had always been recognized as sovereign of each independent dominion. Conferences attended by representatives of the United Kingdom, Canada, Australia, New Zealand, South Africa, India, Pakistan, and Ceylon brought agreement to drop the word *British* and instead to refer to the mutual association of these states as the Commonwealth of Nations. The thorny question of the position of the king was solved when India announced its "acceptance of the king as the symbol of the free association of its independent member nations." The term "head of the Commonwealth" for the monarch was adopted to accommodate India, and by 1953 the designation was common to all the dominions.

As various former colonies or protectorates have obtained their independence, most of them have accepted membership in the Commonwealth. Some did not, such as Egypt, Transjordan, Iraq, Burma, Aden, and British Somaliland. Because of severe criticism of its racial policies by other Commonwealth members, South Africa withdrew its request for continued membership in the Commonwealth when it became a republic. Racial issues and electoral policies were also hotly debated when Southern Rhodesia proclaimed its independence, yet it remained in the Commonwealth as Zimbabwe. Pakistan left the Commonwealth in 1972, the same year that Bangladesh, which seceded from Pakistan in December 1971, joined. At the beginning of 1991 there were fifty members in this association of independent states made up of five indigenous monarchies, twenty-eight republics, and seventeen queen's realms (where Elizabeth II is recognized as monarch).

The British Commonwealth as originally constituted in the late 1920s was composed of predominantly white, English-speaking states. This racial character changed along with the dropping of the designation *British* and the establishment of the Commonwealth. But the use of English as a common language is still an important tie among these diverse states. There are many other such bonds: schools patterned on the British model, British practices of government, British legal codes and procedures (at times even a bewigged judiciary), British trade connections with monetary linkups to the pound sterling, and (not to be underrated) cricket, rugby, horse racing, and the spit and polish of British military training.

The individually sovereign Commonwealth countries are not bound to follow either a common domestic or a common foreign policy or hold to the same laws. At times serious differences have therefore arisen among the members. In 1965, when Britain refused to take armed measures to coerce Rhodesia on the declaration of independence by a white-dominated government, two African members of the Commonwealth—Ghana and Tanzania—cut their diplomatic ties with the United Kingdom. These, however, were soon resumed. Britain's Commonwealth Immigration Act of 1968, which restricted the number of immigrants who had no substantial and close connection with Britain, also stirred protest. The policy of trade preference within the Commonwealth has been continued. Without weakening the association of the Commonwealth, each member participates in other regional groupings. Thus Canada has a special defense agreement with the United States; the United Kingdom, Australia, New Zealand, and Pakistan have special Far East commitments; the United Kingdom and Canada are members of the North Atlantic Treaty Organization; and so forth.

The Experience of Decolonization

Decolonization did not occur without opposition and concern within Great Britain. Yet despite the dislocations and strong feelings involved, the process did not take control of British politics; rather, British politics for the most part asserted its control of the process.

Within the British Conservative party, there were those deeply attached to the imperial experience, as debates over India and economic protectionism revealed. Yet the party had strong and fairly unified leadership during the critical years. It was sufficiently well established not to be dominated by an emotional need to cling to one particular ideological position. Also, the bipolar nature of British politics militated against any individual's defection to the opposition, for the opposition was the Labour party and highly critical of colonialism.

Furthermore, loyalty to "empire" drew upon different constituencies that only moderately overlapped. Some persons were loyal to empire for economic reasons (the Indian connection especially); others, particularly those who had relations in the settler colonies of Africa and the dominions, thought of the empire in terms of kith and kin; still others, citing the British sphere of influence in the Middle East, viewed the empire primarily in terms of prestige. The Commonwealth model was an already proven path to decolonization that preserved more than threatened economic ties. The harsh reality of military expenses and the confusion of Arab politics threw a cold rain on maintenance of empire simply for prestige. Many Britons found themselves out of sympathy with the racial and other attitudes of the settlers in central and southern Africa that were contrary to traditional British conceptions of political democracy.

The Labour party, by socialist ideology not favorable to colonialism, drew substantial support from groups—the working class, religious nonconformists, and others—often excluded from the consensus that had controlled British investments and external policy. Faced by both the military and economic costs of maintaining the empire and challenged by nationalist indigenous populations and the need to rebuild the economy at home, the Labour party would not resist the pressure to decolonize. Indeed, for Labour the more severe political cost would have stemmed from attempting to maintain the colonial relationships and system.

In contrast with the situation in France and the French colonies, decolonization in Britain was further smoothed by another factor. The metropole's fairly well unified political and economic elite proved able for the most part to control the process of change in the colonies (except Southern Rhodesia), whereas settler opposition to decolonization was fragmented. Then, too, British administration in the colonies had been relatively light, and the administrators were well imbued with the tradition of neutrally advancing policy decided upon in London. British economic interests in many of the colonies were complex and well established; small independent farmers were not the dominating influence in most instances. The corporations' major concern was continued peaceful operation. Often this could be achieved better through smooth decolonization than by stubborn resistance to that process, for resistance could provoke labor unrest and the destruction of property.[6]

These reasons and more helped decolonization to be accepted in the home country. If some people found it distasteful or were distressed by the loss of prestige, they nevertheless made the best of the situation. It reflected the theme of Britain's decline in global importance in the postwar years. It was also a price to be paid if the British were to concentrate their energy and fortune on economic modernization, the search for social justice at home, and the definition of Britain's role in the emerging new Europe.

Notes

1. The authors are indebted to the interpretation expressed by Peter Calvocoressi in *The British Experience, 1945–1975* (1978).

2. "Part of the Union," composed by John Ford and Richard Hudson. Published by Fazz Music Ltd., copyright © 1973. Reprinted by permission of the publisher. The song reached the rank of number two on the national popularity lists at the time.

3. *Sunday Times*, May 3, 1981.

4. See Peter A. Hall, *Governing the Economy: The Politics of State Intervention in Britain and France* (1986).

5. As quoted in A. Gamble, "The Decline of the Conservative Party," *Marxism Today* (November 1979), p. 9.

6. The authors are indebted to the analysis provided by M. Kahler in *Decolonization in Britain and France: The Domestic Consequences of International Relations* (1984).

Suggested Readings

Attlee, C. R., *As It Happened* (1954).

Beer, S. H., *Britain Against Itself: The Political Contradictions of Collectivism* (1982).

Calvocoressi, P., *The British Experience, 1945–1975* (1978).

Chamberlain, M., *Fenwomen: A Portrait of Women in an English Village* (1983).

Coxall, W., *Contemporary British Politics* (1989).

Doumitt, D., *Conflict in Northern Ireland: The History, the Problem and the Challenge* (1985).

Eckstein, H., *The English Health Service: The Origins, Structure, and Achievement* (1958).

Eden, A., *Full Circle: The Memoirs of Anthony Eden* (1960).

———, *The Reckoning: The Memoirs of Anthony Eden* (1965).

Gamble, A., *Britain in Decline: Economic Policy, Political Strategy, and the British State* (1983).

Hall, Peter A., *Governing the Economy: The Politics of State Intervention in Britain and France* (1986).

Harris, K., *Thatcher* (1988).

Hewison, R., *In Anger: British Culture in the Cold War, 1945–60* (1981).

Kahler, M., *Decolonization in Britain and France: The Domestic Consequences of International Relations* (1984).

Kavanagh, D., *Thatcherism and British Politics: The End of Consensus?* (1990).

Kelley, K., *The Longest War: Northern Ireland and the I.R.A.* (1982).

Macmillan, H., *Riding the Storm, 1956–1959* (1971).

———, *Tides of Fortune, 1945–1955* (1969).

Mansergh, N., *The Commonwealth Experience* (1969).

Rose, R., *Politics in England*, 3d ed. (1980).

Smith, A., *Poverty and Progress in Britain, 1953–1973* (1978).

Stromberg, R., *After Everything: Western Intellectual History Since 1945* (1975).

Williamson, B., *The Temper of the Times: British Society Since World War II* (1990).

Wilson, E., *Only Halfway to Paradise: Women in Postwar Britain: 1945–1968* (1980).

———, *Women and the Welfare State* (1977).

Young, M., and P. Willmott, *Family and Kinship in East London* (1957).

CHAPTER TEN

France

ॐ

Establishment of the Fourth Republic
The Provisional Government • The Constitution and the French Union

Internal and External Affairs
Economic Recovery • Overseas France: Colonies and Mandates
Alliances and Regional Groups • Political Developments

Establishment of the Fifth Republic

Domestic and Foreign Affairs
Transformation of Overseas France • The Experience of Decolonization
Domestic Policy • Foreign Affairs
Growing Domestic Unrest • Resignation of de Gaulle

Gaullists, Socialists, and the Contest Between Ideology and Pragmatism
Politics After de Gaulle
The Rise, Check, and Reemergence of Mitterrand

Notes

Suggested Readings

In France the loss of life and the fatigue caused by World War I were not overcome in the interwar period. Further great destruction, though fewer casualties, came with World War II. Like Britain, France lost an empire in the years after that conflict. For the French, however, the process was more violent and costly than for their neighbors across the Channel. Yet despite this succession of blows to French resources, the main theme of French history since World War II has been that of recuperation and revival. Starting in the 1950s, recovery began; the economy surged forward, carrying France to the forefront of the European league. This progress was achieved by a judicious mixture of private enterprise and state guidance that drew world attention to French forms of "indicative planning" and that owed much to an excellent body of civil servants.

France also took the lead in bringing about economic unity in the western portion of the Continent, with Jean Monnet and Robert Schuman playing conspicuous roles. France took an equally important part in furthering political unity in the West, particularly during the 1970s, and Franco-German collaboration became a cornerstone of an emerging Europe.

Internally, during the first postwar decade France suffered from severe political instability. General Charles de Gaulle's assumption of power in 1958 inaugurated an era of greater stability and continuity. That approach appeared challenged by student-led demonstrations and political crisis in 1968. In the long run, the changes that ensued were not as great as predicted at the time, and the process of building French prestige in Europe continued. So, too, did efforts toward increased economic, social, and political modernization that, if occasionally pushed to extremes by political pressures, soon returned to a moderate course.

In Britain acceptance of the need to modernize came quickly, although recognition of the extent of the effort and adjustments required did not. Strong debates on how to achieve a modernized society accompanied that recognition. In the two Germanys acceptance both of modernization and the price associated with it was rapid; there could be no clinging to former ways. Moreover, both the Soviet Union and the West were demanding fundamental transformation. In France, however, the situation was very different. Though the political formulation of the Third Republic (1870–1940) was discredited by its shocking collapse before Hitler's war machine, the French way of life was not.[1]

The faith of the French in their life-style along with a desire to protect it through reforms sustained and motivated them during the German occupation. Thus, after the liberation of Paris in 1944, there was a strong move to form a new government and return to the way of life inhibited by the Nazi boot for over four years. Within the wartime resistance movement, some Catholics, Socialists, and Communists favored significant change. The Com-

A Frenchmen weeps as he watches German troops march into Paris on June 14, 1940. Four years later, General Charles de Gaulle (in center, waving) marches down the Champs Elysées in a tumultuous victory parade. He said of the liberation, "Paris! Paris outraged! Paris broken! Paris martyred! But Paris liberated! Liberated by itself, liberated by its people with the help of the armies of France, with the support and help of the whole of France, of France that is fighting, of France alone." Even though few agreed with his description of how France was liberated—especially his omission of the role of British and U.S. troops—the French populace was deeply moved by his words. (Top photo 208-PD-10A-3 from the National Archives; left photo from UPI/Bettmann.)

munists, strong in number thanks to their role in the resistance, relied heavily on the non-French Soviet model of modernization. It is not surprising, then, that the nationalistic French were willing to oppose Communist political success, once they were provided the necessary leadership. Yet they disagreed as to whether to transform French society and, if so, on the method for doing so.

Despite the repudiation of the Third Republic, the Fourth Republic (1946–1958) resembled it in both structure and ideas. The most notable deviation from the pattern was willingness to enter into international economic agreements, such as the Marshall Plan, the European Coal and Steel Community, and the Common Market. Economic necessity more or less forced such steps, which in turn fostered the emergence of advanced industrialization in France. These developments, however, did not bring a major reorientation of the French economy or politics. Military and psychological commitment to empire, especially Indochina and Algeria, symbolized continuing traditionalism among both conservatives and significant groups of the Left, including the Socialists.

De Gaulle, who created the Fifth Republic in 1958 and became its president in 1959, held a vision of a more dynamic, grander France. He was a towering figure, destined to become the most important Frenchman of the twentieth century. De Gaulle saw his country liberated from the burden and distractions of empire that he believed hindered the development of a technically modern France able to play an influential role in continental and global politics. His tools for French society were revived French nationalism, technologically modern military forces, peace, and a new political structure granting authority to the central government in Paris and within that government more authority to one individual. Many supporters of de Gaulle assumed he would reshape France with Algeria as an integral part of that future. That inclusion in the long run did not occur. Yet the key feature of the "revolution" of 1958 that brought de Gaulle to power was the belief held by many that traditional formulas and goals were worn out: A new approach was needed. Change came rapidly in some areas, such as government-supported technology. In education, by contrast, tradition held sway until rattled by the student demonstrators of 1968.

The protests and petitions of students and strikers brought alterations in the Gaullist pattern of modernization. At the core of the upheaval was the request for more autonomy in local decisionmaking, an easing of centralization. Economic growth and change over the preceding years, by their very progress, had choked their own paths of bureaucratic development. During his remaining year in power, de Gaulle initiated turns leading toward a more decentralized system of government. Further transition to a less centralized and nationalistic form of modernization resulted in the release of accumulated energies under the leadership of de Gaulle's immediate successors, Georges Pompidou and Valéry Giscard d'Estaing.

Economic growth in the 1970s and 1980s was more sporadic than continuous yet nonetheless substantial. Per capita income reached enviable heights; technology and service industries expanded. A new, more satisfying life-style adapted more to personal goals than to national aims was aggressively sought by the younger generation in the 1980s. The same decade witnessed experiments with Socialist government and government by a president and a prime minister of different parties. Though the implications of these changes were not immediately clear, they appeared to reflect affirmation of the arrival of advanced industrial society and the blurring of the former sharp distinctions between the policies of Left and Right. The confidence achieved was demonstrated by the calm acceptance in 1990 of the reunification of Germany. Diplomatic campaigns to strengthen ties with their former enemy and to encourage European integration were further indications of renewed French self-assurance.

Establishment of the Fourth Republic

The establishment of the Fourth Republic in 1946 took place after a long, turbulent period. In May 1940 the French army was defeated. The fall of France and the ensuing occupation of the country by the German army constituted one of the darkest periods in French history. During the occupation, two French centers of leadership came into being. One, under Marshal Philippe Pétain, governed from Vichy in south-central France and was known for its collaboration with the Germans. The other—the Free French movement—was organized in London by de Gaulle. In June 1940 the young general spoke by radio to the demoralized French populace, telling it that the battle had been lost but not the war. Underground groups, known collectively as the resistance movement, sprang up in France. They worked to sabotage the Germans and the Vichy government and to protect loyal compatriots from arrest.

By spring 1943 de Gaulle's personal representative, Jean Moulin, had cajoled the resistance groups into forming a National Council of Resistance. After the successful Allied invasion of North Africa, the French National Committee in London merged with the French North African administration to form the French Committee of National Liberation. With the establishment of a provisional Consultative Assembly in Algiers in November 1943, to which the Council of Resistance within France appointed forty delegates, there existed one center around which the anti-Vichy forces could unite.

France was liberated in June 1944. On August 25, 1944, de Gaulle and other dignitaries marched down the Champs-Elysées, amid music and cheers, to mark the return of France to the French. The emotional climate of postwar France, however, was one of despair and confusion. The war and the occupation had devastated the French land and spirit. In an atmosphere of

Jean-Paul Sartre and his lifelong companion, Simone de Beauvoir, were leading figures in existentialism. This philosophical movement gained force in France after World War II, spreading throughout much of Europe and the United States. Sartre—essayist, novelist, playwright, and journalist— spoke to the widely felt sense of crisis and disillusionment. He saw human beings as having to create their own destiny and unable to depend on anyone but themselves. Through his writings and participation in demonstrations, he sought social justice for the working class. De Beauvoir was a novelist of note and a writer on the condition of women in society. In keeping with their rejection of bourgeois society and religion, she and Sartre never married. (Photo from UPI/Bettmann.)

crisis and uncertainty, intellectuals struggled with conflicting ideologies and movements. Old ideological dilemmas seemed irrelevant. Existentialism, a major philosophical movement, took hold first in France and spread throughout much of Europe and the United States. Jean-Paul Sartre—essayist, novelist, playwright, and journalist—became a leading figure in existentialism. He spoke to the sense of crisis, the loneliness, the lack of identity, and the apparent absurdity of existence. He and others repudiated bourgeois society, religion, and all forms of metaphysical belief. In his monumental work *L'Etre et le néant* (*Being and Nothingness*, 1943), Sartre expressed the disillusionment of his world: "Man can will nothing unless he has first understood that he must count on no one but himself; that he is alone, abandoned on earth in the midst of his infinite responsibilities, without help, with no other aim than the one he sets himself, with no other destiny than the one he forges for himself on his earth."[2]

The Provisional Government

On the liberation of France in June 1944, the provisional Consultative Assembly, which was dominated by de Gaulle, moved to Paris and added more representatives from the resistance groups. The leading role of the Communists in the resistance movement gave this party great prestige in liberated France. In September, General de Gaulle named a cabinet as the provisional government of the French Republic. There was thus a clear thread of organizational continuity between de Gaulle's proclamation of the Free French movement and the establishment of the new French government.

For the next fifteen months, de Gaulle and his cabinet governed France largely by executive decree, although important measures were brought before the Consultative Assembly. It was a difficult time. The French economy, particularly the transportation system, lay in ruins. Before the liberation of France, the resistance groups had issued pronouncements in favor of nationalization of important sectors of the economy. The resistance leaders had considerable political power, whereas some of the large industrialists had been guilty of substantial collaboration with the Nazis. Under such conditions, with industry completely disorganized, de Gaulle agreed to undertake a policy of nationalization. From December 1944 to December 1945, the coal mines of northern France, the Renault works, civil aviation, and major commercial banking and credit firms were nationalized. In 1946, after de Gaulle left office, complete nationalization of the coal mines, gas, electricity, and major insurance companies took place.

With Allied help, the provisional government created a respectable French army, and it shared in the final victory. Above all, this army was prepared to take over a zone of occupation, although a specific French zone in Germany and Austria had originally not been planned. With remarkable success, de Gaulle constantly strove to assert France's position as a great power. At the end of 1944, he concluded a twenty-year treaty of alliance and mutual assistance with the Soviet Union. Even while France was still under the provisional government, it again began to share in directing European affairs, although at the Potsdam conference France was not represented.

With liberation, the provisional government began a wholesale arrest of those who collaborated with the Germans. Marshal Pétain was condemned to death, but his sentence was commuted to life imprisonment in view of his great age and his previous distinguished service to France. Pierre Laval, the arch-collaborator among Vichy officials, was condemned to death and shot. The judicial procedure followed in these early trials aroused much criticism; although more trials were held, the many prosecutions that had been expected did not materialize. As in other countries liberated from Nazi occupation, numerous grudges were settled out of court one way or another.

The provisional government from the beginning worked toward broadening its base of support among the people of France. General de Gaulle by decree granted the right to vote to women. A plebiscite was held to determine that the people favored the drawing up of a new constitution. Elections for a National Assembly gave the largest number of seats to Communists, and a combination of leftist parties controlled the chamber. Although de Gaulle was again acclaimed head of the provisional government by the National Assembly, he resigned at the beginning of 1946 over a question of military credits. France was once more on the familiar path leading to a succession of premiers in the following years.

The Constitution and the French Union

In France, even more than in other countries, the constitution is considered a key symbol and political statement of the premises on which the state and its relations with its constituents will be run. As elsewhere, debate over the limits the constitution places on the sovereign power reflects debate over basic principles and the manner in which politics will operate. General de Gaulle soon came out in opposition to the newly drafted constitution. Above all, he objected to the overwhelming power given to the proposed single-chamber legislative body. It was generally feared that this body might come under the control of the Communists, leaving no check to the communization of France.

The constitution was defeated in a referendum. In new elections the Communists only took second place to the Popular Republican Movement (MRP), a right-center party that had the support of the Catholic church. This time the Socialists and the MRP worked together to draft a more traditional constitution. In spite of the continued opposition of de Gaulle, who believed the executive needed greater powers, the French people approved the constitution in 1946 by a majority of over 1 million, thus formally establishing the Fourth Republic. Overlooked at the time were the number of French citizens who did not give their support: 8 million voted against the constitution and 8.5 million abstained. Yet in a period of little over a year, elections were held five times without serious disorder; their results indicated remarkable stability in relative party strength, the Communists polling between 25 and 30 percent of the vote in each election.

The new constitution, which did not differ greatly from that of the Third Republic, provided for a president with nominal powers who was to be elected by Parliament for a seven-year term. A 1951 law prescribed that the National Assembly be directly elected under a modified form of proportional representation. A Council replaced the old Senate. Local government continued to be closely supervised by the strong central administration in Paris.

A new organization for the empire, known as the French Union, was established; it consisted of the republic, overseas departments, and associated territories. The overseas departments were those of Algeria and four newly created ones: Martinique, Guadeloupe, Réunion, and French Guiana. The rest of French possessions were classed as overseas territories except Tunisia, Morocco, and the Indochinese Federation, which were called associated territories and states. At the head of the union was the president of France and a high council of representatives from the French government and each associated state. There was also an assembly; half of its members were from metropolitan France and the other half from overseas. An ingenious governmental arrangement, the French Union reflected the desire of the French to unify and centralize the empire. This was very different from the British practice, in which decentralization continued to be the order of the day. Yet the French Union was not effective in obtaining strong involvement from its colonial participants, and decisions in regard to the colonies were still made by the French cabinet and the French Parliament. The overseas governments were slow to move; not until 1956 did they grant any considerable extension of suffrage to the indigenous peoples.

Internal and External Affairs

Economic Recovery

In the months immediately following the end of the war in Europe, France suffered severely from shortages of food as well as coal for heating and factory production. Both the Soviet Union and the United States provided aid, but it was primarily to the latter that the French turned. In February 1946, the U.S. ambassador in Paris telegraphed home:

> There is little doubt that the political situation in recent weeks has seriously deteriorated. The average man is still cold, hungry, unable to buy what he needs and frustrated by the feeling that not enough progress has been made. Extremists today are not in control. It is in our interest that public discouragement should not reach the point where extremists appear to offer the only chance of improvement in leadership and in material things. . . . To refuse it [a French request for a loan] . . . will pull out one of the last props of substance and of hope from those in France who want to see France remain an independent and democratic country.[3]

Aid was forthcoming, first in terms of loans through the Export-Import Bank and then via the Marshall Plan. But money, coal, and grain alone would not be enough. Given the immense amount of reconstruction required and the need to husband scarce capital, labor, and resources, some coherent

France

approach was needed. At the beginning of 1947 France therefore adopted the Monnet Plan, named for Jean Monnet, the businessman de Gaulle invited to formulate the guidelines. Not an overall economic blueprint, the plan did establish production goals for a four-year period for six key industries: coal, power, steel, cement, agricultural machinery, and transport. Heavy importation of raw materials and of machinery for the rehabilitation and modernization of French industry formed a vital part of the program. A huge power development in the Rhone valley was undertaken. By 1947–1948, production in French industry as a whole equaled or even exceeded prewar levels, and it continued to expand. Prisoners of war made an important contribution to the French labor supply until their return to Germany in 1948.

In subsequent years, government planning became an increasingly important feature of the French economy. It was widely accepted. Former industrial leaders were discredited either by the collapse of France in 1940 or by collaboration during the occupation. Initially, planning consisted of limited industrial programs aimed at eliminating bottlenecks in six industrial sectors. The second plan, for the years 1953–1957, provided detailed production and investment targets for a broader range of industries. The several modernization commissions that did much of the actual planning and supervision increased in number and personnel.

The plans, at least at their inception, were primarily intended to create a favorable climate for industrial development. Goals set were only indicative. Yet the government had means of influencing industrialists to strive for these goals. Capital investment funds became available, but usually only in return for agreement to quasi contracts pledging the industrialists to invest in accord with aims defined by the plans. Price controls existed, and the government regulated bond issues. Even before the Socialist experiment of the 1980s, some 70 percent of French banks were under public control, and all rediscounted their loans through the Bank of France. It in turn was controlled by the Ministry of Finance through the National Credit Council; thus the ministry could influence investment loans and their conditions. The multiplicity of regulations in France, some overlapping or conflicting, meant that industrialists frequently had to apply to the government for relief. The need for exceptions made firms dependent on the goodwill of government officials, who could offer all sorts of inducements for collaboration with the plans. In short, though the planning was ostensibly indirect, it was implemented by a directive industrial policy consonant with the French tradition of etatism, or state control and responsibility for the general welfare.

Les plans had political functions as well as an economic role: development of a consensus in participation in each plan, education of the populace to assure its understanding and support, and promotion of social change. In practice, participation meant essentially private negotiations with key managers. Over the years relationships became close, evolving into a system whereby persons from the private sector would move to government posts and vice versa. This alliance building between government officials and the private sector enhanced implementation of the plans but left the unions in the cold. Their exclusion to a great extent resulted from their encompassing less than a quarter of the labor force. Moreover, the leadership of organized labor was divided between two large union confederations—the first allied with the Communist party, the second with the Socialists. In addition, a smaller group consisted mainly of Catholic unions.

The educative role of the plans focused less on providing a full range of data to the public than on promoting certain aspects of the plans while leaving in the shadows other features, such as the economic adjustments necessary as large firms were favored over small. The efforts succeeded for the most part. The people accepted the arguments of the planners and moved from traditional preferences favoring small-scale enterprises and the status quo to support for bigness, growth, and competition on international markets. The planners' success in building participation, educating the public, and promoting change greatly aided them in softening the tensions created by social dislocations; these dislocations were of course themselves connected with the economic reorganization of French society that the plans entailed.[4]

At the war's end approximately one-third of France's working population was still engaged in agriculture, and its earnings represented about one-fourth of the national income. In the first years, large importations of wheat were necessary, partly because of several poor growing seasons. Since then, considerable mechanization has taken place on French farms. To make use of modern machinery practicable, many of the small, scattered holdings typical of much of France needed to be consolidated; the government therefore appropriated large grants to facilitate reparceling. A rural revolution resulted that, by the 1960s and 1970s, greatly changed the life of the rural population. As that population became more sophisticated in its farming techniques and more aware of market trends, it also became more politically alert and less conservative. Some youth, as well as farmers whose holdings could not be adapted to the new levels of competition, gravitated to the constantly expanding urban centers. The strains placed upon these urban areas, which often could not make the appropriate adaptations in housing, education, and politics quickly enough, contributed to the difficulties experienced in 1968.

A bad financial situation plagued the French economy. The decline in the value of the franc, the need to increase salaries for governmental employees, the financing of reconstruction projects, the rebuilding of the army, and colonial commitments made budget-balancing difficult. New taxes were imposed, but the long-needed thorough revision of the French tax structure did not take place. As a temporary measure, the government obtained large loans from the United States both directly and through the Marshall Plan. Lesser amounts came from other nations. Even though a substantial array of health and welfare programs were implemented shortly after the war, a series of strikes troubled the period. Inflation and rising living costs were the root causes, although some strikes were inspired by Communists to embarrass the government.

Overseas France: Colonies and Mandates

The internal situation in France was further strained by developments in overseas France. Attempts to reestablish control in all its former mandates and colonies involved France in continual armed conflict until 1962. These wars were on a scale for which the Foreign Legion no longer sufficed, and the National Assembly would not allow conscripts to be sent to some areas (for example, Indochina). A heavy toll fell on volunteers, especially in the officers' corps. The French government reluctantly withdrew completely from Lebanon and Syria and recognized the independence of these states. In Indochina efforts to establish a regime of associated states was never really successful and led to severe conflict in Vietnam. India forced the surrender of century-old French enclaves. Belated efforts to reform the colonial administrations in Sub-Saharan Africa only increased demands for more autonomy and self-government. Rising nationalism eventually led to a recognition of the independence of Morocco and Tunis. This withering away of the French empire, together with differences over colonial policy and the costs inevitably associated with it, added to the political instability of the era. Nor did the continuing round of colonial withdrawals do anything to bolster the French ego and the traditional concept of *grandeur*. All this helped to undermine the French Fourth Republic and pave the way for de Gaulle's return to power.

Alliances and Regional Groups

In the early postwar years, France tried to act as a bridge between the Soviet Union, the United States, and Britain. Assured a place in the occupation of Austria and Germany, the French opposed any policy that promised to bring a united Germany into being. French policy favored the internationalization of the Ruhr and the establishment of a weak federal Germany. With perseverance, the French brought about the separation of the Saar basin from the rest of the French occupation zone. This territory was established as an autonomous state (1947) in economic union with France.

As differences between Russia and the West increased, France began to cooperate more closely with Great Britain and the United States. On March 4, 1947, France signed an alliance with Britain at Dunkirk. In 1948 at Brussels this was expanded into a fifty-year alliance with Britain, the Netherlands, Belgium, and Luxembourg, known as the Western Union. A year later France joined in the formation of NATO. France became a member of the Council of Europe, and Monnet and Schuman, the longtime French foreign minister, were largely responsible for establishing the European Coal and Steel Community (see Chapter 3) in 1952. In 1954 France joined seven other Eastern and Western nations to establish a collective security system for Southeast Asia, the Southeast Asia Treaty Organization (SEATO).

France moved cautiously in everything affecting Germany. Having held out for months, France in 1948–1949 consented to merge its occupation zone of Germany with the U.S. and British zones (Bizonia). After the outbreak of the Korean War, the United States advocated rearming Germany in order to strengthen the defenses of Western Europe. To counter the possibility of a reconstituted German national army, France made proposals (the Pleven Plan) for a "European army." These eventually were transmuted into a plan for a European Defense Community.

The proposed EDC aroused widespread criticism in France and failed in the French National Assembly in 1954. Great Britain then took the initiative, developing new arrangements. Agreement was reached on the restoration of German sovereignty, the rearming of Germany, the Saar, and Germany's membership in the Western European Union and in NATO. Ironically, the opposition to EDC by those in France critical of German rearmament, even as part of an international force, led to approval of a German army.

The way was now cleared for furthering the collaboration begun in the European Coal and Steel Community. Domestic recovery, including economic reforms and improved industrial efficiency, helped to dispel fears that France could not compete on international markets. In 1957 France joined with West Germany, Italy, Belgium, the Netherlands, and Luxembourg in establishing the European Economic Community (Common Market) and the European Atomic Energy Community.

In conjunction with their effort to quell movements for independence in their North African holdings, the French adopted an anti-Arab policy. The nationalization of the Suez Canal Company brought close collaboration with Britain and Israel against Egypt. The armed attack on Egypt in October 1956 was one of the most popular military expeditions that France had undertaken in recent years. It was seen as a necessary move to halt Egyptian support for Algerian rebels. The sharp opposition expressed by the United States on this occasion as well as the generally critical attitude of the United States toward French policy in Indochina and North Africa aroused considerable anti-American sentiment in France. But in spite of all differences of opinion, France remained bound to the United States and Britain. Soviet support of the Arabs and Communist aid to anticolonial agitators in French overseas possessions were factors enough to warrant a pro-Western policy and French membership in NATO.

Political Developments

A new electoral law passed in 1951 permitted parties to form coalition lists and modified the prevailing system of proportional representation. The law was devised to cut Communist influence in the National Assembly, and the general elections held in June showed its effect. Although the Communists polled about the same popular vote as before (25.88 percent), they were reduced from 187 to 103 seats. The MRP lost heavily because of the shift of both leaders and membership to de Gaulle's party. Yet de Gaulle did not assume important leadership in the Assembly and, after disastrous losses in the municipal elections of 1953, took his party out of direct participation in party politics. His followers soon split into factions and formed new political groups.

From the time the new constitution came into force (1947) to May 1958, France had nineteen cabinets. Government was steadier than this rapid turnover suggests, thanks to civil servants within the continuing bureaucracy who in accord with French tradition maintained day-to-day activities and stability of performance in most areas. In the series of changing premierships, that of the Radical Socialist Pierre Mendès-France (June 1954 to February 1955) was the most important. He adopted a vigorous foreign policy, bringing the long Indochinese conflict to a close, inaugurating needed reforms in Tunisia, and participating in the agreements that restored sovereignty to West Germany. Mendès-France also introduced important domestic reforms. He tackled the problem of excessive wine and alcohol production and received much publicity as the milk-drinking Frenchman. Yet his notable achievements and efforts to modernize France's international status and domestic economy did not spare him the usual fate of French premiers. A strange coalition of Communist, MRP, and rightist deputies achieved his downfall in a debate on North African policy.

In part Mendès-France was a victim of a system that led critics to refer to the French Parliament as "the house without windows." Deputies seemed too busy arranging complicated political games and playing musical chairs to look outward to the needs of the nation. Anyone who attempted too assertive a program or accepted or assigned responsibility was thought to be violating the rules of the system. To be sure, some dynamic leaders were able to achieve significant change, as was Schuman; but these cases were infrequent. Moreover, the system was all the more difficult to control because of the intractableness of the issues, the fractiousness of the many small parties existing under the proportional electoral scheme, the strength of committee chairs in the National Assembly, and the highly developed skills of interpellation that made politics a series of chess moves and could provoke sudden crises.

The North African problem plagued successive cabinets. A proposed change in the electoral law brought even more serious disputes that resulted in the dissolution of the Assembly before the expiration of its mandate, a rare occurrence in French politics. In elections held in 1956, the Communists emerged as the largest party. A rightist group of small shopkeepers led by Pierre Poujade also won considerable support, especially in small towns and the south of France. The Poujadists, by their votes and advocacy of strikes,

In the French colony of Algeria, a
colonist is arrested while protesting
a French government reform program for North Africa in 1956.
Many French settlers in the region
bitterly opposed legislation that
would diminish their privileged position in Algeria and transfer more
political and economic control to
Arab and Muslim leaders. Other
former imperial powers, such as
Britain and Belgium, also faced
enormous challenges in carrying
out the process of decolonization.
(Photo from UPI/Bettmann.)

rebelled against government taxes, regulations, and interference in their
economic lives; they zealously protected the remains of empire, especially of
Algeria. Threatened by modernization and the effects of rationalization in
large industries, the Poujadists were angry over a perceived loss of status as
prestige and influence in France shifted to the large, technologically modern
industrialists. The rapidity of the rise of the Poujadists would be matched by
their subsequent fall from popularity as modernization continued, for their
reactionary views were out of touch with what was at the time perceived to
be the needs of the developing society.

In view of these gains by the extremist parties, the Socialists—the second
largest group—agreed to participate in a Republican Front government. Since
1951 they had refused to join the cabinet because of differences with center
parties over government aid to private, mostly Roman Catholic schools. On
this point they retained their freedom of action, but the expected legislation
on this issue was not introduced because of more urgent problems. The
Socialist leadership became deeply involved in trying to suppress the Algerian
revolt. It advocated free elections in Algeria but insisted on restoration of
peace and order as a prerequisite for these elections. In spite of ever larger
commitments of French troops, no end could be brought to the Algerian
rebellion. On May 13, 1958, while France was emerging from one of its ever
recurring cabinet crises, French army leaders seized power in Algeria. They
demanded that General de Gaulle be named premier. Instead, Pierre Pflimlin

became head of the government and was granted extraordinary powers by the chambers. The army revolt spread to Corsica, and elements within the French navy joined the dissident generals. Unable to carry out an effective policy, Pflimlin and French president René Coty undertook negotiations with de Gaulle, who took over the government on June 1, 1958, on his own conditions.

De Gaulle had long been demanding that the constitution be changed to give the executive more power. In the existing crisis the National Assembly granted de Gaulle full powers for six months to act by decree in domestic and international affairs; he also won authority to bring constitutional reforms directly before the people for a referendum without first submitting them to the Parliament for approval.

The general made an immediate visit to Algeria and obtained the cooperation of army leaders there. His statement to them, "Je vous ai compris" (best translated as "I have understood you"), was a masterpiece of ambiguity. De Gaulle's policy of federalism and of granting Muslims equal status did not meet with full approval from the European French element, but he seemed to offer better prospects for a "correct settlement" than any other French politician.

Establishment of the Fifth Republic

On assuming power in 1958, de Gaulle set himself two main tasks. One was to offer France a new form of government; the other was to end the war in Algeria. Constitutional reform got under way at once with the appointment of juridical experts who assisted in drawing up the new constitution that the general presented to the nation in an elaborate ceremony in September.

The constitution as proposed did not outline in detail the government of the French republic. Much was left to be regulated by future organic laws. The constitution simply stated, for example, that Parliament was to consist of a directly elected National Assembly and an indirectly elected Senate. The size, method of election, and distribution of seats was left to future determination. Even the exact scope of the Parliament's powers was not stated, but it was clearly not to have as much power as under the Third or Fourth Republic. Under the constitution, the government (cabinet) could ask for power for a limited period of time to implement its program by ordinance, such ordinances becoming invalid if a bill for ratification was not submitted to Parliament before the date for the expiration of the special powers. After the expiration of this period, Parliament possessed the power to modify these ordinances only in those matters lying within its legislative domain. The legislature thus had opportunity to accept or reject the ordinances, but delaying tactics could easily avoid a showdown. The National Assembly (not the Senate) could force the resignation of the premier by a majority vote of its total membership. Motions of censure did have to wait forty-eight hours before they could be voted upon. Thus the effect of surprise tactics or emotional surges could be tempered.

The constitution vested dominant power in a president to be elected for a term of seven years, at first by an electoral college comprising the members of Parliament and representatives of departments, overseas territories, and communal councils. In 1962 a constitutional amendment provided for the direct election of the president, a change the National Assembly opposed but the electorate accepted in a referendum. The significant provisions in the constitution for such referenda, which could approve legislation without parliamentary review, reflected de Gaulle's distrust of political party quibbling and his preference for passing over the politicians and going to the public at large.

The president had the usual executive functions, was granted wide appointive powers, and was specifically given the duty of naming the premier. He could request a rereading by Parliament of any law or parts thereof that were submitted to him for signature and promulgation. After consulting the premier and the presidents of the assemblies, the president could dissolve Parliament. Article 16 gave him the right in case of emergency to assume dictatorial powers by his own decision, but he was required to consult the Constitutional Council on the measures he undertook. During the period when he exercised exceptional powers, the National Assembly was not to be dissolved.

The Constitutional Council was made up of nine members, three appointed by the president of the republic, three by the president of the Assembly, and three by the president of the Senate. The council was to supervise the election of the president and carry out all referendums. Before promulgation, organic (that is, constitutional) laws must, and ordinary laws may, be submitted to the Constitutional Council; it was to decide whether or not they were in conformity with the constitution. A law once promulgated could not be declared unconstitutional by the process of judicial review as practiced in the United States.

In respect to overseas territories, with the notable exception of Algeria, the constitution established a new French Community in place of the highly centralized French Union of the Fourth Republic. In internal affairs all member states of the community were to enjoy autonomy and possess the right to secede. In establishing the community, France was clearly preparing for a major change in colonial policy. Centralized control was to give way to close cooperation among freely associated states. Metropolitan France overwhelmingly approved the constitution in a September 1958 referendum, perhaps more out of fear of civil disorder if de Gaulle should resign than out of support for its provisions.

In a whirlwind tour of the African territories at the end of August, de Gaulle offered all the overseas territories, except Algeria, the alternative of voting for the constitution and becoming a member of the French Community or voting no and securing independence. In the latter case France would end all economic aid, and the territories would lose their privileged position in the French tariff system. The new constitution was approved in all the territories with the exception of Guinea. Although Algeria had not been offered such a choice, the French settlers feared that a negative vote would lead to a separation from France. Consequently, although the constitution did not meet their demands fully, the referendum also showed a favorable majority there.

Thus on October 4, 1958, after twelve years of precarious existence, the Fourth Republic came to an end, and the new constitution came into effect with the establishment of the Fifth Republic. De Gaulle immediately set about implementing the main provisions of the constitution. A new electoral law changed from the system of proportional representation to one of 465 single-member electoral districts. This major reform was expected to reduce the fragmentation of the National Assembly among inflexible political parties and to benefit candidates of whatever label who supported de Gaulle. It also worked against the Communists; their representation fell from 144 seats to 10 in the next elections. On December 21 de Gaulle was elected the first president of the Fifth Republic.

Domestic and Foreign Affairs

Transformation of Overseas France

Settlements had been reached in Indochina, Morocco, and Tunisia before the end of the Fourth Republic, but it was left to de Gaulle to work out new arrangements in Algeria, Sub-Saharan Africa, and various scattered French territories.

The general had been raised to power largely because of the failures of the previous governments in Algeria. By a series of promotions and new appointments to high army commands he was able to break the power of the All-Algerian Committee of Public Safety and bring the government there under the control of Paris authorities. Yet additional troops could not defeat the Algerian guerrillas, and terrorism spread to metropolitan France. In mid-1960 de Gaulle vaguely indicated that he would be willing to enter into discussions with Algerian leaders under certain conditions. The possibility of a negotiated agreement led some prominent French citizens in Algeria to form the Front for French Algeria. They were determined to halt de Gaulle's plans, which they maintained could only separate Algeria from France. Divisions also increased in France. De Gaulle assumed emergency powers, carrying on by decree legislation.

In a plebiscite held in January 1961, de Gaulle won the support of the people of France and Algeria for his Algerian policy, ill defined as it was. The outlook for negotiations seemed improved. The prospect of a compromise settlement led four army generals in Algeria to attempt a coup d'état with the support of other dissident officers, about 20,000 Foreign Legion troops, and 25,000 paratroopers. In the name of the Secret Armed Organization (OAS), they took control of Algiers and some other cities on April 21, 1961. In a forceful speech de Gaulle called on the people to save France from the "partisan, ambitious, and fanatical" officers who threatened a national disaster. He gained widespread support. Reservists were called up in Paris and security forces brought into the city. The army, air force, and navy remained firm, and on the night of April 25–26 loyal forces entered Algiers. The danger of the coup was ended, but the OAS continued to cause serious difficulties.

Talks were begun between the French government and Algerian leaders but soon deadlocked. Shootings, bombings, assassinations, and burnings by the OAS raged on in Algerian and French towns. Finally, on March 18, 1962, a cease-fire was signed at Evian-les-Bains. After eight years of the worst colonial warfare in modern times, and, for the first time since September 1939, France was at peace.

The Evian accords provided for a referendum on independence for Algeria. Meanwhile Algeria was to be governed by a French high commissioner and a twelve-person provisional executive. France promised to continue its financial support after the referendum and to negotiate a continuation of the special preferential tariff, marketing, and other commercial arrangements that were of direct benefit to Algeria. The Saharan oil fields were to be developed and exploited to the mutual benefit of France and Algeria, a provision that led subsequently to some differences. French citizens in an independent Algeria received guarantees, and inhabitants were to choose within three years if they wanted to become Algerians or remain French. France was gradually to reduce its troops but was promised a fifteen-year lease of the Mers-el-Kebir naval base. France actually withdrew from this base in 1978, nine years before the date specified.

The terms were a victory for the Algerian nationalists. The OAS used terrorism to express its bitter hostility to the agreement. The people of both France and Algeria accepted the Evian accords by large margins, yet the outflow of Europeans from Algeria accelerated, as many did not wish to live under Arab rule. It is estimated that in 1962–1963, 900,000 out of the 1 million Europeans living in Algeria fled to France. Housing in France for this influx was inadequate, and in some of the larger cities grave economic and social problems arose. The returnees, termed *pieds noirs* (black feet) by some metropolitan French, also added a dissident element to the political scene, but de Gaulle retained his mass support.

In Sub-Saharan Africa de Gaulle also made concessions to the rising wave of anticolonialism. Most former colonies initially opted for membership in the proposed French Community with all the privileges and aid that entailed. Yet in the early 1960s several African states chose independence. Though the French Community reorganized, it soon lost what little significance it once had, only technically remaining in existence.

None of the former colonies cut themselves off completely from France, and most kept their currencies linked with the French franc. Through bilateral arrangements and grants of aid, France salvaged a leading position in most of the states. It obtained the right to intervene in certain circumstances and to station troops at various bases. These developed into highly trained mobile units that at times have come to the rescue of existing governments, as for example in Chad in 1970 and again in the 1980s.

The Experience of Decolonization

The transformation of France's relations with its former colonies was a remarkable achievement, especially because of the impact the issue of decolonization had upon the politics of metropolitan France. In comparison with the British case, events on the periphery of the empire seemed to affect the process of politics in the metropole more than metropolitan politics affected the course of political events in the colonies.

There were various reasons for this circumstance. One was that the decolonization debate involved not just the position of any particular political party but the republican regime itself. Historically, the empire had not been created by a party of the Right but rather by a coalition of politicians of the Center. Its maintenance and support had generally been advocated by interest groups that found voice across the entire political spectrum, except for the Communist Left. Defeat at the hands of Germany and the effort to maintain the concept of the republic in the empire while Paris was occupied bolstered the link between empire and regime. The matter of relinquishing colonial control thus involved greater emotional overtones than might otherwise have been the case. This was especially true of the early Gaullist involvement. It was also true for the Socialist party (French Section of the Workers' International, or SFIO) by the late 1950s. Demonstrations by Algerian settlers, mutterings by army officers, and insubordination by French civil administrators in Algeria convinced many that the republican regime was endangered; it, above all, had to be supported even if the price were colonial war. An extremist such as Poujade also gained considerable following, especially in North Africa, the south of France, and regions of economic decline where the common people felt their status threatened and clung to the prestige of empire.

Another factor was the presence of a variety of political options for those who disagreed with the positions taken by party leaders. Defections either to other parties or to newly formed parties occurred regularly. De Gaulle himself had profited from this tendency in French politics. Guy Mollet, a leader of

the SFIO, found himself taking a nationalist stance unsupportive of decolonization, thus distinguishing his position from the Communists' and guarding
against defection of his supporters in that direction. The predilection for
fragmentation deprived leaders of the ability to make compromises or to
retain party discipline.

The capacity of the metropolitan Assembly to control events was also
affected by the extensive voice exercised by colonial representatives, especially
those of Algeria, who by virtue of Algeria's status actually held seats in the
Assembly. This voice was not that of indigenous nationalists but of the French
settlers (colons), who strongly favored maintenance of the empire in which
they held a special place. On the whole, the economic development of France's
North African colonies had not brought extensive local industrial development. Most industries that did exist did not pose a challenge to metropolitan
industries, a condition that would have diminished homeland corporations'
support for imperial connections and preferences. Rather, the colonies remained an inexpensive source of raw materials and labor as well as a profitable
market for manufactured goods. Many colons were small farmers; an even
higher proportion were members of the colonial civil service. The latter
would lose both job and status in the process of decolonization. They had
worked long and loyally in collaboration with the French military stationed
in the colonies. Both fonctionnaires (civil servants) and military developed
loyalty to local peoples who assisted them and opposed rebellious nationalist
elements. There were, then, interest groups strongly against decolonization
that did have a voice in metropolitan politics and over which, moreover,
neither the frequently changing occupants of political office nor even the
more permanent central civil service administrators had complete control.

The psychological link between defense of a republican regime and
defense of empire, the presence of political alternatives that weakened the
hand of the governing political elite, the interpenetration of political parties
and the civil and military services by pro-colon sentiments—all were influential in making decolonization difficult for France. Yet slowly the controversy
moved toward resolution. Human and economic losses in colonial wars stirred
feelings of patriotism and renewed determination, but they also led to the
sense that the game might not be worth the expense. As France moved into
a more prosperous period of economic expansion in the late 1950s, the old
colonial ties seemed increasingly outdated, of marginal utility, and even
contrary to the developing global dimensions of world economics and politics.
A newer conception of French nationalism emerged slowly. It was based on
the economic resurgence of the metropolitan regime linked with the global
economy rather than tied to a somewhat backward empire where, especially
in Algeria, the emphasis seemed to be on maintenance of the status quo.
First, Mendès-France led the move to a realistic assessment of the situation
in Indochina and the withdrawal from that conflict; then de Gaulle mediated
Algerian independence.

It is ironic that de Gaulle did this, for he was brought to power by some who thought he would resolve the issue in favor of continued empire. Gaullism immediately after the war was highly nationalist and pro-empire. In his years away from power, however, de Gaulle revised his views on Algeria, though few persons heeded his veiled comments. In training and career, de Gaulle was a metropolitanist and technologist. He had served in the colonies only briefly, and his first concern was the welfare of continental France. The general also knew that the colonial wars were creating a net loss in French power. He apparently viewed the army's preoccupation with these wars as slowing any reorientation of French military power in terms of atomic weapons and weakening France's influence in the European context. A strong nationalist himself, he had to substitute a new sense of pride in the glory of France for the still lingering but outmoded pride in empire. That he succeeded in doing so is a tribute to his skill in inspiring a movement that was loyal more to him than to any ideological posture. It is significant that in the first months of his march to decolonization, de Gaulle's strongest financial supporters were from the most dynamic sectors of banking and industry, in the latter case manufacturers of aircraft and chemicals, the flagship industries of the new economies of the major powers.[5]

The decolonization process played a crucial role in the political and economic modernization of France. It culminated in the creation of the Fifth Republic, the independence of Algeria and other African states, and the cessation of the decolonization issue's paralyzing role in the Assembly. It also substituted a focus on the role of France in Europe and world politics for France's obsession with colonial prestige and power. De Gaulle's traditional nationalism clearly aided him in mediating the change from the "old" France to a the newer France. However, he was not able to move rapidly, and by the end of his years of service the very sectors of the society and the economy that had most significantly supported him and to which he gave important encouragement would be pressing for an accelerated pace of change.

Domestic Policy

As the Fifth Republic came into being, affairs within France were dominated by de Gaulle. Parliament faded in significance as the president assumed emergency powers during the Algerian crisis. In 1962 the Assembly did attempt to assert itself when de Gaulle planned to bypass it by submitting directly to the people a constitutional amendment providing for popular election of the president. After a fifteen-hour debate, the Assembly overthrew the government. De Gaulle promptly dissolved the chamber and won a landslide victory both in the referendum on the constitutional change and in the ensuing parliamentary elections. His party, the Union for the New Republic and Democratic Union of Labor, dominated the returns. The Democratic Center (Popular Republicans, Independents, and others) fared poorly, and the Socialists scarcely better. These last were sharply divided over the Algerian War and by debates over organization and ideology. No Communist-Socialist left front materialized immediately, nor did the Socialists and the Center find sufficient grounds for coalition.

In the second half of the 1960s, some organized opposition to de Gaulle's political supremacy emerged. In 1964 the Communists were hard hit by the death of their longtime leader, Maurice Thorez, and became more susceptible to the notion of working with other leaders of the Left. The following year veteran leftist François Mitterrand challenged de Gaulle in the first direct election of a president. Mitterrand won enough support from both Socialist and Communist parties to force de Gaulle to a second-round runoff ballot. The Assembly elections of 1967 showed that the opposition forces were back in stride when the Gaullists obtained a bare majority. Local elections also indicated growing political opposition.

At the time de Gaulle came to power, the French economy had slowed in comparison with the boom years of 1953–1957. He was confronted with an inflationary situation, a treasury and foreign trade deficit. The war in Algeria was a steady drain on finances. Yet slowly the situation was improved. The franc was devalued and then, in 1960, a new heavy franc at 100 old francs to 1 was introduced. In 1959, for the first time in years, the foreign trade balance was reversed and exports exceeded imports. In part this was the result of free trade with the countries of the Common Market. Gold and foreign exchange reserves steadily increased, very much at the expense of the U.S. gold supply.

France continued to model its economy according to successive modernization and equipment plans. These grew in size and detail, as officials prepared to control a wide range of activities and possibilities. In the early 1960s the plan was extended to include responsibility for the social infrastructure. Projections for more schools, houses, indoor plumbing, and telephones were drafted as research showed that although previous plans had stimulated the economy, the population was reaping little benefit from the industrial growth. Toward the end of the decade, the Fifth Plan encouraged bigness, as de Gaulle sought "national champion" industries that would win victories for France on international markets. Emphasis was put on international competitiveness, on selected firms, and on consolidation of family firms rather than on general growth in all sectors of the economy.

The industrial expansion of France was not as dynamic as that of Germany or Italy, yet France made steady progress. Although industry accounted for about 50 percent of the gross national product, agriculture, in which about 25 percent of the active population was engaged, remained the backbone of the economy. Farmers were hard hit by de Gaulle's efforts to prevent inflation by holding prices level. They blockaded roads and markets with trucks and tractors; surplus products that could not be sold profitably were dumped in government buildings and on streets. Tumultuous demonstrations brought clashes with troops in 1961. The government was forced to take cognizance of the farmers' plight and fell back on an extensive farm goods price support program. It also furnished funds for research and for the modernization and consolidation of farms. It granted tax relief and extended some social benefits to farmers. With most products distributed via Paris, however, little headway was made toward improving the antiquated marketing system. Estimates indicated that the cost of a peach increased by 1,150 percent between the grower and the consumer. A general labor shortage led to the influx of foreign workers, who for the most part filled the more arduous and unpopular jobs. As these workers were not citizens and had no vote, political parties took little interest in them and focused upon the better-paid workers who participated in the franchise; thus even parties of the Left came to have a more bourgeois character.

By a decree issued in January 1959, the whole system of public education was reorganized. It remained nevertheless strongly centralized, with decision-making in Paris, whether on matters of examination questions, curricula, teacher assignments, or student-sponsored social events. Given the other financial pressures on the government, funding could only incompletely address issues of low salaries, crowded classrooms, and insufficient scholarships for secondary and higher education. In 1961, 80,000 teachers in Paris and neighboring departments struck for a 5 percent salary increase. University students in Paris repeatedly demonstrated against the lack of classroom and laboratory space. These demonstrations were particularly turbulent in the spring of 1968 (see the section below on Growing Domestic Unrest).

Foreign Affairs

As in domestic matters, de Gaulle strove to refurbish the glory of France in foreign affairs. France had to be a great power, strong and independent, its sovereignty unblemished. Pacts and alliances had to be a union, not a merger of independent states; Europe had to become not one state but a *Europe des patries* (Europe of national fatherlands). Decisionmaking had to be the result of negotiation; it could not be vested in a body where France could be outvoted or would not have a decisive voice. These basic attitudes governed French policy regarding the Common Market, NATO, the United Nations, and the development of atomic power.

At the time de Gaulle took over, the European Economic Community was well established and on its way toward bringing about greater unity in Western Europe. The market promised to be so advantageous to French farmers and industrialists that de Gaulle had no choice but to continue to cooperate in the organization. But he proved to be a hard bargainer and slowed the progress of integration. He consistently opposed the extension of power of the EEC's Central Commission, with its ever enlarging group of "European civil servants."

When Great Britain applied for entry into the Common Market, de Gaulle and diplomats from other countries questioned the extent of the special conditions the British were requesting to ease their move. But it was the general who in January 1963 bluntly vetoed the admission of Great Britain into the organization. Behind the veto was opposition to the enlargement of the EEC, for British membership would surely have soon brought in several other members of the European Free Trade Association and Ireland as well. Such an expanded organization would inevitably make it harder for France to play a dominant role in its affairs.

Agricultural policy was always a crucial consideration in the Common Market negotiations and led to a crisis in the closing months of 1964. It was resolved only when the other EEC members agreed to the French position. But the agricultural differences were far from settled, and in 1965 France withdrew its members from some of the important EEC committees and also its permanent representative to the European Commission. The dispute ostensibly involved farm subsidy programs and financial arrangements for the joint agricultural market; back of it lay the increased authority these measures would give to the Common Market Commission and the further political integration of Europe that would result. Because all major EEC decisions at that time required the unanimous approval of the members, the French boycott stymied the organization for some while.

Within the Common Market, France attempted to consolidate its position, most notably by an effort to establish close relations with West Germany. Chancellor Adenauer was a firm believer in French–West German ties and was glad to sign a treaty of cooperation with France in 1963 (the Elysée treaty). It provided for regular meetings of the chiefs and foreign ministers of the two countries in order to coordinate their policies within the EEC and in international affairs in general. De Gaulle saw the agreement as a means of strengthening his position against what he considered the growing domination of Europe by Britain and the United States.

De Gaulle maintained a hostile attitude toward NATO, for he considered it too much under U.S. direction and a restriction on French sovereignty. To show his displeasure, he withdrew the French fleet from NATO command in July 1963, and this policy was extended in various degrees to other services and even to the Command Headquarters itself. By late 1964 only two reduced French divisions in Germany and three air wings remained under NATO's Supreme Headquarters. France exploded its first atomic bomb in 1960, and de Gaulle insisted on developing France's own atomic striking force. France did not sign the 1968 treaty on the nonproliferation of nuclear weapons. De Gaulle refused to have any part in developing a NATO multilateral nuclear fleet and never hid his desire to have a general revision of the NATO agreements. On July 1, 1966, he terminated French participation in the NATO command organization and forced the removal of all foreign as well as NATO military installations from French territory by April 1, 1967. He stopped payment of France's 12 percent share of the military expense in 1967. Yet in spite of his uncooperative attitude, he did not withdraw entirely from NATO, and the other members of the alliance chose to put a good face on a bad situation. Without withdrawing completely, he discontinued active participation in the Southeast Asia Treaty Organization and denied any obligation under that treaty with respect to Vietnam as the United States became deeply involved in war in that country.

De Gaulle's attitude toward the United Nations was similar. Such organizations restricted the independence of France, and he considered them ineffective. He opposed the UN Assembly's attempt to bring about a settlement of the Algerian problem. In the Congo crisis he also departed from UN policy and like the Soviet Union refused to pay the assessment for the Congo peacekeeping force. He also refused to contribute to the UN force in Cyprus; instead, he offered his services as mediator. Yet France continued to participate in the many UN agencies, made substantial contributions to some of the voluntary funds, and usually voted with the Western powers on crucial issues.

De Gaulle was far from breaking his ties with either the United States or Britain, but he refused to do anything that might be considered hanging onto their coattails. He cultivated better relations with the USSR and with the states of Eastern Europe and recognized Communist China. He condemned the policy of the United States in Vietnam and called for the neutralization of all Southeast Asia. He made spectacular tours of many countries, including those in Central and Latin America, in an effort improve the image of France and to better trade relations. On a visit to Canada to attend the International Exposition at Montreal in 1967, he overstepped the bounds of courtesy when he encouraged French separatists in Quebec by ending his speech with their slogan, "Vive le Québec libre" ("Long live free Quebec"). Everywhere and at all times he sought, not without some success, to further his own ideas of France's national honor and special glory.

Though diplomats in London, Washington, and elsewhere might complain that de Gaulle was a difficult partner with whom to work, they gave credit to the manner in which he extricated France from the Algerian problem and obtained influence in the Third World. With some foresight, de Gaulle recognized the value of holding a position that enabled him to achieve meaningful dialogue with both sides of the superpower confrontation. By maintaining credibility with the East, West, and Third World nations, he helped to pave the way toward détente well before the term became popular in the media. Nor did his reduction of commitments to NATO mean abandonment of Western concerns. He lent prompt and unequivocal support to U.S. president Kennedy in the Cuban missile crisis of 1962 and facilitated U.S. negotiations with North Vietnam. His criticism of U.S. strategy and tactics in that war was not well received in Washington. But de Gaulle had the courage to say directly what others in Europe were thinking, and this won him their respect.

Although de Gaulle provided France with a strong personal rule, it was designed to preserve, not eliminate, the democratic process. The chambers continued to meet, political parties as well as labor unions remained active, and the French people could still grumble and voice their feelings. Above all they were free to strike, and each year there were actions by all kinds of workers, including civil servants. The government reluctantly acceded to at least part of their demands. Wages increased but did not keep up with the escalation of prices. Housing remained inadequate, and modernization of both household and factory proceeded slowly. On the whole the economy strengthened, and France became one of the most prosperous and high-priced countries of the world. But there were weak spots, and the business boom declined in 1967. This formed part of the background for the serious disturbances that paralyzed France in spring 1968.

Growing Domestic Unrest

The trouble began with student riots at the Nanterre campus of the University of Paris in March and spread to the Sorbonne. Students occupied buildings and challenged government troops with street barricades. Clashes occurred, cars were overturned, and tear gas filled the air. In May the student revolt was joined by a rash of illegal trade union strikes. Although there were some extremists, in general the students wanted only long-overdue reforms and reasonable facilities for education and employment. Their boldness reflected the experience of their own generation. That experience was not one of depression, war, and of a general who had kept the faith and maintained France's honor. Rather, it was one of expecting the opportunities and the material benefits that were arriving in West Germany and elsewhere. Though promised, these had not appeared rapidly enough in a France seemingly dominated by a cautious older generation that had lost its vitality but retained rigid control. Such a case is overdrawn, but in reality overcrowded classrooms and laboratories were a long-tolerated disgrace.

The most salient—and extreme—student leader was Daniel Cohn-Bendit, "Danny the Red." He attacked French capitalism as strong, stultifying, and unjust. The universities he denounced as "factories of privilege":

> The present educational structure ensures that the majority of working-class children are barred not only from the bourgeois society we are trying to overthrow, but also from the intellectual means of seeing through it. . . .
>
> Our struggle was not one against Fascism as such but against bourgeois authoritarianism. The mediocrity of university teaching is no accident, but reflects the life style of a civilization in which culture itself has become a

The fiery eloquence of French student leader "Danny the Red" stirred his followers during the rioting in Paris in May 1968. Students took to barricades to protest conditions in the universities. For a short time, an atmosphere of civil war prevailed, and Paris almost ground to a halt. In the countryside and most other French towns, however, the students aroused little popular support. Although the psychological trauma to France was significant, the students' demonstrations failed to mark the turning point in French history that some observers at the time predicted. (Photos from UPI/Bettmann Newsphotos.)

marketable commodity and in which the absence of all critical faculties is the safest guarantee of profitable specialization of university studies.[6]

The workers for their part were demanding a forty-hour work week, first promised by the Popular Front in 1936; a guaranteed wage of about $200 a month; and retirement at the age of sixty. For some weeks the government seemed inclined to permit the demonstrations to continue. Differences between the workers and the students appeared. The general population, appalled by the disruption of services and the destruction that was taking place, demanded an end to *les manifestations*.

De Gaulle waited. Finally, on May 30, having flown to Germany and secured the support of French army generals in a secret meeting, he addressed the nation. He squashed rumors that he would resign and promised to see matters through. The president dissolved Parliament and issued a decree granting a 35 percent increase in minimum wages, which did much to appease the workers; he also promised educational reforms. Widespread demonstrations supported the head of state, especially in the provinces, where the choice was seen as one between communism and Gaullism. In the June Assembly elections, the Gaullists took 358 of the 487 seats.

De Gaulle appeared in full control, but some within his administration suspected that the general did not fully grasp the seriousness of the crisis or the real nature of the problem. There was need to find both a greater will for modernization and change and the right tools to achieve such change. As Jean-Jacques Servan-Schreiber, a cogent observer of contemporary France and a successful entrepreneur, wrote at the time:

> The Gaullist party is incapable of leading the way ahead. It is too identified with authoritarianism and has never really believed that the French are able to think for themselves. . . . Its official opponent, the ossified French Left, is so firmly rooted in the old system that it is not capable of governing with any credibility. . . . Two urgent tasks confront us: saving France from the disaster of underdevelopment and advancing a true democracy.[7]

Some damage control was achieved, as steps were taken to assuage those who resented de Gaulle's quick and originally secret turn to the army for support. Pompidou, prime minister before the president abruptly retired him following the elections, arranged educational reforms that were quietly approved in October. Though they did not meet all student demands, the reforms broke the stranglehold of government bureaucracy and granted some campus autonomy. Needed expansion of facilities remained to be carried out, but prospects of this change were reduced by financial difficulties. Efforts to increase wages and hold price levels cut profit margins and reduced investments. Austerity measures were introduced, foreign loans acquired, and a highly unpopular sales tax instituted.

Resignation of de Gaulle

In retrospect, it appears that deep-lying concerns were beginning to erode the strength of de Gaulle's position, but this certainly did not seem the case in the wake of the post-riot elections. He had received a strong endorsement, and he determined to make full use of it. For some time de Gaulle had contemplated changing the makeup and role of the Senate, for it no longer served as a check on the Assembly, that role having passed to the president. He now wished to merge the Senate with the Economic and Social Council and allow it only advisory functions. At the same time more power was to be granted to regional councils throughout the country, a decentralization move intended to stimulate more regional economic initiatives. De Gaulle chose to refer the matter directly to the people rather than to submit it first to the Assembly. Such had been the procedure de Gaulle followed when direct election of the president was instituted. Many held it to be incorrect. De Gaulle also had to overcome the long tradition of the Senate in France and the opposition of most existing senators. Choosing to consider the referendum as a vote of confidence, de Gaulle stated he would resign if the people did not approve what he considered an essential political reform. In the election held on April 27, 1969, 46.7 percent supported him whereas 53.2 percent voted against his proposals. True to his word, de Gaulle resigned as president the next day.

Gaullists, Socialists, and the Contest Between Ideology and Pragmatism

Politics After de Gaulle

According to the constitution, Alain Poher, president of the Senate, became interim president. He was challenged in the June 1969 election by Pompidou. The latter had served as de Gaulle's prime minister from 1962 to 1968. A former schoolteacher, he had worked with the general after the liberation of France and also served as a director of the Rothschild bank. At first considered merely a loyal lieutenant of the leader, in time Pompidou was recognized in his own right for his calmness and managerial capabilities. Many French citizens attributed the successful weathering of the storm in 1968 to Pompidou rather than to de Gaulle. In any case, Pompidou was ready to take over power on his own. He won the election handily, de Gaulle vacationing abroad and playing no role in the campaign. (He died November 9, 1970, just short of eighty years of age.)

The transition of power went smoothly. Pompidou announced no radical changes, and the new cabinet could still rely on the Gaullist-controlled chamber. The austerity measures de Gaulle introduced had not solved the currency problem; it became necessary to devalue the franc by 12 percent. This act led to immediate devaluation in fourteen African countries where the currency was pegged to the French franc. It also had severe repercussions in other former French territories such as Algeria, Tunisia, and Morocco, where the currency was less closely related. In France the government was forced to enact various price and wage control measures in an effort to prevent the beneficial effects of devaluation from being dissipated.

The new president achieved the image and the reality of dynamism without effecting radical change. In 1970 he launched a campaign to speed the industrialization of France, with the intent of doubling production in ten years. Profit sharing at Renault and other nationalized industries was approved, thus strengthening worker commitment. Steps were taken to ease the strong tradition of centralization that had made Paris so dominant—and almost unmanageably crowded—to the detriment of regional cities. Other centers expanded. Old road and rail linkages were modernized and special high-speed trains were created. Plans called for replacement of the old centrally controlled agricultural marketing system. The crowded, colorful, and obsolete Parisian food distribution center of Les Halles was transferred to new and far more efficient facilities on the outskirts of the capital, and a large shopping mall took its place. Construction of nuclear energy plants moved forward. The long neglected "rural desert" of southwest France received development funds, as did the previously neglected western portion of the Mediterranean coast.

Although there was no startling change in foreign policy, a greater degree of flexibility became evident. In December 1969, under pressure from other Common Market members and aware of the need for help in balancing the German influence within that market, the French agreed that negotiations should begin with the United Kingdom on the question of its joining that organization. France resumed its seat in the meetings of the Western Union that it had left vacant for fifteen months. Loyalty to NATO was affirmed, and relations with the United States improved.

Pompidou visited the Soviet Union to demonstrate that France saw itself as outside the blocs of either superpower. The strengthening of the French independent nuclear force continued. Pompidou subscribed to de Gaulle's belief in the value of a strike force that, if not powerful enough to obliterate an enemy, would be able to wound it sufficiently to deter it from taking aggressive action. Implied in this was the thought that, whatever the promises it made, the United States would not risk the destruction of its own country to protect European states from limited aggression.

An agreement to sell modern French fighting planes to Libya enhanced the position of France in the Arab world. France continued its arms embargo to Israel, refusing to recognize the right of that country to annex territories it had seized in the Six-Day War of 1967 (land on the West Bank of the

---

Presidents of the Fifth Republic

René Coty	October 5, 1958–January 8, 1959
(continues presidency from Fourth Republic)	
Charles de Gaulle	January 8, 1959–April 28, 1969
Alain Poher	April 28, 1969–June 20, 1969
(interim president)	
Georges Pompidou	June 20, 1969–April 2, 1974
Alain Poher	April 2, 1974–May 27, 1974
(interim president)	
Valéry Giscard d'Estaing	May 27, 1974–May 21, 1981
François Mitterrand	May 21, 1981–

Jordan River, the Gaza Strip, and the Golan Heights). France did support the right of Israel to exist as a state.

Shaken by the loss of Indochina and Algeria, the demonstrations of May 1968, previous economic difficulties, and the departure and death of de Gaulle, French confidence began to revive. Then Pompidou died suddenly, on April 2, 1974. In his career, able as he was at politics, he had lived up to his definition of a statesman rather than a politician: "A statesman is a politician who places himself at the service of the nation. A politician is a statesman who places the nation at his service."

The Gaullists were caught without a well-groomed and publicized candidate in the ensuing presidential elections, as they had assumed Pompidou would continue to lead their movement for some while. The pressures for change that Pompidou had sensed and tried to accommodate and control now worked against the Gaullists. Their candidate was defeated in the first round. The eventual victor was an Independent Republican, Valéry Giscard d'Estaing, considered a centrist and somewhat more liberal than the Gaullists.

By the middle of 1974, France was feeling the brunt of the oil shortage brought by the Arab oil boycott after the Arab-Israeli War of 1973. Construction of nuclear energy plants accelerated. Unemployment and inflation rose simultaneously. International economics had changed the environment for French economic planning; key factors seemed out of the control of even the best planners. Government officials had long taken credit for economic growth. They could not now escape blame for decline. The Seventh Plan, inaugurated in 1974, claimed a reduced role for the state and was more a presentation of budgetary priorities than an actual plan. Even as the plan took a diminished place in guiding the economy, it also appeared to become less of a purely technical effort and to have increased political overtones.

In other areas, quick steps were taken to improve the popularity of the government through major changes in the social security system. In September the Council of Ministers approved a plan designed to give social protection to all French workers by January of 1978. In October agreement was reached between representatives of labor and employers to the effect that a dismissed laborer would receive payments equal to a year's real wages. The voting age was lowered from twenty-one to eighteen years, thus catching up French standards in this matter with those established in many neighboring countries. Despite these breakthroughs, the political Left made substantial gains in by-elections, as French workers, no doubt aided by the new youth vote, demonstrated their concern over the economy. Giscard was aware that his chief opponent in the next presidential election, the leftist Mitterrand, had received 45.4 percent of the vote when running against de Gaulle. Giscard therefore disassociated himself somewhat from the right-leaning Gaullist faction and replaced the Gaullist prime minister, Jacques Chirac, with Raymond Barre, a professor of political economy not known for party connections.

Barre moved to curb inflation, steady the franc, control the money supply, improve the balance of payments in foreign trade, and make French industries more modern and efficient. A new tax program encouraged savings to flow into industrial investment. His administration installed wage and price controls and warned industrialists that, if wage increases over 2 percent were granted, their firms would experience difficulty in obtaining government contracts and loans or protection from foreign imports.

Previously, government policy had been to subsidize import-competing industries that, if developed, could replace foreign imports. It was a popular approach, for it protected jobs. Unfortunately, it was not particularly effective, as whatever structural factors made the French products uncompetitive (scarcity of proper raw materials, high cost of labor, poor quality) remained unchanged, thus forcing subsidies year after year. Now export-oriented industries were stimulated. This path had not been chosen earlier because of the difficulty of identifying which products would sell well at an expanded rate on the international market. It was unusual also in that few political lobbies existed for the yet-to-be-determined industries producing the marketable goods; still, both unions and industrialists had active lobbies calling for protection of the readily identifiable firms being undercut by imports. Though encouraging the export industries, the government hoped that limits on wage increases would hold down the demand for foreign goods, thus further improving the balance-of-payments picture. After the elections of 1978, price controls were eased so that industries could obtain greater profits that could in turn be reinvested for further growth. The government also took control of the ailing iron and steel industry and approved significant layoffs.

The campaign had some positive results. The franc stabilized as trade deficits were sharply reduced; it seemed that French industries were regaining

---

Prime Ministers of the Fifth Republic
(cabinet reformations not indicated)

Charles de Gaulle	October 5, 1958–January 8, 1959
Michel Debre	January 8, 1959–April 14, 1962
Georges Pompidou	April 14, 1962–July 11, 1968
Maurice Couvre de Murville	July 11, 1968–June 20, 1969
Jacques Chaban-Delmas	June 20, 1969–July 5, 1972
Pierre Messmer	July 5, 1972–May 27, 1974
Jacques Chirac	May 27, 1974–August 25, 1976
Raymond Barre	August 25, 1976–May 21, 1981
Pierre Mauroy	May 21, 1981–July 17, 1984
Laurent Fabius	July 17, 1984–March 20, 1986
Jacques Chirac	March 20, 1986–May 10, 1988
Michel Rocard	May 10, 1988–May 15, 1991
Edith Cresson	May 15, 1991–

---

control of the nation's domestic market. This progress had been achieved, however, as much by austerity measures and reduced consumption as by competitive dominance. The government's willingness to tolerate increased unemployment in the name of industrial efficiency and international competitiveness brought criticism. By 1978 the Gaullists were calling for the state to take an even more active role in the guiding of industrial investments. The Socialists condemned the austerity policy of low wages as crippling domestic consumption. Without stimulation from that sector, they argued, the industrialists would simply eat their profits rather than reinvest. So the disputes continued over how to reach a commonly accepted goal—the modernization and reemergence of French industry as a competitive force on domestic and world markets. A second oil supply crisis in 1979 provoked renewed inflation and slowed what industrial growth had previously been stimulated; unemployment and popular dissatisfaction continued. Devaluation of the franc had helped exports. But oil purchases were denominated in dollars. Thus the greater the devaluation of the franc, the greater the trade imbalance in dollars, given the large amount of oil France had to import. Challenged by this difficulty, in May 1979 France reluctantly entered the European Monetary System and pegged the franc to the West German deutsche mark.

The Rise, Check, and Reemergence of Mitterrand

As criticism mounted with the economic difficulties, Mitterrand, the leader of a small left-of-center party (Convention for Republican Institutions) was

François Mitterrand parlayed a position as head of a small leftist party into two terms as president of the Fifth Republic beginning in 1981. A pragmatic and skillful tactician, he purposefully blurred some of the traditional French political doctrinal distinctions in the process of building political support. (Photo courtesy of the Press Service of the French Embassy.)

endeavoring to unite the leftist movement in France. This movement had long been weakened by the multiplicity of parties and differences between the Socialists and Communists.

In 1965 Mitterrand had persuaded the Communist party not to enter a candidate in the presidential election. Mitterrand himself succeeded in forcing de Gaulle into a runoff election and by this feat came to be considered the chief leader of the opposition, a figure that had not existed for some time. Because Mitterrand was not a Socialist, that party did not nominate him for the presidency upon de Gaulle's death. The Socialists lost so badly in the election that they later had to accede to Mitterrand's insistence that small parties be included in the Left's planning; his leadership was acknowledged, and he became the first secretary of the Socialist party in 1971. He worked diligently to rebuild the party so fragmented by the disputes that shook the SFIO in the closing months of the Fourth Republic and the first years of the Fifth.

Despite Mitterrand's efforts, he lost in the presidential elections of 1974. In 1977 the Gaullist Chirac, who had reformed the old Rally for the Republic party (RPR), was able to defeat the United Left in a bitter campaign for the mayoralty of Paris. The Left thereafter split apart as the Communists insisted on the right of workers to request nationalization of their plants whatever their size. This was anathema to the Radical Socialists, who wished to protect small businesses. (Note that the titles of French political parties are sometimes confusing. For example, the Radical Socialists are not to the left of the Socialists in the political spectrum but are rather a bit closer to the center.) Mitterrand struck a compromise posture, calling for the nationalization of nine of the remaining major private industries. The Communists campaigned against the presence of foreign guest workers, whereas the Socialists suggested these should be granted a vote in local elections after five years of residence. Differences also arose over defense posture. Last-minute efforts at cooperation were ineffective, and the Left fared poorly in the 1978 elections. The RPR was the biggest winner, but by then it contained more non-Gaullist than Gaullist elements.

In 1980 the split between the Communists and Socialists was confirmed. Georges Marchais, Communist party leader, visited Moscow, espoused hard-line policies in both domestic and foreign affairs, and made no mention of the 1979 Soviet invasion of Afghanistan, which had been denounced by many Socialists. The trip marked the end of a flirtation with Eurocommunism dating from late 1975. At that time the French Communists had briefly joined with other European Communist leaders to assert the nonmonolithic character of the Communist movement. They had concomitantly emphasized the necessity for Communists in various nations to take independent and different paths according to national heritages and circumstances. The brief Eurocommunism of Marchais was more a tactical move undertaken in the hope of reaping steady electoral successes similar to those achieved by the Italian Communist party than a true conversion. Several party leaders remained skeptical. After Communist victories in municipal elections, their pressure for concessions from the Socialists and the latter's resistance contributed to the Left's failure in the 1978 parliamentary elections.

Mitterrand's efforts gained him the presidency in 1981; he received 52.22 percent of the votes cast in the second round of balloting, defeating Giscard. Many reasons have been put forward for his success. It is clear that Mitterrand's earlier move to the left enabled him to pick up leftist voters whom he held even after the Communist party broke from the United Left and reasserted its earlier Stalinist nature; indeed, he even obtained Marchais's support in the second round of balloting. Mitterrand's breadth of appeal at the same time enabled him to gain some middle-of-the-road voters who had lost confidence in Giscard and saw no other figure to whom to turn. Giscard's own personality visibly changed in his tour of duty. No longer did he seem warm, informed, and approachable. Instead, he appeared remote, less interested in the people; he was accused of running an imperial presidency. News that he and his wife had accepted gifts from Jean-Bedel Bokassa, the former corrupt, self-proclaimed emperor of the Central African Republic, further damaged his candidacy—no matter that the jewels had been sold and the proceeds donated to charities in the African Republic. The populace also chafed under the weight of an increased bureaucracy seemingly indifferent to calls for more local autonomy. Then, too, the Socialists had well-established political organizations in local communities and had long been building a foundation in local elections. The Gaullists, in contrast, had always been more a national than a local party. Their lack of development at the local level stemmed in part from de Gaulle's distrust of political parties that were difficult to budge because they were dominated by local notables.

This was the first presidential election in which about 2.5 million young men and women between the ages of eighteen and twenty-one could vote. Many favored change. The economic downturn, furthered by new oil short-ages, continued. Jobs were scarce and the government was even laying off workers from nationalized industries. Government by right-of-center regimes seemed stale, lacking in new ideas, even cynical. Technological change had lost the promise that it held a few years earlier. The French political system appeared blocked, unable to meet the social and economic challenges with which it was faced.

A large number of the French, not just the youth, were also turning inward in what was called *le repli sur soi* (the withdrawal into privacy). This movement brought renewed concentration on the individual, whether in terms of physical fitness and the new "thinning" cuisine, the pursuit of the ultimate vacation, or the conscious choice to abandon the rat race of upward mobility in favor of a more fulfilling personal and family life. The social aspects of *le repli* in many ways seemed more consonant with the Socialist emphasis on "quality of life" and human goals than the more desiccated formulas of the other parties.[8]

As soon as he assumed office in May 1981, Mitterrand announced he would bring about *le changement* (change). This had been his call for some while: "Syndicates to undertake true negotiations, enterprises to democratize, a plan to master development, a society to decentralize, a better diffusion of knowledge and culture: There will be no socialism without dismantling of the structures that assure the class power of the dominant groups."[9]

National elections promptly held in June brought resounding successes for the Socialists, as they gained a majority of seats in the Assembly. Giscard's Union for French Democracy (UDF), a five-party coalition he had formed in the 1970s to strengthen his political base, and the RPR were both hurt. Despite sustaining severe losses, the Communists were allowed four cabinet ministers, albeit reformist in tendency. Mitterrand and his premier quickly changed a number of the directors of the nationalized railroads, broadcasting system, and rectors in the universities. Nationalization of the remaining eighteen major public banks and two investment houses began. Five major industrial groups were also nationalized; smaller industries were not, in order to avoid angering the Radical Socialists and the Center. The Constitutional Council forced greater compensation to the owners than Mitterrand had initially envisioned. The government now controlled 75 percent of the credits and deposits in the banking system, was involved in management of some 3,500 firms, and employed 23 percent of the industrial workers in France. The minimum wage was raised by 24.7 percent, old-age pensions by 40 percent, housing allowances by 50 percent. The work week was reduced from forty to thirty-nine hours and a fifth week of paid vacation declared. The accepted retirement age shifted from sixty-five to sixty, and some 54,000 public service jobs were created.

Decentralization of the bureaucracy allowed more local autonomy. Despite the centralization implied in the nationalizations of banks and industries, Mitterrand argued that decentralization and the shifting of governmental decisions to local levels was necessary to assure national unity. This Socialist distrust of centralization reflected an important intellectual shift within the party since World War II, as it became critical of Stalin's methods and increasingly concerned with assuring a democratic voice for the individual worker. The 1982 passage of a law proposed by Gaston Defferre, minister of the interior and decentralization, brought extensive reorganization of local government, encouraging local authorities to take more decisions and responsibilities, especially for land use, economic stimulation, and subsidies for new industries.

Most of the steps taken between 1981 and the end of 1983, even the abolition of the death penalty, proved controversial. Especially so was the rearrangement of electoral districts accompanying the decentralization measures. Chirac, the mayor of Paris, forced modification of the plan that he asserted was meant to undercut him. Inflation and deficits mounted and production fell, employers putting the blame on the higher wages and extra week of vacation. Workers became disenchanted with what they considered a failure to carry *autogestion* (worker self-management of industries) as far as promised in the election campaign; plant managers protested the extensive control exercised by the central authorities. Investment capital fled to other countries. Unemployment rose to nearly 16 percent in 1982.

Despite restructuring, broad rather than selective subsidization, and efforts to introduce new technology, the nationalized sector of the economy (now accounting for about one-third of the nation's productive capacity) did not serve as a motor to drive the rest of the economy forward. Indeed, the heavy subsidies, though they helped to preserve jobs, led to increasingly severe budget deficits. Domestic demand for foreign goods rose as French industries failed to reconquer their own market; this in turn led to a worsening trade imbalance and layoffs. The franc fell against other currencies, suffering three devaluations between 1981 and 1983. Brief price and wage freezes proved ineffective, and strikes broke out in the automotive industry and elsewhere. In retrospect, it appears that efforts to substitute French products for imports failed in part because France, like other Western states, had difficulty matching the low prices offered by the up-to-date technology and low labor costs of newly emerging Third World industries. Subsidization of exporting firms, though contrary to the Socialist desire to provide for domestic consumption, might in the long run have strengthened the economy and taken advantage of the low value of the franc.

By 1983 Mitterrand had to take a step back, which he called a second phase of action. Fiscal expansion had not brought recovery; austerity would be the next course. He appointed a new minister of social affairs and introduced a tighter budget. An emergency tax of 1 percent was levied on all incomes; price increases were negotiated on items ranging from rail tickets to bread and tobacco. Further significant change appeared unlikely until the economy recovered; to a great extent that depended upon lower oil prices and the economic performance of other nations, especially of the United States. Large budget deficits in that country continued to force high interest rates that siphoned badly needed investment capital away from France and primed a further decline of the franc.

The economic problems inevitably brought protests and political repercussions. The austerity measures were unpopular and strikes increased. Other difficulties arose. In 1984 the government proposed that even though private schools, mostly Roman Catholic, should continue to receive state funds to pay teachers' salaries, those teachers should be appointed by the state. Demonstrations on behalf of the private schools ensued; the minister of education resigned, claiming insufficient support from his governmental colleagues, and the legislation failed to pass.

Political troubles mounted. In June 1984 the Communist party seceded from the government coalition, criticizing Mitterrand's leadership. It was especially incensed by the president's plans to streamline some of the traditional but inefficient "sunset" (declining) industries and by the cabinet shuffling that accompanied the decision to move in this direction. Support for the Socialists weakened. The March 1985 regional council elections brought a resurgence of centrist and neo-Gaullist groups. The elections also confirmed the growing strength of the extreme right-wing National Front, which garnered 8 percent of the vote in the first round of balloting.

In response to these defeats, Mitterrand moved to alter the Fifth Republic's method of electing representatives to the chambers while he still held a majority there. Anticipating the 1986 parliamentary elections, the government proposed that the system of two-round, winner-take-all elections in single-member districts be replaced by proportional representation determined in one election. Such a system would, politicians predicted, enhance Socialist representation and force some of the centrists to collaborate with Mitterrand rather than allow the extremes of the Left and Right to bring down Socialist-led cabinets. Critics pointed out that the change would erase a key reform made by de Gaulle in the creation of the Fifth Republic, a reform that had helped to end the instability of ministries so typical of predecessor republics. Proportional representation might be more democratic, as the Socialists had argued in their platforms since 1971, but now it would mean larger delegations from extremists such as Maoists on the Left and from what was accused of being the antiforeign, anti-immigrant, and perhaps anti-Semitic Right of the National Front. Despite these objections, the chambers approved the change.

The president was also embarrassed in the summer of 1985 when revelations showed that key government officials were involved in the sinking of the *Rainbow Warrior* in Auckland harbor, New Zealand. This was the flagship of a protest flotilla that the international peace and ecology movement Greenpeace was preparing to send into the forbidden zone around Mururoa Atoll in the South Pacific to protest French nuclear tests. Questions of Mitterrand's control of his own officialdom were raised, and relations with New Zealand suffered.

Mitterrand's foreign policy initially did not reflect significant deviation from that of previous administrations, as he took tough stands critical of Soviet actions in Afghanistan and Poland and backed Britain on the Falkland Islands issue. The president traveled far more readily and widely than his predecessors, even de Gaulle. A trip to Algeria demonstrated his intention of building new and better relations with that state, and a visit to francophone Africa reinforced statements of interest in maintaining close ties with that region. In 1983 (and again in 1986 and 1987) Mitterrand sent troops to intervene in the war in Chad, where it appeared that Libyan dictator Muammar al-Qaddafi was stirring trouble in the hope of gaining territory. In 1983 France participated in the international force sent to Beirut, Lebanon, to help secure peace in the strife-torn city. French troops died as a result of terrorist bombings, and in 1984 the remainder of the detachment was brought home when Italy and the United States also withdrew their troops. Mitterrand worked steadily to improve ties with West Germany and in 1987 took a leadership role in proposing creation of a German-French defense council as a key step toward a European security community.

The Socialists' leading political opposition meanwhile united, as in 1985 the RPR and the UDF pledged to govern together if their coalition ever reached power. They jointly called for a return to the single-member district electoral system, lower taxes and expenditures, and denationalization and deregulation of industry. The pathway envisioned as properly leading to a modernized, postindustrial society clearly differed from Mitterrand's.

Within the Fifth Republic it was long assumed that successful functioning of the government required a similarity of political views between the president and the prime minister. Yet the election of the president by popular vote separate from the parliamentary choice of prime minister based on party coalitions did not assure this. When Assembly elections in spring 1986 favored the RPR-UDF and Chirac became prime minister, speculation arose as to how two persons of such markedly different political persuasions would work together while holding the key governmental positions. The unplanned experiment of "cohabitation" initially operated more smoothly than predicted. With a strong parliamentary majority, however, Chirac did not hesitate to reverse some of Mitterrand's policies. He denationalized segments of the banking and manufacturing industries that Mitterrand had so recently nationalized. Return to single-member districts and majority voting was approved by the Assembly; laws were passed allowing employers to lay off workers without government approval and tightening immigration regulations. The president could only fight a delaying battle.

Yet there were key points of the Socialist program that the RPR-UDF coalition could not safely touch. No politician desiring votes would quickly revoke the fifth week of paid vacation or reduce pension payments. Nor did Chirac succeed in passing legislation late in 1986 that would have reduced access to university education by raising entrance standards and increasing fees for attendance. When students demonstrated, Chirac withdrew the legislation. It offended because it ran counter to the concept of equality of opportunity in a society where access to the good jobs is highly dependent upon education and, for government positions, upon graduation from the right university. Encouragement of small businesses accelerated, for Mitterrand and other leaders had come to believe that the great industries of France were so saddled with structural and competition problems that they could not provide the expanding job opportunities and technological flexibility required by the nation. Construction of nuclear energy plants was also maintained. France depended upon the cheap electricity they produced and the projected revenues from sale of that electricity to Great Britain.

Mitterrand's fortunes proved resurgent as the presidential elections of 1988 approached. Widely referred to by his nickname of Tonton (Uncle), he was more popular personally than his chief opponents, Barre and Chirac. The Socialist had stayed above the university legislation fiasco, which tarnished the latter. The Center-Right was also embarrassed by the popularity of National Front leader Jean-Marie Le Pen. That former paratrooper found wide appeal for his complaint that France was being taken over by immigrants, whom he blamed for increased crime, housing shortages, unemployment for French workers, and overcrowding in hospitals, schools, and welfare support systems. "This vanguard of millions of foreigners will turn itself into an army and then into a flood. . . . France will become an Islamic republic. . . . France is like an old drunken lady whose purse is wide open and who gives money to whoever passes by." A riveting orator, Le Pen drew support from former colons, Vichyites, and anti-Gaullists; he also appealed to the youth and those in lower positions in the economy who, challenged by the immigrants for jobs and status, in former years had voted Communist.

Campaigning on the theme of "France United," Mitterrand won the final presidential ballot with 54.3 percent of the popular vote, gaining a greater margin than in 1981. Chirac resigned as prime minister, and Mitterrand appointed moderate Socialist Michel Rocard in his place. The latter, a technocrat, former leader of the Unified Socialist party, and former minister of agriculture, had long advocated a market-oriented economy; his popularity had increased as Mitterrand's early economic program had faltered.

The ensuing June 1988 elections brought the first hung Parliament in thirty years. The Socialists won 276 seats, 13 short of a working majority. The Right coalition garnered 271. The UDF fared better than the RPR, declining 2 seats to 130, whereas Chirac's group fell from 158 to 128. The Communists won 27 seats (down 8). The National Front, hurt by the single-member electoral system, surprisingly seated only one deputy; Le Pen was himself defeated in Marseilles. The voters seemed to be endorsing middle-of-the-road politics. If the politicians had disliked cohabitation, the people apparently had not found it so distasteful; doctrinal clashes and sharp swings in policy only harmed, rather than helped, the movement toward a modernized economy and society.

Hoping to find a variety of center votes to support a ministry on different issues, the president asked Rocard to form a minority government. Some observers predicted a future of risk and instability for France, but others thought that a newly emerging Center might carry France forward. In subsequent months Rocard would on the one hand be accused by Socialists of not sufficiently backing Socialist legislation and on the other be threatened by a possible coalition of conservatives and Communists on a no-confidence vote. Yet he survived a serious crisis at the end of 1990. Student demonstrations forced a large addition to the education budget. At the same time the social security system, endangered by operating deficits, had to be bolstered by a tax increase opposed both by labor unions and conservatives.

Eventually, even though he held on to his substantial personal popularity, Rocard could no longer maintain his political consensus, and his ministry was hurt by allegations of financial scandals. He resigned in May 1991, perhaps to distance himself from the government prior to running for the presidency in 1995. His replacement was Edith Cresson, the first woman prime minister in French history. Standing to the left of Rocard in her personal politics and more combative in style, she was also known for her strong support of the business community in international trade battles.

The shift of Mitterrand toward pragmatic, realistic economic policies has brought about what one author terms an "unintended revolution."[10] In the 1970s, forced to compete with the Communists for the votes of the Left, Mitterrand and the Socialists clung to ideological positions and concentrated on party political infighting rather than on the changing economic realities of the world about them. A few years in power indicated that good intentions, a sharp rupture with capitalism, and nationalizations would not solve the problems of the French economy. Rather, sound enterprise had to provide the productive economy that in turn could allow increasingly equitable distribution of the benefits of technological modernization. The decline of the electoral fortunes of the Communists in the 1980s, abetted by the unimaginative leadership and contradictory moves of Marchais, enabled the

In 1991 Edith Cresson became the first woman prime minister in French history. Her direct manner and strong opinions even on tangential matters have aroused criticism and for a time brought her the lowest approval rating ever given a French prime minister. But she has attracted the public's attention and won credit for her vigor and courage. (Photo courtesy of the Press Service of the French Embassy.)

Socialists more easily to lay aside the outdated myths of revolution and shift toward policies of gradualism and pragmatic realism. This unintended de-ideologizing of the Socialists has its parallel on the Right. If the Left can no longer claim that only it can properly care for the welfare of the people, neither can the Right assert that it alone offers a democratic form of government that is noncollectivist. Whether this unexpected demythologizing and de-ideologizing trend in French politics will continue remains to be seen.

The overthrow of the East German Politburo in November 1989 and the opening of the barriers between the two Germanys presented an awkward challenge to the French government. It had long supported the concept of self-determination and democracy in Central and Eastern Europe. The specter of a reunited Germany was not, however, a welcome possibility to many French people who remembered German invasions and worried about even greater German economic competition. Mitterrand indicated he "did not fear" the eventual unification of Germany. Yet he also underlined the importance of creating a strong European Community in which Germany could participate without posing a threat to individual countries. Though accepting the reunification of Germany in 1990, he therefore also redoubled his efforts to accelerate progress on the European Monetary Union, which he viewed as a crucial step toward a single European market.

Mitterrand also endeavored to maintain a diplomatic position that would enable him to communicate with both the United Nations and Iraq after the latter nation seized Kuwait in 1990. In doing so, he was within the French tradition of trying not to be completely tied to any one bloc of powers. The president was also relying upon what the French had always viewed as their special relationship with the Arab world and their understanding of Arab concerns. Yet France was unable to mediate the crisis in the Persian Gulf and in fact was criticized for having fueled it by sale of French arms over previous years. The independence with which the Iraqis, Syrians, and other Arabs acted, moreover, demonstrated the obsolescence of the traditional French position. Mitterrand was forced to throw his full support to the United Nations. When war broke out, French planes and troops played a key role in defeating Iraqi forces.

The French military achievements and praise from other members of the UN coalition won Mitterrand great popularity within his own country. This reaction encouraged the president to explore further departures from the posture of strict autonomy in foreign affairs, set years before by de Gaulle, in favor of closer collaboration with the Western Alliance and especially with the EEC. Thus in June 1991 he launched a major disarmament proposal, calling for abolition of biological and chemical weapons and reduction of nuclear arms. At the same time, he indicated that France was prepared to sign the 1968 nuclear nonproliferation treaty, which it had previously shunned. When civil war broke forth in Yugoslavia, the French president encouraged the EC to undertake mediation in search of a cease-fire.

In the years following the great bicentennial celebration of the French Revolution of 1789, the continuing drive toward economic modernization consisted of an amalgamation of Socialist-type welfare policies linked with an economic system geared to encouraging private profit initiative. Government support was forthcoming especially for technological improvements. The cohabitation experience revealed the constitution of the Fifth Republic as flexible and able to preserve political stability. Success of cohabitation suggested further that the process of political and economic modernization had reached the point where the imperatives of such modernization no longer required one dominant political party or figure. Confidence in France and the progress of European integration made German reunification seem less of a threat than in previous decades.

France remained both politically and economically more centralized than its Western European counterparts, yet decentralization and regional autonomy had come a long way since 1945. Long-standing tensions between French individualism and the authority of the state stayed unresolved. The comment the intellectual Raymond Aron wrote in the preface to the 1979 U.S. edition of his book *In Defense of Decadent Europe* still seemed pertinent a decade later:

> The juxtaposition of the words *In Defense of* and *Decadent Europe* in the book's title may startle . . . , but the paradox expressed by these words is part of a theme that has long been debated. Our values, the youth movements,

the struggles for women's rights—all are moving in the same direction: personal freedom. It will be up to historians and philosophers, one day, to decide what was extreme individualism and what was evolutionary historical vitality.[11]

The transition to a modern, advanced industrialized state confident of itself and playing an independent role within Western bloc foreign politics had not been without hesitations and ironies. Economic success was marked by such technological feats as the development with Great Britain of the supersonic Concorde jetliner. Yet the plane required substantial subsidies for many months before it began to operate at a profit. More successful was production of the Airbus, which replaced U.S.-built planes on many routes. France constructed the first commercial-sized, fast-breeder nuclear plant in the early 1980s, adding to the Western world's largest system for production of nuclear power; then a 1986 accident at the Soviet nuclear plant at Chernobyl raised deep questions about reliance on nuclear energy and about plant design. The modernized armed forces continued to take pride in their *force de frappe* (strike force), yet the anomaly remained that, though France had nuclear weapons, it possessed separate from NATO neither the methods to deliver them successfully nor the means to prevent them from being destroyed on the ground should attack occur. Nevertheless, shorter-range missiles such as the Exocet—which France sold to Argentina and which the Argentineans used to sink a destroyer belonging to France's ally, Great Britain, during the Falkland Islands War—gained France renown. They also made the French munitions industry a subject of controversy. France won itself a position of trust with some Third World nations but at times at the expense of firmer relations with its Western allies (for example, when France refused overflight permission to U.S. planes operating against Libyan terrorists in 1986).

Such problems are not unusual. Their linkage with technology demonstrates France's movement into an advanced industrialized society, as did the reduction in the size of the French agricultural population from about one-third in 1945 to less than 8 percent in the late 1980s. The political process of adapting to and controlling the scientific and technological revolution that the political leaders had forthrightly launched and abetted was still under way in the century's last decade. It seemed likely that some shifting of programs would continue as consensus built regarding the correct mixture of centralization and local autonomy, welfare, investment, energy, and defense and foreign policies. Achievement of a technological society was assured and therefore no longer required a single strong political hand such as that of a de Gaulle. For some while the debate had not been about clinging to traditional formulas but rather of ascertaining the right formula for entering the future. Thus even if no consensus were rapidly to emerge in terms of one-party or coalition control and economic doctrine, yet the commitment to a modern, technological economy, military, and society (a key achievement of de Gaulle) remained unchallengeable. Since 1945 France had not only revived; it had also defeated its fears, renewed its economy, found grounds for a positive relationship with Germany, and assumed a leadership role in the European integration movement.

Notes

1. The nature of the several French republics varied. Each was marked by one or more new constitutions, although the Third Republic did not even have a formal constitution. Each had a different organizational structure and witnessed changes in allocations of power. The First Republic was a product of the French Revolution; the brief-lived Second Republic followed the Revolution of 1848.

2. J. P. Sartre, *L'Etre et le néant* (1943).

3. J. Caffery to J. Byrnes, February 9, 1946, *Foreign Relations of the United States, 1946*, 5:412–413.

4. The authors are indebted to the insights of P. A. Hall in *Governing the Economy: The Politics of State Intervention in Britain and France* (1986).

5. See M. Kahler, *Decolonization in Britain and France: The Domestic Consequences of International Relations* (1984).

6. D. Cohn-Bendit, *Obsolete Communism: The Left Wing Alternative*, trans. A. Pomerand (1968), pp. 14, 35.

7. J. J. Servan-Schreiber, *The Spirit of May*, trans. R. Steel (1969), pp. 47–48.

8. The reader may wish to read the analysis of *le repli* in J. Ardagh, *France in the 1980s* (1983).

9. F. Mitterrand, *Ici et maintenant: Conversations avec Guy Clisse* (1980), p. 121.

10. J. Friend, *Seven Years in France: François Mitterrand and the Unintended Revolution, 1981–1988* (1989).

11. R. Aron, *In Defense of Decadent Europe*, trans. S. Cox (1979), p. x.

Suggested Readings

Ambler, J. S., *The French Army in Politics, 1945–1962* (1966).

Ardagh, J., *France Today,* (1988).

Aron, R., *France, the New Republic* (1960).

Bell, D., *The French Socialist Party*, 2d ed. (1988).

Cerny, P. G., and M. A. Schain (eds.), *Socialism, the State and Public Policy in France* (1985).

Cross, G. S., *Immigrant Workers in Industrial France: The Making of a New Laboring Class* (1983).

Crozier, M., *The Stalled Society* (1973).

Duchen, C., *Feminism in France: From May '68 to Mitterrand* (1986).

Ehrmann, H., *Politics in France*, 4th ed. (1983).

Frears, J. R., *France in the Giscard Presidency* (1981).

Friend, J. W., *Seven Years in France: François Mitterrand and the Unintended Revolution, 1981–1988* (1989).

Gaulle, C. de, *Memoirs of Hope* (1972).

Gourevitch, P. A., *Paris and the Provinces: The Politics of Local Government Reform in France* (1980).

Hall, P. A., *Governing the Economy: The Politics of State Intervention in Britain and France* (1986).

Hanley, D. L., *Contemporary France: Politics and Society Since 1945* (1979).

Hirsch, A., *The French New Left: An Intellectual History from Sartre to Gorz* (1981).

Hoffman, S., *Decline or Renewal? France Since the 1930s* (1974).

Hoffman, S., and W. G. Andrew, *The Fifth Republic at Twenty* (1981).

Kahler, M., *Decolonization in Britain and France: The Domestic Consequences of International Relations* (1984).

Ledwidge, B., *De Gaulle* (1982).

Lovenduski, J., *Women and European Politics: Contemporary Feminism and Public Policy* (1986).

Luethy, H., *France Against Herself* (1957).

Machin, H., and V. Wright (eds.), *Economic Policy and Policy-Making Under the Mitterrand Presidency* (1985).

Mitterrand, F., *The Wheat and the Chaff* (1982).

Rioux, J. P., *The Fourth Republic, 1944–1958*, trans. G. Rogers (1987).

Talbott, J., *The War Without a Name: France in Algeria, 1954–1962* (1980).

Williams, P., and M. Harrison, *Politics and Society in de Gaulle's Republic* (1971).

Wright, V., *The Government and Politics of France*, 3d ed. (1989).

CHAPTER ELEVEN

Italy and the Vatican

🍂

Establishment of the Republic
Post-Fascist Governments • The New Republican Constitution

Internal and External Affairs
The Political Kaleidoscope
Economic Recovery • Foreign Relations

The Vatican
Pius XII in the Postwar Era
John XXIII and the Calling of Vatican Council II
Paul VI and the Changing Church
John Paul II

Notes

Suggested Readings

A remarkable transformation took place in Italy after World War II. Before the war Italy had been a poor country, lagging well behind the rest of Western Europe. Because of food and job shortages, it had to send abroad large numbers of workers. It was, moreover, stifled by an oppressive and corrupt Fascist dictatorship. The Second World War brought huge destruction and great loss of life to Italy. Since then, however, the country has made enormous economic progress. By the beginning of the 1990s, Italy's per capita income was slightly ahead of Britain's and not much behind that of France and Germany. Italy has also made its mark in film and design.

This advance has been accomplished in spite of continued governmental instability: The average duration of cabinets is less than one year. It has also continued in spite of the failure to integrate fully Italy's economy and society and to bridge the gap between its prosperous north and backward south. Modernization and prosperity are concentrated largely in the northern third of the country, whereas the southern third still suffers from economic and social underdevelopment.

Following the war, the need for economic and political modernization in Italy was monumental. The massive destruction of housing and factories, the excess population for which there was neither sufficient food nor jobs, the drastic differences between the southern and northern regions, the poorly developed infrastructure of roads, bridges, sewage, power, and water supplies—all called for action. Yet reform was inevitably slow in coming where traditional restraints on change were strong. Cultural, social, and political differences between north and south also hindered change. The people's inherent distrust of central government and their practice of placing political trust elsewhere posed problems, as did their habit of skirting laws and taxes. So, too, did the religious outlook that at times seemed far from conducive to change, especially in terms of altering the status of women.

A major question concerned whether modernization should be directed from the center or achieved more on a regional basis. A second question focused on whether Communists or capitalists should be in charge. Out of a desire to reduce the chance of a Fascist or, later, Communist takeover of the central government, the Western Allies and the Catholic capitalist and democratic parties chose a policy of decentralization. Ironically, in time this policy assisted the Communist buildup at local levels. In their effort to achieve a political voice, the Communists moved far from the Soviet line. But although their program and personnel won support at the regional level, they remained frustrated in their efforts to gain seats in the national cabinet.

Despite the often rough contest between the Left and Right in Italy, despite the arguments over control of welfare funds, over abortion and divorce, and over worker control of industry, modernization occurred. Its pace, however, was erratic. Agreement did exist about much of what needed

The great Italian filmmaker Federico Fellini was influenced by the early postwar Neorealist filmmakers. The Neorealists sought to portray the bleakness and poverty of life in postwar Italy exactly as they were. Fellini's best-known films, La Dolce Vita (1960) and 8 1/2 (1962), are characterized by a freer imagination. He once remarked: "There is no end. There is no beginning. There is only the infinite passion of life." (Photo courtesy of the Italian Cultural Institute.)

to be done. Reconstruction had to be undertaken, inexpensive power supplies found, infrastructure improved, government authority restored in the lands of the Mafia, north-south relations bettered, and good trading relations established with other European countries (without such relations Italy stood little chance of supporting its own population). Ministries changed, but the underlying consensus remained. Modernization must go forward even at times when political leadership seemed confused. Whether the consensus was strong enough for Communists and Christian Democrats to work together fruitfully in a national cabinet was at times debatable; considerable energy was dissipated in political fencing. In addition, it was uncertain if the national government could establish full control in southern Italy and Sicily. Further, question remained whether the government could gain sufficient support to curb the maverick tendencies of both private capitalism and Communist trade unions.

The Roman Catholic church and its leaders in the Vatican, the papal headquarters in Rome, also faced a serious task. Their challenge was to adapt the oldest continuing institution in Western history to the new times while preserving the strengths of tradition and established Catholic dogma. The structure and personnel of church administration were reshaped to reflect more fully the global realities of its constituency. The Vatican II Ecumenical Council in the 1960s created significant change in doctrine and practice. Efforts in later decades, however, focused more on defining the limits of those

Population of Italy (1989 estimate) 57,576,429

Population of Rome conglomeration (1989 census)
2,803,931

Population of Milan conglomeration (1989 census)
1,449,403

Area of mainland Italy, 97,097 sq. mi.

Area of Italy, including Sardinia and Sicily,
116,324 sq. mi.

Area of Vatican City, 108.7 acres

GERMANY

FRANCE

AUSTRIA

LIECHTENSTEIN

HUNGARY

SWITZERLAND
Lake Geneva

S. TYROL

DOLOMITES

A L P S

Trieste

Milan LOMBARDY
Po River

Fiume (Rijeka)

PIEDMONT
Turin

Venice

YUGOSLAVIA

Parma
Reggio

EMILIA-

Genoa

A P P E N I N E S

ROMAGNA

Bologna

SAN
MARINO

Florence
Livorno

THE MARCHES

Ligurian Sea

TUSCANY

M O U N T A I N S

Perugia

Elba

Adriatic Sea

Corsica
(France)

Tiber R.

VATICAN CITY

Rome

ALBANIA

Bari

Naples

PUGLIA

Brindisi

Salerno

SARDINIA

Tyrrhenian Sea

CALABRIA

Cagliari

Ionian Sea

Mediterranean Sea

Messina

Palermo

Reggio di Calabria

Strait of Sicily

SICILY

Syracuse

0   50   100 mi

0   50   100   150 km

AFRICA

Italy

changes than on exploring their ramifications or possible elaboration. Above all, the papacy reasserted the legitimacy of the central authority of the pope and of his control of the modernization process within the church.

Establishment of the Republic

Post-Fascist Governments

On July 25, 1943, the Fascist Grand Council, eager to end both Mussolini's rule and Italy's involvement in the war, forced the dictator's resignation. Marshal Pietro Badoglio, the conqueror of Ethiopia, headed the new government. It was he who signed the armistice terms with the Western Allies in September 1943, and they supported his regime in southern Italy. Mussolini, who had been held captive, was freed by German paratroopers and established a new Fascist Republican regime in northern Italy. This division only sharpened the ever present differences between north and south. Opposition to its Fascist rulers made the north the great center of the partisan movement that, like the French resistance, believed that it should oversee peacetime reconstruction.

The Italian forces in the south were loyal to Badoglio, who brought Italy into the war against Germany as a cobelligerent of the Allies in October 1943. Badoglio, however, was too tainted with fascism for most of the Italians. Four times he reformed his cabinet to take in leaders of the anti-Fascist movement before he gave way himself. The Allied Military Government (AMG), which was merged with the Allied Control Commission (ACC), gradually extended the jurisdiction of the Italian government; by 1946 all northern Italy except the region around Trieste was turned over to Italian authorities.

According to agreements reached when the Italian armistice terms were formulated in autumn 1943, each of the Allies was to have an equal voice in the decisions of the AMG and ACC. Yet Britain and the United States seldom sought Soviet opinion regarding Italy. This established the precedent that the countries whose troops occupied the territory of a defeated enemy would control its political future. This precedent worked in favor of the Soviet Union in Romania, Bulgaria, and Hungary, and of the United States in Japan.

Unlike the situation in Germany, where unconditional surrender brought the disappearance of all central authority, Italy continuously had in place a recognized Italian government headed by the king and cabinet. The first postwar Italian governments faced all the pressing problems of immediate reconstruction. A widespread famine made necessary large shipments of United Nations Relief and Rehabilitation Administration supplies. In addition, the state had to be purged of fascism. Such cleansing meant not only taking action against former leading officials but also making a thoroughgoing examination of many organizations and the whole legal system. One of the first bits of fascism to go by the board were the Italian racial laws. In 1946 elections took place for a Constituent Assembly to succeed the Consultative Chamber that had been appointed by the government the previous year. A referendum favored a republic over continued monarchy. Humbert II, who received the crown following his father's abdication in 1946, withdrew to Portugal. On June 18, 1946, Italy officially became a republic.

The New Republican Constitution

The Constituent Assembly did not set itself seriously to drafting the new constitution until after signature of the peace treaties and the termination of the Allied Military Government in March 1947. At the beginning of the next December, the last British and U.S. troops withdrew from Italy, and that same month the assembly approved the new constitution. As in the other European states, it set the parameters within which most political battles would be fought. It was the expression of an intent to make a new beginning in the establishment of Italy as a modern state. Those persons who did not accept the constitution's terms were automatically cast into the role of outlaws; some of these eventually turned to terrorism.

The constitution and its bill of rights in general represents the views of the Christian Democrats and establishes a conventional parliamentary form of government. The president is elected for a term of seven years by Parliament, which for this purpose is augmented by three delegates from each of the twenty new regions into which Italy was divided. These regions were intended to bring about a lessening of Fascist centralism; they were in turn subdivided into the traditional provinces and communes. Because a number of the local parliaments would almost certainly come under Communist party control, establishment of the regions involved much political maneuvering. Bitter rivalry occurred over the location of the capital, for the new regional offices meant additional jobs, public work contracts, and considerable influence.

The regions served as electoral districts for the Senate, electing a senator for each 200,000 inhabitants by universal suffrage of voters over thirty (twenty-five after 1975) years of age. The term, originally six years, was changed to five years in 1962 to make it coincide with that of the second chamber. The president can additionally appoint five distinguished citizens as senators; ex-presidents become de jure senators for life. The Chamber of Deputies is elected for five years by voters over twenty-one years of age (eighteen after 1975). Preferential voting within a list of party candidates was practiced through 1991, when a campaign to reduce corrupt vote counting led the electorate to approve a reform introducing single-candidate ballots.

The Senate and the Chamber have equal powers and usually do not differ greatly in political makeup; the ministry, which constitutes the real executive, is responsible to them. In an effort to avoid the danger of rule by executive decree, the conditions under which parliament may delegate legislative power are carefully defined. A Constitutional Court decides on the constitutionality of laws and decrees, and it judges disputes between the state and regions and between regions.

The constitution sanctioned the settlement of 1929 with the Vatican. Under this agreement Catholic religious instruction was compulsory in all state elementary and secondary schools. A church marriage ceremony was sufficient for a legal marriage, a civil ceremony being optional, and divorce was prohibited. Although other faiths were to be tolerated, only the Catholic church was to receive state subsidies. Proposals for alteration of this church-state relation caused much political debate in the following decades.

Internal and External Affairs

The Political Kaleidoscope

The April 1948 elections were bitterly contested, with a sense that they would determine the outcome of the Cold War between Western and Eastern Europe. Italians in the United States were urged to write their relatives to vote anti-Communist. The U.S. government gave twenty-nine ships to Italy as a sign of friendship and faith in Italian democracy; some U.S. leaders intimated that all U.S. aid to Italy would cease in case of a Communist victory, and Congress hurriedly passed an interim aid bill for Italy. Britain and the United States took this occasion to announce unilaterally that they favored the restoration of the free territory of Trieste to Italy. France and the United States also promised to support Italy's claim to trusteeship over its former colonies. The Vatican openly supported the Christian Democrats and urged the defeat of Communists. In spite of all the internal and external pressure, the Communists and left-wing Socialists together captured 31 percent of the total vote. In a country where 90 percent of the people are Roman Catholics, this indicated that many Italians pray and vote while facing in different directions. The sizable Communist vote reflected the extreme poverty of a large part of the population and the efforts of Communist-led labor unions.

The election results gave the coalition cabinet, headed by Christian Democratic leader Alcide de Gasperi, a good working majority. Democracy survived, but it was of a conservative flavor and joined with a conservative capitalism that kept wages low and the political voice of workers muted. These conditions only served to strengthen the determination of the Com-

munist worker movement over the next decades. Municipal elections in 1951–
1952 showed a gain for parties on the left and also for a neo-Fascist group.
To prevent a possible deadlock by a combination of extreme left and right
groups, de Gasperi pushed through an electoral reform law in the spring of
1953. It provided that a party or group of parties that obtained 50 percent of
the popular vote would be assigned a considerable majority of seats in the
Chamber of Deputies. The center parties confidently expected that this
arrangement would assure them a resounding victory in the election scheduled for June. However, they won only 49.1 percent of the popular vote and
had to be content with the bare majority of seats they had managed to win.
The Communists and left-wing Socialists accounted for 35.3 percent of the
total.

This time de Gasperi could not form a government because of divisions
in his own Christian Democratic party and the failure of the Democratic
Socialists to support him. The unstable political situation became almost
permanent over the ensuing years, as cabinets fell with astonishing regularity.
This instability is linked with the coalition nature of Italian politics and
reflects what is termed "immobilism" more than rapid change. No party is
strong enough to rule on its own, nor are the coalitions formed sturdy enough
to carry through extended programs of reform. Significant change is therefore
sporadic if it occurs at all, and progress toward economic and political
modernization is slow at best. The basic givens of Italian political life remained
much the same despite the revolving ministries. New cabinets often meant
more a reshuffling of individuals and portfolios than a true change in
administration.

The Christian Democratic party (CDP), founded after the war under
U.S. influence, is a coalition of groups; it finds support in the middle classes
of the northeast and among the rural Catholics in the south. The Christian
Democrats frequently ally with the Republican party on the right. The
Republicans find adherents among the intellectuals; these usually favor reform
and economic planning but are staunchly anticlerical. Also to the right of the
Christian Democrats are the Liberals, who are anticlerical and, despite their
name, conservative. The Italian Socialist Movement (MSI) appears to be neo-
Fascist and has some following, though fascism is banned in Italy. The nearly
extinct Monarchists are pro-church but too conservative to work well with
the Christian Democrats.

To the left of the Christian Democrats stand the Socialists, who are
divided into the Socialist and Social Democratic parties. They coalesce and
separate over a variety of issues. The most difficult of these involves their
relationship with the strong Communist party that for years, either alone or
in cooperation with Socialists of various persuasions, controlled many municipalities. Some Socialists want to carry this cooperation over to the national
level; others argue that their party's practice of collaborating with center
parties at the national level should be extended downward. From 1948 to the

late-1980s, custom held that a national government must resign rather than stay in power with the aid of Communist votes.

The Italian Communist party (PCI) has suffered splits as its majority rejected the Soviet hard line and advocated a moderate course of action. In this it became the leader in the 1960s and 1970s of a movement known as Eurocommunism; its posture won the Italian party the widest support of any Communist party in Western Europe at that time.

The original steps toward the independence of the Italian Communist movement were taken by the longtime party chief, Palmiro Togliatti, when he returned in 1943 to liberated Italy from exile in the USSR. In consonance with the then current Soviet posture of collaboration with the Allies, he announced in a speech at Salerno what came to be called the "Salerno turn": willingness to work with bourgeois forces to achieve the defeat of fascism. After that goal was achieved, he did not abandon the notion of cooperation. In 1946 he called for a new party open to all, Marxists and non-Marxists, believers and atheists, who wished to work for progressive reform. Nor did he preach imitation of the Soviet Communist model of modernization:

> International experience teaches us that in the actual conditions of the class struggle in the whole world, the working class and the advanced masses, in order to reach socialism—that is, in order to develop democracy to its extreme limit which is precisely that of socialism—must discover new paths different, for instance, from those which had been chosen by the working class and the labouring masses of the Soviet Union.[1]

Togliatti renounced old views that the path to socialism necessarily would involve armed conflict; the Italian way would be peaceful, he asserted. Younger Italian Communists, such as Enrico Berlinguer, joined him. They were not exiled under fascism, did not speak Russian, and saw themselves as Italians rather than as supporters of the spread of Soviet communism. They argued that the Greco-Roman heritage, the emphasis on the individual in Western Christianity, the traditions of democracy stemming from the Renaissance and the Enlightenment, and the longer establishment of Western industrialization, all meant that the path to socialism must be different in the West and in Italy than in the Soviet Union. The possibility that bourgeois democracy might be more conducive to social programs than authoritarianism in the Soviet manner was put forward. The Eurocommunists suggested that Westerners simply would not abandon their attachments to democratic values. Religion might bring positive change rather than serve as an alienating or repressive force. Above all, the Italian Communists agreed with Marshal Tito in Yugoslavia and Santiago Carrillo of the Spanish Communist party that communism is not a monolithic ideology. It could have many centers, not just one in Moscow. Togliatti's term for this concept (1956) was *polycentrism*. He and Berlinguer began to separate themselves from Soviet foreign policy.

In the early postwar period, the charismatic Enrico Berlinguer was expected to build a new, dynamic Communist party in Italy, based on the principles of Eurocommunism, which included a commitment to winning power through the electoral process and an abandonment of the concept of the dictatorship of the proletariat. Instead, his early death left the party divided, without clear leadership, and later weakened by the secession of the Red Brigades, a terrorist group. (Photo courtesy of the Italian Cultural Institute.)

Togliatti died in 1964, and the Communist party went through a period of confusion and somewhat divided leadership until Berlinguer took over the top position in 1972. His moderate posture and reasonable and attractive style enabled him to build the party's strength through the 1970s and the early 1980s. As the PCI focused on domestic reform and its leaders spoke out against Soviet actions in Czechoslovakia and Afghanistan, it appeared increasingly like the Socialist party. Berlinguer was forced to counter attacks from the radical wing by reasserting the revolutionary nature of the party; even so, the PCI was vulnerable to charges of being "revisionist" in its Marxism. The double game of Togliatti and his successors of advocating revolution but endorsing revisionist policies, then, initially won new followers to the PCI standard but in the long run left a legacy of division and distrust within the party.

The most radical of Berlinguer's critics, for the most part members of a still younger generation who advocated taking direct action against the establishment and who admired Mao Zedong of China, broke away from the PCI and formed revolutionary Red Brigades. Secretive in their cell-like organizational structure, the Red Brigades funded themselves by kidnappings and bank robberies; they spread fear throughout Italy with acts of terrorism. Berlinguer's stature was such that he provided a strong rallying point for the PCI, caught between the Red Brigades and the Socialists. His unexpected death in 1984 therefore dealt the Italian Communist party a serious blow and left its ideological and political future uncertain.

In succeeding years, the Communists still found their greatest support among industrial workers and used the party labor union, the largest in Italy, to lobby for their goals. Yet party leadership came to reflect the new search for members in the technical trades and government civil service. In the middle 1980s the Communists suffered a setback as the Socialists, under Bettino Craxi, allied with centrist parties at the local level and ousted Communists from mayoralties in key cities.

Further efforts sought to broaden the PCI's electoral basis by enlisting moderate left-wing independents as party candidates in the 1987 elections. This attempt to win middle-class votes was unsuccessful and provoked disgruntlement among party traditionalists. Yet new party leader Achille Occhetto in 1989 continued to lead the party congress away from the tenets of Leninist democratic centralism and toward social democracy and the political center. The PCI had experienced a 17 percent decrease in membership over the preceding two years, a fall to only 21.9 percent of the vote in the 1988 municipal elections, and a steady decline of entry of younger members into the aging party. To meet these challenges, Occhetto and the party granted women a greater voice within the party, took stands on current issues such as the environment and drugs, and negotiated for better relations with the Vatican. Though the Communist party had remained the second largest in Italy after that of the Christian Democrats, the Socialists steadily rejected its offers to cooperate in a "left alternative" government. Older Communists meanwhile complained that Occhetto was turning their party into just another "populist" movement. Finally, in 1991, in consequence of the embarrassments recently suffered by Communist parties in Eastern Europe and to give the party a new image within Italy, the PCI renamed itself the Democratic Party of the Left.

Coalitions are difficult to hold together for long. Though the Christian Democrats share some of the same concern for social reform as the moderate Socialists, the differences of the two parties over the role of the church impede long collaboration. The Liberals are so few in number that their value in coalition with the CDP is limited. The Christian Democrats have a large spectrum within their own party, and the left and right wings will block any tendency for the party to wander too far in the opposite direction in search of political partners. Indeed, the right wing is often opposed to the social reforms sponsored by the party's left wing. Because the Italian Parliament for many years used secret balloting almost exclusively, members of the chamber could vote against their own party or cabinet with anonymity, thus increasing governmental instability. Only in 1988 was the freedom of the "snipers" trimmed, as agreement was reached that budgetary votes would be public; votes on constitutional and personnel matters and those of conscience (such as divorce and abortion laws) would remain secret. Given these political realities, Italian cabinets often cannot show decisive leadership, instead remaining immobile while busying themselves with minor legislation.

The difficult political situation is made worse by the long-standing "southern problem." When Italy was established from the 1850s to 1870, the process was more an expansion of the kingdom of Sardinia-Piedmont than one of unification. The governmental system imposed was that of the northerners, who had little interest in sharing power with the population of the south. The differences of the nineteenth century have continued into the twentieth. The north, especially the region of the Po River valley, is industrialized, cosmopolitan, oriented toward Western Europe, experiencing growing prosperity, and not closely tied to the church in much of its thinking. The south remains poor, rural, traditional, loyal to its Catholic beliefs, and oriented toward the Mediterranean; agriculture is the mainstay of the southern economy, yet it suffers from infertile soil and drought. In addition, racial stock, dialects, and customs are substantially different.

For decades northern officials tended either to ignore the south or to exploit it. Roads, electric lines, and railroads expanded far more in the north than south of Rome. Unification meant an end to internal tariffs within the peninsula, enabling northern factories to dominate and eventually to eliminate nascent industries in the south. Rome itself for decades stood in second place to Milan as a center of business, industry, and modern culture. It is not surprising that the Mafia was able to establish extensive influence in the south.

Though efforts to develop the south in a coherent and meaningful manner began in the 1950s and accelerated in subsequent decades, not until the 1980s did the government make a major attempt to curb the influence of the Mafia bosses. Before immigration laws were changed in the United States and elsewhere, many southerners with initiative emigrated, thus reducing the potential for good local leadership. Since the 1970s, southern youth have found their best chances for employment either abroad or in the government bureaucracy. In the latter positions, their traditional conservatism as well as the old adage "to get along go along" prevent them from showing initiative, thus contributing to governmental immobilism. This attitude is slowly changing. In 1991 a large voter turnout overwhelmingly supported a popularly initiated referendum for electoral reform aimed at reducing the influence of party and Mafia bosses on voting procedures.

Another factor that has negatively influenced governmental effectiveness is the "uncivic culture."[2] Italians tend to set personal, family, or local group interests well ahead of municipal and national concerns. Foreign powers occupied Italy for centuries. During that period certain habits became ingrained: lack of civic interest, the attitude that only a fool would be careful to obey laws of the foreigners whereas the foxy would skirt them, and the centering of respected authority in the head of the family rather than in governmental officials. The cynical view toward government and politics was

The differences between the agrarian south (above) and the industrialized north (left) have long created problems for Italy. South of Naples, land redistribution after World War II proved difficult because estate owners resisted changes that would alter their social standing. The impoverished population, unable to purchase manufactured goods to any substantial degree, slowed development of a domestic market for Italy's industries. In the north, the prosperity of the industrial Milan-Turin-Genoa triangle is illustrated by the Alfa-Romeo assembly line in Milan. These cars are purchased by the wealthy, in Europe and elsewhere, not by the average Italian. (Top photo courtesy of the Library of Congress; left photo courtesy of the Italian Cultural Institute.)

reinforced by the experience of Mussolini's corrupt regime. Many Italians, especially in the south, feel alienated from the political system and will not throw their support behind it. Others, especially bureaucrats, note that there are multitudes of laws that govern every activity. Many laws conflict, and any innovation can be easily and legally stymied by those who do not favor the change. In the economic realm, considerable activity goes unreported, evading government regulation and, of course, taxation. During the postwar years this underground economy burgeoned substantially, with many of its practitioners more intent on obtaining its benefits than on working to modernize the prime industries. Estimates in the 1980s indicated that goods produced in this manner amounted to 10 to 30 percent over and separate from the nation's official output.

The search for governing coalitions that would provide leverage for effective governmental initiative led the Christian Democrats to make an "opening to the right" (coalition with Republicans, Liberals, and Monarchists) in the late 1950s. In February 1962 Pietro Nenni, the venerable Socialist leader, renounced his former policy of "unity of action" with the Communists. Premier Amintore Fanfani of the Christian Democrats therefore shifted to an "opening to the left," and although the Socialists did not actually join the cabinet, they supported it. Elections in early 1963 brought a setback to the Christian Democrats, as their popular vote dropped to 38.3 percent whereas the Communists' rose to 25.3 percent.

It was clear that the "opening to the left" had to be maintained. After much negotiation, by the end of 1963 a four-party coalition of Christian Democrats, Socialists, Democratic Socialists, and Republicans formed under Premier Aldo Moro, with Nenni as vice-premier. Angered by Nenni's decision to participate in the government, a left-wing faction broke away (January 1964) from the Socialists and formed the more radical Socialist party of Proletarian Unity. Differences arose within the Christian Democrats, and on one occasion the Socialists (briefly reunited) withdrew from the cabinet. Yet various coalition governments dominated by the Center but leaning left remained the norm.

As a church-oriented party, the Christian Democrats were reluctant to embrace a divorce bill, but they were forced to do so by their partners to the left. Although this was a question that cut across party lines, the Socialists in general supported the enactment of legislation permitting divorce. Without divorce, many Italians struck up permanent liaisons with congenial partners. Children born to such unions were regarded by law as illegitimate and were not considered for family allowances. A strong argument for a divorce law was that such parents could free themselves from their former spouses, remarry, and thus legitimize their offspring. The Vatican consistently opposed all divorce legislation and maintained that a divorce law violated the Concordat of 1929, a treaty negotiated between the papacy and Mussolini. It had regularized and calmed the formerly hostile relationship that had existed between Italy and the Vatican since 1870, when the Italians in unifying their country wrested control of Rome from the pope.

A limited divorce law was eventually passed, becoming effective in December 1970. It permitted divorce only after waiting periods of five to seven years, depending on the nature of the separation and whether the applicant was judged to be at fault. Yet the law provoked strong opposition from the Right and a campaign for a referendum. Reflecting its internal divisions, the Christian Democratic party, after first sponsoring the legislation, now sided with the MSI against it. The May 1974 referendum showed that the CDP was out of touch with the country, as the law was upheld by a three-to-two margin.

As the CDP lost face in this incident, the governing coalition also appeared to be losing control over the country. Strikes became a way of life. Italian manufacturers lost three times as many days of productive labor because of strikes as did British firms and more than sixty times as many as German industries. These strikes were encouraged by a workers' autonomy movement. Formed about the time of the student strikes of 1968, this mass movement reflected distrust of authority and eagerness to assert worker control of society, if not of the state. Bombings and political kidnappings by extremist groups of right and left increased. Especially active were the Red Brigades.

The 1975 regional elections weakened the CDP, as its percentage of the vote fell to 35 and the Communists' rose to 33. The Communists now controlled some twenty-three major cities and a belt of six regional governments across north-central Italy. Four factors seemed associated with this political development. First, Parliament had lowered the voting age from twenty-one to eighteen years for local and national chamber elections; the voting age for the national Senate was lowered to twenty-five years. Approximately 60 percent of the 3 million new local voters supported the Communists, apparently rejecting the Christian Democrat leadership as aging and ineffective in dealing with Italy's economic difficulties. Second, the political indifference of earlier years was disappearing, as educational work by the unions and the wave of terrorism stirred political concern in the populace. Third, economic crisis aggravated by the oil shortage provoked by the 1973 Arab-Israeli War caused further upset. Finally, the growth of terrorism sparked demands that something more be done.

Plagued by continuing inflation, rumors of payoffs to governmental officials by the American Lockheed Corporation (which was eager to sell arms to Italy), student violence, an earthquake in Friuli, and more kidnappings, the CDP-Republican coalition cabinet held on. Inability to mount a strong economic modernization campaign mirrored the failure to break away from the political traditions of coalitions and immobilism. Instead, austerity measures were pressed. The legal marriage age was raised to eighteen and legal equality was established between marriage partners, thus altering the

Aldo Moro, several times prime minister of Italy, was known for his skill in political brokering. He attempted to break the governmental paralysis caused by inter- and intraparty factional strife, inefficient and demoralized bureaucracies, and continuous economic crisis. Negotiator of a "historic compromise" between the Christian Democrats and the Communists, he became a victim of terrorism. Seized by the Red Brigades, Moro was executed when the government refused to negotiate for his release. (Photo courtesy of the Italian Cultural Institute.)

previous position of the Italian husband as the family despot. The cabinet fell in January 1976, when the Socialists withdrew their parliamentary support, asserting that the CDP paid too much heed to the Communists. The Socialists soon forced elections that only saw the Communists increase their share of the vote whereas the Socialists' declined.

Formation of cabinets proved even more difficult over the next several years, as both Socialists and Communists demanded concessions. Efforts continued to keep Communists out of the cabinet. At first Giulio Andreotti won tacit acceptance by the Communists of a minority Christian Democratic cabinet. He did this by agreeing that many funds for health, education, and welfare be turned over from Rome to the regional and local administrations; in many cases these were Communist dominated or controlled.

In 1977 the Communists demanded actual participation in the national government. The United States pressured Andreotti to keep Communists out of the cabinet, and after the longest ministerial crisis since the war— eight weeks—Andreotti succeeded himself. The Communists, though not in the governing ministry, were formally acknowledged as part of the governmental majority. The opposition of the Red Brigades to such "bourgeois" compromise was soon demonstrated. Aldo Moro, architect of the compromise and several times prime minister and the current president of the Christian Democratic party, was kidnapped March 16, 1978, and put on "trial" by the Brigades. His body was found May 9 in the trunk of a car symbolically placed halfway between the Communist and the Christian Democratic party head-quarters in Rome. Regional elections a few days after Moro's funeral reflected the people's shock and favored the CDP at the expense of the Communists.

The new cabinet shepherded an abortion bill to passage despite strong church opposition. Women over eighteen years of age could receive free abortions during the first ninety days of pregnancy if they demonstrated that their mental or physical health would be endangered by childbearing. Physicians were not required to perform these operations, and many Catholic nurses and doctors chose not to do so. In the aftermath of the Moro affair, a number of Red Brigade leaders were arrested, tried, and imprisoned. Loss of Moro harmed communication between Communists and Christian Democrats. The government fell in 1979, and new elections brought losses for the Communists whereas the CDP held its own.

Cabinets continued to form and fall. Terrorism wracked the country: There were about 1,600 terrorist acts in the first six months of 1979; the president of Sicily's regional government was killed in January 1980. In 1980 Parliament passed an emergency law permitting the government to jail suspected terrorists for twelve years without trial and to conduct wiretaps and searches without warrants. In a few months over 700 leftist terrorists and 260 rightists went to prison; yet eighty-four people were killed in the Bologna railroad station in a bomb explosion attributed to rightist elements.

A 1981 referendum on the abortion issue supported the legislation two to one, with even the Catholic south in favor despite papal opposition. That same year, for the first time since the war, a cabinet was formed not led by the Christian Democrats but rather by a Republican, Giovanni Spadolini. Discovery that public servants, contrary to law, were members of a secret lodge of Freemasons called P-2 proved an embarrassment. The lodge allegedly participated in both rightist terrorism and tax evasion. Even the Vatican was implicated as the Vatican investment bank admitted links with failed banks in turn connected with P-2. Eventually, a governmental decree officially dissolved the lodge. One of the few positive achievements of the period came in January 1982, when special Italian police forces rescued U.S. Brigadier General James Dozier, a NATO officer kidnapped by the Red Brigades the preceding month.

Economic problems required Spadolini and his Christian Democrat successor, Fanfani, to attempt austerity measures. These had little effect except to alienate the Socialists. Elections only muddled the picture further, as various small parties increased in size at the expense of the larger parties, thus making coalition forming even more difficult. The Socialist Craxi took his turn at heading a cabinet, but Christian Democratic resurgence in 1985 forced the Socialists to sacrifice control of the presidency on the grounds that the two key posts in the realm could not both be held by Socialists. The Italians' readiness to accept this notion contrasted sharply with the excitement of the French a few months later when elections brought about a similar division of the two key posts in France.

Despite the various governmental changes, a major crackdown on the expanding Mafia continued. U.S. authorities, desirous of reducing the drug trade in which the Mafia is believed to be deeply involved, had urged action. In 1982, following the assassination of the prefect of Palermo in charge of the investigation, Parliament ruled that membership in the Mafia constituted a crime. Through the middle years of the decade, numerous arrests were matched by occasional retaliatory assassinations.

In October 1985 a new crisis developed as Spadolini, minister of defense and leader of the Republican party, which held twenty-nine of the 630 seats in the Chamber, resigned over Craxi's handling of the hijacking of the *Achille Lauro* cruise liner by Palestinian terrorists (the incident also put strains upon Italo-U.S. relations). That the leader of a party controlling less than 5 percent of the seats in the Chamber could provoke a cabinet change is as good a demonstration as any of the coalition nature of Italian politics. And the eventual reformation of essentially the same continuing coalition of Socialists, Republicans, CDP, Social Democrats, and Liberals in the next cabinet showed the stability existing beneath the churning surface waters of Italian national politics. Craxi, although he established a record for longevity as prime minister in postwar Italy, could not hold on forever. The peculiarity of claiming the most seats in the chamber but not controlling the premiership rankled the Christian Democrats. Following a ministerial crisis in 1986, Craxi agreed to surrender the lead position in the cabinet to a Christian Democrat the following year and to let the parliamentary elections of 1988 determine the future.

The bargain did not hold, and Craxi resigned in early 1987. After the Christian Democrats failed to form a government, President Francesco Cossiga invited the president of the Chamber of Deputies to form a government. This was a double first, in that Nilde Iotti was both the first Communist and first woman ever offered such an opportunity in Italy. The quick failure of her effort again demonstrated the Communists' inability to obtain control of a national government. An election had little effect other than to strengthen the Socialists vis-à-vis the Communists, who suffered from lack of strong leadership. Eventually a cabinet formed consisting of the same five parties as before under Christian Democrat leadership. Differences between the wings of the Christian Democrat party, especially over how close its relationship should be to the Vatican, provoked changes of the first minister; yet the coalition continued. It would finally be slightly altered in the spring of 1991 as the perennial minister, Andreotti, dropped the Republicans while forming the fiftieth Italian government since the end of World War II.

The pattern thus remained one of compromise for stability in the midst of ostensible change. Intraparty differences at times were more significant than interparty disputes in the five-party coalition. The Communists stayed

Socialist Bettino Craxi, shown here with Vatican Secretary of State Cardinal Agostino Casaroli in 1984, demonstrated his political skill by holding on to the post of prime minister for several years. He moved energetically to curb inflation and to take legal action against the Camorra and Mafia. Craxi was less successful, however, in forcing powerful economic interests such as the Mafia into the light of public scrutiny. (Photo courtesy of the Italian Cultural Institute.)

outside the national government, their local preeminence slowly waning as well. Craxi's period of leadership produced real achievements: increases of production, decreases in inflation, progress in the battle against the Mafia and terrorists. Nevertheless, the need for governmental leadership less inhibited by political bartering and more able to take strong modernizing action seemed evident. Whether the multifaceted postwar political structure would be altered to that of two blocs remained to be seen. An equally significant issue is the as yet undetermined result of the contest against the Mafia in the south and the government's attempt to exert true control in that region. Important also are two other questions. Has the long growth of Communist power in local elections come to an end? Will local politics in time have greater impact on national politics and policies than they have had in previous decades?

Economic Recovery

After World War I journalists and diplomats often spoke of "have" and "have-not" powers. Italy was classed among the "have-nots" because it possessed few raw materials and its economy could not take care of the expanding population. World War II only aggravated this problem. Postwar discovery of rich methane gas deposits and some oil, notably in Sicily, has added to Italy's supply of power. The ever expanding electric power industry was nationalized in 1962. Italy, however, remains a country with too many people for its capital, arable land, energy, and material resources. During the decades around the turn of the century, approximately 30 percent of the natural increase in population emigrated. This produced a large influx of gold to Italy, for the emigrants sent generous gifts of money back to their relatives. Over the ensuing decades, other countries have restricted immigration. Some, such as Germany and France, have continued to admit numbers of guest workers, but these often are not allowed to bring their families along and are the first to be laid off in a recession.

In 1953 a parliamentary committee investigated the poverty in which many Italians lived. It reported that the housing of nearly 3 million families, 24.1 percent of the population, was subnormal. In southern Italy 57 percent of the population maintained a low or subnormal standard of living. Housing projects have forever been high on the list of many cabinets' modernization programs, but housing still remains inadequate. Industry has grown, and since 1952 the number of Italians engaged in manufacturing has exceeded the number in agriculture. In spite of the stream of agricultural workers to the city, there was not enough land to support those who remained behind. All the easily available land was reclaimed, although the government continued with new projects. In 1950 a moderate agrarian expropriation program was enacted for certain districts in southern Italy; since then it has been extended to other regions. Breaking up large estates into smaller tracts stifled some social unrest; it also raised economic considerations. Increased mechanization, which is sorely needed, is usually not adapted to an agricultural system based on many tiny holdings. More is to be gained both by the greater use of fertilizers (for Italy's yield per acre is still low) and by shifting from wheat to more intensive crops. Moves along these lines have brought about progress.

The manufacturing plants of the great northern cities survived well the last days of conflict. But even here much unemployment or partial employment prevailed for a considerable period. A policy of spreading available work existed, and industries kept on the payroll people who might well have been let go. Outright grants as well as loans from the United States bolstered the economy. Aid under the Marshall Plan along with subsequent economic and military assistance did much to improve conditions. Great advances took place, and the Italians, in referring to the expansion of the years 1958–1962, speak of the economic miracle. By the time the economy had begun to level off, unemployment that had long hovered around the 2 million mark had fallen to around 750,000. Foreign trade expanded, but Italian imports regularly exceeded exports. The trade deficit was in large part covered by the increasing influx of tourists. The Italians did much to lure the auto traveler. Superhighway links were constructed from Milan to the toe of Italy and to

Bari and Brindisi on the Adriatic. The modernization of infrastructure has greatly aided the shipment of industrial goods.

In order to lessen the traditional differences between northern and southern Italy, the government undertook a special fifteen-year development program, subsequently extended, for southern Italy, Sicily, and Sardinia. Special five-year plans beginning in 1964 called for unprecedented state intervention in a continued attempt to liquidate the imbalances between north and south, industry and agriculture, urban and rural areas. Unfortunately, the impressive industrial development of the Milan-Turin-Genoa triangle has thus far not succeeded in absorbing the surplus population exiting from the countryside and the south. Pollution is an increasing problem, and large sectors of Mediterranean coastline have become unsafe for swimming. Historic monuments crumble from the effects of acid rain. The problems became so acute in the 1970s that the government began appropriating substantial sums for preservation work. A special bill passed in 1973 provided sinking Venice with funds to help protect against flooding.

The chief problems of the 1970s and 1980s involved the meeting of workers' wage demands, an imbalance of trade, government deficits, energy shortages, inflation, and unemployment. During the radical wave that traversed Europe in the "hot autumn" of 1969, student activists stimulated virulent worker strikes in Italy. These strikes led to wage increases later blamed for higher industrial costs and reduced production in following years. Italy had hardly begun to emerge from recession and its accompanying unemployment when the Arab oil boycott following the Arab-Israeli War of 1973 brought renewed economic difficulties. Austerity measures and price and wage freezes had little success in ending the economic distress. The tradition of an underground economy continued to cost the government tax revenues and, because of its size, frustrated some of the government's domestic economic policies.

In 1975 the IMF provided a loan of $936 million. Measures were taken to reduce tax evasion, a widespread sport that costs the state billions of dollars each year. Yet austerity measures could not be well enforced because of the instability of the governing coalitions and the established practice of ignoring inconvenient laws. In 1977 the IMF again had to be approached. It laid down strict requirements before granting a $500 million loan. Workers were forced to accept reductions in the escalator clauses of their contracts (which theoretically protected them against inflation and led them to be callous in this regard) and lost five paid holidays. Still, inflation raged at 20 percent in 1979 and unemployment mounted. The lira suffered in comparison with other currencies and was officially devalued. The famous Italian automobile industry went through setbacks; Maserati production ceased and that of Fiat was reduced.

By 1981 the governmental budget deficit was 8.4 percent of production, far higher than in most countries. Job programs did not prevent growth of unemployment, and the P-2 lodge scandal brought a crisis in the Milan stock market and its closing for five days. Inflation, unemployment, and union pressure for higher wages all continued in the next months, as did various governmental austerity programs. Professional economists pronounced Italy a hopeless case, yet the country continued to produce and to keep its economy going.

The mid-1980s brought encouraging change, however. In 1985 a growth rate of 3 percent was reached, somewhat better than that of the rest of Western Europe. The inflation rate fell from 15 percent to about 5 percent by 1987, as oil prices declined and Prime Minister Craxi held to his program of reducing the *scala mobile* (the indexing of wages to inflation) in the face of a Communist attempt to block him in an unsuccessful 1985 referendum. Even more remarkable, tax collection improved and traditional evasion practices were curbed. Unemployment, especially among youth, remained high. So did the annual budget deficit, which by 1989 reached 11 percent of the gross domestic product. Soaring oil prices during the Kuwait crisis the following year crimped expansion. Yet despite all the difficulties, Italy was incorporating new techniques in its businesses, improving production and trade, and distributing the benefits thereof more widely through all sectors of society. In short, modernization was being achieved.

Foreign Relations

Italy's application for membership in the United Nations became linked with those of Hungary, Romania, Finland, and Bulgaria, all of which failed to receive the support of the permanent members of the Security Council until December 1953. Carlo Sforza, minister of foreign affairs in the immediate postwar years, gave Italy a distinctive Western orientation that has been followed ever since. In spite of the noisy opposition of the Communists, Italy joined the Marshall Plan, NATO, the Council of Europe, and the European Coal and Steel Community and was willing to share the burdens of the European Defense Community. When France defeated this plan, Italy participated in the London conference that brought agreement on the restoration of full sovereignty to Germany and the entrance of Italy and Germany into the Western European Union. Italy has been a staunch member of the European Economic Community and the European Atomic Energy Community. It supported Britain's application to the Common Market and has favored policies designed to further European integration. The Common Market has greatly promoted Italian prosperity. West Germany was Italy's chief trading partner for a number of years. By 1986 Libya held that position, thanks to oil imports that were, however, reduced for political reasons as the West criticized Libya's support of terrorism.

Numerous reasons, both ideological and practical, explain Italy's support of European unity. Some of these were voiced by the politician de Gasperi in the late 1940s when his country was struggling, not very successfully, to achieve political and economic modernization in the face of tradition, poverty, and lack of commitment by its entrepreneurial class.

> I must have a united Europe to absorb in her vast bosom three problems we Italians alone will never be able to solve and on which our future depends. One is the presence of the Church among us, a state within the state, oil and water. It has interfered with Italian internal affairs since the unification and made the creation of a well-governed and law-abiding nation more difficult. Two. We want to hand over to Europe our two million chronic unemployed and God knows how many of our underemployed. In the larger context of Europe, the percentage of our unemployed would become insignificant. Three, the percentage of the Communist votes, dangerously high here, would reassuringly decrease in a United Europe until they would no longer represent a frightening menace.[3]

As a result of the war, Italy lost its African possessions of Libya, Eritrea, and Somaliland. Under the peace treaty of 1947, a free Territory of Trieste was created. Zone A (86 square miles, or 223 sq km; population 298,000, mostly Italians), which included the city proper, was to be administered by Britain and the United States, whereas Zone B (199 square miles, or 575 sq km; population 73,500, mostly Slovenes and Croats) was to be under the charge of Yugoslavia. As early as 1948, Britain, the United States, and France, without consulting the Soviet Union (also a party to the peace treaty), announced that Trieste should be returned to Italy. Marshal Tito of Yugoslavia protested. After much negotiation, in 1954 Zone A, minus about 5 square miles (13 sq km), was handed over to Italy; Yugoslavia gained Zone B plus the small addition from Zone A. The city of Trieste retained its status as a free port and the political, cultural, and economic rights of ethnic minorities were safeguarded.

Italy has not played a spectacular role in the higher policy of the powers. The traditional ties of friendship with Britain have been reknit; relations with the United States have been friendly. In 1967 President Nikolai V. Podgorny of the USSR paid an official visit to Rome, the first Russian head of state to visit Italy since Czar Nicholas II in 1909. He even conferred with the pope. The visit furthered new Italian-Soviet accords covering cultural, economic, scientific, and technical fields. The Italian Fiat Company obtained the right to manufacture automobiles in the Soviet Union, and Air Alitalia inaugurated service between Italy and Moscow. These strengthened ties to the USSR did not keep the Italian government from criticizing Soviet Near Eastern policy, Soviet actions in Czechoslovakia in 1968, or the Soviet invasion of Afghanistan in 1979. Nor did Italy welcome the growing Soviet naval presence in the Mediterranean.

Italy has met its UN obligations and cooperated fully in NATO. Its role in that alliance is enhanced by Italy's significant Mediterranean location, as demonstrated by the United States' successful effort to station in Italy the F-16 warplanes withdrawn from Spain in 1988 because of Spanish political pressures. In 1979 the Italian Parliament supported NATO deployment of U.S. missiles in Western Europe. Reluctant for trade reasons to make a sharp break with Libya in the late 1980s, the Italians could not condone apparent Libyan support of terrorism. Aware of U.S. pressure to take some action, the Craxi government condemned Libya, cut back oil purchases, and bought up the 15.9 percent of Fiat stock that Libya had acquired in 1976. This last move freed the Italian government of an embarrassment and opened the way for Italian firms to compete for U.S. Strategic Defense Initiative research contracts.

Only with Austria has there been dispute. In establishing the region of Trentino-Adige, Italy united the predominantly German-speaking southern Tyrolese province of Bolzano with the predominantly Italian-speaking province of Trento. Austria charged that this action, along with other policies, deprived the German-speaking Tyrolese of the autonomy envisaged in the 1946 Austro-Italian agreement. Activists among the inhabitants resorted to bombing of electric power lines and other terroristic acts. After much controversy, agreement was reached in 1969 on dissolution of the merger of Trentino and Bolzano, with the German-speaking province again being known officially as South Tyrol. At the time the population ratio was about 230,000 German-speaking to 130,000 Italian-speaking inhabitants. South Tyrol gained a substantial increase in local autonomy. Its chief administrative officials are locally appointed, and there are many safeguards in respect to the use of German in schools and in administrative and judicial procedures.

The passage of divorce and abortion bills strained relations with the Vatican, which asserted that these actions as well as the revision of the laws governing the family and marriage were in violation of the Concordat of 1929. Basic agreement was reached on a new concordat in 1977. The deaths of both Pope Paul VI and John Paul I in 1978 slowed movement on the matter; Pope John Paul II then requested time to review the terms and reasons for the proposed accord. It was finally ratified by Italy and the Vatican in 1985. The new concordat confirmed the independence of Vatican City, but the Roman church was no longer considered the state church of Italy. State subsidies for the clergy were to end in 1990; tax deductions would be allowed to Italians who contributed to priests' wages. Equal standing was given to both church and civil marriages, and the legality of divorce and abortion under certain circumstances was recognized. If parents requested it, religious education would be available in state schools; it would no longer be a compulsory subject.

Italy contributed 2,000 troops to the multinational (U.S., French, Italian) force sent to Lebanon in 1983 to bolster peace there. They were withdrawn at the same time U.S. and French troops left in early 1984. At first reluctant to become involved in the Persian Gulf dispute between Iran and Iraq in 1987, Italy eventually forwarded naval detachments to protect neutral shipping after an Italian merchant ship was attacked. The nation's support for the U.S.-Soviet arms control treaty of 1987 was enthusiastic. During the Persian Gulf War in 1991, Italy participated in the United Nations coalition force but did not play a major role.

The Vatican

Pius XII in the Postwar Era

The Vatican, as the focal point of spiritual leadership for a great segment of the European population, a stalwart opponent of Communist atheism, and a clarion for human rights in the world and in such different nations as Spain and Poland, has played a significant role in European society since World War II. Cordial relations have existed between the Italian government and the Vatican, and the papacy has overtly supported the Christian Democratic party, which has steadily been a member of the ruling coalitions. This support is in line with the Vatican's general policy of backing Catholic parties in those continental countries where there are substantial numbers of Catholic believers.

In Eastern Europe this policy led to direct conflict with the Communist governments, which, following their united-front policy, were bent on establishing single-party states. In certain countries the governments closed convents and confiscated church lands in the process of carrying out their programs of land distribution. Another major issue in these countries was the complete secularization of the school systems. In general, religious education in the schools was handicapped, though not universally abolished, but private religious schools were closed. Notable conflicts between the Catholic church and the state centered on the imprisonment and trial of Archbishop Stepinac in Yugoslavia in 1946 and of Cardinal Joseph Mindzenty in Hungary in 1949. Under pressure from the Soviet government, the Uniate churches of Ruthenia and the former provinces of Poland in 1946 declared their allegiance to the patriarch of Moscow. The Uniate churches of Romania were later (1948–1949) incorporated into the Romanian Orthodox church. The papacy naturally deplored the loss of these Eastern-rite Christians who for so long had pledged allegiance to the pope, and thus the conflict between the Vatican and communism grew more intense.

In the summer of 1949, as the governments in Czechoslovakia and Poland began drastically to curb the privileges of the Roman Catholic church, the papacy excommunicated all persons who were Communists or in any way aided the cause of communism. In Czechoslovakia the government answered by declaring it would charge any priest with treason who tried to enforce the papal edict. In Italy, France, and most Western countries, the priests made no particular effort to enforce the ban, although it was universal in its application. Relations between the papacy and the churches behind the Iron Curtain, although far from satisfactory, slowly improved; leading church officials were permitted to visit Rome, and in time the pope visited Iron Curtain countries. In 1964 the Vatican signed a treaty with Hungary in which the Hungarian government recognized papal appointments to the Hungarian hierarchy.

During the immediate postwar years, the pope issued many statements asking for reconciliation among the peoples of the world and for an advanced social solution of the problems of industry. The Catholic church, however, refused to cooperate in the World Council of Churches, formally constituted in 1948 by delegates representing 147 churches from forty-four different countries. New dioceses were created. The first local hierarchies in Africa in fourteen centuries were formed in 1950, and Norway, for the first time since the Reformation, received a hierarchy in 1953.

John XXIII and the Calling of Vatican Council II

The death of Pius XII in 1958 brought to a close one of the most significant pontificates in recent times. It also remains controversial, as criticism of its posture toward Hitler's Germany and his treatment of the Jews mounted as the years passed.

Angelo Giuseppe Cardinal Roncalli, patriarch of Venice, became the 262d official successor of Saint Peter. As John XXIII, he strengthened the administration of the church by filling several long-vacant posts; he broke with tradition by increasing the size of the College of Cardinals. The Italians, who lost their majority in 1948, became an even smaller fraction, as many of the new cardinals came from African and Eastern churches.

John XXIII, nearly seventy-seven years old, reigned slightly over four and one-half years. He was an innovator and a man of action; he initiated a revision of canon law and sent forth eight encyclicals. Most important of all, in January 1959 he announced his intention to convoke an Ecumenical Council of the Church, the first to be held since the Vatican Council of 1870. He issued a call for *aggiornamento*—the updating of theological teachings and discipline—because he wished to bring an inner renewal of the church, to open its windows to "the winds of change."

Pope John presided over the first session of Vatican II in late 1962 as over 2,500 cardinals, archbishops, bishops, and heads of the major religious orders, as well as representatives from Protestant churches and of the Orthodox church in the USSR, attended the council. The meeting did much preparatory work. Pope John pointed the way by decreeing the first change in the canon

Pope John XXIII signs the call for Vatican Council II, which took place from 1962 to 1965. Vatican II, as it came to be called, did much to adapt the church to modern values such as secularity, ecumenism, and pluralism. It is generally acknowledged that the discussions held during Vatican II shaped the current Catholic church, but the exact nature of their impact is still debated. (Photo from UPI/ Bettmann Newsphotos.)

of the mass since the early seventh century, inserting the name of Saint Joseph, the spouse of the Virgin Mary, into one of the prayers.

Paul VI and the Changing Church

John XXIII died in June 1963. Few, if any, popes achieved the admiration and love accorded him by people of all faiths, ranks, and conditions of life. He was succeeded by Giovanni Battista Cardinal Montini of Milan, who took the name of Paul VI. A noted scholar and intellectual, he carried forward with the second session of the council that fall. The council endorsed the principle of collegiality, which maintains the collective governing and teaching authority of the bishops: the bishops, as successors of the apostles, share with the pope in the government of the church. It also sanctioned the use of the vernacular in the administration of the sacraments and in parts of the mass. At this session, as already at the previous one, a cleavage between the so-called progressive and conservative groups became evident.

When Pope Paul VI made the pilgrimage to Jerusalem in 1964, he was the first supreme pontiff to leave Italy since 1814 and the first to visit the Holy Land. Orthodox Patriarch Athenagoras made a visit to Jerusalem at the same time, and the meeting between the leaders of the two churches—the first in over 500 years—was a landmark in ecumenical cooperation. The pope continued to travel new paths, visiting Bombay and then New York to address the United Nations Assembly.

At the third session of the council in the fall of 1964, collegiality again received a strong affirmative vote. In closing the session, the pope decreed the statement on ecumenism approved by the council. He also proclaimed the formulation of the constitution of the church, although amending the text somewhat. In this constitution the principle of collegiality was accepted, yet the doctrine of papal infallibility and primacy was reaffirmed:

> But the College or body of bishops has no authority unless it is understood together with the Roman Pontiff the successor of Peter as its head. The Pope's power of primacy over all, both pastors and faithful, remains whole and intact. In virtue of his office, that is as Vicar of Christ and pastor of the whole church, the Roman Pontiff has full, supreme and universal power over the church. And he is always free to exercise this power.[4]

At the fourth and final session of the council in the fall of 1965, the pope announced his decision to establish a synod of Catholic bishops "for consultation and collaboration" with him in the government of the church.

At this session of the council, two more constitutions (that is, formal significant doctrinal statements) were added to those already proclaimed on the liturgy and the church. They were on Divine Revelation and the church in the modern world. Decrees dealing with practical matters of church affairs were formulated regarding monastic orders and seminaries, on the apostolate of the laity, and on missions and priestly life. Declarations, which are statements of principle, were adopted on the relationship of the church and non-Christian religions, on Christian education, and on religious liberty. The declaration that renounced the continuing responsibility of Jews for the death of Christ attracted worldwide attention. The pope in his own decision revised the role of the four-century-old Sacred Congregation of the Holy Office, which deals with issues of heresy, retitling it the Congregation for the Doctrine of the Faith; he further stated that its tribunals must operate under canon law rather than by secret procedures.

The papacy continued to update church practices and administration. In 1966, fasting was made obligatory for Latin rite Catholics only on Ash Wednesday and Good Friday. Friday abstinence (no eating of meat) remained, but national conferences of bishops were given the power to abrogate this, and many have. An apostolic constitution set new norms for obtaining indulgences and the practice of referring to them in terms of years and days was dropped. The calendar of saints was revised (1969) and some saints of doubtful authenticity dropped. The rules on mixed marriages eased slightly. In 1970 the practice of permitting the laity to receive both bread and wine at communion was extended, and local conferences of bishops were to decide whether this practice was to be followed in their dioceses. Regulations regarding cooperation and worshiping with Protestants were liberalized.

The first synod of bishops was held in Rome in 1967, and in 1968 a major reorganization of the curia went into effect. In general, the various national conferences of bishops became more active and created more diversity within the church. The Dutch hierarchy, for example, sponsored a new catechism (1966) that aroused much attention and criticism from Vatican theologians. At the second synod of bishops in 1969, the pope agreed the synods should meet every two years rather than irregularly and promised to listen carefully to bishops' proposals regarding agenda items.

On a visit to Uganda in 1969, the pope gave his blessing to the creation of a loose confederation of the twenty-eight episcopal conferences of Africa. His statement on that occasion summarized the conflict between unity and diversity that confronted the Catholic church at the end of the twentieth century and also reflected on the wide problem of Christian unity. Bidding the African bishops and all African Catholics to be "missionaries to yourselves," he went on to say:

> A burning and much-discussed question arises concerning your evangelizing work, and it is that of the adaption of the gospel of the church to African culture. Must one church be European, Latin, Oriental, or must she be African? Your church must be first of all Catholic. That is, it must be entirely founded upon the identical, essential, constitutional patrimony of the self-same teaching of Christ, as professed by the authentic and authoritative tradition of the one true church. This condition is fundamental and indisputable.
>
> The expression, that is, the language and mode of manifesting this one faith, may be manifold; hence it may be original, suited to the tongue, the style, the character, the genius and the culture of the one who professes this one faith. From this point of view, a certain pluralism is not only legitimate but desireable.

Two major issues have brought forward differences among the various national conferences of bishops, the Vatican, and individual clergy. One is the continuance of the church rule on celibacy for the clergy. This practice applies to the priests of the Roman rite but not to those of the Oriental rites in the Catholic church. Many would relax the prohibition and believe that to do so would help relieve the growing shortage of priests. The issue has been widely debated, and groups among the clergy have openly advocated it. The Vatican, however, reaffirmed its traditional policy on celibacy. Nevertheless, there has been an increasing number of withdrawals from both the secular and regular clergy by members who are no longer in accord with this teaching. Here again the Dutch hierarchy is in advance of others in trying to devise methods of keeping the services of priests who marry, permitting them to preach and conduct prayer services but not to say mass.

Opposition to celibacy was nothing compared to the upheaval engendered by the papal stand on a second issue, that of birth control. This problem had been up for study by ecclesiastical officials ever since the close of Vatican II. There were some indications that the church's teachings—in view of the burgeoning demographic problems facing the world—would be modified. Instead, the pope, in the encyclical *Humanae Vitae* of 1968, again proclaimed the church's prohibition against all forms of artificial birth control. Various national conferences of bishops, notably in Austria, Belgium, Canada, France, Germany, and the Netherlands, issued statements pointing out that the encyclical was not a dogmatic utterance and in their interpretation left latitude to the consciences of individuals in applying the doctrine.

The last half of the approximately fifteen-year pontificate of Paul VI witnessed a sharpening of the debate between those who favored furtherance of liberalization tendencies inherent in the actions brought by the Vatican Council and those who opposed additional change. The pope, though supportive of movements for social justice, held to a conservative position on theological matters and papal authority. Pressure for ordination of married individuals continued, and the practice of wearing lay clothing spread among priests and members of religious orders. In 1972 the Dutch were warned that their new catechism must be revised. The following year marked the beginning of an extended controversy with Swiss theologian Hans Küng of the University of Tübingen (West Germany), whose writings suggested that the truth of the church was not bound to particular historic formulations of dogma. This view enabled the professor to question the doctrine of papal infallibility.

The plight of the poor and oppressed drew increasing attention throughout the 1970s, especially in the Latin American and African branches of the church. The 1971 synod of bishops meeting at the Vatican pressed for more vigorous action on social change. Another problem that confronted Paul VI was the status of the church within Communist-dominated countries. Unpalatable as communism is to the papacy, the latter nevertheless has a duty to ensure the continuing existence of the church in those states. In 1971 Cardinal Mindzenty abandoned his fifteen-year self-exile in the U.S. embassy in Budapest and came to Rome, thus easing Vatican relations with Hungary. Steps toward a modus vivendi with Communist states did provoke reaction, as bishops of the Eastern-rite Ukrainian Catholic church decried Vatican moves to improve relations with the USSR. The papacy avoided making many direct statements regarding the war in Vietnam, yet Paul VI repeatedly called for world peace, upheld peaceful negotiation of differences, and warned of the dangers of nuclear war.

John Paul II

Paul VI died August 6, 1978. Albino Cardinal Luciani of Venice was chosen to succeed him, the cardinals apparently considering him a compromise candidate acceptable to both conservatives and reformers. Some new popes follow the practice of assuming the name of a predecessor whose person and policies they admire. Luciani confirmed the impression that he wished to draw together the branches of the church by taking the title of John Paul I. The sixty-five-year-old man had little opportunity to act, for he died unexpectedly after only thirty-four days in office. The following papal election produced surprise, as a split among the Italian cardinals and the appointment of many cardinals from other regions of the world over previous decades had their impact. The new pope, the first non-Italian in 455 years, Karol Cardinal Wojtyla of Krakow, Poland, took the title of John Paul II.

He soon proved a dynamic occupant of the chair of Saint Peter. Within the first year of his papacy, he toured the world, pleading on behalf of the poor in Mexico, for peace in Northern Ireland, and for religious and human rights in Poland. His June 1979 visit to his native land stirred millions of listeners and was later considered a key factor in stimulating the unrest that led to the formation of the Solidarity trade union. A second visit to Poland in 1982 was postponed by Polish authorities for a year as a possible threat to internal stability. When he again traveled there in 1983, the pope implicitly criticized the imposition of martial law on December 13, 1981, and stressed the concepts of Polish nationalism and human rights, themes displeasing to the Soviet bloc.

John Paul II easily became the most widely traveled pope in history. Everywhere he was received by joyous thousands, although at times, notably on his visit to the Netherlands, Belgium, and Luxembourg in May 1985, he was to hear criticism of certain church policies and demands for reform. A request for a more significant role for women in church affairs was among the more important changes his critics advocated.

John Paul II's first encyclical, *Redemptor Hominis* (1979), indicated a Christocentric view of the church and deep concern for the sacredness of human life. At the same time that he spoke strongly in favor of social justice, he took steps indicating that he did not support some of the more liberal theological reformers. Küng was censured and barred from teaching as a Catholic theologian. The pope opposed the activity of priests in politics and ordered Father Robert F. Drinan, a priest from Boston, Massachusetts, not to run for a sixth term in the U.S. Congress.

On May 13, 1981, an assassination attempt was made on the pope by Mehmet Ali Agça, a fugitive from Turkey. Despite allegations of connections between Agça and Bulgarian authorities, the trial of Agça produced no evidence of such complicity. John Paul II recuperated well and pursued his world travels with vigor. As legislation legalizing abortion passed in numerous countries, the pope leant his support to "right-to-life" movements. Pressure from within the church for a more lenient policy regarding artificial birth control and married clergy continued but was resisted.

By the 1980s a new challenge appeared in the form of a "liberation theology" taking root in Latin America. The term came from a volume published in 1971 by Father Gustavo Gutiérrez of Peru, *A Theology of Liberation*. Roughly put, the new theology supports the rights of the oppressed and the poor and advocates political change. It asserts that the church is bound to the elite rich and argues that instead it should be based on the masses and alert to their needs. Gutiérrez emphasized "horizontal" human-to-human relationships rather than the "vertical" human-diety dimension. Another liberationist, Brazilian Franciscan Leonardo Boff, in the early 1980s stressed the concept of a "people's church." Critics of liberation theology charge that it links Marxist revolutionary class struggle ideas with those of Christian charity; they see it as placing the concept of a people's church in conflict with the existing hierarchical church. The concern in the Vatican is that in its most militant form the theology implies the validity of Marxism and puts the mantle of religion over armed struggle, whereas Christianity ought to stand for peace and nonviolence. In 1984 and 1985 John Paul II issued stern warnings on this matter and formally silenced Boff for an indefinite period. Yet the pope had to be diplomatic to reduce chances of losing the support of village priests concerned for the welfare of their poverty-stricken parishioners.

In Nicaragua several priests, despite the pope's ban on involvement in politics, participated in the Sandinista overthrow of the dictatorship of Anastasio Somoza in 1979. At the beginning of 1985 those who still served as officials in the Marxist-oriented Sandinista regime were ordered to resign or lose the right to perform sacerdotal duties.

To those who asserted that John Paul II was liberal on issues of social concern but conservative in matters of theology, politics, and discipline, the pope replied that Christian doctrine is of one piece, not to be subdivided in any way. His anticommunism was well recognized. The Vatican gave a thundering condemnation of the murder in 1984 of a priest noted for his sympathy for the Solidarity movement, the act committed by members of the Polish secret police (who at their trial asserted they were acting on their own). Debate continued between conservatives and liberals, much of it focusing on the precise meaning of Vatican II. Its major reforms had been implemented, and conservatives believed that enough change was achieved. Liberals within the church argued that the overriding message of the council was one of openness to continuing change.

In order to resolve this issue and to demonstrate his leadership, John Paul summoned an extraordinary synod of bishops in 1985 to consider formally if proper implementation had been given to the decisions of the Second Vatican Council, which had come to its conclusion precisely two decades earlier. At the gathering, the presence of bishops from some thirty-four African, seventeen Asian, and twenty-two Latin American and Caribbean countries joined with a modified one-country–one-vote organization assured that the import of the Third World for the church was recognized. Liberation theology found its defenders as well as its critics. The collegial rules of the church that permitted more autonomy to national gatherings of bishops than members of the Vatican curia occasionally wished to grant also had their advocates. Few major issues were resolved, but the spirit of ecumenicity and of willing dialogue within the Roman church was enhanced. Another such conference held two years later focused primarily on the role of the laity within the church.

Throughout these years, the pope extended his travels, speaking on behalf of the poor and oppressed and, in 1987, denouncing the treatment of the church in Czechoslovakia. Calls continued for an enhanced role for women in the church, perhaps including ordination; so, too, did pressure for ending the celibacy requirement for priesthood and changing church policy on birth control. In a 1987 visit to the United States, John Paul, aware of the strong diversity in U.S. Catholic views, admonished the faithful that they could not select only those aspects of Christian teaching with which they were comfortable; the doctrine of faith is unified and seamless. The Vatican further had to remonstrate with U.S. bishops who advised their flocks to use protective devices (forms of birth control) to avoid contamination in the spreading AIDS epidemic. Yet 163 theologians who favored reconsideration of the church's ban on artificial birth control issued in 1989 a declaration at Cologne, West Germany, protesting papal authoritarianism in using the general teachings of the New Testament to support a specific teaching.

Challenges came from conservatives as well. French Archbishop Marcel Lefebvre began founding ultratraditionalist seminaries in 1970 under the leadership of his Society of Saint Pius X, named for a conservative pope. Lefebvre's insistence on continued celebration of the Latin tridentine mass reflected not just differences with Rome over liturgy but also over the concept of authority of the priest, authority he claimed was undermined by the ecumenical council. He also opposed the "satanic influence of liberalism" that led Vatican II to such modernist heresies as attempting to reconcile the true faith of Roman Catholicism to other religions. Though enjoined by the pope not to consecrate four of his followers as bishops, Lefebvre did so in 1988 without papal authorization, thus automatically bringing excommunication and creating the first schism in the church since 1870. Such excommunication Lefebvre held of no value because it was decreed "by modernists, by people who should themselves be publicly excommunicated," and in one of his letters to his bishops he claimed that "the chair of Peter and the posts of authority in Rome are occupied by antichrists."

Although debate over various issues did not lull, the activity of John Paul II and the attention his travel and pronouncements attracted demonstrated that the Roman church had a meaningful role to play in modern society and that the Vatican did not intend to shrink from the opportunity. The pope roundly condemned racism and apartheid. In 1989 he received Polish Solidarity leader Lech Walesa at the Vatican. Even before the June 1989 elections so favorable to Solidarity, the Polish Parliament granted the Roman church legal status within Poland; it was the first East bloc nation to do so. The church regained the right to own property and operate media outlets, and Poland soon joined 116 other nations who had diplomatic relations with the Vatican. In Ukraine, advocates of autonomy for that region called for legalization of the Ukrainian Uniate church, which had been suppressed in 1946. The subject no doubt was one among many touched upon in an unprecedented meeting of Soviet leader Gorbachev with John Paul II toward the close of 1989. Moderation of the Soviet attitude toward religion, a concept Gorbachev said the Soviets had previously treated in "too simplistic a manner," appeared to pave the way for improved Soviet-Vatican relations. Negotiations with Anglicans over possible reunification of the two churches foundered, however. There were several problem issues, among them serious differences over the consecration of a woman bishop by a U.S. Anglican diocese. If some Catholics still protested that the papacy was moving too slowly on internal church matters, there was no denying that the Vatican was a major participant in the creation of a new Europe.

Notes

1. P. Togliatti, "La nostra lotta per la democrazia e il socialismo," in *Il Partito* (1973), p. 56, as quoted by D. Sassoon, *Contemporary Italy: Politics, Economy and Society Since 1945* (1986), p. 233.

2. This term and parts of the present analysis are based on Michael Roskin, *Other Governments of Europe: Sweden, Spain, Italy, Yugoslavia, and East Germany* (1977).

3. Quoted in Luigi Barzini, *The Europeans* (1984), pp. 191–192 and passim.

4. This quotation is from chapter 3 ("On the Hierarchical Structure of the Church and in Particular the Episcopate") of the constitution. It appeared in "Text of Vatican Council's Constitution 'De Ecclesia,' as Proclaimed by Pope Paul VI," *New York Times*, November 23, 1964, p. 19.

Suggested Readings

Bull, G., *Inside the Vatican* (1983).

Clough, S., *The Economic History of Modern Italy* (1964).

Cornelison, A., *Women of the Shadows* (1977).

De Grand, A., *The Italian Left in the Twentieth Century: A History of the Socialist and Communist Parties* (1989).

Filippelli, R. L., *American Labor and Postwar Italy, 1943–1953: A Study of Cold War Politics* (1989).

Gatt-Rutter, J., *Writers and Politics in Modern Italy* (1979).

Giammanco, R., *The Catholic-Communist Dialogue in Italy* (1989).

Graham, R. A., Jr., *Vatican Diplomacy* (1959).

Greeley, A. M., *The Making of the Pope, 1978* (1979).

Hughes, H. Stuart, *The United States and Italy*, rev. ed. (1965).

Kogan, N., *A Political History of Italy: The Postwar Years* (1983).

Lange, P., and S. Tarow (eds.), *Italy in Transition* (1980).

Leonardi, R., *Italian Christian Democracy* (1989).

Leonardi, R., and P. Corbetta, *Italian Politics*, vol. 4: *A Review* (1990).

Leonhard, W., *Eurocommunism: Challenge for East and West* (1980).

Mack Smith, D., *Italy: A Modern History* (1969).

Mammarella, G., *Italy After Fascism: A Political History, 1945–1965* (1966).

Miller, J. E., *The United States and Italy, 1940–1950: The Politics and Diplomacy of Stabilization* (1986).

Nichols, P., *The Politics of the Vatican* (1968).

Noel, G., *Anatomy of the Catholic Church* (1980).

———, *The Pope's Divisions* (1981).

Ranney, A., and G. Sartori, *Eurocommunism: The Italian Case* (1978).

Rynne, X., *Vatican Council II* (1968).

Sassoon, D., *Contemporary Italy: Politics, Economy and Society Since 1945* (1986).

Sciascia, L., *The Moro Affair and the Mystery of Majorana* (1987).

Stehle, H., *Eastern Politics of the Vatican, 1917–1979* (1981).

Templeman, D. C., *The Italian Economy* (1981).

Urban, J., *Moscow and the Italian Communist Party: From Togliatti to Berlinguer* (1986).

Zuckerman, A., *The Politics of Faction: Christian Democratic Rule in Italy* (1979).

CHAPTER TWELVE

The Small States of
Western and Northern Europe

Austria
Governmental Reorganization • *Economic Development* • *Foreign Affairs*

Switzerland
Politics and Economy • *Foreign Affairs*

The Lowlands
Reestablishment of Governments
The Economy and International Relations • *Political Development*

Ireland
Severance from Britain • *Relations with Ulster*

The Scandinavian States
The Political Scene • *Social Legislation*
Economic Developments • *Foreign Affairs*

Finland
Political Development • *Economy*

Notes

Suggested Readings

T he history of the small states of Europe after World War II in many ways reflects the history of the great powers. The colonial empires of Belgium and the Netherlands dissolved as did those of Italy, France, and Great Britain. All European states followed more or less a common foreign policy in joining the United Nations (Switzerland is the sole exception, and even it adheres to some of the UN-related organizations), and such regional pacts as the Council of Europe, the Common Market, the EFTA, and NATO. All countries large or small are subject to much the same current economic, social, religious, and political stresses, but not necessarily to the same degree. In the decades after the Second World War, Western Europe became increasingly more of a piece than ever before. The smaller Eastern European countries also developed more linkages and similarities, although on a much lesser scale. In the early 1990s new Eastern European openness and increased desire for trade relations with the West suggested a continuation of the process of integration.

Yet the histories of the small states are significantly different from those of the great powers. Their problems are unique, and they make a singular contribution to modern civilization. The small powers have a style of their own that deserves study and evaluation, particularly if history is considered to be more than power politics. Developments in some of these states—for example, the cooperation of the Benelux nations, the alteration of regime in Spain, or the revolution in Portugal—have had significance well beyond the borders of those countries, affecting European economic integration, defense planning, and decolonization.

The small countries considered in this and the following chapter present substantial diversity as a whole. They include the wealthiest countries of Europe and the poorest; many belong to NATO, but some of the most important (Sweden, Switzerland, Austria, and Finland) are neutral. Certain trends, nevertheless, prevail within each group.

The Scandinavian countries and Switzerland were, even before World War II, among the richest in Europe; the events of the war generally enhanced their position. Their continued prosperity, political stability, and social homogeneity have enabled them to set up welfare states that are greatly admired in other parts of the world. In the last two or three decades they have been joined by Austria and Finland, countries formerly suffering from poverty and authoritarian governments. By virtue of their geographic locations, both of the latter countries were of special significance in the Cold War and consequently had to conduct their foreign affairs with great care. The Low Countries reached a similar level of economic and social prosperity. Moreover, in establishing the Benelux union, Belgium, the Netherlands, and Luxembourg pioneered a model for European integration.

The poorer countries—Spain, Portugal, and Greece—have two very impressive achievements to their credit. They have succeeded in casting off their former authoritarian governments in favor of democracy, with a smoothness that has amazed outside observers. And they have integrated their backward economies and societies into the European Community. Ireland has made a similar transition, but this is proving more difficult for Turkey; Cyprus remains wracked by internal ethnic conflict.

Austria

The questions and challenges facing Austria at the war's end were legion. Could Austria achieve its own identity separate from Germany? Separation would surely be required by the victorious powers and by all Austrians shamed by their country's participation in the atrocities of the Third Reich. Yet maintenance of a separate identity had been the subject of debilitating division and debate since at least the 1890s. Could an acceptable modus vivendi be worked out with each of the ethnic minorities? Could longstanding animosities between the rural populations and the urban workers of Vienna and other cities be reconciled? Could a truly independent foreign policy be established between the opposing blocs of the superpowers? And could all this be done while moving the Austrian economy, so sickly in the interwar years, toward advanced industrialization and modern agricultural techniques?

Governmental Reorganization

The attainments reached in each of these areas by the 1990s were unimaginable in 1945. At that time, the first task was simply that of creating an official Austrian national government, a missing entity since the annexation (*Anschluss*) by Germany in 1938. On April 29, 1945, three weeks after the Soviet armies entered Vienna, Karl Renner announced formation of a provisional government. An old, respected Socialist leader, Renner had played a key role in establishing the Austrian republic after World War I. The Soviets immediately recognized the Renner government, which was a coalition of Socialist, Communist, and People's (Catholic, later Christian Democratic) party leaders. All laws dating from the Hitler period were abolished, and from the start the Austrian government assumed responsibility for denazification. Each major member of the victorious coalition, including France, took over individual occupation zones; a small district in the center of the city of Vienna was reserved for joint control by the occupying powers. In October the Allied Control Council officially recognized the Renner government. Thus, unlike Germany, Austria from the first had one central government of its own that operated under the supervision of the Allied powers.

In order to broaden the basis of his government, Renner called a meeting of representatives of the Austrian provinces. They endorsed his government and his program of returning to the constitution of October 1920, as amended in 1929. The meant that Austria was again to have a president elected by Parliament, which consists of an upper chamber chosen by the provincial diets and a lower chamber elected directly by the people. In the November 1945 elections, the conservative People's party won eighty-five seats, the Socialists seventy-five, and the Communists four. Renner was elected president, and a member of the People's party became chancellor at the head of a three-party coalition cabinet. The occupation authorities in January 1946 announced their recognition of Austria as a state, with the frontiers of 1937, pending a final delimitation. This meant that Austria could establish a diplomatic corps and begin again to conduct foreign relations. Soon a new control plan permitted Austrian laws (other than constitutional provisions) and international agreements (other than those with the four occupying powers) to go into effect unless unanimously disapproved by the Allied Control Council. This plan did much to strengthen the Austrian government and prevented many one-power vetoes.

The Austrian government extended its administration over all Austria, although it ran into hindrances in some zones. Although there were differences between the occupying powers, they did not approach in seriousness those which developed among the four powers in Germany. The Austrian government was always able to focus attention on Austria as a whole. Its efforts to win back the southern Tyrol from Italy failed, but it played a part in rebuffing Yugoslavia's claims for frontier rectifications.

The level of confrontation between the Eastern and Western powers was reduced in Austria in part because both sides saw Germany and Berlin as more significant foci for dispute. After the West brought the German Federal Republic into its sphere of influence, the Soviets recognized that achievement of complete dominance in Austria was beyond their reach, especially during the leadership adjustment period in the USSR following Stalin's death. The incorporation of the German Federal Republic into the Western defense system did, however, call for extensive Soviet countermeasures. These took the form of an effort to obtain the formal neutralization of such strategic countries between the two blocs as Yugoslavia, Austria, and Germany. In this scheme Austria played a particularly important role as a stage for a spectacular demonstration of the new Soviet policy. In the spring of 1955, the Soviet government therefore made known its willingness to negotiate a settlement and invited representatives of the Austrian government to Moscow. Following later discussions with the other governments concerned, the Austrian State Treaty was signed on May 15, 1955.

Judged in the light of Soviet demands over the past decade, the terms of this treaty were lenient. The Yugoslav territorial claims had long since been abandoned, and the principal price Austria paid was the settlement of the

Soviet claims to German assets. More important was the Austria's obligation to declare its neutrality. This provision meant that Austria could not be brought into the Western defense system and established, with Western approval, the principle of neutralizing the uncommitted countries between the two blocs. Austria undertook never to enter into any military alliances or to permit a foreign power to establish military bases on its territory. Austria did gain permission to have its own army. Political or economic union between Germany and Austria was specifically forbidden. It remained for subsequent negotiations among the four great powers to determine the role that the idea of neutrality would play.

As it turned out, neutralization did not extend beyond the case of Austria. That country joined the United Nations without difficulty in 1955. When it applied in 1961 and again in 1963 for associate membership in the European Economic Community, the Soviet Union protested that a neutralized state should refrain from political, economic, and cultural ties with other states as well as from military ties. Austria persevered and won associate membership in the EEC in 1972 notwithstanding Soviet objections. Austria's orientation both economically and politically has been toward the West, and the Soviets for the most part have appeared willing to accept this in return for official and military Austrian neutrality.

In domestic politics, the postwar parliamentary elections up to 1970 resulted in a slight edge for the People's party over the Socialists, with a few seats going to minor groups. When the Communists withdrew their representative from the cabinet in 1947 as a protest against a currency measure, the succeeding governments consisted until 1966 of a coalition of the two major parties. Leaders of both these parties wisely shunned the possibility of governing through an alliance with a minor group. By agreement, the two parties shared in appointments to public office; the chancellors were for some while members of the People's party. An electoral shift gave the People's party sole control in 1966, but in 1970 the Socialists achieved a reversal, and Bruno Kreisky became the first postwar Socialist chancellor, heading a minority government.

Kreisky's electoral success appeared to be in part due to his appeal to younger voters (the minimum age for voting had just been lowered from twenty to nineteen years). Even more so, it was the result of a new image that he gave his party, as he abandoned several traditional Marxist positions for a more moderate stance. Because of these changes, the Roman Catholic church ceased automatically to endorse the People's party; in 1971 an accord was reached between the Vatican and the Austrian government that Austria would pay 100 percent rather than 60 percent of the teachers' salaries in the approximately 100 Roman Catholic schools in the country. Though the Socialists' margin grew only slightly in subsequent elections, they remained in control through the mid-1980s; at times they formed coalitions with the small Freedom party and then, when that party turned markedly to the far

Austrians took pride when Kurt Waldheim served with distinction as secretary general of the United Nations. But their pride turned to dismay when, during Waldheim's 1986 campaign for the Austrian presidency, it was disclosed that he had concealed his knowledge of Nazi crimes against Jews while serving as an officer in the German army during World War II. These revelations opened up old wounds regarding Austrian participation in Nazi Germany's war of aggression but were not enough to prevent Waldheim's election to the presidency. (Photo from Reuters/Bettmann.)

right, with the Christian Democratic party once again in 1987. Legislation generally moved through Parliament smoothly. This included a series of laws on linguistic rights and on the family; in 1976 wives and husbands formally obtained equal status. In the early years of the 1990s, the coalition partners focused their concerns on environmental issues and European integration. Austria clearly sensed a major responsibility for assisting the newly emerging democracies of Eastern Europe in establishment of market economies, enhancement of social welfare, and environmental protection.

The Austrian president is elected to a six-year term by popular vote; in these elections the Socialists regularly carried the day, as they also have in the city elections in Vienna. When Franz Jonas had to resign the presidency for reasons of health in 1974, Kreisky put forward his foreign minister, Rudolph Kirschläger, who was known more as a nonparty specialist than as a Socialist. He won, and in a good example of what some experts call "consociational politics," he won again in 1980 when the major opposition, the People's party, chose not to run a candidate against him.

Controversy arose, however, in 1986, when Kurt Waldheim, former foreign minister and secretary general of the United Nations, ran as an independent candidate but with the support of the People's party, challenging the Socialist nominee. During the campaign, the World Jewish Congress charged that Waldheim, as a German officer during World War II, had participated in anti-Jewish acts and war crimes. This he denied. Nationalist sympathies against outside intervention were aroused, and Waldheim won the balloting. Some nations subsequently refused to invite him for official state visits, causing brief periods of diplomatic hard feelings. The Austrians asked an international panel of historians to study all available documents. It found, in the words of its chairman, "no personal guilty behavior nor participation in war crimes" by Waldheim. Yet it pointed out that he was "excellently informed" of the acts and did nothing about them and that he had concealed his war record in later years. The president claimed he was vindicated but admitted he had kept silent during the war because "I wanted to survive. . . . I have the deepest respect for all those who resisted. But I ask understanding for all the hundreds of thousands who didn't do that, but nonetheless did not become personally guilty." The issue did not go away, for it stimulated further discussion of anti-Semitism within Austria; it also helped to expose the myth that most Austrians had only unwillingly participated in the Nazis' Third Reich. In the fall of 1991, Waldheim announced he would not attempt to run for a second term.

Although the republic was firmly established and universally accepted, the position of the Habsburgs remained a political question for some while. In 1962 the Supreme Administrative Court confirmed the legality of Arch-duke Otto's renunciation of membership in the imperial house of Habsburg-Lorraine and his declaration of loyalty to the Austrian republic. These were prerequisites for the end of his exile and return to Austria. Although the People's party leaned toward accepting the court's ruling, the Socialists raised a clamor. The issue became involved in a cabinet crisis; by agreement between the two parties the decrees barring Otto from Austria remained in effect, finally to be relaxed in 1983.

Economic Development

After World War I Vienna required large food shipments, and the Austrian economy relied upon large international loans for its revival. The same was true after World War II. The United Nations refugee relief agency furnished much aid, and the United States provided even more in outright gifts. While the French and Soviet occupying forces, at least in the first years, lived off the land, Britain and the United States supplied more than their own rations. The cost of the occupying armies was a heavy drain on the Austrian budget. In 1947 the U.S. government returned most of the payments it had received and agreed that henceforth the United States would pay its own occupation costs. Some years later the Soviet Union, Britain, and France followed suit. Because the Austrian economy had been so closely linked with Germany, serious repercussions were felt from events in that country. Inability to obtain replacement parts for broken-down machinery alone constituted a real problem. Rupture of trade relations with southeastern Europe posed a serious handicap.

Several orderly currency reforms helped to stabilize the economy. Austria participated in the Marshall Plan, and a good part of the funds paid for erection of dams and expansion of heavy industry in the Western Zones. Although there were differences as to controls in the four zones and movement among them was not always free, the Austrian economy in general functioned as a unit. The State Treaty of 1955 restored to Austria control over its oil fields and provided for Austrian repurchase of the Danube Shipping Company. The terms of the payment and the agreed deliveries of oil and other goods to the Soviet Union over a period of ten years constituted a heavy burden, yet they were so much more reasonable than previous demands that Austria accepted them willingly. The USSR subsequently agreed to further reduction of oil deliveries and Austria's obligations to the Soviet Union under the treaty were proclaimed fulfilled in 1964. Hydroelectric power was greatly expanded and an excellent network of superhighways constructed. In general the economy flourished. Austria successfully integrated the refugees who remained there after the war and again after the Hungarian revolt of 1956 and the Czechoslovakian crisis of 1968. Economic growth even led Austria to recruit workers from nearby frontier countries.

Austria was an original member of EFTA (formed in 1960); in 1972 Austria also achieved associate membership in the European Economic Community. Previous efforts to join the EEC had been frustrated by questions concerning Austria's neutral status, internal EEC politics, and difficulties with Italy over South Tyrol. Resolution of the last issue enabled Italy to support Austria's bid for EEC membership. Agreements reached in 1972 provided for the gradual elimination of most industrial tariffs between Austria and sixteen other countries by July 1977. The year 1972 marked the inauguration of a value-added tax that bolstered state revenues (it was required by membership in the EEC, which received the returns of the first percent). Austrian imports from Common Market countries tripled over the next thirteen years, and exports to the European Community grew over 400 percent. Thus by 1987 two-thirds of Austria's imports came from the EEC, and 60 percent of its exports flowed to Common Market states. Plans for the creation of a single European market by 1992 and increasing efforts at collaboration between EEC and EFTA countries heightened Austrian interest in full membership in the community. Formal application was again made in 1989, with the proviso that Austria's neutral status should be preserved. At the same time, additional bilateral trade agreements with Comecon nations were explored in the atmosphere of flexibility that *perestroika* was initiating in international economics.

Events in Eastern Europe in 1989 and 1990 proved an economic boon for Austria, as the small country's exports to reunified Germany increased sharply. Austria's industries, many of them export-driven, expanded rapidly and were supported in this growth by a corresponding expansion in the investment sector of the economy. Tourism also grew, favorably affecting Austria's overall balance of trade. The likelihood was strong that Austria would be accepted into the EEC after that organization had completed formation of its single internal market in 1992. Austria also looked forward to participation in the wider market of the proposed European Economic Area.

The oil crises of the 1970s and 1980s had, however, hurt the Austrian oil refining industry and economy. Austria came to rely on hydroelectricity; the one nuclear plant constructed was never put into operation. In 1986 an explosion at the Soviet Chernobyl nuclear plant released radioactive clouds over much of Europe, and two major, well-publicized chemical spills polluted the Rhine. These events deepened Austrian fears that economic modernization could bring dangers for the environment and for the people. On this wave of public concern, the ecologically oriented United Greens party for the first time won sufficient votes to enter Parliament. Steps taken at the close of the 1980s strengthened Austria's competitive position within the European economy. Taxes were cut and shares of oil, high-technology, and banking firms were placed on the market. Such privatization, according to Foreign Minister Alois Mock, formed "part of a larger process of structural reform that aims at modernizing the Austrian economy."[1]

Foreign Affairs

Austria joined the United Nations as one of the sixteen countries in the so-called package deal of 1955. Since then it has been a firm supporter of that organization and has served terms as an elected member of the Security Council. As a participant in the Council of Europe, the OECD, the GATT, and the EFTA, Austria undertook a progressive lowering of tariffs. Over 50 percent of Austria's trade is with Common Market countries. When associate membership in the EEC was finally achieved in 1972 (full membership was not consonant with Austria's neutrality, the USSR held), steps taken to assuage Soviet concern led to a formal economic cooperation accord signed the following year. Beginning in 1960 Austria undertook a modest foreign aid program, much of it devoted to putting Austria's excellent scientific and educational facilities at the disposal of underdeveloped countries.

Difficulties arose with Yugoslavia in the mid-1970s, as that nation became concerned for the rights of Slovenes and Croats in Austrian Carinthia. By a law of 1976, minority groups who made up 25 percent of the population in a given region were granted the right to use their language in schools, businesses, courts, and on street signs. In 1979 the great buildings of the Vienna International Center were completed and rented to the United Nations as an agency headquarters for a schilling a year. Austria's service as a relocation center for refugee Jews en route to Israel led to some difficulties with Arab terrorists. Israel appreciated these services but protested Austrian recognition of the representatives of the Palestine Liberation Organization (PLO) to the UN agencies in Vienna.

Neutrality, far from being a hindrance to Austria's development, has enhanced it. Austrians were spared the costs and difficulties of hosting troops from either bloc and allowed to develop economic ties with the prosperity of the Common Market. Made aware by their history of the dangers of internecine feuding, and far from anxious to be the object of competing advances from either West or East Germany, the Austrians were able for the first time in decades to focus on being Austrians. By the 1990s the amelioration of ethnic and social disputes and the effort, not uncommon in countries ravaged by war, simply to improve the level of daily existence led to a resurgence of a modern Austria more unified and economically viable than that of the prewar and early postwar years.

Switzerland

The Austrians, recognizing the divisions of the interwar years, the ignominy of defeat as part of the Third Reich, and the suffering of invasion and deprivation, accepted the need for change. By contrast, the Swiss, who had enjoyed the relative prosperity of the interwar years and had successfully weathered World War II as part of a neutral country, believed that change should be taken cautiously and only with extensive popular support. Because of these and other factors, the conservative Swiss played a minor role in the postwar development of Europe.

Politics and Economy

During the war the activity and power of the federal government in Switzerland expanded rapidly. Rationing, price control, and all the other things that go with the supervision of a nation's economy had to be done on a federal rather than on a cantonal (state) level. With the end of hostilities, Swiss opinion divided over the question of whether these state controls should be retained. In 1947 a series of amendments to the constitution were approved by national referendum, giving the federal government wide powers to control the nation's economy under certain conditions and for certain ends. The people also approved an old-age security and insurance plan to be administered by the federal government. The federal government retained its emergency taxing powers for a while, but in 1953 a referendum returned them to the cantons.

Postwar elections reflected no striking changes in party alignment, although the leftist parties, as everywhere, gained a few seats. The Communist party, which had been banned in 1940, was permitted to participate in the 1947 elections and won seven out of a total of 196 seats. Subsequent elections saw Communist seats reduced. Communism has no great appeal to the Swiss, and the party has no members in the upper house of the Federal Assembly, which represents the cantons. Since 1959, a four-party coalition made up of the Social Democratic party, Radical Democratic party, Christian Democratic People's party, and the Swiss People's party has always garnered enough votes to control the Federal Assembly. The presidency rotates annually among the leadership of these four parties. Elections are held every four years.

Swiss political parties exercise little discipline, allowing members to vote as they wish. Conflicts within a party are settled by compromises acceptable to the minority. This system helps to define policies that will retain the support of Switzerland's diverse linguistic, religious, and economic groups. (In the late 1980s about 65 percent of the total population spoke German, 18 percent French, and 12 percent Italian, though some of these were not nationals. Only 1 percent spoke the fourth officially recognized language, Romansch, a tongue of ancient Latin origin. About 55 percent were Protestants and 45 percent Roman Catholics.) The system at the same time works against substantial or sudden change and promotes conservative political behavior.

Proposals giving women the right to vote in federal elections, to be elected to the Parliament, and to be appointed to the Supreme Federal Court passed the chambers in 1957–1958. As constitutional amendments, they were subject to a referendum in 1959, in which the voters rejected them. Not until 1971 was legislation giving women the right to vote and run for national offices approved by referendum. Women's suffrage in cantonal affairs was left for each canton to decide. Progress was slow. Only in November 1990, as a result of a federal court ruling, did the last half-canton reluctantly relinquish its position as the only remaining area in Europe that denied women the vote. The cause of women's rights was bolstered in 1981 with the approval by national referendum of a constitutional amendment stating that men and women have equal rights, in the family and at work, and that laws require equal pay for equal work. A 1985 referendum abolished a group of laws that had assured male supremacy within the institution of marriage.

Despite these developments, social change has come slowly in Switzerland. The pace has not been quickened by the practice of submitting many items of legislation to referendum. Some important changes have been made; for example, in 1973 a referendum removed the constitutional ban on the Jesuits and on the establishment of other religious orders. In 1979, after years of wrangling, a twenty-third canton, Jura, the first created since 1848, split from the German-speaking Bern canton. Referenda have rejected the lowering of the voting age below twenty or the granting of a substantial loan to the International Development Association of the World Bank. A surprising amount of popular support (35 percent) was given to a failed proposal to abolish Switzerland's armed forces (every able-bodied male must undergo military training).

At the beginning of the 1980s, predominantly young persons took part in numerous demonstrations against the conservatism of what was called the governing elite, lack of housing and women's rights, crowding of universities, and the manner in which they thought Switzerland was becoming an armed camp that profited well from the sale of weapons. In 1986, environmental activists demonstrated after the Sandoz chemical plant twice poured toxic materials into the Rhine, killing aquatic organisms as far as 200 miles (322.6 km) to the north. Concern about the safety of nuclear energy plants and disposal of their wastes stimulated a referendum in 1990 that banned construction of any new nuclear plants through the end of the century. The five existing facilities, which provide nearly 40 percent of Swiss electrical power, were allowed to continue operation.

Switzerland's economy has traditionally been strong. In the 1980s the nation ranked second in the world, behind Kuwait, in terms of per capita value of gross national product. Tourism brings substantial revenues, as does the banking industry, long known for the privacy and service it renders to wealthy depositors from many lands. Switzerland continues to be a location of choice for large and competitive industries in such fields as chemicals, pharmaceuticals, and machinery; it is also a headquarters of international organizations and for multinational conferences. Switzerland was a founding member of EFTA and has trade pacts with most countries of both Western and Eastern Europe. Commerce, however, is primarily with the countries of the EEC, especially Germany. Switzerland applied for associate membership in the Common Market and after some delay participated in 1972 in treaties signed with sixteen other nations, including Austria, intended to create a Western European free trade area. The relative prosperity of Switzerland, the limited unemployment, and the volatility of monetary events outside the country has led the government to take a variety of measures to guard against inflation and to ensure the continuing strength of the Swiss franc. These have included increased regulations affecting deposits by foreigners in Swiss bank accounts.

The influx of foreign workers poses a special problem. These workers now number well over 1 million in a country with a population of about 6.5 million. Two-thirds come from Italy and many from Spain, both predominantly Catholic countries; some Swiss see in this a danger of upsetting Switzerland's historic social and religious balance. Swiss industrialists insist that foreign labor is badly needed, yet in 1970 the number of workers admitted each year was limited to 40,000. The influx of political refugees in the mid-1980s renewed nationalist backlash against foreigners. Anti-immigrant sentiment has played a role in several referenda intended to limit the percentage of foreign residents in Switzerland; these have been defeated but regularly reappear in new forms. Civil rights have not been extended rapidly to alien workers, and seasonal workers still must wait several years before they may bring their families with them, receive social security, or live outside special residence halls. In 1987 voters strongly supported a plan that limits admission of political refugees yet grants some preference to those from "traditional countries." Critics have suggested that this vote reflected a larger European bias against immigrants from the Third World.

Foreign Affairs

In the spring of 1946, Switzerland resumed diplomatic relations with the USSR, which had been suspended since 1919. Extended negotiations took place between the Swiss and Allied governments over the return of German assets secreted in Swiss banks. The Swiss for a long time refused to meet the Allied demands. They finally agreed to turn over 50 percent of the Nazi funds to the Inter-Allied Reparation Agency for the rehabilitation of countries devastated by Germany and in 1952 terminated the matter with a large lump-sum payment.

In no way a joiner, Switzerland did not become a member of the Council of Europe until 1963. The Swiss government accepted the invitation to collaborate in the Marshall Plan with a reservation safeguarding its traditional neutrality but did not actually receive any Marshall Plan funds. It regularly appropriates aid to developing countries. Though Switzerland is a member of the International Court of Justice and many of the UN specialized agencies, for a long time it expressed little interest in joining the United Nations. Conservatives, who feared such a move, were among those who backed a referendum in 1977 approving a law that requires all treaties for national defense or for membership in international organizations to be submitted to popular ratification. In late summer 1982, however, the government reversed its attitude toward participation and proposed to the Federal Assembly that Switzerland seek membership in the UN, the IMF, and the World Bank. Parliamentary approval followed slowly, but the referendum held in 1986 rejected membership in the UN by a margin greater than three to one. In keeping with its neutrality, Switzerland has continued to be a locus for international conferences. It has also served a useful role in representing interests of countries not in formal diplomatic contact, as, for example, it represented the United States in talks with Cuba and Iran.

The Lowlands

At the close of the war, the three low countries, Belgium, Luxembourg, and the Netherlands, took positive steps to improve their future. Primarily, they agreed to cease their former debilitating economic competition in favor of international trade agreements and the development of economic integration. They supported Western defensive unity against the Soviet bloc and opposed any possible German military resurgence. In this context, the Belgian government provided a major benefit to Western security by granting the United States and Britain first option for a number of years on a rich uranium source in the Belgian Congo. The United States and United Kingdom paid well for this atomic energy fuel; proceeds from a special tax on the ore substantially funded development of a Belgian atomic energy program and plant.

Consensus on economic modernization and foreign relations did not, however, beget consensus on local social, ethnic, and religious issues. In all three countries there were endless debates on domestic problems, although these took different forms in each state. They were especially divisive in Belgium, where they mixed with the volatile question concerning the right of King Leopold III to rule. Some observers suggested that Belgian citizens favored a united Europe because such a Europe diminished the importance of Belgium's own internal divisions.

Reestablishment of Governments

Belgium and Luxembourg were completely liberated in September 1944, although sections of both were temporarily overrun in the Battle of the Bulge that December. Most of the Netherlands remained in enemy hands until the very last. Luxembourg had been incorporated directly into Germany in 1942, but with liberation the government-in-exile returned and took over direction of affairs without difficulty. In Belgium Prince Charles, the younger brother of King Leopold III, became regent in 1944, inasmuch as Leopold was still held captive in Germany. Parliament for a time continued this arrangement after the war. Many Belgians objected to the king's capitulation in 1940, his subsequent marriage to a commoner, and his supposedly authoritarian leanings. Leopold's cause intertwined with the Flemish question, for his wife was a Fleming and Flanders is the stronghold of the Catholic party, which supported him. The Flemish movement had grown during the German occupation. The return of the king was an issue in the elections of 1949, in which women voted for the first time. The Catholic party made notable gains, and, in a special referendum in 1950, 57.7 percent of the voters favored Leopold's resuming the throne. On Leopold's return to Belgium in July 1950 after six years of exile, the Socialist opposition approached revolutionary proportions, becoming so virulent that Leopold agreed to retire at once and to abdicate in 1951 when his son Baudouin would become of age. This solution was accepted. In August 1950 Baudouin was invested with the royal power, formally ascending the throne the following year.

The reestablishment of the government in the Netherlands after the war occurred without undue political strife. Many collaborators were arrested, and the execution of two of them marked the first break since 1854 in Holland's abstention from capital punishment. After celebrating her fiftieth anniversary on the throne in 1948, Queen Wilhelmina abdicated in favor of her daughter, Juliana. She in turn abdicated on her seventy-first birthday in 1980 and was succeeded by her daughter Beatrix.

The Economy and International Relations

By the time the Netherlands could start rebuilding, the economy of Belgium was functioning again and earning valuable foreign exchange through services to the Allied armies. Belgium soon ranked as the most prosperous of the European states that had been at war. Recovery in the Netherlands was slower, but by the end of 1945 all the flooded areas were drained and a real beginning had been made on the rehabilitation of agriculture, the most important Dutch occupation. The revival of the German market benefited the Lowland countries, for Germany has always accounted for a large share of their exports and imports. In 1954 an Amsterdam-Rhine canal opened, cutting shipping time from the German border to Amsterdam to twenty hours. Both Belgium and the Netherlands pursued an aggressive policy of extension and modernization of their internal waterway systems, and in 1963 they undertook a new canal joining the Antwerp and Scheldt rivers with the Rhine. Modernization and expansion, especially of tanker-servicing facilities, made Rotterdam the world's busiest port.

In the eyes of Dutch diplomats, the Netherlands' empire in Indonesia qualified their country as a middle power. They sought recognition as such and were angered when plans for the United Nations did not grant an explicit role for middle powers or reserve a permanent seat for them on the Security Council. U.S. criticism of colonialism and interest in an economic open door in Indonesia also aroused Dutch ire. Unlike the Belgians, the Dutch for a while opposed any Western pacts outside the United Nations, thinking them likely to offend the Soviet Union. The Dutch altered this position and supported the Brussels treaty of 1948 as a means of enhancing their own position within the councils of the West. They were also influenced by the commitment of the United States to European security as expressed through the Truman and Marshall plans. For Belgian and Dutch foreign policy, the 1948 Communist coup in Prague had only modest impact, as the direction of their policy was already set. The Dutch nevertheless briefly considered not participating in NATO as a means of forcing the United States to end its opposition to Dutch colonial policy and military actions in Indonesia.

The granting of independence to the Dutch colonies in the East Indies (1949) and to Belgian colonial territories in the Congo (1960) necessitated many adjustments. For a country the size of the Netherlands, the loss of Indonesia constituted a severe economic blow. During the interwar years, the sale of Indonesian raw goods to the United States had brought many dollars to the Netherlands and been a key source of Dutch prosperity. Yet the ending of the colonial war, which for so long had economically and psychologically drained the Netherlands, did have some good effects. Energies and resources were promptly turned to the rapid expansion of the domestic economy, especially of the shipping facilities central to the Netherlands' role as an entry port to Europe.

The Congo became independent only with extensive difficulties involving loss of life and financial holdings. Belgium also suffered embarrassment as the United Nations intervened. Since 1960 the Belgians have put considerable effort and financial aid into their continuing relations with the new nation of Zaire, and they still have extensive investments there.

The colonial conflicts were costly, both in terms of investment losses and in human terms. Returning colonials had to be absorbed into the economy at home. In Belgium an austerity program reducing social insurance benefits and increasing taxes brought a rash of strikes. To alleviate some of the grievances the government passed a national insurance law in 1963 that covered more than two-thirds of the population. It set up a rate of standard fees (raised after a doctors' strike) for medical care and provided free treatment for invalids, orphans, and widows.

Discovery in 1961 of natural gas and oil in the coastal waters of the Netherlands added greatly to the limited supply of natural resources. In 1967 the Netherlands, Belgium, and West Germany agreed to build a $100 million fast-breeder nuclear reactor capable of generating 300 megawatts of electricity. The Dutch economy performed well for most of the succeeding years but reflected strain in the 1980s as increasingly large sums devoted to social welfare programs forced taxes upward just as the European economy sagged.

In the Grand Duchy of Luxembourg, the effect of this economic decline on ARBED, one of the largest European steel conglomerates formed after the war, was balanced by the phenomenal growth of the international banking industry. By the middle of the decade, Luxembourg ranked as the third largest banking center in Europe, after London and Paris. It was the hope of the duchy that it would become the permanent seat of the European Parliament, but by 1983 it had lost its bid to Strasbourg.

Meeting in London in 1944, representatives of the Dutch and Belgian governments agreed to adopt a common customs policy after the war. In 1946 a council was established to integrate the two tariff systems, a difficult task because the Belgian tariffs were relatively high and specific, whereas the Dutch rates were low and levied on an ad valorem basis. The compromise substantially increased Dutch rates. As Belgium and Luxembourg had already formed an economic union in 1921, this new agreement became the basis of the Benelux Union of Belgium, the Netherlands, and Luxembourg, which went into effect on January 1, 1948. Benelux was to play a major role in the future development of the three Low Countries and serve both as a model and stimulus for further European integration.

The accord provided a common tariff against outside states, but it did not bring free internal trade. Varying excise taxes remained that were collected when goods passed from one country to another. Salt, for example, bore an excise in the Netherlands but not in Belgium, and the reverse was true of matches and vinegar. Complete economic union, originally planned for 1950, was not then achieved, primarily because of wage differences and agricultural costs; but economic integration constantly increased in the 1950s. In 1958 a series of agreements establishing the Benelux Economic Union was signed. The treaties, which went into effect November 1, 1960, and are to run for fifty years, consolidated the arrangements that had gradually been achieved. These arrangements freed all trade between the countries from tariffs and liberated about 97 percent of trade from restrictions on volume. They also reduced tax differences, set up a common trade and payments policy toward other nations, and established a single labor market with free movement of workers. Negotiations for trade agreements with other countries now take place on a joint Benelux basis. The agreements are administered by a committee of ministers. It makes major decisions that are then referred to their respective national parliaments for ratification. There is an Inter-Parliamentary Advisory Council (twenty representatives each from Belgium and the Netherlands, nine from Luxembourg) and a secretariat general. Benelux economy has benefited greatly from the establishment of the Common Market.

The original Benelux agreement was purely an economic one, yet the three states have tended to carry their cooperation over into the political field; indeed, their own cooperation has to an extent been a model for subsequent larger collaboration efforts. Two Belgian politicians, Paul van Zeeland and Paul-Henri Spaak, the first a conservative, the second a Socialist, became active spokesmen for a united Europe even before the end of the war. Some Belgians expressed concern that their small country might be severely overridden in a large treaty organization such as NATO. Spaak, who would serve as NATO's secretary general from 1957 to 1961, argued the need for a common front:

> Let us end our timid efforts, which at best show vague good will more than a closer awareness of realities, and let us accept the consequences of the plain fact that the fate of all of us in the West is inextricably linked. The atom bomb leaves no room for neutrality or separate national policies. The West is condemned not only to wage war together but to create policy together. . . . The Atlantic Alliance is a great thing.[2]

The willingness of the Low Countries to further efforts toward international cooperation in Europe became increasingly evident. They participated in the Brussels Pact (1948) leading to the Western European Union (1955), the OEEC (1948), the Council of Europe (1948), NATO (1949), the

The socialism of Paul-Henri Spaak (right) of Belgium was inspired by a strong sense of justice and concern for the common individual. It moved from radicalism to a belief that capitalism, instead of being overthrown, should be used to improve the lot of all citizens, especially the working class. As foreign minister of Belgium before World War II, Spaak was the architect of its independent foreign policy. After the war he became a leading advocate of international cooperation and European integration, and his diplomatic skills won him the sobriquet of "Mr. Europe." Here he is shown in 1967 with one of the authors of this volume, Jonathan Helmreich. (Photo courtesy of Allegheny College.)

ECSC (1952), the EEC (1958), and EURATOM (1958). When de Gaulle forced the withdrawal of Supreme Headquarters of the Allied Powers Europe (SHAPE) from France in 1967, it was shifted to Castreau, Belgium, and the headquarters of NATO to a town just south of Brussels. It can safely be said that over time the Benelux states have tended to follow a common line on questions of foreign policy.

The issue of stationing U.S. intermediate-range nuclear missiles in Europe provoked severe debate in the middle 1980s. Although political leaders of all the major parties approved the NATO plan and recognized the necessity of accepting the missiles on their soil, antinuclear groups protested with vehemence. This was especially true in the Netherlands, where street demonstrators found sympathy in the chambers. In 1985 the Belgian Parliament voted to accept a limited number of missiles. The debate in the Netherlands was more intense. The government approved deployment in some years' time, but the controversy that would have accompanied actual deployment was averted by the Soviet-U.S. intermediate-range missile disarmament pact of 1987.

Political Development

In all three countries the first postwar elections indicated an increase in the strength of the Catholic parties. They were, however, unable to command a clear majority and therefore cooperated with other parties, including the Socialists. In the Netherlands the presence of numerous minor parties offsets the ideological clash between Clericals and Socialists. The Dutch Catholic church has been at the forefront of the movement to modernize the Catholic church and has been open to change in political spheres as well. The rather pure proportional representation system in the Netherlands has at times caused problems, as coalition cabinets are often required to incorporate a wide spread of parties to obtain a parliamentary majority. During the 1970s there was talk of a constitutional revision and a shift to single-member elected districts, but nothing came of it despite the 208 days required to form just one cabinet in 1978.

In Belgium three great political issues clouded the scene. One was the question of Leopold III's return, which aroused much strife before it was settled. The second was the old problem of state subsidies for Catholic-controlled schools. These grants increased when pro-Catholic cabinets were in power; under a Socialist-Liberal cabinet in 1955, there was a substantial reduction in state subsidies to Catholic schools in an effort to strengthen state schools. Unrest and mass demonstrations resulted. When the three major parties—Christian Socialists, Socialists, and Liberals—finally reached an agreement, Parliament passed an education law in 1959 that allayed the controversy. A special fund was created to overcome the shortage of state schools; these would be established if a sufficient number of parents in a district requested one. Church schools were given the same subsidies as public schools, and parents were free to choose which type of school their children should attend. Payments of fees for secondary education were abolished.

The third great political issue in Belgium, the conflict between the Flemings and Walloons, is of long standing and has many facets. The coal industry, the mainstay in the economy of the Walloon sections, has become obsolete, and the newer industries have shifted to the Flemish regions. The balance between the two groups has been affected by the higher birthrate among the Flemings, who now outnumber the Walloons by more than a five-to-three ratio. Politically, Flanders constitutes the stronghold of the Christian Socialists; the Socialists and Liberals are numerous in the less clerically minded Walloon areas. As so often happens, nationality conflicts come to center on linguistic differences. A law of 1932 required the exclusive use of the predominant language in each community. To determine which language predominated was not easy, and traditional practices were continued, which usually gave an advantage to French. Under pressure the government drew a dividing line in 1962, subsequently revised, that provided for the administrative division of the country into unilingual Flemish and Walloon regions, with greater Brussels remaining bilingual. This meant doing away with former bilingual administrative and educational systems in many localities. Additional laws provided for a completely bilingual state administration, extending even to the diplomatic service. Feeling ran high on these measures, and there were many public demonstrations. The Catholic University of Louvain was located inside the Flemish linguistic border; beginning in 1965 the Flemings demanded that it become an entirely Flemish teaching institution. Riots erupted, and the bishops divided along nationality lines in an unsuccessful attempt to find a way out. This led to a government crisis in 1968 and further measures to ensure absolute parity between Flemings and Walloons in all spheres of national life. Henceforth there were to be dual ministers for education, culture, and community relations. An agreement reached in 1970 divided the universities of Louvain and Brussels into separate French- and Flemish-speaking universities.

Increasingly it appeared that the only solution to the linguistic issue would be the establishment of a federated Belgium made up of Flanders (Flemish- or Dutch-speaking), Wallonia (French-speaking), and Brussels (bilingual). Legislation to that effect failed in 1970, but the following year extensive reforms were approved. Autonomy in cultural matters was granted to the two linguistic groups and the boundaries and status of bilingual Brussels further defined. Special regional councils were to implement this legislation, and the German-speaking district in the east was to be administered by the ministry of interior. A two-thirds majority in Parliament had to approve specific powers for the regional councils. Because such a majority could not be mustered, nonelective consultative councils were created in 1974. Cabinet after cabinet fell on the issue.

In 1980 a different autonomy plan created parliaments for Wallonia and Flanders. No agreement could be reached on Brussels. The capital remained a French-dominated enclave in the Flemish-speaking region. The Flemings did not wish to see it expand but, because of the presence of many Common Market institutions and the nearby headquarters of NATO, its growth was inexorable. Ministerial instability was further increased by economic difficulties. Unemployment grew in measure with the energy crisis and the decline of the fortunes of Belgium's textile and steel mills, which could not meet foreign competition. Severe austerity measures in the 1980s brought street demonstrations, yet there seemed no other economic course for the government to follow. Linguistic controversies in the last years of the decade forestalled progress in budget control and tax reform. The king finally charged his ministers with devising further constitutional revisions to resolve disputes on language-related issues. In 1989 a regional government was formed for Brussels. About one-third of the national budget, including funds for roads and communication, education, and scientific research, shifted to the three regions for their direct administration. A new constitutional court was also established to deal with conflicts arising from the progressive devolution of central government powers to the three regions.

Thus the imperatives of political modernization seemed to call for continuing decentralization of authority in Belgium, yet this very decentralization created additional expenses and got in the way of economic and military efficiency. At the same time, such decentralization did achieve a broader distribution of governing power, and the range of social services funded by the central government worked toward the same end in the economic sphere. Achievement of what was at least a temporary modus vivendi on the linguistic issue allowed some controversial social issues to be addressed. In 1990 the age of majority was dropped to allow eighteen-year-olds to marry without parental permission, the minimum age for divorce was lowered from twenty-three to twenty, and abortions were made legal under certain restrictions.

Ireland

The post–World War II years for Ireland were dominated by the same three issues that had throbbed so strongly in the interwar years: relations with Great Britain, desire to unite the six counties of Northern Ireland with the southern region, and economic survival. The issues were interrelated and were all the more awkward to deal with because Irish political sensitivities called for distancing Ireland from Britain, whereas Ireland's economic needs required cooperation with the United Kingdom. Roman Catholic–Protestant differences and the long history of animosity between Ireland and Britain only made resolution of the problems more difficult.

In 1914 the Irish had finally won the right to home rule from the British Parliament. The onset of World War I caused the British to postpone implementation of home rule, much to the anger of many Irish; the most militant of them staged an unsuccessful rebellion on Easter Sunday in 1916. There were Irish, however, in the northern six counties of the island (a region commonly referred to as Ulster) who did not want to sever ties with Great Britain. The residents of these predominantly Protestant and industrial counties feared that their way of life and interests would suffer if they were submerged in a political entity dominated by the larger, strongly Roman Catholic and agricultural region of southern Ireland. The northerners laid in a goodly supply of arms.

In the south, the republican political organization Sinn Fein gathered arms as well. In 1918 it called a National Assembly and proclaimed Ireland a republic. The British tried to reestablish their control and were challenged by the guerrilla warfare of the newly organized Irish Republican Army. After months of civil war, a new Government of Ireland Act was passed in London in 1920. It prescribed that separate parliaments be established in the northern and southern parts of Ireland. The next year the British offered Ireland dominion status and persuaded the government that the southern Irish had formed to negotiate on that basis. The result was a treaty, signed in December 1921, granting southern Ireland dominion status as the Irish Free State. Ulster continued under the existing arrangements.

Militant Irish nationalists in the south, led by Eamon de Valera, opposed this solution and continued to fight for full separation from Britain and for membership of Ulster in the Irish Free State. De Valera's campaign eventually won him the presidency of the Dail, the Irish parliament, in 1932. From this position he pushed forward his program of breaking off the remaining legal ties with Britain. In 1937 a new constitution was accepted by a national plebiscite. It changed the name of the free state to Eire but, although it contained many provisions asserting the independence of Eire, did not go so far as to declare a republic. The position of the king in Ireland was not clearly defined; the office of the governor general, traditionally the representative of the king in a dominion, was henceforth held by the Irish president.

Severance from Britain

Ireland remained neutral during World War II, the only dominion of the British Commonwealth to do so. This meant it was not classed as one of the peace-loving states and hence was not one of the charter members of the United Nations. Membership was finally achieved in 1955, as part of the so-called package deal when sixteen states were admitted at once. In 1948 the Parliament of Eire repealed the "External Relations Act" (signed a decade earlier to regularize relations with Westminster) and broke the last legal ties connecting Eire with Britain. In commemoration of the Easter rebellion of 1916, this act went into effect on Easter Monday, April 18, 1949. The name of Eire officially changed to the Republic of Ireland, and Ireland ceased to be a member of the Commonwealth. Every effort was made to persuade the six northern counties of Ulster to join with Ireland. Yet elections there seemed to show that the majority wished to remain a part of the United Kingdom (the validity of voting procedures has been challenged). The government in London recognized Ireland as no longer belonging to the king's dominions. It refused, however, to class it as a foreign state, and relations with the republic are handled by the secretary for Commonwealth affairs, not by the foreign minister. The British nationality act inaugurated in 1949 created three types of citizens: United Kingdom citizens, Commonwealth citizens, and Irish citizens. It provided that members of the three categories would enjoy equal rights and privileges in the United Kingdom, rights not enjoyed by citizens of any other countries. Citizens of the Irish republic who live in a British constituency, for example, are entitled to be included in the registry of electors and can vote. Whatever they would be, it was clear that the Irish were not yet considered foreigners in Britain, although there could be no doubt how the Irish of the republic considered themselves.

The economies of the two countries remain closely linked. Both countries shifted to decimal currencies in 1974. The one-for-one link between the Irish and British pounds was broken in 1979; as a result of market forces, the workings of the European Monetary System required intervention to strengthen the Irish pound. A 1966 free trade agreement between Ireland and Britain provided for gradual reduction of import duties in both countries until their abolition in 1975. Ireland is economically dependent on Britain, which in 1982 accounted for approximately 38.8 percent of Ireland's exports and 48 percent of its imports. In addition to trade ties, Ireland and Great Britain concluded a reciprocal social security agreement (1961). When Britain applied for membership in the Common Market, Ireland followed suit. Both suffered a French veto, primarily because French president de Gaulle wished to limit Anglo-Saxon influence on the Continent but also because French agriculture would suffer in competition with cheaper Irish products. After British and Irish applications to the EEC were approved in 1971, a referendum in Ireland the following year endorsed entry of the country into the Economic Community. In subsequent years, as the Irish economy has suffered setbacks, the EEC has provided help in the form of loans.

Relations with Ulster

In 1959 de Valera, who had held the office of prime minister six times, gave up his post and ran for the presidency, a post he easily won. He served until retirement in 1973 at the age of ninety-one and died two years later. Relations with Northern Ireland gradually improved. The IRA, which had sought to force unity through a policy of terrorism, in February 1962 announced the end of its campaign. This step eased the international position and domestic economy of the Irish republic. For the first time since partition, the prime ministers of Ireland and Ulster held a conference in 1965, and similar meetings have taken place since then.

In spite of more contacts between the two countries and more cooperation on the governmental level, antagonism between the Irish of the republic and the Irish of Ulster continued to flare. Within Ulster, violent confrontations between Protestants and Catholics took place with increasing frequency; the loss of life mounted. The IRA, far from abandoning its efforts, reconcentrated them in the form of waging a civil war within Northern Ireland, retreating over the border for rest and safety in the south when necessary. Prime ministers in the republic were faced with a ticklish task in terms of their posture regarding the civil war to the north. Jack Lynch, a leader of the Fianna Fail party (Party of Destiny) who served as prime minister on several occasions, supported the reunion of Ireland but only by peaceful means. This position seemed inadequate to some Irish nationalists, Anglophobes, and opponents of Ulster Protestants. As the number of terrorist acts within the republic mounted, Lynch and the Dail in 1972 attempted to crack down on the IRA; special three-judge courts were created to try terrorists, as juries seldom brought any verdict but acquittal (perhaps out of fear of retribution).

Lynch's successor, the more moderate Liam Cosgrave of the Fine Gail (United Ireland) party, even met with British prime minister Heath and Prime

Minister A. Brian Faulkner of Ulster at the Sunningdale conference in 1973 to plan the creation of a Council of Ireland. This, like other proposed arrangements, proved abortive. In 1985 British prime minister Thatcher and Irish prime minister FitzGerald agreed once more on a joint body that would be called the British-Irish Intergovernmental Conference. It was intended to give the republic some voice in Protestant-Catholic relations in Ulster; FitzGerald in return formally acknowledged the desire of Ulster to be ruled by Britain. It was his hope in the long run to bring about peaceful union by so shaping the republic that it would appear attractive to the northerners: "If we could create a state down here which they could accept, and they could find the civil and religious liberties in which they believe, they would be willing to think again." The difficulties he would experience in such an effort were reflected in the electorate's vote in 1983 declaring abortion unconstitutional, the opposition of the Roman church to a barely passed 1985 measure making contraceptive devices available to persons over eighteen, and the populace's rejection the following year of a proposal to permit divorce under extensive restrictions. Continuing guerrilla tactics of the militant Provisional IRA in the north, Britain, and even Gilbraltar also indicated the unlikeliness of any prompt, peaceful compromise on the Ulster issue.

Concern for a united Ireland and the question of what policies to follow in achieving it remain the major political issue in the republic. Since the middle 1970s, the issue has been joined by another serious one: the economy. Ireland was hit hard by many of the factors that had negative influence upon the European economy as a whole in these years. Offshore gas and oil explorations did not produce nearly the yields expected; meanwhile, inflation and unemployment mounted. Wage freezes could not be maintained for long, and sharp increases in the value-added tax could not meet the costs of social services demanded by the populace. Cabinets fell over economic issues; yet each successor could only prescribe additional austerity measures, which in turn threatened popular welfare programs. Thus, although the need for economic modernization seemed clear and although some leaders argued for political and social restructuring as the best path to unification of the Irelands, no clear consensus supportive of decisive action developed.

The Scandinavian States

The four Scandinavian states—Denmark, Iceland, Norway, and Sweden— have a long history of close relations and speak variants of what is in effect a common language (linguistically distinctive Finland is usually not considered part of this group). Iceland and Norway had been under the rule of Danish kings since the fourteenth century, until Norway was ceded to Sweden in 1814. In 1905 Norway seceded from Sweden to become an independent state. In 1918 Iceland in the North Atlantic became an independent state sharing a common sovereign with Denmark, and in 1944 it declared its independence as a republic.

The three Scandinavian states in Europe—Denmark, Norway, and Sweden—emerged from the war with differing experiences. Sweden benefited from its neutrality, not only by avoiding destruction but also by selling industrial goods to both sides of the conflict. Denmark and Norway were both occupied by the Germans, and they were forced to submit to Nazi rule and to contribute to the German war effort. They regained their traditions as liberal monarchies, however, as soon as the war was over. Denmark and Norway became original members of the United Nations, and Sweden and Iceland were admitted in 1946. Norway and Denmark sent contingents to serve in the British zone in Germany.

The Political Scene

Only the Norwegian government was in exile during the war, and it promised from the very beginning to resign immediately upon its return to Norway. A new cabinet consisting partly of old officials and partly of resistance leaders was formed without a political crisis. In both Denmark and Norway, collaborators were arrested by the thousands, and the leaders (among them the notorious Nazi-supported Norwegian dictator, Vidkun Quisling) were executed. Elections in all these states showed a remarkable continuation of the prewar pattern. The Communists' influence was at its height in the immediate postwar elections but has since declined.

In Denmark the Social Democrats, except for brief interludes, headed the governments until 1982. Various non-Socialist—often minority—governments have ruled since then. For a while, frequent but calm cabinet reshufflings became a feature of the Danish political scene. The Social Democrats' continuing control of a number of seats in the Folketing (the Danish unicameral parliament) enables them to act as a brake on government economic programs and efforts to trim social welfare expenses.

In Norway the Labor party dominated for thirty years but in 1961 lost its majority in the Storting (the Norwegian national assembly) elections. It stayed in power for two more years by working with other parties and then gave way to a Conservative-Liberal coalition. Since then the two groupings have alternated in control of the government, occasionally maintaining minority cabinets dependent upon the votes of the opposition to stay in power. In Norway as in several other countries, the Socialists no longer proclaim adherence to the Marx-Engels ideology and have adopted a gradualist-reformist attitude.

A major debate broke forth in 1990, as increasing numbers of Norwegians came to believe their country should join the European Community. The agrarian Center party, however, rejected EC membership, for it would require abandonment of Norway's concessionary laws restricting foreign ownership

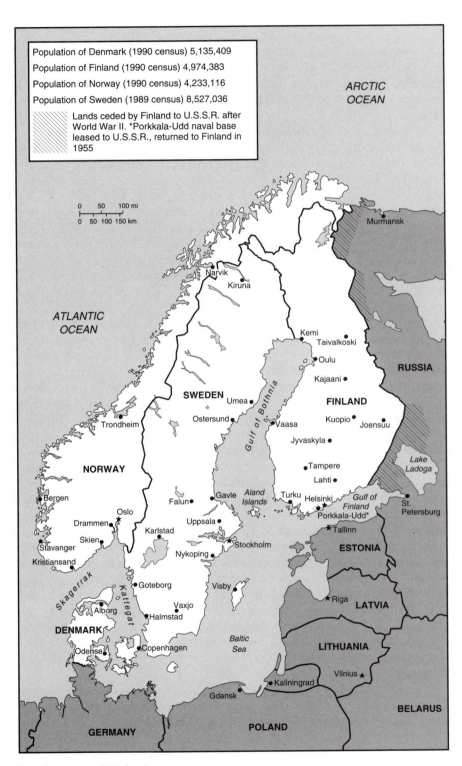

Population of Denmark (1990 census) 5,135,409
Population of Finland (1990 census) 4,974,383
Population of Norway (1990 census) 4,233,116
Population of Sweden (1989 census) 8,527,036

Lands ceded by Finland to U.S.S.R. after World War II. *Porkkala-Udd naval base leased to U.S.S.R., returned to Finland in 1955

0   50   100 mi
0 50 100 150 km

ARCTIC OCEAN

ATLANTIC OCEAN

Murmansk

Narvik
Kiruna

Kemi
Taivalkoski
Oulu
Kajaani

RUSSIA

SWEDEN   Umea
Ostersund
Vaasa
Trondheim

Kuopio
Joensuu
Jyvaskyla

FINLAND

Lake Ladoga

NORWAY

Tampere
Lahti

Bergen
Falun
Gavle
Aland Islands
Turku   Helsinki
Gulf of Finland
Porkkala-Udd*

St. Petersburg

Oslo
Drammen
Skien
Stavanger
Kristiansand

Karlstad
Uppsala
Nykoping

Stockholm

Tallinn

ESTONIA

Goteborg
Visby

Riga   LATVIA

Skagerrak
Kattegat
Alborg
Halmstad
Vaxjo

DENMARK

Odense
Copenhagen

Baltic Sea

LITHUANIA

Vilnius

Kaliningrad
Gdansk

BELARUS

GERMANY   POLAND

Gulf of Bothnia

Scandinavia and Finland

of businesses, financial institutions, and property in Norway. The non-Socialist governing coalition of which the Center party was a member therefore came apart. It was replaced by a minority Labor cabinet that favored eventual entry into the EC and received support on this point from various other parties as well.

For most of the postwar years Swedish politics were dominated by the Social Democratic party, with its emphasis on full employment and a strong social welfare program. A coalition of Moderates (formerly called the Conservatives), Liberals, and representatives of the Center party (formerly called the Agrarian party) took over in 1976 but disintegrated over the volatile issue of nuclear energy. A minority Liberal government soon fell, as did two more coalition cabinets before the Social Democrats resumed power in 1982. They were led by Olof Palme, a principal advocate of the welfare state and a leader of the nonaligned nations. His assassination in 1986 disrupted the peaceful evolution of Swedish politics; after years of inquiry, no direct connection could be found between the act of his alleged assassin and Palme's policies and views.

In the 1980s the Left party (Communist) retained only slightly more than 5 percent of the voters and spoke out critically against Soviet actions in Afghanistan and Poland; it traditionally has given tacit support to Social Democratic cabinets. In 1988 an environmental Green party for the first time achieved enough votes to hold seats in the Riksdag (the Swedish unicameral parliament). Though out of office, the Moderates slowly increased their following, as business, professional, and young voters were drawn to their program of free enterprise, reduced growth of the public sector of the economy, and closer ties with the West.

Discontent over high (for Sweden) unemployment, soaring inflation, trade deficits, and taxes that consumed some 57.7 percent of the Swedish gross national product—the highest percentage for any Western nation—eventually brought repudiation of the Social Democrats. Prime Minister Ingvar Carlsson proposed an austerity budget in 1990. The Left party refused to accept a wage freeze; the plan fell, and the government with it. No viable political alternative to Carlsson proved available, and so he returned to power. With the aid of Left party votes, he guided through the Riksdag legislation that provided freezes on rents and prices but none on wages. He advocated joint application by the Nordic nations to the EC and criticized Norway for snagging talks between the Nordic Council (a consultative council involving the Scandinavian states plus Finland) and the EC over the creation of a European Economic Area for free trade. But in the elections of 1991, the Social Democrats suffered their worst defeat since 1928.

The victorious Moderates, Liberals, Center, and Christian Democrats, all groupings of the Center-Right, nevertheless could not form a majority government without the support of a dissident right party, New Democracy.

This new grouping was not content with the prospect of minor reductions in the welfare state but rather demanded that it be dismantled. A Moderate-led minority government was therefore formed, with the New Democrats abstaining on the vote of confidence. It appeared that government policy would shift to the right, but just how much Socialist programs would be reduced remained uncertain. The volatility of the issues and the wider division of view within the Riksdag gave promise in any case that sharp debates and more political battles lay in the future.

In all three countries monarchy remains an accepted and popular institution. Some constitutional revisions have been achieved, however. Denmark accepted a new constitution in 1953 that introduced a unicameral legislature and provided for direct representation in that body from Greenland and the Faeroe Islands. The voting age dropped from twenty-five to twenty-three, and female succession to the throne was recognized. Norway in 1952 passed an electoral reform bill rectifying the overrepresentation of rural districts. Sweden inaugurated a major constitutional change in 1970–1971, replacing the bicameral system with a 350-member unicameral parliament elected for a three-year term. Like the West Germans, the Swedes adopted measures to curb splinter parties that often result from proportional representation.

Social Legislation

A key aspect of modernization involves the dispersion of the benefits accrued from the scientific and technological revolution to all sectors of the population. The intention is that the benefits not accumulate to the advantage of only one segment of the society or, worse yet, fail significantly to affect society at all. The Scandinavian states take pride in the manner in which progress has been shared throughout their societies. Social insurance legislation has been regularly extended in all three nations. In 1954 agreements were reached among Denmark, Norway, and Sweden covering the principal fields of social security; workers thereafter could go from country to country without losing their benefits. The agreements, along with the abolition of earlier work permits, did much to establish a common labor market. Iceland and Finland joined in the movement for labor cooperation on a more limited scale. In Denmark, government-subsidized health insurance programs cover about 80 percent of the population on a voluntary basis. The obligatory health insurance program was expanded in Norway in 1956 to cover all Norwegians. Further expansion of Norway's social welfare system took place in the 1980s, financed by revenues obtained from exploitation of newly developed oil and natural gas reserves.

Denmark has long enjoyed a rich cultural life, and in 1961 a ministry of cultural affairs was created as part of a government policy to spread and democratize cultural life and to enrich the citizens' leisure. In the 1970s protest movements, even street demonstrations, were recognized as cultural events because the government wished to encourage social change. In the 1980s, however, a less bold policy was followed. Budgetary problems slowed the extension of the program, yet in 1987 Denmark was spending approximately $52 per capita on cultural matters, primarily in support of libraries, museums, theaters, and films.

Sweden has long been known for its tradition of the "middle way," that is, the combination of private capitalist enterprise with extensive government involvement in the economy and a developed system of social welfare. A landmark in this involvement is the system of social security, which grew significantly in the postwar decades. On January 1, 1955, a universal health insurance plan went into effect. An extension of older programs, it was financed by premiums paid by the insured (44 percent), contributions from employers (29 percent) and from the state (27 percent). By another law the famous Bratt liquor-rationing system was ended in 1955. The state retained the monopoly of all sales of spirits, wines, and strong beers. Consumption is discouraged by imposing high taxes; for example, taxes make up 89 percent of the price of a bottle of aquavit. Restaurants can dispense spirits only under a strict licensing system, and driving under the influence of liquor is heavily penalized. The government also sponsors an active temperance program. Serious differences arose in Sweden in the fall of 1957 over whether an additional old-age pension plan should be obligatory or voluntary. This dispute led to a cabinet crisis, and in a referendum the compulsory plan advocated by the Socialists won over the voluntary plans advocated by the the Agrarians and Liberals. Old-age pensions have also been increased in Norway and Denmark. Sweden guarantees a place in its public child-care system for all children between two and six years of age, and beginning in 1989 it required upper secondary education of all teenagers.

The provision of such extensive welfare services as offered in Sweden is costly, and by the decade of the 1990s the system was facing severe challenges. Citizen groups called for reduction of taxes yet insisted that program benefits be maintained. Indeed, there was need for program expansion in order to deal with the increasing drug-abuse problem. The percentage of the population over sixty-five years of age was growing (Sweden has a high life expectancy rate) and requiring health and pension services. Shortages of places in day-care programs and public old-age homes have caused complaints. Advanced medical services are overburdened, and the waiting period for certain elective and highly technical procedures such as cataract and heart bypass surgery is long. The birthrate has been low, thus bringing a decline in the number of workers paying into the programs compared with the retired population drawing benefits. Record levels of immigration have augmented the working population, but this, too, proves a problem, as the integration of immigrants and their families into the welfare program has burdened the system.

Economic Developments

A mixed economy, with government ownership or control dominating the utility and public services industries, continues to be the rule in Scandinavia. To help pay for imports through shipping services Norway rebuilt its merchant fleet so that it ranked third in the world as compared to fourth before the war. In 1952 the Norwegian government launched a ten-year economic development plan for northern Norway. The development of water power in this region was keyed to the rich ore deposits in neighboring Sweden. All the states became more industrialized, and the high quality of Swedish products gained world renown. Agriculture, however, suffered a relative decline. The number of farms is steadily diminishing as more mechanization takes place. Today only some 20 to 26 percent of the Scandinavian population is fully employed in agriculture. Agricultural exports in the form of dairy products are most important in Denmark.

At meetings of the foreign ministers of Denmark, Iceland, Norway, and Sweden in 1947 and 1948 it was decided to set up a Committee on Economic Cooperation with a permanent secretariat. This committee investigated the possibilities of establishing a common tariff schedule, reduction of inter-Scandinavian customs duties, limitation of quantitative trade restrictions, and in general an increase in economic cooperation among the Scandinavian states. In 1952 a consultative Nordic Council was founded made up of representatives from the above four states. Finland was invited to join but did not participate until 1955, when the Soviet Union no longer objected to Finnish cooperation in the council. Attended by cabinet and parliamentary representatives, the council has discussed and planned a wide variety of measures envisaging greater cooperation among the northern powers.

In 1957 the Committee on Economic Cooperation submitted a detailed report to the governments outlining a draft convention for a customs union. The plan for a Scandinavian tariff union was superseded by the conclusion of the European Free Trade Association in 1960, in which the three Scandinavian states were joined by Austria, Britain, Portugal, and Switzerland. Finland joined the group as an associate member in 1961 and as a full member in 1986. In a national referendum held in 1972, Norway rejected membership in the European Economic Community. Denmark was admitted to the Common Market in 1973, but its Greenland province chose to withdraw in 1982. As the only Nordic state in the EC, Denmark plays a key role as a bridge between the two regions. Sweden, always more concerned to preserve its strict neutrality because of its proximity to the USSR and Finland, held aloof from direct ties with the EEC until 1967, when it sought associate membership. In 1969 the governments of Denmark, Norway, Sweden, and Finland released plans for the economic integration of the four countries into a Nordic Economic Union.

The costs of the social welfare programs in the Scandinavian states have grown more rapidly than state revenues. This has resulted in what is known as the crisis of the welfare state, shared to some extent by Great Britain and West Germany. In the decades immediately after World War II, the problem was not acute, for the Scandinavian states were able to expand their gross domestic production fairly rapidly and enjoyed good competitive position in terms of exports. Sweden, in particular, developed its successful export industries before the other European states had regained their economic strength. But more recently, with stronger competition and in the context of the European recession stimulated by the oil shocks of the 1970s, it faced a serious crisis of constrained exports and increased unemployment. Policies of economic austerity were introduced, devaluations aided exports, and industry recovered as automobile exports soared.

In Denmark in the early 1980s, the deficit in the state budget amounted to almost one-tenth of the gross national product and was the highest per capita deficit in the world. Policies of fiscal restraint improved the situation by the close of the decade, yet long-term structural problems, including high taxes, low mobility within the labor market, and a large foreign debt, remained to be solved. Norway had the weakest economy following the German occupation and the destruction of World War II but in recent decades has fared much better. A modern maritime fleet, a strong market for its metals and chemicals, and especially oil resources brought into production in the mid-1980s have strengthened its position.

Sweden remains one of the world's wealthiest countries. An industrial nation (agriculture now constitutes only 3 percent of its gross domestic product and employs under 5 percent of the labor force), it nevertheless must steadily reinvest in new machinery and plants if it is to continue successfully to export one-third of its production. The move toward a single Europe by 1993 posed a threat to that trade, and many industrialists wondered if Sweden needed to interpret its neutrality so narrowly as to remain outside the European Community. By 1991 the Swedes were urging a joint application of the Nordic states to the EC, but Norway remained reluctant. Sweden moved ahead with its own application, and it appeared that Norway and Finland might follow. Norway's reservations regarding fishing rights were resolved, and the EEC and EFTA nations completed drafting the provisions for a European Economic Area.

Nearly 88 percent of the Swedish work force is unionized and will not take lightly to any moderation of consumption or wage increases in order that investment may be achieved. Political debate over the proper path of future change remains strong. The Moderate party advocates reduced public expenditure and lower taxes that will make possible higher private profits that can be reinvested. The New Democrats want a far greater reduction of taxes and of the welfare system. The Social Democrats defend the programs they have developed over the years. They also advocate a system of wage-earner funds and worker codetermination, whereby union investment funds obtain equity in Swedish industry and workers gain influence in management decisions. Whatever course is followed, the Swedes are determined to protect their environment. Though coal and oil must be imported, after both a referendum and a vigorous parliamentary debate, in 1980 they decided to phase out all nuclear power reactors by 2010, beginning in 1996. As nuclear production accounted for 44 percent of their power in 1987, further expansion of the already large hydroelectric system is contemplated.

Foreign Affairs

The Scandinavian states by virtue of their location as well as their resources were of vital strategic import to both sides of the superpower conflict. The policy of each has been affected by its location relative to the Soviet Union or the Western powers. The Finns and the Swedes have chosen neutrality, with Finland concomitantly signing treaties of friendship with the USSR. Norway, Denmark, and Iceland are part of the Western defense bloc. To avoid irritating the Soviets, Norway decided not to stock nuclear weapons during peacetime nor to allow foreign forces to be stationed on its soil unless it has been directly threatened. Sweden in particular chose a delicate course: Its neutral posture relieved Soviet anxieties, although Sweden maintained close trade and cultural relations with the West. Only in the early 1990s, as the Soviet threat diminished, did the Swedes favor application for full membership in the EC. More remarkable, although Sweden was one of the few Western countries that had acknowledged Soviet annexation of Estonia, Latvia, and Lithuania in 1991, it supported the Baltic republics in their campaign for independence. Sweden was joined by the other members of the Nordic Council, and they were among the first to recognize the independence of the Baltic states.

Attempts to negotiate a Scandinavian defense pact collapsed in the spring of 1949 because the negotiations touched the defense plans of the Western powers. Sweden, which had not been at war since the French revolutionary era, preferred to adhere to its traditional neutrality. To have reversed this policy would almost certainly have brought greater Soviet pressure on Finland, which the Swedes wished to avoid. Norway, having been confronted with the delicate task of refusing a Soviet pact of mutual assistance, found no alternative but to cast its lot with the Western powers in the Atlantic pact, as did Denmark and Iceland. Indeed, U.S. concern for Norway was a strong factor in accelerating negotiation of NATO. By a twenty-year treaty of 1951, the United States obtained air and naval bases in Greenland that were used by other NATO powers as well. Denmark in 1956 reestablished normal trade relations with the USSR—the last of the northern states to do so.

During the 1980s the Soviet Union actively developed its naval capabilities in the Baltic Sea and the North Atlantic. On more than one occasion its submarines penetrated Swedish territorial waters, and in 1985 it conducted massive naval exercises off the coast of Norway. These exercises were, apparently, a rehearsal for actions to prevent NATO aid to Norway, and for a Soviet landing in Norway, in case of war.

The Nordic Council, an excellent example of a regional group within the United Nations, although engaged largely in furthering economic and social cooperation among its members, at times does devote its attention to broader international affairs. Thus in 1954 a resolution was adopted advocating the admission of the People's Republic of China to the United Nations. Norway, as the second largest user of the Suez Canal, was greatly affected by the Suez crisis in 1956. It cooperated in the peaceful solution of this problem and in the arrangements for the United Nations forces that took over the area. After the closing of the Suez Canal resulting from the Six-Day War between Arabs and Israelis in June 1967, Norwegian shipowners immediately placed orders for large supertankers to share in the profitable oil route around the Cape of Good Hope.

The Scandinavian countries have consistently supported United Nations efforts to further peace, and Sweden has furnished contingents for peacekeeping operations in the Congo and in Cyprus. U.S. policies in Vietnam came under severe criticism in all three countries, but particularly so in Sweden. Sweden granted asylum to numerous defectors from the U.S. armed forces and in 1968 granted official recognition to North Vietnam. More recently, Swedish opinion has taken a less critical view of the United States.

Finland

Finland was conquered by Russia in 1809, after some six centuries of Swedish rule, and enjoyed a privileged status with home rule under the empire. In 1917 Finland proclaimed its independence and, after a civil war, became a respected member of the international community. Finland has been closely associated with the Scandinavian states, although it has an entirely different language and heritage. It fought in World War II as a bitter enemy of the USSR and also of Germany after September 1944. Following the war it contended with a vigorous Communist party yet managed to maintain both a neutral policy in foreign affairs and political democracy at home. The relative freedom of action retained by Finland, at a time when the Soviet Union annexed the Baltic states and established tight control of all Eastern Europe except Yugoslavia, may be explained by two factors. One of these was the desire of the Soviet government to retain the neutrality of Sweden. Soviet annexation of Finland would probably have driven Sweden into the arms of the West, and this the Soviets wished to avoid. Moreover, the cost to the USSR was not high, as Finland did not represent a route of invasion and it could, in any case, be occupied in the event of a crisis. The second factor that accounts for Finnish freedom is the vigor with which the traditional leaders of the country have resisted attempts at Communist infiltration. Ever since the civil strife following World War I and the struggles of World War II, Finland's rulers have had a realistic view of communism, and the Soviets, in turn, had a healthy respect for the determination of the Finns.

Finland's postwar relations with the Soviet Union were founded on the armistice terms and the peace treaty, which were severe but not unbearable. Some 12 percent of Finland's land area went to the Soviet Union, and heavy reparations were paid. The armistice terms called for the trial of war criminals, and early in 1946 eight prominent wartime cabinet ministers received prison sentences of from two to ten years. They were released well before the end of their sentences, however, and the whole procedure was characteristic of the independent spirit of the Finns. Similarly, when in 1948 the Soviet government invited Finland to negotiate a ten-year treaty of friendship and mutual assistance, the Finns insisted on terms confirming their sovereign rights. Unlike the Soviet treaties with the other states of Eastern Europe, this treaty explicitly recognized Finland's neutral position. Military cooperation was provided for only in case of an attack by Germany or a state allied with Germany, and the two states were to confer before the treaty went into operation.

Political Development

Finland thus stood outside the Soviet alliance system and was not a member of the Warsaw Pact. In 1955, during the period of relaxation in Soviet-Western relations in which the Austrian State Treaty was concluded and the summit conference was held at Geneva, the Soviet government terminated its fifty-year lease of the naval base at Porkkala-Udd; at the same time, the treaty of mutual assistance was extended for another twenty years. A year later the Karelo-Finnish SSR, one of the sixteen constituent republics of the USSR, was demoted to the status of an autonomous republic of the Russian Socialist Federated Soviet Republic (RSFSR). This republic, bordering on Finland and including territories annexed from that country in 1940, was inhabited largely by Finns. It had been created in 1940 under circumstances that led most observers to conclude that it was designed to serve as a base for annexing the whole of Finland, or at least as an ominous reminder to the Finnish government. Its dissolution consequently seemed to signify a further relaxation of pressure on Finland. Otto Kuusinen, the veteran Finnish Communist leader who had headed the Karelo-Finnish SSR from the start, was now given an honorary position on the Politburo of the Communist party of the Soviet Union. This new relaxation of Soviet-Finnish tension permitted Finland to join the Nordic Council. Finland also gained admission to the United Nations, after a ten-year deadlock resulting from East-West difficulties.

Urho Kekkonen served as president of Finland from 1956 to 1981. A staunch anti-Communist who fought against the Bolsheviks in 1917, he withdrew from politics in opposition to peace terms imposed on Finland by the Soviets following the Winter War (1939–1940) between the two countries. Reentering the political arena in 1944 with more realistic views, he served as foreign minister and prime minister before becoming president. Kekkonen firmly defended Finland's independence vis-à-vis the Soviet Union, albeit at the cost of pledging that his country would follow a neutral policy and not allow troops of foreign nations on its territory. (Photo courtesy of Information Service of Finland.)

In domestic politics, the struggle with communism was, on the whole, more strenuous than in the realm of foreign relations. After the war the Communists joined with other left-wing groups to form the Democratic Union; in the election of March 1945 this party won a quarter of the seats in the Eduskunta (Diet). On the basis of this electoral strength, the Communists played a prominent role for three years in a coalition cabinet with Social Democrats and Agrarians, working hard to gain control of the key ministry of interior. They failed because of the astuteness and vigor of the rival parties; when the electoral strength of the Democratic Union fell to 19 percent in 1948, the Communist members were not included in the cabinet. The following year widespread Communist-led strikes almost paralyzed the government, but in the end they also failed.

During this period the Soviet government refrained from giving the Finnish Communists overt material support, and the latter did not have sufficient domestic strength to obtain their objectives. For practical purposes, the Social Democrats and the Agrarians shared political power throughout the postwar period, although they represented rival interests within the country. Juho Paasikivi, the veteran nonparty leader, served as president from 1946 to 1956, when he was succeeded by Urho Kekkonen, the leader of the Agrarians. The Communist-led Democratic Union retained close to 20 percent of the vote in the decade after 1948, but when its strength rose to 23 percent in 1958 the delicate balance between the Agrarians and the Social Democrats was upset. Kekkonen was now able to form a predominantly Agrarian government with Communist support in the Parliament, and the Soviet government quickly took advantage of its new opportunity. In 1958–1959 and again in 1961–1962, the USSR brought great pressure to bear on Finland by means of demands and threats. It in effect agreed to favor Kekkonen's government in return for economic concessions as well as his assurance that political leaders unfriendly to the USSR would not receive government positions.

The predominance of centrist and leftist parties continued under Kekkonen's leadership until his retirement in 1982. He was succeeded by Mauno Koivisto, head of the Social Democratic party. He became Finland's first left-wing president, but the cabinet continued to include representatives of Center parties, and no significant changes in Finland's policies resulted.

Electoral sentiment shifted to the right by 1987. The Conservative party's gains in voting that year enabled it to claim ministerial seats for the first time since 1966 in an unprecedented coalition with the Social Democrats. The Communists of the Democratic Union had by this time suffered the loss of one splinter party, the Democratic Alternative, and would soon experience another schism as the Communist Labor party broke away.

The governmental change brought only small shifts in policy. Minor constitutional reforms already in the works were approved. A few powers moved from the president to Parliament, and a system of popular advisory voting, somewhat like a referendum, was created. Finnish voters would also cast direct ballots for the presidency as well as votes for an electoral college in the 1988 election. Koivisto was reelected, but because he did not obtain a pure majority in the multicandidate race, the final decision was made by the electoral college. The general election of March 1991 brought a surprise, however, as the ruling "Blue-Red" coalition of the Conservatives and Social Democrats lost seats. The Greens made gains and the Center party became the leading party of the country, replacing the Social Democrats, who had held that distinction since 1962.

Changes in the status of the Cold War and changes of leadership in the Soviet Union brought improved relations between the two countries in the latter half of the 1980s. In a visit to Helsinki in October 1989, Soviet president Gorbachev praised Finland as a locus of neutral stability in Europe and made clear that the Soviet Union no longer claimed any moral or legal right to invade its neighbors. Finland also tightened its ties with the West, as earlier that year it became the twenty-third member of the Council of Europe. Finnish links with Estonia were always close. In 1991, under pressure from its own population, Finland's government moved toward more outspoken support of its neighbor's independence efforts and in August recognized the three Baltic states.

Economy

Throughout the postwar years, Finland labored under a heavy economic burden. The delivery of materials for war reparations to the USSR, reduced by Moscow in 1948, was completed in 1952. These payments approximately equaled in value the budget of the Finnish government for one year. In addition, there was extensive war destruction to be repaired, not the least of which was caused by the retreating German troops. More difficult was the resettlement of some 56,000 families from territories ceded to the USSR. The government took full responsibility for this operation. Place was found for all by subdividing existing landholdings and opening up new lands. During the 1950s, as much as one-third of the gross national product of Finland was reinvested each year in permanent agricultural and industrial installations. Although this placed a great burden on the Finnish people and no doubt accounts for some of the social unrest, the rapid investment resulted in a significant growth of the Finnish economy. Many industries, such as shipbuilding, expanded rapidly; the pace of industrialization was reflected in the growth of the urban share of the population from one-third in 1950 to two-thirds in the 1980s. As a member of the Nordic Council and an associate member of the EFTA, Finland more than doubled its foreign trade in the 1950s and 1960s, with the USSR accounting for about 15 percent of its imports and exports. By the onset of the 1990s, the government's chief economic concern was to cool the overheated expansion of production sufficiently to avoid inflation. Consumers, however, enjoyed prosperity and continued to buy. The economic development of Finland since the war's end and the skilled tightrope walking of its diplomats amid the pitfalls of the Cold War won the admiration of other countries, which saw these achievements as evidence of the independence and moderation of the Finnish people.

Notes

1. *Journal of Commerce*, August 11, 1988, as quoted in *Austrian Information*, 41, 8 (1988):2.
2. P. H. Spaak, "The Atomic Bomb and NATO," *Foreign Affairs*, 33 (April 1955):359.

Suggested Readings

Austria

Bader, W. B., *Austria Between East and West, 1945–1955* (1966).
Bauer, R. A., *The Austrian Solution: International Conflict and Cooperation* (1982).

Gruber, K., *Between Liberation and Liberty: Austria in the Post-War World* (1955).
Hankel, W., *Prosperity Amidst Crisis: Austria's Economic Policy and the Energy Crunch* (1981).
Shell, K. L., *The Transformation of Austrian Socialism* (1962).
Steiner, K. (ed.), *Tradition and Innovation in Contemporary Austria* (1982).
Sully, M., *Political Parties and Elections in Austria* (1981).

Switzerland

Bonjour, E., H. Offler, and G. L. Potter, *A Short History of Switzerland* (1952).
DeSalis, J. R., *Switzerland and Europe* (1971).
Gretler, A., and P. E. Mandl, *Values, Trends, and Alternatives in Swiss Society* (1973).
Hughes, C. J., *The Parliament of Switzerland* (1963).
Schimel, C. L., *Conflict and Consensus in Switzerland* (1981).

The Lowlands

Arango, E. R., *Leopold III and the Belgian Royal Question* (1963).
Coleman, J. A., *The Evolution of Dutch Catholicism, 1958–1974* (1979).
Dutt, A. K., and F. Costa (eds.), *Public Planning in the Netherlands* (1984).
Eyck, F. G., *The Benelux Countries: An Historical Survey* (1969).
Fitzmaurice, J., *The Politics of Belgium: Crisis and Compromise in a Plural Society* (1984).
Griffiths, R. T. (ed.), *The Economy and Politics of the Netherlands Since 1945* (1980).
Helmreich, J. E., *Belgium and Europe: A Study in Small Power Diplomacy* (1976).
Lijphart, A., *Politics of Accommodation: Pluralism and Democracy in the Netherlands*, 2d, rev. ed. (1976).
———— (ed.), *Conflict and Coexistence in Belgium: The Dynamics of a Culturally Divided Society* (1981).
Mallison, V., *Power and Politics in Belgian Education, 1815 to 1961* (1963).
Marque, P., *A Short History of Luxembourg* (1974).
Riley, R. C., and G. Ashworth, *Benelux: An Economic Geography of Belgium, the Netherlands, and Luxembourg* (1975).
Vandenbosch, A. J., *Dutch Foreign Policy Since 1815: A Study in Small Power Politics* (1959).
Voorhoeve, J.J.C., *Peace, Profits and Principles: A Study of Dutch Foreign Policy* (1979).
Wels, C. B., *Aloofness and Neutrality: Studies on Dutch Foreign Relations and Policy Making Institutions* (1983).

Ireland

Ayearst, M., *The Republic of Ireland: Its Government and Politics* (1969).
Bell, J. B., *The Secret Army: The I.R.A. 1916–1979* (1979).
Bowman, J., *De Valera and the Ulster Question, 1917 to 1973* (1982).
Chubb, B., *The Government and Politics of Ireland*, 2d ed. (1982).
Dangerfield, G., *The Damnable Question: 120 Years of Anglo-Irish Conflict* (1983).
Fanning, R., *Independent Ireland* (1983).

The Scandinavian States

General

Anderson, S. V., *The Nordic Council: A Study of Scandinavian Regionalism* (1968).

Derry, T. K., *A History of Scandinavia* (1979).

Heckscher, G., *The Welfare State and Beyond: Success and Problems in Scandinavia* (1984).

Lindgren, R. E., *Norway-Sweden: Union, Disunion, and Scandinavian Integration* (1959).

Wuorinen, J. H., *Scandinavia* (1965).

Denmark and Iceland

Fitzmaurice, J., *Politics in Denmark* (1981).

Horton, H. H. (ed.), *Iceland* (1983).

Lauring, P., *A History of Denmark* (1960).

Tomasson, R. F., *Iceland: The First New Society* (1980).

Norway

Allen, H., *Norway and Europe in the 1970s* (1979).

Bourbeuf, A., *Norway: The Planned Revival* (1958).

Kuhnle, S., *Party Programs and the Welfare State: Consensus and Conflict in Norway, 1945–1977* (1981).

Lafferty, W. M., *Participation and Democracy in Norway* (1981).

Olsen, J. P., *Organized Democracy: Political Institutions in a Welfare State—The Case of Norway* (1983).

Sweden

Abrahamson, S., *Sweden's Foreign Policy* (1957).

Oakley, S., *A Short History of Sweden* (1966).

Rosenthal, A. H., *The Social Programs of Sweden* (1967).

Rustow, D. A., *The Politics of Compromise: A Study of Parties and Cabinet Government in Sweden* (1955).

Tögil, S., *Sweden and World Society: Thoughts About the Future* (1980).

Tomasson, R. F., *Sweden: Prototype of Modern Society* (1971).

Finland

Jakobson, M., *Finnish Neutrality: A Study of Finnish Foreign Policy Since the Second World War* (1969).

Mazour, A. G., *Finland Between East and West* (1956).

Wuorinen, J. H., *A History of Finland* (1965).

CHAPTER THIRTEEN

The Iberian and Aegean States

❧

Isolation and Reemergence:
The Iberian States
Spain • Portugal

Economic Progress and Political Turmoil:
The Aegean States
Turkey • Greece • Cyprus

The Small States in Perspective

Notes

Suggested Readings

T he smaller European states of the Mediterranean region (Andorra, Liechtenstein, Malta, and Monaco are not considered here because of their limited impact on international affairs) shared many of the same problems as did their northern neighbors. Yet these smaller states experienced a lower level of industrial development and economic prosperity than the states discussed in the previous chapter; for that reason alone, as well as for others, they faced great challenges in the years after World War II.

Isolation and Reemergence: The Iberian States

The two Iberian states, Spain and Portugal, lagged behind many other European nations in modernization. Their conservative political regimes proved wary of taking forward steps. Mindful of the disruption and chaos brought by previous revolutions in their countries, the Spanish and Portuguese governments seemed little interested in political, economic, or social change at the close of the war. While other nations talked about greater economic integration and political cooperation, the Iberian countries withdrew into themselves and sought to control all developments within their borders. The situation was exacerbated by the rejection shown by other countries that disliked the Fascist nature of the Eanes and Salazar regimes.

Both emerged from this position, Spain by peaceful revolution, Portugal by more violent means. In each instance the reemergence demonstrated a desire to move to different political and economic models and, in fact, was stimulated by a shift in attitudes and needs. This trend was partly a direct result of outside forces, such as the development of the Cold War, better relations with neighboring states and the Common Market, the changes in the posture of the leadership of the Roman Catholic church, and the growth of nationalism in colonial territories. Internal factors also played a major role. Expansion of the middle classes, pressure for autonomy from various groups, demands for true political parties, discontent and disaffection in the military, concern among the lower clergy for the welfare of their congregations, and economic growth all reflected substantial passages in the histories of the Iberian states.

During the war years, the economies of Spain and Portugal, which were neutral states, were closely linked to the economy of the Axis, although the two states also traded with the Western powers. The rupture of the Axis connections, the unprecedented drought in the early postwar years, and the reluctance of some states to return to normal trade relations caused a severe economic crisis. Spain, which formerly exported food, was forced to buy

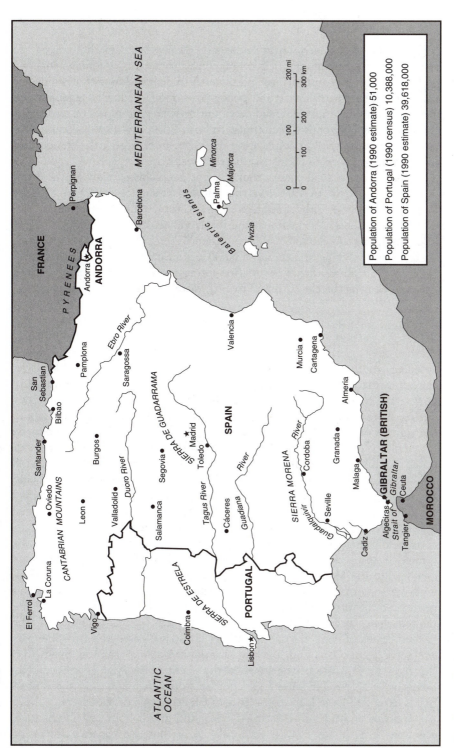

The Iberian Peninsula

Population of Andorra (1990 estimate) 51,000
Population of Portugal (1990 census) 10,388,000
Population of Spain (1990 estimate) 39,618,000

high-priced Argentinean wheat under a credit arrangement that helped the regime of Generalissimo Francisco Franco to survive. In 1948 France opened its frontier to trade with Spain, and Spanish trade, notably with Britain, also increased. The Spanish wartime policy of economic autarky gradually fell away, resulting in unprecedented economic growth and improved trade with the European Economic Community. In both Spain and Portugal the population increased rapidly, complicating the problem of raising the standard of living through more equal distribution of wealth.

Significant political change took place in both states following the death of Franco of Spain in 1975 and the relinquishment of power in 1968 by Portugal's longtime authoritarian premier, António de Oliveira Salazar. Liberalization of the governments in the Iberian states made them more acceptable as military and economic allies of other Western European governments. Portugal was an original member of NATO, but Spain was not admitted until 1982. In 1986, after years of negotiation, promises, and hesitations, Spain and Portugal became the eleventh and twelfth members of the EEC.

Spain

At their first meeting in San Francisco, the members of the United Nations voted to bar the Franco regime permanently from participation. Its Fascist character, dictatorial framework, close relations with Hitler and Mussolini during the Spanish civil war, and trade relations with Germany and Italy during World War II made Spain, despite its official neutrality, non grata to the signers of the Atlantic Charter and to the Soviet Union. In 1946 the Assembly of the United Nations passed a resolution requesting all member states to withdraw their diplomatic representatives from Madrid. But in 1948 an active bloc in the assembly, led by South American states, urged that Spain be admitted to the United Nations. As the lines of the anti-Communist conflict became more sharply drawn, Western hostility to the dictatorial Spanish regime lessened. The Soviet Union, alone of the great powers, consistently maintained an anti-Franco policy, but Spain squeezed into the United Nations under the package admission deal of 1955. Spain was not admitted to the Marshall Plan nor asked to join in forming NATO. In 1953, with the somewhat reluctant assent of Britain and France, the United States negotiated a mutual-aid agreement with Spain. Under this agreement, the United States furnished Spain military and economic aid; in return, the United States gained joint use of military and naval bases in Spain. The pact was subsequently renewed, but not without difficult bargaining. Spain won the right to veto use of the bases in the event of an Arab-Israeli or U.S.-Soviet war. Nuclear missiles could not be stored in Spain, and the United States extended large loans to assist Spanish economic development.

U.S. expenditure on the bases, loans, and grants bolstered the Spanish economy. U.S. policy toward Spain also contributed to Spain's decreasing isolation in international affairs. In 1958 Spain joined the IMF, the World Bank, and the Organization for European Economic Cooperation. Spain's initial requests for membership in NATO and for associate membership in the EEC failed primarily for political reasons. The change on that scene was so great, however, that by the time Spain did gain admittance to NATO, there was some question whether the socialist government of that country desired the sort of close alliance envisioned by the other members. Admission to the Common Market was slowed by the very real problem of integrating Spanish agriculture, especially the low-priced olive oil and wines, into the troubled and heavily subsidized Common Agricultural Policy of the EEC. The large Spanish shipbuilding industry and subsidized steel industry, areas in which the Common Market countries already had surplus capacity, raised further difficulties. Compromises included a transition period of seven to ten years to allow Spain and Portugal to adapt to EEC free trade policies. Trade relations with Eastern European countries also expanded, albeit cautiously. Spain negotiated its first direct trade agreement with the Soviet Union in 1966 and since has established links with other Eastern European states and with Communist China.

Tangier, which Spain had occupied in 1940, again came under international control in 1945, when Spanish troops were forced to withdraw. This city, as well as northern Spanish Morocco, was transferred to the sovereignty of the kingdom of Morocco in 1956, after that state achieved its independence from France. Ceuta and Mellila, both ancient Spanish coastal enclaves in North Africa governed as parts of Spanish provinces, were not affected by the transfer. Subsequent clashes occurred between a self-styled, irregular Liberation Army of the Moroccan Sahara and Spanish troops in the Spanish colonies along the West African coast. In 1958 Spanish south Morocco—a desert region of some 10,000 square miles (25,900 sq km)—was transferred to Moroccan jurisdiction. The small enclave of Ifni went to Morocco in 1969, and in 1976 Spanish Sahara was also relinquished. Equatorial Guinea (known as Spanish Guinea before 1963) gained its independence in 1968, ending 104 years of Spanish rule. Repeated restrictive measures levied against Gibraltar in the late 1960s failed to bring Britain's surrender of that bastion. Negotiations continued sporadically in the 1970s, as the Spanish complained of British violations of Spanish air space. Talks broke off and did not resume until early 1985, at the same time final negotiations were under way concerning Spain's entry into the EEC. The discussions achieved some positive results and the frontier between Gibraltar and Spain was again opened to intercourse and trade. Britain, however, continued to refuse to return Gibraltar to Spain.

In spite of early postwar opposition, General Franco maintained his rule without serious changes. He hinted his views as to succession with laws in 1947 that abolished the republic and proclaimed Spain a monarchy. At the same time Franco was assured life tenure as chief of state. These steps were confirmed in a new constitution approved in a 1966 national referendum.

Generalissimo Francisco Franco, shown here on the left, took the title of El Caudillo (the Leader) while assuming personal control of Spain in the late 1930s. Shunned for his pro-Fascist views by the democratic Allies during and immediately after World War II, he eventually won better relations with them because of his staunch anticommunism. The slow industrial development of Spain that accompanied provision of Western aid helped to make obsolete the conservatism of Franco's regime. (Photo from UPI/Bettmann.)

Hailed as introducing a more liberal regime, the constitution actually changed little. About one-fourth of the members of the Cortes (Spain's parliament) were to be elected directly, and married women were given the right to vote. But political parties were not recognized as legal institutions, and the people had little more than the liberty of approving government-sponsored lists of candidates. In 1969, amid great fanfare, Franco designated Prince Juan Carlos of Bourbon, the grandson of Alfonso XIII (who left Spain without abdicating in 1931), as his successor as chief of state. This choice was an obvious rebuff to the more liberal Don Juan of Bourbon, son of Alfonso XIII and father of Prince Juan Carlos, who continued to claim his right to the throne. In 1953 a concordat with the Vatican recognized Roman Catholicism as "the only religion of the Spanish peoples" and provided for the nomination of bishops by the Spanish government. The state appropriated money for the Catholic church, and the church exercised a controlling hand over Spanish schools. The Spanish church remained in the hands of a conservative hierarchy, but the split between liberal and conservative forces in the church grew steadily. Many priests and some bishops sided with students and workers in their strikes for reform. Progressive churchmen also attacked the provision of the concordat that gave the government a deciding voice in the nomination of bishops. In this protest they were backed by the Vatican, which at various times indicated its desire to update the church in Spain.

Terrorism grew, especially that of the Euzkadi ta Azkatasuna (Basque Country and Freedom, or ETA), an organization founded in 1959 and dedicated to achieving separate status for the four Basque provinces in northeast Spain: Alava, Navarra, Guipuzcoa, and Viscaya. Some Basque priests supported Basque autonomy, whereas many younger priests were supportive of Catholic workers' brotherhood movements that undertook illegal strikes. Franco, for his part, wished Spanish courts to hold jurisdiction over priests. He therefore pursued negotiations with the Vatican regarding revision of the concordat, but these talks did not lead to an agreement.

Over 99 percent of the Spanish population is Roman Catholic; the minority religions constitute a minuscule group in a population that by the beginning of the 1990s numbered nearly 40 million. For years the religious minorities suffered under many legal as well as extralegal discriminations. Their places of worship could not be marked, they were not allowed to hold public processions or services of any kind, they had no legal status as corporate bodies, their marriages celebrated by their clergy were not recognized by the state, they could not have their own schools or publications, and they were discriminated against in all public service appointments. In 1955 a Spanish court did rule that civil marriage between a baptized Catholic and a Protestant (a mixed marriage) could be contracted, although the decision was not free from qualifications. A gradual relaxation of restrictions became discernible in the early 1960s, and in 1965 Franco surprised everyone by stating that he favored "the exercise of freedom of conscience." A law to implement this more liberal policy, drastically revised under the influence of the hierarchy, was finally passed by the Cortes two years later. It still did not bring full equality or liberty to Spain's religious minorities. Yet on December 16, 1968, the 462-year-old ban on Jews in Spain was ceremoniously lifted on the occasion of the opening of the first new synagogue in Spain in 600 years.

Long termed a Fascist state by outside critics, Spain under Franco did differ from Fascist Italy and National Socialist Germany. In Spain no Fascist party held control, for the influence of the Falange (a prewar, authoritarian— nearly Fascist—grouping) was submerged in the national movement that Franco created to bolster his political power. Nor was the Spanish economy modern enough to support the sort of economic organization or military ambitions that emerged in both Italy and the Third Reich. Nevertheless, emphasis on the leader and his authority and Fascist implications for civil liberties were strongly present in Spain. Occasional student riots, increasing in number and virulence after 1965; a large number of labor strikes; and even critical articles in the clerical press indicated popular dissatisfaction with the regime.

As the Roman church went from staunch to lukewarm support—and even at times to criticism—of Franco, one of the three traditional pillars of the regime weakened. The second pillar was the army. Like the church, it held a generational split. The senior officers who had fought under Franco were dying off, and the younger officers, drawn from a wider range of society, felt held down by the gerontocracy. Underpaid, they often took part-time jobs in the civilian economy; no longer did the junior staff consider itself as an elite caste, nor was it oblivious to the complaints of society as a whole. The third pillar, the National Movement (into which the Falange and other parties had been merged in 1937), had by the 1970s long since lost whatever ideological cohesiveness it had; indeed, Franco had purposefully stripped it of influence some while ago. The regime hung on, in part because there were no groups confident and organized enough to challenge Franco and his protégés. Yet Franco's very success in spurring the economic development of his country created more entrepreneurs eager to move to the less repressive styles of government evident in the countries with which they traded. Pressure for change from the Common Market countries, even the influx of millions of tourists whose spending bolstered the economy, fed the growing sense that changes would soon have to occur.

Franco had long managed to control the many factions supporting his regime by balancing them against one another, never allowing any one to hold preeminence for long. In 1969 he appeared to abandon this tactic by giving nearly half the positions in his cabinet to a group he may have hoped would prove a new and strong pillar of support. This was the Sacerdotal Society of the Holy Cross and Opus Dei (Work of God), founded in Spain in 1928. An association of Roman Catholic laymen and priests, its purpose is to bring religious practice into its members' daily lives and work. The association gained no real foothold until after the end of the Spanish civil war and World War II, when the Vatican formally approved it as the first secular institute authorized to operate throughout the world. Opus Dei comprises both celibate and married members, many of them highly educated and dedicated men. Although the core membership is not large, it has a wide circle of adherents in Spain. In keeping with its aim of helping Christians to be better people, Opus Dei has established a considerable number of educational, social, sport, and recreational centers. Its members have infiltrated and gained a leading role in a large part of Spain's banking, insurance, construction, and communication industries. In the cabinet shifts in 1969, Opus Dei members achieved virtual domination of the government.

The political activity of Opus Dei, its secretive ways (many members do not disclose their affiliation), and its quiet monopolization of key business and government posts provoked controversy and suspicion. Its confidence in modern business techniques, capitalist enterprise, and rationalization of economic regulations did much to spur the Spanish economy and justified the rise of Opus Dei to cabinet-level influence. But the society was soon scandalized by the disclosure of business fraud involving cabinet members and government money. By the mid-1970s it had lost its leading position to Catholic Action, a center-right movement supportive of democracy and a source of an emerging Christian Democrat political party.

Juan Carlos of Bourbon assumed ruling power after the death of Franco in 1975 and was officially crowned king of Spain on November 22 of that year. Though little was expected of him, he surprised many with his vigorous leadership, guiding his country from an era of right-wing dictatorship to genuine democracy while retaining the loyalty of the army and the various political parties. (Photo courtesy of the Information Department, Embassy of Spain.)

As the aging Franco found that his deteriorating health would not permit him to carry out his duties fully, he increasingly delegated responsibility to Admiral Luis Carrero Blanco, a longtime aide Franco appointed prime minister in 1973. Carrero Blanco's policies were conservative, and some observers assumed that though Juan Carlos might be Franco's titular successor, Carrero Blanco would hold de facto power. Such speculation ended with the assassination of Carrero Blanco by ETA terrorists on December 20. Carlos Arias Navarro was his successor. Aware of pressures for reform, he announced an "opening" of the regime the following January. By mid-July 1974, Franco's illness had progressed to the point that he began to hand over the reins of power to Juan Carlos. Franco lingered in poor health until his death on November 20, 1975, two weeks short of his eighty-third birthday. Juan Carlos, thirty-seven, was crowned two days later.

By the time of the king's accession, demands for change had greatly increased. An opposition Democratic junta had formed. ETA terrorism mounted, resulting in the arrest and execution of five terrorists, sentences that brought protests from many of the European countries Spain was courting in hope of joining the EEC. Arias promised reforms but did little; by mid-1976 it was evident that a new premier was needed. By the Organic Law of 1967, Franco had arranged that the Council of the Realm would propose three names to the king, from which list the king would choose a prime minister. The original members of the council were aging Francoists, but shortly after taking the throne, Juan Carlos was able to appoint a personal friend, a presumed conservative, as head of the group. Thus the king was assured that individuals acceptable to him would be nominated. His choice for prime minister was a moderate reformer, Adolfo Suárez González. Men in their forties rather than their sixties dominated the cabinet; they were primarily Christian Democrats and favorable to gradual reform. Juan Carlos I had shown himself more of a leader, more of a reformer, and more politically astute than anyone had expected.

Suárez led the Cortes to permit political parties (except the Communists) to function again, and he pardoned a number of political prisoners. In November 1976 the Cortes passed a Law of Political Reform that reestablished democracy and terminated the Cortes as then organized. It was to be replaced by an elected congress (350 members) and a senate (207 elected members, 40 appointed by the king). Of the two chambers, the congress was to be dominant. A December referendum overwhelmingly approved the change. The following April the Communist party was legalized, and in June 1977 the first democratic election in Spain since 1936 took place. A multitude of parties presented candidates. The Union of the Democratic Center (a center-left coalition led by Suárez), and the Socialist Workers' party emerged as the chief winners, gaining 165 and 118 congressional seats, respectively.

Changes continued, with self-government granted to Catalonia. Announcement of preautonomy status for the Basque regions did little to curb the terrorism of the ETA, however. The new congress drafted a constitution that freed Spain of the strictures of Franco's constitution of 1966 and Organic Law of 1967. Under the new constitution, the king is the supreme commander of the armed forces and has the power to appoint the prime minister and to dissolve the Cortes. He may grant pardons and must approve all laws. Religious freedom is guaranteed, yet a continuing close relationship with the Roman Catholic church is also mentioned. Trade unions are permitted and the "right of autonomy of the various nationalities and regions" assured. Capital punishment of civilians and torture are banned. This new constitution was approved by the congress, by the people in a referendum, and by the king by the close of 1978. Suárez had achieved great change, and across the political spectrum the king was applauded for his role.

Under the leadership of Santiago Carrillo, even the Communists altered their orientation in 1978. "Leninist" was dropped from the party's self-description as it turned toward the sort of Eurocommunism foreshadowed by Carrillo's words of 1976:

> We had our pope, our Vatican and we thought we were predestined to triumph. But as we mature and become less of a church, we must become more national, closer to reality. . . . [A] person's preference of friends, of music and literature, whether to be religious or atheist, has nothing to do with the party. The party can only be concerned with problems of politics

and social struggle. . . . We want a type of socialism with universal suffrage, alternation of government, not control of power for the communists but an alliance of forces that in no way would allow a communist monopoly.[1]

Social change accompanied political change. Most striking was the alteration of the status of women. Previously constrained by legislation embodying the concept of *permiso marital*, women had to obtain the permission of their husbands to take jobs outside the home, hold their own bank accounts, or undertake many other activities. Those laws evanesced after Franco's death. In 1981 a new law permitted divorce by mutual consent following two years of separation; in 1985 abortion became legal, although many doctors would refuse to perform the procedure. Standards of permissibility in literature changed, and scantily clad female figures appeared in advertisements. Although most citizens appreciated the new freedoms, some worried about increases in pornography.

Economic difficulties could not be avoided. Sharply rising oil prices in 1980 curtailed economic growth and fostered both inflation and unemployment, which in turn sparked labor unrest. In January 1981 Suárez resigned. While efforts were under way to form a new ministry, a group of dissident civil guards seized the parliament building and briefly appeared to be achieving overthrow of the short-lived democracy. King Juan Carlos remained cool and in a well-phrased radio speech urged the populace to support the new institutions. The military in the main remained loyal to the king; the coup aborted. Some officers were subsequently dismissed and the office of chief of staff reorganized. The king emerged with new respect in all quarters and enhanced control over the army. Leadership of the government was confided to Leopoldo Calvo Sotelo, noted for his experience in economic affairs and his efforts to win membership for Spain in the EEC. He immediately proposed limitations on wage increases and continuation of the growing nuclear energy program; despite Socialist opposition, he also pushed through Parliament legislation supporting Spain's application for membership in NATO.

Unexpected major political change occurred in 1982, when the Socialist Workers' party (PSOE), led by the young (aged forty) and dynamic Felipe González Márquez, won 201 of the 350 seats in the congress. The Union of the Democratic Center fell apart and won only twelve seats. The Communists also lost badly, and the aging Carrillo was replaced as party leader by Gerardo Iglesias. The Popular Alliance, a right-wing coalition led by Manuel Fraga Iribarne, a former Franco reformist minister, fared well, winning 106 seats. Descent into conflict between Left and Right seemed again possible, as rumors of a military coup to avert a Socialist government were rife. Yet González peacefully became the first Socialist head of government since the defeat of the republic.

In his campaign González had questioned Spain's adherence to NATO; after assuming office, he did not take steps to withdraw from the alliance, but movement toward meaningful participation was frozen. By 1986 González was convinced that the economic progress of Spain was dependent upon maintaining ties with the NATO membership. Prior to a national referendum on the issue, he argued that quitting NATO would mean regressing into "backwardness, poverty, unemployment, and third-worldism." He and his government were supported by a 52.5 percent vote in favor of staying in the defense organization. Though he advocated continued membership in NATO, González promised the electorate a diminution of U.S. military presence in Spain; he therefore firmly negotiated the withdrawal of a contingent of U.S. warplanes in 1988. Spain also declined to place its troops under NATO command. It did, however, take responsibility for the waters between the Canary Islands in the Atlantic and the Balearic Islands in the western Mediterranean. Upon coming to office González quickly moved to modernize the army and establish better civilian control of it; he simultaneously raised military pay. The civil service, long used to short hours and to lining its own pockets, was similarly subjected to streamlining; a new conflict-of-interest law was enforced and longer office hours required.

González vigorously pursued the union with the Common Market so badly needed by the Spanish economy. Steps toward the granting of autonomy to the Basque regions, such as the creation of an autonomous Basque police force, did not halt the terrorism of the separatist ETA. Rumors persisted that the armed forces might be politically unreliable despite his efforts to win them over. In 1984 Spain's largest holding company was nationalized, but huge losses quickly led the government to plan to return it to the private sector and dampened interest in further nationalizations. Indeed, the government soon encouraged private investment in growth industries and closed down or sold unprofitable state-owned firms. In turn, it was gratified by increased exports, signs of support in the military, and a bull market on the Madrid stock exchange stimulated by confidence based on entrance into the EEC and the results of the NATO referendum. Nevertheless, unemployment rates among the young stayed persistently high. Lax drug laws led to an epidemic in heroin use and a crackdown in 1987. These factors, joined with an effort to increase university fees and tighten admission standards, brought student demonstrations. In 1988, militant leftists within the Socialist General Union of Workers broke with the government over budget ceilings. Long the protestors themselves, the Socialists were now faced with the liabilities of being "the establishment."

Despite achievement of a remarkable rate of growth in its gross domestic product (around 4.5 percent) in 1987—Spain's own "economic miracle"— unemployment remained seriously high (19.8 percent). Discontent spread among the labor unions, which staged "an extra-parliamentary vote of no-confidence," that is, a general strike, in 1988. The Socialist General Union of Workers failed to support the Socialist Workers' party in the 1989 parliamentary elections. González's new cabinet was barely approved by the Cortes, and in many cities a new coalition of conservatives and centrists replaced Socialist control. In Spain, as elsewhere, the challenge of expanding the economy while holding down inflation and enhancing the price competitiveness of Spanish goods on the world market presented political difficulties. A continuing economic growth rate of about 5 percent, spurred by membership in the EC, nevertheless enabled González to maintain his position. Thus in 1991 he was able to push through legislation that raised to sixteen the age of mandatory schooling, briefly reducing the flow of new workers into the marketplace. This reform was linked, over conservative protests, with another that made optional the Roman Catholic religious instruction long formerly required in the schools.

Over the years, the pattern of governance and of change in Spain changed remarkably. Franco based his initial efforts to unify and move Spain forward after World War II on close alliance with the army and church, opposition to Socialists and political parties in general, political centralization, and economic autarky. The very success of his program brought the necessity of change, the need to reach out to new markets and to take new approaches. A Socialist head of government in the 1980s led his state into the Common Market, granted limited autonomy to separatist groups, diminished the role of the church (which itself had been a key factor in creating a more modern society, concerned for all classes), and then soft-pedaled traditional Socialist emphases on nationalization and economic planning. Changes accelerated. The Spain of the 1990s differed markedly from the Spain of 1945 in terms of adaption of technology to industrial and agricultural processes, development of political parties and multifaceted political relationships, and economic capacity. Individual rights had expanded enormously; social integration had also progressed, although much remained to be achieved, including some arrangement with the separatist Basques.

Portugal

Following World War II, António de Oliveira Salazar, a former economics professor, maintained a firm grip on the government that he had joined as finance minister in 1928 and had controlled as prime minister since 1932. Asserting that he was following a middle course between those forces which naively and sometimes irrationally advocated change and those which blindly rejected innovation of any kind, Salazar claimed he was founding a new state based on corporatism. His system emphasized functional groups and the family rather than the individual. Pluralism and individual concerns were sacrificed in favor of the unity of the state and of stability. As time wore on, Salazar's rule became increasingly dictatorial. Some opposition did persist. In 1959 an opposition candidate campaigned on the premise of having Salazar replaced as prime minister and received 20 percent of the vote. Salazar's response was to have the constitution of 1933 amended so that henceforth the president would be chosen by an electoral college made up of the National Assembly, the appointive Corporative Chamber, and representatives from the municipalities and overseas legislative councils. Antigovernment demonstrations continually occurred but were not permitted to get out of hand; Portugal remained a dictatorial state.

In spite of his authoritarian government, Salazar was generally accepted by the Western states, and Portugal would have been admitted to the United Nations long before 1955 had it not been for the Soviet veto. Portugal participated in the Marshall Plan, is a member of NATO, and belonged to the European Free Trade Association (Outer Seven) until joining the Common Market in 1986. During the war the United States and Britain made use of the Portuguese Azores as an air base, and postwar negotiations extended some of these privileges. The old Portuguese-British alliance continued and played its part in establishing Portugal's postwar international position.

Portugal undertook a number of relatively successful six-year plans to expand basic industries. Yet Portugal continued to have one of the lowest standards of living in Europe and a high rate of illiteracy. In 1951 the status of Portuguese overseas possessions was changed from "colonies" to "overseas territories," but they continued to be administered in much the same old authoritarian fashion. In the African territories there was practically no secondary or higher education for natives, forced labor was utilized, and only a few thousand natives were given *assimilado* status. To obtain this status, legally equal to that of Europeans, the natives had to meet certain rather rigorous educational, occupational, and other requirements.

For a time it seemed as if Portugal's overseas territories might escape the rising tide of native nationalism and anticolonialism. In 1955 diplomatic relations with India were severed as a result of a dispute over Portugal's tiny colonial outposts in India, which Portugal refused to surrender. India's blocking of the right of passage from one Portuguese colony to the other over Indian territory was taken to the International Court of Justice for settlement, where the ruling (1960) was in India's favor. Portugal turned a deaf ear to India's repeated demands for a negotiated surrender. Finally, in 1961, the Indian government sent troops into the colonies and incorporated them into the Indian union. Portugal complained to the United Nations, but division among the great powers forestalled any investigation or official censure of India.

It was not until 1961 that serious nationalist uprisings, triggered by events in the neighboring Congo, broke out in Portuguese Angola. The Portuguese sent in more troops and more or less continuous fighting ensued. In 1963 nationalist guerrilla warfare spread to Portuguese Guinea. Mozambique was less affected, but here, too, uprisings occurred in 1964. The bitter fighting in Angola led the UN Assembly to adopt a resolution calling upon Portugal to cease repressive measures against the people of Angola. Portugal denied the competence of the UN to deal with these disturbances because they were internal affairs, the overseas territories being an integral part of the unitary state. Portugal claimed there was no question of granting these peoples independence, as they were already free and held equal status with the Portuguese homeland in Europe. Needless to say, this euphemism was not accepted by the vast majority of the indigenous population in the African territories, nor by most members of the UN.

In 1968, a cerebral hemorrhage incapacitated Premier Salazar after forty years in power. President Américo Tomás appointed Marcello Caetano as his successor. A law professor, the latter had long been associated with Salazar; on taking office, he announced that he would continue his predecessor's policies. Portugal would fight to retain its territorial possessions in Africa, communism would be suppressed and public order maintained. There was some indication that the rigid censorship of the past would be relaxed and more political activity permitted. These changes did not materialize, and a report of the Council of Europe in 1970 stated that despite a certain liberalization by the new regime, Portugal was not yet eligible for membership in the council, which admits only democratic states. It cited serious limitations on individual rights, the ban on political parties, the continued censorship, and the absence of universal suffrage.

On April 25, 1974, officers belonging to the Movimento das Forças Armadas (Armed Forces Movement, or MFA) revolted, overthrowing Caetano. There was only limited consensus within the group, based on dissatisfaction with the continuing wear of colonial warfare, its concomitant negative effects upon the Portuguese economy, and resentment of the low pay and status of the armed forces. Numerous political parties covering a wide spectrum of views sprang up, including a vocal Portuguese Communist party that looked to Moscow for leadership. Over the next two years, six different provisional governments briefly held office. General António de Spínola, a key figure in the initial bloodless revolt, resigned in 1974 in protest over growing Communist influences. A failed coup attempted by rightist military officers in 1975 led to Communist ascendancy for several months. The Junta of National Salvation formed the preceding year was dissolved and power placed in the hands of a new Supreme Revolutionary Council on which key military leaders and the president sat.

The Socialist party, upset by the treatment given the Socialist press by the government and by Communist unions, soon withdrew from the government coalition. Pressure from various moderate political parties and segments of the MFA forced General Vasco dos Santos Gonçalves, known for his pro-Communist sympathies, to resign as premier. On November 25, 1975, leftist paratroopers seized four military bases and the national television network; other military units remained loyal to the government and the coup failed. In its aftermath many leftist military leaders were expelled from their positions and deprived of political rights for twenty years. The MFA and the political parties then reached a new pact that envisioned the withdrawal of the military from politics over a four-year transition to civilian government.

The form of that prospective government was prescribed by a Constituent Assembly elected in April 1975. The constitution it drafted took effect on April 25, 1976, when balloting for a new parliament was held. The Constituent Assembly, though it was elected at a time of considerable Communist influence in the provisional government, was dominated by moderate parties and especially the Socialists. Its product, the constitution of 1976, proclaimed Portugal a republic "engaged in the formation of a classless society." Extensive protection was given to individual civil rights. The Supreme Revolutionary Council was renamed the Council of the Revolution and continued to hold considerable power. The military figure who led the opposition to the leftist coup, António Ramalho Eanes, was readily elected president of the new republic in 1976 and reelected to a second term in 1980. The influence of the Roman Catholic church, the European Economic Community to which Portugal with its troubled economy looked for aid, and conservative groups in the north of the country nudged the government toward a less radical stance and weakened the influence of the extreme leftists and Communists. Because the old dictatorship was ended and democratic elections had been held, Portugal was finally allowed to join the Council of Europe in 1976. The NATO nations, which over the preceding two years had withheld strategic information from Portugal for fear it would be leaked to the Soviet Union, began again to take Portugal into their confidence. Especially important to them were the Azores, for as a U.S. military adviser would comment a decade later, "Controlling the Azores means control over most of the North Atlantic."

Coalition politics prevailed, with the Socialist party at first taking the lead in forming governments. In 1979 a coalition of the Social Democratic party and the Popular Monarchist party, known as the Democratic Alliance, won a majority of seats in the Parliament. Francisco Sá Carneiro, prime minister, president of the Social Democratic party, and the leader of the alliance, was killed in a plane crash at the end of 1980. Yet the alliance held together sufficiently long to achieve, with the aid of the Socialists, a major constitutional revision in 1982.

Much of the Marxist rhetoric disappeared in the new version of the constitution. The Council of the Revolution, on which President Eanes and other military officers sat and which had used its veto power to block legislation favorable to the private economic sector, also was eliminated. Free enterprise gained more latitude, Communist-sponsored "agrarian reform" was ended, and civilian control of the military was prescribed. The president serves as commander in chief and is elected by universal and direct suffrage for a five-year term. The president, guided by the Assembly election results, appoints the prime minister and the Council of Ministers. The president can veto legislation, but this veto may be overruled by the Assembly. Deputies are elected to the Assembly by a system of proportional representation. There is a Supreme Court and an advisory Council of State, consisting of five members chosen by the president, five selected by the Assembly, and five key civilian officeholders. This council, now dominated by civilians rather than by the president and military, succeeded to some of the responsibilities of the former Council of the Revolution. The president protested to no avail the diminution of his powers under the constitution of 1982.

The Democratic Alliance collapsed shortly after the passage of the constitutional revision, and the Socialists once again took the lead in forming coalitions, turning first to the Social Democrats. These drove a hard bargain in 1984, as they achieved promises that labor legislation would be changed and that private industry might be allowed back into the fertilizer, cement, and banking industries, which had been nationalized after the 1974 revolution. Stability of government and a firm coalition were much to be desired; therefore Socialist Prime Minister Mário Soares was willing to make these concessions.

A prime goal of Soares and of preceding governments was the rehabilitation of the Portuguese economy. The revolution of 1974 had affected it greatly. The formerly dominant large financial-industrial groups were broken up at that time. A wide range of utilities and firms in the transportation, banking, and construction industries had been nationalized; others were subjected to close governmental control. The return to more moderate government attitudes in the 1980s brought a reopening of the economy to private investors. Many dispossessed landowners regained their farmlands, and the number of worker-run companies declined substantially. Various austerity programs were attempted during the late 1970s and early 1980s, but parliamentary squabbling and the inflation provoked by rising oil prices prevented them from being fully effective. More export trade was needed. Resolution of difficulties concerning agricultural subsidies and the consequent agreement by the European Economic Community that Portugal could become a member on January 1, 1986, were therefore welcome. Entrance brought major social aid and regional development funds from the EEC, as Portugal's per capita income was only about one-quarter of the EEC average and the jobless rate was over 11 percent. Nearly $5 billion of EEC funds helped to upgrade Portugal's neglected infrastructure over the next five years.

Soares had prevented the revolution from being captured by left extremists or advocates of right-wing dictatorship and had gained Portugal's acceptance into the EEC. His achievement was recognized in his election in 1986 as the first civilian president of Portugal since 1926. Prime Minister Aníbal Cavaco Silva of the Social Democrats continued with efforts to stimulate the economy through market incentives, reduction of protectionism and state intervention in the economy, privatization of portions of the public sector, and streamlining of the bureaucracy. When the minority government was balked by parliamentary opposition, Soares called for elections in 1987 rather than turn to a left coalition involving the Moscow-oriented Communists.

The voters resoundingly supported Cavaco Silva, giving him an absolute legislative majority. The way was clear for decisive action along the modernization path Cavaco Silva defined. Government-owned firms were partially reprivatized. Next, a 1989 revision of the constitution permitted full denationalization of industries and sale of a majority, rather than a minority, of government shares in a firm. The new version of the constitution also proclaimed Portugal's goal would be construction of "a free, just and united society" rather than a "classless society."

In elections held in 1991, the center-right premier and the Social Democrats won a solid majority of the popular vote and of the seats in Parliament. A steady economic growth rate of 4.5 percent, a construction boom that lowered unemployment, foreign investment eager to take advantage of a low wage scale, and the embarrassment of the still hard-line Communist party by events in Eastern Europe all contributed to this success.

Discontent with the unending colonial wars had much to do with the occurrence of revolution in 1974. Though the territories did have economic significance for Portugal, quick steps were taken by the revolutionaries to grant them full independence. Guinea-Bissau was recognized as independent in 1974. The next year Angola, Cape Verde, and Mozambique all achieved that status. By the end of 1976, the Azores were autonomous, possessing their own governments and legislatures; Timor had been seized by Indonesia. In 1987 an agreement with the People's Republic of China provided for transfer of rule of Portugal's last colony, Maçao, to China in 1999. The revolution, which despite its hesitancies and vagaries avoided both Communist and military dictatorships, thus brought significant changes: divestment of colonies, emergence of a more democratic form of government, and initiation of new economic patterns and policies that in turn led to participation in the European Economic Community. This last linkage initially benefited both the Portuguese economy and the democratic cause within the country. In the first years of the 1990s, Portugal relinquished to Greece the position of poorest member of the EC. Yet much modernization remained to be done, especially in housing, literacy, and in the heart of the state's economy—textiles and agriculture—if Portugal were to hold its own upon the demise of all trade barriers within the EC.

Economic Progress and Political Turmoil: The Aegean States

Turkey

Turkey's strict neutrality until almost the end of World War II was born of its disastrous experiences in the many European wars in which it had participated in the past. The Turkish government considered that it could best protect the country's interests by remaining neutral. This was especially true because both Germany and the USSR had designs on Turkey's independence. For Germany, Turkey was important both as a means of outflanking the Soviet Union and as a route to the Arab countries and oil fields. In the Soviets' view, Turkey occupied an important strategic position that blocked the way to the Mediterranean; they feared Turkey would be controlled by enemies of the Soviet regime if it were not controlled by the Soviet Union itself. While the war was in progress, the Turkish government succeeded in preserving a good balance between these two pressures; it refrained from joining the United Nations coalition until March 1945.

With the defeat of Germany, however, the danger to Turkey inherent in the Soviet aims became more immediate. Early in 1945, when the defeat of Germany was imminent, Moscow denounced the Soviet-Turkish nonaggression pact of 1925 on the ground that a reconsideration of its terms was necessary. It soon became clear that the USSR not only wanted to participate in the defense of the Turkish Straits but also desired to annex a small strip of territory in northeastern Turkey. This pressure was vigorously resisted by Turkey, which rejected subsequent Soviet proposals regarding the straits as "not compatible with the inalienable rights of sovereignty of Turkey or with its security." Receipt of U.S. military supplies under the Truman Doctrine of 1947 (see Chapter 3) bolstered the Turks' determination not to give way.

Between the two world wars, Turkey had experienced a significant economic and social transformation under the leadership of Mustafa Kemal Atatürk, a remarkable statesman who served as president from 1923 to 1938. Under the People's party that he founded, Turkey was administered by a one-party system that drew on the autocratic heritage of the Ottoman Empire of which Turkey had been the core in the centuries before World War I. President Ismet Inönü continued this mode of governance after 1938, but with the end of the war, the forces of pluralism began to assert themselves with a demand for greater political freedom. The Democratic party founded by Celal Bayar finally came to office in 1950 after winning a landslide electoral victory. This was the first time in Turkish history that a government had been changed as a result of free elections, and it was generally regarded as a step in the direction of democratic government as known in the West.

Turkey's development efforts after the war were greatly assisted by extensive U.S. aid, which continued into the 1990s. The new government elected in 1950, with Bayar as president and Adnan Menderes as prime minister, made many important gains during its long tenure of office. Economic growth in particular was greatly stimulated. In the decade after 1948, agricultural production was doubled and industrial production increased by about one-half. In such specialized fields as electric power, road building, and merchant shipping, expansion was much more rapid. Turkey extended its international ties by joining NATO in 1952, the Balkan Alliance in 1953,

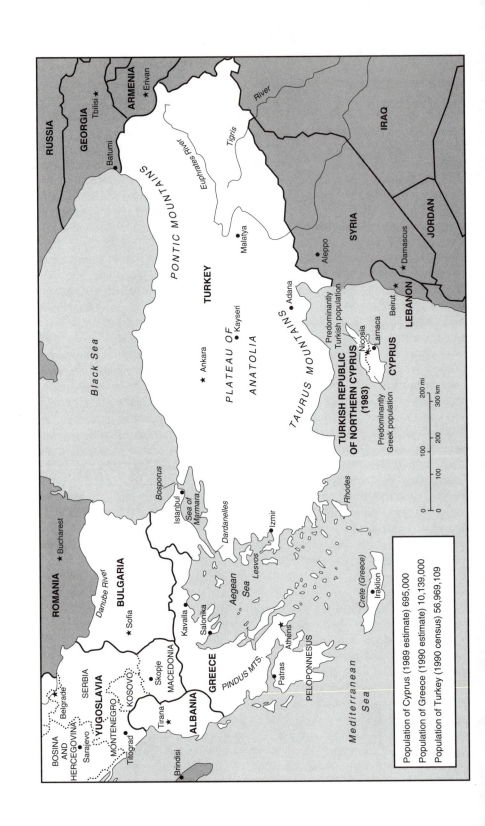

RUSSIA

GEORGIA

Tbilisi ★

ARMENIA

★ Erivan

● Batumi

PONTIC MOUNTAINS

Euphrates River

Tigris River

River

IRAQ

SYRIA

★ Damascus

JORDAN

● Aleppo

Malatya ●

TURKEY

PLATEAU OF ANATOLIA

★ Ankara

Kayseri ●

● Adana

TAURUS MOUNTAINS

Predominantly Turkish population

Nicosia ●

Lamaca ●

Beirut ★

LEBANON

TURKISH REPUBLIC OF NORTHERN CYPRUS (1983)

Predominantly Greek population

CYPRUS

Black Sea

Bosporus

Istanbul ●

Sea of Marmara

Dardanelles

Izmir ●

Lesvos

Rhodes

200 mi

300 km

200

100

200

100

0

0

ROMANIA

★ Bucharest

Danube River

BULGARIA

★ Sofia

Kavalla ●

Salonika ●

Aegean Sea

Crete (Greece)

Iráklion ●

SERBIA

★ Belgrade

YUGOSLAVIA

MONTENEGRO

KOSOVO

Skopje ●

MACEDONIA

BOSINA AND HERCEGOVINA

Sarajevo ●

Titograd ●

Tirana ★

ALBANIA

GREECE

PINDUS MTS.

Athens ★

Patras ●

PELOPONNESUS

Mediterranean Sea

Brindisi ●

Population of Cyprus (1989 estimate) 695,000
Population of Greece (1990 estimate) 10,139,000
Population of Turkey (1990 census) 56,969,109

and in 1954 the Middle East Treaty Organization (known until 1959 as the Baghdad Pact and thereafter as the Central Treaty Organization, or CENTO). Turkey was also active in the Council of Europe and in the United Nations. In the latter connection it participated in the Korean War with a brigade of 4,500 troops, which fought bravely in some of the most bitter battles. Despite incessant Soviet pressure, Turkey stood firm in defense of its independence and was respected as a strong and progressive state.

These gains by the Democratic regime were nevertheless bought at a high price. In the economic sphere, Turkish investments in industry and transportation greatly surpassed the country's ability to pay for them. Unlike Greece, Turkey built up a large indebtedness to West European creditors that it could pay for only with U.S. economic aid. The Democrats believed that Turkey was so vital to NATO that the United States would continue to pay its debts. Yet the United States refused to expand its aid to this extent, and by the end of the 1950s Turkey found foreign credit very difficult to obtain. The import of consumer goods and raw materials was severely restricted, industrial production was cut down, inflation increased, and popular discontent grew.

As its domestic situation became more troublesome, the Democratic regime took increasingly harsh measures against its political opponents. Starting in 1953, the government adopted laws restricting freedom of speech and of the press and jailed prominent members of the opposition on flimsy charges. Thanks in part to such measures, and in part to its success in winning the support of the peasantry, which the People's party had neglected, the Democrats remained in office. In the elections of 1954 they kept their large parliamentary majority, but in 1957 they received only 48.5 percent of the popular vote as against 41 percent for the People's party. Owing to the peculiarities of the Turkish electoral system, the Democrats still retained a large parliamentary majority. Their policies, however, provoked increasing criticism at home and abroad. This growing discontent with the policies of Menderes culminated in a coup d'état on May 27, 1960, by a group of army officers under the leadership of General Cemal Gürsel.

The action of the military leaders responded to widespread discontent in a period of great turbulence in Turkish affairs. A new constitution was drawn up and a civilian government was again elected to office in 1961. Despite rapid economic growth, there was continuing political unrest and violence. In 1980 the Turkish army under General Kenan Evren again established military rule. Another constitution was drafted and approved by referendum in 1982. Former political party leaders were also banned from politics for ten years, apparently in an effort to end old rivalries and gain a new start. Following elections held in 1983, a civilian government headed by Turgut Özal of the new Motherland party, took office, but it continued to function under military guidance with General Evren as president. Özal's principal challenge was to reduce unemployment and inflation at the same time, and he sought to do this through rigid economic and political controls. A

After a career as a government bureaucrat, Turgut Özal emerged as the key civilian Turkish politician of the 1980s. His economic reform program, the January 24 (1980) Measures, laid the foundation for his later efforts to end Turkey's paralysis and to catch up with Western industrial nations. Austerity, a switch from import-substitute manufacturing to promotion of exports, adjustment of controls on foreign exchange, privatization of state enterprises, and reduction of subsidies to state businesses were central to a curbing of inflation and the formation of a more stable economic environment. Yet resurgent inflation in time undercut Özal's popularity. His great achievement in domestic policy was the formation of the Motherland party, which broke the hold of traditional parties in Turkey because of Özal's economic successes, his avoidance of ideological identification, and his appeal to the middle classes. (Photo by Jodi Levinson.)

particular problem was the economic depression in Western Europe, where many Turkish workers had been employed. Not only was the income that they contributed markedly reduced, but their return added to unemployment.

A referendum in 1987 lifted the ban on former politicians, and Özal quickly called an election. His economic measures had experienced moderate success, and his party triumphed over the Social Democrat Populist party and the True Path (sometimes called Correct Way) party. But in his second term Özal encountered intractable inflation and unemployment, difficulty in assimilating some 300,000 Turks who fled to Turkey from mistreatment in Bulgaria as well as Kurds fleeing from atrocities and genocide in Iraq, and a Kurdish rebellion at home. He greatly hoped that entry into the European Community would ease Turkey's economic problems, winning it development aid and increased access for its surplus workers to European jobs. But the vast differential between Turkey's economic basis and that of the more Western states and the strain Turkey's membership would place on the EC's Common Agricultural Policy led to critical review of Turkey's application; it was essentially rejected by the EC in December 1989. By that time Özal had been elected president of Turkey. As the popularity of the Motherland party faltered, strife between its liberal wing and its rural-based Islamic fundamentalists grew.

Despite disappointment over their application to the EC, the Turkish leaders remained loyal to the West during the Persian Gulf crisis. They closed two key oil pipelines from Iraq at considerable cost to their own economy in order to back United Nations sanctions against Iraq. When actual fighting broke out, they permitted NATO air bases in Turkey to be used to launch United Nations coalition attacks against Iraq, disregarding criticism from segments of their Muslim population. Though the forces of Iraqi dictator Saddam Hussein were defeated by those of the United Nations, they remained strong enough to put down renewed Kurdish rebellion in the northern regions of Iraq. Thousands of Kurds fled across rugged mountains to seek safety in Turkey. Without jobs, food, or shelter available for the refugees, and unwilling to see their numbers swell those of restless Kurds within Turkey, President Özal denied them entrance. The United States and the United Nations then made belated efforts to provide for the fleeing Kurds within Iraq. The episode was ironically unfortunate for Özal, as he had recently taken steps to ease relations with the Kurdish population in his own country, including lifting of a ban on the speaking of Kurdish. Such action may well have been a partial response to criticisms of Turkey's human rights record that had hindered the European Community's consideration of Turkish application for membership in the EC.

Later in 1991 the Turkish air force launched raids against what were claimed to be bases of the hard-line Marxist Kurdish Workers' party just over the border in northern Iraq. The Ankara government also proclaimed a 3-mile-deep (4.8-km) buffer zone along the 220-mile (355-km) border, in Iraqi territory, to defend against guerrilla attacks. Such firm action hardly impressed Özal's critics. The Motherland party suffered reverses in the fall 1991 elections. Suleyman Demirel, leader of the True Path party and a former prime minister six times over, took charge of forming a new governmental coalition. In the campaign he had denounced Özal's relaxation of restrictions on Kurds in Turkey and apparent softening of the Turkish stance regarding Cyprus. An inflation rate of 71 percent and alleged corruption and nepotism in Özal's regime also drew fire. Demirel announced that once in power he would not rest until the president was forced to resign; Özal said he would hold firm. Thus the political future of Turkey held potential for further instability, ethnic controversy, and weakening of efforts to obtain admission to the EC.

The ideology of the new Turkey established by Atatürk rested on concepts of nationalism, secularism, state control, and reliance on the West for support in terms of ideas, technology, and finances. But this model of modernization, known as Atatürkism, has been challenged by a course of events ranging from the rise of Muslim fundamentalism in the Middle East to the stimulus of ethnic nationalists in the neighboring Soviet Union drawn from Gorbachev's *perestroika*. Turkey's turbulent political record since the 1950s may be attributed to both domestic and international conditions. At home, the effort to implement a pluralistic system of government in a country accustomed to autocratic rule over the centuries is only part of the problem. The Kurdish minority holds strong grievances and expresses them through terroristic acts. Muslim religious leaders are resentful of the secular system established by Atatürk. In addition, political radicals, at times supported in part by the Soviet Union, have sought to destabilize the government. In the international arena, Turkey's position on the border of the Soviet orbit and as guardian of the outlet of the Black Sea to the Mediterranean, as well as its continuing controversy with Greece, place it under constant pressure. Failure to gain admittance to the European Community has also been a disappointment for some and raises doubts about the course and continuing growth of the nation's economy.

Greece

Unlike Turkey, which had been governed in a relatively stable and progressive fashion from the 1920s to the 1960s, Greece has suffered intermittent civil strife since World War II. The country has been torn by conflict between royalists and republicans and among conservatives, moderates, and radicals. From 1936 to 1941 the Greek monarchy under King George II was governed by an authoritarian regime headed by Ioannis Metaxas, who died as his country was being overrun by Axis forces in 1941. The king escaped to Egypt and formed a government-in-exile, which remained under the influence of extreme nationalist elements. In occupied Greece, at the same time, a powerful coalition group, known as the National Liberation Front (EAM), was formed with a view to organizing resistance to the Axis occupation forces. Although democratic leaders were among its members, the EAM gradually came under the domination of the Communists as a result of their well-developed, united-front infiltration techniques. By the end of the war, the EAM had under its command an armed force sufficiently powerful to seize control of the government if necessary. The moderate democratic leaders, who would normally have had the support of a majority of Greeks in peacetime, were now divided in their loyalty between the government-in-exile and the EAM. Just before the end of the war, however, the moderates managed to form a government of national unity under Georgios Papandreou, a Social Democrat, that included representatives of the EAM. It was this government that returned to Greece upon the liberation of that country in October 1944, accompanied by British troops. The king remained in exile, pending the establishment of a stable government.

Following a prolonged period of civil strife, elections were held under international supervision in 1946 that brought to office a conservative government. In a subsequent plebiscite, the country voted by a modest majority in favor of the return of King George II. When the king died in 1947, his brother, Paul, took the throne; Paul's son in turn took his place in 1964 as Constantine II.

The difficulties Greece faced in returning to normal life after the war were considerably alleviated by financial and technical assistance from the United States. Britain, which had taken primary responsibility for the security of the eastern Mediterranean in the postwar period, had announced that the financial burden was too great. Greece therefore turned to the United States, and in March 1947 President Truman declared that the security of Greece was crucial to U.S. national interests. This policy, which was known as the Truman Doctrine and embraced Turkey as well as Greece, was the starting point of the very substantial U.S. program of financial and military assistance in this region. In 1947 no more than $300 million in U.S. aid was designated for Greece, but by 1956 some $2.5 billion dollars had been advanced in economic and military aid. The needs of war-devastated Greece were so great, and its position as a line of defense against possible Soviet expansion so important, that this aid program was widely hailed as a vital enterprise.

In purely economic terms, Greece made remarkable gains in the period after 1947. Production of wheat and rice greatly expanded, and the profitable tobacco business was restored. By 1950 agricultural production had passed the prewar level, and by 1955 it had increased again by one-half. Similar gains were scored in industrial production, which by 1956 had reached almost double the prewar level. These gains were made possible primarily because of the shipment of modern equipment to Greece and the technical advice provided by the U.S. economic mission. Accompanying this growth in production was an extensive road-building, irrigation, and electrification program. Within a few years, a revolution was produced in Greek internal communications, and electricity was brought to several hundred villages. Two principal long-term economic benefits resulted from this aid: Production now began to expand more rapidly than the population, thus raising the hope of a steady improvement in living standards; and for the first time Greece was able to raise enough food to feed itself without imports.

Through the 1950s and into the 1960s, Greece enjoyed a continuity of policy and a steadily rising standard of living. Greece joined NATO in 1952, and as an associate member of the European Economic Community in 1962 participated in Europe's new affluence. Continuing U.S. military aid and extensive capital investments from Western Europe were important elements in this period of prosperity. At the same time, this new affluence was purchased in good measure by acceptance of unpopular Western policies. The stationing of NATO forces, including nuclear weapons, on Greek territory met with much opposition. More particularly, the opposition of the Western allies to Greek annexation of Cyprus (see the section on Cyprus below) was especially unpopular.

With the growth of political participation in this period, Greek opinion was increasingly divided by the tension between relying on the Western allies for capital and trade and resentment of Western opposition to Greek national aims. A conflict between Papandreou, who served as prime minister from 1963 to 1965, and King Constantine II led to a prolonged political crisis that was terminated in 1967 by a military coup by Greek colonels. They established a military dictatorship that drove the king into exile, withdrew from associate membership in the EEC, and sought to take Cyprus by force. A return to civilian rule was finally negotiated in 1974. A democratic government under Konstantinos Karamanlis sought to steer a difficult course between asserting an independent Greek policy and continuing reliance on Western aid and investments. Normal political life was resumed and a plebiscite led to the establishment of a republican form of government. At the beginning of 1981 Greece joined the EEC. Elections later that year failed to give the government a majority.

The new Parliament brought to power the U.S.-trained economist Andreas Papandreou, son of Georgios Papandreou, as head of the Pan-Hellenic Socialist movement (PASOK). Papandreou now sought to implement a much more decisive reallocation of resources to social welfare, and his rhetoric was vigorously defiant of NATO policies and of U.S. bases in Greece. He was reelected by a large majority in 1985, but shortly after the election he was forced to recognize that his social policies had led to increased indebtedness, unemployment, and inflation. Despite his nationalistic rhetoric, he remained loyal to NATO because Western support was not only essential for the economy but also strengthened Greece in its conflict with Turkey.

The longer Andreas Papandreou stayed in office, the more turbulent Greek politics became. In 1987 he proposed legislation that would permit the

Widely recognized as Greece's senior statesman during the latter half of this century, Konstantinos Karamanlis has been elected member of Parliament twelve times since 1935 and has held the post of prime minister for a total of fourteen years. In 1974 Karamanlis headed a national unity government responsible for the restoration of democracy following the collapse of the military regime. One of the first European leaders to promote the idea of a united Europe, Karamanlis was the architect of Greece's accession to the European Community in 1981. (Photo courtesy of the Greek Press and Information Office.)

government to take over the property of the Greek Orthodox church. Bishops and priests protested. Even a modified law drew vehement criticism; eventually government-church negotiations achieved a compromise on the issue. Meanwhile increasingly substantive charges of corruption were levied against the government and cabinet. Many officials, from high to low station, seemed to be on the take. Papandreou's personal life also became a distraction, as the septuagenarian took up with a much younger woman and divorced his wife of thirty-eight years. Though the long-standing state of war with Albania was ended in 1987, renewed difficulties with Turkey flared in subsequent years over Cyprus and sea and air rights in the Aegean.

Corruption charges and the circus atmosphere surrounding the prime minister's personal life led to the decline of the PASOK's fortunes in two parliamentary elections in 1989. Before the elections, the PASOK altered voting rules in a manner that increased the difficulty of any one party achieving a majority of seats in the Parliament. Thus, though the opposition New Democratic party made substantial gains, it had to settle for a leadership role in an all-party coalition that did not include Papandreou. That government struggled with a huge budget deficit, rocketing inflation, and increasing strikes. After still another election in 1991, the New Democrats held exactly half of the seats in Parliament and won approval of their cabinet, thanks to the vote of one center-right deputy. It is clear that no formula for political stability and coherent economic growth was readily available for Greece. Instead, gyrations in both economic and political affairs worked against the

*Andreas Papandreou, leader of the Pan-Hellenic Social-
ist Movement, initially won support by giving raises to
Greek government workers, condoning other forms of
government spending, and criticizing the United States
(this last garnering the approval of Greek nationalists).
His popularity eventually declined because of the high
rate of inflation, a large foreign debt that burdened the
economy, and especially because of his own comport-
ment and accusations of corruption by the opposition,
which failed to result in a court conviction. (Photo
courtesy of the Greek Press and Information Office.)*

achievement of stability and successful modernization in either area; this
volatility was in part, of course, a reflection not only of personal political
agendas but also of the social dislocation associated with modernization
efforts.

Cyprus

The extension of U.S. aid to Greece and Turkey under the Truman Doctrine
brought these two countries more closely into the Western orbit, and their
admission to NATO in 1952 led to their cooperation in defense of the eastern

Mediterranean. This unity of purpose and interest was soon fundamentally disturbed, however, by controversy over the Mediterranean island of Cyprus.

Cyprus, under British rule since 1878 and a crown colony since 1925, had played an important role as a British base in World War II. Nearly 80 percent of its population of 655,000 was Greek, and for a generation there had been an active movement in Cyprus as well as on the Greek mainland favoring Greece's annexation of the 3,572-square-mile (9,251.5-sq-km) island. The Turks, for their part, pointed out that 18 percent of the population of Cyprus was Turkish. Moreover, the island is only 40 miles (64.5 km) from Turkey, whereas it is some 660 miles (409 km) from the Greek mainland. Great Britain's use of Cyprus as a major military base was also an important consideration. Valuable as a site for airfields, it was the only remaining location in this area where the British could freely maintain sizable armed forces. In the postwar period, Cyprus thus became a bitter issue not only between Greece and Great Britain but also between Greece and Turkey.

After the war the Labour government in Britain took steps to give the Greeks a more active role in the government of Cyprus and to improve economic conditions. These efforts met with hostility, however, and were further complicated by the strife in Greece itself. Once the Communists in Greece were defeated, Cyprus became the major issue for Greek nationalists. The Communists also seized on this issue as a means of salvaging some of their popularity. The situation in Cyprus deteriorated rapidly, with the Greeks resorting to terrorism and the British replying with martial law. Initial British proposals for a compromise met with failure, as did the efforts of the Greeks to obtain support for their point of view in the United Nations. At the same time Greek-Turkish relations rapidly became embittered. In 1960, after several thousand lives had been lost in civil strife, the Greek and Turkish governments negotiated a compromise under which an independent Republic of Cyprus was created. The constitution of this new state, which was under the joint guarantee of Britain, Greece, and Turkey, provided for a Greek president, a Turkish vice-president with coequal powers in vital matters of policy, and a ratio of seven to three for the two nationalities in the assembly and in the public services.

This arrangement had some of the elements of a genuine compromise of the issues under dispute, but it left both sides discontented. Religious rivalry between the Orthodox Christian Greeks and the Muslim Turks did not die down. The Greeks in Cyprus remained dissatisfied because they had placed great hopes on reunion with Greece. They were also concerned that the Turks, with only 18 percent of the population, should have a 13 percent representation in the government and a veto on major policy matters at the executive level. The Turks, for their part, did not believe that the Greeks sincerely intended to implement the 1960 compromise; they were especially concerned about the rights of the Turks in the five major cities where the population was mixed. Before long these disagreements and misunderstandings led to the collapse of the compromise and to renewed civil strife on a large scale.

Early in 1964 the United Nations established a peacekeeping force in Cyprus to maintain order. Calm conditions were preserved until the military government that came to power in Greece in 1967 began to adopt a more aggressive policy; for a while it seemed again that war might break out between Greece and Turkey over possession of the island. A compromise was nevertheless finally reached under which Greek and Turkish troops were withdrawn from the island, and the UN force was given a predominant role in preserving order. This settlement collapsed in 1974 when the Greek military regime sought to overthrow the republic in an effort to annex Cyprus to Greece. The Turkish government responded with a large-scale landing on the island that ended with Turkish troops' occupying a substantial portion of northern Cyprus and forcing the evacuation to the south of some 200,000 Greek Cypriots. Despite continuing negotiations under UN supervision, the Cyprus problem remained unresolved into the 1990s. The Republic of Cyprus administers the Greek portion of the island, and it is internationally recognized as the legitimate government of Cyprus. The Turkish portion is administered by the "Turkish Republic of Northern Cyprus," recognized only by the Turkish government.

The Small States in Perspective

The variety of experiences of the small states of Europe since World War II, even without consideration of the smallest states such as Andorra, Malta, Monaco, and Liechtenstein, is wide-ranging. Each has modernized in its own way, with those least damaged by the war initially experiencing the slowest pace of evolution. Yet even these, including conservative Switzerland, have had their share of change. Those that attempted to hold most stubbornly to the formulas of the past—Spain and Portugal—were, in fact, those that eventually experienced the greatest alteration of their governments and societies.

In contrast, some of the Scandinavian states that explored most fully the possibilities of the welfare state have recently been forced by economic factors to take a step back from their most ambitious plans. In these states new thinking, spurred by environmental concerns, has led to reconsideration of exactly what should result from adapting to the revolution in science and technology. The use of new technology, even if it may bring cheaper electricity to run more household appliances and medical equipment, is no longer thought a goal in itself; this is because the technologies involved may destroy the environment or make hostages of future generations. Hence the banning of nuclear plants in Sweden and renewed interest in small and moderately sized industries.

Nationalism has played a role. In some countries it has furthered a sense of national identity and commitment of effort, as in Ireland. In others, it has divided the population and slowed or made more costly the progress of economic achievement, as in Belgium. In some instances, it has brought diversion of funds and efforts to military support of nationalist quarrels, as in the Aegean states. Yet almost universally the imperatives of economic and political modernization have worn down some of the corrosive edges of nationalism. They have led observant nationalists as well as persons of international orientation to recognize that often national interests can best be served by forms of international cooperation.

In terms of integration, the small states are in a peculiar position that forces them to take a stop-and-go pace. Through integration, they may be able to enjoy markets and to apply technologies that they simply could not gain otherwise; leadership in international cooperation can also give a small state influence and prestige it otherwise would not have. Yet many smaller states, even Belgium, which has done perhaps the most in this regard, are sensitive to the danger that their interests could be smothered by those of the greater powers. The need is therefore always present for them to work with the United Kingdom, the United States, Germany, France, and the Soviet Union and its successors to persuade them that great-power interests can be served by paying attention to the needs and concerns of the smaller states.

Religion has worked to heighten both national identity and commitment to given policies (e.g., Ireland); it has also been divisive (e.g., Belgium, Cyprus, the Netherlands). In some regions, it moved from being a conservative force to being a key factor in facilitating change and modernization. Consider, for example, the role of the church and Opus Dei in Spain. Yet in some other areas, as in the Netherlands, the Roman church has been accused of opposing change because of its stance on birth control and women as priests; note, too, the differing views regarding church-backed antiabortion legislation and women's rights in the several small states.

In international affairs, small states over the years have earned the reputation of tendering their friendships in a manner that augments rather than counters any imbalance of power between two security systems. Since World War II this has not been nearly as predominant a pattern as has the influence of geographic location and the effort to keep communications open with both superpower blocs. Neutrality does not necessarily mean that a small state always chooses to stand halfway between the contestants; it may lean one way or another (compare the orientations of Finland and Switzerland). But in some cases it proves a useful tool in reducing areas of conflict (Austria, Finland, Sweden).

Above all, the balance sheet for the small states of Europe since 1945 shows that the trend has inexorably been one of commitment to economic and political modernization, either consciously chosen or forced by circumstances. This trend has been accompanied by substantive moves toward increased democracy, whether in the form of democratic elections in once authoritarian states or in the form of increased involvement in decisionmaking by all sectors of the public in states that were already well along the democratic path before the war.

Notes

1. Flora Lewis, "Spanish Red Likens Revolt Against Soviet to Luther's," *New York Times,* July 7, 1976, p. 2.

Suggested Readings

The Iberian States

Arango, E. R., *Spain: From Repression to Renewal* (1985).

Baklanoff, E. N., *The Economic Transformation of Spain and Portugal* (1978).

Braga de Macedo, J., *Portugal Since the Revolution: Economic and Political Perspectives* (1981).

Bruneau, T. C., *Politics and Nationhood: Post Revolutionary Portugal* (1984).

Bruneau, T. C., and A. Macleod, *Politics in Contemporary Portugal: Parties and the Consolidation of Democracy* (1986).

Carr, R., and J. P. Fusi, *Spain: Dictatorship to Democracy,* 2d ed. (1979).

Clark, R. P., *The Basques: The Franco Years and Beyond* (1979).

Coverdale, J. F., *The Political Transformation of Spain After Franco* (1979).

Graham, L. F., and H. M. Makler (eds.), *Contemporary Portugal: The Revolution and Its Antecedents* (1979).

Graham, L. F., and D. L. Wheeler (eds.), *In Search of Modern Portugal: The Revolution and Its Consequences* (1983).

Kay, H., *Salazar and Modern Portugal* (1970).

Newitt, M., *Portugal in Africa* (1981).

Payne, S. G., *The Franco Regime, 1936–1975* (1987).

———— , *A History of Spain and Portugal,* 2 vols. (1973).

Porch, D., *The Portuguese Armed Forces and the Revolution* (1978).

Preston, P., *The Triumph of Democracy in Spain* (1986).

Pridham, G. (ed.), *The New Mediterranean Democracies: Regime Transition in Spain, Greece and Portugal* (1984).

Raby, D. L., *Fascism and Resistance in Portugal: Communists, Liberals and Military Dissidents in the Opposition to Salazar, 1941–1974* (1988).

Robinson, R.A.H., *Contemporary Portugal: A History* (1979).

Sullivan, J., *ETA and Basque Nationalism: The Fight for Euskadi, 1890–1986* (1988).

The Aegean States

Turkey

Ahmad, F., *The Turkish Experiment in Democracy, 1950–1975* (1977).
Bianchi, R., *Interest Groups and Political Development in Turkey* (1984).
Davison, R. H., *Turkey* (1964).
Dodd, C. H., *Politics and Government in Turkey* (1969).
Hale, W., *The Political and Economic Development of Modern Turkey* (1981).
Hershlag, Z. Y., *The Contemporary Turkish Economy* (1988).
Karpat, K. (ed.), *Social Change and Politics in Turkey* (1973).
Ozbudun, E., *Social Change and Political Participation in Turkey* (1976).
Ozbudun, E., and A. Ulusan (eds.), *The Political Economy of Income Distribution in Turkey* (1980).
Rustow, D. A., *Turkey: America's Forgotten Ally* (1987).
Weicker, W., *Political Tutelage and Democracy in Turkey* (1973).

Greece

Kousoulas, D. G., *Modern Greece: Profile of a Nation* (1974).
Mouzelis, N. P., *Modern Greece: Facets of Underdevelopment* (1978).
O'Ballance, E., *The Greek Civil War, 1944–1949* (1966).
Psomiades, N. J., *The Eastern Question: The Last Phase, A Study in Greek-Turkish Diplomacy* (1968).
Woodhouse, C. M., *The Rise and Fall of the Greek Colonels* (1985).
Xydis, S. G., *Greece and the Great Powers, 1944–1947* (1963).

Cyprus

Denktash, R. R., *The Cyprus Triangle* (1982).
Hitchens, D., *Cyprus* (1984).
Polyvious, P. G., *Cyprus: Conflict and Negotiation, 1960–1980* (1980).
Volkan, V. D., *Cyprus—War and Adaptation: A Psychoanalytic History of Two Ethnic Groups in Conflict* (1979).

PART FOUR

Conclusion

CHAPTER FOURTEEN

A New Europe

Europe's Destiny

The European Crisis

Toward a New Europe

Whither Europe?

Suggested Readings

The year 1992 marks an anniversary of great significance for Europe—the 500th anniversary of the discovery of America. To be sure, "America" had been discovered before—by the Vikings around the year 1000 and by the nomads of Inner Asia (mistakenly called "Indians" by the Europeans) many thousands of years earlier—but it was the discovery in 1492 that was to be so crucial for Europe. It was crucial because the America that loomed only dimly on the western horizon of Europe at the end of the fifteenth century was in due course to challenge the world preeminence that Europe had held for so long.

Europe's Destiny

This European preeminence has been explained in part by environmental and societal advantages. In *The European Miracle*, the economist Eric Jones notes the benefits accruing to Europe from its mild climate, the relative absence of natural disasters, and its endowment of fertile soil and other natural resources. A social system evolved in Europe that encouraged relatively lower birthrates than those in other parts of the world and permitted a greater per capita investment in material welfare. Equally important in Jones's analysis is the variety of political systems in Europe and the absence of centralized empires, which in Asia were inclined to become more of a burden than a stimulus to economic development and social change.

These European advantages would have been passive, however, had it not been for a more critical factor—the growth of a rational, scientific attitude toward the material world. This advancement of knowledge gave individuals and societies the possibility of exploiting the human environment in ways unimagined in Europe before the sixteenth century and unknown to most other parts of the world until the nineteenth and twentieth. It underlay the scientific revolution and its technological spin-offs that would later transform the human condition.

In late medieval and early modern Europe, in a process that has been replicated many times in societies that modernized thereafter, those who benefited from traditional institutions and values felt threatened by the evolving rational approach to human affairs and sought to block it at every turn. This struggle of the old against the new permeated all aspects of European society, and in some respects it is still continuing. The French Revolution of 1789 was a great symbolic victory for the modern outlook, although many of its achievements were soon overturned and had to be fought for again.

It was in this context that the opening up of the New World played such a crucial role. Although the first travelers to the newly discovered American

For more than a century, the Eiffel Tower has stood as a symbol of modern Europe's highest aspirations. It was built in 1889, at the height of European self-confidence and optimism, in celebration of the French Revolution of 1789, which had brought the powerful ideals of individual liberty and social justice to the rest of Europe. Here, in 1989, the Eiffel Tower displays a dazzling illumination for its own centennial and bears mute witness to the beginning of a new era in European history, an era largely inspired by those very same revolutionary ideals of 1789. (Photo courtesy of the Press Service of the French Embassy.)

continent were mainly explorers and adventurers, it began to attract settlers who were willing to face the risks of moving to a new and dangerous environment. The dominant motives for this courageous venture were the desire to escape from the limitations imposed by Europe's stratified way of life, to gain freedom from the intellectual, religious, and political constraints of the Old World, and to form a society where freedom and rationality would prevail.

The philosophy underlying this search for a new society was succinctly stated in 1816 by Thomas Jefferson, when he wrote that

> laws and institutions must go hand in hand with the progress of the human mind. As that becomes more developed, more enlightened, as new discoveries are made, new truths disclosed, and manner and opinions change with the change of circumstances, institutions must advance also, and keep pace with the times. We might as well require a man to wear still the coat which fitted him when a boy, as civilized society to remain ever under the regimen of their barbarous ancestors. It is this preposterous idea which has lately deluged Europe in blood. Their monarchs, instead of wisely yielding to the gradual change of circumstances, of favoring progressive accommodation to progressive improvement, have clung to old abuses, entrenched themselves behind steady habits, and obliged their subjects to seek through blood and violence rash and ruinous innovations, which, had they been referred to the peaceful deliberations and collected wisdom of the nation, would have been put into acceptable and salutary forms. Let us follow no such examples.

America, which began as an outpost of Europe, became its rival and then in many respects its leader. By the twentieth century, the United States was the benchmark by which other societies were measured. It possessed to an even greater degree many of the environmental and economic characteristics that help to explain Europe's preeminence in the modern era. More important, America did not have the burden of transforming a previously feudal society. Like the other countries of the New World, its political system and social structure were open to innovation. By 1950 the United States, with 6 percent of the world's population, accounted for some 40 percent of the gross world product—more than twice the share of the twelve countries that later formed the European Community.

In the meantime, another rival outpost of European civilization—Russia—began to loom large on Europe's eastern horizon. As early as 1835, the French sociologist Alexis de Tocqueville had predicted, in effect, that the United States and Russia would one day eclipse Europe:

> There are at the present time two great nations of the world, which started from different points, but seem to tend toward the same end. I allude to the Russians and the Americans. . . .

All other nations seem to have nearly reached their natural limits, and they have only to maintain their power; but these are still in the act of growth. All the others have stopped, or continue to advance with extreme difficulty; these alone are proceeding with ease and celerity along a path to which no limit can be perceived. The American struggles against the obstacles which nature opposes to him; the adversaries of the Russian are men. The former combats the wilderness and savage life; the latter, civilization with all its arms. The conquests of the Americans are therefore gained by the ploughshare; those of the Russian by the sword. The Anglo-American relies upon personal interest to accomplish his ends, and gives free scope to the unguided strength and common sense of the people; the Russian centres all the authority of society in a single arm. The principal instrument of the former is freedom; of the latter, servitude. Their starting-point is different, and their courses are not the same; yet each of them seems marked out by the will of Heaven to sway the destinies of half the globe.

Tocqueville's remarks about Russia referred, of course, to czarist society, which was undergoing the same struggle of tradition versus modernity that was engaging Europe—but under circumstances in which those favoring traditional institutions and values were much more firmly established and resistant to change than in Europe. The Russian Revolution of 1917 was another great symbol of victory for the modern outlook. True, the Soviet Union that was created in its wake resembled the prerevolutionary society in many ways. It has often been argued that the use of force, the centralization of authority, and the servitude of the people were as characteristic of the Soviet Union as of the czarist Russia Tocqueville described. Yet in the 1930s the progressive rhetoric of the Soviet five-year plans presented a challenge to a Europe that was plagued by depression and disunity, and there was considerable support for the view that socialist planning was the answer to Europe's problems. It was therefore not surprising that in the early postwar years many observers were inclined to believe that the Europe that had for so long led the world in the advancement of knowledge, in the development of political institutions, in industrialization, in social mobilization, and in literature and the arts had finally lost its predominant role.

Interpreters of Europe's decline agreed that its explanation had to be sought in the disjuncture between European political and economic systems. The European states had failed to cope with the forces unleashed by economic growth and social change. In spite of the human benefits that were derived from this progress, the cost of European greatness was nevertheless profoundly disturbing both socially and psychologically. After 1850 the European states had dealt effectively with these forces, providing their citizens with transportation, loans, and education and eventually with security against sickness and unemployment. The states also developed national philosophies that gave coherence to their citizens' lives. Individuals thus came to be largely protected from the whirlwinds of change. The national states, however, could afford this protection only as long as their policies could encompass the relevant economic factors. Their insecurity was reflected in the uneasy imperialism of the 1880s and 1890s and in the search for security in alliance systems during the first decade of the twentieth century.

It was at this point that the elements of economic and social change—natural resources, labor, capital, and markets—began to expand beyond the reach of the national policies of the European states. The increasing difficulty of providing the extensive services now required by integral nationalism caused the European states to seek through imperialism and alliances the security that only a few decades earlier had been primarily a domestic problem. The economic system, which at the start of the nineteenth century had been largely a matter of local and provincial concern, had now expanded beyond national frontiers and was reaching regional and in some respects global proportions. The European states were not flexible enough to cope with these developments; their inability to adjust was revealed in many forms, including the trauma of two world wars.

By the middle of the twentieth century, the Europeans began to question whether the organization of their society into relatively discrete sovereign national states did not lie at the heart of their decline. Pessimism had been voiced since the First World War, and many observers conceded the gloomy predictions of Oswald Spengler's *Decline of the West* that the great urbanization and materialism of European society would soon lead to its decay. Others were influenced by Arnold Toynbee, who in his *Study of History* sought the key to the ills of the West in a comparative study of the rise and fall of earlier civilizations. Although Toynbee offered some hope that people might learn from past experience, the sociologist Pitirim Sorokin, in *Social and Cultural Dynamics*, presented a view of history as a series of unalterable fluctuations between spiritual and secular ages. Later, William H. McNeill, in *Rise of the West*, introduced a positive note in his reply to Spengler. He suggested that, because most of the world had adopted European institutions and values, the West had conquered the minds of other peoples even if it had relinquished political control over them.

More influential and substantive were the observations of the German social scientist Max Weber, one of the founding fathers of modern sociology. His emphasis on the role of rationality as a primary characteristic of the modern era saw it as the basis of economic and political action, expressed in particular by bureaucracies as the most efficient means of organizing human affairs. At the same time, he was concerned that the increasing bureaucratization and nationalism resulting from the First World War would crush the freedom of individuals motivated likewise by rational purposes. Although Weber died in 1920, this aspect of his work may be interpreted as foreseeing the dictatorships that arose in the Soviet Union, Italy, Germany, and elsewhere.

Weber was not alone in this concern. Many others expressed fears of "massification"—a condition in which atomized individuals would form an undifferentiated "mass" and be easily swayed by demagogues and turned to destructive ends. They were concerned that the gradual weakening of intermediate political institutions, like municipal councils, and social organizations would result in the accumulation of overwhelming power by national governments. Under these circumstances the only culture to survive would be that which appealed to the instincts and understanding of the lowest common denominator. The creative minority responsible for the flowering of modern knowledge would then be suffocated in the popular quicksand.

Another popular critique of European society in the interwar years came from the Marxists. Although Karl Marx had died thirty-four years before the end of the First World War, the influence of his writing had grown over the decades. His underlying critique was that the wealth produced in industrialized societies was being used irrationally—it was being employed not for the general welfare but for the benefit of the owners of the means of production at the expense of the workers. In 1848, in his *Communist Manifesto*, Marx had issued a call for a revolution by the working class, but by the twentieth century his followers had become divided into numerous conflicting programs of action. The Soviet program of Marxism-Leninism took the term *revolution* literally and advocated a radical program of transformation of what was still a predominantly peasant society. In retrospect, it is difficult to overstate the appeal that this alternative path to modernity held for many Europeans, not to mention for developing countries in the non-Western world.

In Western and Central Europe, both the Social Democratic and the Communist branches of the labor movement considered themselves to be Marxist, and their struggles with each other and with conservatives and moderates took many forms, including violence on each side. From the perspective of the 1990s, when a large share of the gross national product of all industrial societies is allocated to consumption and welfare, it may seem strange that the idea of a welfare state should have aroused so much controversy. The contest of ideas and political programs involved complex ideological components, including differences regarding such basic matters as the nature of humankind. It also had its international implications. One of the principal sources of support for Hitler's National Socialist movement came from those who believed it was Germany's destiny to defend Europe against the Communist threat from the East.

The European Crisis

In more concrete political terms, there were really two different issues involved in the crisis that Europe faced as it emerged from World War II. The first had to do with the domestic political economy—the equitable distribution of goods and services—and the second with relations among the European countries.

Would the evolution of human relations toward a more just and equitable society be achieved by moderate means—the absorption of the workers into the middle class by the redistribution of goods and services through democratic processes? Or would it come about by radical means—a violent revolution of the workers against the middle class, just as the middle class had overthrown the privileged elites in the French Revolution and in subsequent decades? As the speculation of Europeans about this dramatic crisis evolved in the postwar period, it tended to gravitate around two poles: a liberal outlook, using this term broadly to include the range from Christian Democrats to Social Democrats, and a Marxist-Leninist outlook.

A leading representative of the Western liberal tradition was the German philosopher Karl Popper. Although his major work was in the field of political theory and was not concerned with specific societies or schemes of periodization, Popper established strong negative and positive positions that had direct implication for the way that Europeans thought about their future. In *The Open Society and Its Enemies*, he argued against the view that history, and hence the future, was predetermined by immutable laws. He favored the view that individuals are free to create their own history and future. History had no meaning in itself; instead, it had the meaning that people gave it. Popper argued for piecemeal social engineering, for the redressing of specific inequities in an open society in which institutions are attuned to the rational and critical processes of thought and action. Popper's work does not suggest a specific near future, but it carries the implication that one can and should work for open societies in which pragmatic solutions to functional problems are sought by rational means.

Other contemporary writing in the Western liberal tradition that defended the claims of open as against closed societies, to appropriate Popper's terminology, was concerned principally with the English-speaking and Western European societies. It also assumed that the values of the Western liberal tradition would prevail in other societies if they were skillfully supported against the threats that beset them.

This attitude of piecemeal social change stands in sharp contrast to that of the Marxist-Leninists. For them the future was a matter of major concern that played a vital role in determining the conduct of policy and in the justification of the heavy sacrifices that were demanded of citizens. In a manual entitled *Fundamentals of Marxism-Leninism*, edited during the Khrushchev administration by a committee headed by O. V. Kuusinen (a Finnish member of the Soviet Politburo), the near future is seen as a struggle between two world systems, capitalist and socialist. In this struggle the socialist leaders are confronted with a twofold task: They must "build socialism" within the societies they control to the fully developed form known as "communism," and they must take advantage of situations in the rest of the world that are conducive to the success of the inevitable (as they see it) proletarian revolutions in capitalist societies. It is on this issue, among others—the costs and prospects of a policy of supporting revolutions—that the Soviet and Chinese leaders became engaged in an acute ideological struggle. Although both sought to avoid a general nuclear war, the Chinese leaders were at that time much more optimistic than the Soviets regarding the prospects of early and relatively inexpensive revolutions. Nevertheless, both the Soviet and Chinese parties were agreed that when the struggle with capitalism was concluded, the possibility would exist of creating something approximating a perfectly balanced society, in which both high levels of production and a corresponding level of social justice would be reached in tandem. Their economically deterministic view of history itself gave them confidence in this vision.

Nevertheless, by the 1970s a revolution had occurred in Soviet thinking that reversed many of these previous assumptions. The key to this new approach was the view that not the class struggle but the advancement of knowledge—the revolution in science and technology—was the engine of history. Whereas the earlier view saw the Soviet Union in the forefront of human development, as the first country to undergo a proletarian revolution, the new view saw it as behind the West and having to catch up.

By the late 1980s, with the well-known problems facing most socialist states, liberals and Marxist-Leninists had much more common ground than in the 1950s in their approach to the European dilemma. Leaders reflecting the two schools of thought were concerned primarily with the political, economic, and social development of their societies—the allocation of resources primarily toward consumption and investment, with as little as possible going to defense. The two views, in differing degrees to be sure, were inclined to balance the use of central bureaucracies in domestic affairs with greater emphasis on local initiative and privatization. More important, both increasingly recognized that the industrial societies as a whole were moving toward ever greater interdependence.

The second aspect of the European crisis had to do with the relations among individual European countries. Would they continue to pursue discrete and autarkic policies relying on tariffs and force, or would they devise institutional means to regulate their political and economic relations? Many serious students of the European experience tended to be pessimistic. In *The Passing of the European Age*, for example, Eric Fischer's concern with the transfer of European civilization to non-European centers led him to ask why civilizations declined. Fischer suggested that military defeat might in some cases mark the end of civilizations, but in his view these defeats would never have been decisive if disintegration had not already been far advanced. In the case of Europe, national differentiation and political friction had become marked in the twentieth century, and the resulting tensions were apparent to all. Fischer's interpretation was not only brief and general, but it also avoided dogmatism. He acknowledged that the parallels with past civilizations

Soviet demonstrators carry a banner depicting a mock tombstone that proclaims the death of communism. As communism died in its champion country, one could be sure that the old empire known as the USSR was finished. What one could not know is what would follow. But there can be no doubt that Europe faces many difficult challenges, and that ethnic clashes, economic problems, and political tensions may characterize Europe's future as much as the promise of the emerging European Community and the normalization of relations between the countries of East and West. (Photo courtesy of Paul Christensen.)

were not close, and he did not necessarily maintain that the European age had already passed. But Fischer was inclined "to regard Europe's great period as near its closing moment." He believed that the decline of European civilization had only been accelerated by the German effort to unite the Continent under its rule, and that if Germany had been victorious in the Second World War, the civilization of Europe would not have survived the destruction of so many of its creative centers. Fischer's hopes for the survival of European civilization lay in its transfer to other centers, such as the United States and the Soviet Union, and also to Europe's former overseas possessions.

Arguing along somewhat similar lines in *The Rise and Fall of Civilization*, Shepard Clough recognized the expansion of production in nineteenth-century Western Europe that resulted from the mechanization of industry, the exploitation of raw materials, the agricultural revolution, and the growth of trade. This expansion of production had been sufficient to provide not only a rising standard of living for a rapidly growing population but also a surplus adequate for great artistic and intellectual achievements. If Clough had his doubts regarding Western culture, it concerned rather its success in establishing control over its human environment. However remarkable their achievements in the social sciences, the societies that made up Western culture had been plagued both by domestic social tensions between "haves" and "have-nots" and by international tensions resulting from extreme forms of chauvinism that threatened to drain their resources and undermine their civilization.

Clough noted that whereas the United Kingdom, Germany, France, Belgium, Italy, and Sweden had produced 61 percent of the world's manufactures in 1870, as compared with 23.3 percent for the United States and 3.7 percent for Russia, the corresponding figures for 1936–1938 were 29.7, 32.2, and 18.5 percent. He therefore suggested that as a center of intellectual and artistic achievement Western Europe would have to cede to societies with greater economic development. He believed the United States and Canada to be the natural heirs, as they provided the most favorable conditions for economic development in relation to their populations.

Even more pessimistic was Hajo Holborn. In his volume on *The Political Collapse of Europe*, published six years after World War II, he asserted flatly that Europe was "dead and beyond resurrection." He noted the relative stability of the European political institutions established after the defeat of Napoleon, which prevented a major war for 100 years. He traced the development of the balance-of-power system, which continued to play a significant role during the nineteenth century, and described the workings of the concert of states that kept a firm hand on European affairs from 1815 to the middle of the century. He then described the gradual breakdown of this system under the impact of nationalism and the industrial revolution. He went on to show how the European states came to seek national security through military force rather than political compromise, and how this development culminated in the open conflict of the great wars in which the entire world was eventually involved. Holborn pointed out that after the First World War a primarily European political system was never reconstructed. The more general institutions relying on continued U.S. participation in European affairs and on the League of Nations had, he argued, failed to assure the security of the European states. The search for security continued through a series of local arrangements, but these were soon swept away by the Great Depression that undermined the political institutions of the continental states. No political system was left to preserve the peace when Hitler's challenge came.

Toward a New Europe

How different from Holborn's view of Europe as "dead and beyond resurrection" Europe seemed to its people only a few decades after the end of World War II. When the twenty-one-year span of peace between the two world

wars was equaled, Europeans already felt a sense of achievement; by the time
the fortieth anniversary of peace was celebrated in 1985, peace in Europe
seemed sufficiently secure to allow détente and disarmament to become the
predominant concerns. The most remarkable feature of postwar Europe was
the absence of war itself. For centuries the Continent had been the battle-
ground of nations and empires, and the two world wars of the first half of
the twentieth century were among the most devastating in world history. Yet
in the early 1990s, France, Britain, Germany, Italy, and the smaller European
states were cooperating closely on many issues, military and economic alike,
and it was inconceivable that they would resort again to war against one
another. This change was by all odds the most dramatic development in
Europe's long history.

    Moreover, despite the problems the various European states had—eco-
nomic, social, and otherwise—the European record in the half century since
World War II is impressive. All the European countries possess a higher
standard of living than in the prewar period, although there are many
differences among them. For many years the Western European countries
devoted more of their resources to consumption than did those in the East.
Although the latter might have enjoyed a somewhat more equitable distribution of income, the Western European states were still able to make up for
their shortcomings with government-sponsored welfare programs. Indeed,
the two superpowers have experienced more difficulties with income distribution than most European states, in part because of the heavy burden of
military expenses. At the end of the 1980s at least 20 percent of the Soviet
population lived in poverty, according to later revelations by Soviet economists. Within the big Soviet cities, the beggars encountered in subways and
railroad stations increased in numbers during the economic difficulties at the
beginning of the next decade. In the United States, about 15 percent of the
population was considered poor, although the standards by which poverty
was measured were much higher in the United States than in the Soviet
Union. There is a sharp contrast between the United States, where the
homeless and beggars are frequently seen in public, and the Western European
countries, where poverty rarely falls below a livable level despite wide
differences in income.

    If European achievements since 1945 are substantial, it is also true that
many references to these are based upon distinctions that often seem ambig-
uous and even artificial. After all, the long period of peace that Europeans
enjoyed after the Second World War was facilitated not by Europe's unity
but by its division. Peace was maintained on the basis of a balance of terror
between the two blocs, between NATO and the Warsaw Pact. It was a
situation in which one side's threat to use weapons of mass destruction against
the other was enough to ward off wars of territorial expansion and aggression.
Then, too, when observers spoke of "Europe's achievements" in the past,
they usually meant *Western* Europe. The lands to the east under Soviet

domination were much less well known and were chiefly objects of idle curiosity for their wealthier, considerably more prosperous cousins in the West. Indeed, when many Western European intellectuals and politicians spoke of the virtues of European political and economic integration, it rarely occurred to them to think of the states in the Soviet bloc.

Thus the events of 1989 and 1990 marked a major turning point in European history. For the first time in decades, all Europeans, theoretically, could come together again as one entity. Optimism, and euphoria as well, replaced pessimism. Nonetheless, many Europeans, in the East and West alike, were unsure how to deal with the many challenges that lay before them.

Whither Europe?

What will be the nature of Europe in the beginning years of the twenty-first century? The upheavals and changes that occurred in 1989, 1990, and 1991 clearly indicated the end of the equilibrium that had characterized the decades immediately preceding. Yet there were no obvious signs of what the future would bring. The scenarios available to the Continent were more numerous and implied more possibilities than those in any other period since the years just after World War II.

For example, the idea of eventually including all of Europe in a common market might seem a natural consequence of the EC's drive for a single Europe. But would that single Europe include Poland, Hungary, Czechoslovakia, Yugoslavia, perhaps Bulgaria and Romania? What of the disintegrated Soviet Union? How well would the sovereign states within the new Commonwealth interrelate, and what role would they collectively and individually play in international affairs?

The immersion of the German Democratic Republic into the EC in 1990 was facilitated by huge subsidies furnished by the Federal Republic. Everyone could see that task would not be so easy for the other countries in the Eastern bloc. The possible economic integration of all of Europe poses a legion of problems. How could convertibility of currencies be best achieved? What of common accounting, employment, and social benefit systems? Changing economic systems implies changing ways of life and even recalibration of value scales. Many Eastern Europeans, shortly after they had concluded their revolutions, were therefore asking themselves what they had lost. Had it been worthwhile to lose the more relaxed pace of life under socialism, with its guarantee of certain securities such as jobs, housing, and health care—inadequate as they might have been—for competition and the risk of unemployment but also greater opportunity for personal advancement, physical comfort, and political freedom? Should one automatically welcome a society that accepts economic inequality as ethical as opposed to a society that professes to reject such a view?

Even though most experts associate economic integration with economic growth and thus with modernization, the early 1990s were colored by much debate and uncertainty about political integration as well. From the 1960s to the first part of the 1980s, Eastern Europe was characterized by much more political coherence than was the West. Constitutions and state forms all followed the Soviet model with considerably less variability than the Western European states followed the Social Democratic model. In this sense, the events of 1989–1991 implied not a pulling together of the Eastern European states but essentially a greater separation, as each sought to find its own way into the post-Communist world. In calling for democracy and departing from Leninist democratic centralism, the populations of the various Eastern European countries and the former Soviet Union were asserting not only their right to govern themselves in their own manner but also their own national identities. But what did this mean? It suggested that as Western Europeans were acknowledging the need to soft-pedal their ethnic identities in order to achieve greater economic and social integration, the Eastern Europeans were going in a slightly different direction. They emphasized nationality and separateness as key features of their efforts to achieve political modernization (i.e., self-rule, independent of the influence of the old, Soviet-style elites that had been imposed upon them from without).

This Eastern European nationalism was both stimulated and abetted by the growth of ethnic identification to such an intensity that it challenged the stability of the Eastern nation-states. Ethnic rivalries broke into open hostilities not only in Eastern Europe (especially Yugoslavia), where such feelings had been the bane of democratic governments in the interwar years, but also in the USSR. There—following the example set by the Baltic peoples— Moldovans, Georgians, Armenians, Uzbeks, and numerous others asserted the right to govern their regions with ever increasing autonomy. Most notably, leaders of the Russian republic—by far the largest component of the union— threatened to secede unless the lines of the union were redrafted. To meet these challenges, as we have seen, Gorbachev showed in the period before the August coup that he was willing to risk even the success of his reform program as he raised the specter of the use of forceful presidential rule— virtual dictatorship. Naturally, he was fully aware of the contradiction this represented, and he therefore also showed signs of flexibility. If extreme restrictions were to be imposed politically, then how could the initiatives necessary for the economic revitalization of the USSR flourish? Would Western financial aid continue to be forthcoming? Historically speaking, this problem was not new at all. It was related to one of the long-standing, traditional difficulties of czarist and Soviet modernization: the contradiction of attempting to stimulate independent economic initiative from below while demanding political obedience by fiat from above.

As the Eastern Europeans and the Soviets were grappling with these problems, they were scarcely beginning to address the even more ominous question of how European security was to be guaranteed. True, the speeches delivered on the occasion of the signing of the Charter of Paris in 1990 were hopeful in their visions of a Europe that had outgrown the internecine conflicts of earlier times. But as the military arm of the Warsaw Pact was abolished in 1991 and NATO was deprived of its last clearly defined enemy on the Continent, one had to wonder what concrete force was to bind the Europeans together. Some Western Europeans began to look hopefully for a state that was willing to play the role of a new leader in continental affairs, providing guidance and vision regarding new European objectives and undertakings. Perhaps it was not surprising that with German reunification already under way, many thought the new, larger Federal Republic might somehow fit into such a role; were not the Germans finally in a position to translate their tremendous economic power into political power and responsibility as well? Yet there were two major problems with the image of Germany as an emerging superpower. Even after four decades in which the FRG had been allowed to prove its democratic credentials, some of the country's neighbors in both Western and Eastern Europe refused to be convinced that the Germans could be counted upon to act in the Continent's best interest. The other problem, ironically, was that even the Germans themselves were uncertain about wanting to assume such a position. The financial and psychological travails of reunification alone were enough to focus the attention of many of the Federal Republic's best-known politicians exclusively on the demands of domestic politics.

An equally pressing issue to emerge as a result of the collapse of the Warsaw Pact, the replacement of the Soviet Union by an only vaguely defined commonwealth, and the new uncertainties within NATO had to do with how Europeans on both sides of the once divided Continent would relate to one another. Could the Western European powers, most of whom were already integrated into the Atlantic alliance, easily make common cause with their former adversaries to the east? And if so, with which ones? Would the North Atlantic Cooperation Council, created at the end of 1991 by NATO ministers as a vehicle for discussions with their counterparts in former Eastern bloc nations, be successful? What of the future of all the various republics that had once comprised the Soviet Union? And what of their proliferating nuclear weapons? Would Gorbachev's "new thinking" of the late 1980s carry through to cause future generations of policymakers, like those surrounding Russian president Yeltsin, to deal with their European neighbors in cooperative ways? Or would the return to nationalistic themes in emerging powers like the Russian republic instead lead their politicians to turn back to the chauvinism and xenophobic tendencies of earlier times?

None of this is to say that all the future European trials and problems are to be found exclusively in the East. In the wake of the collapse of

Jubilant young Germans, still exhilarated despite a night of celebration after tearing down parts of the Wall the day before, throng about and upon the Berlin Wall on November 10, 1989. The division of Berlin had come to an end and the reunification of Germany would soon follow. Probably more than any other single European country, Germany had personified both the terrible wounds of the war it had unleashed and the long awaited healing of peace and freedom. (Photo from Reuters/ Bettmann.)

communism in Eastern Europe and the USSR, many of the most populous states of Western Europe were faced with the onslaught of hundreds of thousands of would-be emigrés from the East who regarded the "golden West" as a possible source of employment for themselves and perhaps better futures for their families. What many of these people found upon their arrival in the major metropolitan centers of Germany, France, and the Benelux countries in the early 1990s, however, was not simply untold affluence and luxury but also blatant racism and equally strong xenophobic sentiments. In part, some Western Europeans merely feared that their own jobs and livelihoods would be jeopardized in the face of competition from cheaper labor. But in addition, the presence of such dark tendencies was a reminder that even higher levels of industrialization and education were not sufficient in the modern age to guarantee that people would display civility toward forces they considered alien to their own experience.

Beyond these problems, it was also clear that both parts of the Continent were bound to share certain anxieties about the complexity of the modern world. As the final decade of the twentieth century began, for example, few persons in Western or Eastern Europe questioned the need to modernize, to bring the advances of the Western scientific and technological revolution to all of their populations. But did the arrival of computers and rapid systems of information transfer permit more individualism, or did these developments require and create greater homogeneity? How should nationalism, ethnic identification, and economic and possibly even political integration interrelate? Which step was the right one, and where would it lead? In Great Britain, the ruling Conservatives balked at the notion of a full-scale European Monetary Union (partly to protect the role of sterling in the world's markets), whereas continental leaders hailed the possibility of developing a European currency more powerful than any other on the globe. But would this lead to economic wars with other regions? The confrontation in the Persian Gulf in 1990–1991 between Iraq on the one hand and the European states and their U.S. and Arab allies on the other did not bode well. It implied a future of further conflicts with the rest of the world that might cut Europe off from its former fields of influence and resources.

Debate regarding the best course of modernization at the international level has been paralleled in domestic issues as well. There was, for example, the matter of priorities. How should consumption, investment, and defense be ranked? The Western European countries have been determined to give priority to social welfare, but in due course the high cost of the social programs has led to budgetary deficits and confronted leaders with what Harold and Margaret Sprout, in *The Context of Environmental Politics*, described as "the statesmen's dilemma." Based on an earlier study of Great Britain, the Sprouts reached the conclusion that the demands called for by modernizing economic and social reforms challenged leaders with increasingly difficult choices among priorities. Britain and Denmark in particular have reached "the crisis of the welfare state." They faced difficult alternatives: reducing welfare programs or defense expenditures in order to balance their budgets, or raising taxes and thus decreasing the availability of investment funds for stimulating economic growth. The Soviet Union and the United States encountered similar crises in the 1980s.

The environment is currently recognized as a serious issue. Since the onset of the industrial revolution, and more especially since the mid-nineteenth century, the application of increasing amounts of energy to increasingly massive production facilities was assumed to improve the lives of everyone. But at the end of the twentieth century, populations and political leaders— not just members of the environmentalist Green parties—were questioning this article of faith. Pollution that turned lakes into dead seas, acid rain that killed forests, fluorocarbons that destroyed the ozone layer of the atmosphere, and pesticides that created cancer warned that technology by itself might not be leading humankind toward a better life. It might be that such advances were in fact poisoning life and endangering future generations. Technology would have to be used, but in a different manner and with greater understanding than in the past.

Regardless of the fall of communism, questions also continued to be raised about the role of governments in promoting economic growth. At the turn of the century, according to some measures, governments had played a comparatively minor role in economic development and social change. In the major Western European countries for which information is available, government expenditures ranged from 5 to 10 percent of gross national product in 1900 and from 10 to 15 percent in 1930. By 1980 this share had risen to 40 or 55 percent. In that decade some 20 percent of the labor force in the OECD countries was employed by governments.

To some extent, the postwar expansion of the role of government in Europe was ideological. When Labour replaced the Conservative government in Great Britain in 1945, for example, it undertook a major program of nationalization of industry and social services. Socialist parties generally tended to use the state as the principal instrument for the achievement of social equality through the redistribution of wealth. By the 1980s, however, ideology was no longer a major factor in Western Europe, and both moderate and socialist leaders came to assume that government should play a large role in society. This was still not the view of conservatives, many of whom thought governments should reduce involvement in the economy. Though the debate was often couched in the simple terms of either-or, in fact nearly all Western economies had become complex "mixed economies." Government-run enterprises and privately owned firms operated side by side, and between these extremes there were many way stations, including state funding or tax relief for private firms, state regulation of production or price levels, subsidies for exports or tariffs on imports, state authorization of private cartels regulating a given industry, complex administrative codes, nonprofit corporations, and more.

Though most citizens accepted a positive role for government, experience tended to reveal the shortcomings of government intervention along the Western European model. On the economic side, overcentralization led to inefficiency in business administration. Governments were inclined to support uneconomic enterprises in order to maintain employment. Lack of competition was held accountable for lax management, and nationalized companies found it difficult to expand on an international scale. On the welfare side, the effort to administer all health services, to provide the unemployed substantial incomes (sometimes for life), and to support the aged in comfortable circumstances led to a level of taxation that the economy could not support. Not only did government debts begin to rise, a factor leading to inflation, but the taxpayers began to revolt against the system. It would seem that once government expenditures rise to over one-half of the gross national product, the burden would become greater than the benefits. The peoples of Western Europe were not less eager to achieve the goals of equality and welfare, but they came to realize that societies had to be much more productive than they were in the 1980s if the governments were to take responsibility for such a wide range of needs.

In the last years of the century, therefore, it seems possible that Europe will move toward more domestic decentralization and privatization of the economy. At the same time, some trends may work for wider (involving more countries) and deeper (involving more areas, such as banking and health insurance in addition to trade) integration on the international level. These shifts would not be contradictory but would complementarily further the process of modernization. The easing of restrictions in the flow of people, technology, patents, and ideas over state borders would enhance the spread and advancement of knowledge. The application of the fruits of this expansion in a pluralistic manner could in turn accelerate political development, economic growth, and individual change.

The issue of social change remains a difficult one, however, as all Europeans search for new means to transcend age-old conflicts. To what extent should ethnic or religious rights be subordinated to the demands of a larger entity or principle? How is one to define the larger entity or principle? To what extent should linguistic divisions be allowed to complicate the administration of Belgium, Czechoslovakia, or the successor parts of the Soviet Union?

What, too, of costs? The advancement of knowledge does not come cheaply or necessarily imply that all of society's means will be used to apply all new developments to all segments of society. In Britain, for example, the current decision is that kidney dialysis will not be available for older citizens under the National Health Service. Similarly, pressure for the application of technical advancements to all of society will vie with traditional expenditures such as national defense. So also the costs of environmental control conflict with industrial profitability and employment prospects. The human drive for a better way of life, usually associated with a desire for an increasingly equitable application of what is perceived as justice, has long been a force for change and modernization. The possibility that environmental concerns may require a perceived reduction in living standards—for example, the acceptance of cooler homes, smaller cars, less travel, inconvenient recycling, and higher food costs—may dull this drive. In turn, the shortage of funds and the debate over how such resources should be used lead increasingly to discussions of fairness and to examination of taxing procedures. These issues relating to social change can, and surely will, influence the speed and nature of European growth over the coming years.

One way or another, the debate over the pace and character of Europe's development, and especially over the sort of social and personal changes that can be achieved, will occur in a far different environment than that which

Leonard Bernstein conducts Beethoven's Ninth Symphony in Berlin in December 1989 in joyous celebration of the dismantlement of the Berlin Wall a few weeks earlier. The orchestra and chorus for the performance of this majestic work consisted of citizens from both parts of the once-divided Germany. To heighten the symbolism of the concert, Bernstein changed the words in the last movement from An die Freude (ode to joy) to An die Freiheit (ode to freedom), giving musical expression to the exuberant sense of rebirth sweeping all of Europe. (Photo from Reuters/Bettmann.)

prevailed in the first forty-five years after the end of World War II. The decline of many aspects of the military confrontation between the super-powers appears to have lessened the pressures of military costs for the European states. Already, many of these countries had in any case only reluctantly and only partially met their defense preparation assignments. Equally important, the financial and trade difficulties of the United States and USSR have caused these old superpowers to refocus their attention on domestic issues. Other problems, such as those of the Middle East, have distracted their attention from European affairs. The economic and ethnic problems of the former Soviet Union in particular are so severe that it seems likely that those who replace the old Soviet leadership will not be able to repeat—even should they so desire—the kind of heavy-handed attempts to influence their European neighbors that were so common in the first postwar years. Ironically, the decline of Soviet influence in Europe also reduces that of the United States, which can no longer use the threat of Soviet and Communist subversion as a justification for its own dominant role in leading the West.

The interrelation of domestic and foreign affairs; the debate over social priorities and justice; the balancing of the benefits of government intervention against the values of decentralization, privatization, and ethnic identity; and the search for a new security order are all bound to take Europe in fundamentally new directions in the closing years of the twentieth century. In 1945 Europe was devastated, without sufficient means to support itself. It was sharply divided, devoid of confidence, and stripped of much independence of action. Now Europe, or at least a great part of it, is economically sound, possessing a modern infrastructure and confident in its own ability. If Europe remains divided, the old dividing line has shifted eastward and its ultimate location remains uncertain. Perhaps the economic and social distinctions that accompanied the former military division between East and West will also be reduced. Though the future is unclear, Europe stands independent, potent, and part of a polycentric rather than a bipolar world. Its many states are now in a position to direct their own destiny. After years of travail, Europe has been reborn.

Suggested Readings

Aho, C. M., and M. Levinson, *After Reagan: Confronting the Changed World Economy* (1988).

Albrecht-Carrié, R., *One Europe: The Historical Background of European Unity* (1965).

Clough, S. B., *The Rise and Fall of Civilization: An Inquiry into the Relationship Between Economic Development and Civilization* (1951).

De Porte, A. W., *Europe Between the Superpowers: The Enduring Balance* (1979).

Fischer, E., *The Passing of the European Age: A Study of the Transfer of Western Civilization and Its Renewal in Other Countries* (1948).

Gilpin, R., *The Political Economy of International Relations* (1987).

Graubard, S. R. (ed.), *A New Europe?* (1964).

Holborn, H., *The Political Collapse of Europe* (1951).

Inkeles, A., and D. H. Smith, *Becoming Modern: Individual Change in Six Developing Countries* (1974).

Jones, E. L., *The European Miracle: Environments, Economies, and Geopolitics in the History of Europe and Asia* (1981).

Kennedy, P. M., *The Rise and Fall of the Great Powers: Economic Change and Military Conflict from 1500 to 2000* (1987).

Kuusinen, O. V. (ed.), *Fundamentals of Marxism-Leninism*, 2d ed. (1963).

Laqueur, W., *Europe Since Hitler: The Rebirth of Europe*, rev. ed. (1982).

Lukacs, J. S., *The Decline and Rise of Europe* (1965).

McNeill, W. H., *The Rise of the West: A History of the Human Community* (1963).

Morse, E. W., *Modernization and the Transformation of International Relations* (1976).

Olson, M., *The Rise and Decline of Nations: Economic Growth, Stagnation, and Social Rigidities* (1982).

Popper, K., *The Open Society and Its Enemies*, 4th ed. (1962).

Richta, R. (ed.), *Civilization at the Crossroads: Social and Human Implications of the Scientific and Technological Revolution*, 3d ed. (1968).

Schmidt, H. A., *Grand Strategy for the West: The Anachronism of National Strategies in an Interdependent World* (1985).

Schroeder, G. E., and I. Edwards, *Consumption in the U.S.S.R.: An International Comparison* (1981).

Sorokin, P. A., *Social and Cultural Dynamics*, 4 vols. (1937–1941).

Spengler, O., *The Decline of the West*, 2 vols. (1926–1928).

Sprout, H., and M. Sprout, *The Context of Environmental Politics: Unfinished Business for America's Third Century* (1978).

Taylor, C. L., and D. A. Jodice, *World Handbook of Political and Social Indicators*, 3d ed., 2 vols. (1983).

Toynbee, A. J., *A Study of History*, 11 vols. (1934–1959).

Ullman, R., *Securing Europe* (1991).

Van der Wee, H., *Prosperity and Upheaval: The World Economy 1945–1980* (1987).

Weber, M., *Economy and Society*, rev. ed., 3 vols., (1968).

Chronology

1945

JANUARY 11   Soviet forces capture Warsaw.

JANUARY 20   Hungarian government at Debrecen signs armistice.

FEBRUARY 4–12   Franklin Roosevelt, Winston Churchill, and Josef Stalin meet at Yalta.

FEBRUARY 19–MARCH 17   U.S. forces win the battle for Iwo Jima.

MARCH 4   Finland declares war on Germany, retroactive as of the previous September.

MARCH 12   Stalin turns over northern Transylvania to Romania.

APRIL 12   Roosevelt dies; Harry S Truman becomes president.

APRIL 13   Soviet troops take Vienna.

APRIL 21   USSR and Polish provisional government sign a twenty-year treaty of mutual assistance.

APRIL 25–JUNE 26   San Francisco conference draws up United Nations Charter.

APRIL 29   Partisans execute Benito Mussolini.

APRIL 30   Adolf Hitler commits suicide in a bunker of the chancellery in Berlin.

MAY 7   The provisional government of Germany surrenders unconditionally.

MAY 8   The war in Europe ends; V-E Day is declared.

MAY 29   Czechoslovakia cedes Ruthenia to the USSR.

JULY 17–AUGUST 2   Truman, Stalin, and Churchill (later replaced by Attlee) meet in Potsdam.

JULY 26   The victory of the Labour party in British general elections held July 5 is announced.

AUGUST 6   The United States drops the first atomic bomb on Hiroshima.

AUGUST 8   USSR declares war on Japan.

AUGUST 9   The United States drops the second atomic bomb on Nagasaki.

AUGUST 14   The Japanese surrender unconditionally.

AUGUST 15   The Allies declare victory in Japan; V-J Day is celebrated.

SEPTEMBER 2   Japan signs a formal surrender aboard the U.S.S. *Missouri* in Tokyo Bay.

OCTOBER 20   The Allied Council for Austria recognizes the Austrian provisional government, established April 25.

NOVEMBER 20   The Nuremberg trial of twenty top Nazi leaders opens.

DECEMBER 16–27   First session of the Council of Foreign Ministers meets in Moscow.

1946

MARCH 5   Churchill delivers his "Iron Curtain" speech at Westminster College, Fulton, Missouri.

APRIL 18   League of Nations Assembly holds its final session in Geneva.

APRIL 25–JULY 12   Second session of the Council of Foreign Ministers meets in Paris.

JUNE 3   An Italian plebescite rejects the monarchy.

JULY 1   Foreign ministers in Paris delimit the Italian-Yugoslavian boundary.

JULY 29–OCTOBER 15   Delegates from twenty-one nations meet in Paris to consider drafts of peace treaties with Italy, Romania, Bulgaria, Hungary, and Finland.

SEPTEMBER 8   Bulgaria rejects the monarchy in a plebiscite and is proclaimed a people's republic September 15.

SEPTEMBER 28   George II returns to Athens as king of Greece.

OCTOBER 13   The French approve a new constitution.

OCTOBER 16   Ten leading Nazis are executed as a result of their conviction in Nuremberg; Hermann Goering, former holder of key positions in the Third Reich, including chief of the Nazi air force, commits suicide.

NOVEMBER 4–DECEMBER 12   Third Session of the Council of Foreign Ministers meets in New York.

1947

JANUARY 1   Britain and the United States establish Bizonia, an economic merger of their occupation zones in Germany.

FEBRUARY 10   Allied powers sign peace treaties with Italy, Finland, Romania, Bulgaria, and Hungary in Paris.

MARCH 4   France and Britain sign a fifty-year treaty of alliance.

MARCH 10–APRIL 24   Fourth session of the Council of Foreign Ministers meets in Moscow.

MARCH 12   The Truman Doctrine is announced; the president asks Congress to aid Greece and Turkey.

JUNE 5   In an address at Harvard, Secretary of State George Marshall suggests a plan for rebuilding Europe.

JUNE 30   The United Nations Relief and Rehabilitation Administration is officially ended.

JULY 12   Representatives of sixteen European states meet in Paris to lay the basis for the Marshall Plan, the Soviet Union refusing to cooperate.

AUGUST 15   British rule in India ends; the dominions of India and Pakistan come into being.

OCTOBER 5   Formation of a Communist Information Bureau (Cominform) with headquarters in Belgrade is made public, the bureau to include the Communist parties of the USSR, France, Italy, Poland, Czechoslovakia, Hungary, Romania, Bulgaria, and Yugoslavia.

OCTOBER 30   Twenty-three nations under UN auspices sign a trade agreement that becomes the origin of the General Agreement on Tariffs and Trade.

NOVEMBER 25–DECEMBER 15   Fifth session of the Council of Foreign Ministers meets in London.

DECEMBER 30   King Michael of Romania abdicates.

1948

JANUARY 1   Benelux Customs Union is inaugurated.

JANUARY 30   Mahatma Gandhi is assassinated.

FEBRUARY 25   Communists take control of the government of Czechoslovakia.

MARCH 17   France, Britain, the Netherlands, Belgium, and Luxembourg sign the fifty-year Brussels Pact, forming the Western Union.

APRIL 16   Organization for the European Economic Cooperation is formed.

MAY 15   British mandate in Palestine expires; the state of Israel is proclaimed.

JUNE 18   Currency reform in three Western-controlled zones of Germany.

JUNE 19   Soviet authorities start the Berlin blockade, which develops into a general blockade between the Eastern and Western zones.

JULY 5   Labour government's broad health and social security program goes into effect in the United Kingdom.

DECEMBER 27   Hungarian government arrests Joseph Cardinal Mindzenty and sentences him to life imprisonment February 8, 1949.

1949

JANUARY 20   Nineteen Middle and Far Eastern countries meet in New Delhi to discuss Asian affairs.

APRIL 4   NATO agreements are signed in Washington, D.C.

APRIL 18   Eire officially becomes completely independent as the Republic of Ireland.

APRIL 21-27   British Commonwealth prime ministers convene in London; India agrees to remain in what is to be known as "the Commonwealth of Nations," with the king at its head as the symbol of the free association of its members.

MAY 5   United States, Britain, France, and USSR agree to end the blockade between Western and Eastern zones (including Berlin) on May 12.

MAY 5   Ten European states sign the Statute of the Council of Europe in London; they choose Strasbourg as seat of the council.

MAY 8   Parliamentary council at Bonn adopts the final draft of a constitution for West Germany, the German Federal Republic.

MAY 23-JUNE 20   Sixth session of the Council of Foreign Ministers convenes in Paris.

JULY 13   The papal ban of excommunication of all Communists is published.

SEPTEMBER 19   United Kingdom devalues its currency; similar action follows in many other states.

SEPTEMBER 23   Truman announces U.S. knowledge of the successful Soviet test of an atomic bomb.

OCTOBER 7   German Democratic Republic (Soviet zone) is proclaimed.

NOVEMBER 22   UN Assembly reaches a decision on Italian colonies of Libya and Somaliland.

DECEMBER 16   British Parliament Act of 1911 is revised to further restrict the power of the House of Lords.

DECEMBER 27   The independence of the United States of Indonesia under the Dutch crown is officially proclaimed.

1950

JANUARY 6   Great Britain recognizes the Communist government of China.

JANUARY 26   India is formally declared a republic.

JANUARY 26   United States and South Korea sign a pact for U.S. arms aid.

MARCH 12   Referendum in Belgium favors the return of King Leopold.

APRIL 1   Italy takes over trusteeship of Somaliland.

MAY 9   The French foreign minister formally proposes a plan for integration of Western European coal and steel production.

JUNE 25   North Korean forces invade South Korea, leading to UN intervention spearheaded by the United States.

JULY 8   General Douglas MacArthur is appointed commander of combined UN forces in Korea.

SEPTEMBER 19   European participants in the European Recovery Program agree to form the European Payments Union.

OCTOBER 4, 5   Turkey and Greece accept an invitation to join NATO, their membership to become effective in 1952.

NOVEMBER 28   Poland and East Germany ratify the Oder-Neisse line as their common frontier.

DECEMBER 19   General Dwight D. Eisenhower is appointed supreme commander of NATO forces in Europe.

1951

FEBRUARY 1   UN General Assembly declares Communist China guilty of aggression in Korea.

FEBRUARY 2   France cedes Chandernagore to India.

APRIL 11   MacArthur is dismissed as commander of UN forces in South Korea.

APRIL 30   Iranian Senate approves an oil nationalization bill, leading to controversy with Great Britain.

SEPTEMBER 1   United States, Australia, and New Zealand sign the Pacific Security Agreement.

SEPTEMBER 8   Forty-nine countries sign a peace treaty with Japan.

OCTOBER 24   United States proclaims the end of the state of war with Germany.

DECEMBER 24   Libya proclaims its independence.

1952

MARCH 1   Helgoland is restored to the Federal Republic of Germany.

APRIL 28   Japanese peace treaty and U.S.-Japanese security pact take effect; Allied occupation ends.

MAY 27   France, Germany, Italy, and the Benelux countries sign the European Defense Community treaty and related protocols.

JULY 25   European Coal and Steel Community treaty enters into force.

NOVEMBER 4   Eisenhower is elected president of the United States.

1953

FEBRUARY 12   Britain and Egypt sign an agreement recognizing self-government for the Anglo-Egyptian Sudan.

FEBRUARY 28   In Ankara representatives from Greece, Turkey, and Yugoslavia sign a treaty of friendship and collaboration.

MARCH 5   Stalin dies at the age of seventy-three; Georgi Malenkov succeeds him as premier.

JUNE 2   Elizabeth II is crowned in London.

JUNE 17   Riots in East Berlin are put down by Soviet troops.

JUNE 18   Egypt proclaims itself a republic.

JULY 26   Representatives of North Korea and a sixteen-country UN force meet at Panmunjom to sign a Korean armistice, to enter into effect July 27.

DECEMBER 4–8   Eisenhower, Churchill, and Premier Joseph Laniel of France meet in Bermuda to discuss relations with the USSR and issues related to Germany.

1954

JANUARY 25–FEBRUARY 18   The Big Four come together in Berlin to discuss Germany, Austria, and European security; deadlock results.

APRIL 2   Turkey and Pakistan sign a mutual defense agreement.

APRIL 26–JULY 21   Geneva conference on Korea and Indochina takes place.

APRIL 29   India and Communist China sign an eight-year nonaggression pact in Beijing; Tibet is recognized as part of China.

MAY 7   French garrison surrenders to the Viet Minh at Dien Bien Phu.

JULY 21   Indochina cease-fire agreements are signed in Geneva.

AUGUST 5   Iran initials an agreement with oil companies settling an oil dispute.

AUGUST 9   Yugoslavia, Greece, and Turkey sign a twenty-year military alliance.

AUGUST 10   An agreement ending the Netherlands-Indonesian Union is signed in The Hague.

AUGUST 30   French National Assembly rejects the European Defense Community treaty.

SEPTEMBER 6–8   The Southeast Asia Defense Conference is held in Manila; the United States, Britain, France, Australia, New Zealand, Pakistan, Thailand, and the Philippines sign the Southeast Asia Collective Defense Treaty and Pacific Charter to create the Southeast Asia Treaty Organization.

SEPTEMBER 28–OCTOBER 3   A nine-power conference meets in London to discuss West German sovereignty and rearmament.

OCTOBER 5   Italy, Yugoslavia, the United States, and Britain reach an initial agreement dividing the territory of Trieste between Italy and Yugoslavia.

OCTOBER 11   The Soviets and Chinese settle the Soviet evacuation of Port Arthur and various other matters.

OCTOBER 19   Britain and Egypt agree on the transfer of the Suez Canal to Egypt, with full evacuation of the British garrison by June 1956.

OCTOBER 21   France agrees to turn over its remaining Indian stations (Yanaon, Pondicherry, Karikal, Mahé) to India.

OCTOBER 21   Nine-power meeting (Brussels pact nations, United States, Canada, Federal Republic of Germany, Italy) approves accession of the Federal Republic and Italy to the Brussels pact; the Western European Union is created.

OCTOBER 23   France and West Germany agree on the Europeanization of the Saar and sign protocols on the sovereignty and rearmament of Germany.

DECEMBER 2   The United States and Nationalist China sign a mutual defense treaty.

DECEMBER 29–30   French Assembly approves West German membership in NATO and modification of the Brussels pact.

1955

FEBRUARY 8   Malenkov resigns as president of the USSR and is succeeded by Nikolai Bulganin.

APRIL 5   Churchill resigns as prime minister of the United Kingdom and is succeeded by Anthony Eden.

APRIL 18–24   An Asian-African conference is held in Bandung, Indonesia.

MAY 5   The Federal Republic of Germany becomes a sovereign state as the 1954 Paris agreements go into effect.

MAY 7   USSR cancels friendship treaties with France and Britain.

MAY 11–14   Leaders of eight Eastern European states sign the Warsaw Pact.

MAY 15   Britain, France, the Soviet Union, the United States, and Austria sign the Austrian State Treaty, to go into effect July 27.

JULY 18–23   Heads of state from Britain, France, the Soviet Union, and the United States meet for a summit conference in Geneva .

OCTOBER 4   Foreign ministers from the Big Four gather in Geneva.

DECEMBER 14   A package deal results in the admission of sixteen new members to the UN.

DECEMBER 18   Saar elections are won by pro-German parties.

1956

JANUARY 1   Sudan becomes an independent republic; the Anglo-Egyptian condominium ends.

JANUARY 26   USSR returns Porkkala naval base to Finland.

FEBRUARY 14   Khrushchev attacks Stalin and the "cult of the individual" at the Twentieth Communist Party Congress in Moscow.

APRIL 16   The Cominform is dissolved.

JUNE 13   The last British troops leave the Suez Canal, ending seventy-four years of British occupation.

JUNE 23   Gamal Nasser is elected president of Egypt.

JUNE 28–30   Over 100 workers are killed as the Polish army, with Soviet officers, quells riots in Poznan, Poland.

JULY 19   The United States withdraws its offer to aid Egypt in construction of the Aswan Dam.

JULY 26   Egypt nationalizes the Suez Canal.

OCTOBER 19   Japan and the USSR end the state of war and renew diplomatic relations.

OCTOBER 21   The Polish Communist Central Committee elects a new Politburo, with Wladyslaw Gomulka as first secretary; modest reforms lead to a Polish "spring in October."

OCTOBER 24   Start of the Hungarian revolution, suppressed by the USSR.

OCTOBER 29   Israel invades the Sinai Peninsula of Egypt.

OCTOBER 30   France and Britain issue an ultimatum to Egypt and attack by air the next day.

NOVEMBER 7   Cease-fire in Egypt results from UN actions.

DECEMBER 22   French and British forces complete their withdrawal from Egyptian territory.

1957

JANUARY 1   Saar becomes the tenth state of the Federal Republic of Germany.

JANUARY 10   Harold Macmillan succeeds Eden as prime minister of Great Britain.

MARCH 4   Israel orders withdrawal of troops from the Gaza Strip and Gulf of Akaba area.

MARCH 9   The Eisenhower Doctrine is announced: The United States will aid Middle Eastern countries requesting help in combating Communist aggression.

MARCH 25   France, the Federal Republic of Germany, Italy, and the Benelux nations sign the treaties of Rome, creating the European Economic Community and the European Atomic Energy Community; the treaties are to take effect January 1, 1958.

MARCH 29   The Suez Canal is reopened after having been blocked since November 1, 1956.

MAY 7   Soviet production is reorganized: Ninety-two economic regions are established.

JUNE 20   UN report indicts the USSR for crushing the Hungarian uprising and replacing Imre Nagy's legal government.

JULY 3   Malenkov, Vyacheslav Molotov, Dmitri Kaganovich, and Lazar Shepilov are ousted from the Central Committee of the Communist party.

OCTOBER 4   USSR launches the first earth satellite, *Sputnik I.*

1958

JANUARY 31   The first U.S. satellite, *Explorer I,* is orbited by the army

FEBRUARY 1   Egypt and Syria form the United Arab Republic, later approved by plebiscites.

MARCH 2   Yemen affiliates with the United Arab Republic.

MARCH 27   Nikita Khrushchev becomes president of the USSR but remains first secretary of the Central Committee of the Communist party.

MAY 13   An army coup occurs in Algeria, its leaders calling for Charles de Gaulle's return to power.

JUNE 1   De Gaulle becomes premier of France and is granted wide powers.

JULY 14   The monarchy is overthrown in Iraq, the king and prime minister assassinated.

JULY 15   The United States sends marines to Lebanon in response to a request for aid by the president of Lebanon.

JULY 17   British paratroopers land in Jordan at the request of King Hussein.

AUGUST 21   In a special session, the UN General Assembly unanimously adopts a resolution facilitating early withdrawal of U.S. forces from Lebanon and British forces from Jordan.

SEPTEMBER 28   The French people approve the constitution of the Fifth Republic, drafted under de Gaulle.

OCTOBER 9   Pope Pius XIII dies; Angelo Giuseppe Cardinal Roncalli, patriarch of Venice, is elected his successor on October 28, becomes John XXIII.

OCTOBER 27   France revalues its currency and joins with the United Kingdom (and those countries that tie their currencies to the British pound), West Germany, the Benelux countries, Italy, Norway, Sweden, and Denmark in widening currency convertibility.

1959

FEBRUARY 19   Turkey and Greece agree to establish Cyprus as an independent republic, effective August 16, 1960.

MARCH 24   Iraq withdraws from the Baghdad pact.

MAY 11–JUNE 20 and JULY 13–AUGUST 5   Foreign ministers from the Big Four meet in Geneva to discuss the German problem; they agree to form the ten-nation Disarmament Committee.

AUGUST 15–27   Khrushchev visits the United States.

OCTOBER 8   Conservative party sweeps British elections.

NOVEMBER 20   The Outer Seven—Austria, Denmark, Norway, Sweden, Portugal, Switzerland, and the United Kingdom—form the European Free Trade Association (Stockholm treaty); the EFTA will be formally established May 3, 1960, upon ratification of the treaty by participating countries.

1960

FEBRUARY 13   France explodes its first atomic bomb.

MAY 1   The Soviets shoot down a U.S. U-2 reconnaissance plane.

MAY 16   Eisenhower, Macmillan, de Gaulle, and Khrushchev attend a summit conference in Paris, Khrushchev lashing out against the United States with a speech on the U-2 incident.

JUNE 30   Belgian Congo becomes the independent Republic of the Congo; riots and civil war follow.

JULY 14   Security Council authorizes sending UN forces to the Republic of the Congo.

AUGUST 12   UN forces enter Katanga province in the Congo.

NOVEMBER 9   John F. Kennedy is elected president of the United States.

DECEMBER 14   Agreements are signed changing the Organization for European Economic Cooperation to the Organization for Economic Cooperation and Development, effective September 30, 1961.

1961

JANUARY 3   United States severs diplomatic relations with Cuba.

MARCH 1   United States establishes the Peace Corps.

APRIL 12   Yuri A. Gagarin of the Soviet Union becomes the first human to orbit the earth.

APRIL 17   U.S. involvement in an attempt of Cuban rebels to invade Cuba leads to the Bay of Pigs incident.

MAY 31   South Africa severs ties with the Commonwealth and becomes a republic.

JUNE 3–4   Kennedy and Khrushchev confer in Vienna as the crisis over the status of Berlin mounts.

AUGUST 13   German Democratic Republic erects a wall between East and West Berlin.

SEPTEMBER 18   Dag Hammarskjöld, secretary general of the UN, is killed in an airplane crash in Northern Rhodesia.

DECEMBER 10   USSR and Albania sever diplomatic relations.

DECEMBER 18-19   India forcibly takes over Portuguese Dao, Damo, and Din.

1962

FEBRUARY 20   John Glenn becomes the first U.S. astronaut to orbit the earth.

MARCH 18   French and Algerian leaders sign a cease-fire agreement, ending seven years of war in Algeria.

APRIL 8   French voters in referendum approve the Algerian peace settlement.

JULY 1   Algerians vote overwhelmingly for independence.

AUGUST 15   Dutch-Indonesian agreement on West New Guinea is reached.

OCTOBER 11-DECEMBER 6   First session of Vatican Council II takes place.

OCTOBER 22   USSR is involved in the U.S.-Cuban crisis over missile bases.

1963

JANUARY 14   De Gaulle rejects Britain's application for membership in the Common Market; the application is officially vetoed at the EEC meeting in Brussels January 29.

JANUARY 22   French-German treaty of friendship and reconciliation is signed.

APRIL 10   John XXIII issues the encyclical *Pacem in Terris* calling for a world community to ensure peace.

MAY 23-26   A summit conference of African powers in Addis Ababa leads to the Charter of African Unity.

JUNE 3   Pope John XXIII dies and is succeeded by Paul VI.

JUNE 20   The United States and the USSR decide to establish a direct Washington-Moscow telephone line to reduce the chance of a nuclear war.

AUGUST 5   The United States, USSR, and United Kingdom sign the first nuclear test ban treaty.

SEPTEMBER 29-DECEMBER 4   Second session of Vatican Council II takes place.

NOVEMBER 22   Kennedy is assassinated; Lyndon Johnson is sworn in as president.

DECEMBER 21-24   Clashes between Turkish and Greek Cypriotes lead to a prolonged crisis in Cyprus.

1964

JANUARY 4-6   Pope Paul VI visits the Holy Land, meeting with Patriarch Athenagoras of the Eastern Orthodox church.

JANUARY 27   France recognizes Communist China.

MARCH 6   King Paul I of Greece dies and is succeeded by Constantine II.

JUNE 30   Last UN troops leave the Congo.

SEPTEMBER 14-NOVEMBER 21   Vatican Council II meets for its third session.

OCTOBER 10-15   Khrushchev is deposed; Leonid Brezhnev succeeds him as first secretary of the Communist party, Aleksei Kosygin becoming chairman of the Council of Ministers.

OCTOBER 15   Labour wins British elections; Harold Wilson becomes prime minister.

OCTOBER 16   People's Republic of China explodes its first atomic bomb to become the world's fifth nuclear power.

DECEMBER 1   UN session is hamstrung by U.S.-Soviet dispute over payment of assessments for peacekeeping operations.

1965

JANUARY 21   Indonesia withdraws from the UN.

JANUARY 24   Churchill dies at age ninety-one.

FEBRUARY 24–MARCH 2   Walter Ulbricht, head of East Germany, visits the United Arab Republic, leading to a crisis between West Germany and the Arab states and the exchange of ambassadors between West Germany and Israel.

APRIL 28   The United States lands marines in the Dominican Republic during a governmental crisis.

SEPTEMBER 14–DECEMBER 8   Fourth and final session of Vatican Council II convenes.

NOVEMBER 11   Rhodesia proclaims its independence but is not recognized by Great Britain.

DECEMBER 9   Nikolai Podgorny succeeds Anastas Mikoyan as Soviet president.

1966

JANUARY 30   The EEC nations bow to de Gaulle's wishes and agree to retain requirement of a unanimous vote on significant issues in the EEC Council of Ministers.

APRIL 1   The Labour party under Prime Minister Wilson obtains a ninety-seven-seat majority in British parliamentary elections.

DECEMBER 3   U Thant is reelected as UN secretary general for a five-year term.

1967

MARCH 17   French Somaliland decides to continue association with France rather than become independent.

MARCH 21   Svetlana Alliluyeva, daughter of Stalin, defects to the West.

APRIL 19   Konrad Adenauer, former chancellor of West Germany, dies at age ninety-one.

APRIL 21   A military dictatorship is established in Greece.

MAY 15   Delegations to the General Agreement on Tariffs and Trade reach a settlement on the reduction of import duties.

JUNE 5–10   Israel defeats the Arab states in the Six-Day War; the UN Security Council adopts a cease-fire resolution.

JUNE 17   Communist China explodes its first hydrogen bomb.

JUNE 23–25   Soviet premier Kosygin and U.S. president Johnson confer in Glassboro, New Jersey.

JULY 1   European Commission of the EEC is formed, combining the executive commissions of the EEC and EURATOM and the High Authority of the ECSC.

JULY 24–26   De Gaulle pays an official visit to Canada and in a speech in Montreal calls for a "free Quebec."

AUGUST 4   West Germany and Czechoslovakia establish diplomatic relations on a consular level.

DECEMBER 13–14   King Constantine of Greece goes into exile in Rome after an unsuccessful attempt to remove the military junta.

1968

JANUARY 5   Alexander Dubcek is elected first secretary of the Communist party in Czechoslovakia, replacing Antonin Novotny, who remains as president.

MARCH 1   Great Britain curtails immigration of British subjects of Asian ancestry into Britain.

MARCH 30   General Ludovik Svoboda replaces Novotny as president of Czechoslovakia.

MAY   Student riots and industrial strikes rock France.

JUNE 30   Gaullists win a large majority in National Assembly elections in France.

JULY 1   The United States, Great Britain, the USSR, and fifty-eight nonnuclear states sign a nuclear nonproliferation treaty.

JULY 29   To widespread opposition, Pope Paul VI issues an encyclical condemning artificial methods of birth control.

AUGUST 21   After a series of negotiations, troops of the USSR, Poland, Hungary, Bulgaria, and East Germany invade Czechoslovakia to halt the liberalization program.

SEPTEMBER 27   Marcello Caetano replaces the critically ill António de Oliveira Salazar as premier of Portugal.

OCTOBER 4   Czechoslovak leaders accede to Soviet demands on ending liberalization and agree to the stationing of Soviet troops on Czech soil.

OCTOBER 30   A law is enacted establishing a Czech and Slovak federal state effective January 1, 1969.

NOVEMBER 5   Richard Nixon is elected president of the United States.

1969

FEBRUARY 17–20   At a conference in Namey, Niger, some thirty French-speaking countries agree to establish an agency in Paris to facilitate cultural and technological cooperation and exchange.

MARCH 5   Despite East German harassment, West Germany holds an election for its president in West Berlin; Gustav Heinemann, a Socialist, is elected.

APRIL 17   Gustav Husak replaces Dubcek as first secretary of the Communist party in Czechoslovakia.

APRIL 28   De Gaulle resigns the presidency of France following the rejection of constitutional reforms in a referendum.

JUNE 10   Pope Paul VI addresses the International Labour Organisation in Geneva and visits headquarters of the World Council of Churches.

JUNE 16   Georges Pompidou defeats Alain Poher in the French presidential election.

JULY 20   The United States successfully carries out the first landing of humans on the moon.

JULY 29   For the second time in as many months, the Geneva Disarmament Conference raises its membership (to twenty-six, up from twenty in May, and eighteen earlier).

DECEMBER 2   The EEC agrees to open negotiations in 1970 on British membership.

1970

MARCH 5   The nuclear nonproliferation treaty goes into effect.

MARCH 19   Chancellor Willy Brandt of the German Federal Republic and Premier Willi Stoph of the German Democratic Republic meet in Erfurt for the first conference of chiefs of government of West and East Germany.

MARCH 26   The United States, Britain, France, and the USSR hold the first four-power talks on Berlin since 1959.

JUNE 18   Under the leadership of Edward Heath, the Conservative party sweeps the British elections.

AUGUST 12   The Federal Republic of Germany and the USSR sign the Moscow treaty of reconciliation and peaceful cooperation.

SEPTEMBER 28   President Nasser of the United Arab Republic dies and is succeeded by Anwar Sadat.

OCTOBER 9   Cambodia is formally proclaimed a republic.

NOVEMBER 9   De Gaulle dies.

DECEMBER 7   West German–Polish treaty of reconciliation is signed.

DECEMBER 15–19   Increases in food prices trigger serious uprisings in Gdansk and other Polish cities.

DECEMBER 20   Edward Gierek replaces Gomulka as first secretary of the Polish Communist party.

1971

FEBRUARY 15   Britain adopts decimal currency.

JUNE 17   United States agrees to return Okinawa to Japan by 1972.

JUNE 23   Agreement is reached on terms of British entry into the Common Market.

JULY 15   Nixon announces that he will visit Beijing before May 1972.

AUGUST 23   France, the USSR, Britain, and the United States accept a draft agreement on the status of West Berlin.

OCTOBER 20   West German chancellor Brandt is awarded the Nobel Peace Prize.

OCTOBER 28   Parliament approves British entry into the EEC.

1972

JANUARY 22   Kurt Waldheim succeeds U Thant as secretary general of the UN. The United Kingdom, Ireland, and Denmark join the EEC.

MARCH 13   The United Kingdom and China resume full diplomatic relations after a twenty-two-year hiatus.

APRIL 10   The United Kingdom, the United States, and the Soviet Union, with forty-six other nations, sign a convention outlawing biological weapons.

MAY 17   The West German Parliament ratifies treaties with the USSR and Poland.

MAY 22–26   Nixon travels to Moscow for the first visit of a U.S. president to the USSR; the two countries sign the SALT I treaty May 26.

JUNE 3   A four-power agreement on Berlin is signed.

AUGUST 26–SEPTEMBER 11   At the Olympic Games held in Munich, eleven Israeli athletes are killed by Arab terrorists.

1973

JUNE 1 The Greek military regime abolishes the monarchy and establishes a republic; a new constitution is approved by referendum August 19.

JUNE 6–22 Brezhnev visits the United States for a summit conference with Nixon.

JUNE 21 UN Security Council approves admission of East and West Germany to the United Nations.

SEPTEMBER 5–9 A summit conference of nonaligned nations is held in Algiers.

OCTOBER 6–24 Yom Kippur War follows Egyptian and Syrian invasions of Israel.

OCTOBER 16 Henry Kissinger and Le Duc Tho are awarded the Nobel Peace Prize for their attempts to negotiate an end to the Vietnam War; Le Duc Tho rejects his award.

1974

FEBRUARY 27 Sweden adopts a new constitution reducing the king to a figurehead.

FEBRUARY 28 Following a general election in Britain, Heath's Conservative government resigns and is succeeded by a minority Labour government headed by Wilson.

APRIL 2 French president Pompidou dies in office; Valéry Giscard d'Estaing succeeds him in May.

MAY 6 Brandt resigns; Helmut Schmidt takes over as West German chancellor on May 16.

JULY 15 President Michael Makarios of Cyprus is overthrown in a coup led by the Greek military.

JULY 20 Turkish forces occupy northern Cyprus.

AUGUST 8 Nixon resigns as president and is succeeded by Gerald Ford.

OCTOBER 10 Wilson's Labour party wins the British general election.

NOVEMBER 17 Konstantinos Karamanlis and his New Democratic party win first general election in Greece in ten years.

NOVEMBER 24–25 A summit meeting between Brezhnev and Ford takes place in Vladivostok.

DECEMBER 7 President Makarios returns to Greece.

1975

FEBRUARY 13 Turkey proclaims a separate state in northern Cyprus.

FEBRUARY 28 EEC concludes a five-year trade agreement (Lomé convention) with forty-six developing nations.

MARCH 12 Armed Forces Movement seizes power in Portugal.

APRIL 23 Socialist leader Mário Soares comes to power in Spain after the first free election in fifty years.

APRIL 30 South Vietnam surrenders to the Vietcong, who are backed by North Vietnamese forces; the last U.S. officials leave Saigon.

JUNE 5 In the first British referendum, electors vote two to one in favor of remaining in the EEC.

JULY 17 U.S. *Apollo* and Soviet *Soyuz* spacecrafts dock in outer space.

JULY 30–AUGUST 1 Leaders of thirty-five nations meet in Helsinki to discuss European security; they sign the Final Act.

OCTOBER 9   Soviet scientist Andrei Sakharov is awarded the Nobel Peace Prize.

NOVEMBER 10   Angola achieves independence from Portugal after 500 years of colonial rule.

NOVEMBER 30   Francisco Franco dies in Spain and is succeeded as head of state by King Juan Carlos I.

1976

FEBRUARY 14   Iceland breaks off diplomatic relations with Britain over a fishing dispute.

APRIL 15   James Callaghan succeeds Wilson as British prime minister and head of the Labour party.

JUNE 1   Britain and Iceland sign an agreement ending the fishing dispute.

SEPTEMBER 9   Mao Zedong dies in China; Hua Guofeng succeeds him.

NOVEMBER 2   Jimmy Carter is elected president of the United States.

1977

JANUARY 27   The eleven members of the Council of Europe sign the European Convention on the Repression of Terrorism.

APRIL 5   Deng Xiaoping becomes paramount leader in China.

MAY 24   Brezhnev succeeds Podgorny as president of the Soviet Union.

JUNE 15   In the first Spanish election in forty years, the Democratic Center Union party led by Adolfo Suárez comes to office.

SEPTEMBER 1   The World Psychiatric Association condemns the USSR for abusing psychiatry for political purposes.

NOVEMBER 5   The United States withdraws from the International Labour Office.

NOVEMBER 20   Sadat of Egypt addresses the Israeli Parliament and agrees to negotiate with Israel (November 27).

1978

FEBRUARY 3   EEC and China sign their first trade agreement.

MAY 23   UN General Assembly begins a five-week special session on world disarmament.

JULY 25   Heads of eighty-six nonaligned nations meet in Belgrade.

AUGUST 6   Pope Paul VI dies and is succeeded by Pope John Paul I.

SEPTEMBER 5-17   Carter, Sadat, and Israeli premier Menachim Begin, meeting at Camp David, produce the framework of a peace treaty between Egypt and Israel.

SEPTEMBER 28   Upon the death of Pope John Paul I, Karol Cardinal Wojtyla of Poland becomes Pope John Paul II.

OCTOBER 27   Sadat and Begin receive the Nobel Peace Prize.

NOVEMBER 21-22   Warsaw Pact countries hold a summit meeting in Moscow.

DECEMBER 15   The United States announces establishment of diplomatic relations with the People's Republic of China as of January 1, 1979, and withdrawal of formal diplomatic relations with Taiwan.

1979

JANUARY 16   Shah Mohammed Reza Pahlevi and his family leave Iran and go into exile.

FEBRUARY 1   Ayatollah Khomeini returns from fifteen-year exile to become paramount leader in Iran.

MARCH 15   Pope John Paul II, in his first encyclical, attacks both Western and Communist models of society.

MARCH 26   Sadat and Begin sign a peace treaty after thirty years of war.

MAY 4   After Conservative electoral victory, Margaret Thatcher becomes the first woman prime minister in Britain.

JUNE 2   Pope John Paul II arrives in Poland for the first visit of a pope to a Communist country.

JUNE 15–18   Carter and Brezhnev hold a summit meeting in Vienna that results in the SALT II treaty.

JUNE 28   OPEC members meet in Geneva; the price of oil rises to $34 a barrel.

SEPTEMBER 3–8   The sixth summit conference of nonaligned nations meets in Havana.

NOVEMBER 4   Students occupy the U.S. embassy in Iran and seize over fifty hostages.

DECEMBER 25   USSR occupies Afghanistan.

1980

FEBRUARY 12   Former German chancellor Brandt presents a report to the UN secretary general calling for dramatic reshaping of relationships between rich and poor countries.

MAY 5   President Tito of Yugoslavia dies after thirty-five years in office.

JULY 19–AUGUST 3   The United States and forty other nations boycott the Olympic Games being held in Moscow to protest the Soviet invasion of Afghanistan.

AUGUST 31   The Polish government and Lech Walesa, leader of the Solidarity movement, sign the Gdansk agreement granting extensive rights to trade unions.

SEPTEMBER 12   Following months of violence, a military coup topples the Turkish government.

NOVEMBER 2   The Iranian Parliament votes to release U.S. embassy hostages.

NOVEMBER 4   Ronald Reagan is elected president of the United States.

1981

JANUARY 3   Greece is admitted to the EEC as the tenth member.

JANUARY 20   Iran releases the remaining fifty-two U.S. hostages in Tehran.

FEBRUARY 9   General Wojciech Jaruzelski, chief of staff, becomes prime minister of Poland.

MAY 10   François Mitterrand defeats Giscard d'Estaing in French presidential elections.

MAY 13   Pope John Paul II is seriously wounded in an assassination attempt by Turkish terrorist Mehmet Ali Ağca.

OCTOBER 6   Sadat of Egypt is assassinated in Cairo; Husni Mubarak succeeds him.

OCTOBER 14   The Nobel Peace Prize is awarded to the UN High Commission for Refugees.

OCTOBER 18   Andreas Papandreou wins general elections and forms the first Socialist government in Greek history.

DECEMBER 1   U.S.-USSR nuclear arms talks open in Geneva.

DECEMBER 13   Martial law is declared in Poland.

1982

APRIL 2   Argentine forces invade the Falkland Islands, a British colony for 150 years.

MAY 30   Spain becomes the sixteenth member of NATO.

JUNE 6   Israel invades southern Lebanon.

JULY 14   The Argentine military commander surrenders to the British in the Falkland Islands.

SEPTEMBER 17   Schmidt's government is defeated in the West German Parliament; Helmut Kohl becomes the new chancellor.

OCTOBER 8   The Polish Parliament votes to ban Solidarity.

NOVEMBER 10   Brezhnev dies in office; Yuri Andropov is named as his successor.

DECEMBER 10   UN Convention on the Law of the Sea is signed by 119 nations but rejected by the United States, United Kingdom, Italy, Belgium, and eighteen other industrialized nations.

DECEMBER 15   Javier Perez de Cuellar succeeds Waldheim as secretary general of the United Nations.

DECEMBER 31   Martial law is suspended in Poland.

1983

MARCH 7   The seventh summit conference of nonaligned nations opens in Delhi.

JUNE 9   Thatcher's Conservative party wins general elections in Britain.

JUNE 16   Pope John Paul II, on his second visit to Poland, holds talks with General Jaruzelski and Solidarity leader Walesa.

SEPTEMBER 1   Soviet fighter planes shoot down a South Korean Boeing 747 airliner over Soviet territory.

OCTOBER 1   A five-year U.S.-USSR agreement on grain sales takes effect.

OCTOBER 5   The Nobel Peace Prize is awarded to Walesa.

OCTOBER 25-28   U.S. forces occupy the island of Grenada.

NOVEMBER 25   USSR walks out of nuclear arms reduction talks in Geneva without setting a date for their resumption.

1984

JANUARY 17   Thirty-five-nation conference on disarmament in Europe, attended by NATO and Warsaw Pact foreign ministers, is held in Stockholm.

FEBRUARY 9   Andropov dies in Moscow and is succeeded by Konstantin Chernenko.

JUNE 6   Heads of state of eight allied nations attend ceremonies marking the fortieth anniversary of the D-Day landing in Normandy.

JULY 28-AUGUST 12   The USSR and all Eastern European countries except Romania boycott the Olympic Games held in Los Angeles.

SEPTEMBER 26   Britain and China sign a final agreement for the transfer of Hong King to Chinese rule in 1997.

1985

MARCH 10   Chernenko dies in Moscow and is succeeded by Mikhail Gorbachev.

MARCH 12   U.S.-Soviet arms negotiations are resumed in Geneva.

JUNE 2   Greek Socialist leader Papandreou wins a second term in an electoral victory.

JULY 15–26   The UN World Conference of Women, with 2,200 delegates, meets in Nairobi.

SEPTEMBER 22   France, the Federal Republic of Germany, Great Britain, Japan, and the United States officially form the Group of Five to influence international currency matters.

NOVEMBER 15   Great Britain and the Irish republic sign an agreement giving Ireland a consultative role in the governing of Northern Ireland.

NOVEMBER 19–21   Reagan and Gorbachev hold a summit meeting in Geneva.

DECEMBER 10   The International Physicians for the Prevention of Nuclear War receive the Nobel Peace Prize.

1986

JANUARY 1   Portugal and Spain join the EEC.

JANUARY 20   The British and French governments agree to construct a railroad tunnel under the English Channel.

FEBRUARY 17   Nine members of the EEC sign the Single Europe Act, with Denmark, Greece, and Italy to adhere later.

FEBRUARY 28   Olof Palme, prime minister of Sweden, is assassinated in Stockholm; Ingvar Carlsson succeeds him.

APRIL 26   Fallout from an explosion of a reactor at the nuclear power plant in Chernobyl, USSR, results in widespread pollution in northern and central Europe.

MAY 6   The Group of Five is expanded to include Canada and Italy.

OCTOBER 11–12   Reagan and Gorbachev hold a summit meeting in Reykjavik, Iceland.

DECEMBER 9   The Palestinian revolt (*intifada*) begins in the Israeli occupied territories of the West Bank and Gaza.

DECEMBER 17   Milos Jakes replaces Husak as first secretary of the Czechoslovak Communist party.

1987

JANUARY 25   The Christian Democratic party, led by Kohl, is elected for a second term in West Germany.

JANUARY 27   The United States establishes diplomatic relations with Mongolia.

JUNE 19   Thatcher's Conservative party wins a third term, unprecedented in Britain since the 1820s.

DECEMBER 8–10   At a summit meeting in Washington, Reagan and Gorbachev sign the Intermediate-Range Nuclear Forces (INF) Treaty.

1988

FEBRUARY 8   An international panel of historians finds that Waldheim was aware of war crimes perpetrated by his unit during World War II but did not himself commit any crimes.

FEBRUARY 27   Armenian nationalists suspend demonstrations in the Soviet Union when assured Gorbachev will examine their grievances.

MARCH 4   Ethnic fighting erupts in Azerbaijan.

APRIL 14   Afghanistan and Pakistan sign accords on settlement in Afghanistan.

MAY 8   The Socialist party, led by Mitterrand, is elected to a second term in France.

MAY 15   Soviet forces begin withdrawal from Afghanistan.

MAY 28   At the Communist party conference, Gorbachev proposes reform of the political system and strengthening of the post of president.

MAY 29–JUNE 2   Reagan and Gorbachev hold a summit meeting in Moscow and exchange ratifications of the INF Treaty.

SEPTEMBER 30   UN Peacekeeping Forces are awarded the Nobel Peace Prize.

SEPTEMBER 30   Andrei Gromyko resigns as Politburo member and as president of the USSR; three others are ousted, and four supporters of Gorbachev are appointed to the Politburo.

OCTOBER 1   Gorbachev succeeds Gromyko as president of the USSR.

NOVEMBER 8   George Bush is elected president of the United States.

DECEMBER 1   The Supreme Soviet approves constitutional changes for the USSR.

DECEMBER 7   A major earthquake devastates Soviet Armenia.

1989

JANUARY 18   The Central Committee of United Workers (Communist) party in Poland recommends legalization of the Solidarity trade union.

JANUARY 25   Soviet troops begin final withdrawal from Afghanistan.

MARCH 23   Rioting occurs between police and ethnic Albanians in the Kosovo province of Yugoslavia.

MARCH 26   Many Communist party regulars are defeated in elections for 1,500 seats in the new Soviet Congress of People's Deputies; later, 750 more seats are filled by party and other organizations.

APRIL 5   The Polish government and the opposition, led by Walesa, agree on a new structure for government, with bicameral legislature; the government recognizes the Roman Catholic church.

APRIL 9   Georgian nationalists riot in Tbilisi.

APRIL 25   As Gorbachev strengthens his position, 110 old-time officials, including seventy-four members of the Communist party Central Committee, resign.

MAY 2   Hungary dismantles fencing along the 150-mile (241-km) border with Austria.

MAY 25   The new Congress of People's Deputies elects Gorbachev president.

MAY 27   Soviet Congress of People's Deputies elects 542 of its 2,250 members to form the new Supreme Soviet.

JUNE 3–4   The military crushes student prodemocracy demonstrations in China.

JUNE 4, 18   In Polish elections, Solidarity supporters win 99 of 100 seats in the Senate and all 161 seats allotted to the opposition in the Sejm.

JUNE 13   Gorbachev and Kohl sign a declaration that every state has the right to choose its own social and political system.

JUNE 24   The Communist party in Hungary establishes a collective presidency.

AUGUST 24   Tadeusz Mazowiecki, member of a small Catholic party, becomes Polish premier after the Communist premier is unable to form a cabinet.

SEPTEMBER 11–14   Thirteen thousand East German refugees travel through Hungary to Austria and the Federal Republic of Germany.

SEPTEMBER 20   Gorbachev strengthens his position in the Politburo and cautions against separatism in the Baltic republics and Ukraine.

OCTOBER 7   Hungarian Socialist Workers (Communist) party renames itself the Socialist party, dedicated to democratic socialism.

OCTOBER 9   Demonstrations begin in Leipzig, East Germany, and will grow in size over the next week.

OCTOBER 18   Erich Honecker is removed as head of the East German SED and replaced by Egon Krenz as head of state, party, and chair of the Defense Council.

OCTOBER 18   The Hungarian People's Republic is renamed the Republic of Hungary.

OCTOBER 23   Soviet foreign minister Eduard Shevardnadze says the Soviet 1979 invasion of Afghanistan was illegal.

OCTOBER 23   Demonstrations in Leipzig become huge.

OCTOBER 25   The Soviet foreign minister vows Soviet noninterference in Polish affairs.

NOVEMBER 9   East German travel restrictions are ended; the Berlin Wall falls.

NOVEMBER 10   Todor Zhivkov resigns as Bulgarian president and secretary general of the Communist party.

NOVEMBER 13   Hans Modrow is elected premier in GDR.

NOVEMBER 24   Czech Communist party leader Jakes resigns.

NOVEMBER 29   After weeks of demonstrations, the Czech Parliament removes from the constitution a phrase granting the Communist party a leadership role in society.

NOVEMBER 30   The 240-mile (387-km) border between Czechoslovakia and Austria is opened.

DECEMBER 1   The East German Parliament removes a constitutional clause granting a leading role to the SED party; Pope John Paul II and Gorbachev meet at the Vatican.

DECEMBER 2–3   Bush and Gorbachev confer at Malta.

DECEMBER 3   Amid revelations of corruption, leaders of the SED resign.

DECEMBER 5   Honecker is arrested in East Germany.

DECEMBER 6   Krenz resigns from his remaining posts in the GDR.

DECEMBER 8   Zhivkov's allies are removed from key posts in Bulgaria.

DECEMBER 10   Czech president Husak resigns; a non-Communist coalition government is formed.

DECEMBER 14   Andrei Sakharov, Soviet physicist and dissident, dies.

DECEMBER 16   SED renames itself the Socialist Unity Party of Germany–Party of Democratic Socialism (SED-PDS). Demonstrations in Timisoara, Romania, are repressed by troops.

DECEMBER 18   Turkish application to the EEC is essentially rejected.

DECEMBER 20   Lithuanian Communist party declares itself independent of the USSR Communist party.

DECEMBER 22   A coalition of officials, officers, and students form the National Salvation Front in Romania.

DECEMBER 25   Romanian president and Communist party leader Nicolae Ceausescu is executed in the midst of civil war.

DECEMBER 26   Gorbachev denounces actions by the Lithuanian Communist party and opposes secession by any Soviet republics.

DECEMBER 29   The Czech Parliament elects a non-Communist, Václav Havel, as president; Dubcek is elected speaker of the Federal Assembly.

1990

JANUARY 11   Martial law is lifted in the People's Republic of China, but new restrictive civil laws are put in place. Soviet Armenia declares its right to overrule Soviet laws affecting Armenia.

JANUARY 12   Romania outlaws the Communist party.

JANUARY 15   Soviet troops are sent to Azerbaijan to quell ethnic fighting. Bulgaria ends the Communist party monopoly of power. Demonstrators in East Germany sack the headquarters of the secret police.

JANUARY 23   Yugoslavia ends Communist party monopoly of power as Serb, Slovene, and Albanian ethnic differences mount.

JANUARY 29   Polish United Workers (Communist) party disbands; a new Social Democracy party is formed, hard-liners creating the Social-Democratic Union.

FEBRUARY 15   Local party and government leaders resign after riots in the Tadzhik-istan republic of the USSR.

MARCH 11   Lithuania declares independence from the USSR.

MARCH 13   Soviet Congress of People's Deputies votes out Article 6 of the constitution granting the Communist party a leading role in society; it approves a strong presidency, elects Gorbachev president (March 15), and sets popular presidential elections for 1995.

MARCH 14   Mongolian Communist party drops its constitutional monopoly of power.

MARCH 18   In East German elections, conservative parties favoring reunification win 48 percent of the vote; Social Democrats fare half as well, and former Communists do poorly.

MARCH 22   A Soviet military convoy enters Vilnius, capital of Lithuania.

APRIL 2   The Supreme Soviet passes rules for secession of republics, including the requirement of approval by a two-thirds majority in a referendum in the affected area.

APRIL 3   The Bulgarian Communist party changes its name to the Bulgarian Socialist party.

APRIL 12   Lothar de Maizière (CDU leader) becomes prime minister in East Germany.

APRIL 18   Soviets cut the flow of oil to Lithuania.

MAY 4   The Parliament of Latvia votes in favor of independence from the USSR.

MAY 5   Foreign ministers of the USSR, United Kingdom, France, United States, and the two Germanys hold their first meeting to discuss resolution of German issues.

MAY 7   Estonian Parliament declares an Estonian republic.

MAY 16   Enforcement of independence laws is suspended by the Lithuanian government.

MAY 30–JUNE 2   Bush and Gorbachev meet in Washington to sign a trade treaty and an agreement on limiting long-range nuclear missiles.

JUNE 13   The Romanian government summons riot police and miners to rout student demonstrators in Bucharest.

JUNE 30   Soviets allow export of oil to Lithuania to resume.

JULY 1   Economic union of East and West Germany takes place.

JULY 6   Prodemocracy riots in Albania are repressed.

JULY 12   Boris Yeltsin leaves the Communist party of the USSR.

JULY 16   Gorbachev and Kohl reach an agreement on German unification; the new Germany may remain in NATO.

AUGUST 2   Iraq invades Kuwait.

SEPTEMBER 12   The two Germanys, France, Britain, the USSR, and the United States sign the Treaty on Final Settlement with Respect to Germany.

OCTOBER 3   Germany is reunited.

NOVEMBER 12   Kyrgyzstan becomes the last of the fifteen Soviet republics to declare its sovereignty.

NOVEMBER 21   The Charter of Paris is signed by leaders of thirty-four nations at the Conference on Security and Cooperation in Europe.

NOVEMBER 24   Thatcher announces her resignation from leadership of the British Conservative party.

NOVEMBER 28   John Major becomes British prime minister.

NOVEMBER 29   UN sets deadline of January 15, 1991, for Iraq to withdraw from Kuwait.

DECEMBER 2   Kohl is victorious in the first elections held in the united Germany.

DECEMBER 9   Walesa is elected president of Poland.

DECEMBER 13–14   Demonstrations occur in Albania.

1991

JANUARY 5   Comecon announces plans for its dissolution.

JANUARY 13   Soviet troops kill demonstrators in Vilnius, Lithuania.

JANUARY 16   UN forces, led by the United States, launch a war to drive Iraq from Kuwait.

JANUARY 31   Czechoslovakia is accepted as a member of the Council of Europe.

FEBRUARY 9   A nonbinding plebiscite in Lithuania favors secession from the USSR.

FEBRUARY 20   The Parliament of the Slovenian republic approves legislation that would allow the republic to assume functions previously held by the Yugoslavian central government, as the movement for disassociation from Yugoslavia strengthens.

FEBRUARY 25   Members of the Warsaw Pact announce dissolution of its military, though not political, dimension by March 31.

FEBRUARY 27   Victorious UN forces declare an informal cease-fire in Kuwait.

MARCH 15   Boris Jovic, chair of the Yugoslav collective presidency, resigns as his call for martial law is rejected.

MARCH 21   Britain announces the phasing out of its controversial poll tax by 1993.

APRIL 2   Prices in the USSR increase sharply as state controls are eased.

APRIL 23   Leaders of nine of the fifteen Soviet republics reach tentative agreement on tactics to ease the economic crisis; they also agree that the republics will be granted a greater governing role.

JUNE 12   Yeltsin is chosen president of the Russian republic by direct popular election.

JUNE 25   Croatia and Slovenia proclaim their independence from Yugoslavia.

JUNE 28   Comecon is to be phased out over ninety days.

JULY 1   The Warsaw Pact is officially ended.

JULY 17   U.S. and Soviet leaders reach agreement on START; the Group of Seven meets with Gorbachev.

JULY 30   United States extends most-favored-nation trading status to the USSR during a Moscow summit.

JULY 31   Bush and Gorbachev sign the Strategic Arms Reduction Treaty.

AUGUST 19   Vice-president Gennadi Yanayev of the Soviet Union assumes the role of president, announcing that Gorbachev has been "hospitalized"; Yeltsin denounces the coup, calling for a general strike; demonstrators erect barricades to protect Russian government offices.

AUGUST 20   Estonia declares immediate full independence; other republics follow suit.

AUGUST 21   Soviet coup leaders (the Committee of Eight) disband; Soviet Parliament affirms Gorbachev as president; Yeltsin is popularly considered a hero.

AUGUST 22   Yeltsin disbands Communist party cells in Soviet armed forces on Russian republic territory.

AUGUST 24   Gorbachev resigns as head of the Soviet Communist party, disbands the Central Committee, and places party property under control of the Soviet Parliament.

AUGUST 29   Supreme Soviet votes to suspend all activities of the Communist party in the USSR.

SEPTEMBER 5   Soviet Congress of People's Deputies approves a new system of state relations.

SEPTEMBER 6   New Soviet State Council of Republic Leaders recognizes the independence of Estonia, Latvia, and Lithuania.

SEPTEMBER 11   Gorbachev announces Soviet troops will be withdrawn from Cuba.

SEPTEMBER 13   United States and USSR announce an accord to discontinue military aid to rebel and government forces in Afghanistan.

SEPTEMBER 15   Swedish elections end the long period of government by the Social Democratic party.

SEPTEMBER 20   Extended fighting between Serbian forces of the central army and Croatian troops in Yugoslavia erupts into full-scale war despite EC efforts to arrange a truce.

SEPTEMBER 27   Bush announces unilateral reduction of U.S. tactical nuclear weapons.

OCTOBER 18   Eight Soviet republics sign a treaty of economic union; Ukraine is not among them.

OCTOBER 22   Negotiators for the EC and EFTA announce plans for joint formation of the European Economic Area (EEA).

DECEMBER 1   Following elections that overwhelmingly support the move, Ukraine declares itself an independent nation.

DECEMBER 8   The presidents of Russia, Belarus, and Ukraine declare the Union of Soviet Socialist Republics dead and announce the formation of a Commonwealth of Independent States and invite other former Soviet republics to join them.

DECEMBER 11   The leaders of the EC nations, meeting at Maastricht, The Netherlands, sign a treaty providing for the creation of a common EC currency and central bank by 1999, if not earlier.

DECEMBER 21   Presidents of eleven former Soviet republics meet at Alma Ata (Georgia does not participate) and declare the end of the USSR and the creation of a Commonwealth of Independent States. They announce that they will respect mutual borders and that the UN Security Council seat formerly held by the Soviet Union should fall to the Russian Republic. Gorbachev is dismissed as commander-in-chief of military forces and temporarily replaced by the Russian Republic minister of defense.

DECEMBER 22 Fighting breaks out in the Georgian Republic as dissidents attempt the overthrow of the president.

DECEMBER 25 Gorbachev resigns as president of the now defunct USSR; the Russian Republic's white, blue, and red flag replaces the red flag with hammer and sickle over the Kremlin.

About the Book & Authors

Rebirth: A History of Europe Since World War II examines, from the perspective of the historic events of 1989–1991, the transition of Europe from a period of crisis to an era of political confidence and economic strength. As the title suggests, the pervasive theme of the book is that of rebirth. The most recent decades are set in the context of modern European history as a whole. The authors trace the disillusionment and uncertainty that overcame Europe at the turn of the twentieth century, which culminated in the devastation of the Second World War. In their analysis of the political and economic causes of the renaissance that has followed the demise of the Cold War, the authors highlight the themes of national integration and economic modernization.

The chapters are uniquely organized to present both international and domestic developments in Europe as coherent wholes, as well as the importance of their interaction. The initial analysis of key international developments in the twentieth century helps students to understand the relationship between foreign and domestic events and provides background for the substantial discussion of the major European countries that follows in chapters devoted to each national experience. The political and economic histories of these nation-states are considered in terms of their individual traditions and challenges, and the authors explore difficult issues such as the overall costs and benefits of the scientific-technological revolution, the pursuit of social justice, the proper role of the state and of political parties, and contrasting national paths of economic and political development.

Rebirth is designed as a text for use in courses on modern European history—especially twentieth-century Europe—and for students of comparative politics who are seeking a substantial consideration of the historical factors of European politics.

Cyril E. Black was professor of history and international affairs emeritus at Princeton University. **Jonathan E. Helmreich** is professor of history at Allegheny College, Pennsylvania, and **Paul C. Helmreich** is professor of history at Wheaton College, Massachusetts. **Charles P. Issawi** is professor emeritus, and **A. James McAdams** is professor of political science, both at Princeton University.

541

Index